An International Dictionary of
Adult and Continuing Education

An International
Dictionary
of Adult and
Continuing
Education

PETER JARVIS

ROUTLEDGE
London and New York

First published 1990 by Routledge
11 New Fetter Lane, London EC4P 4EE

Simultaneously published in the
USA and Canada
by Routledge
a division of Routledge, Chapman and
Hall, Inc.
29 West 35th Street,
New York, NY 10001

Typeset by J&L Composition Ltd, Filey,
North Yorkshire
Printed and bound in Great Britain by
Mackays of Chatham PLC, Chatham, Kent

*British Library Cataloguing in
Publication Data*
Jarvis, Peter, *1937–*
    An international dictionary of adult
    and continuing education.
    I. Title
    374
    ISBN 0–415–02421–8

*Library of Congress Cataloging in
Publication Data*
Jarvis, Peter.
        An international dictionary of adult
    and continuing education/
    Peter Jarvis.
        p.   cm.
    ISBN 0–415–02421–8
    1. Adult education—
Dictionaries. 2. Continuing
education—Dictionaries. I. Title.
LC5211.J37 1989
374'.005—dc20   89–33895

Preface

Adult and continuing education is changing at a tremendously rapid rate in this contemporary, urban world. Indeed, by the time this dictionary is published some of the information will already be obsolescent. This is a feature of today's society. It might be wondered, therefore, if this is an opportune time to prepare such a dictionary. Obviously, the cliché that there is never an opportune time is as valid here as it ever is. That some of the information might be less valid because of change only reflects the dynamic nature of society and the manner in which adult and continuing education is adapting to respond to these changes.

However, adult and continuing education is still a complex field to enter and it is hoped that this dictionary will at least act as a guidebook to those who wish to find their way through it. Naturally, it reflects one person's understanding of the field and consequently it contains its own limitations. If any colleague is prepared to send me corrections and changes, these will be incorporated in any new edition.

This selection of information must necessarily be my own and, consequently, it reflects my own understanding of the field. It will be seen, for instance, that there are many references here that could have come from initial education. This is because I understand the field of education to be a single field with many common elements across the different forms, rather than a number of separate fields. It will also be noted that there are terms from a variety of the social science disciplines because I understand education to be field of study which in its practical form utilizes their knowledge bases.

As the field is international I have tried to record some information about the wider world of adult and continuing education. This is useful because it enables us to compare what is happening in our own society with that occurring elsewhere. We can learn from this and it may enrich both our own understanding and practice of education. However, spelling presented a problem. I have therefore tried to give as much information as I can and, consequently, I have included the expressions, titles, and so on in their first language, wherever this has been possible.

Words that appear in italics can be cross-referenced in the dictionary and so I have not repeated information from different references, unless it seemed appropriate to do so.

I owe a great debt to all scholars in the field whose work I have read and who have influenced my understanding of the field. I have not included a bibliography of works consulted for this dictionary because it could not be complete. I can but express my appreciation for all that I have learned from them, often my friends and colleagues, who have helped me so much. One colleague who has known about this project from its inception, has encouraged me throughout, and has done me the honour of reading some of it, is Alan Chadwick. I have been most grateful to him for his support. Without the constant support of my wife, Maureen, and my children, Frazer and Kierra, who are often only aware of my presence at home because they are aware that I am in the study, I can only once again express my love and gratitude.

During the preparation of this volume for publication Emma Waghorn has been diligent in her proof reading and copy editing, far beyond the call of duty; but because of her careful work and patience many errors have been avoided. I am most grateful to her for all that she has done throughout this period.

When I started this undertaking, I understood something of its magnitude. On completion of this phase of it, I realize that I underestimated it. The field is very wide and ever-changing. I can only hope that students of adult and continuing education who consult this book will find it useful. While many people have helped me and provided me with information, the mistakes are my own.

Peter Jarvis

AAACE Newsletter The newsletter of the *American Association for Adult and Continuing Education* which has been renamed *On-Line.*

Abendgymnasium German *evening high school* adult education institution which provides opportunities for adults to take courses leading to the *Abitur* which it is necessary to pass before entrance to a university in West Germany. This is known as the *second route (2 Bildungsweg)* and it consists of two and a half years of evening study – some 20 hours a week, followed by one and a half years study fulltime, in order to complete the normal four-year *Abitur.* During the part-time period fees are minimal and the students work but during the full-time period students are supported by the state.

Abendschule German *evening school* sponsored by either industry or local government to provide *general* and *vocational education.*

Abend-techniken Swiss *adult education* institution.

ability A person is said to have this if he/she can carry out a mental, emotional, or physical task with or without instruction. The extent to which ability is a product of *learning* rather than being innate is a debatable question.

Abitur The high school diploma in the Federal Republic of Germany, necessary in order to enter university. Adults can also sit the Abitur later in life, if they did not gain it whilst at school, by enrolling in an *Abendgymnasium.*

abstract 1. A synopsis of a paper, often occurring at the start of a paper in an academic journal, but also included in some journals which contain only lists of abstracts. 2. A concept which has no reference to material objects.

abstract ideas These form the basis of theory; they are concepts and generalizations that relate to specific and concrete phenomena but are not congruent with them.

Abteilung Erwachsenenbildung Fachbibliotek The Austrian adult education department library which contains a large collection of books and periodicals about *adult education.* Current address: Wallnerstrasse 8, 1014 Vienna, Austria.

academic 1. Relating to a place of *learning.* 2. One who spends time studying. 3. Often contrasted to the practical in the sense of being theoretical, e.g. 'That person is not academic.' 4. A member of the teaching/research staff of an educational institution, i.e. the academic staff as opposed to the *support staff.*

academic education The classical and liberal subjects of the *curriculum* in both school and post-school education.

academic failure One who may be regarded as having failed in *initial education.* A great deal of *adult education* is directed towards supporting those who, having been regarded as failures, seek to return to the educational system later in life.

academic freedom 1. Freedom of academic institutions to decide upon the courses that they will teach, the processes that they will employ to teach, and the areas that they will research without coercion from outside bodies. 2. The individual freedom of the academic to teach and of students to study without coercion or restriction by others. This is sometimes referred to as the autonomy of the professoriat in the United States.

academic year The period of the school/university year, usually September through to the beginning of July, but varying from country to country, and even in some cases among institutions in the same country, e.g. the *Open University* academic year in the United Kingdom begins in February rather than September and ends in October/November rather than June/July.

Academie of the Third Age This is an informal group of elderly people in the Copenhagen area which was started in 1986, and which meets in members' homes for study. In many ways it is similar to the *Institute for Retired Professionals* in the United States. Current address: c/o The Danish Cultural Institute, Kultorvet 2, 1175 Copenhagen, Denmark.

academy A place where *academic* pursuits are practised, e.g. either a school, college, or learned society.

Academy for Educational Development American association. Current address: 680 Fifth Avenue, New York, New York 10019, USA.

acceptance An uncensuring attitude towards a person's behaviour and attitudes and recognition of that person's worth as a human being without either condemning or condoning those actions or attitudes.

access A variety of meanings have been given to this term, including: access to the opportunity to acquire entrance qualifications, usually for *higher education*,

e.g. *second chance education*; the opportunity to acquire qualifications that are regarded as equivalencies to recognized qualification; access to a particular course that leads into an institution of *higher education*. See *access courses*.

access courses These courses are especially organized to prepare unqualified adults for *higher education* without pursuing the traditional routes. Usually they are mounted by educational institutions in liaison with specific universities, polytechnics, etc. They were originally established for teacher training and social work training but they have subsequently developed much more widely.

Access to Information Technology (AIT) A scheme in which the *Manpower Services Commission* makes grants towards courses of up to 30 hours to encourage the use of existing training capacity during times when it would be otherwise underutilized, to enable existing employed adults to increase their awareness of *information technology*. (Note: MSC changed its name to the *Training Commission* and then to the *Training Agency* in 1988.)

Accion Cultural Popular (ACPO) A *cultural action* project in Colombia, Latin America. It was the first Catholic Church-sponsored *radio school* project in Latin America, starting in 1951. It is a technique of using a *cultural circle* approach to listen to a radio broadcast and then study textbooks produced by the project, with the support of a local teacher/volunteer who is trained but has also received a higher level of education than the local population participating in the programmes. Current address: Carrere 39A No 15–81, Bogotá, Colombia.

accommodation 1. The tendency to alter cognitions to fit structures and objects that are encountered during the process of living. 2. A form of *learning*. 3. The physical premises in which *teaching* and *learning* is conducted.

accommodator A *learning style* in which people respond to problems in a trial-and-error manner and people learn through discussion with other people.

accountability The fact of being responsible to someone for action or decision. This has become more prevalent in *adult education* in recent years as organizations have had to become more self-sufficient financially. See also *educational accountability*.

accreditation 1. The process whereby recognition is given to an educational course by a statutory body or by an accrediting agency. 2. The system of granting credit, i.e. placing some recognized standard on a course, so that the ensuing certificate can be used towards a further qualification at a later date in the same or a different educational institution. 3. *Accreditation Associations* seek to determine the value of a course.

Accreditation Associations Associations that assess the value of a course. There are regional associations throughout the United States.

Accreditation Council for Continuing Medical Education The professional body in the United States which accredits *continuing medical education*, including that which a physician may undertake in order to gain a *Physicians Recognition Award*. Each state has its own accreditation council and its own procedures.

accreditation of prior learning Schemes for giving students formal *credit* for *prior learning* as an alternative method of demonstrating *entry requirements*, or as a method of being granted remission of part of the *course requirements*.

accredited correspondence education In the Netherlands *correspondence education* has been brought under the ambit of the law; from 1 August 1973 institutions have to meet certain specified conditions in order to gain accreditation from the Ministry. See *Wet Erkenning Schriftelijk Onderwijs*.

accredited training centre Centres, 44 originally created, often within *further education* provision which have been approved by the *Manpower Services Commission (MSC)* to provide qualifying courses for *trainers*, often short *continuing education* courses which are themselves funded by the MSC. *Managing agents* for *youth training schemes* in *approved training organizations* are expected to attend such courses. (Note: the MSC changed its name to the *Training Commission* and then to the *Training Agency* in 1988.)

Accrediting Commission on Graduate Education for Hospital Administration An American accrediting body for hospital administrator education. Address: One Dupont Circle NW, Washington DC 20036, USA.

acculturation A *socialization* process whereby a person or persons learns the *culture/subculture* of a group or nation.

achievement Level of performance.

achievement need The psychological state in which people feel constrained to be successful, to satisfy their drive towards success.

achievement orientation An approach to studying which is competitive, so that study methods are organized in order to gain success.

achievement test An examination that seeks to test the extent to which a *learner* has acquired *knowledge* or *skill*, usually as a result of specific *teaching*.

ACSET See *Advisory Committee on the Supply and Education of Teachers*.

ACSTT See *Advisory Committee on the Supply and Training of Teachers*.

act A performance. Often used in teaching, e.g. *role play*.

Act of Adult Education The Parliamentary Act on *adult education* in Norway, passed in 1976 and operative from August 1977. The act specifies the financial provision that the state should make to *adult education* although it leaves the decisions about the provision to local and regional bodies. The act endeavours to create equality of access to education for all groups of people in the community, although it does not make it a statutory right that people should be entitled to education throughout their lives. It does, however, specify that participants in *adult education* should have a right to reasonable influence on the content and methods of their class/group.

Act on the Protection of Participants of Extra-Mural Study (Fern USG) Passed in 1976 and became effective in 1977 in the Federal Republic of Germany, which regulates extra-mural study examination regulations throughout the whole country. Additionally, it provides for all courses offered on a fee-paying basis to be checked and regulated by state authority. See *Central Office for Extra-Mural Study*.

action State or process of doing. See *action learning*.

action–centred leadership Leadership courses developed in the United Kingdom which involve small group work.

Action for Independent Maturity (AIM) A retirement education series produced by the *American Association of Retired Persons*, useful for those who organize retirement courses.

Action for Special Groups *Manpower Services Commission* provides courses of *training* for special groups, which include disabled adults, ethnic minorities, and women. Courses for the disabled are provided at four residential colleges and through eight other specialist providers in the United Kingdom. (Note: the MSC changed its name to the *Training Commission* and then *Training Agency* in 1988.)

action learning Learning through doing, either in *simulation* or in the actual situation. It is a *learning process* involving the learner's *reflection* upon, or *memorizing* of, the action *experience* and its results.

action research A form of research in which the researcher is a participant in the phenomenon under scrutiny, and the actual process of the action is itself the subject of the research.

active learning Methods by which learners actively participate in the learning process, e.g. *discussion group, problem-solving education, experimentation,* etc.

activism Action in pursuit of a chosen cause, which occurs in *community action* and in some other forms of *community education*. Some community educators consider that educators should take a stance in social situations about which they teach, but this is not a view which is universally accepted by *adult educators*.

activity methods Many *teaching* and *learning methods* in *adult education* are participative; thus these are methods through which learners learn by doing. See *action learning*.

activity-orientated learning Those who enrol in a formal educational course for reasons related to the activity rather than the content of the learning. One of *Cyril Houle's* three types of learning. See also *goal-orientated learning; learning-orientated learning*.

adaptive further training The term used in West Germany to refer to that form of *continuing education* which prepares members of the workforce to handle new techniques, processes, and organizational forms. It is not regarded as preparation for career advancement, but training so that the present job can be undertaken more efficiently.

Addams, Jane Founder of one of the early *settlement houses* in the United States, Hull House in Chicago, in 1889.

Adequacy of Provision The title of a report of research conducted by *The National Institute of Adult Education* and addressed to the Department of Education and Science in 1970 about the level of organized provision of educational opportunities for mature people in the United Kingdom. The report was published as volume 42 no. 6 of the journal *Adult Education*.

Adiseshiah, Malcolm Vice Chancellor of Madras University, chairman of the Indian Institute for Development Studies, and the first president of the *International Council for Adult Education*. He was Deputy Director-General of *Unesco* and has also been chairman of the board of Unesco's *International Institute for Educational Planning*.

adjunct professor A part-time, or contract, teacher in an American college or university.

Adler, Alfred (1870–1937) Well-known psychologist whose pioneering work included studies of the inferiority complex.

Adler, Mortimer J. One of the originators of the *Great Books Movement* in the United States. He was a professor and assistant director of the *People's Institute* and then co-operated with *Robert Hutchins* at the University of Chicago on the Great Books programme. In it he espoused the type of *liberal adult education* that he had learned with *Everett Dean Martin*.

admission Formal acceptance to a course or programme.

admissions tutor The academic member of staff in *higher education* who is responsible for processing applications and interviewing applicants for specific courses in an academic department.

adolescent A *young adult*, someone between the ages of biological and social maturity. Similar to the American term *pre-adult*.

Adolf-Grimme Institute Under the jurisdiction of the *German Adult Education Association*, it is concerned mainly with working with the media, including training *adult educators* to work in this sphere, to organize groups of people to judge the television programmes broadcast within the Federal Republic and to prepare educational programmes. Address: Adolf-Grimme Institute, Eduard-Weitschweg 25, Marl, North Rhine-Westfalia, Federal Republic of Germany.

adult 1. The legal age of adulthood in the United Kingdom is 18 years. 2. The concept of adult has troubled a number of adult educators because it underlies the question of whether adults and children learn differently. However, adulthood is socially constructed since the age of entry into adulthood varies among different countries of the world. Hence, in educational terms it is perhaps best regarded as the age at which a person feels him/herself to be an adult and at which that person is also treated as one by his/her social group. Thus it is a combination of the social and the individual, but relative to society and not necessarily biologically determined. This therefore raises questions about the extent to which adults' *learning* differs from children's.

adult armchair education Associated with *Leon Howard Sullivan* in America who discovered that many who were on feeder programmes to the *Opportunities Industrialization Centers* learned better in informal surroundings and at times convenient to themselves. He started an adult education programme which is known as the adult armchair programme.

adult basic education 1. In nearly all the developed countries of the world this has become a crucial part of the *adult education* service. The three main components are skills in language (reading, writing, speech), number, and social living. 2. The Dutch have incorporated it into their state regulations which came into effect in 1986 in which they specify that adult basic education entails education that enables people to function in everyday life and to develop as persons. In addition, it specifies that cultural minorities should have the opportunity of full participation in Dutch society through adult basic education programmes.

Adult Basic Education Program
(ABE) Established in the United States in 1965, launched by the US Department of Education as a result of the Economic Opportunity and *Adult Education* Acts, it is administered at state level by state education agencies. This programme includes not only the normal *adult basic education*, but also *English as a second language*. Current address: Division of Adult Education, Office of Vocational and Adult Education, 400 Maryland Ave. SW, Washington DC 20202, USA.

adult Christian education This is *adult religious education* conducted by the Christian Churches to teach people about their Churches' specific doctrines and practices.

adult continuing education This fusion of two concepts, *adult education* and *continuing education*, as in the *National Institute of Adult Continuing Education*, is an attempt to end the historic division between *adult liberal education* and *vocational education* and to illustrate that both are about the *education of adults*. Conceptually this is valid, but it was seen by some as a sign that *liberal adult education* had little future. This was not so, although in the United Kingdom there are policy changes that have been significant in this respect.

adult development The multi-disciplinary study of the physical, psychological, and intellectual changes in people during adulthood. A study frequently undertaken by adult educators reading for higher degrees in adult education, especially in the American programmes. Some psychologists suggest that development is attained through a series of stages. See *Jean Piaget, Lawrence Kohlberg* and *James Fowler*.

adult distributive education
Instruction of a basic and post-basic nature within *professional education* designed to prepare people to work and make progress within the marketing and distributive occupations.

adult education 1. The term is first used in *Thomas Pole*'s *History and Origins and Progress of Adult Schools*. The concept is among the most problematic in the field. It tends to be used to refer to *liberal education* for adults in the United Kingdom, whereas in the United States, for example, it has the wider connotation of the *education of adults*, whether it be vocational or otherwise. If education is a planned process of learning or a programme, then adult education refers to those planned processes of learning for adult participants. Some scholars wish to restrict education to certain forms of planned process, such as those having a humanistic basis, but other scholars would wish to restrict the process to certain types of learner, e.g. willing and voluntary, etc.
2. *Unesco* defines it as 'the entire body of organized educational processes, whatever the content, level, or method, whether formal or otherwise, whether they prolong or replace initial education in schools or colleges, and universities as well as in apprenticeship, whereby persons regarded as adult by the society to which they belong develop their abilities, enrich their knowledge, improve their technical or professional qualifications, or turn them in a new direction and bring about changes in their attitudes or behaviour in the two-fold perspective of full personal development and participation in balanced, independent, social, economic, and cultural development'.
3. In Eire the *Murphy Committee* defined adult education as 'the provision and utilization of facilities whereby those who are no longer participants in the full-time school system may learn whatever they need to learn at any period of their lives'.
4. In Dutch law it is defined as 'the promotion of one's personal development and function in society

through extension of knowledge, insight and attitude, as well as social, cultural, and technical skills'.

5. The study of this area of practice was formalized first at the University of Nottingham, UK, having the first Department of Adult Education in 1920 with *Robert Peers* as director and first professor. There were a few awards of doctorates in adult education in other universities in England, such as the University of London, but these were not part of a formalized adult education programme.

6. Columbia University in the United States had the first course in 1922, the first Department of Adult Education in 1930, the first degree programme and the first doctorates awarded in 1935. See also *Institute of Adult Education*.

Adult Education 1. The journal of the *National Institute of Adult Continuing Education*, first published in Britain in September 1926 as *The Journal of Adult Education*. It is the longest-running journal in adult education. It was a bimonthly journal but from June 1981 it became a quarterly journal for practitioners. It was discontinued in 1989 and replaced by *Adults Learning*. 2. This is the title of the journal of the *Adult Education Association of the United States of America*, which changed its name at the start of 1984 to *Adult Education Quarterly*. 3. The title of the journal started in 1982 by the *Adult Education Association of Zambia*. 4. *Adult Education* (Erwachsenenbildung) is the quarterly journal of the *Federal Catholic Workshop for Adult Education* in the Federal Republic of Germany. See *Catholic education organization*.

Adult Education: A Plan for Development The full title for The *Russell Report* published in 1973 in the United Kingdom. This was a crucial report in the United Kingdom and led to a number of developments in the field but the climate in the country changed before all its recommendations could be adopted.

Adult Education Act Promulgated in America in 1966 as part of the Elementary and Secondary Education Act. Its purpose was to expand educational opportunities for adults below college level. It established a national *adult basic education* programme in the United States with some federal funding on submission of satisfactory proposals to the Secretary of Education. In addition, the act allows costs for staff training, research, and development. It has been amended on a number of occasions since its inception.

Adult Education Action Council American association. Current address: 4201 Cathedral Avenue NW, Suite 1205 East, Washington DC 20016, USA.

Adult Education and Development This journal is published twice a year by the *German Adult Education Association*. It is a practical journal, publishing short articles about adult education and development from all parts of the world.

Adult Education and Older Adults An *International Council for Adult Education* network. Current address: 6 Parkside Gardens, London SW19 5EY, UK.

Adult Education and New Technology An *International Council for Adult Education* network. Current address: Department of Extra-Mural Studies, Chinese University of Hong Kong, 67 Chatham Road South, 13F Kowloon, Hong Kong.

Adult Education and Peace An *International Council for Adult Education* network. Current address: Peace Education Institute, Fredrikinkatu 82B, 00100 Helsinki 11, Finland.

Adult Education and Primary Health Care An *International Council for Adult Education* programme. Current address: Consejo de Educación de Adultos de América Latin, Casilla 6257, Correo 22, Santiago, Chile.

Adult Education and the Library A newsletter published by the American Library Association between 1924 and 1930 which was read beyond the library profession.

Adult Education as an Emerging Field of University Study The famous *Black Book*, edited by Gale Jensen, A.A. Liveright, and Wilbur Hallenbeck, published by the *Adult Education Association of the United States of America* in 1964. It is a landmark book which American adult educators regard as crucial in the development of *adult education* as a field of study. In it the editors point to ways in which the field may be studied from the perspective of the different academic disciplines.

Adult Education Association of Israel See *Israel*.

Adult Education Association of the United States of America. Established in May 1951 at a conference at Columbus, Ohio, as a result of a merger between the *American Association of Adult Education* and the *Department of Adult Education of the National Education Association* and continued until it became one of the constituent members of the *American Association of Adult and Continuing Education* in 1982. It was the national association for individuals and associations concerned with the *education of adults* in America. It published two journals, *Adult Education* (not to be confused with the one published in the United Kingdom), and *Lifelong Learning: The Adult Years* and was located at 810 Eighteenth Street NW, Washington DC 20006.

Adult Education Association of Zambia Founded in 1968, this association has been supported by the *German Adult Education Association*, the *Norwegian Adult Education Association* and is itself a member of the *African Adult Education Association*. Membership is associational and individual. The association publishes its own journal. Address: P.O. Box 50232, Lusaka, Zambia.

Adult Education Bulletin The *National Education Association* issues a regular publication about *adult education*.

Adult Education Clearinghouse Newsletter The international newsletter from the *National Adult Education Clearinghouse*, published monthly.

adult education conferences *James Stuart*, founder of the *university extension movement*, probably held the first adult education conference in Sheffield in 1875 in order to discuss the problems of the recently formed *university extension movement*.

Adult Education, Development and Peace Journal started by the *National Association for Total Education* in Sri Lanka and sponsored by the *German Adult Education Association* and the *South Pacific Bureau of Adult Education*.

Adult Education Guided Independent Study See *AEGIS*.

Adult Education Handlist A quarterly listing of periodical articles and books, distributed by the *East Midlands Institute of Adult Education* in the United Kingdom in co-operation with the Derbyshire County Council.

Adult Education in Canada Published in 1935, a national survey of *adult education* in Canada.

Adult Education in Finland An English language quarterly journal aimed at giving foreign readers a wide perspective of Finnish *adult education*, established in 1963 and obtainable from the Society for Popular Culture, Museokatu 18 A, 00100 Helsinki 10, Finland.

Adult Education in Ireland Known as the *Murphy Report* after its chairman, a very important report on adult education commissioned by the Minister of Education for Ireland.

Adult Education in Nigeria The adult education journal of the *Nigerian National Council for Adult Education*.

Adult Education Information Notes Published quarterly by *Unesco* in English, French, Spanish, Arabic, Russian, and Chinese, containing information about *adult education* activities of Unesco, including some recent publications and news of events. Previously called *Literacy – a newsletter*, which was started in 1973. Address: Unesco, Adult Education Section, Division of Primary Education, Literacy and Adult Education, 7, place de Fontenoy, 75700 Paris, France.

Adult Education Journal The title assumed by the *Journal of Adult Education* of the *American Association of Adult Education* in January 1942. It retained this title until it was merged with the *Adult Education Bulletin* in 1950.

adult education legislation There has been legislation about *adult education* in many countries of the world and the following illustrate some recent enactments. 1. In Denmark, the Act of Leisure Time Education for Adults 1968 has been amended on many occasions, but makes it compulsory for counties to establish courses leading to examinations at school leaving level, and the Act on Folk High Schools, Continuation Schools and Home Economics Schools was passed in 1970. 2. Adult education law was passed in the Federal Republic of Germany in 1970 in which it is treated as the fourth dimension of the education system and equal to the others. It is funded differently, by municipalities with state assistance, so that it does not have to compete with other educational provision as it does in the United Kingdom. 3. Legislation in Eastern bloc countries relates to the workers' right to have educational opportunity to take secondary school-leaving examinations.

Adult Education News The official newsletter of the *Australian Association of Adult Education*. Current address: AAAE Newsletter, Council of Adult Education, 256 Flinders Street, Melbourne, Victoria, 30000, Australia.

adult education officer (AEO) The officer of the Local Education Authority in England and Wales responsible for the *adult education* provision and funding in that LEA area. See also *local authority advisor*.

adult education policy community Analysts of government policy refer to the group of organizations which are interrelated in terms of government policy as a policy community. The adult education policy community is that group of organizations which advocates on behalf of *adult education*.

Adult Education Quarterly (AEQ) Formerly *Adult Education*, it adopted its new name at the start of 1984. It is a quarterly academic journal of the *American Association of Adult and Continuing Education*.

Adult Education Regulations Published in 1924 by the Board of Education, these were the first official regulations in England for *adult education*. *Responsible Bodies* were first established by these regulations.

Adult Education Research Conference (AERC) Established in the United States in 1960, this is an annual conference of *adult educators* involved in research in North America, who meet in a different North American city each year. Publishes its proceedings. In 1988 the first joint conference with *Standing Conference on University Teaching and Research in the Education of Adults* and the *Canadian Association for the Study of the Education of Adults* was held in the United Kingdom.

Adult Education Research Institute Russian research institute. See *Institut obscego obrazovanija vzroslych*.

Adult Education Research Society The only national scientific society in *adult education* in Finland, and it has a wide membership. The society both promotes and launches research in the field. Holds public lectures and publishes its own journal *Adult Education*

(Aikuiskasvatus) in conjunction with the *Society for Popular Culture*. Address: Tampere University, Hämeenkatu 6A, 33100 Tampere 10, Finland.

Adult Education: The Challenge of Change The *Alexander Report* published in 1975 as a report upon leisure time *adult education* in Scotland. It made significant recommendations about the future of adult education in that country.
Published by Her Majesty's Stationery Office, Edinburgh.

adult educator One who is involved either in the *teaching* of *adults* or in the organization and administration of the *education of adults*. It is important to recognize that at the present time some would define the term by the teaching function and others by the administrative one. Others would perhaps define it by a combination of the two.

Adult Leadership An *adult education* journal published by the *Association of Adult Education of the United States of America* between 1952 and 1977, when it was replaced by *Lifelong Learning: The Adult Years*.

adult learner See *adult*. Any definition of adult learner must relate to an understanding of *adult*. However, generally and imprecisely it refers to those who have completed their *initial education* and who have returned to *education*.

Adult Learning The first journal of the *Canadian Association for Adult Education*, which was published between 1936 and 1939. It was followed by *Food For Thought*.

Adult Learning Programming Service of the Public Broadcasting Service Established in 1981, this service seeks to provide educational institutions in the United States with access to a wide range of telecourses through co-ordinating the activities of *public broadcasting* stations and distributing educational material.

Adult Learning Strategies and Approaches (ALSA) The successor to *Teaching Adults*, a publication for practitioners from *National Institute of Adult Continuing Education* in the United Kingdom. It is intended for all engaged in the education of adults, especially *part-time tutors, volunteers, organizers, and trainers* and covers all aspects of *teaching, training, and learning*.

adult library service So-called as it is the provision of a library service by an educational institution for adults who are not members of that college or university in the United Kingdom.

adult literacy A precise definition of *literacy* is problematic, for *adults* especially so. Definitions generally refer to the *ability* to handle written information, i.e. to read and write, though many point out that ability is itself difficult to define and measure. *Adult basic education* is now the term most commonly employed to refer to adult literacy.

Adult Literacy and Basic Education Specialist American quarterly journal and the official journal of the US Commission on *Adult Basic Education*.

Adult Literacy and Basic Skills Unit (ALBSU) Established in April 1980 in the United Kingdom from the *Adult Literacy Unit* and charged with developing within the general education service a basic education service designed to improve the standards of proficiency for adults whose first or second language is English, in literacy, numeracy, and basic coping skills. Its first director was Alan Wells and it was located at the same offices as the *Adult Literacy Unit*. It functions under the auspices of the *National Institute of Adult Continuing Education*. Current address: 229–231 High Holborn, London WC1V 7DA, UK.

Adult Literacy Campaign 1. The term used in the United Kingdom to promote *adult literacy* during the 1970s. The number of people receiving help rose from 6,000 to 60,000 within the first year of the Campaign, reaching 100,000 within ten years. 2. In Spain an official decree in August 1963 established an Adult Literacy Campaign which was terminated in 1973 when a permanent *adult education* programme was introduced in the country. 3. Many countries in the world have organized similar campaigns in recent years.

Adult Literacy Centre The Tanzanian centre for *adult literacy*. Current address: P.O. Box 1141, Mwanza, Tanzania.

Adult Literacy Initiative Established on 7 September 1983 in the United States by President Reagan to facilitate collaboration between national groups and to recruit new resources and support for *adult literacy*. Current address: Adult Literacy Initiative, US Department of Education, 400 Maryland Avenue SW, Room 4145 FOB-6, Washington DC 20202, USA.

Adult Literacy Organization of Zimbabwe (ALOZ) This organization trains literacy teachers and conducts the literacy campaign in Zimbabwe by running classes, producing teaching material, and sponsoring some small projects. Current address: P.O. Box 4480, Harara, Zimbabwe.

Adult Literacy Resource Agency (ALRA) Established in 1975 in the United Kingdom by the *National Institute of Adult Education* to respond to the problems of adult literacy which had become apparent during the 1970s. It received its first government grant for the financial year 1975–76. The first director was W.A. Devereux. Its work was terminated when the *Adult Literacy Unit* was established in 1978.

Adult Literacy Support Services Fund Established as a registered charity in the United Kingdom, it was responsible for much of the early activity in the adult literacy movement. It ceased to function as such in 1980, changing its function and name into *Broadcasting Support Services*.

Adult Literacy Unit (ALU) Established under the auspices of the *National Institute for Adult Education* in 1978 in the United Kingdom with a remit for three years to provide adult literacy tuition, excluding *English as a second language*, and the provision of immediate post-literacy education. Its director was Alan Wells and its address was 52–54 High Holborn, London WC1V 2RL. In 1980 it became the *Adult Literacy and Basic Skills Unit*.

adult nutrition education A *community education* programme offered to poor people in developing countries.

Adult Performance Level Program (APL) A five-year programme, commissioned by the US Department of Education in the early 1970s to cater for the *needs* of those who have not been successful in the traditional educational programme. It is *competency-based*, starting with a pre-programme test, and includes a *life skills* element. There is also an individual element built into some of these programmes. The final test contains 67 items in a *multiple choice* test. Considerable debate has ensued about the success or validity of the programmes.

adult religious education There has been a growth in interest in this field in *adult education* in recent years, but there are a number of different forms: 1. *Lay training*, in which people are educated to work in the church, synagogue, etc. 2. That form of education which is confessional, e.g. teaching and learning about Catholicism, Judaism etc. 3. That form of education which seeks to help people to understand the established religions of the world. 4. That form of adult religious education which concentrates upon the personal, the learner's own responses to life – more of an *experiential* approach to education.

Adult Residential Colleges Association An association of the 27 residential colleges in adult education in the United Kingdom which offer short courses to adults. These are non-profit colleges offering a wide variety of educational opportunities for adults throughout the year. Address: The Secretary, 19B De Montfort Street, Leicester LE1 7GE, UK.

adult returner An adult who returns to formal study later in life. Often it is these potential students who require courses in *study skills* in order to make the most of their return to a learning environment.

adult school A separately organized school for adults and young people beyond the age of compulsory schooling. The first adult school was established in Britain in 1798, in Nottingham, with the aim of teaching men and women to read the bible. Another early adult school was in Bristol, founded in 1812 by William Smith. Gradually the schools offered a wider syllabus and they are now of a more general educational nature. The schools are independent, although there is a *National Adult School Organization*.

Adult School Hymn Book Issued in 1909 as the official hymn book of the *adult school movement*.

Adult School Lesson Handbook See *Lesson Handbook*. First published in 1911 and continued until 1918, when it changed its name to *Study Handbook* and adopted a thematic title for each year.

adult school movement There has been an organization with a variety of different names (see elsewhere under *adult school*) seeking to co-ordinate *adult schools* in Britain since the foundation of the *Friends First-Day School Association* in 1847.

Adult Schools Association (*Studieförbundet Vuxenskolan*) One of the ten *educational associations* sponsoring *study circles* in Sweden, it is related to the Liberal political party and collaborates with the *folk high schools*. It trains its group leaders and is concerned with working with the handicapped.

Adult Services Division Formed in 1957 in the United States from the *Board of Adult Education and the Library* but still retains a major role in the

American Library Association for *adult education*.

Adult Teacher A monthly magazine started by the General Board of Education of the Methodist Church in the United States in 1945.

Adult Training Promotions Unit This unit provides all the publicity for *PICKUP* in the United Kingdom. Current address: Room 2/14, Department of Education and Science, Elizabeth House, York Road, London SE1 7PH, UK.

Adult Unemployed Programme (*REPLAN*) A programme funded by the *Department of Education and Science* and administered through the *National Institute for Adult Continuing Education, Further Education Unit*, and the *Open University* to facilitate change in the provision of *adult education* for the unemployed. It is a programme of pump-priming rather than sponsoring in order to relate education more closely to the lives of the unemployed, especially in such areas as education and training with respect to community, economic and social health and well-being. It is involved in both *vocational* and *non-vocational* aspects of education and has field officers working in the regions to oversee its programmes.

adult vocational education Education that is designed to provide either *training* or *retraining* for adults in order to assist them in gaining employment or advancement.

Adult Vocational Guidance Service The first *educational guidance service* in the United Kingdom was established in Northern Ireland in 1967 under this name, but was later retitled the *Educational Guidance Service for Adults*.

adulthood Some definitions restrict this to biological age, e.g. 20 years old, or to the legal definition, e.g. 18 years old. Others would seek to define it in terms of maturity and/or independence, while other definitions combine the two. See *adult, early adulthood, middle adulthood, late adulthood.*

Adults Learning In 1989 the *National Institute of Adult Continuing Education* in England and Wales discontinued the journal *Adult Education* and started publishing this new magazine for adult education practitioners.

advance standing The system of crediting students with parts of the *course requirements* with respect to their *prior learning.*

advanced course 1. Courses that follow an introductory or foundation course. 2. In the United Kingdom, those *further education* courses that are so designated as having advanced status.

advanced courses pool A financial system in the United Kingdom whereby all *local education authorities* subscribed funds to a central pool, controlled by the Department of Education and Science; colleges and polytechnics could receive funding for the approved advanced courses that they operated. This was sometimes referred to as pooling, It operated because not every *local education authority* was in a position to offer every advanced course so that students were forced to travel to different local education authority colleges. It became defunct in 1986.

advanced diploma Usually a post-graduate qualification in the United Kingdom, often a step towards a higher degree qualification.

advanced further education *Higher education,* not normally available to those under 18 years of age. It covers certificate, diploma, and degree-level studies. See also *non-advanced further education.*

advanced graduate standing A recognition that a student has reached a stage in the process of reading for a higher degree in the American university system.

advanced organizer A short introduction to prepare readers or listeners for the thesis or argument that is to follow, so that they can adjust themselves mentally in order to comprehend more clearly what follows.

Advanced Placement (AP) A programme of examinations of 24 college courses in 12 fields, administered by the *College Board* in the United States, and designed to measure college-level work undertaken in high schools.

advanced placement test A test designed to appraise whether a student can bypass an initial course in a college and commence at a more advanced level.

advisement An American term for supervision of *graduate students.*

advisor 1. In the United Kingdom, the term is used for a *Local Education Authority* person who is employed to advise teachers, e.g. an adult education advisor. The advisor acts as an inspector and is involved in the selection of new academic staff. 2. In the United States, the term is used to refer to one who advises students about the selection of courses and about the direction of their research.

advisory centre A centre in which educational guidance can be offered to adults.

Advisory Committee on Development Education Established to advise the government of the United Kingdom on this topic, the committee published a major report on the subject in 1978, and was abolished by the Conservative government in 1979.

Advisory Committee on Non-Award Adult Education in South Australia. Established in 1987, it published a report recommending that a Standing Committee be established to advise government, that a register of providers be established, and that a *training* *programme* for *adult educators* be established, *inter alia*.

Advisory Committee on the Supply and Education of Teachers (ACSET) See *Advisory Committee on the Supply and Training of Teachers*.

Advisory Committee on the Supply and Training of Teachers (ACSTT) A committee under the chairmanship of *J.N. Haycocks* which reported on the training of full-time and part-time tutors in *further education* and *adult education*. The report is often referred to as the *Haycocks Report*. In 1977 it recommended a two-tier two-year part-time course for fulltime further education teachers, the first year being more classroom-orientated and the second year more theoretical, leading to a Certificate of Further Education award. In addition, in 1978 it recommended a three-stage course of training for part-time adult education teachers; the first part being a short introductory course (ACSTT I), a second stage (ACSTT II) which was similar to the *City and Guilds 730, Further Education Teachers' Certificate*, and a third stage (ACSTT III) being similar to the second stage of the FE course leading to a Certificate of Education award. This latter scheme is similar to one introduced into the East Midlands in 1969. Later its name was changed to *Advisory Committee on the Supply and Education of Teachers (ACSET)*, and it was abolished by the Conservative government in the early 1980s.

Advisory Council for Adult and Continuing Education (ACACE) Established in 1977 in the United Kingdom initially for a period of three years, subsequently renewed for a further three years, to advise the Secretary of State in the fields of adult and continuing education. During its short life it published many documents and commissioned a great deal of research. The Committee was first proposed as a Development Council by the *Russell Report*. It ceased to exist in 1983 when some of its functions were assumed by the *National Institute of Adult Continuing Education*.

Advisory Council for the Education of Romany and other Travellers (ACERT) Exists in the United Kingdom to provide expert advice about education for travelling people.

advocacy To speak out on behalf of another. Often *adult educators* need to perform this role or to prepare others to perform it. The use of advocacy sometimes occurs in *human resource development*, especially when alternative strategies are being examined.

AEDNET An experimental electronic network initiated by the Adult Education Department at Syracuse University using BITNET. Electronic mail address: AEDNET @SUVM.

AEGIS This stands for *Adult Education Guided Independent Study*, the doctoral programme organized by Teachers College, Columbia University, in New York, for experienced professionals working in *adult* and *continuing education*.

aesthetics Study of the nature of art forms in society from a variety of perspectives. Both a sub-discipline of philosophy and an occasional subject on *programmes* in *adult education*.

aetiology Examination of the causes and derivations of psychological and social states.

affective domain The aspect of life that relates to the emotions or affections. Adult educators have concentrated upon this domain more systematically than have those working in *initial education*.

affective education The education of the emotions, sometimes referred to as *experiential education*, although this is a restrictive use of the concept of *experience*.

affective learning Aspects of *learning* that have been gained through emotional experiences rather than intellectualism, whether in a formal educational setting or otherwise.

affirmative action A concern of *adult education*, it is the process whereby positive action is taken in respect of minority groups and women.

African Adult Education Association The association of adult education associations in the continent of Africa which was formed in 1965 as a result of a proposal at a conference in Tanzania in 1964. It ceased to exist in 1984 when it merged with the *Afrolit Society* to form the *African Association for Literacy and Adult Education*.

African Adult Education Association Newsletter The newsletter of the *African Adult Education Association*.

African Association for Distance Education This is a pan–African association, but it does not have its own offices. Contact address: The Secretary, c/o College of Adult and Distance Education, P.O. Box 92, Kikuyu, Kenya.

African Association for Literacy and Adult Education Formed in 1984 as a result of a merger between *Afrolit Society* and the *African Adult Education Association*. Current address: P.O. Box 50768, Nairobi, Kenya.

Afrolit News The journal of the *Afrolit Society*, which acted as a communication link for literacy workers in Africa. Published in English and French.

Afrolit Society A non-governmental, non-political association of literacy workers founded in 1968. It offered a consultative service to *adult literacy* workers, developed research and provides seminars, and published a quarterly newsletter. It merged with the *African Adult Education Association* in 1984 to form the *African Association for Literacy and Adult Education*.

Age Concern This is a British national elderly people's welfare council; it publishes literature, advises clients and lobbies on behalf of the elderly. Current address: Burnard Sunley House, 60 Pitcairn Road, Mitcham, Surrey CR2 3LL, UK.

Age Concern Scotland This is the Scottish counterpart to *Age Concern*. It is concerned with the education of older people although its remit is much wider. Current address: 33 Castle Street, Edinburgh EH2 3DN, UK.

ageing Spelled 'aging' in the United States. It is the lifelong process of becoming old and a great deal of *adult education* study has been devoted to this process, so that *adult development* is a major course of study in adult education courses in *higher education* in America. The process can be controlled to some extent through physical and mental activity, so that education for ageing has become a focus of adult education. It should be noted that it is a developmental process rather than a process of decline. See *gerontology*.

Agence de Coopération Culturelle et Technique. Current address: 13 quai André Citroen, 75015 Paris, France.

Agence Nationale pour la Développement de l'Education Permamente French national association concerned with the development of *lifelong education*. Current address: Tour Franklin, Cedex 11, 92081 Paris la Défense, France.

agency 1. An organization, usually working in the *community*. Hence a *community education* organization might be referred to as agency. 2. In some studies it refers to a person or organization initiating action, as opposed to the social structures that might inhibit it. See also *agent*.

Agency for International Development Sometimes referred to as USAID. It was formed in 1961 from the *Point Four Program*. This is a US agency which is concerned with *development* of Third World countries and sends out many *adult educators* to assist with development programmes.

agenda Something to be done; a prepared list of topics to be discussed during a meeting.

agent One who acts. It could refer to one who takes the initiative in social/community activities. In sociological literature it need not be an individual but an organization which takes the initiative.

aggression A form of behaviour apparently intended to cause harm to self or others, although aggressive behaviour may stop short of actually causing harm.

Aging International The quarterly journal of the *International Federation on Aging*.

agogy Used in Europe in a similar manner to *pedagogics*. Concerns the study of *teaching and learning*.

agology Theories of agology are theories of *community education* and *development*. Term used in Belgium.

agribusiness and agricultural production The study of the production and propagation of crops and all the related business, including mechanics, marketing, and processing.

Agricola Agricultural Open Learning Agency in the United Kingdom, based at Riseholme Hall, Lincolnshire, and the Welsh Agricultural College, this is a *Manpower Services Commission* initiative to provide *open learning* and *flexi-study* for farmers and growers. Current address: Agricola, Riseholme Hall, Lincoln LN2 2LG, UK. (Note in 1988 the Manpower Services Commission changed its name to the *Training Commission* and then to the *Training Agency*.)

agricultural college A college that provides studies in agriculture. See also *land grant colleges* in the United States.

agricultural development This is the main aim of the *Cooperative Extension Service* in the United States.

agricultural extension See *Cooperative Extension Service* with reference to the United States. In the Federal Republic of Germany there is an agricultural extension service – a *continuing education* for farmers. It is based in fifty-nine offices throughout the country to which farmers are invited to participate in monthly *seminars* led by staff members of the Service. In the Federal Republic of Germany this service is free by law and all costs of the service are provided by the State.

Agricultural Extension Act See *Smith–Lever Act*.

agricultural extension agent An *adult educator* who is employed by the *Cooperative Extension Service* to act as an adviser to farmers. See *extension agent*.

Agricultural Extension and Rural Development Centre Based at the University of Reading, United Kingdom. One of the few centres in the United Kingdom which are concerned with *agricultural extension*. Current address: University of Reading, Reading RG6 2HU, Berks, UK.

agricultural school See *home economics school* in Denmark and *agricultural college* in the United Kingdom as nearest equivalents. In Denmark there are thirty-two agricultural schools and two horticultural ones. See also *Danish Association of Agricultural Schools*.

agricultural science The study of agriculture.

Agricultural Training Board The industrial training board responsible for agriculture and horticulture. Current address: Bourne House, 32–34 Beckenham Road, Beckenham, Kent BR3 4PB, UK.

aids See *audio-visual aids*.

aim The broad philosophical *goal* of the *curriculum*, or of a specific course. General statement of intention by teachers or educational organizations. See *objective*.

Aker, George Professor of adult education at Florida State University and president of the *Adult Education Association of the United States* from 1969 to 1970, Aker contributed a great deal to the development of *adult education* in Latin America. He was killed in a car accident in Panama in March 1987.

Aker Memorial Fund This fund was established after the death of *George Aker* in 1987 in his memory and is administered by Florida State University.

Akina The newsletter of the *New Zealand Association of Continuing and Community Education*, published quarterly since 1983.

Albert Mansbridge College A residential college at Leeds University named after *Albert Mansbridge*, the founder of the *Workers Educational Association*.

Alexander Report 1. See *Adult Education: The Challenge of Change*, a major report on *adult education* in Scotland. 2. A further *education* report in 1964 by this name was concerned with public relations.

Alfabetización Integral (ALPIN) The Peruvian literacy programme which is not only involved in *literacy* education, but also seeks to sustain people's ethnolinguistic personality and to raise awareness of their cultural history.

alfalit Term sometimes used to refer to the type of literacy which studies words in isolation from their social context.

Algeria The centre for *adult literacy* in Algeria is the Centre National d'Alfahabetisation. Current address: BP 251, El Biar, Algeria.

alienation A concept of self-estrangement which was made popular by the writing of Karl Marx, although it was not used first by him. It is a learned state of powerlessness, isolation, and estrangement.

alimiyah Doctoral degree in higher Islamic culture.

All-Russian Extraordinary Commission for Elimination of Illiteracy Established in Russia in 1920 to seek to eradicate illiteracy in Russia. It organized a large literacy campaign, started many schools for literacy, and published a journal, *Down with Illiteracy*.

All Union Society for the Spread of Scientific Knowledge See *Znanie*.

Allama Iqbal Open University The *Open University* of Pakistan. Established in 1974 to provide educational facilities for people who could not leave their homes or their jobs, to provide a wider education for the people, to prepare school teachers, and to offer a *vocational education* programme. It uses books and broadcasting for its courses. Many of the students are sponsored by their employers and pay no fees but there is a general policy to keep the fees as low as possible for all students. It has regional offices and uses *study centres*. The university is located in Islamabad.

Allaway, Albert John (1902–83) Professor of *adult education*, at Leicester University in the United Kingdom, an active adult educator most of his life, and author of the main study of the *Educational Centres Association*, of which he was president.

Alliance for Citizen Education An American association concerned with citizen education, which also publishes its own quarterly bulletin. Current address: Room 810, 401 North Broad Street, Philadelphia, Pennsylvania 19108, USA.

Allport, Gordon. (1897–1967) American psychologist whose work on *personality* and *prejudice* remain important in the study of adult behaviour.

alma mater An individual's old school, college, or university.

altenacademie Similar to the *University of the Third Age* and established in 1975 at the University of Dortmund, Federal Republic of Germany, about the same time as its more famous French counterpart, it offers a range of informal classes and activities.

alternative adult education The form of *adult education* designed to help the *learners* question the most fundamental values and purposes of any system and to enable them to recognize the manner by which the social system operates. See also *radical adult education*.

alternative attendance patterns Patterns of timetabling at different times each day, week, etc. to ensure that students who are prevented from attending some sessions of a course can attend others.

altruism The practice of putting the *needs* of others before one's own. Important principle in *humanistic adult education*.

alumni college Programme of studies provided by a college or university for its alumni.

alumnus/alumna (plural: alumni/ alumnae). Former student of a school, college, or university. Word more frequently used in the United States.

American Assembly of Collegiate Schools of Business An *accrediting body* in the United States. Current address: 1755 Massachusetts Avenue NW, Washington DC 20036, USA.

American Association for Adult and Continuing Education (AAACE) Formed in 1982 at the San Antonio Annual Conference, it is the result of a merger of the *Adult Education Association of the United States of America* and the *National Association for Public Continuing and Adult Education*. This has become the national association for *adult education* in the United States. It sponsors *Lifelong Learning* and *Adult Education Quarterly*, produces a regular newsletter, and organizes a national conference. It is also active in lobbying on behalf of *adult education* in the United States. Current address: 1112 16th Street NW, Suite 420, Washington DC 20036, USA.

American Association for Adult and Continuing Education Newsletter Published by *AAACE* ten times a year, then changed its title to *On-Line*. It was formerly called *Pulse of Public Continuing and Adult Education*.

American Association for Adult Education (AAAE) The *Carnegie Corporation* initiated a programme of *adult education*; in order to implement this policy a panel of experts was called in 1924 to advise the Corporation on adult education. They recommended a national organization, which was established in 1926. The first director was *Morse Cartwright* and Carnegie sponsored it until 1941. In 1951 it merged with the *Department of Adult Education of the National Education Association* to form the *Adult Education Association of the United States of America*.

American Association for Higher Education Current address: One Dupont Circle NW, Suite 780, Washington DC 20036, USA.

American Association for Vocational Instructional Materials A national institute which has pioneered a variety of instructional materials, including those on *competency-based education* for administrators. Address: 120 Driftmier Engineering Center, Athens Georgia, 30602, USA.

American Association of Colleges for Teachers Education Publishes the journal *Teacher Education* and organizes the dissemination of knowledge about teacher education in a variety of ways. Current address: One Dupont Circle NW, Washington DC 20036, USA.

American Association of Colleges of Nursing Current address: One Dupont Circle NW, Washington DC 20036, USA.

American Association of Colleges of Pharmacy Association of colleges of pharmacy in the United States. Publishes a directory of all approved colleges.

American Association of Community and Junior Colleges (AACJC) An association of community and junior colleges, active in a number of educational areas, including *literacy*. It is also involved in national discussion programmes such as the *National Issues Forum*. Publishes its own journal and a free monthly newsletter about co-operation between work, education, and the labour unions. Current address: One Dupont Circle NW, Washington DC 20036, USA.

American Association of Counselling and Guidance A professional association formed in 1952 which also maintains a large library for members. Current address: 5999, Stephenson Avenue, Alexandria, Virginia 22304, USA.

American Association of Dental Schools Current address: 1625 Massachusetts Avenue NW, Washington DC, USA.

American Association of Engineers A professional and qualifying body. Current address: 8 South Michigan Avenue, Chicago, Illinois, USA.

American Association of Land Grant Colleges and State Universities Professional association of *extension agents* as well as the formal association for agricultural extension.

American Association of Medical Colleges American co-ordinating association, involved in disseminating information about medical education. Current address: One Dupont Circle NW, Washington DC 20036, USA.

American Association of Museums Established in 1905. Whilst it has an *adult education* function, it was slow to recognize this speciality. Current address: 1225 Eye St NW, Washington DC, USA.

American Association of Retired Persons An American association which publishes its own news bulletin, the *AARP Bulletin*, and seeks to represent the interests of the elderly. Current address: 1909 K Street NW, Washington DC 20006, USA.

American Association of Sex Educators, Counselors and Therapists Address: 11 Dupont Circle NW, Washington DC 20036, USA.

American Association of State Colleges and Universities Established in 1961, this association seeks to improve standards within these institutions through corporate planning and co-operation. Current address: One Dupont Circle NW, Suite 700, Washington DC 20036, USA.

American Association of University Women Formerly *Association of Collegiate Alumnae* but changed its name in 1921. It organizes study groups for women graduates for which members of the national staff provided study guides and institutes research. Current address: 2401 Virginia Avenue NW, Washington DC 20037, USA.

American College Founded in 1922 by Solomon Huebner, this college offers a full degree programme to the life and health insurance industry of the United States. It has a single campus but many off-campus sites throughout America. Its courses are accredited by the Middle States Association of Schools and Colleges. Address: The American College, Bryn Mawr, Pennsylvania, USA.

American College of Nurse Midwives Current address: 1522 K Street NW, Washington DC, USA.

American College Testing Program Established in 1959. Provides services to secondary and post-secondary schools to support career planning, college evaluation and planning, academic and staff development programmes, and student financial aid programmes.

19

Publishes a free quarterly newsletter. Current address: 2201 North Dodge Street, Iowa City, Iowa 53343, USA.

American Council on Education (ACE) The major American organization in the field of *higher education*; most institutions of higher education are affiliated to it. Organizes a Testing Service for *General Education Development*. Its *Office on Educational Credit and Credentials* became the *Center for Adult Learning and Educational Credentials* in 1987. Current address: One Dupont Circle NW, Suite 800, Washington DC 20036, USA.

American Council on Education for Journalism Accrediting body for education in journalism. Current address: 563 Essex Court, Deerfield, Illinois 60015, USA.

American Council on Pharmaceutical Education The nationally recognized accrediting agency for education in pharmacy in the United States. It also monitors *continuing education* in the profession. Current address: 77 West Washington Street, Chicago, Illinois 60602, USA.

American Education Research Association Leading educational research association in the United States. Publishes the journal *American Educational Research Journal* and organizes conferences. Current address: 1126 16th Street, Washington DC 20036, USA.

American Educational Research Journal The journal of the *American Educational Research Association*.

American Federation of Labor/ Congress of Industrial Organizations Department of Education (AFL/CIO) These two national organizations merged in 1955. They share a department of education whose function it is to assist all affiliated organizations to develop their educational programmes. Current address: 815 17th Street NW, Washington DC 200006, USA.

American Foundation for Continuing Education Formerly the *American Foundation for Political Education*, this foundation has developed materials for discussion programmes for adults interested in public issues and political, economic, and ideological themes. It has worked closely with university extension in some parts of the United States.

American Foundation for Political Education Founded in 1951 but subsequently renamed *American Foundation for Continuing Education*.

American Institute of Industrial Engineers A professional association and *accrediting body*. Current address: 25 Technology Park, Atlanta, Georgia 30071, USA.

American Institute of Sacred Literature Established in 1889 by William Rainey Harper to provide *adult Christian education* to adults through a variety of means.

American Issues Forums Organized in 1975–76 by the *National Endowment for the Humanities* in order to provide an opportunity for public debate about national issues. It was one of the bicentennial programmes to give an intellectual basis for the celebrations. See also *National Issues Forums*.

American Journal of Distance Education Established in 1987, this journal focuses upon delivery systems in higher and continuing education for adults. Issued three times a year. Current address: Pennsylvania State University, Rackley Building, University Park, Pennsylvania 16802, USA.

American Labor Education Service Established in 1927 as a loose federation to co-ordinate workers' summer schools, but subsequently broadened its activities to help co-ordinate labour education generally, especially among white-collar workers.

American Library Association The American professional association for librarians. It has more than 40,000 institutional and individual members, and has been very active in *adult education*, especially in *adult literacy*. It established its own division of adult education in 1957. It organizes its own programmes to teach *literacy* skills and has responsibilities for *training librarians* to work with adult education. Current address: 50 East Huron Street, Chicago, Illinois 60611, USA.

American Library Association Bulletin Carries articles on adult education and the library service.

American Management Association Established in 1923, involved in all aspects of management education and training. Current address: 135 West 50th Street, New York, New York 10020, USA.

American Medical Association, Council on Medical Education Accrediting association. Current address: 535 North Dearborn Street, Chicago, Illinois 60610, USA.

American Museum Association Current address: 2233 Wisconsin Avenue NW, Washington DC 20007, USA.

American Personnel and Guidance Association Established in 1952. The professional association for counsellors. Current address: 1607 New Hampshire Avenue NW, Washington DC 20009, USA.

American Public Health Association Involved in all aspects of public health including accrediting educational programmes at *graduate level*. Current address: 2010 Massachusetts Avenue NW, Washington DC 20036, USA.

American Society for Engineering Education Current address: One Dupont Circle NW, Washington DC 20036, USA.

American Society for the Extension of University Teaching (ASEUT) In existence between 1890 and 1916, it convened the first meeting on university extension in the United States in 1891.

American Society for Training and Development (ASTD) The professional society of all who are interested in *human resource development*, especially those in industry and commerce. It has a large resource centre and publishes its own journal and newsletter. Current address: 1630 Duke Street, Box 1443, Alexandria, Virginia, USA.

American Society of Training Directors Established in 1945 to provide a service to those whose work is training in business and commerce. Runs conferences, publishes *Journal of the American Society of Training Directors*, and is organized on the basis of local chapters.

American Studies The interdisciplinary study of aspects of the life, culture, geography, etc. of America.

American Vocational Association Established in 1925 and concerned with *vocational education* throughout America. Current address: 1510 H Street NW, Washington DC 20005, USA.

Americanization education Education of immigrants into the American way of life. This began when there was pressure to educate immigrants in the early years of the twentieth century. In 1917 Congress demanded *literacy* as a requirement of naturalization. In 1918 the *Carnegie Corporation* commissioned a series of ten books on Americanization Studies: The Acculturation of Immigrant Groups into American Society. Americanization became almost synonymous with *adult education* for a period, with the result that *evening schools* gained more state support.

analysis of variance (ANOVA) Statistical technique to determine whether the differences from the mean of different sets of observations might have occurred by chance.

analytical marking The form of marking whereby an assessor checks carefully all aspects of the content and seeks to assess the overall quality of the work from an analysis of the elements assessed. See *global marking*.

Anderson, John, (d. 1796) A professor at Glasgow University who gave lectures in the city of Glasgow in applied science for the benefit of the townspeople. *Anderson's Institution* was named after him and established from his estate.

Anderson's Institution Founded in Glasgow in 1796 from the estate of *John Anderson* who sought to establish a rival university to Glasgow. It became the Glasgow Royal College of Science and Technology. See also the *mechanics institutes*, whose history is related closely with this institution.

Andhra Pradesh Open University A *distance teaching* university in India. See also the *Indira Gandhi Open University*, which is an Indian national university.

andragogee The *adult learner*.

Andragogical Centre Situated in Zagreb in Yugoslavia, this is an independent, national institution which specializes in research and programming in socio-cultural work, research for the *people's universities*, and other educational bodies. It is also concerned with the dissemination of information about adult education. Current address: 41000 Zagreb, Vojnovićeva 42/11, Yugoslavia.

andragogical cycle A system of procedures which evolve in different stages of the educational process. It has been suggested that there are six stages: study of *needs* and motives, planning the educational process, programming the educational content, preparing and organizing the process, implementing and evaluation of the process, and the product of the exercise. The andragogical cycle is a *programme-planning* exercise.

Andragogija The Yugoslavian journal of *Andragogy*, which began in 1969. Prior to that it was called *Obrazovanje odraslih*, and before that *Narodno sveučilište*, commencing originally in 1954. Its aim is to provide systematic guidance in the practice (whilst developing the theory and scientific thinking) of *adult education*.

andragogue An *adult educator* who employs *andragogic* methods in the teaching and learning transaction.

andragogy 1. First employed by a German school teacher, Alexander Knapp, in 1833 and derived from the Greek word for man. Ever since there has been a debate as to whether adults learn differently from children, and whether andragogy differs from *pedagogy*. 2. In the United States this term has been popularized by the work of *M. Knowles*, who defined it as the art and science of helping adults learn, and who originally maintained that andragogy was a process different from pedagogy. His definition has been disputed by many scholars, but remains quite potent in adult education literature. 3. In Holland andragogy means the overall study of social work, community organization, and adult education, which is similar to the manner in which it is employed in other parts of Europe, especially Eastern Europe. There the term refers not to the process of adults learning but to the field of study of *adult education*. 4. In Yugoslavia andragogy departments have been established in the universities and bachelors, masters, and doctoral degrees are awarded in andragogy. It will be noted that in Yugoslavia, where these departments have been established, various forms of andragogy have emerged and the term is now used in a similar manner to *education* in the United Kingdom. See, for instance, *penal andragogy*.

andragology The Dutch employ the term for the study or science of *andragogy*. The term was first used in the Netherlands when Ten Have published an article in the periodical *Volksopvoeding* in 1960. In the same article he also employed the term *social agogy*.

Andrew Norman Institute Established in 1981 in the United States with a grant from the Andrew Norman Foundation, this institute was founded for the advanced study of geriatrics and gerontology and is located in the *Andrus Gerontology Center.*

Andrus Gerontology Center (Percy Ethel Andrus) Situated in the University of Southern California, this is one of the leading centres for the study of *gerontology.* Considerable work in *educational gerontology* has emanated from this centre.

animateur One who is involved in *animation,* a *facilitator* of learning, but regarded as distinct from one who is a *trainer.* Usually employed in *popular education* in France.

animation Short for 'animation socio-culturelle' it means socio-cultural *community development* but is usually used in the abbreviated form. It is a form of *community education* in France.

Annan Committee Report submitted in March 1977 which recommended that the proposed fourth channel on British television should contain a large proportion of educational broadcasting, including the broadcasts of the *Open University.* This proposal was never put into operation as the Committee had proposed.

annotated bibliography A *bibliography* which contains notes on each item within it.

anomie The condition of normlessness, in which one feels out of touch with the surrounding norms and values. A sociological concept which has been used within educational theory.

Antigonish Movement Started by *Father James Tompkins* but made famous by *Moses Coady* in 1928, on the establishment of the *extension service* of St Francis Xavier University in Nova Scotia when *Moses Coady* became director. It was a blending of Christian

ethics, *adult education,* and social justice in which the poor fishing people of Nova Scotia were encouraged to discuss their own problems, engage in *self-help* and create their own co-operation movement.

Antigua and Barbuda Adult Education Association Current address: c/o Department of Extra-Mural Studies, University of West Indies, P.O. Box 142, St. John's, Antigua, West Indies.

Anti-Poverty Program Educational and other programmes undertaken in America in order to help relieve poverty.

anti-racism training A form of *affective education* which seeks to make people aware of racist attitudes and prejudices. See *racism awareness training.*

anxiety 1. A general state of *stress,* unease, etc. 2. In learning theory the term refers to a conditioned drive which functions to motivate avoidance responding (a movement away from an unpleasant goal), so that avoidance response is reinforced by the reduction in anxiety.

AONTAS The Irish National Association of Adult Education, established in 1969. Current address: 14 Fitzwilliam Place, Dublin 2, Republic of Ireland.

Aontas Review The journal of the Irish association *AONTAS,* launched in 1979. Published twice a year.

Apex Trust An organization which runs educational day centres throughout the United Kingdom for persons released from prison. Current address: 31–33 Clapham Road, London SW9, UK.

a posteriori A proposition which can only be known to be true or false by reference to a known actuality.

Appalachian Regional Development Act Passed in 1955 in the United States to make federal funds available for *vocational education* in the poor regions of Appalachia.

applied research Research activities designed to investigate specific problems for which immediately applicable findings are required.

appraisal An estimation of an adult education procedure, an evaluation of a person's performance, e.g. on an annual basis and conducted by either a peer or a superior within an employing organization.

appreciation classes Adult classes organized to help adults learn to appreciate the *arts*, i.e. to learn about their qualities. It should be recognized that there are a number of facets to this and they include the artistic skill of the artist and the subjective exercise that relates to learning to appreciate *high culture*.

apprentice libraries Such *libraries* were established in New York and Boston about 1820 and associated with the mechanics schools that were founded there.

apprenticeship Derived from the Latin *apprehendere*, to learn. It has always referred to the method whereby a young person was attached to a master craftsman in order to learn a trade or an occupation. Hence it became known as 'sitting by Nellie', because it was basically a matter of copying the expert. It was one of the earliest forms of *vocational education*, primarily of the poor, and although it was vocational there was often opportunity provided to learn to read and write. In recent years the traditional methods employed in apprenticeship have been criticized by those having more preparation in the skills of educating adults.

approved training organization An organization which is approved by the *Manpower Services Commission* in the United Kingdom to mount *youth training scheme* courses. (Note: in 1988 the *Manpower Services Commission* changed its name to the *Training Commission* and then to the *Training Agency*.)

a priori Knowledge arrived at without reference to experience. It is often the premise from which *deduction* begins.

aptitude 1. *Skill* or ability that assists in the *learning process*. 2. In *mastery learning*, the time required to *learn* a specific task to a given level under ideal conditions.

aptitude test An examination designed to measure a person's potential to learn to perform certain forms of activity.

Arab Educational, Cultural and Scientific Organization A regional council for *adult education*, affiliated to the *International Council for Adult Education*. Current address: Mohammed V Street, P.O. Box 1120, Tunis, Tunisia.

Arab Literacy and Adult Education Organization (ARLO) The Arab regional literacy organization. Current address: 113 Abu Nawas Street, Baghdad, Iraq.

Arbeitsstelle der Deutschen Evangelischen Arbeitsgemeinschaft für Erwachsenenbildung The *Protestant Association of Adult Education* in West Germany. One of the main *adult education providers* with programmes covering a wide range of the humanities and social sciences, with some few in science and technology. Offers over 100,000 programmes a year to more than 3 million participants. Works closely with the *Catholic Association of Adult Education*. Current address: Schillerstrasse 58, 7500 Karlsruhe, Federal Republic of Germany.

archives The historical records of an institution.

area college A *college of further education* in the United Kingdom which offers some *advanced work*. Some now call themselves colleges of further and higher education.

area co-ordinator An *adult educator* who co-ordinates the provision of *adult* *education* throughout a geographical area, often a section of an area *adult education institution*.

area principal The *principal* of an *adult education institute* which is situated on a number of different sites within a given geographical area. This idea of area institutions has often resulted from the merger of local institutions by local government in the United Kingdom to try to make *adult education* provision by *local education authorities* more cost-effective.

area vocational education school A department of a *community college, university* or high school in the United States which provides occupational preparation in at least five different occupations, and which acts under the supervision of the State Board.

Argentina *Adult education* in this country is organized by the Ministry. Current address: Dirección Nacional de Educación del Adulto, Ministerio de Cultura y Educación, Belgrano 637, 1092 Buenos Aires, Argentina. See also *Documentación e informatión, Centro multinacional educatión adultos.*

Argentine Association of Distance Education A national association involved in the dissemination of information about *distance education* to all its members. It is also involved with the training of teachers, assistance to providers, and research into distance education. Current address: ULSA Educación a Distancia, Independencia 338, C.C.P. 9, 1653 Villa Ballester, Argentina.

Argyris, Chris (b. 1923) Professor of Education and Organizational Behavior at Harvard University and author (and co-author with *Donald Schon*) of many influential books on *learning, reflection,* and *action.*

Aristotle (384–322 BC) Greek philosopher, born in Stagira and pupil of *Plato*, although later in his life he seems to have diverged a little from his Platonic basis. He was concerned with *reasoning*. Much of his philosophy has survived intact but little usage has been made of it as yet in the *philosophy of adult education*.

arithmetic mean Statistical measure of central tendency. Usually referred to as the *mean*.

Arkleton Trust Awards mid-career fellowships to people involved in *rural development* and *education*. Address: Unstone, Oxford OX7 4HH, UK.

armed forces education A great deal of the *education of adults*, of both a *vocational* and *non-vocational* nature occurs within the armed services, but in some countries – such as the United Kingdom – the initial qualification for an education officer tends to be that of school teacher rather than *adult educator*.

Armed Services Vocational Attitude Battery (ASVAB) The military services in the United States are no longer recruiting entrants who do not have *General Education Development*, but there is an alternative route in which recruits are required to take this series of tests.

Army Bureau of Current Affairs (ABCA) Established in 1941 in the United Kingdom and continued until 1951, this bureau issued bulletins on current affairs and information about the progress of the war. The information provision was itself a major form of *adult education*.

Army Continuing Education System (ACES) A comprehensive programme of education from *adult basic education* through to higher degrees. It also involves skills and counselling. It is administered to all army service members in the United States.

Army Education Corps Corps in the army devoted to the education of personnel in the United Kingdom.

Arnold Report Published in 1960 in the United Kingdom, it recommended the introduction of specific certification, including *Ordinary* and *Higher National Certificates and Diplomas*. These were replaced in the 1980s.

Art for the People Started in 1935 by the *British Institute of Adult Education*, it was an exhibition accompanied by experts who initiated informal teaching sessions with those who came to view. It resulted in the formation of the *Council for the Encouragement of Music and the Arts*. The scheme was taken over by the *Arts Council* in 1949.

artificial intelligence The capacity of a machine or other device to perform functions that are normally associated with human *intelligence*.

artificial language Created languages, such as Esperanto, to foster international communication.

artist 1. One who is engaged in creative and performing arts. 2. A painter, one who draws.

arts The arts usually refers to drama, film, literature, music, painting, poetry, and sculpture – what some sociologists would call *high culture*. However, there is not general agreement on its constitution although there is more agreement on the fact that the arts are a *social construct*.

Arts and Humanities Program Concerned with the improvement of education in these areas both in schools and in the education of adults in the United States, organized by the *National Center for Educational Research and Development*.

Arts Council of Great Britain Established in 1946 by royal charter as a result of the successful efforts of the *Council for the Encouragement of Music and the Arts* during the Second World War. The charter was renewed in 1967 to develop and improve knowledge of the arts, increase their accessibility, and to advise national and local government about the arts. Its members are government-appointed. It is responsible for much innovation in the *arts* and support of many established enterprises. It has its own education unit and publishes its own *Education Bulletin*. It works through local regional councils. Current address: 105 Piccadilly, London W1V 0AV, UK.

Ashby Committee The Ashby Committee was appointed in June 1953 to investigate the organization and finance of adult education in England and Wales, under the chairmanship of Sir Eric Ashby, with special reference to *Responsible Body* funding. The Committee considered that the funding arrangements were satisfactory and it recommended that the automatic grant of 75 per cent should be abolished and a grant not exceeding 75 per cent of teaching costs should be fixed annually for each Responsible Body a recommendation which was accepted by the government in office.

Ashby Report Published in 1954. See *Ashby Committee*.

Asian and South Pacific Bureau of Adult Education (ASPBAE) A regional international adult education organization having members from different national adult education organizations in the South Pacific. The secretariat is based in Colombo, Sri Lanka. Current address: c/o The National Association of Total Education, 30/63A Langden Place, Colombo 7, Sri Lanka.

Asian Resource Centre Established in Birmingham in 1977, this centre encourages *self-help* in a run-down area of the city. It seeks to encourage Asian projects which promote a sense of community and ethnic pride. It is a *community development* resource centre.

Asociación Costarricense de Educación de Adultos Costa Rican association of adult education. Current address: Heredia Costa Rica Avda, 8 CS 6–8 Heredia, Costa Rica.

Asociación de Educadores de Adultos de Nicaragua Nicaraguan association of adult educators. Current address: Departmento de Educación de Adultos, Ministerio de Educación, Publica Escuela Normal Barrio La Fuente, Managua, D.N. Nicaragua.

Asociación de Educatores de Adultos del Paraguay Association of *adult educators* of Paraguay. Current address: Fulgencio R Moreno casi Mexico, Asuncion, Paraguay.

Asociación para la Enseñanza de la Mujer (Association of Women's Education) Founded by the *Free Institution of Education* in Spain but its activities ceased with the Civil War. See *Instituto de la Mujer*.

Asociación Pro Educación de Adultos The *adult education* association of Honduras. Current address: Calle La Fuente 720, Frente Embajada Alemana, Tegucigalpa D.C., Honduras.

assertiveness training A technique to help people understand the effects of their socialization upon them and so free them from it in order to enhance personal relationships and renegotiate social situations. It promotes self-confidence and well-being. Used in some forms of *professional education* and in women's groups.

assessment The process of placing a value upon, deciding the degree of excellence of, adjudging standard(s) of, or deciding the correctness of an artefact, piece of academic work, performance, or procedure. The process is largely subjective although the degree of subjectivity depends upon the condition of knowledge underlying the work, procedure, or performance, etc. For instance, the level of correctness of simple mathematical knowledge may be assessed much more objectively than the social skills expertise of a professional practitioner. There have been many attempts to make assessment more objective, e.g. the use of *multiple choice questions* and the preparation of

assessment criteria, but the extent to which the subjectivity has been removed is debatable.

assessment of prior learning (APL) The measurement of learning that has been acquired outside of formal educational institutions and is uncertificated.

assessment pack Often prepared to accompany *study packs* by *distance learning* institutions, they consist of a series of *computer marked assignments, self-assessment questions*, etc.

assimilation The tendency to absorb, distort, or alter encounters to make them fit existing cognitive structures.

assimilator A *learning style* in which people prefer to learn from the abstract rather than from people.

assistant professor The first rank of university teacher in the United States. Equivalent to a university lecturer in the United Kingdom.

Associação Portuguesa para a Cultura e Educação Permanente Portuguese adult education association. Current address: Rue de S. Domingos á Lapa – 111–3, 1200 Lisbon, Portugal.

Associació d'Educació Permanent d'Adults (AEPA) Catalonian (Spanish) *adult education* association. Current address: Francesc Cambó, 14 8 F, 08003 Barcelona, Spain.

associate degree An award for the successful completion of studies requiring at least two years fulltime college-level study but less than the four years required for a *bachelor's degree* in the United States.

associate professor The second level of university professor in the United States, somewhat closer to senior lecturer in the United Kingdom.

associate student Term used in the *Open University* in the United Kingdom for a learner who is registered as a student with the university but paying the full course fee for an individual credit/half-credit course, although not registered for the full degree programme. See also *guest student*.

Associated Resource Centers in Adult Education (ARCAE) A group in the United States seeking to promote networks and create relationships among adult education resource centres, both nationally and internationally.

association A term used to refer to the type of learning that occurs through the connection of two or more diverse ideas or events. A form of *synthesis*.

Association for Community-Based Education A US national membership organization and force linked to *community development*, founded in 1976. Formerly called *Clearinghouse for Community Based Free Standing Educational Institutions*. Members of this organization tend to serve the educational *needs* of people which are not being met by established educational institutions. The association offers technical advice to members, acts as an advocate for *community education* in America, establishes standards, awards scholarships to needy recipients, organizes a loan assistance programme, has a publishing programme, and organizes conferences and workshops. *Adult literacy* features highly in its work. Current address: 1806 Vernon Street NW, Washington DC 20009, USA.

Association for Continuing Education, Malaysia Formed in the early 1980s to encourage further involvement in *continuing education*, to serve as a centre for research, provide and disseminate information, and organize programmes, conferences, and seminars. Current address: c/o Faculty of Education, University of Malaya, Kuala Lumpur, Malaysia.

Association for Continuing Higher Education (ACHE) A national association in America concerned with *continuing education* within *higher education*. It has no fixed address but moves to the university at which its officers are employed. Current address: University of Tennessee, 451 Communication Building, Knoxville, Tennessee 37916, USA.

Association for Continuing Professional Education An American association concerned with the development of *continuing education* in *higher education*. Its address moves to the universities in which its officers are employed. Current address: 402 Graham Hall, Northern Illinois University, De Kalb, Illinois 60115, USA.

Association for Cultural and Social Development (CODECAL) A Latin American association concerned with *popular education*. It runs courses, publishes literature, conducts research, and offers an advisory service. Current address: Apartado Aéreo, 20439 Bogotá, Colombia.

Association for Educational Activities Founded in 1943 in Finland, it is involved in *lifelong education*, organizes some *study centres*, and disseminates knowledge about *adult education* generally. Publishes its own journal *Study Circle Member* (Opintokerholainen). Address: Pohj. Rautatiekatu 23B, 00100 Helsinki 10, Finland.

Association for Educational and Training Technology (AETT) Concerned with instructional technology, this voluntary body holds conferences, stages exhibitions and courses, and has a number of regular publications. Current address: BLAT Centre, BMA House, Tavistock Square, London WC1H 9JP, UK.

Association for Educational Communication and Technology Formerly the *Department of Audio-Visual Instruction* of the National Educational Association. Concerned with *education, training*, and *educational technology*.

Current address: 1126 16th Street NW, Washington DC, USA.

Association for Educational Gerontology Formed in the United Kingdom in 1985. It has within its membership English and international adult educators. Its purpose is to promote the study of education and ageing. It publishes a biannual journal, *Journal of Educational Gerontology*, and organizes an annual conference. Current address: c/o Dept of Adult and Continuing Education, University of Keele, Keele, Staffs ST5 5BG, UK.

Association for Field Services in Teacher Education American association with concerns in *adult education*. Current address: Indiana State University, Division of Continuing Education, Terre Haute, Indiana 47809, USA.

Association for Folk High School Work in the Netherlands See *Vereniging voor volkshogeschoolwerk*.

Association for Free Cultural Activities Established in 1978 in Finland to work mainly with young adults in the fields of *adult education* and culture. Politically non-committed. Current address: Simonkatu 12A, 00100 Helsinki 10, Finland.

Association for Gerontology in Higher Education Addresses the increasing concern for the study of gerontology in *higher education* in the Western world as the population ages. Current address: 1835 K Street NW, Suite 305, Washington DC 20006, USA.

Association for Hospital Medical Education An American association concerned with the development of *medical education* in hospitals. Current address: 1911 Jefferson Davies Highway, Suite 905, Arlington, Virginia 22202, USA.

Association for Liberal Education Established to promote views about liberal education in the United Kingdom.

The association holds conferences and publishes a magazine.

Association for Media and Technology in Education in Canada Professional group of academics in Canada. Current address: c/o Faculty of Education, Queen's University, Kingston, Ontario, Canada.

Association for Part-Time Higher Education (APHE) Established in 1987 to serve as a national forum and lobby group for those concerned with part-time *higher education*. Its aims are to exchange information regarding practices and problems, help improve the effectiveness of part-time higher education, and promote the interests of those involved within the field. Current address: 43 Gordon Square, London WC1H 0PD, UK.

Association for Popular Education: Scandinavia–Latin America Established on 3 March 1988 at the *Nordic Folk Academy*. The concerns of the association are human rights, the situation of women, problems of minority groups, etc. Membership is open to any individual living in Scandinavia or Latin America. Current address: c/o Nordens Folkiga Akademi, P.O. Box 1004, S-442 25 Kungalv, Sweden.

Association for Recognised English Language Teaching Establishments in Britain Current address: 125 High Holborn, London WC1V 6QD, UK.

Association for Recurrent Education (ARE) Established in 1975 to promote and disseminate views about *recurrent education*. The association has an individual membership, and publishes a newsletter and a number of discussion papers. In addition, it holds an annual conference. Current address: c/o Centre for Research into the Education of Adults, Cherry Tree Buildings B, University Park, Nottingham NG7 2RD, UK.

29

Association for the Encouragement of Popular Scientific Knowledge Established in 1912. This marked the beginning of many *popular universities* in Holland.

Association for the Establishment of Folk High Schools Formed in Holland in 1931 with the express intention of developing and renewing popular culture through the formation of *folk high schools*, where there could be residential education rather than the more formal lecture-type education offered by the *popular universities* and the *folk houses*.

Association for the Study of Medical Education A professional body of medical educators in the United Kingdom. Current address 150b, Perth Road, Dundee, DD1 4EA, UK.

Association Française pour la Formation Professionnelle des Adultes French professional adult education association. Current address: 13, Place de Villiers, 93103 Montreuil Cédex, France.

Association Méditerranienne d'Éducation des Adultes The Mediterranean Association of Adult Education. Current address: Rue St Maur 108–110, 75011 Paris, France.

Association Nationale pour la Formation Professionelle des Adultes (AFPA) The French national association for professional *adult education*. Current address: 13 Place de Villiers, 93108 Montreuil Cedex, France.

Association Nationale pour le Développement de Education Permanente (ADEP) Current address: Tour Franklin, Cedex 11, 92081 Paris le Défense, France.

Association of Adult and Continuing Education The professional association for people who work full time in *adult education* and *continuing education* in the United Kingdom. In 1984 it amalgamated with the *National Association for Teachers in Further and Higher Education*.

Association of Adult Education Centres Finnish organization. Its membership consists of municipalities and sponsoring organizations of *adult education* centres. Established in 1919, it is involved in looking after the interests of the centres, training activities, and some research. Publishes a journal, *'Adult Education Centre Journal'* (Opisto-lehti), eight times a year. Current address: Cygnaeksenkatu 4B, 00100 Helsinki, Finland.

Association of Adult Religious Educators Established in 1984, this association emerged from the National Board of Religious Inspectors and Advisors of the Roman Catholic Church in England, and is now an autonomous professional Roman Catholic group. Contact address: The Catechetical Centre, St Vincent's, The Roman Way, West Denton, Newcastle upon Tyne NE15 7LT, UK.

Association of American Colleges Current address: 1818 R Street NW, Washington DC 20009, USA.

Association of American Medical Colleges This association is involved in research into the principles of adult learning and endeavours to apply them to the *continuing education* of health care professionals. Current address: One Dupont Circle, Suite 300, Washington DC 20036, USA.

Association of Boards of Evening Schools in the Netherlands See *Vereniging van besturen van avondscholen en avondscholengemeenschappen in Nederland*.

Association of British Chambers of Commerce National body co-ordinating the local chambers, concerned with *education* and *training*. Current address: 68 Queen Street, London EC4N 1SN, UK.

Association of British Correspondence Colleges Central

body of the *correspondence colleges* in the United Kingdom. It seeks to enhance their prestige. Current address: 6 Francis Grove, London SW19 4DT, UK.

Association of British Travel Agents Training Board (ABTA) This board is responsible for training within the travel industry in Britain. Current address: Waterloo House, 11–17 Chertsey Road, Woking, Surrey GU21 5AL, UK.

Association of Centres of Adult Theological Education (ACATE) One of the Christian *adult education* associations in the United Kingdom. It publishes its own journal, the *Journal of Adult Theological Education.*

Association of Colleges for Further and Higher Education A national association concerned with *tertiary education* in the United Kingdom. Current address: Doncaster Metropolitan Institute of Higher Education, High Melton, Doncaster DN5 7SZ, UK.

Association of Collegiate Alumnae Established in 1862, it changed its name in 1921 to *American Association of University Women.* It was established for many reasons, including that of raising standards of education for women in higher education.

Association of Community Workers UK organization open to all people interested in *community work*, including *adult educators*. It has its own publications and networks. Current address: Grindon Lodge, Beech Grove Road, Newcastle upon Tyne NE4 2RS, UK.

Association of Danish Evening and Youth Schools The Danish association which voices the professional concerns of teachers of adults in Denmark. Address: Christiansborggade 1, DK-1558 Copenhagen V, Denmark.

Association of Finnish Adult Education Organizations Established in 1969, it is the co-ordinating body of organizations working in the field of adult education in Finland. It also

assumes an international role on behalf of Finnish adult education and is involved in policy-making, It arranges training and disseminates information about Finnish adult education. There are eight national organizations associated with this body. Address: Hietalahdenkatu 8, 00180 Helsinki, 18 Finland, or Museokatu 18 A 9, SF-001000 Helsinki, Finland.

Association of Hungarian Teachers Established in 1979, this is the association of those who work in *cultural houses* as *adult educators* in Hungary.

Association of Independent Colleges and Schools American association concerned with *adult education*. Current address: 1730 M Street NW, Suite 401, Washington DC 20036, USA.

Association of Institutes for Correspondence Education The Dutch association for *accredited correspondence education* institutions. See *Vereniging van instellingen schriftelijk onderwijs.*

Association of Laity Centres An association of Christian *adult education* centres in the United Kingdom. Membership is open to centres, organizations, and individuals and is ecumenical.

Association of Media-Based Continuing Education for Engineers A non-credit educational organization which utilizes the educational satellite network in America to provide updated courses for engineers.

Association of Northern Ireland Education and Library Boards This is the national association of *local education authorities* in Northern Ireland. Current address: City Hall, Belfast BT1 5GT, UK.

Association of Nurse Education This is a professional association for nurse tutors in Britain. Current address: The Royal College of Nursing, Cavendish Place, London, UK.

Association of People's and Workers' Universities Each state in Yugoslavia has its own association in which all the *people's universities* and *workers' universities* are represented. There are eight separate associations in the country.

Association of Polish Adult Educators Established in 1981 to integrate Polish adult educators and their *andragogical skills* with the formation of ideological, social, and moral attitudes. Current address: Association of Polish Adult Educators, ul Nowogradzka 31, pok. 413, 00–511 Warazawa, Poland.

Association of Principals and Teachers of Day/Night Schools in the Netherlands See *Vereniging van rectoren/directouren en docenten aan dag/avondscholen.*

Association of Recognised English Language Schools National association of independent language schools. Current address: 43 Russell Square, London WC1B 5DH, UK.

Association of Social Research Organisations UK association. Current address: Overseas Development Institute, Regent's College, Inner Circle, Regent's Park, London NW1 4NS, UK.

Association of Teacher Educators Established in the United States in 1921 for those involved in teacher education. Current address: 1201 16th Street NW, Washington DC 20036, USA.

Association of Teachers in Colleges and Departments of Education (ATCDE) The professional association for those concerned with teacher training in the United Kingdom until it merged with the *Association of Teachers in Technical Institutions* to form the *National Association of Teachers in Further and Higher Education* at the time when the monotechnic colleges of education were being merged with other institutions of *higher education.*

Association of Teachers in Technical Institutions (ATTI) Professional association for teachers in *colleges of further education* which merged with the *Association of Teachers in Colleges and Departments of Education.*

Association of Teachers of Lip-Reading to Adults An association which accredits those who wish to teach lip-reading. Has its own journal. It can be contacted: c/o Central London Adult Education Institute, The City Literary Institute, Stukeley Street, Drury Lane, London WC2B 5LJ, UK.

Association of Tutors in Adult Education Formerly an association of those academic adult educators who worked in *university extra-mural departments* in the United Kingdom.

Association of University Evening Colleges (AUEC) Established in 1939, it has been a significant body in the development of *adult education* in the United States. It has been associated with the establishment of the *Center for the Study of Liberal Education for Adults.*

Association of Women's Studies Programs for Latin America Formed in 1981 and based in Mexico. Contact address: c/o Third World Center for Economic and Social Studies, Coronel Porfirio Diaz 50, San Jeronomo Lidice, Mexico 20 D.F.

Association to Promote the Higher Education of Working Men Established by *Albert Mansbridge* in 1903 as the precursor of the *Workers Educational Association.* The association was formally launched at the Oxford Extension Summer Meeting in August of that year, with Mansbridge as secretary. The association's name was changed in 1905 to *Workers Educational Association.*

associative learning See *association.*

Associazione Italiana di Educazione degli Adulti (AIDEA) An Italian association of adult education which was formed in 1983 and publishes its own newsletter, *Notizie*. Current address: Via Thailandia 12, 00144 Rome, Italy. See *Italy*.

Aston Training Scheme A two-year course of preparation for the ministry of the Anglican Church in the United Kingdom, organized on a part-time basis, using educational material devised by the *Open University, National Extension College*, and some of its own. The course includes residential weekend study, and has a handbook and newsletter.

Athabasca University Founded in 1970, but not formally established until 1978, in Alberta, Canada to explore and institute new procedures in curriculum organization and instruction. It has become a *distance teaching* university offering undergraduate programmes, but also offers preparatory courses for adults returning to study at university level. Additionally, it offers higher degree programmes as well. The university uses a system of learning centres, similar to *study centres*, and has a number of regional offices throughout Canada. Current address: Athabasca University, Suite 120, 1040–7 Avenue, SW, Calgary, Alberta, Canada T2P 3G9.

attention The ability to concentrate upon one phenomenon and exclude other possible phenomena from the immediate perception.

attention span The length of time that a person can continue to concentrate without distraction.

attitude 1. An orientation towards some phenomenon, having cognitive, affective, evaluative, and connative components. 2. A combination of a perception and a judgement which often results in an emotive orientation towards a phenomenon. 3. Attitudes often occur as the third dimension of *syllabii* in *professional education* curricula, along with *knowledge* and *skills*.

attitude scale Ranking scale designed to measure traits of *personality*.

attitude survey The use of survey techniques using *attitude scales* to measure *attitudes*. Useful in *needs assessment, human resource development*.

attitude test An examination designed to assess the *attitudes* held by an individual or a group towards some particular phenomenon.

Attleborough Experiment A *community education* project in the town of Attleborough in Norfolk, United Kingdom, it was an ambitious attempt to discover the learning needs of an entire rural community and to meet them. There was a substantial degree of media involvement and the project is well-documented.

attrition rate Drop-out rate.

Atwater Library of Montreal Founded in 1828 as the *Montreal Mechanics Institution*, it was the first *mechanics institute* to be established in Canada.

audience reaction team A group of persons who are primed to interrupt a speaker in order to assist in clarifying points that might appear obscure.

audio–cassette A prepared cassette containing *learning material* which might be included in a *study pack* prepared for either *distance learning* or *self-directed study*.

audio–conferencing A telephone networking system that enables a group of *learners* to interact simultaneously with the *teacher* and with each other. Used in some forms of *distance education*.

audio–recording 1. A research technique that uses a tape recorder to record answers to questions or any other form of audio-data. 2. A teaching technique that employs audio-recordings to stimulate *discussion*, transmit information, etc.

audio–typing The ability to type directly from a prepared *audio cassette*.

audio-visual aid (AVA) A device to assist in the teaching and learning process using drawings, diagrams, models, or technical machines.

audio-visual instruction Teaching which employs a variety of media in the presentation, i.e. the use of *audio-visual aids*.

audit Literally, the correction and presentation of financial statements detailing the activities of an organization. It has come to assume a meaning in education relating to the collation of an assessment of an occupational performance.

Aulas de Cultura – Boletin Informativo de Educación de Adultos A biannual Spanish newsletter, established in 1985, about *adult education*.

aural learner One who learns best through listening.

Australian Association of Adult Education The professional association for *adult education* in Australia. Formed in 1960, its first secretary was Dr Desmond William Crowley, a New Zealander who settled in Australia. The association publishes a newsletter and organizes a national conference. Current address: G.P.O. Box 1346, Canberra, A.C.T. 2604, Australia.

Australian Association of Community Education Current address: c/o Continuing Education, Chisholm Institute of Technology, Mcmahons Road, Frankston, Victoria 33199, Australia.

Australian Consortium on Experiential Education A consortium of individuals working in all forms of education, schooling, colleges, universities, business, industry, and the public services, all devoted to the promotion of *experiential learning*. Current address: c/o P.O. Box 187, Rozelle, New South Wales, 2039, Australia.

Australian Council for Adult Literacy The official body in Australia to deal with *adult literacy* provision, implementing the government's proposed national campaign of 1987–88. Current address: c/o Council of Adult Education, 256 Flinders Street, Melbourne 3000, Australia.

Australian Highway The journal of the Australian *Workers' Educational Association*. See *Highway*.

Australian Institute of Training and Development (AITD) Australia's professional institute for *training officers*. In Australia there is a separate division in each state.

Australian Journal of Adult Education The journal of the *Australian Association of Adult Education*, published three times a year since 1961.

Australian Securities Institute The professional institution, awarding degrees and professional qualifications for all those who work in stockbroking and other securities occupations in Australia.

Australian Technical and Further Education Council (TAFE) This body has established a clearinghouse with computerized information about research, curriculum developments, feasibility studies, etc. Current address: 296 Payneham Road, Payneham 5070, Australia.

Austrian Association of Folk High Schools Current address: Wienytaubengasse 13, A 1020 Vienna, Austria.

author/authoress One who composes a book, article, paper, or other piece of written work.

authoritarian personality Associated with the work of T. Adorno, the authoritarian personality both receives and obeys legitimate authority but also acts in an authoritarian manner when placed in a position of *authority*.

authoritarianism The exercise of *authority*, often in an insensitive manner. An ideology of teaching in which the 'teacher knows best' and presents the material for the students to learn in an uncompromising, non-democratic manner.

authority A form of legitimized power. Within the education of adults, it is perhaps the authority of the teacher that requires some clarification. As an employee of an educational institution, the teacher exercises authority by virtue of the contractual relationship between the employing institution and the employee/teacher. In this instance the teacher is *in* authority. As a professional, the teacher has a professional authority vested in him/her by virtue of the judgement of both peers and students, who acknowledge the level of professional expertise demonstrated in knowledge and practice. In this instance the teacher is *an* authority.

authority figure A person who is perceived by others to be in or to have authority as a result of a dominant presence.

autobiographical method See *life history* method of research, whereby the researcher seeks to understand a phenomenon, like *learning*, through the study of autobiography.

autocrat One who exercises great power with sole authority.

autocratic Action which is *authoritarian* and allows for little opportunity for discussion.

autodidact A person who is self-taught. See *self-directed learning*. There was a long history of autodidacticism in England among the working-class movement until the growth of the secondary school system, which has apparently resulted in a decline in the number of self-taught individuals.

Autoeducación – Revista de Educación Popular Popular education review, published in Spanish in Peru three times a year since 1981.

autonomous learner 1. See *self-directed learner*. Although these terms are not quite the same conceptually, since the word *autonomy* has distinct connotations, they tend to be used synonymously. 2. One who has the capability to learn independently and to choose the mode of *learning* best suited for the learning task.

autonomy The philosophical idea that the individual's will and actions are governed only by his/her own principles and laws rather than by external constraints. This is a philosophical position espoused by *humanistic adult educators*. See *freedom*.

auto-tutorial devices Aids that can be employed by the *autodidact* or by other learners independently of a teacher.

Avalon College See *Ruskin College*, the name that it assumed in 1900.

average The *arithmetic mean* is the usual measure of average although both the *mode* and the *median* are measures of average.

aversion therapy A form of therapeutic *learning* which seeks to eliminate undesirable behaviour by *conditioning* a person to associate the behaviour to be changed with unpleasant experiences.

Avoncroft College Established in 1921 in the Vale of Evesham in the United Kingdom. Moved to Stoke Prior in Worcestershire in 1935. One of the residential colleges founded by the Cadbury Trust, having an agricultural bias. See also *Woodbrooke College*.

award 1. A student prize. 2. A grant towards fees. 3. Formal recognition, such as a certificate, diploma, etc. indicating the successful completion of a course of study.

award unit The amount of credit that is given to a specific course of study, e.g. a *credit hour*.

awareness day Started in December 1986 in the United Kingdom, sponsored by the *Manpower Services Commission*. Mixed groups of *participants* who attend a college to get a taste of a subject area. (Note: the *Manpower Services Commission* changed its name to the *Training Commission* and then to the *Training Agency* in 1988.)

Awareness List The *International Bureau of Education* publishes these lists in a variety of educational topics to help scholars and libraries keep abreast with recent publications in specific areas.

B.A. Bachelor of Arts.

baccalaureate 1. The French school-leaving examination, taken at the end of secondary school in order to achieve qualification for university entrance. 2. When referring to a degree, it is the first-level degree. It is always used this way in French-speaking universities, some European universities, and occasionally in the United States.

bachelors degree The first level of degree award by universities. It may be awarded in a variety of subjects, from education to the arts, sciences, etc. In some countries, such as the United Kingdom, it is awarded as a result of a three-year course of study, whilst in other countries, such as the United States, it is the result of a four-year programme of study.

Bacie Journal The journal of the *British Association for Commercial and Industrial Education*, published six times per annum.

B.Ad.Ed. Bachelor of Adult Education. Degree awarded by the University of Zimbabwe through courses run in its Adult Education Department. Students are expected to specialize in one area of: design and delivery on instruction; administration and supervision of personnel in adult education; research and local investigation.

Badger, Colin R. Founder of the Council of Adult Education in Melbourne and the director of Adult Education in the State of Victoria, Australia.

Bahamas Adult Education Association Founded in August 1982. Current address: c/o Continuing Education and Extension Service, College of the Bahamas, P.O. Box N4912, Nassau, Bahamas.

Bahrain Current address: The Directorate of Adult Education, Ministry of Education, Bahrain.

Bangladesh Saksharata Samity Bangladesh adult education association. Current address: 59 Rajabazar Tejaon, Dhaka 15, Bangladesh.

banking education 1. Professional education of those people who work within banking, administered in UK by the *Institute of Bankers* which awards qualifications at the level of Associate of the Institute of Bankers. A Diploma of the Institute of Bankers is currently under consideration. 2. *Paulo Freire* employs this term to refer to that form of education in which information is merely memorized in an uncritical manner.

bar chart Data presented in the form of rectangles, often horizontal. Useful for comparative purposes.

Barbados Adult Education Association Current address: No. 3 3rd Avenue, Belville, St Michael, Barbados, West Indies.

Barnaparichaya The Bengali title means 'An introduction to alphabets'. A fortnightly magazine, founded in 1979 and published in Calcutta, India, which focuses upon *adult education, non-formal* *education, women's education*, and *rural development education*.

Barnett, Canon Samuel (1844–1913) Anglican clergyman and first warden of *Toynbee Hall* from 1884 to 1896, where he was involved in a variety of *adult education* activities such as establishing a *University Extension Society* which introduced many different cultural activities into the East End of London.

barriers to participation A great deal of research has been undertaken to discover why adults do not *participate* in *adult education* activities, this term has been used to refer to the obstacles which appear to prevent adults from joining such activities. It has been recognized that there are three sets of barriers: situational, due to position within the social structure; institutional, which refers to the types of procedures and time-tabling of educational institutions that are less orientated to certain groups of people than they are to others; and dispositional factors, which refer to the negative *attitudes* of *non-participants* towards education.

Barrow, Dame Nita A former president of the *International Council for Adult Education* and the ambassador of Barbados to the United Nations.

Basic A computer language.

Basic Choices An influential educational group in North America concerned with commitment, social and political, which was founded by P. Ohliger. The group issues a newsletter by the same name, the first edition being published in November 1985.

Basic Education 1. See *adult basic education*, where it refers to programmes of courses designed to give the *learners* a proficiency to utilize language, numbers, and literacy in everyday life. 2. Proposed journal in 1980 from the *National Extension College*. It was to be published three times a year, but did not survive.

Basic Education after Independence A policy adopted in India after independence to provide education of a *formal* and *non-formal* kind throughout life for the Indian peoples in their villages. It was not successful with the tribal peoples, with whom considerable efforts are still being made.

Basic English Devised in 1948. An attempt to limit vocabulary to 850 basic words. This has led to the development of graded vocabularies.

basic human needs These are defined in terms of the individual's consumption of food, shelter, and clothes, and in terms of people's access to social services, health care, public transport, and educational and cultural opportunities. In recent years there has been a variety of 'hierarchies of needs' such as *Maslow's hierarchy*, in which there is a progression from bodily needs to those of the self. In addition, others have suggested similar hierarchies such as: first-order needs (bodily); second-order *self-expression*; third-order (luxury). Adopted as one base-line for development education.

basic mathematics There was a growing awareness in the 1970s that *numeracy* was almost as great a problem as *literacy*. Thus there emerged a movement to teach adults basic mathematics, which became incorporated in the *adult basic education* curriculum.

basic research Research activities designed to test *theory*.

basic skills See *Adult Literacy and Basic Skills Unit*. This relates to the types of social and other skills that are required to function in contemporary society, e.g. listening, speaking, reading, writing, and mathematics.

basic skills test Examinations designed to assess the competency of people in the use of *basic skills*.

basic tests Produced by the Associated Examining Board in the United

Kingdom. A set of tests for *basic skills*, e.g. maths, English, life skills, etc.

Bayley, Rev. R.S. Founder of the *People's College* in Sheffield in 1842, where he was minister of the Independent Chapel. The college continued until 1874 and was a considerable influence on *F.D. Maurice* and the London *Working Men's College*.

B.D. Bachelor of Divinity.

Beard, Charles An American, and one of the founders of *Ruskin College* in the United Kingdom. See also *Walter Vrooman*.

Beat the Street A literacy programme in Canada which uses the talents of street people to tutor others who are homeless.

B.Ed. Bachelor of Education.

Behaviorally Anchored Rating Scales (BARS) A method of *appraisal*, it is a US system in which the users, rather than individuals in a hierarchical perspective, develop the rating scales for assessing their behaviours. These provide the basis upon which future *learning/training* might be planned. The group itself defines the dimensions of the work task and then decides upon a rating scale.

behaviour 1. An observable act. 2. A response to a stimulus. Important to some forms of *learning theory*. See *behavioural objectives*.

behaviour modification Techniques employed to change behaviour in therapy and some forms of *experiential learning*, based upon *conditioning*. See *behaviourism*.

behaviour patterns Human behaviour is not entirely free and haphazard; behaviour patterns seem to occur which are chains of shorter acts that are repeated in a variety of situations.

behaviour therapy Forms of therapy that assume that through learning/behaviour change, certain forms of disorder may be eliminated.

behavioural learning model An approach to learning based on the idea that *learning* is a change in behaviour as a result of experience or practice. It is a theory that has been criticized a great deal by some *humanistic adult educators*.

behavioural objectives Associated with *behaviourism* in as much as these are behavioural learning *goals* specified for individual sessions/lessons. This relates to a definition of *learning* that assumes it to be a change in *behaviour*.

behavioural science Studies in those subjects which are concerned with human actions, either as individuals or in groups. Psychology and sociology, for instance, are usually referred to as behavioural sciences.

behaviourism A theoretical approach in psychology associated with J.B. Watson and *B.F. Skinner* in which experimental psychologists opposed introspective methods assuming that humans and animals can be understood by *objective* study.

Belgium See *Le Conseil Superieur d'Education Populaire* and *Vlaams Centrum voor Volksontwikkeling, Ministerie van de Vlaamse Gemeenschap* and *Ministère de la Communauté Française*. Belgium has two major cultures, each with its own professional association for the education of adults.

Belgium Adult Education Association See *Le Conseil Superieur*.

belief A principle accepted as true but without sufficient evidence to prove it. This is a form of ideology, often taken as knowledge, but it is not verifiable by the normal means of verifying knowledge.

bell-shaped curve The shape of a normal distribution diagram in statistics.

Benin The organizing authority for *adult education* here is the Ministère de la Jeunesse Culture Populaire et des Sports, BP. 65 Porto-Novo, République de Bénin.

Bergevin, Paul American *adult educator* who was professor of adult education at Indianna University. He wrote one of the earliest philosophies of adult education and was concerned with *adult religious education*.

Berlitz Schools of America Inc. Foreign language schools organized in the United States. Address: 866 3rd Avenue, New York, New York 10022, US.

Berlitz Schools of Language A commercial school for language teaching which has achieved international prominence. Address: 31 Boulevard des Italiens, Paris, France.

Bertolt, Oluf (1891–1958) *Folk high school teacher*, active in the field of workers' education. He became secretary of the *Workers Educational Association* of Denmark in 1925, a year after its foundation, and one of the founders of the *Danish Council for Adult Education*.

Berufsschulen The day release colleges established in the Federal Republic of Germany and administered by local government (Länder).

Beth Johnson Foundation This foundation sponsors and encourages work with over-60-year-olds locally and nationally. Current address: Parkfield House, 64 Princes Road, Hartshill, Stoke-on-Trent ST4 7JL.

Bettelheim, Bruno (b. 1903) Psychologist interested mostly in disturbed children.

bibliography List of academic papers, books, etc. consulted which should appear at the end of every academic piece of writing, whether essay, paper, or book, referencing sources that the writer employed.

bilingual education Teaching and learning in two languages.

Bilingual Education Act An education act in the United States in 1968 that ensures that children of limited ability in English should receive an education appropriate to their linguistic abilities, amended in 1973 to support both new programmes and additional research.

bimodal distribution A statistical distribution in which there are two peaks in the distribution curve, indicating that there is more than one maximum frequency.

Birhan Published monthly in Amharic since 1981, an adult literacy journal in the Gondar Province of *Ethiopia*. See also *Ediget*.

Birkbeck College Formerly the *London Mechanics Institute* and founded in 1823, now a constituent college of the University of London devoted to offering part-time courses of both undergraduate and post-graduate level for *adult students*. In recent years its future has been threatened because of the fact that British universities have traditionally been funded on a full-time student basis. However, when the University of London reorganized *adult education*, the College incorporated the *Extra-Mural* department into it. Current address: Birkbeck College, Malet Street, London, UK.

Birkbeck, George (1776–1841) After graduation as a medical doctor he went, as Professor in Natural Philosophy, to *Anderson's Institution* in Glasgow, where he gave public lectures. In the early 1800s he settled in London where he was one of the main founders of the *Mechanics Institute* movement in England. He is generally regarded as the founder of the *Mechanics Institute*. He was also involved in the London Mechanics Institute which was later to be renamed *Birkbeck College*. He was involved in the founding of the University of London and other educational enterprises.

Birotehnika One of Yugoslavia's three main *distance teaching* institutions, providing courses at both *secondary* and *higher education* level. It also has its own publishing house, which publishes course material and a wide range of items. It is situated in Zagreb. See also *Workers Correspondence University, Correspondence Education Centre*.

bivariate analysis A simple form of research, used in some forms of *adult education* research in which there are only two variables, the independent and dependent. See also *multivariate analysis*.

Black Book See *Adult Education as an Emerging Field of University Study*.

Black Studies The study of the society, culture, economy, and language of black people, especially in the United States. This field of study is becoming increasingly common and significant in other countries of the world.

blackboard Formerly a black slate board on which the teacher could write with chalk so that a class could all see; now frequently green and rarely of slate but serving the same purpose. *Adult educators* are sometimes critical of the *teaching methods* that use 'chalk and talk'. See also *chalk board, white board*.

blind Educationally, the blind are those people who must rely on hearing and touch as their main means of receiving information and stimuli in order to learn.

B.Litt. Bachelor of Letters.

block release A system in the United Kingdom and elsewhere whereby employees are released from their work for a period of time in order to further their studies. Often a form of *continuing professional education*, pioneered by the trade unions.

block release course A course which is divided into blocks of practice and blocks of theory, usually having less than 18 weeks a year of the latter.

Bloom's Taxonomy of Educational Objectives Initially this was posited only in the *cognitive domain* but subsequently the *affective* and psychomotor domains were also discussed. The latter was not really analysed within the context of Bloom's original research or that of his original team. Benjamin Bloom was the leader of a group of educational researchers, including David Krathwohl, concerned with *objectives in examinations*. They suggested a six-level hierarchy of *knowledge: knowledge, understanding, application, analysis, synthesis*, and *evaluation*. While this has not gone uncriticized, it has provided stimulus for a considerable amount of research into *examination* techniques, etc.

B.Mus. Bachelor of Music.

Board of Advisors to the Fund for the Improvement of Post-secondary Education (FIPSE) Established in 1972 as an advisory committee to the secretary of Education of the United States, who also appoints the membership.

Board of Education An elected or appointed group of people responsible for the administration and evaluation of a school system.

Board of Governors of State Colleges and Universities in Illinois degree program (BOG degree) A degree programme designed for older adults, using innovative evaluation and instructional techniques, and utilizing the resources of the five institutions within the state of Illinois (Chicago State, Eastern Illinois, Governors State, Northwestern Illinois, and Western Illinois). Students can be *assessed for prior learning* using the standards adopted by the *Council for the Advancement of Experiential Learning*. The programme commenced in 1973.

body The physical aspect of the *person*, perhaps neglected in the study of *adult education* but developed in some social psychological studies. Since education places such emphasis upon *knowledge* it is not surprising that body is neglected as a topic for study.

body language *Non-verbal communication* by means of physical posture and movements of parts of the body.

body of knowledge 1. The total accepted *knowledge* about any field of study. 2. The amount of knowledge that a teacher seeks to impart or help students learn during a course, or other learning encounter.

Boletim Bibliográfico do Mobral The bibliographic bulletin of *MOBRAL*, published in Portuguese three times a year since 1973. It focuses upon *adult literacy* and other aspects of *adult education*.

Bond van Nederlandse volksuniversiteiten (Federation of Dutch People's Universities). Current address: Laan van Meerdervoort 90, 2517 AP Den Haag, The Netherlands.

book box A small library of recommended reading, usually contained in a box, which is often supplied with university *extra-mural classes*. It was also used in the *adult school movement* in the United Kingdom.

book club Started when a small group of people joined together to purchase books for mutual benefit. Among the first occurred as early as 1735 in Salisbury, Wiltshire in England.

bookmobile Travelling library.

Boston Literary and Historical Association Founded in 1901, a radical black *literary association* aimed at educating black people about their own rights. *Adult education* was its central purpose.

Botswana The Department of Non-Formal Education. Current address: Ministry of Education, Private Bag 0043, Gaborone, Botswana.

Botswana National Adult Education Association Current address: Private Bag 0045, Gaborone, Botswana.

Boyd–Apps Model This is a three-dimensional model of the field of *adult education*, proposed by Robert Boyd and Jerold Apps, in which they suggest that there are three dimensions to the field of study: the client, the system, and the transaction. In addition, they suggest that each of the three dimensions has three facets. The model has not been widely accepted within the field of adult education.

B.Phil. Bachelor of Philosophy.

brainstorming A problem-solving technique in which members of a group suggest solutions to problems without interruption or discussion by other members of the group.

brain train This is the title given to some courses, study circles, or *self-help* learning groups that have been established on commuter trains in the south of England. This was started in 1976–77. See *Commuter Study Clubs*.

brainwashing Literally, to wash the brain clear so that it can be reprogrammed according to the *attitudes, views* of those who were in control or teaching. It is a form of *conditioning*.

Branching Out The newsletter of the Indiana Association of Adult and Continuing Education.

Brandt Report Published in the early 1980s, this report was entitled *North-South: A Programme for Survival*. It examined the poverty and political weakness of the developing (south) countries. Adult educators concerned with development and the Third World have paid great attention to this report.

Bray, Thomas (1656–1730) One of the founders of the *Society for Promoting Christian Knowledge* (SPCK). He was concerned with making books available to both clergy and gentry and, hence, the introduction of libraries of religious and secular books. He also founded the Society for Propagating the Gospel (SPG) and created the 'Associates of Dr Bray', a group which is still active.

Brazil See *National Foundation for the Education of Youngsters and Adults*.

Bread Winners College Founded in 1898 in New York to disseminate knowledge to working people. No longer in existence.

Breakaway Course Organized by the *Young Women's Christian Association* for women who wish to widen their horizons by education and employment. These are organized at local centres.

bridging course A course designed to prepare students to commence another one at a more advanced level.

Brier, Nabila Nabila Brier was employed by UNICEF and a member of *International Council for Adult Education* involved in women's education in Palestine. She was assassinated in December in 1986 in the war in Lebanon because of her educational work. See *Nabila Brier Award, Nabila Brier Fund*.

British Accreditation Council An independent organization composed of representatives of higher and further education in the United Kingdom. It exists to define, monitor, and improve standards in independent further and higher education. Current address: 114 Chase Side, London N14 5PN, UK.

British and North American Network for Adult Education (BANANAE) Established in the mid-1980s with a grant from the *Kellogg Foundation*, which resulted in the exchange visits of some American scholars to the United Kingdom and vice versa in 1985 and 1986. From this occurred a joint *AERC–SCUTREA–CASAE* conference at the University of Leeds in 1988.

British Association Founded in 1831 as a learned society with the objective of making it easier for scientists to meet.

British Association for Literacy in Development Current address: Agricultural and Rural Development Centre University of Reading,

16 London Road, Reading RG1 5AQ, UK.

British Association for Service to the Elderly (BASE) An association that offers an educational programme for and about the elderly as a part of its overall programme. Current address: 119 Hassell Street, Newcastle-under-Lyme, Staffs ST5 1AX, UK.

British Association for the Promotion of Co-operative Knowledge Founded by the early co-operative movement in 1829. It gained the support of a number of leading radical thinkers as it sought to serve as a co-ordinating organization for the movement, but the association only lasted until 1931.

British Association of Commercial and Industrial Education (BACIE) Established in 1919 and specializing in a broad range of areas subsumed within its title. It also publishes a journal and sponsors conferences. Involved with *PICKUP*, it operates the *Secondment File*. Current address: 16 Park Crescent, London W1N 4AP, UK.

British Association of Settlements and Social Action Centres *Settlements* have a long history in social action in Britain and much of this has been associated with *adult education*. This is the national association of these organizations. Current address: 13 Stickwell Road, London SW9 9AU, UK.

British Broadcasting Corporation The BBC has an educational remit and recognizes that it is involved in *adult and further education*. It published a brochure to inform people of its educational activities. More recently, it has created a *Continuing Education Department* which publishes a newsletter, *Insight*, giving information on all forthcoming *continuing education* programmes. Current address: 76 Portland Place, London W1N 4AA, UK.

British Centre Founded in Stockholm in the early 1950s by the Stockholm

University Extension Service, it has been instrumental in taking teachers of English from England and placing them in teaching posts, for adults as well as children, throughout Sweden.

British Council An educational and cultural organization with some 200 offices in about 80 different countries. Devoted to fostering international co-operation and support in these areas. There is an adult education specialist employed by the British Council and it continues to support a number of initiatives in the field. Current address: 9 Spring Gardens, London SW1A 2BN, UK.

British Council of Churches This organization, of which most British Christian churches are members, has been involved in *adult religious education* for many years. Current address: 2 Eaton Gate, London SW1W 9BL, UK.

British Educational Management and Administration Society Learned society for those involved in these areas.

British Federation of Film Societies Established in 1945 as a federation of *film societies*. It has its own magazine, *Film*, and acts in an advisory role nationally. Current address: 81 Dean Street, London W1V 6AA, UK.

British Institute of Adult Education Founded in 1921 by *A. Mansbridge* and Haldane. It survived until 1949 when it merged with another national body, the *National Foundation of Adult Education*, to become the *National Institute of Adult Education*.

British Institute of Management Current address: Africa House, 64–78 Kingsway, London WC2B 6BL, UK.

British Journal of Educational Technology Published three times a year, the journal of the *Council of Educational Technology*.

British Journal of Guidance and Counselling Started in 1980, a professional journal for this field of work.

British Library The national library of the United Kingdom, established in 1973 by an Act of Parliament.

British Theatre Association Offers a variety of courses to adults, in evening classes, short courses, and short fulltime courses. Current address: 9 Fitzroy Square, London W1P 6AE, UK.

Broadcast Education Association An American association concerned with education and the media. Current address: 1771 N Street NW, Washington DC 20036, USA.

brokering See *educational brokering*.

Bryan, Tom (1865–1917) First warden of *Fircroft College*. Trained for the Congregational ministry, became active in both the early Labour party and the *Settlement* movement.

Bryson, Lyman L. (1888–1959) Born in Nebraska and became a journalist. Thereafter, one of the leaders of American *adult education* during the first half of the twentieth century. He was director of the *California Association of Adult Education* and also the *Des Moines Public Forum* before he became professor of Education at Columbia University's Teachers College. He was also chairman of Columbia Broadcasting System's adult education board and author of some of the early theoretical studies of adult education, including *Adult Education*, published in 1936 (the first textbook of *adult education*) and *The Drive Towards Reason: An Approach to a Philosophy of Adult Education*, published in 1954. He was also involved in the *Readability Laboratory* at Columbia University.

B.Sc. Bachelor of Science.

BTEC Certificate Awarded for part-time courses by the *Business Technical Education Council*

BTEC Diploma Awarded for full-time courses by the *Business Technical Education Council*.

BTEC First Award A one-year course award by the *Business Technical Education Council*.

BTEC Higher National Award A three-year course award by the *Business Technical Education Council*.

BTEC National Award A two-year course award by the *Business Technical Education Council*.

B.Tech. Bachelor of Technology.

Buber, Martin (1878–1965) Jewish philosopher who settled in Palestine in 1938. Famous for his study on human relationships, he was also president of the Israel Academy of Science and the Humanities. Additionally, he was concerned about *adult education* in Israel, where there is a Martin Buber Institute for *adult education*; current address: Mt Scopus, Jerusalem 91905, Israel.

Bulgaria See *Georgi Kirkov Society for Dissemination of Scientific Knowledge*.

Bulletin de Liaison de l'Institut Canadien d'Education des Adultes The magazine of the *Institut Canadien d'Éducation des Adultes*. Founded in 1966 and published five or six times a year.

Bureau for UK Education Launched in 1988, this bureau seeks to provide a national service of advice and guidance, assisting with the application process and a placement service for both school-leavers and adults who seek *training* and access to professional courses. Current address: The St Thomas Centre, Ardwick Green, Manchester M12 6FZ, UK.

Bureau of Adult, Vocational and Library Programs A unit of the US Office of Education, co-ordinating a wide range of adult and vocational education including *curriculum development and evaluation*. Address. US Office of Education, Washington DC, USA.

bureaucracy A sociological concept which is in many ways the antithesis of *professional*, in that it relates to organization and has such characteristics as centralization, standardization, and formalization. Hence it has come to relate to the procedures of organization and inefficiency, although it was postulated by Max Weber as the most efficient way for an organization to function.

Burnham Further Education Committee The body which negotiates the pay of teachers in *further education*, including *adult education*, in England and Wales.

burnout A cluster of exhaustion reactions which occur in people whose occupation involves helping others. See also *stress*.

bursary A scholarship or grant made to a student.

Burundi See *Direction de l'Education Parascholaire*.

Burwalls The residential adult education centre organized by the University of Bristol *Extra-mural Department* in the United Kingdom.

Business and Technical Education Council (BTEC) Formed from a merger of the *Business Education Council* and the *Technical Education Council* in 1983. Provides and validates courses of *vocational education* at national and higher levels in these areas and ensures that the courses retain a high standard through a system of moderation. Its courses have replaced the *ordinary* and *higher national diplomas*. In addition, its general certificate and diploma awards are regarded as roughly equivalent to the *general certificate of education*. Courses are run in *polytechnics, colleges of further education*, etc. Address: 76 Portland Place, London W1N 4AA, UK.

Business Council for Effective Literacy Inc. (BCEL) A publicly-supported foundation, established in late

45

1983, to foster greater corporate awareness of adult *functional literacy* and to increase business involvement and support in the *adult literacy* field. It publishes a newsletter, bulletin, and monographs and, in addition, provides technical assistance to the business community in a variety of ways. Current address: 1221 Avenue of the America, New York, New York 10020, USA.

Business Education UK journal published three times a year since 1980.

Business Education Council (BEC) Established in 1974 with the objective of establishing a national scheme of awards in *business studies* and administration. Later united with the *Technical Education Council* to form the *Business and Technical Education Council*. Address: 76 Portland Place, London W1N 4AA, UK.

business studies Studies in commercial and management subjects, often taken as an undergraduate but also in management courses. Some companies, like Rank Xerox, award scholarships in this field.

buy-in The process of employing personnel on a part-time basis when there is insufficient time or expertise among the full-time staff for the work to be conducted to a satisfactory standard.

buzz group A teaching and learning technique in which members of a class or seminar briefly discuss in small groups a point that has been raised during the session. Similar to, but not the same as, *brainstorming*.

CAAE Manifesto The manifesto of the London Conference of the *Canadian Association of Adult Education* in May 1943 which committed the Association to democratic reconstructionist policies for Canada after the Second World War. These were more radical than the government of the day wanted. It became both a moral and an ideological base for the Association.

cable television Television system delivered by cable, i.e. narrow casting, rather than by being broadcast.

Cadbury, Barrow (1862–1958) One of the Cadbury family, Quakers by religious persuasion, who became involved in *adult education* through the *adult schools* movement. He was a member of the *National Council of Adult Schools* from its inception and president of the *National Adult School Union* between 1926–27.

Cadbury, George (1839–1922) Long associated with the *adult school movement*, like many of the Cadbury family and many Quakers, and was probably responsible for the growth of the movement in Birmingham, England.

Cadbury, George (1878–1954) Like other members of the family, a Quaker who was involved with the *adult school* movement, but he is chiefly remembered for his involvement in the start of *Fircroft College* in 1909 and *Avoncroft College*, which was more devoted to agricultural education. Both were residential adult colleges.

Cadbury, Richard (1835–99) Like other members of his family, a Quaker and associated with the *adult school* and the Sunday School movements.

Cahiers de l'Annimation, Les The magazine of the *Institut d'Education Populaire* in France. It was started in 1972 and is published five times a year.

California Association of Adult Education The first state association in the United States and, like the *American Association of Adult Education*, it received some of its initial funding from the *Carnegie Corporation*.

calisthenics Rhythmical method of physical education without the use of apparatus.

calligraphy The art of beautiful handwriting; a popular *adult education* course.

Cambridge University *University extension* in England was effectively started by the University of Cambridge when *James Stuart* delivered a series of lectures to the *North of England Council for Promoting Higher Education for Women* in 1867. However, it was not until 1873 that the University actually agreed officially to sponsor *extension* lectures and this only for a trial period.

Cambridgeshire village colleges See *village college*.

Campaign for Adult and Continuing Education The proposed successor to *Save Adult Education Campaign* in 1982 in the United

Kingdom, but it never really became an effective force.

campus The site of a school, college, university, or any other educational establishment. Some colleges and universities do not have campuses because there are many different semi-independent colleges, whereas others have a number of campuses but only one central administration.

Campus Conference Network A *teleconferencing* network in the United States linking affiliate campuses. The organization's central office undertakes all the programming for the network.

Canadian Association for Adult Education (CAAE) Established in 1935 at St Anne de Bellevue in Quebec. Its founding director was *Ned Corbett*; *J. Roby Kidd* was his successor. This organization is the practitioner association in Canada and has always been very active in initiating innovations in *adult education*. Its journal is called *Food for Thought*. See also *Institut Canadien d'Education des Adultes*. Current address: CAAE, 29 Prince Arthur Avenue, Toronto, Ontario, Canada M5R 1B2.

Canadian Association for the Study of Adult Education (CASAE) Academic association for the study of *adult education* in Canada which was formed in 1980. It organizes a national conference and publishes a journal twice a year. Its aims are to promote the study of and research into *adult education*, to disseminate that research knowledge, and to develop effective communication and co-operation between those involved in this study and research.

Canadian Association for University Continuing Education (CAUCE) National association in Canada which universities having an *adult education* commitment may join. It has over 50 affiliated institutions and has conducted a number of surveys of the types of provision for adult education offered throughout the country.

Canadian Association of Departments of Extension and Summer Schools Established in 1951 to co-ordinate the work of these departments in both *credit* and *non-credit* education. Address: c/o The Extension Department, University of British Columbia, Vancouver, British Columbia, Canada.

Canadian Association of Directors of Extension and Summer Sessions Established in 1954.

Canadian Association of Distance Education A Canadian association based at the Centre for Distance Education, Simon Fraser University. The association publishes the *Journal of Distance Education*. Current address: Centre for Distance Studies, Office of Continuing Education, Simon Fraser University, Burnaby B.C. Canada V3A 1S6.

Canadian Citizens' Forum Established in 1943 by the *Canadian Association of Adult Education* as study and action groups using radio broadcasts as the study material. The association believed the popular initiative could lead to the formation of post-war policies that would result in a better and more democratic Canada. This was a part of the reconstructionist educational programme of the *Canadian Association for Adult Education*, following the *Report of the Special Program Committee* of 1943.

Canadian Citizenship Council Started by leading *adult educators* in Canada as the *Canadian Council for Education and Citizenship* in 1940. It concentrated on immigrants and their education.

Canadian Congress for Learning Opportunities for Women Founded in 1972 to promote and advocate learning opportunities for women. It publishes its own journal, *Women's Education des Femmes*. Current address: 47 Main Street, Toronto, Ontario, Canada, M4E 2V6.

Canadian Council for Education and Citizenship See *Canadian Citizenship Council*.

Canadian Council for International Co-operation A council with an international perspective to emphasize overseas development. Established in 1968. Current Address: 75 Sparks Street, Ottawa, Ontario, Canada.

Canadian Council for International Development Address: 3212, Chapel Street, Ottawa, Canada, K1N 7Z2.

Canadian Education Association Established in 1981. Current address: 252 Bloor Street West, Toronto, Canada, M5S 1V6.

Canadian International Development Agency (CIDA) This agency is concerned with all aspects of development including education for adults in Third World countries.

Canadian Journal for the Study of Adult Education A biannual refereed journal, publishing in English and French, committed to the dissemination of research and theory in adult and continuing education. The journal emanates from the Department of Adult Education, OISE, 252 Bloor Street West, Toronto Canada, M5S 1V6.

Canadian Journal of University Continuing Education Academic refereed journal, established in 1973, published twice a year by the *Canadian Association for University Continuing Education*.

Canadian Library Association Current address: 151, Sparks Street, Ottawa, Ontario, Canada.

Canadian Society of Rural Extension Established in 1960 for those interested in rural and agricultural aspects of *adult education*. Its forerunner was a sub-group of the Canadian Society of Technical Agriculturalists.

Canadianization education A fairly rare concept but it refers to the education offered to many of the immigrant labourers in the forest and railways camps of Canada by *Frontier College*, helping them to become Canadians.

candidature The first two years of the five year degree course in Belgian universities. See *licentiture*.

Canelo de Nos, El The first *folk high school* in Latin America, opened in Chile in 1988. It has been developed in order to create a meeting place for *adult educators*, where theory and practice can converge with action and reflection in order to work for a more humane society. It is situated about 20 kilometres from Santiago.

Canfield Learning Style Inventory This consists of thirty items, each with four options and the respondents are required to rank them in order of preference. Each option contributes to a different scale, with every fifth option referring to the same scale. There are problems with the relationship between the findings and the theory and it has been criticized because some respondents associate some of the items with schooling rather than adult learning.

capitation fee The amount of money that an educational institution may have to pay to a central body per student fee.

Captrends The quarterly publication of the *Center for Performance Assessment* in the United States.

Cardenal, Fernado Jesuit priest and leader of the Nicaraguan literacy crusade. He was a nominee for the Nobel Peace Prize. Former professor of philosophy at Managua Catholic University and Minister of Education in Nicaragua.

career 1. A path through life, or through an organization, e.g. through a period of academic study. 2. The occupation/profession chosen as one's lifetime avocation.

career education 1. A process designed to relate the *curriculum* to the demands of society. 2. A form of education in which a person is prepared for his/her own occupation.

careers officer An employee of an educational institution or authority responsible for providing information and guidance about *careers* to students.

Careers Research and Advisory Centre A UK organization. Current address: Sheraton House, Castle Park, Cambridge CB3 0AX, UK.

careers service This service was commenced to assist school-leavers with advice about future work opportunities, but the service throughout the United Kingdom has expanded its work and frequently offers a service to adults as well.

Caribbean Community Secretariat Current address: P.O. Box 10827, Georgetown, Guyana.

Caribbean Regional Council for Adult Education Established in 1982. Its first general assembly was held in the Bahamas in April 1983. Address: c/o The Extra-Mural Unit, University of West Indies, St Augustine, Trinidad and Tobago.

Caritas Roman Catholic charitable organization which organizes *adult education* in many parts of the world, with its international organization, Caritas Internationalis, situated in Rome. 1. In India it was initiated in 1962 and provides both education and research in order to promote human development through education. Current address: Caritas India, CBCI Centre, Sashok Place, (Gole Dakhana) New Delhi, 110001, India. 2. In Hong Kong Caritas provides a large *adult education* programme and runs adult education centres throughout the area. Current address: Caine Road, Hong Kong.

Carnegie Corporation Established in 1911. In the period between 1925 and 1941 this foundation made many grants to *adult education* in the United States and the *American Association of Adult Education* was largely funded by it during the whole of this period. Address:

437 Madison Avenue, New York, New York 10022, USA.

Carnegie Foundation for the Advancement of Teaching Established in 1905 to assist college teachers. Address: 437 Madison Avenue, New York, New York 10022, USA.

Carnegie Report A report on American *higher education* which called for considerable reforms to the system. It was formally entitled 'Less Time, More Options'. Presented in 1971.

Carnegie Unit A standard unit of measuring secondary school subject matter in the United States, it refers to a year's study in a subject, being at least 120 one-hour class periods.

Cartwright, Morse A. (1890–1974) First executive director of the *American Association of Adult Education* from 1926 to 1949. He was an educational liberal who steered the Association through its early years and to some extent helped to shape the direction of the field of study during this period. He was co-editor of the *Journal of Adult Education* when it was first published in 1929.

Carver, George Washington (b. 1863) He was born a slave in Missouri, but managed to acquire an education. Appointed as director of Agriculture Research at *Tuskegee Institute* in 1896, he built his reputation as a scientist, but also as an *extension worker*. It was he who first provided the inspiration for the *Farmers' Cooperative Demonstration*. As part of his extension work he wrote many pamphlets giving advice and guidance to farmers.

case analysis Discussion of either an actual or a prepared *case study* which helps *participants* understand more deeply the problems and issues of *professional practice*.

case history An educational *aid* consisting of a written description of an event, incident, or situation used as a basis for *discussion* and *problem-solving*. See also *case study*.

case study The type of *project* often employed in *professional education* in which the *learner* selects (or has selected) an actual situation in professional practice and has to prepare a *report* upon it for *discussion* and/or *assessment*.

Castren, Zachris (1868–1938) Finnish *adult educator* who was lecturer in *adult education* at the *College of Social Studies* before it became the University of Tampere. He prepared the state report in 1929 that became one of the foundations of government policy for adult education in his country. He was later a Member of Parliament and held other influential positions.

Castrol educational programme In the United Kingdom Castrol have prepared three learning programmes for adults about car maintenance and publish a newsletter. Address: Castrol Educational Division, Athena Ave, Elgin Estate, Swindon, Wilts SN2 6EQ, UK.

catechesis The process whereby the Roman Catholic Church seeks to *educate* all who have been baptized as members of the church into a fuller *knowledge* and understanding of what it means to practise Christianity according to the tenets of that denomination. See also *lay training*.

catechist One who has the designated role of preparing members of the Roman Catholic Church in the catechism, that is the body of knowledge professed by the Catholic Church.

category A logical grouping.

caterbase A project launched by the *Hotel and Industry Training Board* which is a modularized system of training in work-based situations for accreditation in the industry.

Catholic Association of Adult Education A large West German provider of *adult education*. See *Katholische Bundesarbeitsgemeinschaft für Erwachsenenbildung*.

Catholic Countrywomen's Associations in the Netherlands See *Federatie katholieke plattelandsvrouwen Nederland*.

Catholic education organization In the Federal Republic of Germany the churches are major providers of *adult education*. Each area has an organization for Catholic *adult education* although the curricula are usually much wider than a traditional church's. There is also a national organization; see *Katholische Bundesarbeitsgemeinschaft für Erwachsenenbildung*.

Catholic Fund for Overseas Development This fund promoted *development education* and sponsors some projects. Current address: 2 Garden Close, Stockwell Road, London SW9 9TY, UK.

Catholic Summer School of America Established in 1892 to enable those whose occupation did not allow them to attend university to have a university-type experience. See *summer schools*.

Catholic Women Workers' League The largest voluntary organization in Flemish Belgian with an *adult education* remit. It publishes its own monthly journal, *Vrouw & Wereld*. Current address: Poststraat 111, 1210 Brussels, Belgium.

Catholic Workers College Established by the Catholic Social Guild in 1921 at Oxford to provide training in the social sciences for working men and women at a residential college on the *folk high school* model.

Cattell, Raymond B. (b. 1905) A research professor in psychology at the University of Illinois whose work on intelligence has emphasized that there are both *crystallized* and *fluid* forms of *intelligence*, thereby making an important contribution to understanding *adult learning*. In a sense this might be viewed as part of the nature-nurture debate in the social sciences.

causality The theories that seek to explain the relationship between cause and effect.

Cave, Parable of An episode in *Plato's Republic* in which he points to the fact that there may be a better way of social organization than that which most people experience. This is perhaps significant for adult education since it points to the fact that educators have always looked to a better world and that *adult education* is often regarded as a means to this end.

CBI Education and Training Bulletin Published four times a year. The education and training journal of the *Confederation of British Industry Education, Training and Technology Directorate*.

CEDEFOP See *European Centre for the Development of Vocational Training*.

C.Eng Chartered engineer (UK qualification).

Center for Adult Learning and Educational Credentials Formerly, the *American Council on Education's Office on Educational Credit and Credentials*. It provides professional services for *higher education* to a large number of private industries in the United States. Current address: Center for Adult Learning and Educational Credentials at the American Council on Education, One Dupont Circle NW, Washington DC 20036, USA.

Center for Alternatives to Higher Education An American *clearinghouse*. Current address: 1118 S. Harrison, East Lansing, Michigan 48823, USA.

Center for Community Education An American *clearinghouse* with *community education* as its focus. Current address: c/o American Association for Community and Junior Colleges, One Dupont Circle NW, Suite 410, Washington DC 20036, USA.

Center for Education and Work An American *clearinghouse* concerned with the issues relating to education and work.

Current address: c/o National Manpower Institute, 1211 Connecticut Avenue NW, Suite 301, Washington DC 20036, USA.

Center for Helping Organizations Improve Choice in Education (CHOICE) American *clearinghouse*. Publishes its own free bulletin. Current address: Department of Higher/Post-Secondary Education, 227 Huntington Hall, Syracuse University, Syracuse, New York 13210, USA.

Center for International Extension Education (CIED) Founded in 1982 at the University of Maryland, College Park, within the Department of Agricultural and Extension Education to further international activities. It publishes occasional papers on a variety of aspects of its work. Address: College of Agriculture, University of Maryland, College Park, Maryland, USA.

Center for Learning and Telecommunication Established with a grant from the *Carnegie Corporation* in Washington, within the ambit of the American Association of Higher Education. Its function is to monitor the range of *post-secondary* technology-based education in the United States and provide both educators and policy-makers with information.

Center for Museum Education American *clearinghouse* concerned with museums and museum education. Current address: George Washington University, Washington DC 20052, USA.

Center for Performance Assessment This center studies assessment techniques through the use of tests, problem-solving, comparison of direct and indirect writing assessment methods, and assessment programs generally in areas of lifeskill problem-solving. Publishes a quarterly called *Captrends*. Current address: Northwest Regional Educational Laboratory, 300 S.W. Sixth Avenue, Portland, Oregon 97204, USA.

Center for Personalized Instruction
American *clearinghouse*. Current address: Georgetown University, Washington DC 20057, USA.

Center for the Study of Liberal Education for Adults Established in 1951 in America with a grant from the *Fund for Adult Education* with three major objectives: improving university programmes in *liberal adult education*; developing improved methods of teaching adults; and building a climate of support for *liberal adult education* generally. It was situated at Boston University and had the general purpose of helping *American higher education* relate more effectively to *adult liberal education*. It had only three directors throughout its life: J.S. Diekhoff, J.B. Schwertman, and A.A. Liveright. It was dissolved in 1968.

Center for Vocational Education
American *clearinghouse* concerned with all aspects of *vocational education*. Current address: Ohio State Univerity, 1960 Kenny Road, Columbus, Ohio 43210, USA.

Central American Institute for the Extension of Culture The Costa Rican association for *popular education*. Current address: Apartado 2948, San José, Costa Rica.

Central Board for Workers' Education Established by the Indian government in 1958. It provides *training* for all types of workers and is also concerned with *population education* and *adult education*. Current address: 1400 West High Court Road, Gokulpeth, Nagpur 440010, India.

Central Broadcasting and Television University The Chinese *distance teaching university*, probably the largest institution of its kind, with over 800,000 students registered for its courses.

Central Bureau This UK organization provides information, some funding, and advice on educational visits and exchanges. Current address: Seymour Mews House, Seymour Mews, London W1H 9PE, UK.

Central Committee against Illiteracy Established in Greece in 1954 and renamed *Central Committee for Popular Education* in 1965. There were also county committees against illiteracy which functioned at local level.

Central Committee for Popular Education Established in Greece in 1965 from the *Central Committee against Illiteracy*. There are also county commitees of popular education, which function at local level, having representation from adult education, trade unions, and local government, and responsible for the local organization and for employing adult educators.

Central Council for Education and Training of Social Work The central professional body for social work in the United Kingdom. It validates the professional qualification for social workers, *Certificate in Qualification in Social Work*. Address: Derbyshire House, St Chad's Street, London WC1, UK.

Central Educational Library The main educational library of Romania. Address: Biblioteca Centralá Pedagogică, 70714 Str. Zalomit nr 12, Bucuresti 1, Romania.

Central Labour College Early college for working people in England. Regarded as a left-wing competitor to *Ruskin College* since it was founded in 1909 in Oxford as a result of the internal disputes within *Ruskin College*.

Central Office for Extra-Mural Study (ZFU) A controlling body for extra-mural, i.e. leisure-time *adult education* in the Federal Republic of Germany. Among its tasks is that of evaluating courses offered to the general public. It is located in Cologne. See also *Act on the Protection of the Participants of Extra-Mural Study*.

central tendency A statistical concept referring to the fact that most frequency distributions appear to be around a mid-point score.

Centre d'Etudes et de Réalisations pour l'Education Permanente French centre concerned with research and documentation in *lifelong education*. Current address: 12–14 rue de l'Eglise, 75739 Paris, Cedex 15, France.

Centre de Documentation de la Direction Générale de la Jeunesse et des Loisirs General documentation centre in French-speaking Belgium for *adult education, leisure* and *young adults*. Current address: 28 Galérie Ravenstein, 1000 Brussels, Belgium.

Centre de Télé-enseignement Universitaire Many French universities offer *distance teaching* courses and have their specialist centres for this activity.

Centre de Télé-promotion Rurale This organization seeks the *training* and development of people in rural areas of France through the use of *distance education* techniques. The problems that it has faced include the use of popular broadcasting time when other more popular programmes are scheduled. Current address: Rhône-Alpes-Auvergne, BP47X, Centre de Tri, 38040 Grenoble, France.

Centre for Adult Educators This is both a national and international centre in Sweden in which a forum is provided for *adult educators* from all aspects of society to exchange theory and practice in *adult education*. It arranges seminars, conferences, provides a consultancy service and is also building an information and documentation base concerning adult education. Current address: Kanslihuset, Kaserngaten 34, 582 28 Linkoping, Sweden.

Centre for Andragogical Research Established in Belgium with the aim of establishing, stimulating, and sustaining studies and research in *adult education* and cultural work in the Flemish community. Current address: Liedtsstraat 27–29, Brussels, Belgium.

Centre for Educational Research and Innovation (CERI) Created in June 1968 by the Council of the *Organization for Economic Co-operation and Development* with the help of grants from the Ford Foundation and the Royal Dutch Shell Group. Initially the centre was founded for three years and its life has subsequently been extended. The objects of the centre are: to promote research and innovation within the educational systems of the member countries and to promote co-operation between them. Current address: OECD, 2 rue André Pascal, 75016 Paris, France.

Centre for Health and Retirement Education A centre in the United Kingdom which aims at examining issues of health that relate to early retirement, retirement, and redundancy. It is initially funded by a grant from the *Health Education Authority* and is based within the Extra-Mural Department, University of London. Current address: 26 Russell Square, London WC1B 5DQ, UK.

Centre for International Briefing This was established in 1953. It is an independent organization which provides courses for people going from the United Kingdom to live and work in other countries, organizes courses about the United Kingdom for international visitors, and organizes business seminars for people involved in international work. Current address: The Castle, Farnham, Surrey GU9 0AG, UK.

Centre for Information on Language Teaching and Research (CILT) This organization has established a network so that language teachers, including those in *adult education*, can make contact with each other. Current address: Regent's College, Inner Circle, Regent's Park, London NW1 4NS, UK.

Centre for Policy on Ageing Organization in the United Kingdom concerned with research into the needs of older people, including *educational gerontology*. Current address: 25–31 Ironmonger Row, London EC1V 3QP, UK.

Centre for Teachers in Adult Education (Voksenpædagogiske Centre) There are eight such centres in Denmark which provide in-service training for *adult educators*.

Centre for the Study of Education in Developing Countries The universities of the Netherlands established this centre in 1963 as one which is concerned with international co-operation and development. It contains a large documentation centre and supplies, free of charge, lists of publications on request. See *Dr J. van Baal.* Current address: Badhuisweg 251, PO Box 90734, 2509 LS The Hague, The Netherlands.

Centre for Vocational Guidance and Professional Practice These have been established in the Netherlands since 1978 to provide guidance to job seekers, who for social and cultural reasons have little chance of gaining paid employment. They also provide opportunities to acquire the necessary *knowledge* and *skill* to gain employment, and assist people to join *training* programmes.

Centre for World Development Education National centre in the United Kingdom concerned with *development*, provides resources and a curriculum development service and is a resource base for development issues. Current address: Regent's College, Inner Circle, Regent's Park, London NW1 4NS, UK.

Centre for Youth and Adult Studies Established in 1986 at the *Open University* in the United Kingdom, concerned with the professional development of those who are involved in *post-compulsory education*.

Centre National d'Enseignement par Correspondence A French *distance teaching* institution offering correspondence courses at all levels throughout the country.

Centre National d'Etudes Agronomiques A French national centre providing both *initial education* and *continuing education* in agriculture and husbandry in hot climates. Current address: CNEARC, Agropolis, Départment Formation Continue, Domaine de Lavalette, Avenue de Val de Montferrand, BP5098, 34033 Montpellier, Cedex, France.

Centre pour le Développement de l'Information sur la Formation Permanente Documentation centre in France about the developments in *lifelong education*. Current address: Tour Europa – Cedex 07, 92080 Paris la Défense, France.

Centre Universitaire d'Information, de Recherche et de Documentation sur l'Education Permanente (CUIDEP) A national documentation centre for *lifelong education* in France. Current address: 2 Place de l'Etoile, 38000 Grenoble, France.

Centro de Documentación, Instituto Nacional de Cooperación Educativa This is the national documentation centre in Venezuela and is concerned with *adult education* and professional preparation. Current address: Avenida Nueva Granada, Edifico Sede, Piso 12, Caracas 104, Venezuela.

Centro de Investicación y Desarrollo de la Educación (CIDE) This is a centre for educational research and development in Chile and *Red Latin Americane de Información y Documentación en Educación* (REDUC) is located here. Current address: Erasamo Escala 1825, Casilla 13608, Santiago 1, Chile.

Centro Europeo Dell'Educazione (CEDE) See *European Centre for Education*.

Centro Latinamericano de Educación de Adultos (CLEA) A Latin American centre for *adult education*. Current address: Avenida Providencia 2093, 2 Piso, Casilla 16417, Santiago, Chile.

Centro Nacional de Documentación e Información Pedagógica The Cuban documentation and information centre.

Current address: Obispo no 160 esq. a Mercaderes, Havana, Cuba.

Centro Regional de Educación de Adultos y Alfabetización Funcional para América Latina (CREFAL) Formerly the Latin American literacy centre, but in 1979 it became a centre of the Mexican government for *adult education* training and research. Address: Patzcuaro, Mexico.

Centrum voor Andragogisch Onderzoek, VZW This is the Flemish centre for research and documentation of *adult education*. Current address: Liedtsstraat 27–29, 1030 Brussels, Belgium.

Ceres The bimonthly publication of the *Food and Agricultural Organization* in Rome.

Certificat en andragogie An undergraduate-level award of the University of Montreal since 1969, when it was the first French-speaking university in Canada to recognize *andragogy* as a field of academic study. In addition, the University offers masters degrees and doctorates in *andragogy*.

certificate 1. A legal document allowing a person or agency to perform services. 2. The university award of a certificate is usually regarded in the United Kingdom as equivalent to one year's full-time undergraduate study, although there is also a post-graduate certificate awarded by some British universities. There is also some debate as to whether it is a certificate course for post-graduate students, or a one-year post-graduate level course, or one that serves both functions. There is a post-graduate certificate of education which is a school teacher qualification, and the University of Surrey in the United Kingdom awards a post-graduate certificate in the education of adults for *educators of adults* who have completed a one-year full-time course.

Certificate for Vocational Preparation Tutors Issued by the *Royal Society of Arts* in the United Kingdom as a means of certifying a range of relevant experience and training in vocational preparation. It is based upon a log book specifying 19 skills relevant to vocational preparation. Tutors can register with the Society and complete the *profile* in the course of their attachment at a registered centre. Once it is accredited, they may thereby be eligible for certification.

Certificate in Training and Development A certificate of qualification in *training* offered by the *City and Guilds of the London Institute* in conjunction with *The Institute of Training and Development*.

certificate of attendance A document certifying attendance of the bearer at a course, often issued when the course has no certifying agency other than the organizers. See *certificate of completion*.

certificate of competency A document specifying that the bearer has reached a certain specified standard and has demonstrated it by test or examination.

certificate of completion See *certificate of attendance*. A document issued specifying that the bearer has completed a part or whole of a course. It does not have to specify that the bearer has been tested for *competency*.

Certificate of Education (Cert. Ed) 1. The award of a one-year full-time, or two-year part-time course in *further* or *adult* education, which is equivalent to ACSET III. It is not yet a mandatory qualification for teaching in these areas. 2. Earlier it was the qualification of school teachers before school teaching became a graduate profession. In this instance it was awarded after two and, later, after three years of full-time study.

certificate of high school equivalency A formal document issued by the *State Department of Education* in the United States certifying that the bearer has met the requirements for high school graduation on the *General Educational Development* tests. It is an official document accepted by colleges, universities, and employers.

Certificate of Pre-Vocational Education (CPVE) Introduced in the United Kingdom in 1986. A one-year course for a wide ability range at 16 years and over who do not intend to progress to *General School Certificate Advanced Level*. Offered by different educational institutions and awarded by the *British and Technical Education Council* and *The City and Guilds of the London Institute* operating together as a *Joint Board for Pre-Vocational Education*. *Profiling* is a normal mode of assessment used in this course.

Certificate of Qualification in Social Work (CQSW) The professional qualification for social workers in the United Kingdom. It is validated by the *Central Council for Education and Training of Social Work*.

certificate renewal The re-issue of a certificate at a given time when the previous one has expired. The bearer has to demonstrate that the conditions for renewal have been met.

certification The process whereby an awarding agency grants a credential to a person.

chain In *learning* theory, the series of responses and stimuli arising from an initial stimulus.

chain learning See *chain*.

chain of response model (COR) A theoretical model of *participation* in organized education developed by Patricia Cross, incorporating a number of factors that stem from other research. It is a theoretical model designed to identify relevant variables and to hypothesize their interrelationship.

chalk and talk A rather derogatory term to refer to the teaching method whereby the teacher uses his/her own speech and writing on a chalkboard/whiteboard as the only *teaching aid* accompanying the

teacher's input, having little or no student participation.

chalk board A board upon which a teacher can write in chalk so that all the class may see what has been written. Similar to a *blackboard*, although this term is not used as frequently nowadays since many newer boards are another colour, often green or brown.

Change The newsletter of the *Singapore Association for Continuing Education*. It was started in 1982 and is published twice a year.

change See *social change*.

change agent 1. It is argued that social structures are changed as a result of the action by agents, and that it is a function of *community education* to provide a form of education that liberates individuals so that they can become agents of change. 2. *Adult educators* are sometimes regarded as change agents because the educational process is seen as one which produces change.

Channel 4 Education Department Responsible for all educational broadcasting on Channel 4 on UK television, including that aimed at an adult audience. Current address: Channel 4, 60 Charlotte Street, London W1P 2AX, UK.

channels of communication 1. A term that is used to refer to the fact that people receive their sense experiences through a number of different senses, or channels, so that there can be a compensation if one of the senses is in any way defective. 2. In organizational terms, this refers to those routes through which messages go to reach the different people.

charisma A sociological term that is used to describe a person or leader who has the characteristic of inspiring others to follow. It is not necessarily a personal characteristic that is shared by each person, since the actual *authority* of charisma ultimately resides in the followers and they can both give or withdraw their allegiance.

57

charitable foundation An organization established to administer a fund which is subject to the laws of charities.

Charities Year Book A directory of UK-based *charitable foundations*, which includes *educational trusts*.

Charles, Thomas (d. 1814) A Methodist minister in Wales who became involved in the early *Sunday School* movement. He started to organize them in 1787 and established over 100. However, he recognized the reluctance of some adults to learn with children and so he started *adult schools* in 1811. He was also one of the founders of the British and Foreign Bible Society.

Chartered Institute of Public Finance and Accountancy Professional association and accrediting body in the United Kingdom. It was previously called the *Institute of Municipal Treasurers.* Address: 1 Buckingham Place, London, UK.

Chartered Insurance Institute Professional association and accrediting body in the United Kingdom. Address: 20 Aldermanbury, London EC2V 7HY, UK.

Charters, Alexander A leading American *adult educator* who established the archival collection at Syracuse University and who, for many years, was one of the leading exponents of *international adult education* in the world. He was vice-president of Syracuse University, responsible for its *continuing education* programme.

Chartists A movement of working people in the early part of the nineteenth century, mostly in the midlands and north of England, in which *adult education* was widely used as a means of propagating their ideas. This was used especially with the Christian Chartist groups. See *William Lovett, Feargus O'Connor*, and *Thomas Cooper.*

Chautauqua Established in 1874 on the shore of Chautauqua Lake in the United States as a summer school programme for Sunday School teachers by *Dr John Vincent* and Lewis Miller but this soon expanded beyond Sunday School teachers. By 1878 a general adult education programme was offered on a national scale through the newly established *Chautauqua Literary and Scientific Circle*. Chautauqua also spread to Canada.

Chautauqua Institution The contemporary outcome of the *Chautauqua* movement.

Chautauqua Literary and Scientific Circle (CLSC) Established in 1878 to offer a national programme in general adult education through home reading in conjunction with *self-help* groups in each local region. It grew and broadened its educational programme for many years. Many local and regional models followed its pattern. In 1879 it initiated its first *correspondence education*, which became very successful. Although not now so prominent, CLSC provides its members with significant non-fiction books so that they can continue their education.

Chautauquan A monthly magazine started in 1880 and sent to all members of the *Chautauqua Literary and Scientific Circle*. Discontinued in 1914.

checklist A pre-specified list of topics to be covered or areas researched. Useful planning tool.

Chi square A statistical test of association, used to see if association occurs by chance.

Chicago College of the Air Sometimes called the Television College. Established in 1956 with the assistance of the *Ford Foundation* as one of the pioneering colleges using the media for teaching students at a distance. Its work was influential in the development of this form of education.

chief education officer The senior administrative officer for *Local Education Authority* educational services in the

United Kingdom. Will have a senior officer responsible to him/her whose responsibilities include *adult education*, and possibly another officer who will be responsible for *further education*.

Chile See *Comisión Coordinadora de Educcación Popular de Chile.*

Chimo The newsletter of *Frontier College* which was first published in 1973.

China See *National Association of Adult Education of China.*

Chinook Learning Center Established in 1972 in the United States, this center was founded by Fritz and Vivienne Hall. Inspired by the Iona Community, this is an educational and religious centre in which people can consider and act upon their understanding of the world. It has a covenant membership, which meets annually although members do not necessarily live at the Center. There is also an associate membership. The educational programme contains five dimensions: the earth (nature), the inner, the community, the cultural, and the service. Situated in Clinton, Whidbey Island, in the Puget Sound.

Ch.M. Masters degree in surgery. Sometimes written *M.Ch.*

Choice The magazine of the *Pre-Retirement Association of Great Britain*. Publishes articles on a variety of topics relevant to the older citizen.

Christelijke plattelandsvrouwenbond An organization with more than 300 branches throughout the Netherlands. Attached to the Calvinist churches and conducts *non-formal adult education* through the meetings and courses. Current address: Prinsegracht 78, 2512 GC Den Haag, The Netherlands.

Christian Aid A service agency for the British Council of Churches, concerned mainly with support for Third World countries. Publishes its own newssheet, *Next Step*, which is a part of its educational outreach in the United

Kingdom. This organization does have its own *adult education* officer. Address: PO Box 1, London SW9 8BH, UK.

Christian Association for Adult and Continuing Education (CAACE) Inaugurated in 1979, an interdenominational association of Christians in the United Kingdom concerned about *adult religious education*. Current address: c/o Ammerdown Centre, Radstock, Bath, Avon BA8 5SW, UK.

Christian League of Countrywomen Dutch organization. See *Christelijke plattelsandsvrouwenbond.*

Christian Socialism A nineteenth-century movement in the Christian Church in England which was involved in *adult education*. See *F.D. Maurice, the London Working Men's College.* The movement was theologically liberal and concerned with a social gospel.

Church of England Board of Education A body which oversees the educational work of the Church of England in the United Kingdom. It has a division responsible for *adult education*. Address: Church House, Dean's Yard, Westminster, London SW1, UK.

Church Women United, Community Services National American association concerned with *adult education*. Current address: Box 134 Manhattanville Sta, New York, NY 10027, USA.

circulating library The first commercial circulating library to be established in England was started by *Allan Ramsay* in Edinburgh in 1726. It is claimed that circulating libraries tended to issue fiction, whilst the *subscription libraries* were of a more serious disposition. See *library, subscription library.*

circulating schools See *Welsh circulating schools.*

Circulation Welsh Charity Schools See *Welsh circulating schools.*

59

Citizen Action in Education The quarterly free bulletin of the *Institute of Responsive Education* in the United States.

Citizen Education Bulletin The monthly bulletin of the *Alliance for Citizen Education*.

Citizens Advice Bureaux An information, advice, and counselling service offered throughout the United Kingdom. These bureaux carry much information concerning local *adult education*.

Citizens' Educational Association (Medborgarskolan) A Swedish educational association sponsoring *study circles*, and associated with the conservative wing of politics in that country. Concerned with a cultural and broad education. Established in 1940.

Citizens' Forum See *Canadian Citizens' Forum*.

Citizens Leagues Commenced in the United States in Minneapolis–St Paul in 1952, the Leagues have developed in the 1970s and 1980s in a number of cities. They stress citizen research and debate, using community issues as the agenda. They are both a form of *participative research* and *community education*. Financed by membership fees and sponsored by some foundations, although they tend to be independent of each other.

citizenship education Associated with new immigrants in the United States. See *Americanization education*, in which immigrants learn to become citizens of a new country. It is also related to education for responsible citizenship generally. See *Council for the Advancement of Citizenship*.

Citizenship Education News A newsletter issued quarterly by the *Council for the Advancement of Citizenship*.

City and Guilds of London Institute Established in 1879 with the express purpose of making grants, at the same rate as the *Science and Art Department* on successes in non-engineering subjects. After the formation of Technical Instruction Committees in the 1890s the Institute ceased to make grants but it continued to serve as an examining body and also as a provider of courses and syllabuses in a wide field of technical subjects, including education. The Institute provides these services in many areas where there are no *professional associations* to provide them. See *Technical Instruction Act*. Current address: 76, Portland Place, London W1N 4AA, UK.

City and Guilds of the London Institute Further and Adult Education Teachers' Certificate (730) A course of preparation for adult and further education teachers, organized by the *City and Guilds* and roughly equivalent to the ACSTT I and II preparation courses for adult educators.

City and Guilds of the London Institute Further and Adult Education Teachers' Certificate (942) A pilot course devised and tested in the London area of preparation of teachers of adults, roughly equivalent to ACSET I and II. See *City and Guilds of London Institute 730*.

city college A *community college* in the United States.

Civic College In Finland, the first college to establish a lectureship in *adult education* in 1929. Now *Tampere University*.

civic education 1. See *citizenship education*. 2. Used sometimes in *adult education* to refer to the study of local government administration.

civic university A name used to refer to those provincial universities created in the United Kingdom during the end of the nineteenth and early twentieth centuries in which the university adopted the name of the city in which it is located but remained independent of it.

civil engineering The design and building of construction works.

Civil Service College The professional college for *continuing education* in the civil service in the United Kingdom. Address: Sunningdale Park, Ascot, Berkshire, SL5 0QE, UK.

civilization 1. The culture of a particular society. 2. Culture generally that differentiates humankind from the animal kingdom.

clarify To make clear or easy to understand.

Clark, Septima (1898–1987) A pioneer for adult literacy and civil rights among black people in the United States, leader in the Southern Christian Leadership Conference, director of education at *Highlander* and recipient of a 'Living Legacy Award' from the president of the United States in 1979.

class 1. A teaching method in which a group of people meet with a *teacher* to study a specific subject for a predetermined length of time. 2. See *social class*.

class meeting A Methodist Church institution in which groups of church members meet to engage in study. During the nineteenth century it was closely associated with *self-help*. See also *study circle*.

classical conditioning The process of behaviour modification whereby the person learns to associate the presentation of a reward with the stimulus which appears fractionally prior to it, so that behaviour is adjusted to the stimulus in anticipation of the reward. This is associated with the work of *I.P. Pavlov*.

classroom climate The atmosphere or ethos established in the class, usually as a result of techniques and *teaching style* of the teacher. This climate can relate to teacher–student relationships, interrelationships between students, group *motivation*, etc.

classroom ecology A branch of educational research which has not been developed in *adult education* in which the classroom is itself the centre of the research, e.g. interactions within it. See also *ecology*.

classroom interaction The study of interaction within the classroom. See *interaction, classroom ecology*.

classroom observation techniques Forms of research in the classroom, not well developed in *adult education*.

Claxton, Timothy (1790–1848) Born in Bungay, Suffolk, England. The founder of the *Mechanics Institution* in London in 1817. He spent a period of his life in America where he was associated with the founding of other *mechanics institutes* and with *Josiah Holbrook*. On his return to Suffolk he founded other *mechanics institutes*.

clearinghouse A centralized agency for the collection and distribution of information and materials, commonly used within American education.

Clearinghouse Adult Education and Lifelong Learning (ADELL) A relatively new American *clearinghouse* concerned with all aspects of *lifelong education*. Current address: Informatics Inc., 6000 Executive Boulevard, Rockville, Maryland 20852, USA.

Clearinghouse for Community-Based Free-Standing Educational Institutions The original name of the *Association for Community-Based Education* in the United States. Current address: 1806 Vernon Street NW, Washington DC 20009, USA.

Clearinghouse on Adult Education Functions to link the adult education community in the United States with the resources in *adult education*. It provides information, acts as a broker, and publishes lists of materials in a variety of areas of *adult education*. Address: US Department of Education, Office of Vocational and Adult Education,

Division of Adult Education,
400 Maryland Avenue SW, Washington
DC 20202–5515, USA.

**Clearinghouse-Resources for
Educators of Adults** Based at Syracuse
University, which houses one of the
largest collections of *adult education* in the
world. Current address: 224 Huntington
Hall, Syracuse University, Syracuse,
New York 13210, USA.

client-centred therapy A form of
therapy pioneered by such psychologists
as *Carl Rogers*, which concentrates upon
the client's own perceptions. Has
influenced *adult education* method.

clinic An extended series of meetings in
order to diagnose *needs*. This term is not
frequently used in *adult education*.

clinical experience The professional
practice that a trainee nurse, or other
health-related trainee professional,
receives. However, it can also refer to the
experience a professional practitioner has
acquired throughout the whole period of
the career.

clinical method Techniques of *clinical
psychology*.

clinical nurse teacher A trained nurse
in the United Kingdom who has also
undertaken a course of preparation in
teaching, so that (s)he can work with
student nurses in the clinical area to help
them gain in clinical nursing expertise.
The first training programme was in
1958. Training for this role was
discontinued in the 1980s when it was
decided that all *nurse teachers* should be
clinically based. See also *practical work
teacher, field work teacher*.

clinical psychology A branch of
psychology concerned with the
recognition and treatment of mental
disorder.

closed circuit television (CCTV) A
method of employing a video camera and
recorder in teaching adults to record and
play back recorded events so that

participants can learn from viewing the
event. Frequently used in tutor training.

closed communication structure A
structure of communication within an
organization in which members may
interact only with specific personnel,
often only a named central person, about
the functioning of the organization.

closed further education A term
employed in the Federal Republic of
Germany relating to certain forms of
further education which are offered to
specific clientele, such as the trade
unions, etc. See also *open further education*.

closed question The type of
examination *question* that restricts the
respondents' response by asking for
specific information. See also *open
question*.

closed test The type of test that may be
used only by those personnel especially
trained to administer it, such as some of
the psychological tests that are available.

closure 1. Term used in *Gestalt
psychology* to indicate that a client has a
tendency to perceive closed figures more
readily than open ones. 2. To bring to an
end.

**Clothing and Allied Products
Training Board** Responsible for
training within these industries in the
United Kingdom. Current address:
80 Richardshaw Lane, Pudsey, Leeds
LS28 6BN, UK.

Club and Institute Union (CIU) This
UK association is a co-ordinating body
for clubs and institutes and has a large
membership. It also has an education
committee which links with both the
Workers Educational Association and the
Co-operative Union Education Department.
However, *adult education* now plays only
a small part in the life of many affiliated
clubs.

cluster Refers to a group of scores that
fall close together in a correlation matrix
in statistical analysis.

cluster analysis A statistical technique relating to *factor analysis* examining intercorrelations in a correlation matrix.

cluster sample A selection of whole groups or categories within a *sampling frame*, the cluster to be randomly selected.

clusternet The network within the *National University Teleconferencing Network* in the United States which has the ability to uplink its productions with the orbitting satellite network so that live and interactive programmes can be transmitted.

coach 1. A *teacher* or *tutor* who prepares students for examinations. 2. To give tuition or *instruction* to a student. 3. This form of teaching is also associated with expert advice in sports preparation by one who is often called a *trainer*.

coach and student method A *teaching method* in which a pair of students teach each other a procedure, skill, etc. that has been introduced to them by an *instructor*.

Coady, Moses (1882–1959) Jesuit priest and leader of the *Antigonish Movement*. He was a radical social reformer and adult educator, and the founder and first director of the St Francis Xavier University Extension Department.

Coady International Institute Named after *Moses Coady*. Offers a programme to train leaders for social development in the Third World. Current address: St Francis Xavier University, Antigonish, Nova Scotia, Canada B2G 1CO.

Coalition for Alternatives in Post Secondary Education An American grouping. Current address: 1211 Connecticut Avenue NW, Suite 301, Washington DC 20036, USA.

Coalition for Literacy An alliance of many of the organizations in the United States concerned with *adult literacy*. It provides information and focuses attention upon the problem of illiteracy.

It is also concerned with *volunteer training*. Current address: 50 East Huron Street, Chicago, Illinois 60611, USA.

Coalition of Adult Education Organizations (CAEO) A loose coalition of adult education organizations in the United States, established in 1973 as a result of the *Galaxy Conference of Adult Education Organizations*. It seeks to focus attention upon major issues in *adult education*, exchange information at a national level, plan joint projects, and lobby for support from government, foundations, etc. In 1975 it created an *International Associates* group to further its aims on an international basis. Current address: 810 18th Street NW, Washington DC 20006, USA.

code 1. A list of procedures or rules that has been drawn up. 2. The accepted form of behaviour within a social group. 3. Statistical symbols for the conversion and analysis of data in quantitative research. 4. A style of language.

code of ethics A *profession's* statement of the standards of behaviour and occupational performance that it expects of its members. This is often regarded as an essential prerequisite to an occupation being regarded as a *profession*.

coding The system of rules and regulations that have to be *learned* before an activity can be performed. See *decoding*.

coding frame The system that is constructed in quantitative research to enable *questionnaire* data to be translated into the statistical symbols necessary for analysis.

coding schedule The form containing the identification symbols by which the data from quantitative research can be transcribed into the form by which it can be analysed.

coding system In interview research, a prepared system of symbols which the researcher employs to record answers in order to ensure confidentiality of the replies.

coefficient of contingency The degree of association between two variables when each is expressed in several categories or qualities.

coefficient of correlation Provides the measure of the degree of linear association present between two variables. There are two major types of correlation coefficient used in educational research: *Pearson's Product Moment Coefficient of Correlation* and *Spearman's Correlation Coefficient*.

cognition Thought, as distinct from the *emotions* or the *psycho-motor*. See *cognitive mode*.

cognitive development The development of various capacities of thought, associated with the work of *Jean Piaget* with children. However, some psychologists have argued that the process of cognitive development continues throughout adulthood. Different psychologists have made various suggestions about the developmental process in *adulthood*, such as the ability to ask or discover important questions; increasing use of reflective thought; the ability to think about one's own theories and thought processes. However, other scholars have doubted whether these abilities are unique to *adulthood*.

cognitive dissonance This concept relates to the fact that an individual experiences discomfort when he/she holds logically inconsistent thoughts about an object or an event. The person is motivated to reduce the dissonance by an attitude or another form of cognitive change.

cognitive domain See *cognitive mode*.

cognitive learning The acquisition of *knowledge*, principles, beliefs, etc. Some philosophers wish to limit the field of *education* to the cognitive.

cognitive learning theorists Those who seek to explain *learning* only in cognitive terms.

cognitive map Schemes constructed by individuals as a result of a variety of *learning experiences* about phenomena.

cognitive mode The mode of thought that concerns *learning knowledge* rather than *skills*.

cognitive skills What a person knows, perceives, and understands and the manner in which these are used in subsequent *learning* and *problem-solving*.

cognitive strategy Method by which a person uses his/her *knowledge* and *skills* in future *learning*. See *cognitive skills*.

cognitive structure The general framework of thinking, similar to *ideology, world-view*. Something that might alter with experience.

cognitive style The characteristic manner by which a learner approaches the task of learning, perceiving, gathering, and processing information. A variety of different styles have been identified, usually in terms of opposites, e.g. *convergent/divergent*. See also *learning styles*.

cohort Term used in research to refer to a specific group being studied, e.g. an age cohort being a number of subjects of a specific age being researched.

Cole, George Douglas Howard (1889–1959) Professor of Social and Political Theory at the University of Oxford, well-known tutor for the *Workers Educational Association*, and early advocate of *continuing education*. He was also a very early advocate of the recruitment of mature students to university study.

co-leader One whose responsibilities are to assist the leader of a *group* or organization.

Coleg Harlech Founded in 1927 and located in Wales, this is a residential college for adult students providing non-vocational education to men and women over the age of 21 years. The College is funded by the Department of Education and Science and the Welsh Office, and receives support from local education authorities within Wales. The first warden of the college was Sir Ben Bowen Thomas. Current address: Coleg Halech, Harlech, Gwynedd, LL46 2PU, UK.

collaborative assessment A form of assessment which is a negotiation between teacher and learner about assessment method, criteria, grades, etc.

Collage The magazine of the *Christian Association for Adult Continuing Education* in the United Kingdom.

collection An accumulation of information resources, books, papers, etc. such as the archives at Syracuse University.

College Board A national American non-profit agency with a membership of over 2,500 educational institutions, involved in helping with all forms of education. It has an *Office of Adult Learning Services*. Current address: 988 Seventh Avenue, New York, New York 10106, USA.

college boards Examinations prepared by the *College Level Examination Board* in the United States.

Collège d'Enseignement Général et Professionel Colleges established in Quebec in the 1960s as an intermediate stage between school education and either the workforce or university. They also provide *vocational education* for adults.

college diploma An award made by a college itself rather than one accredited by an institution or university.

College for Living The programme offered by the Center of Continuing Education at Colorado State University in the United States for the disabled adult. Established in 1974.

College Level Examination Board A non-profit association of over 2,500 colleges and universities in the United States. It is also a testing organization which administers, among other tests, the *College Level Examination Program*, and the *Advanced Placement*. In addition, it has established an Office of Adult Learning Services to improve access to continuing education for adults. Current address: 45 Columbus Avenue, New York, New York 10023, USA.

College Level Examination Program (CLEP) Located in the United States and administered by the *College Board*, this programme seeks to serve people who have acquired knowledge outside of the formal educational institution. The programme and examinations are designed to measure knowledge gained in the first two years of college. There are five general CLEP examinations and they are currently set in 47 different subjects.

college of advanced education A *tertiary* level educational institution established in Australia in the 1960s. Both *vocational* and *general education* are offered in these colleges. *Adult education* programmes are run in some of them, including the training of teachers of adults.

college of advanced technology Colleges of advanced further technological education, many of which gained university status in the United Kingdom in the 1960s.

college of education 1. A school teacher training college in the United Kingdom prior to the mid-1970s, when monotechnic educational institutions were discouraged and thus many diversified or amalgamated with other types of *higher educational* institution. See *college of higher education*. 2. A college in an American university devoted to the preparation of school teachers and to the study of *education*. Most departments of *adult education* are located in these colleges.

college of further education Located in the United Kingdom, they provide courses for post school-leaving students, often part-time and having a vocational bias although this is not always the case. Some students use this type of college as a route to *higher education*, but the colleges themselves have expanded their role from working mainly with 16–19 year-olds to colleges with a *lifelong education* orientation, especially in relation to *continuing professional education*. As some of these colleges have sought to expand their role into *higher education* they have changed their titles to *colleges of further and higher education*.

college of further and higher education See *college of further education*.

college of higher education The title adopted by some of the *colleges of education* which diversified in the 1970s in the United Kingdom.

College of Lifelong Learning Established in 1973 in the United States to meet the educational needs of people who were unable to attend formal classes at Wayne State University, offering both credit and non-credit education, and a *community education* programme in the Michigan area. Current address: College of Lifelong Learning, Wayne State University, 6001 Cass Avenue, Suite 253, Detroit, Michigan 48202, USA.

Colleges of Mid-America One of the consortia of colleges formed in the United States to offer combined degree programmes.

College of Preceptors Established in the nineteenth century, it is the oldest examining body in England. It offers qualifications in *teaching* and has a *further education* staff training course among its teacher training. Current address: 130 High Holborn, London WC1V 6PS, UK.

College of Radiographers Responsible for the professional training and examination of radiographers in the United Kingdom. Address: 14 Upper Wimpole Street, London W1M 8BN, UK.

college of technology A *college of further education* in which *technology* is regarded as central to its *curriculum*.

College of Telecommunications Engineering Professional college for training personnel for the National Air Traffic Services in such subjects as navigational aids, radar, communications, etc. Run by the Civil Aviation Authority. Address: Bletchley Park, Bucks, UK.

College of the Sea Established by *Albert Mansbridge* in 1938 as part of an *adult education* service he wished to offer to seamen. It offers a full programme for seamen including *vocational education* and some *general education*. It also organizes the Seafarers Educational Service, and offers *educational, counselling*, and *guidance* services.

College Proficiency Examination (CPE) An American *equivalency examination* introduced by the University of the State of New York in which academics prepare curricula, study guides, examinations, and mark the examinations which indicate knowledge equivalent to a university course.

College Work-Study Program As a result of the *Secretary's Initiative on Adult Literacy* in the US Department of Education, in conjunction with 18 colleges and universities, granted funds in the financial year 1984 for pilot projects in which students were trained and paid to assist in a variety of ways in local projects. This number was extended in subsequent years. All other 3,400 colleges having work-study programmes were also encouraged to utilize some of their funds for *adult literacy* work.

colloquy A modification of the *panel* approach to *teaching and learning* in that a group of six to eight persons are selected, some to represent the experts and some to represent the audience. The latter ask questions of the former in the presence of an actual audience.

Cologne Appeal Launched in the autumn of 1985 within Europe in order to establish a specific agenda of joint action between the North and the South. Among its educational activities was the concern to develop a critical approach to world citizenship and to further *development education* throughout Europe.

Colombia The official organization for *adult education* in this country is the Ministry of Education. Current address: Ministerio de Educación Nacional, Educación No Formal y de Adultos, Piso 4, Centro de Administración National, Bogotá, Colombia. See also *Accion Cultural Popular* and *Fondo de Capacitación Popular*.

Comenius, John Amos (1592–1670) A bishop of the Moravian Church, Comenius was a theologian, linguist, educator and author of many books, including 'The Great Didactic'. He advocated that all children should be educated in all branches of learning, that teaching methods should be effective and that education should be the key to peace and prosperity. He considered that the goal of human life on earth consisted of *knowledge*, virtue and piety, since only through education could mankind discover a harmonious relationship with God. He was an early exponent of student led curricula emphasizing that teachers should teach less and learners should learn more.

Comisión Coordinadora de Educación Popular de Chile The *adult education* co-ordinating body in Chile. Current address: Brown Sur 247, Nuñoa, Santiago, Chile.

Comité Venezolano de Educación Permanente This is the Venezuelan committee for *lifelong education*. Current address: c/o Centro Al Servicio de la Acción Popular (CESAP), Parroquia Altagracia – Apartado 4240, Caracas 1010-A, Venezuela.

Commission of Professors of Adult Education Commenced in the early 1950s in the USA under the sponsorship of the *Adult Education Association of the United States of America*, this organization has now become the professional association of university professors of adult education and its annual meeting usually precedes the annual conference of the *American Association for Adult and Continuing Education*.

Commission on Adult Education Commission set up to investigate the provision of education in Eire. Published a report in 1984 known as the *Kelly Report*.

Commission on Higher Education and the Adult Learner Established by the *American Council on Education* to focus upon issues of public policy, institutional *self-assessment* and co-operation among associations concerned with *adult learners*.

Commission on Non-Traditional Study Established in 1971 in the USA by the *College Level Examination Board* and the *Educational Testing Service*, with the support of the *Carnegie Corporation* of New York to study aspects of *non-traditional education*. It had a two year life and made three reports, the most well known being *Diversity By Design*.

Commission on the Library and Adult Education Convened by the *American Library Association* in 1924, its purpose was to study both adult education and the work of libraries. Its report 'Libraries and Adult Education' was published in 1926.

Commission on Voluntary Service and Action An American association. Current address: 475 Riverside Drive, New York, New York 10027, USA.

committee A small group of people appointed or elected to perform a task that cannot be undertaken so efficiently by the whole organization.

Committee for Study and Research in Comparative (International) Adult Education Established in 1987 by the

International Council for Adult Education and the *International Congress of University Adult Education* to examine international adult education.

Committee for Workers' Education in Amsterdam This was formed in 1910 in the Netherlands in order to create a cadre of well-trained activists in the trades union movement; it was the first step in the direction of creating an *Institute for Workers' Education*.

Committee on Adult Education 1. Set up in 1970 in Scotland to consider the future of *adult education* in that country. 2. In Eire, the Murphy Committee was also given this title. The committee published the *Murphy Report* – an interim report was published in 1970 and the final report in 1973 – which concerned the state of adult education in Eire.

Committee on Continuing Education Sometimes called the *Venables Committee* after its chairman, *Sir Peter Venables*, it produced a report on continuing education commissioned by the Open University in UK and published in December 1976.

Committee on Methods Testing in Adult Education A government-appointed research committee in Sweden which has investigated various aspects of the *study circle*.

common knowledge The mutual understanding that makes *communication* possible.

common skills See *life skills*. BTEC suggests that these fall into the following categories: self-development skills; communicating and working with others; problem tackling, decision-making and investigating; information, quantitative, and numerical skills; practical skills.

Common Welfare Educational Establishment Established in 1972 in the Rederal Republic of Germany by the trades union federation to increase its educational facilities and to give it a more common basis.

Commonwealth Association for the Education and Training of Adults An organization formed in the 1980s, its inaugural meeting was held in 1987. It is sponsored by the Commonwealth Foundation and concerned with professional development programmes of those engaged in the education and training of adults in the Commonwealth. Membership is individual and associations may have associate membership. At present, it is operated from the University of Reading, UK.

Commonwealth Fund for Technical Co-operation (CFTC) Founded in 1971 this Fund was established to ensure that the principles of the British Commonwealth would become a reality. Its task is to provide technical assistance, rather than financial aid, to all developing countries within the Commonwealth. Current address: Managing Director, Commonwealth Secretariat, Marlborough House, London SW1Y 5XH, UK.

Commonwealth Institute Established in the UK in 1887 as the *Imperial Institute* but assumed its present name in 1958; it has educational programmes and is also related to the *Commonwealth Association for the Training and Education of Adults*. Current address: Kensington High Street, London W8 6NQ, UK.

Commonwealth of Learning Established in 1988 by the Commonwealth governments to promote co-operation in *distance education* in order to promote human resource development within the Commonwealth. Further Information from: The Commonwealth Secretary-General, Marlborough House, Pall Mall, London SW1Y 5XH, UK.

Commonwealth Relations Trust Formerly the *Imperial Relations Trust*, this Trust offers a bursary for an experienced adult educator, between 28 and 50 years of age, to study adult education in some part of the Commonwealth. The applications are administered by the *National Institute of Adult Continuing Education*.

Commonwealth Secretariat Current address: Marlborough House, Pall Mall, London SW1Y 5HX, UK.

communication The production and reception of messages, sharing and exchanging information, feelings and meanings. A dynamic process between two or more persons. There are a variety of means of communication and communication studies comprise an important element in many courses of preparation and education. See also *channels of communication*.

Communication The newsletter of the *International Bureau of Education*, published in English.

communication pattern A systematic arrangement which defines the origin, direction, and structure of *communication* within a *group*.

communication system Means of exchanging information.

communication technology The technology through which much *communication* occurs.

communications The subject matter, or the study, of *communication*.

communicative competence The ability to communicate ideas to people irrespective of the grammatical correctness of the language used.

Communidad INEA The monthly newsletter of the Mexican association, *Instituto Nacional para la Educacíon de los Adultos*.

community There are said to be over 90 different definitions of this word in sociology. However, in *adult education* the word seems to have five different basic meanings: 1. A group of people who either live or work together. 2. Any geographical area in which people live. 3. A geographical area where people live and interact. 4. An educational activity beyond the walls of the educational institution. 5. An ideal arrangement of people living and working in harmony. This last is the picture that was presented in the 1960s and 1970s of life in the past in areas where people lived, worked, and interacted in close relationship, e.g. 'the world that we have lost' – an ideology that had a great deal of prominence for a period. Some of these different meanings are to be detected in the ideas of *community education* and others of the following concepts.

community action Residents of a locality who organize to take action on some matter of local or national concern. Regarded as the *radical* element in *community education*.

Community Action Program The term sometimes used in the United States to refer to the *Economic Opportunity Act* of 1964 from which a number of *adult education* programmes resulted.

community activator One who alerts people in the community to adult educational possibilities.

community activist One who takes direct action in the community to achieve desired ends. There is a debate within some areas of *community education* as to whether the *community educator* should also be an activist.

community animateur One who intervenes in the community in order to assist groups or organizations to achieve their desired goals, usually on behalf of the whole community.

community arts The activity of artists in a variety of different art forms working in local communities in an educative manner and involving the members of that community in creative *art*. See also *community theatre*.

community association Voluntary, geographically-based association in which local people participate in its organization and administration. See also *community-based organization*.

community-based organization An organization which is representative of and controlled by members of a local community, involved in a variety of social activities and concerns.

community care A system whereby people who need support and might normally reside in an institution live in the *community* and are cared for by health, social welfare, and educational organizations.

community centre A local centre organized by people who live in the *community*, mainly having a social purpose but also often having *adult education* programmes.

community college 1. An institution in the United Kingdom which provides both secondary education and adult education, similar in concept to a *community school*. 2. In the United States the community college, or *junior college*, offers a two-year programme in higher education for local high school graduates in line with the needs of the locality. Usually they are only two-year degree programmes, some leading to an *associate degree*, although some others do run four-year degree programmes. They also run *continuing education* programmes and community service.

community development The process of enriching the social, cultural, economic, political, and educational life of a geographically demarcated area, often through the processes of *community action, community education* and *development education*.

Community Development Journal: An International Forum A community development journal published by Oxford University Press.

community development officer An employee of a community development project. This term was used especially in relation to people who were employed as *community educators* in the project that the Open University ran to promote *community education* in England.

community education There are a variety of meanings to the term *community*, so that the term *community education* is used in many different ways in adult education. It is frequently used to refer to educational processes beyond schooling: education that occurs outside of the educational institution; education that takes place in a *community school* or *community college*; education that occurs for *community development*; education for *community action*. Thus the term spans the ideological perspectives from the conservative to the radical. It has been claimed that there are six aspects to community education: a supportive relationship between a *community school* and the community; a sharing of facilities between school and community; a community-orientated curriculum; lifelong education; community involvement in the management of the community school; and *community development*.

Community Education This journal succeeded the *Scottish Journal of Youth and Community Work* in 1978.

Community Education Advisory Council (CEAC) Established in 1974 as an advisory committee to the Secretary of Education of the United States who also appoints the membership. Current address: Regional Office Building 3, Room 5622, 7th and D Streets SW, Washington DC 20202, USA.

Community Education Association A UK association for those concerned with *community education*. Current address: P.O. Box 63, Briton Road, Coventry CV2 4LF, UK.

Community Education Journal The quarterly journal of the *National Community Education Association*.

Community Education Today See *Today*, the tabloid newspaper of the *National Community Education Association*.

community education tutor 1. A teacher who has educational responsibilities within the community even though he/she is based within a school or college. 2. See also *community educator*.

community educator One who is involved in teaching and learning with people outside of the formal educational system in order to achieve desired educational goals within the community.

community learning *Learning* that is related to the exercise of civic responsibility in the public interest through community political structures.

community problem-solving project A form of *community education* in which the residents of a local area are helped to solve a particular problem by engaging in relevant learning activities and then putting their learning into practice.

community programme A programme organized by the *Manpower Services Commission* in the United Kingdom to provide work experience for long-term unemployed adults by financing their employment in community projects on a one-year parttime basis, and to help them return to work. Three aims are claimed for this programme: the project should contribute something of practical benefit to the community; the work should be undertaken by local unemployed people; each project should improve the employment prospects of those who work on it. Community programme workers are encouraged to join in the *Wider Opportunities Training Programme* in their free time. (Note: in 1988 the *Manpower Services Commission* changed its name to the *Training Commission* and then to the *Training Agency*.

community reading centre Part of the *non-formal education* programme in Sri Lanka is to provide *reading rooms* in communities where people will be able to read newspapers, periodicals and books. It is planned that these rooms should become distributive centres of knowledge. There is some similarity here to the *manner* in which *adult education* developed in England and the United States.

community school The current version of the *village college* in the United Kingdom, the community school seeks to provide education, recreation, and cultural activities for the whole of the locality within which it exists. The school may also be a base for *community development*, or even some forms of *community action*. In addition, it will usually be managed by representatives of the major groups who utilize its facilities. See also *community education*.

community service 1. The type of educational service to the local community that academics in American universities might be expected to provide. 2. Work, usually of a voluntary nature, carried out to assist in *community development*.

community studies The analysis of the way in which communities function. Frequently applied to specific localities by those involved in the study. See *community development*.

community survey A survey, often conducted by learners, of a geographical location, obtaining data about the area, opinions of its residents about the area and its resources, problems, etc.

community television The type of television programme made by members of a community about a local concern of that community.

community theatre The use of drama in an educative manner to assist in *consciousness-raising* within *community education* and *literacy crusades*. See also *community arts*.

community theory An American approach to community that seeks to ensure that people in a local community, usually having a single or major ethnic origin, are encouraged to learn the culture of the ethnic group as well as that of American society.

community tutor The teacher or member of the academic staff in a school or even *community school* whose responsibilities relate to educational work within the *community*.

Commuter Study Clubs Started in the United Kingdom in 1977 by De Pamela Le Pelly with the support of British Rail. Courses are organized on railway trains, provided the journey is longer than 30 minutes in a wide variety of subjects. Occasionally the courses have a tutor, sometimes a volunteer; some are free and others are fee paying. Groups meet once or twice a week in a pre-arranged carriage on the train. See *brain-train*. Current address: Commuter Study Clubs, 18, Victoria Park Square, London E2 9PF, UK.

Company Directors Diploma An award for the successful passing of the examination at the end of the company directors' course organized in Australia for those who hold senior executive positions in industry and commerce.

comparative adult education The study of *adult education* systems and policies in order to learn about them and from them, and to compare them and their origins. This is an empirical form of research rather than a normative one. Comparative adult education can occur within a country or internationally. It is also different from *international adult education* in which no comparison is made.

Comparative Adult Education Newsletter This is a newsletter produced by the *comparative adult education* group of the *Standing Conference on University Teaching and Research in the Education of Adults* (SCUTREA) in the United Kingdom.

comparative need The gap that exists between the services received by individuals of similar characteristics. Term more frequently used in the welfare services than in *education* but has become more prevalent in *adult education* as it is viewed as a social service.

comparative professional education Little research has been undertaken to

examine the approaches of different professions to their educational problems, although this is beginning. The study of *professional education* is still in its infancy with few major studies. However, one of the purposes of comparative studies is the improvement of educational practice and this could also result in this instance.

compensation The process of emphasizing the strengths of learners and de-emphasizing the weaknesses. Hence in examinations good scores may be used to compensate for poor ones.

compensatory education Based on the ideal of giving all adults the opportunity to remedy the deficiencies in their *initial education* later in life. This was an idealist position of the 1960s and early 1970s, but it has not been so prevalent in the latter part of the 1970s nor the 1980s. See *recurrent education, adult basic education*.

competence 1. The level of *skill* and *knowledge* (and sometimes *attitude* is also specified) necessary to perform work efficiently, according to the *standards* accepted by a profession or occupation at a given time. 2. The ability to perform at an agreed level of proficiency, consisting of knowledge, skill, attitudes and professional *values*. 3. Some definitions of competence omit knowledge and regard it as only being skill-based.

competence-based learning Approaches to *learning* which make the outcomes explicit in terms of *competences* which are to be taught and assessed.

competency An ability or capability demanded in the succesful performance of a specific occupational role. It is regarded as being related to a demarcated occupational area and is something that can be measured.

Competency-Based Adult Education Network Established in 1982 to assist *adult educators* involved in *competency-based education*. Current address: Room 5610, ROB 3, 7th D Street SW, Washington DC, USA.

competency-based education This is an *educational process* in which the pre-specified objectives are *competencies*, usually of an occupational nature. As this form of education is normally modular and *self-paced* it does allow for the course of study to be completed in varying lengths of time, and also for there to be a *'roll-on/roll-off' curriculum*. Sometimes called community-based adult education. (CBAE)

competency-based vocational education That form of *competency-based education* in which the occupational task is sub-divided into a number of *competencies* and each comprises a module in the *vocational preparation*. See also *training*.

competency test An examination to assess a *competency*.

competition Rivalry that leads to participants endeavouring to achieve the highest/first place. This is sometimes encouraged in *initial education* as a means of *motivation*, but is less encouraged in *adult education* where co-operation between students is favoured as a more *idealistic* and *realistic* approach to classroom and other group dynamics.

complementary studies The minor subject of study.

completion question The type of question where the learners are required to finish an incomplete statement.

complex In psychoanalytic theory it is a descriptive device to convey a psychological state, but the term has also pathological overtones, e.g. inferiority complex.

component behaviour In *learning* a *skill*, the skill is often sub-divided into elements, or components, so that each can be learned separately.

composition 1. The end product of putting together the parts. 2. An essay.

comprehend To understand.

comprehension 1. A process of understanding. 2. A form of test to assess whether learners have understood – used in language teaching.

comprehension orientation An approach to studying in which the *learner* seeks to relate the ideas being learned to the wider society and actual life experience.

comprehension test A form of assessment designed to examine the extent to which *learners* have understood the meaning of what they have read or what they have learned.

Comprehensive Employment and Training Act (CETA) The United States federal government's response to high unemployment has been to provide funds to create jobs and training for the unemployed through this Act. Many *adult education* initiatives have been taken through this scheme, which is administered through the US Department of Labor.

comprehensive high school A secondary school in the United States having both academic and vocational programmes.

comprehensive manpower serivce program A programme in the United States to develop and create job opportunities and the provision of *training, education*, etc. to enable people to obtain and hold employment.

computer-assisted learning (CAL) The use of a computer to assist in the presentation of teaching materials or to assist learners to work through an already prepared learning programme. There are advantages in allowing learners to pace their own learning and to do so without a teacher being present. Hence it may be seen as a form of *distance education*.

computer-based training (CBT) This is an approach to training that uses a computer program to simulate the main functions of an industrial process and enables trainees to work through most of the likely situations that occur in the process in a 'safe' situation.

computer literacy The level of *knowledge* and *skill* necessary to understand a computer program. However, at present no real agreement exists about a more precise definition.

computer-marked assignments These are often *multiple choice questions* set in *distance learning* by the educational institution, e.g. the Open University. Students complete specially prepared multiple choice answer papers and return them to the centre to be marked by computer.

computer-mediated instruction See *computer-assisted learning*.

Computers in Adult Education and Training An international journal, published three times annually, launched by the University of Keele, UK, in October 1988.

conation The aspect of mental processes relating to volition. Not in frequent current use.

concentration 1. The ability to become absorbed in a task. 2. In analyses of distribution, the number of times a few scores occur in relation to the total number of occurrences.

concentration span The length of time an individual can remain absorbed in a task. It is used especially in relation to the use of the *lecture*, where it is generally agreed that the listeners' concentration span is frequently shorter than the allocated time for a lecture.

concept 1. An abstract idea or thought. 2. A term used to contain a family of phenomena having similar characteristics. E.g. *education* is used in this manner without reference to any of the specific types or forms of education.

concept formation The process of developing *concepts*. See the work of *Piaget*.

concept learning One of the later stages in *Gagné's hierarchy of learning*.

conceptual style See *cognitive style*.

concrete experience Specific *primary experience*, which results frequently in *concrete operational thought* in the early stages of thought but which can lead to *reflection*. See *Kolb's learning cycle*.

concrete operational thought One of the earliest of *Piaget's* stages of conceptual development. It is also essential in understanding some of the theoretical ideas of *experiential learning* since these start with the idea of *concrete experience* and the thought processes that are associated with it. See *Kolb's learning cycle*.

conditioned reflex A *response* to a *stimulus* that occurs without thought or volition. See the work of *Pavlov*.

conditioning The process of behavioural modification that occurs as a result of external forces and without the intelligent, or critically aware, consideration of behaviour being changed. There are two types: *classical* and *operant*.

conductive education A form of education which teaches mastery of the disordered movements of the disabled body to a degree that enables independent functioning. Well-known and developed at the Peto Institute in Budapest, where children and adults have been treated for motor disorders. The first institute for this form of education in Britain was started in September 1987 in Birmingham, sponsored by the Foundation for Conductive Education, University of Birmingham, Birmingham B15 2TT, UK.

conductor One who practises *conductive education*.

Confederación Española Aulas de Tercera Edad (CEATE) The Spanish confederation of *universities of the third* *age*. Current address: Ciudad Puerta de Sierra 1, Penalara 12, 1.B 28230 Las Rozas, Madrid, Spain.

Confederation of British Industry Education, Training and Technology Directorate The CBI committee for education and training in the United Kingdom. Publishes its own bulletin, *CBI Education and Training Bulletin*. Current address: Centre Point, 103 Oxford New Street, London WC1A 1DU, UK.

confer The name of a computer conferencing system in the United States featuring electronic mail and notice board facilities, based at Wayne State University and accessed by a variety of systems and organizations, including the *National University Teleconferencing Network*.

conference 1. A formal meeting of two or more people to confer, consult, and exchange opinions. 2. A meeting of an academic or professional association, often annually.

conference call Telecommunication between more than two persons, which enables *group discussion* to occur. Used in some *distance education* provision.

conference centre A large, usually residential, centre especially equipped to mount conferences. Many hotels in the United States have conference facilities of this nature.

Conference for Independent Further Education An association of independent colleges of further education in the United Kingdom, recognized by the *British Accreditation Council*. These colleges prepare adults and young adults for statutory examinations. Current address: The Secretary, Lovehayne Farm, Southleigh, Colyton, Devon EX13 6JE, UK.

confidence level A statistical measure used to determine whether the differences between two findings might have occurred by chance. E.g., 5 per cent

confidence level suggests that such a difference could have occurred by chance only five times in every 100.

conflict In psychology, conflict refers to opposition between human drives; in sociology, it refers to the type of analysis of society in which change is regarded as occurring as a result of conflict. This latter approach tends to be *Marxist* and has been utilized in the analysis of *adult education* by some *radical* theorists.

conformity Compliance with accepted knowledge, values, standards of behaviour or performance, skills. One of the generally expected outcomes of certain forms of *education* and *training*.

Congo The official organization for *adult education* in this country is Direction de l'Alphabétisation, BP, Brazzaville, Congo.

congregation An academic assembly.

Congregational Work Association of the Evangelical Lutheran Church of Finland Established in 1919 to be involved in *lay training* in the Finnish church. Obtained the right to run its own *study centre* in 1981 and has 26 organizations participating in its work. Current address: Vuorikatu 22 A 00100 Helsinki 10, Finland.

Congress of Adult Education of Trinidad and Tobago Current address: c/o Extra-Mural Unit, University of the West Indies, St Augustine, Trinidad and Tobago, West Indies.

Congress of Industrial Organizations (CIO) Formed in 1938 in the United States. Established its own department of education, offering an educational service to its member unions and emphasizing staff development in political and social action. Merged in 1955 with the AFL to become the *AFL-CIO*; its education department was merged with that of the AFL.

Connect A newsletter published in a number of languages on international environmental education. Available from *Unesco*.

Connecticut The Division of Evening and Continuation Schools was created in the Department of Education in this state in 1917, the first *adult education* department within any state in the United States. Other states followed soon afterwards.

connectionism According to *E.L. Thorndike, learning* is connecting. He regarded the mind as the sum total of the connections between perceptions and memories of situations. *Learning* was for him, the creation of a connection between a *response* and a stimulus.

conscientization *Paulo Freire* has adapted this term to refer to the process by which people, as knowing subjects rather than passive recipients, achieve a deepening awareness both of the socio-cultural reality that shapes their lives and of their own capacity to act back upon the world and transform it.

consciousness-raising The process of helping people to become aware of the social processes that have resulted in the present social situation and of making people aware of their responsibility in active participation in the social processes. See also *conscientization*.

Conseil de l'Éducation Continue des Adultes (CECA) The *continuing education* council of Geneva, Switzerland. Current address: 6 rue Prévost Martin, 1205 Geneva, Switzerland.

Conseil de l'Education Permanente The *University of the Third Age* attached to the Free University of Brussels. It was founded in 1975 and is an official institution of the University. Current address: c/o Free University of Brussels, 30 Avenue Antoine Depage, Brussels, Belgium.

Conseil Superieur d'Education Populaire Translated, the High Council of Adult Education. It is the professional association for adult education in Belgium. See also the Flemish centre, *Vlaams Centrum voor Volksontwikkeling*, which relates to it. Current address: Galerie Ravenstein, 78–1000 Brussels, Belgium.

Consejo de Educación de Adultos de América Latina (CEAAL) The *Latin American council for adult education*. Current address: Casilla 6257, Correo 22, Santiago, Chile.

Consejo Nacional de Educación de Adultos de Nicaragua The Nicaraguan council for adult education. Current address: c/o Director General de Educación de Adultos, Ministerio de Educación, Apartado 509, Managua, Nicaragua.

consensus An agreement between a group of people, usually as a result of concessions of minority viewpoints, in order for the group to function.

Consortium for Public Library Innovation American *clearinghouse* on innovations in *public libraries*. Current address: 300 Nicolet Mall, Minneapolis, Minnesota 55401, USA.

Consorzio per l'Università a Distanza A consortium of six universities in Italy which offer *distance education*.

construct A mental creation, a concept. E.g., a personal construct, a social construct, in which a person's conceptualization is related to either the individuality/personality or to his/her social situation.

Construction Industry Training Board Responsible for overseeing *training* within this industry within the United Kingdom. Current address: Radnor House, London Road, Norbury, London SW16 4EL, UK.

constructivism The process whereby *perceptual experience* is more than a direct response to the stimulus.

Consultative Group for Training and Education in Agriculture (CGTEA) Comprised of representatives of all the major educational bodies which serve agriculture and horticulture in the United Kingdom. Publishes its own newsletter. Its database is also available through *MARISNET*. Current address: East Close, Ditcheat, Shepton Mallet, Somerset BA4 6PS, UK.

consumer education The aims of consumer education are twofold: to help consumers learn their rights, and to be discriminating. It is a form of education espoused by the Co-operative Movement and other groups. Recently it has been included in more *community education* programmes.

Contact The journal of the *International Association of Universities of the Third Age*, established in 1987.

contact hour A measure of time in which the *teacher* and the *learners* interact formally in a teaching and learning situation. The duration is actually often only 50 minutes.

CONTACT Literacy Center Based in Nebraska, United States, this is a telephone referral network with extensive contacts with literacy programmes throughout America. It is also a national *clearinghouse* for information about *adult literacy*. Current address: P.O. Box 81826 Lincoln, Nebraska 68501, USA.

content Usually refers to the *knowledge, skills*, and *attitudes* that learners are expected to explore or acquire during a lesson, course, etc. It is an element of the *curriculum*.

content analysis The analysis of data contained in documentation, often in a qualitative manner. A research technique that is occasionally employed in *adult education*.

content mastery All aspects of proficiency in respect to the specified content of the *course* or *curriculum*.

context dependent question The type of question that often occurs in a professional examination when the field of practice, e.g. a *case study*, forms the basis of the question which elicits either a response relating to the theoretical, the practical, or a combination of both.

Continental Classroom An early *credit course* run and televised by the National Broadcasting Corporation in the United States.

contingency table A statistical table in which two or more variables are categorized.

continuation schools Mainly for young people in Denmark who have left school (folkeskole) but are too young to attend the *folk high school*. These are private, independent, and residential and function as an alternative to the upper end of secondary education. See also *Home Economics Schools*. There is a periodical published by the association of these schools. Current address of the association: Secretariat of the Continuation Schools, Vartov, Farvergade 27, DK–1463 Copenhagen K.

continuing education (CE) 1. Either those learning opportunities that are taken up after fulltime schooling has finished, or those learning opportunities that are taken up after the completion of initial education. It is an all-embracing term that has assumed currency in the 1980s, although *continuing professional education* is also employed in the case of *post-basic vocational education*. 2. The *German Education Council* define it as 'the continuation or resumption of organized learning after the completion of an initial educational phase of varying length'.

continuing education for women (CEW) Part of the American adult education programme for women, it initially concentrated upon women returners to education and more recently has developed outreach programmes. See *New Opportunities for Women* (*NOW*) and *Wider Opportunities for Women* (*WOW*) for similar initiatives in the United Kingdom.

Continuing Education in New Zealand Established in 1968, the journal of the *National Council of Adult Education* in New Zealand.

Continuing Education in Northern Ireland: A Strategy for Development Report published by the Northern Ireland Council for Adult Education in November 1980. See *Strategy Report*.

continuing education record card Some professional groups issue members with record cards on which they are required to keep a record of their *continuing education*. Some of them demand that it is submitted on occasions to the professional association to be monitored.

Continuing Education Standing Committee A standing committee on *continuing education* that reports to both the National Advisory Body and the University Grants Committee, the two bodies that were responsible for *higher education* in the United Kingdom until the formation of *University Funding Council* and the *Polytechnic Funding Council* in 1988.

continuing education unit (CEU) Recognition given to participants for ten *contact hours* within formal *continuing education*. It is becoming widely used in America. See also *Council on the Continuing Education Unit*.

continuing engineering education The first world congress of *continuing education* in engineering was held in Mexico in 1979.

Continuing Higher Education Review The journal of the *National University Continuing Education Association*.

Continuing Library Education Network and Exchange (CLENE) An American association concerned with the use of libraries in *distance education*.

Established in 1975 and initially funded by ten different agencies. It was anticipated that it would eventually be supported by membership fees alone.

continuing medical education The definition used by both the *American Medical Association* and the *Accreditation Council for Continuing Medical Education* in America is that it consists of those educational activities which serve to maintain, develop, or increase the *knowledge, skills*, and professional performance and relationships that a physician uses to provide services for patients, the public, or the profession. The content of this form of education falls within the medical sciences but it is also recognized that certain of the social sciences may be appropriately included within this definition.

continuing professional development The development of the professional practitioner after initial training through staff development plans such as *continuing professional education*, guidance on the job, career counselling, etc.

continuing professional education (CPE) Those learning opportunities which are taken up after the completion of basic vocational preparation. See also *mandatory continuing education*.

continuing vocational education *Continuing education* is often used as if it were synonymous with continuing vocational education, which refers specifically to *education* and *training* that occurs after initial preparation for the vocation during an individual's career. The philosophical debate about distinctions between education and training are rarely referred to in this context, although this may be because the academic study of *vocational education* is still in its infancy.

continuing vocational training See *continuing vocational education*.

continuous assessment The process of assessing students throughout the whole of their course rather than at the end of the course only. It is often claimed that this is a less stressful form of *assessment* but evidence is mixed about this. Continuous assessment is often confused with *course work assessment*. See also *formative assessment*.

continuous education This term is sometimes used in the same way, but without the political connotations as *recurrent education*, i.e. education that recurs throughout life as learners consider it to be necessary to them.

Continuous Learning Established in 1976, the original title of *Learning*, a journal published by the *Canadian Association for Adult Education*.

Continuum The journal of the *National University Continuing Education Association*. Published three times a year. It is refereed but also commissions papers in order to have an expanded discussion on a specific topic.

contract research Research carried out under contract, often short-term, by a researcher or university for another organization. A method of fund-raising that universities of the United Kingdom have increasingly employed. The *Advisory Council for Adult and Continuing Education* engaged in some contracting out of research during its brief period of activity.

controlled experiment A research enterprise in which the majority of independent variables are held constant while only one or two are altered in each stage of the research.

convention An assembly of members, delegates, or representatives from the local branches of an organization.

Convention 140 of the International Labour Organisation Adopted in 1974, this urged member countries to grant workers leave for educational purposes and was a major contributor to the growth of *paid educational leave*.

Convergence Founded in 1968, the quarterly journal of *The International Council of Adult Education*.

convergent thinking The process of thinking characterized by synthesizing ideas, information, or knowledge to solve a problem. This is a *cognitive* or *learning style*. See the opposite kind of thinking, *divergent thinking*.

conversations A method of engaging people in public debate about contemporary issues, first employed in America by Margaret Fuller Ossoli in the early nineteenth century. She charged an admission fee for the series. An organized discussion group led by one person.

conversion course A course taken to equip people for a post or course when previous study has only partially prepared them to perform it.

convocation The assembly of graduates of a university.

Coomasie, Alhaji Ahmadu (b. 1908) One of the pioneers of *adult education* in Nigeria. He was born in Ghana in the Islam tradition, and worked in Northern Nigeria with other Islamic people to encourage *adult literacy*.

Coombe Lodge The UK *further education* staff college. Publishes reports on a variety of topics. Current address: Coombe Lodge Further Education Staff College, Blagdon, Bristol BS18 6RG, UK.

Cooper, Peter (1791–1883) Founder of the Cooper Union, a self-educated craftsman who later made a fortune in numerous commercial interests. He may have been the first American to direct his personal fortune towards the *education of adults*.

Cooper, Thomas A *Chartist* and largely self-educated working-class leader, living in Leicester in England. A social reformer, he occupied a number of different positions in life, many of an adult educational nature. His autobiography is called *The Life of Thomas Cooper*.

Cooper Union for the Advancement of Science and Art Established in New York in 1859 by *Peter Cooper* to provide education in science and arts for the practical business of living. Initially he provided a large set of premises for *instruction, reading,* and other learned pursuits. Tuition was free for *evening classes* and other educational activities. In addition, he provided finance and space for the establishment of a Female School of Design within the Union. Over the years many well-known adult educators have been associated with this institution. Currently it offers a wide programme including degree-level courses.

Cooperative Assessment of Experiential Learning See *Council for Adult and Experiential Learning*.

Co-operative College A UK residential adult education college and a centre for community training and research offering courses that lead to a University of Nottingham award. The college is also an independent international business school, recognized by the Department of Education and Science. Current address: Stanford Hall, Loughborough, Leicestershire LE12 5QR, UK.

Co-operative College of Canada Established in 1973 as a national college, it has developed a resource base for co-operatives in Canada. It is also a teacher-accrediting institution and provides a variety of *curricula* material. Receives some funding from the federal government, especially for its work with the Third World and the Inuit. See also *International Co-operative Institute* and *Western Co-operative College*.

co-operative education A form of education in which the school and the occupational field co-operate in order to provide a joint educational programme with alternate attendance in both school and work. A concept used in American education. See *co-operative programme*.

Cooperative Education Association Seeks to provide a forum for those involved in *co-operative education* in the United States. Contact address: c/o Drexel University, 32nd and Chestnut Street, Philadelphia, Pennsylvania 19104, USA.

Co-operative Education Materials Advisory Service Seeks to improve the quality of *co-operative education* in developing countries and to facilitate the supply and exchange of information through seminars and workshops. It publishes its own bulletin quarterly. It is a section of the *International Co-operative Alliance* and located at the Alliance's headquarters.

Cooperative Education Research Center American *clearinghouse*. Current address: 408 Churchill Hall, Northeastern University, Boston, Massachusetts 02115, USA.

cooperative extension See Cooperative Extension Service.

cooperative extension agent First employed in 1906. An educational organizer working in *cooperative extension* and jointly employed by the US Department of Agriculture and the university offering the extension service.

Cooperative Extension Service The term 'co-operative' stems from the fact that it is a co-operative arrangement funded by county, state, and the federal government in the United States. Established in 1914 in the *Smith-Lever Act*, it is among the largest adult education enterprises in the world since the United States is a largely agricultural society. Each state receives a federal grant annually on production of a satisfactory plan, which is usually in co-operation with a *land grant college*. These colleges receive general guidelines from the Department of Agriculture, which also monitors their performance. Its functions include assisting farmers in the efficiency of agricultural production; conservation and use of natural resources;

management of farm and home; family living; leadership development; community improvement; assisting farmers and others in relation to public affairs. No educational program run by co-operative extension leads to a university degree; it is essentially a practical educational service. See also *4-H movement, cooperative extension agent.* Headquarters address: US Department of Agriculture, Washington, DC., USA. See also *agricultural extension.*

cooperative program US equivalent of the *sandwich course* in the United Kingdom, where a student spends blocks of time in an educational institution and blocks in the workplace. Courses of this nature are usually either at professional qualification or undergraduate level.

Co-operative Society Founded in Rochdale, England in 1844. Many of the branches of the movement devoted as much as 2.5 per cent of their profits of the movement to educational purposes. Hence, throughout the history of the movement there has been a great concern for the *education* of underprivileged groups of people.

Co-operative Women's Guilds Established in 1883 in England to help women take their place within the *Co-operative Movement.* Provides both a social and educational programme; also involved in *consumer education.*

Coördinatiegroep projecten volwasseneneduucatie The Dutch national co-ordinating body for *adult* and *continuing education.* Current address: Postbus 1004, 3700 BA Zeist, the Netherlands.

coping skills The ability to deal successfully with personal, social, and work-related problems. See *life skills.*

Corbett, Edward Annaud (1889–1964) Corbett, like many others in *adult education,* was influenced by his religious beliefs and training. He was director of the Extension Department of the University of Alberta, and became the first director of the *Canadian Association of Adult Education* in 1935. He was a very influential figure in Canadian *adult education.*

core curriculum 1. Generally regarded as that part of the *curriculum* which is essential studying for every student. See also *option units.* 2. In the United States, it is also sometimes regarded as the basic programme to which other credits can be added. See also *required course.*

corporate classroom Large industrial and commercial companies are now organizing a great deal of their own *continuing professional education.* These institutions are commonly known as corporate classrooms.

corporate culture The values and beliefs that are shared by members of an organization that help to shape management style and the employees' behaviour.

Corporation for Public Broadcasting An American corporation involved in the production and the stimulation of production of high–quality educational television programmes. Current address: 1111 16th Street NW, Washington DC 20036, USA.

correction The process of *assessing* students' work and highlighting the faults. In adult education it is usually suggested that this process should be undertaken in a positive manner so that the *self-concept* of the *adult learner* is not threatened but positively enhanced as a result of the feedback.

correctional education Education that takes place within penal institutions. See also *penal andragogy, prison education.*

Correctional Education Association The professional association of educators working in penal institutions in the United States, it publishes its own journal, *Journal of Correctional Education,* and yearbook. Current address:

1400 20th Street NW, Washington DC 20036, USA.

Correctional Institutions Unit A committee of the *American Association for Adult and Continuing Education*.

correlation A tendency of two or more variables to change in accord with each other. Often mistaken for *causality*. Used a great deal in statistical analysis.

correspondence college An educational organization that tutors its students through the medium of correspondence usually to prepare them for some examination.

Correspondence College of the German Trades Union Federation Provides both *political* and *vocational education* for members by *distance study*. A member of the Workshop of Correct Distance Study in the Federal Republic of Germany.

correspondence education A form of education organized through the written medium, begun in Britain as early as 1840 when *Pitman* started teaching shorthand through correspondence. It increased in popularity in England towards the end of the nineteenth century. In America, there were attempts to introduce correspondence education in 1873 but it really began with *Chautauqua* in 1879. See *correspondence tuition*.

Correspondence Education Centre One of Yugoslavia's three main *distance teaching* institutions, providing both *secondary and higher education*. It also has its own publishing house which produces material other than that prepared for the courses. Located in Belgrade. See also *Workers Correspondence University* and *Birotehnika*.

correspondence school See *correspondence college*. 1. In the United States, a large number of such schools were established after the success of *Chautauqua*, especially the *International Correspondence Schools*. 2. The first correspondence school opened in Yugoslavia in 1926.

correspondence tuition The form of student–teacher relationship in which the medium of teaching is correspondence, an early popular form of *distance education*. In the United States, its first major success was with *Chautauqua*.

Correspondence University In 1883 an unsuccessful attempt was made to start correspondence education in America with the formation of this organization at Ithaca, New York.

correspondence workers' universities *Workers' universities*, or merely *correspondence colleges* established in Yugoslavia.

cosmopolitan Used in the study of occupations for practitioners whose *reference group* is the whole of the occupation rather than the local employing agency. In a sense this term is used in a similar manner to *professional*. See also *locals*.

Costa Rica See *Central American Institute for the Extension of Culture* and *Associación Costarricense de Educación de Adultos*.

Council for Adult and Experiential Learning (CAEL) Started in 1974 in the United States as a project of the *Educational Testing Service*, it is now an independent non-profit institution devoted to the recognition that learning occurs in all types of situations, so that *assessment of prior learning* and other aspects of *experiential learning* are its major focus among adults. In 1974 it was known as *Cooperative Assessment of Experiential Learning*; in 1977 it became independent and was then called *Council for the Advancement of Experiential Learning*; in 1985 it assumed its present name. It publishes a bimonthly newspaper, organizes national meetings, and is involved in a number of research projects in this area. It has an individual and associational membership. Address: 10840, Little Patuxent Parkway, Suite 203, Columbia, Maryland, 21044, USA.

Council for Business Education
Established in 1956, an American
organization. Address: 725 15th Street
NW, Washington DC 20005, USA.

**Council for Education in World
Citizenship** An institution that seeks
through education and the dissemination
of information to promote world
citizenship. Current address:
19–21 Tudor Street, London EC4Y 0DJ,
UK.

Council for Educational Technology
(CET) Established in 1973 in the United
Kingdom as a successor to the *National
Council for Educational Technology*. This
council is involved in the use of and
advice on all forms of curriculum
planning and educational technology,
and includes a micro–computer
support unit for educators. It is also
concerned with all aspects of *open
learning*, publishing a newsheet, and a
variety of material providing advice or
guidance. Current address:
3 Devonshire Street, London W1N 2BA,
UK.

**Council for Environmental
Education** National body in the United
Kingdom concerned to increase
awareness of the significance of the
environment. Current address:
24, London Road, Reading RG1 5AQ,
Berks, UK.

**Council for National Academic
Awards** (CNAA) Granted a royal
charter in 1964, this is the accrediting and
degree-awarding body of all non-
university *higher education* in the United
Kingdom. It has gradually developed a
more relaxed policy towards some of the
polytechnics so that while they still
award CNAA degrees, they have more
autonomy. The CNAA has also been
involved in developments for *credit
transfer*. It succeeded the *National Council
for Technological Awards* although its
concern has been much wider than the
National Council's. Address:
344–354 Gray's Inn Road, London WC1,
UK.

**Council for Small Industries in Rural
Areas** The aim of this council is to
regenerate rural areas of England. It
provides training courses in a range of
skills necessary for rural life. Address:
141 Castle Street, Salisbury, Wilts
SP1 3TP, UK.

Council for Technical Co-operation
Established by Commonwealth
Members to promote technical education
but now merged with the *Council for
Technological Education and Training for
Overseas Countries.*

**Council for Technological Education
and Training for Overseas Countries**
Founded in 1962 in the United Kingdom,
this body seeks to enhance *vocational
education* in Third World countries.

**Council for the Accreditation of
Correspondence Colleges** Established
in the United Kingdom in 1969, it has its
own code of conduct. Current address:
27 Marylebone Road, London NW1 5JS,
UK.

**Council for the Accreditation of
Teacher Training** (CATE) The
statutory body in England and Wales that
reviews and accredits courses proposed
by institutions of higher education
offering training for school teachers.
Established in 1984 for a limited period
to ensure that all courses follow national
criteria. The Council itself does not offer
an award, but without its accreditation
no course can be given leading to
qualified teacher status. Current address:
CATE, Department of Education and
Science, Elisabeth House, York Road,
London SE1, UK.

**Council for the Advancement and
Support of Education** An American
association. Current address: One
Dupont Circle NW, Suite 530,
Washington DC 20036, USA.

**Council for the Advancement of
Citizenship** (CAC) Created in the
United States to foster *citizenship
education* nationally. It is a consortium of
national, state, and local organizations.

Current address: 1724 Massachusetts Avenue NW, Suite 300, Washington DC 20036, USA.

Council for the Advancement of Experiential Learning See *Council for Adult and Experiential Learning*. Current address: American City Building, Suite 208, Columbia, Maryland 21044, USA.

Council for the Encouragement of Music and the Arts (CEMA) Established in 1939 to ensure that the appreciation of music and the arts was not lost during the Second World War. Its origins lie in the fact that the *British Institute of Adult Education* successfully started *Art for the People*. In 1946 it was reconstituted as the *Arts Council of Great Britain* and granted a Royal Charter.

Council for Licensed Conveyancers Body responsible for the *training, examination*, and licensing of professional conveyancers in the United Kingdom. Current address: CLC, Golden Cross House, Duncannon Street, London WC2N 4FJ, UK.

Council for Museums and Galleries in Scotland The national council in Scotland which offers professional advice and guidance for the benefit of museologists. It is partially funded by government grant.

Council for Non-Collegiate Continuing Education An American association concerned with *continuing education* outside the educational system. Current address: 6N 6th Street, Richmond, Virginia 23219, USA.

Council for the Education of Adults in Latin America (CEAAL) This council represents more than 60 national groups in all the countries in Latin America. It is an associated organization of the *International Council for Adult Education*. Address: Consejo de Educación de Adultos de America Latina, Casilla 6257, Santiago, Chile.

Council of Engineering Institutions The professional body which establishes the standards of engineering education in the United Kingdom. Current address: 2 Little Smith Street, London SW1, UK.

Council of Europe This body has concerned itself with both *adult education* in its formal sense and in *cultural* activities in the wider sense and has issued a number of reports on these subjects. Address: Council of Europe, F-67006 Strasbourg Cedex, France. It has a separate division for Out-of-School Education with the following address: Education Committee BP 431 67006, Strasbourg, Cedex France.

Council of Graduate Schools in the United States American body concerned to co-ordinate the work of graduate education. Address: One Dupont Circle NW, Washington DC 20036, USA.

Council of Legal Education The professional body for the education of barristers in the United Kingdom. Address: Gray's Inn Place, London WC1, UK.

Council of National Organizations Formed in 1952 in the United States to co-ordinate the work of national *adult education* organizations. Member organizations had to have a national remit and an educational philosophy compatible with that of the *Adult Education Association of the United States of America* of which it was constitutionally related.

Council of National Organizations for Adult Education Formed as an independent organization from the *Council of National Organizations* in 1959. Current address: 810 18th Street NW, Washington DC 20006, USA.

Council on Library Resources The American body concerned with academic libraries. Address: One Dupont Circle NW, Washington DC 20036, USA.

Council on Non-Collegiate Continuing Education Seeks to impose standards and regulations on organizations that offer *continuing education* outside of the traditional educational setting.

Council on Post-Secondary Accreditation (COPA) A private, non-profit national organization in America whose main aim is to support, co-ordinate, and improve non-government *accreditation* schemes at post-secondary level. Current address: One Dupont Circle NW, Suite 760, Washington DC 20036, USA.

Council on Social Work Education An American professional association concerned with *education* within social work. Current address: 111 Eighth Avenue, New York, New York, USA.

Council on the Continuing Education Unit American organization establishing principles of the use of the *continuing education unit*. It has published guidelines and principles of use for the unit. Current address: c/o Evening College and Summer Session, Shaffer Hall, Johns Hopkins University, Baltimore, Maryland 21218, USA.

counselling A generic term which is used to cover a number of processes, such as interviewing, advising, guiding, and even providing therapy in areas of personal problems. There are different techniques, such as *non-directive counselling*.

county agent The *adult educator* working in the *Cooperative Extension Service* who is an agricultural specialist and who acts as an advisor to agriculturists and farmers generally. Like the *home demonstration agent*, this agent is usually based in the extension section of an Agricultural College of a *land grant university* in America.

Courrier de l'ADEP, Le The magazine of the *Agence National pour le développement de l'Education Permanente*. It was started in 1977 and is published three times a year.

course 1. A specified number of lessons and assignments to be studied. 2. The content to be studied during a specified number of lessons.

course manager The administrator who is concerned with the production of a course. This job is especially important in the production of *distance education* courses.

course meeting A gathering of academic staff and students on a course to discuss the progress of the course and to allow the students and all the academic staff an opportunity to participate jointly in both the content selection and the process of the course.

course requirements The obligations and demands imposed upon the student before the award of a certificate to signify satisfactory completion of an academic course of study.

course team The team of academics and other professionals such as educational broadcasters and designers if involved in *distance education*, who prepare an educational course.

course team assistant An administrative assistant involved in undertaking many of the minor administrative tasks in the production of a course, especially useful in *distance education*.

course team chairman Where the course team is large, due to its multi-disciplinary or multi-media nature, it is necessary to have an administrative chairman. This occurs in the UK *Open University* courses where one of the academic staff usually fulfils that role; often it is the member of staff who originally proposed the course under preparation. However that member of staff often relinquishes the post when the course has been prepared and is being taught.

course tutor 1. A teacher to a course of study. 2. A part-time tutor to a course of study with the *Open University* in the United Kingdom.

course work assessment The process of using students' work during the course as part of their final assessment. This is sometimes referred to as *continuous assessment* although it need not be, since there may still be a *summative assessment*.

courses by radio See *Funkkolleg*.

courses for young entrepreneurs Organized by the *Manpower Services Commission* for young entrepreneurs between the ages of 18 and 25 years. (Note: the *Manpower Services Commission* changed its name to the *Training Commission* and then to the *Training Agency* in 1988.)

court The governing body of a university in the United Kingdom.

co-variance A statistical concept which refers to the manner in which two variables change in relation to each other.

cow college See *land grant college*.

craft education Learning traditional and modern crafts has become a major area of *adult liberal education*. It is also *vocational education* for the few who still work in these areas.

Crafts Council Established in the United Kingdom to promote crafts. It is aware of the significance of *adult education* in the fulfilment of its aims, having commissioned research into this area of adult education. Current address: The Education Section, Crafts Council, 12 Waterloo Place, London SW1Y 4AU, UK.

Cranage, Rev. D.H.S. (1866–1957) Dean of Norwich Cathedral. Prior to that he served as an *extension lecturer* for the University of Cambridge. Thereafter, he was Lectures Secretary to the University of Cambridge Syndicate and, later, Secretary to the Board of Extra-Mural Studies of the University, where he remained for 26 years. He was responsible for the erection of *Stuart House* as the headquarters for the Board.

creative Innovative, producing new approaches.

creative learning *Learning* through synthesizing and *reflecting* so that new ideas and meanings are created in the *learning process*. See *creativity*.

creative writing The art of writing in an imaginative manner.

creativity The process of bringing something new into existence. A much valued concept among adult educators, especially those who adopt a more humanistic perspective. Some psychologists regard it as one of the outcomes of divergent or lateral thinking. Some adult educators might regard it as a learning outcome of critical or reflective thinking of which everyone is capable. It should include elements of transformation, innovation, novelty, etc. and should include the development of the learner's own *self*, as well as the product of the learning.

credit The unit of value awarded for successful completion of *courses* of study, or other *learning experiences*, which count towards the final award. See *Carnegie units, credit hour*.

credit accumulation A system whereby learners accumulate credit for the successful completion of recognized *modules* of learning, so that the learner determines to a considerable extent the overall pattern of his/her study and the constitution of the subjects studied for an award.

Credit Accumulation and Transfer Scheme (CATS) Launched in the United Kingdom in 1986 and administered by the *Council for National Academic Awards*, it is a scheme which accredits courses run by education and educational departments in industry and commerce as fractions of a degree. An undergraduate degree is worth 360 points and courses are awarded points to designate how much credit can be gained for successful completion of each course. In addition, individual students can be offered advice and register with the scheme, so that they can design their own course of study leading to whatever award they elect to follow. Address: Registrar, Council for National Academic Awards, 344–354 Gray's Inn Road, London WC1X 8BP, UK.

credit by examination *Credit* earned by the successful completion of a test designed to indicate that the candidate has mastered content that would be taught on a *course* of study.

credit course A course of study that is recognized for specific credit by an award-giving educational agency, such as a university.

credit exemption The recognition by an educational award-giving agency, such as the *Open University* of the value of previous study undertaken by the student in another context and the award of specific *credit* towards the educational qualification for which the learner is studying. See also the *assessment of prior learning*.

credit hour Unit of academic time used in American universities. E.g., a course may be worth three hours, which is usually equivalent to 30 actual hours of study.

credit transfer The ability to transfer *credit* gained in one educational context to another. One university will accept as creditworthy the courses followed in another, similar institution.

credit unit The unit of value that is awarded for the successful completion of a course or part-course, e.g. a *credit hour*, a *Carnegie unit*.

crisis education Community learning when a local crisis, such as a workers' strike, provides opportunity for study and discussion. Frequently utilized in *study circles* in Scandinavia.

criterion Recognized standard or level of performance against which individual achievement might be compared.

criterion-referenced testing An approach to *assessment* that is based upon judging against pre-selected standards or criteria, rather than against the performance of others. See *norm-referenced testing*.

critical consciousness The process of becoming aware of the social processes operative within society and of acquiring distance from one's own thought processes to reflect upon them.

Critical Education Association A provider of *general adult education* in Denmark, but attached to some of the popular grassroots movements and pressure groups.

critical incident technique A technique used in *human resource development* in which a collection of reports about action or behaviour relating to a specific incident that is crucial to the functioning of an organization are gathered and analysed.

critical pedagogy An approach to teaching that encourages the *learners* to use their own reality as a basis for understanding and analysis. See *emancipatory education, radical education*.

Critical Pedagogy Networker A publication on critical social issues in education from the School of Education, Deakin University, Australia. It began in February 1988 and there are four issues per annum.

critical theory An analytical perspective that owes its origin to the Frankfurt School, especially to the work of *Jürgen Habermas*. There are elements of *Marxist* thought combined with *Freudian* perceptions within this theoretical analysis. It does not accept the positivist, value-free approach to the analysis of social phenomena but rather asserts that no interpretation of a social fact is value-free. Hence, it is possible to analyse the values which underlie social action and the methods through which interpretation is socially constructed.

This process, claim the critical theorists, is *emancipatory*. It is important to distinguish critical theory from *critical thinking*.

critical thinking The ability to analyse propositions and to assess the extent of their validity. A thought form very much valued by *adult educators*. See also *reflection*.

critical value The value in a statistical test which determines acceptance or rejection of a *null hypothesis* in quantitative research.

criticism The process of analysis and assessment.

critique A critical analysis of an argument, case, position, etc.

Cross, K. Patricia (b. 1926) Well-known American psychologist and professor at Harvard University whose writing has concentrated upon *adult learning* and *higher education*.

Cross–Culture Learner Centres Founded in Canada in the late 1960s, these centres exist to help Canadians understand the dominant issues of Third World development, colonialism, and racism. They are funded both by government and by membership fees.

cross–sectional study A research process that studies different groups or categories at the same point in time. See *longitudinal study*.

Crowther Fund A fund established by the *Open University* in the United Kingdom to make grants or Open University graduates who wish to undertake a minor research, one which does not necessarily have to lead to a *higher degree*.

Crowther Report Published in 1959, a report on the educational provision needed for teenage people in the United Kingdom. It recommended the establishment of continuation colleges throughout the United Kingdom. The report was never implemented.

crystallized intelligence That form of *intelligence* that is related to experience and education rather than biology. See *fluid intelligence*.

Cuba The Ministry of Education controls *adult education* in Cuba. Current address: Obispo No 160 esq Mercaderes, La Habana Vieja, República de Cuba.

cultural action An aspect of *radical adult education*, often following the ideas and methods of *Paulo Freire*, in which oppressed people are helped to understand their own position in the socio–political world through a dialogic process of teaching and learning. This then enables them to take social or political action to improve their social situation. Many radical Catholic adult education developments have occurred in Latin America which might be classified as revolutionary.

cultural activity Term usually restricted to the performing, visual, and literary arts and crafts. In this sense *culture* is being used in the sense that sociologists would use 'high culture'.

cultural animation A term used for some aspects of *adult education* in countries such as Yugoslavia. It refers to the fact that if people are to manage the whole of their lives, they have to be encouraged and taught to participate in cultural development, cultural policies, creation of works of art, etc. In Yugoslavia each commune has its cultural parliament where such decisions are made and in which citizens may participate equally.

cultural centre 1. Residential centres of adult education in Holland run by the religious denominations. 2. In Belgium these centres are similar to the *maison de la culture* in France. They provide *adult education* and a variety of other cultural activities for a specific geographical area. There is an association of cultural centres in Belgium that relates directly to the *Vlaams Centrum voor Volksontwikkeling*.

cultural circles An informal method of teaching and learning by establishing groups to discuss relevant social topics, such as nationalism, development, etc. A method of teaching and learning utilized widely in some parts of the Third World. See *study circle*.

cultural development The process of enriching the cultural context in which an activity occurs.

cultural development project An educational project designed to enrich the culture of a community or a society.

cultural disadvantage Persons whose backgrounds or *socialization* differ from the norm of a social group to such an extent as to disadvantage them culturally within it.

cultural enrichment The development of *cognitive*, *perceptual*, and *verbal skills*.

cultural heritage The *culture* of one generation that it seeks to preserve and pass on to the succeeding generation. This has been seen by some scholars as the basis for much compulsory education.

cultural house Local cultural centres found throughout Hungary. There are about 2,600 such institutions throughout the country and a national conference of cultural houses is held occasionally. See also *Institute of Culture*.

cultural invasion An aspect of imperialism whereby one society and its culture dominates that of another society, often to the extent of quashing it.

cultural transmission The transmission of aspects of an established *culture* to those who have not already acquired it. It is regarded critically by some sociological analysts (see *critical theory, radical adult education*) but seen by others as essential for the survival of society by those with a more *functionalist* perspective.

culture 1. A sociological concept with a number of different meanings, but when used within the framework of adult education it usually refers to the sum total of *knowledge, beliefs, attitudes, values,* etc. of a social group. 2. In common speech, however, it usually refers to the established arts, such as classical music, art, etc. This is sometimes known as the elite theory of culture.

Culture The journal of the French *adult education* association *Peuple et Culture*. It was started in 1982 and is published three times a year.

culture of silence A social situation in which oppressed peoples are unable to exert any control in the decision-making processes affecting themselves and their own society. A concept popularized in *adult education* by the work of *Paulo Freire*.

culture shock The trauma experienced by a person entering a new *culture* or *subculture*.

cumulative frequency The sum of the *frequencies* of a *distribution*.

current expenditures per student per hour per course meeting Current expenditure for *adult/continuing education* divided by the aggregated student hours. A useful measure with part-time students.

curriculum A relatively common concept in initial education. Rare, until recent times, in adult and continuing education, with terms like *programme* being more commonly used. Some scholars deny that adult education has a curriculum, often because they adopt one specific approach to the concept, although there are many. Curriculum tends to mean the entire range of learning experiences provided by an educational institution, including *the hidden curriculum*. Such a definition is close to the meaning of *programme* as it is used in the United Kingdom and the United States.

curriculum design The construction of a *curriculum* to embody specific principles, e.g. as a response to a *needs analysis*.

curriculum development The implementation of the *curriculum design*.

curriculum vitae See *résumé*. The statement of the biographical details of a person, used most frequently in applications for jobs.

cut-off point The number or score which is used to distinguish one category or *grade* from another.

cybernetics A branch of science concerned with control systems through feedback and subsequent systems modification in electrical or mechanical devices and the relationship between these and *communications* in man-made and biological systems.

CYCLOPS The UK Open University computer programme through which computer data can be transmitted via telephone to a visual display unit in another place.

Cyprus See *Pan-Cyprian Committee for Adult Education*.

Cyprus Adult Education Association Current address: PO Box 4019, Nicosia, Cyprus.

Czechoslovakia There are two major institutes in this country: Institute of Adult Education, Blanick 4, 120 00 Prague 2, Czechoslovakia; and Adult Educayion Institute in Bratislava, Námesti Slovenské no nárohmiho povstá ni, 12, 811 06 Bratislava, Czechoslovakia.

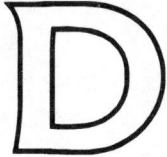

DACUM A system developed by the Canadian Department of Manpower whereby the *competencies* of an occupation may be specified prior to constructing a *curriculum* for vocational preparation.

Danage See *Landsforeningen Aldre Sagen*.

dance The creation of physical movement to express natural, emotional, or other phenomena, often in time to music. It is the language of gesture. There is a vast range of dance movements and dance is a popular *adult education* pursuit. There is also currently a growth in interest in dance education.

Danish as a second language In common with many other developed countries, Denmark has become the host nation for many immigrants. Hence it has become important to teach the national language and adult educators have been engaged in this task.

Danish Association of Agricultural Schools The co-ordinating association of the 32 *agricultural schools* in Denmark. There are also two horticultural schools within the Association. Current address: The Secretariat, Agricultural Information Office, Danish Association of Agricultural Schools, Tune Agricultural School.

Danish Council for Adult Education Founded in 1941, the co-ordinating body for voluntary *general adult education* in Denmark. This organization co-operates with the international bodies in *adult education*. Current address: Roemergarde 7, DK-1362 Copenhagen K, Denmark.

Danish Engineers' Post-Graduate Institute (DIEU) An independent non-profit educational institution located in the Technical University. Established in 1975 by two engineering unions, this organization employs professional staff from all over the world to work with its small professional team, organizing courses and conferences. It is also engaged in research projects, mostly in management and technology. Current address: The Technical University of Denmark, Building 208, Lyngby, Box 326, DK 2800 Lyngby, Denmark.

Danish Institute Established to inform other countries of the cultural developments in Denmark and to establish cultural co-operation internationally. It organizes conferences and courses each year on *adult education* and related subjects, and also organizes study tours. It has offices in Edinburgh and some European countries. Current address: Det Danske Selskab, Kultorvet 2, DK-1175, Copenhagen K, Denmark.

Danish Leisure Education Act Passed in 1968 the act upon which *adult education* in Denmark is financed. It also specifies that teachers of adults should have qualifications for teaching adults.

Danish Parliamentary Resolution On 30 May 1984, the Danish government adopted a ten-point resolution to act as a guide to the development of *adult education* and *popular education* in coming years. This resolution lays out a futuristic plan which includes expansion of both adult and popular education, the right to *paid educational leave*, development of *vocational education*, the *assessment of prior* *learning,* the creation of a fund for education, and support for experimentation and innovation. See *adult education legislation.*

Danish Research and Development Centre for Adult Education
Established in 1984 by Act of Parliament and funded by the state. The centre collects and stores information on new activities in adult education, has its own library, publishes newsletters and other publications, and provides public lectures and information in a variety of other ways. Additionally, it will undertake externally-funded research and information activities. Current address: Tordenskjoldgade 27, 1055 Copenhagen K, Denmark.

Danish Voluntary Education Act In 1968 the Danish Parliament passed legislation which guaranteed two-thirds funding by national and municipal authorities for *adult education* classes of at least 12 persons, for most subjects, and that funding would be made available to any provider approved by the municipal authorities. There are, consequently, a large variety of *evening schools* in Denmark. The act was more generous to the disabled. Classes are free and can run with a minimum of five students. Immigrant education is governed by separate legislation.

Dansk Aften–og Ungdomsskoleforening (DAUF) The Danish trade union for people teaching in evening, adult, and youth programmes. It is also interested in establishing contact with educators in other countries, and to this end it organizes joint study programmes. Current address: Christiansborggade 1, DK-1558 Copenhagen V, Denmark.

data (singular: datum) General term for raw research material or information stored on a computer.

day folk high school (Daghøjskoler) Recently started in Denmark as daytime *adult education* institutions with fulltime staff, rather than being run on the lines of the *evening school.*

day release A feature of some *paid educational leave* whereby workers are allowed a specified period of time each week to follow a course of study. Pioneered by the trade unions for shop stewards in the United Kingdom but practised in a great deal of *vocational education.*

day training centre Established in the United Kingdom in 1972 as a result of the Criminal Justice Act which can require offenders to attend on a probation order.

D.B.A. Doctor of Business Administration.

D.D. Doctor of Divinity.

deaf Persons whose ability to hear has been impaired so that it affects their learning performance even with the aid of amplification. They have to use other senses to receive information and stimuli. See *hard-of-hearing.*

deaf-blind People who have both visual and hearing impediments so that they are unable to learn under normal circumstances and require special educational provision.

dean An academic office in a university or other *institution of higher education* in the United Kingdom. The dean is the chairman of the faculty or responsible for a wide-ranging area of the university's work. In an American university the dean runs the college. In all educational institutions the dean is responsible for work beyond that of a single department.

death education Consists of two elements: preparing members of the caring professions to cope with death and dying; and helping individuals to come to terms with their own feelings about their own transience. This form of education is becoming a more established part of *adult education* programmes.

death instinct Freud called this the 'thanatos instinct' (Greek θανατος) which was for him an innate tendency to destroy and to possess an orientation towards death itself.

debate A teaching method whereby two or more people make opposing *presentations* so that the breadth of an issue may be examined.

decay Concept in research into *memory* which relates to the fact that *recall* becomes less efficient over time.

decile Statistical term for one-tenth of the *population* under consideration. Used frequently in graphic illustrations.

decimal classification The library system for classifying books devised by Melvil Dewey and more frequently known as the *Dewey decimal classification system*.

decision dynamics training A system of management training developed at Strathclyde University, Scotland.

Declaration of Persepolis In 1975 there was an international symposium for literacy in Iran and the final declaration is known as the Declaration of Persepolis. It was published by the Food and Agricultural Organization in Rome in 1975.

Declaration on Citizenship and Adult Learning Following a draft declaration in 1985, the *Canadian Association of Adult Education* issued this declaration in 1986. Its purpose was to incite a nationwide debate on active citizenship and a recognition that *adult education* and, therefore, *adult educators* have a significant part to play in the formation of Canadian society and the development of its communities and the country as a nation.

decoding The system of rules and regulations that have to be understood before an activity can be interpreted and given meaning. This can often be regarded as a form of *problem-solving* learning. See *coding*.

deculturation A term used in anthropology and ethnography to describe the loss of a *culture*, often because of the influence of a more dominant one.

D.Educ. Doctor of Education, sometimes used in the United States in preference to *Ed.D.*

deduction An argument that commences with general principles and reaches specific conclusions. In philosophical thought it is impossible to assert the premises and deny the conclusion without being contradictory. See *induction*.

deductive method A teaching method which follows the techniques of *deduction*, that is by starting with the general and moving to the specific.

deductive thought The application of general principles to specific situations.

deep processor A *learning style* which refers to the process of acquiring *knowledge* at a deep level, that is seeking meaning and relevance rather than just the facts. See *surface processor*.

defence mechanism Mechanism to protect the *ego* against painful experiences.

Defense Activity for Non-Traditional Education Support (DANTES) A military service educational programme for American servicemen serving outside of America, offering high school completion and a catalog of correspondence courses.

deference Term used when one person defers to another, relevant in some *peer assessment* studies where people of lower status accord higher achievement to those of higher status.

deficiency model An approach to the analysis of *adult education* which begins with the assumption that the potential learner comes below a norm in some aspect of learning, or has a deficiency which may be remedied through education. See *needs*, since this is one element in the deficiency model of *adult education*.

deformalize Since education may be seen as both *formal* and *non-formal* and it is recognized that it is relatively easy for the latter to evolve into the former, the question has been asked whether the process can be reversed.

degree An award conferred by a college or university as an official recognition of successful completion of a programme of studies.

degrees of freedom Statistical concept to indicate the number of changes that can be made to a group of figures whilst still satisfying the external requirements. This number relates to the number of unrestricted variables within the total score.

delegacy The body responsible for administering an aspect of the work of a university or college. Some *extra-mural* provision has been administered by delegacy in the United Kingdom.

deliberate discussion A technique to ensure that groups pay careful attention to statements made during discussions. It involves having the group deliberate, discuss, and decide what to say next in response to another statement made by a previous group. When the group decides on its best statement it is tape-recorded and played back to the original group to respond to. This is continued until some agreement is reached.

delivery system The process whereby *learning materials* are made available to the *learner*, e.g. a *learning package* in some forms of *self-directed learning*.

Delphi Technique Developed in the early 1950s, this is a technique designed to obtain group opinions, especially expert opinion. There are usually three or four rounds of questionnaires to each respondent, with feedback from each round so that respondents can reconsider their opinions in the light of the feedback. It has been used in *adult education research*.

demand Frequently confused with the concept of *need*. In a market model of *adult education provision* demand is the willingness to enrol in educational courses at the fee charged. Whilst this has been practised in the United Kingdom for many years, often under the guise of a *needs-meeting approach*, it became more obvious in the 1980s as the government of the day curtailed financial support for *liberal adult education*. Alternatively, it refers to the requests made for courses to be provided in specific subject areas.

democracy Literally, the power of the people. An arrangement of government whereby the people's will can be exercised, although the criteria for such action have varied throughout history and it is debatable whether any country has really achieved fully such a state. Educational philosophers have recognized that this has special reference to educational procedures and outcomes, especially within *adult education*, where *andragogic/humanistic* procedures are regularly practised as democratic. See especially the work of *John Dewey*.

democratic leadership A form of leadership in which the leader takes into consideration the views and opinions of those who are being led. Important in *group* techniques in *adult education*.

democratic methods Teaching methods which encourage learners to participate in the planning of the teaching and learning process.

demography The study of population statistics.

demonstration A *teaching method* in which an expert shows precisely how she/he believes procedure should be carried out.

demonstrator One who demonstrates; often employed to give demonstrations in education but not to teach.

D.Eng. Doctor of Engineering.

Denman College The college of the *National Federation of Women's Institutes* in the United Kingdom. It takes about 4,500 students each year for short courses on a residential basis; usually the students have to be members of the WI. It is named after Lady Denman who was the first chair of the organization, a position she held until 1946. Current address: Marcham, Nr Abingdon, Oxfordshire OX13 6NW, UK.

department In a college or university, a department is usually a subsection of the organization devoted to one specialist area of work, or to teaching and research in one particular field of knowledge.

Department of Adult Education of the National Education Association Merged with the *American Adult Education Association* in 1951 to form the *Adult Education Association of the United States of America.*

Department of Education Act Passed in 1867 in America and became the first federal education office in Washington. Changed its name in 1869 to US Office of Education.

Department of Education and Science UK department of government responsible for all educational provision in the country, except that which is administered privately outside the scope of compulsory schooling. It is responsible for Local Education Authority *adult education* provision and university *extra-mural provision*. Address: Elizabeth House, York Road, London SE1 7PH, UK.

Department of Education of the AFL–CIO Established in 1938 by the Congress of Industrial Organizations (CIO) in the United States, it provided the same service for CIO unions as did the *Worker Education Bureau* for the AFL. They were able to combine in 1955 when the two sets of labor organizations merged.

Department of Science and Art See *Science and Art Department.*

dependency 1. The condition in which one needs to rely on another person or something else, e.g. drugs, in order to satisfy *wants* or *needs*. Some adult educators have argued that there should be no dependency in normal *adulthood,* or that one of the aims of *adult education* should be to foster *independence.* 2. A condition of being causally linked with another phenomenon.

dependent variable A variable whose value is subject to change as the result of changes in *independent variables.*

depository library A library that houses the complete documentation of a particular governmental body.

deprivation A state of being deprived. Can refer to cultural or other forms of stimulation. Many *adult educators* regard *adult education* as *remedial* in the sense of seeking to provide *needs* attributable to the deprived state.

depth psychology See *psychoanalysis.*

depute Scottish term for deputy.

D.E.S. Doctor of Engineering Sciences.

Des Moines Forum This community-wide forum programme in Iowa initiated a new approach to *adult education* in that it was the first programme that sought to provide *adult education* for all members in the community, rather than just for organizational members.

deschooling movement A movement popularized by *Ivan Illich* emphasizing that *education* might be best conducted in less formal settings than the *school* since formal organizations are themselves barriers to *participation* for some people.

descriptive research Research seeking to gather *data* that enable the researcher to provide an overall picture of the phenomenon being researched, as opposed to *analytical research.*

descriptor A term used to characterize a subject area.

desk training *Vocational education* on the job.

deskilling The adaptation of methods used to perform a task in order to lower the level of *skill* required to perform it. This has occurred a great deal with the introduction of automation and has affected *craft* and *vocational education*.

determinism A philosophical theory that suggests that human action is not entirely free but controlled by external forces acting upon the will. A view that is contrary to the *humanistic* philosophy of much *adult education* theory.

Deutsches Institut für Fernstudien (German Institute for Distance Studies) Established at the University of Tübingen in 1967 and initially funded by the Volkswagen Foundation, this is technically a private foundation funded by the government and state authorities. It is involved in projects for the updating of teachers, *radio college* (*Funkkolleg*), and *newspaper college* projects. Most of the major disciplines are taught through *distance teaching* in projects undertaken by this Institute. It is also a research institute. Certification is undertaken by the state and not the Institute.

development 1. The process of people achieving their potential through, in this case, education. *Growth* is another term used by *humanistic* adult educators.
2. The process by which a country modernizes. See *development education*. However, it should be recognized that some theorists relate development to modernizing in the Western sense whilst others regard it as a process of achieving a country's independence so that it can progress in its own direction. A problem with the latter approach is that no country is isolated from the rest of an interdependent world.

Development Alternatives with Women for a New Era (DAWN) Founded in 1984, this organization has been concerned that women suffer most from *development* policies. This movement has been actively following these aims ever since. Current address: c/o Instituto Universitario de pequisas do Rio de Janeiro, Rua Paulino Fernandes 32, Rio de Janeiro, R6, Brazil.

Development Centre for Popular Education and Adult Education Funded by the Danish government, this centre has been established in Copenhagen with a number of remits: to document new developments in *popular education* and *adult education*; to build up a consultation service to assist in innovative experiments; and to keep an account of what is actually occurring in the field in Denmark.

development community A community within a larger grouping that works for and advocates development within the larger body, e.g. a pressure group.

development education Term that gained currency in the 1960s for education which is aimed at increasing awareness in the plight of people in the Third World; and helping people in the Third World to understand the reasons for underdevelopment and, subsequently, to develop their own societies. It is significant to note that while development is often regarded in economic terms, *Freire*, among others, disagrees, claiming that this is *modernization* since *development* must first relate to people. See *Advisory Committee on Development Education*.

development education group A network of groups throughout the United Kingdom that are concerned about *development education*. They meet together, occasionally have their own centres, newsletters, etc. In the UK they are usually affiliated with the *National Association of Development Education Centres*.

development method A teaching method whereby *learners* are taken through each stage at a time in ascending order of difficulty.

developmental task The tasks for which satisfactory completion is necessary in order to proceed to the next stage of human *development*.

Dewey, John (1859–1952) American *pragmatic* philosopher and educationalist. His *progressivism* in education has influenced all educational theory tremendously. Whilst his work was not directly related to *adult education*, he has been perhaps the most influential of all educational theorists in both theory and practice. For instance, he influenced *Eduard Lindeman* who also taught at Columbia University in New York, and Lindeman's writings have had a wide influence in *adult education*. Dewey was a prolific writer and his writings are gradually being discovered by *adult educators* throughout the world.

Dewey decimal classification system The library classification system used extensively and devised by Melvil Dewey, librarian at Teachers College, Columbia University, New York towards the end of the nineteenth century. A system whereby the subjects are classified into ten main areas and then further subdivided in tenths.

diagnosis of needs In *learner-centred adult education* it is generally maintained that the *needs* of the learner should be determined by the teacher at the outset of the teaching and learning *transaction*.

diagnostic appraisal The initial process of diagnosis which is essential to preparing teaching to respond to learning *needs*. See *diagnosis of needs*, *formative evaluation*.

diagnostic teaching Teaching designed to reveal learner *needs*.

diagnostic test Tests designed to reveal the nature of an educational need or a mental disorder.

Dial Our Learning Listening Library (DOLLY) This facility has been started by Central Piedmont Community College in North Carolina, USA It consists of a 24-hour service in which people can telephone the college and have one of a wide selection of educational audio tapes played over the telephone. The tapes are accessed by a telephone operator, Each lasts from between one and 15 minutes, They are generally of a *non-credit* nature although faculty at the College tend to use some of the material to supplement their own prepared teaching.

dialect The form of language that is spoken in specific geographical regions.

dialectic A logical argument, used from the Greek thinkers onward. It has had several slightly different variations in meaning.

dialectical materialism Those who hold this view contend that materialism is fundamental and that thoughts emerge from it. They also argue that the laws that govern matter are *dialectical*.

dialectical thought The ability to think logically and critically to assess and evaluate propositions.

dialectics 1. The art of assessing the truth of a proposition or theory by discussion and logical disputation. 2. Logical argument.

dialogical education An approach to education in which the teacher enters genuine discussion with the learners in order to understand how they perceive reality, so that the teacher and learner can grow together in the *teaching and learning* process. This is a process in which the learner becomes teacher and the teacher has to learn to listen to the learners. It is a concept that has been introduced by *Paulo Freire* although the method is not unique to him.

diary Written records of events, made during *fields visits* etc. See also *learning log*.

didactic teaching A form of teaching in which the teacher presents information, as the authority. The word *didactic* comes from the Greek word διδαχε meaning 'teaching' or 'doctrine'.

didactics The art and science of teaching

dietetics Science of diet and food.

differential psychology Branch of *psychology* concerned with differences.

differential sampling A form of sampling which is deliberately biased in a specific direction.

differentiation The increase in the number of mental *skills* developed by individuals as they learn and develop.

difficulty score Score which indicates the highest level of difficulty obtained on a given variable.

diffusion The process of extending awareness, e.g. the diffusion of knowledge.

diploma 1. A formal document certifying successful completion of a recognized course of study. 2. The university award of diploma in the United Kingdom is usually regarded as being equivalent to at least one, and sometimes two, years of fulltime undergraduate study, or one year of post-graduate study.

diploma disease The excessive concern in the acquisition of educational qualifications in order to enable the holder to proceed to the next stage in the career.

Diploma in Adult Education 1. A higher award granted by some universities in the United Kingdom for higher-level study in *adult education*. This is often a part-time course of study. 2. (DAE) In the University of Zimbabwe, the diploma is the first-line award in adult education and programme candidates may be university graduates or non-graduates with practical experience in the field. See also *B.Ad Ed. M.Ad.Ed.*

Diploma in Education A higher-level award in the study of *education* granted by some universities in the United Kingdom.

Diploma in Further Education A higher-level award granted by universities in the United Kingdom in *further education*. This might include the study of *adult education* since it is sometimes regarded as technically part of *further education*.

Diploma in Health Education 1. An award granted by universities in the United Kingdom for the further study of *health education*. This is usually a part-time course of study. 2. In *Zimbabwe* it is the award of the national university, as a result of co-operation between the departure of adult education and medicine.

Diploma in Management Studies (DMS) A higher-level award granted by institutions of *higher education*, including universities, in the United Kingdom for the study of management. This is often a part-time course of study.

Diploma in Nursing An advanced qualification in nursing, awarded by institutions of higher education in the United Kingdom, for a part-time course of study. It is the normal entry requirement for teachers of nurses.

Diploma in Nursing Education 1. A university award that qualifies nurses to become teachers of nursing in the United Kingdom. There are other qualifications such as a *Certificate in Education*, or *Post-Graduate Certificate of Education of Adults* at an approved college or university. This is normally a full-time course. Another route entails gaining a certificate at an unapproved college and a year's service under supervision. 2. In *Zimbabwe*, an award of the University of Zimbabwe at which the departments of adult education and medicine co-operate to run a joint course.

Diploma in Pedagogics (Diplom-Padagogik) An award made by many West German universities on the successful completion of a four-year course, in which *adult education, social education*, etc. can be studied during the last two years.

Diploma in Technology (Dip. Tech) An award made by the *National Council of Technological Awards* in the United Kingdom from the middle of the 1950s until the Council ceased to exist.

Diploma in the Practice of Higher Education One of the first advanced awards to be made by a British university for the study of *higher education*. Introduced at the University of Surrey by *distance learning* for overseas students.

Diploma of Art and Design The professional qualification in art and design in the United Kingdom, awarded by Colleges of Art. Now superseded by the award of first degrees as the colleges have amalgamated with institutions of higher education.

Diploma of Higher Education (Dip H.E.) An award proposed in the United Kingdom in the 1970s on the recommendation of the James Report, which addressed the future of teacher education in the United Kingdom. The award was to be equivalent to two years study in *higher education*. At that time it was envisaged that it would be similar to the two-year degree in the United States and students could then transfer, if they so desired, to a university or polytechnic in order to complete the bachelor's degree. A few of the colleges adopted it, but to a great extent it did not gain credibility in the United Kingdom.

Diplôme d'Etat relatiff aux Fonctions d'Animation (DEFA) French diploma organized by the Ministry of Leisure in conjunction with the Ministry of Social Affairs in *animation*.

Diplôme d'Etudes Appronfondies A French diploma taken after the first year of advanced study to permit a student to continue to gain an academic qualification by research.

Diplôme Supérieur au Travail Social (DSTS) French diploma in social work which has an option in *animation*.

direct action A form of *community action* that seeks to deal directly with the problem.

direct costs Costs that increase directly with increases in the scale of operation. See also *fixed costs*.

direct returns to education See *rate of return to education*.

directed experiential learning A method of *teaching* and *learning* that seeks to provide the *learner* with the opportunity to learn *knowledge* and *skills* by having an experience of the situation in which they are normally utilized. See *professional practical placement*.

directed observation Observation guided by a teacher, who might also assist with the interpretation.

directed private study See *directed study*.

directed study A *teaching method* whereby the *learner* seeks to develop *skills* or acquire *knowledge* in direct relationship with a *resource person* who may or may not actually undertake teaching.

directed teaching A form of teaching which is teacher-directed; not always acceptable within the education of adults.

Direction de l'Education Parascholaire The adult education body of Burundi. Current address: BP 2264, Bujumbura, Burundi.

Directory of Social Change UK organization which is an educational charity. It undertakes research and provides information and training with *voluntary organizations* in a variety of aspects of education for adults. Current

99

address: 9 Mansfield Place, London
NW3 1HS, UK

disabled persons People who because of
ill health, physical incapacity, or mental
illness, are unable to function effectively
in one or more spheres of everyday life.

disadvantaged Refers to persons who,
by reason of physical or social handicap,
have not had equality of opportunity to
achieve their potential through
educational means. See *educational
disadvantage*.

discipline The classification of
knowledge into specific subjects, or
disciplines, based upon the conceptual
structure and the methods and
approaches necessary to understand and
research that branch of knowledge.

discipline of adult education Scholars
tend not to regard *adult education* as a
separate discipline, but to see it as a *field
of study* and an area of practical *knowledge*
that can be studied from the perspectives
of some of the academic disciplines.

discourse 1. An academic treatise.
2. The language of academic statements.

discourse analysis A form of analysing
and categorizing the structure of talk,
often carried out in the *teaching and
learning* situation. Still more common
with *initial education* research than with
research into *adult education*.

discovery learning A learning situation
within which the content to be learned is
not given to the learners; they have to
discover it for themselves. Frequently
used within *adult education*, often in the
form of *problem-solving*.

discovery methods The utilization of
teaching methods that enables *discovery
learning* to occur.

Discrepancy Evaluation Model An
evaluative tool in which the difference
between what should occur and what
actually occurs is assessed. Used in *human
resource development*.

discrete variable 1. A statistical term to
refer to a variable that can only change
by whole units. 2. A separate quantity in
a piece of research.

discretionary grant In the United
Kingdom the government awards two
forms of grant to assist students in
pursuing further study: *mandatory* and
discretionary, This latter form is one in
which Local Education Authorities may
choose whether to use their funds to
support students following specified
courses but do not have to do so by law.
A number of *adult education* courses have
come into this category since there has
been no statutory requirement for
teachers of adults to have a teaching
qualification prior to employment.

discrimination The ability to identify
differences between phenomena,
arguments, etc.

discussion group A teaching method
whereby the group is divided into small
units in order to share interests,
concerns, insights or to solve problems.
A common teaching method in *adult
education* since it enables the expertise of
all the course *participants* to be utilized,
provided they are willing to participate.
It is also assumed that *adult educators* have
the necessary *skills* to practise this
technique.

discussion group leader A participant
in the group whose main task is to help
the group work together towards the
achievement of its goals. The group
leader may be a *task-orientated leader* or an
expressive leader.

discussion pack Often prepared by a
distance learning institution, this is a set of
discussion topics for *discussion groups*,
sometimes to accompany *study packs*.
Such packs contain information,
suggestions as to how the group might
use the material, and cover a number of
different topics.

disengagement A concept with a
number of meanings that relate to the
ageing process: disengagement from

work, from social life, and ultimately from life itself. It has tended to relate to a lifestyle among the elderly that is relatively uninvolved with the wider society.

dispersion A statistical term which refers to the spread or concentration of values around a given point.

displaced homemakers centers The first was established on the campus at Mills College, Oakland, California in May 1976, to assist women who are divorced, separated, or no longer eligible for aid for dependent children. They provide counselling, job training, assistance in finding employment, etc.

displacement Psychological term referring to the displacement of a real cause of anxiety by a substitute one.

disposition Potential state of readiness to perform in a certain manner.

dissertation A written thesis, often required for a higher degree.

distance education 1. This concept covers a variety of forms to teaching and learning at various levels of education but the main feature is that the learning is not under the continuous, immediate supervision of tutors who are present with the learners in the place of study. However, students may have access to tutors if and when they need and at specified times. 2. The generic term for forms of education in which the teachers and students are separated by geographical distance and communication is through correspondence or other forms of technology, e.g. satellite, computer, electronic mail. The *Open University* in the United Kingdom is often seen as the epitome of this form of education although there were many countries in the world which had *distance teaching universities* before its foundation.

distance teaching A method of instruction in which the *teacher* and *students* perform their roles in different

geographical locations and the content of the study is transmitted through technological means.

distance teaching universities Throughout the world there has been a growth in the development of these universities, all offering degree programmes. There is a real sense in which the *Open University* in the United Kingdom acted as a catalyst in the formation of these institutions, with many of them being founded in the 1970s and 1980s. However, the first university to engage in distance teaching was the University of Queensland in Australia, which began its distance education programme in 1911. In the 1950s the University of New England in Armidale, Australia had included within its charter a *distance education* remit. This latter has become the model upon which some other universities have developed. In addition, the German Democratic Republic instituted it as early as June 1950, and subsequently at least 20 of its 53 universities have *distance education* programmes.

distinguished professor An American term to refer to a high-ranking professor. A few *adult educators* have gained such a title within their universities.

distribution A statistical term to refer to the *frequency* of occurrence of a set of values in a *population*.

distributive education programme A programme of occupational instruction in the areas of marketing and distributive trades designed to prepare individuals for any level of the occupation. See *adult distributive education*.

district agriculturalist The Canadian term for *county extension agent*.

divergent thinking The process of thinking characterized by moving laterally away from the direct response to a problem. Often associated with creativity. See its opposite *cognitive style*, *convergent thinking*.

Diversity by Design A report by the *Commission on Non-Traditional Study* in the United States, which reviewed innovative schemes throughout America. Published in 1973.

Division of Eligibility and Agency Evaluation A unit in the *United States Department of Education* whose main function is to determine the eligibility of *post-secondary education* institutions and programmes for Department of Education funding.

divisional inspector Senior member of *Her Majesty's Inspectorate* responsible for the educational inspection of an area of the United Kingdom.

D.J. Doctor of Jurisprudence.

D.Litt. Doctor of Letters.

D.M.A. Doctor of Musical Arts.

D.Mus. Doctor of Music.

doctor's degree The highest *earned degree* that a university awards, usually based upon the ability to perform scholarly research.

Documentación e información. Centro multinacional educación adultos The Argentine information and documentation centre, which was started in 1972. Current address: 1166 Lamadrid 676, 1426, Buenos Aires, Argentina.

documentation centre A resources centre which stores and makes available documents for academic study. See *clearinghouse*. There are a number of such centres for adult education in Europe.

dogma A belief or opinion regarded as authoritative, but not verified *knowledge*.

dogmatic Characterized by making *authoritarian* assertions. Often the inability to consider another's viewpoint.

Dokumentationssystem Erwachsenenbildung (DOKEB) A computerized adult education documentation and information service in Austria. Current address: c/o Institut für Erziehungswissenschaften, Garnisong, 3/8, 1090 Vienna, Austria.

Dolff, Helmuth (1929–83) Leading West German adult educator and director of the *Deutsche Volkschoschul Verbands* for over 20 years, during which time he helped the German association take an international perspective on *adult education*. He became well known for his work internationally as well as nationally. He also served as president of the *European Bureau of Adult Education* for several terms and was associated with the founding of the *International Council for Adult Education*.

Domestic Policy Association The association which has sponsored the *National Issues Forums* and, like it, is located in Dayton, Ohio.

dominance 1. In psychology, the preferred use of one or the other side of the brain. 2. In sociology, the results of the exercise of power. See *dominant ideology*.

dominant culture The *culture or subculture* of the most powerful group or social class within *society* or a social grouping and which is assumed by some to represent the culture of the whole group. It is often this culture that controls the content of the educational curriculum for all age groups.

dominant gene The gene which always expresses the hereditary characteristics.

dominant ideology The *ideology* of the dominant group which appears to represent the group as a whole.

Dominican Republic The *adult education* association is currently located at: Associación de Educadores do Adultos de la Republica Dominicana, Costa Rica No 20, Santo Domingo, Dominican Republic.

dottore Title given to a graduate of an Italian university.

double loop learning A concept used frequently by *C. Argyris* and *D. Schon*. The opposite of *single loop learning*, which suggests that when this form of learning occurs, it results in changes to the social context within which the learner has learned. In a sense this is a matter of problematizing the situation in which the problem occurs.

double session Two periods of *teaching and learning* in the same subject that run consecutively.

Down With Illiteracy The title of the journal that was started in 1920 with the creation of the literacy campaign in Russia. See also *All-Russia Extraordinary Commission for Elimination of Illiteracy*.

downward mobility Social mobility in a downward direction, e.g. from middle class to working class.

D.Phil. Doctor of philosophy. This degree can be obtained in a variety of subjects, including education and *adult education*.

drawing rights See *individual entitlements*.

dream analysis Method used in psychoanalysis to obtain information about the subconscious and emotions of a person.

drill Repetitious *training*.

drive Term with many uses in psychology, can refer to a motivation state which is produced by deprivation of a needed substance or a noxious stimulus, such as an explosion. There are similarities here with the way in which the term *need* is used in *adult education*.

drop-out One who fails to complete schooling, or fails to complete any other course of study.

drug addiction A state of dependence upon drugs.

D.Sc. Doctor of Science.

D.Tech. Doctor of Technology.

dualism A philosophical theory that sees everything in terms of two opposites, e.g. mental and material, good and evil, etc.

dualist A *learning style* which is similar to *surface processing* in that it seeks to acquire facts and, in addition, sees everything in terms of correctness or incorrectness, right or wrong.

Dumazedier, Joffre one of the founders and the first chairman of *Peuple et Culture*.

D.Univ. Doctor of the University. This is usually an honorary degree which a university awards to a distinguished person.

Dunlop W.J. Director of *university extension* at the University of Toronto in 1934, he convened the seminar that resulted in the formation of the *Canadian Association of Adult Education*. At that seminar there were 86 delegates from 46 organizations.

Durkheim, Emile (1858–1917) French sociologist and educationalist; one of the founding fathers of sociology. His theories have resulted in functional analyses of education.

Dutch Association of Countrywomen See *Nederlandse bond van plattelandsvrouwen*.

Dutch Association of Housewives See *Nederlandse vereniging van huisvrouwen*.

Dutch Open University (Open Universiteit) Commenced operations in October 1984. Current address: Open Universiteit, Heerlen, The Netherlands.

dyad A pair.

dysphasia Defective symbol behaviour, A dysphasic may have difficulty in dealing with speech, reading, writing, gestures, pictures, numbers etc. Working with dysphasics is one of the elements of *adult basic education*.

E

each one teach one The phrase which describes the *Laubach* literacy method.

early adolescence Stage in human development, usually from about 12 to 16 years of age.

early adulthood The ages of about 22 to 40 years, when a person learns to choose, create, and maintain his/her own life structure.

early adult transition The ages of about 17 to 22 years comprise the transition in the *life cycle* to *early adulthood*. See *pre-adulthood*.

earned degree Term used in America to refer to a degree awarded by a college or university as a result of successful completion of an accepted course of study. See *honorary degree*.

East Midlands Educational Union (EMEU) A regional examining body in the United Kingdom which administers examinations in *further education*.

East Midlands Regional Advisory Council Training Scheme A scheme of training for part-time tutors in *further* and *adult education* which was introduced in the 1970s in the United Kingdom in which there was an introductory stage, a second level, and a third level equivalent to a full-time year's study. This scheme formed the basis of the *Haycocks Committee*'s recommendation for a national training scheme in England and Wales. See *Advisory Committee for the Supply and Training of Teachers*.

East Midlands Regional Institute of Adult Education An adult education group established in 1972 and supported by *Local Education Authorities*, which has a regional base and seeks to draw together adult educators in the region. It organizes regional seminars and conferences which are supported by the *Department of Adult Education, University of Nottingham*. Information about the Institute can be obtained from the Department, at 14–22 Shakespeare Street, Nottingham NG1 4FJ, UK.

Ebbinghaus, Hermann (1850–1909) German psychologist who investigated *memory* experimentally and devised the forgetting curve for nonsense knowledge.

Echeverria, Louis Second honorary president of the *International Council for Adult Education* and former president of Mexico. An international statesman concerned with issues of national development.

Echo The title of the newsletter of the *World Confederation of Organisations of the Teaching Profession*.

école-atelier Swiss secondary school providing *vocational education*.

école nationale French institution of *higher education*.

école technique supérieure Swiss institution of *higher education* which is distinct from the university system.

ecology The study of the relationships between living organisms and their environment. Also used with human ecology, which is the study of the relationship between groups of human beings and their environment. Hence, social ecology is also used. See also *classroom ecology*.

Economic Opportunity Act (1964) Legislation in the United States under which the *Adult Basic Education Program* was established. Under this act the poor and educationally disadvantaged were to be assisted and the *Job Corps* was established.

economics The study of the production and consumption of commodities and services.

Ecuador *Adult education* is organized through a department in the Ministry. Current address: Dirección Nacional de Educación Compensatoria, Ministerio de Educación y Cultura, Edificio Bolivar, Bolivar y Venezuela 268, Quito, Ecuador.

Ed. D. The doctorate of education degree awarded by many universities in the United States, often in *adult education*. It is generally regarded as a mixture of a taught and research degree and slightly lower than the Ph.D. degree, which is also awarded.

Ediget Published twice a year since 1982 in Amharic and concerned with family life, this is an *adult literacy* journal of the Bahir-Dar Province of *Ethiopia*.

Edinburgh Walk-In Numeracy Centre (EWINC) Established in February 1982 as a voluntary organization and a registered charity to provide numeracy help for anybody who wishes to use its services.

Ed. M. Master of Education award in some American universities.

educable One who is capable of being educated. Usually used in relation to those who are mentally retarded.

Educación a Distancia Established in 1982 and published twice a year in

Spanish in Chile, it contains information about *adult education* and *distance education*.

Educación Permanente Published twice a year since 1973 in Spanish, this is a Colombian *adult education* journal.

educand One being educated; student.

education Refers to a variety of approaches. 1. The *Unesco* definition is the 'organized and sustained instruction designed to communicate a combination of *knowledge*, *skills* and understanding valuable for all the activities of life'. This definition relates to the concept of *lifelong education* which Unesco has espoused but might be flawed in that it omits attitudes and includes the concept of 'communication', which may be restrictive. 2. Some philosophers, such as Richard Peters, consider that the phenomenon is too complex to define, but others disagree and produce a variety of definitions. 3. One of these definitions is: any planned series of incidents, having a humanistic basis, directed towards the participants' learning and understanding. 4. The organized ways of learning from the experience of others. 5. The social institution in which formal teaching and learning processes are performed. 6. The study of teaching and learning. 7. The subject matter concerned with the study of teaching and learning.

Education Act (1944) This legislation in the United Kingdom made it a statutory requirement that Local Education Authorities provide fulltime and parttime education and also provide organized cultural training and recreative activities for those over compulsory school-leaving age. The act was a milestone in legislation for school education in the United Kingdom.

Education and Criminal Justice Programme A programme sponsored by the *International Council for Adult Education* with five main thrusts: 1. To introduce, develop, and gain acceptance for an educational approach in the field of criminal justice. 2. To persuade educational authorities to assume a role in this area. 3. To persuade national governments to adopt a policy of recognizing the humanity of prisoners and to encourage their human growth and development. 4. To persuade university departments to undertake research in this area of education. 5. To persuade governments to amend the United Nations Resolution on minimum roles for prisoners in accordance with the *ICAE* resolution.

Education and Libraries Act
Legislation in Northern Ireland in 1972 that established five education and library boards to be responsible for education, library, and youth services.

Education and Library Board The *Local Education Authority* in Northern Ireland. There are five in the whole of Northern Ireland.

Education and Training 1. A monthly magazine published by the Association of Business Executives, 14 Worple Road, Wimbledon, London SW19 4DD, UK. 2. A bimonthly magazine established in 1959 and published in the United Kingdom by MCB University Press. It covers subjects from qualifications and career choice to current policy.

Education and Work A magazine published in America every two weeks by Capitol Publications of Washington.

Education Benefit A proposal that *young adults* (16–19 year age group) should be given financial support whilst attending fulltime education.

education by doing An expression used to refer to a form of *experiential education* in which the learners are expected to undertake the designated task and learn from it.

Education Centre at Ebernburg A residential centre run by the *Farmers' Union* in Rhineland-Palatinate in the Federal Republic of Germany.

Education et Societé The journal of the *Institut National de Formation et de Recherche en Education Permanente*.

Education for Aging A free bimonthly bulletin published by Hunter College, New York, USA.

Education for All An aim of *Unesco's medium-term plan, 1984–89*, in which adult education was specified as one of the areas in which education and work, education and citizenship, education in leisure and culture, and education and later life were all highlighted. Other aspects of the programme included women's education, and education and rural development.

Education for Kagisano The title of the 1977 Education Act in Botswana, 'kagisano' meaning social harmony. It is concerned with all aspects of education, including the *education of adults*. It discusses *extension education, continuing education, vocational education*, and cultural and social programmes.

education for liberation An approach to education that regards learning as freeing the learners from the constraints of their socio–cultural environment. This approach often takes a political perspective (see especially the writings of *Paulo Freire*), and it is also an element in *critical theory*.

Education for Reconstruction Conference Conference held in Quebec, Canada in September 1943 when the *Canadian Association of Adult Education* led the way in that country towards the creation of a 'better society' after the Second World War, in opposition to the government of the country. It resulted in the creation of the *Citizen's Forum*.

education for self-management The educational programme in Yugoslavia to help prepare people to undertake *self-management* in all aspects of daily living and working.

Education for Self-Reliance In Tanzania in 1966 President Nyerere announced a national philosophy of African socialism and followed it with a national education programme called Education for Self-Reliance.

education from above An approach to education which assumes that the curriculum and the form of teaching is imposed upon the *learners* from above, i.e. from those who exercise control, so that education functions as an agency of social and cultural *reproduction*. See *education of equals*.

education index A library index for educational publications, authors, and classifications.

education of adults This wide term tends to be used to refer to all *education* of *adults* rather than the more restricted term, *adult education*. Hence its meaning relates to the conceptual understanding of both *education* and *adult*.

education of equals An approach to education which is *egalitarian* in nature and which presupposes certain *curriculum* practices. It is a form of *education* which is espoused by many in *adult education*. See *education from above*.

education officer In some of the professions there are professional officers responsible for overseeing and advising on the educational processes in professional preparation and in *continuing professional education*.

education para-professional An aide to a teacher, usually to assist in the classroom. This term is used in North America.

éducation permanente The French term for *lifelong education*. French law specifies that higher education must be open to former students as well as mature students who have not previously had the opportunity of higher education, even if they do not have the necessary entrance qualifications (i.e. to a system of lifelong education).

Education Permanente 1. A journal published four times a year in France by the organization Education Permanente since 1969. Carries articles on all forms of *adult education*. Address: 21 rue du Fauberg Saint-Antoine, 75550 Paris Cédex 11, France. 2. A Swiss quarterly published by the *Swiss Federation of Adult Education* about *adult education* in general.

education-related military experiences Those military-based experiences which have particular significance in relation to a person's subsequent learning. It is a form of *prior learning* recognized in America, where a booklet has been issued indicating the creditworthiness of specific experiences.

education shop A number of experiments have been attempted in the United Kingdom to reach people with advice and guidance, e.g., a drop-in advisory centre was initiated by Oldham Local Education Authority. The venture includes a shop in which parents can purchase local school uniforms and where they can also learn about events in children's education and receive educational advice.

Education Support Grant A financial grant awarded by the Department of Education and Science in the United Kingdom within *REPLAN* to a college or educational institution in order to help it develop an educational project.

education week A period of time devoted to publicizing the *adult education* courses being offered in a local area in the United Kingdom. This often occurs at the start of the academic year in order to encourage enrolments.

Education with Production Established in 1981, the biannual journal of the *Foundation for Education with Production*. The journal represents a wide range of views relating to the role of education in developing more just, equal, and democratic societies. Address: The Editor, P.O. Box 20906, Gaborone, Botswana.

educational accountability *Responsibility* for achieving certain results in the *teaching* and *learning* process.

educational advisory services A service which offers help, support, and guidance to adults seeking advice concerning their own educational *needs* in the United Kingdom. See *educational guidance service for adults*.

educational aid See *audio-visual aid*.

educational association In Sweden 11 national associations are recognized by the government (Riksdag) as organizers of *study circles*.

Educational Association for Unions of Salaried Employees Established in 1978 in Finland, started its *study centre* work in 1980. Its main task is to promote the educational activities of union officials and civil servants, but it is also involved in wider training activities through *study circles*, courses, lectures, and by organizing other cultural activities. Current address: Asemamiehenkatu 4, 00520 Helsinki 52, Finland.

Educational Association of the Swedish Church (Sveriges Kyrkliga Studieförbund) An educational association which sponsors *study circles*, in Sweden to provide leisure time study and a wide variety of other educational opportunities. Dates back to the 1930s.

Educational Association of the Temperance Movement (Nykterhetsrörelsens Bildningsverksamhet) An educational association sponsoring the *study circles* in Sweden concerned with member training and cultural activities. This is the earliest *educational association* in Sweden and can be traced back to the late nineteenth century.

educational broadcasting In the United Kingdom, this term refers to broadcasts through radio and television with specific educational aims. In the United States the term refers to non-commercial broadcasting in which educational and community organizations have participated.

Educational Broadcasting Corporation American public television station distributing educational programmes to non-commercial television stations throughout America. Address: 304 W 58th Street, New York, New York, USA.

educational brokering agency An organization which offers counselling and guidance services. At the same time it directs clients towards that educational activity which best suits their *needs*. There are a great number of these throughout America. See *Educational Exchange of Greater Boston*. They offer a broad array of *learning* opportunities, advertise their services, assess likely students, and offer a wide range of counselling opportunities. They appear in a number of different forms; some are independent whilst others are attached to larger educational organizations. Currently a *National Center for Educational Brokering* exists.

educational centre Used to refer to a single location for adult education; it might be one site of an *Adult Education Institute*. Often the centre has a head who is either a full-time or part-time member of the staff. See also *Educational Centres Association*.

Educational Centres Association Formerly, the *Educational Settlements Association*. This United Kingdom association offers its members an opportunity to relate to each other in a national conference. It is an association for students, teachers, and administrators in adult education. Address: National Secretary, ECA, Chequer Centre, Chequer Street, Bunhill Row, London, EC1Y 8PL, UK.

educational clearinghouse An organization that offers information and related services to people in order to help them address an educational problem. See *clearinghouse*.

educational climate The social and contextual qualities of an *educational institution*, as perceived by the *students*, *participants, and learners.* It is often considered to have four components: ecology, milieu, social system, and culture. Considerable research has been undertaken in school education but less in *adult education* although some of the assumptions underlying *andragogy* relate to it.

Educational Considerations The education journal of Kansas State College. Whilst a College of Education journal, it does occasionally publish articles and whole issues that are concerned with *adult education*.

educational consortium A grouping of two or more independent organizations combining either to offer teaching or other services, or to conduct research.

Educational Counselling and Credit Transfer Information Service (ECCTIS) A national computer-based operation in which all courses leading to a recognized qualification in advanced further and higher education throughout the United Kingdom (including some further education qualifications) are stored, so that credit transfer between courses is possible. It also endeavours to assess educational equivalency between courses. Educational guidance counsellors may also access this information in order to assist their clients in choosing the right course for their projected careers. This is not a counselling service in the traditional sense. Address: P.O. Box 88, Walton Hall, Milton Keynes MK7 6DB, UK.

educational disadvantage Refers to the state of having been disadvantaged for a variety of reasons, including social position, health, and educational opportunity. See *disadvantage.*

Educational Exchange of Greater Boston First known *educational brokering service,* begun in 1923 in the United States.

Educational Film Library Association American society of organizations involved in film and other visual aids

within the educational context. It was one of the five associations that helped create the *Joint Committee for the Study of Adult Education Policies, Principles and Practices* in 1946.

Educational Foundation for Visual Aids Established in 1948 in the United Kingdom as an educational trust, it offers advice to those involved in producing visual aids for educational purposes, as well as producing its own. In addition, it has its own centre and library. Current address: 35 Queen Anne Street, London W1, UK.

educational games Methods employed to facilitate *learning.* See *games.*

educational gerontology The study and practice of education among and about the elderly. A growing field of study as the demographic features of Western societies move in the direction of a greater proportion of senior citizens.

Educational Gerontology A specialist American journal published bimonthly by Hemisphere Publishing Corporation, 1010 Vermont Ave. NW, Washington DC 20005, USA. See also *Journal of Educational Gerontology.*

Educational Grants Advisory Service UK advisory service for students enquiring about sources of funding for courses. Current address: 501–505 Kingsland Road, London E8 4AU, UK.

educational guidance Increasingly, adult educators have recognized the need to provide a counselling and advice service to guide adults through the complexities of the post-school education system. However, adult educators themselves are not always aware of all that is being offered. This, the initial stage, is a collation of all the information about educational opportunities for *mature students.*

educational guidance service for adults Some of these services are run by volunteers while a few have paid part-time staff. All seek to provide educational guidance at local level for adults. The first one to be established in the United Kingdom was in Belfast in 1967. See the *National Association of Educational Guidance Services for Adults*.

educational ideology The term 'ideology' has so many different connotations that it is difficult to define this concept precisely. However, it broadly refers to a system of beliefs that gives a general direction to the educational policies and practices of educators and those who make policy for education.

educational management The theory and practice of managing the educational services. It was recommended by the third *Haycocks Report* in the United Kingdom that there should be more training for management in *adult education*, but this has not yet occurred to any great extent. Since many full-time members of staff have a great deal of management responsibility, this remains a *training need* that should be met.

Educational Media Council Founded in 1960, it is an American clearinghouse for national associations involved in media education. Current address: 1346 Connecticut Ave. NW, Washington DC 20036, USA.

educational need Term frequently used synonymously with *learning need*, but more correctly it refers to either the necessity for additional *education* or to a deficiency which can be rectified by education.

educational objectives The short-term desired learning outcomes of the *teaching and learning process*. See *objectives*, *behavioural objectives*, *expressive objectives*.

Educational Opportunities Scheme Established in Eire on an experimenal basis in 1986, it allows those who are over 25 years old, who have been unemployed and received unemployment benefit for more than one year, to pursue a one-year full-time education course without loss of benefit.

educational planning 1. A management exercise in which plans are drawn up for future educational provision. 2. Planning for a course or a teaching and learning session. See *program planning*.

educational process A planned and institutionalized process of *learning*, often under the guidance of a *teacher*.

educational psychology Adult education literature has been dominated by psychological literature applied to adults, especially in the fields of *learning theory* and *adult development*. However, educational psychology encompasses: 1. the study of the psychological processes that occur within education; 2. the study of behaviour within the educational setting; 3. psychological practice within the educational context.

educational research Research into any aspect of the theory and practice of education.

Educational Resources Information Center (ERIC) An information system that has been in operation since 1966, sponsored by the Office of Educational Research and Improvement, US Department of Education. It provides users with access to English-language literature dealing with education. There is a central unit in Washington and 16 *clearinghouses* situated throughout the United States, each focusing on a different area of education. That which is concerned with *adult* and *vocational education* is located at Ohio State University. Each clearinghouse offers a database, abstracts journals, microfiche, computer searches, document reproduction, and analyses. Current address: Clearinghouse for Adult, Career and Vocational Education, Ohio State University, 1960 Kenny Road, Columbus, Ohio 43210, USA.

educational settlements See *university settlements*. The Society of Friends opened a number of non-residential settlements in the United Kingdom in 1909, and the *adult school movement* continued this with additional non-residential settlements in 1914.

Educational Settlements Association
The original name of the UK-based *Educational Centres Association*, founded in 1938 in order to promote permanent centres of *adult education*.

educational sociology An aspect of the sociology of education which consists of the study and practice of those aspects of sociological theory that can assist the *educational process*.

educational support grants Grants made by the Department of Education and Science in the United Kingdom to local educational institutions for specific educational purposes.

educational technology Originally this referred to *audio-visual aids* and similar hardware but more recently it has come to mean the software as well, Therefore it now also relates to the design and implementation of systems of *teaching* and *learning* and the field of study associated with it.

educational telephone network A telephone-based instructional system, a form of *distance education*, in which the telephone is the means of communication among students and between them and their tutors. This system has been used fully in the state of Wisconsin, United States in group *continuing education*.

educational television The transmission of material that is either especially designed for educational purposes or which may be used for that end. See also *closed circuit television, educational broadcasting*.

Educational Television Broadcasting Act American legislation of 1962 which made federal funds available for educational broadcasting.

Educational Testing Service (ETS) American research and testing organization that provides established tests and assessment services to

educational institutions. Current address: CN 6403, Princeton, New Jersey 08541–6403, USA.

educational theory The body of accepted knowledge about education.

educational thought See *philosophy of education*.

educational trust A charitable foundation established to support educational enterprises. Directories of these trusts are in circulation, e.g. *Charities Year Book*.

Educazione degli Adulti Nell'Area Mediterranea Mediterranean association of *adult education* which was formed in October 1981. Current address: Cattedra di Educazione degli adulti, Università degli studi, Via di Parione, 50123 Firenze, Italy.

Effect, Law of One of *Edward Thorndike*'s laws which states that satisfaction serves as a reinforcer of the *stimulus–response* bonds.

effective student hour A method of funding introduced into grant-aided *adult education* in the United Kingdom in the 1980s. This measures actual hours of course contact rather than *enrolment* number. It is an approach to cost-effective *adult education*.

egalitarianism A philosophy that maintains the equality of people. Important philosophy underlying many theories in *adult education*, especially those with a *humanistic* basis.

ego 1. From the Latin for 'I' or 'self'. 2. Part of *Freud*'s three elements of the person, it relates to those aspects of the *personality* which mediate between the drives of the *id* and the constraints of the *superego*.

ego consciousness A form of self-awareness.

ego-development The emerging awareness of the *personhood* of the person. See *self-development*.

111

ego ideal Slightly different from the *superego* in as much as it refers to the idea of what a person would like to be.

ego integrity Refers to Erikson's final *stages of man* and is important in studies of *adult development* and *educational gerontology*. It is the state of acceptance of old age and death.

ego needs In occupational psychology, this term relates to the *needs* of the person in the performance of a job and, where fulfilled, will result in *job satisfaction*. See *needs*.

ego trip Any pattern of behaviour engaged in by a person for the purpose of boosting his/her sense of self-importance. *Teaching* can often be perceived in this way.

egocentricism Preoccupation with the *self*; being *self-centred*.

egoism Being motivated by self-interest.

Egypt *Adult education* is organized by a central council. Current address: Supreme Council for Adult Education, Ministry of Education, Falaki Street, Cairo, Egypt. In addition, information can be obtained from: Nile Centre for Information Training and Education, 1 Domiat Street, Agouza, Cairo, Egypt.

eidetic Images in the mind that are imagined and unreal but which are so vivid that they are mistaken for reality.

Eighteen Plus Groups As a result of a survey by the Carnegie UK Trust in 1939, entitled 'Disinherited Youth', self-supporting groups, rather like *study circles*, came into being. These had the objectives of helping young adults between 18 and 30 understand and appreciate life, develop a deep personal philosophy, and become engaged in public affairs. They developed their own national federation.

El Salvador The national *adult education* association is the Associón de Educatores de Adultos de El Salvador. Current address: Extensión Universitaria, Universidad Nacional de El Salvador, San Salvador, C.A. In addition, the ministry has a separate department. Current address: Dirección de Educación de Adultos, c/o Ministerio de Educación, Edif, Biblioteca Nacional, San Salvador, C.A.

elaborated code The speech form that Basil Bernstein discovered which is used mostly by the middle classes. His work was done with children but his findings probably relate to *adult* speech codes as well. It is the type of speech which is abstract and complex, and uses long sentences. Those who employ elaborated speech codes are also able to understand and use *restricted codes*, although the reverse is not true.

eldergogy A term that has been used to imply the need for a systematic approach to teaching older people. See *gerontology*.

elderhostel A residential educational provision for elder citizens in the United States to study on university campuses in vacation time. It began in 1975 and was pioneered in New Hampshire, it has more recently become an international network. Based on the belief that retirement should not mean withdrawal from the world, but should provide the opportunity to discover new avenues of involvement and sources of satisfaction. The movement has become a registered charity, so it cannot become a profit-making organization.

elderstudy A precursor to the formation of the *University of the Third Age* in the United Kingdom. *Age Concern* established a working group in 1979 to investigate the possibility of an *elderhostel* type of provision.

elective An optional *module* chosen by the learner during a course of study.

Electronic University A private organization which offers both *credit* and *non-credit* courses through electronic techniques. The founder is Ron Gordon, former chief executive of a computer company, who has produced a special *modem* and software package which can be sold to students so that they can participate in the university.

element In *personal contruct theory* an element is a single aspect abstracted from the environment by use of a special construct.

elementarism A philosophical theory which maintains that complex phenomena may only be understood by reducing them to their basic parts.

elementary education The first school for young children.

Élet és Tudomány (Life and Science) The weekly magazine of the *Scientific Educational Association* of Hungary.

elite The select few, used in Marxist theory to refer to those who hold power.

elitism 1. A theory that holds that the exercise of power by a select few is essential to the maintenance of group cohesion. 2. A theory that maintains that those who are most able will always rise to the higher ranks of hierarchy.

Elsinore Conference The first post-Second World War international conference on *adult education* sponsored by *Unesco* and held at Elsinore, in Denmark in June 1949.

emancipatory education See *liberation education*. The idea is present in the writings of *Freire* and *Habermas*. However, it was prevalent in *adult education* as early as *Robert Owen*. It refers to the educational process which results in learners becoming critically aware of the social processes which made them, the learners, what they are and which located them in the position that they occupy in the social structures.

emancipatory literacy *Adult literacy* programmes founded upon a revolutionary ideology which claims that oppressed people can participate in the

building and transformation of their own society in a *democratic* manner. See *Freire*.

embedded figures test A form of testing for *cognitive style* in which the subject is presented with a complex figure and requested to identify other simpler figures within the complex figure. However, one of the weaknesses with this test is that it measures ability to perform, rather than cognitive style.

embourgeoisement The theory that as the working classes become affluent they assume middle–class lifestyles and values.

Emile Published in 1762 and written by *Rousseau*, this book has been regarded by many as the starting point for *progressive education* theories which have also found their way into *adult education* theory.

emotion A term with a variety of meanings but essentially an affect-laden state which results in certain predispositions to behave in specific ways and feel certain orientations towards or away from a phenomenon. See *affective domain*.

emotional maturity The state of emotional reactivity considered appropriate for a stable adult within a given society. In discussions about *adulthood* within the debate about *adult education*, this might be relevant.

emotive imagery Imagery that provokes emotional response.

emotive learning *Learning* through the emotions.

empathy A state of identification with the attitudes and feelings of other people.

Empire State College Founded in 1971 as part of the State University of New York to provide educational opportunities for the people of New York. An autonomous *non-traditional*, *adult education* institution which grants *external degrees*. It is accredited by the Middle States Association of Colleges and Secondary Schools. In 1979, it created a *distance teaching center* known as the Center for Distance Learning. This institution has used some of the *Open University*'s (UK) material. Current address: Saratoga Springs, New York, USA.

empirical Derived from experience rather than *a priori* premises.

empiricism The theory that all *knowledge* of facts is based upon *experience*. Hence the natural sciences are regarded as the model by which knowledge is discovered. *Knowledge*, in this sense, is distinct from *ideology*, which cannot be verified in this manner.

Employment and Training Act The Act of Parliament in 1973 which led to the establishment on 1 January 1974 of the *Manpower Services Commission* in the United Kingdom. (Note: in 1988 the *Manpower Services Commission* changed its name to the *Training Commission* and then to the *Training Agency*.)

Employment Protection Act Passed in the United Kingdom in 1975, this Act of Parliament gave trade union shop stewards the right to a reasonable amount of *paid educational leave* so that they could be *trained* for their role. In addition, the government made a grant to the unions so that they could support workers on approved educational courses.

employment training A scheme introduced by the *Training Commission*, formerly the *Manpower Services Commission*, in the United Kingdom to introduce high-quality *training* for unemployed people through a national scheme based upon local networks of training agencies and training managers, as from September 1988. It replaced a variety of other schemes that had been operating previously. However, the trade unions failed to support the scheme and the government was forced to re-think its policy in this matter. (Note: in 1988 the *Manpower Services Commission* changed its name to the *Training Commission* and then to the *Training Agency*.)

empowerment A concept used in different ways, but generally regarded as an outcome of the educational process. *Radical adult educators* use the term in relation to providing a social class, e.g. the working classes, with the awareness and knowledge to act in and upon the social structures so that people can restructure society in a more egalitarian manner. More conservative and *progressive* adult educators use the term to refer to equipping and raising the confidence of individuals so that they can be more successful in the world.

encoding The process of putting meanings into words.

encounter group A small group involved in intensive personal *interaction*. Frequently used in some aspects of *affective education*, emphasizing the emotions and the present rather than the cognitive and the intellectual.

endorsement Additional qualification(s) added to an initial one.

Engineering Council The council responsible for the education and *continuing education* of engineers in the United Kingdom. Current address: 10 Maltravers Street, London WC2 3ER, UK.

Engineering Design Education and Training Journal published by the Design Council in the United Kingdom. Originally it was not concerned with *industrial training* and *continuing education* but in 1988 it expanded its remit to cover these areas.

Engineering Industry Training Board Responsible for training in engineering in the United Kingdom. Current address: P.O. Box 176, 54 Clarendon Road, Watford WD1 1LB, UK.

engineering science The principles and practice of engineering.

Engineers' Council for Professional Development An American professional association and *accrediting* agency.

English as a foreign language (EFL)
See *English as a second language*; this, however, is not *adult basic education* in quite the same way. EFL is organized for those who wish to come to live in an English-speaking country or those whose work necessitates their use of English. There are qualifications in the United Kingdom for teaching this subject. Many private language schools and *colleges of further education* offer courses in EFL.

English as a second language (ESL)
See *English as a foreign language*. ESL, however, is a concern in *adult basic education*. It really began in the United Kingdom in the mid–1960s with the increase in immigration but has a longer history in countries such as the United States which have a long history of receiving immigrants. ESL consists of courses mounted for immigrants whose native language is not English to assist them to live within English-speaking society. In England, as a result of a Home Office circular in 1966, financial grants are made to *Local Education Authorities* which employ staff to teach those whose language and customs differ from the rest of the community.

English Heritage Education Service
Provides educational information about a range of sites that it administers. Address: Education Service, English Heritage, 15 Great Marlborough Street, London W1V 1AF, UK.

English Language Proficiency Survey
Commissioned by the *United States Department of Education* and conducted by the Bureau of Census in the fall of 1982. Written tests were conducted in private homes with a national sample of some 3,400 adults aged 20 years and over. It was estimated that between 17 million and 21 million US adults were *illiterate*, about 13 per cent of the population.

English National Board Learning Resources Unit The English National Board for Nursing, Health Visiting, and Midwifery has established a *learning resources unit* at the Sheffield Polytechnic. It is a resource centre for all those

engaged in nurse education. Current address: National Centre for Developments in Nurse Education, 55 Broomgrove Road, Sheffield S10 2NA, UK.

enquiry-based learning Alternative spelling for *inquiry-based learning*. See *discovery learning*.

enrichment programme A course or mixed programme designed to compensate those who have been culturally or socially deprived. A form of remediation.

enrolment The act of joining an *adult education* class, indeed registering for any class.

enrolment week A period, often a week, set aside at the start of each academic year by many *adult education institutes* to enrol students for the new year.

Ente Nazionale Acli Istruzione Professionale (ENAIP) Italian *adult education* in the United Kingdom. Current address: 69 Union Street, Bedford, Beds, UK.

entertain To divert, amuse, or cause someone's time to pass agreeably. There is a relationship between *adult education* and entertainment in as much as some teachers are entertainers; there is a possibility that the entertainment value of *adult education* might influence some forms of student *assessment* of teachers and courses. The same value might be very useful in some forms of *adult education* work.

entry requirements The level of academic competency expected before one can be considered as a suitable candidate for another course of study.

environmental education The protection of the environment has become a more significant feature in adult education programmes. There is a *Council for Environment Education* in the United Kingdom.

episodic memory *Memory* which is stored within the context of the situation in which it was acquired, e.g. something that was learned at a specific event. See also *semantic memory*.

epistemology The theory of *knowledge*. It is the branch of *philosophy* that studies *knowledge*.

Epsilon Sigma Phi Fraternity A professional association in America for *extension agents* of ten or more years' experience.

equal opportunities In recent years a number of organizations have recognized the need to introduce equal opportunities, not only between sexes and races but also between age groups, health groups, etc. A number of codes of good practice about equal opportunities have now been accepted in *adult education*.

Equal Opportunities Commission This commission established by the United Kingdom government has an educational function. Current address: Overseas House, Quay Street, Manchester M3 3HN, UK.

equalitarianism A movement in England in the nineteenth century seeking to make *higher education* less exclusive.

Eradication of Ignorance Campaign Campaign conducted in Israel in the 1960s, using girl soldiers as teachers in one-to-one teaching and learning situations, to help immigrants from the Moslem countries to improve their educational attainments. The campaign lasted several years.

Erasmus, Desiderius (1466–1536) Dutch thinker. Major figure in the growth of *humanism* and very much concerned with the growth and spread of learning in Europe.

ergonomics The study of the person's physical and mental relationship with the environment, especially at work and with the use of occupational equipment. See also *human engineering*.

ERIC Clearinghouse on Adult, Career and Vocational Education See *Educational Resources Information Centre*.

Erikson, Erik (b. 1902) Psychologist concerned with the development of the person. Has also written about *adolescence*.

escapism The desire to evade the present reality and escape, perhaps, into an imaginary world.

Esperanto An artificial language created to try to overcome the problems of international communication. Its component parts come from the European languages.

espoused theory A concept used by *C. Argyris* and *D. Schon* to refer to a theory of action to which a respondent gives allegiance and which, upon request, she/he communicates to others. This differs from the theory of action to which they refer as *theory in use*.

essay An extended form of prose composition.

essentialism 1. A philosophical position emanating from *Plato* that behind all physical objects there are perfect abstractions. 2. A philosophical theory propounded by *Aristotle* that all phenomena have certain essences without which they could not exist. Hence in education there are certain activities, *knowledge* and *skills*, that form the very nature of education.

Essert, Paul L. (d. 1985) Perhaps the first full-time professor of adult education, he was on the faculty of Teachers College, Columbia University, New York from 1947. Prior to that he had been an *adult educator* and the author of a number of early books in the field.

ethics 1. The study of moral philosophy. 2. A code of personal behaviour. 3. A statement of professional standards, usually referred to as a *code of ethics*.

Ethiopia *Adult Education* is co-ordinated by the Adult Education Department in the Ministry of Education. Current address: Ministry of Education, Adult Education Department, P.O. Box 2996, Addis Ababa, Ethiopia.

ethnic studies The study of distinct cultural and racial groups.

ethnocentricism the tendency to assess social behaviour and values against those of one's own group. This often results in certain forms of *prejudice* occurring in people who are ethnocentric.

ethnography The branch of anthropology that deals with the description and comprehension of individual human societies, Its methods of research involve *participant observation* and *interviewing*. These methods have been employed in research into *educational institutions* and *educational climates*.

ethnology The comparative study of human cultures. See *anthropology*.

ethnomethodology The sociological study of methods by which ordinary people understand and produce co-ordinated social interaction. This approach to the study of social behaviour has been employed in research into school children's behaviour but not a great deal with *adult students*.

ethology The study of human character and cultural customs.

eugenics The study of genetic inheritance.

Europe Institute Situated at Munsbach Castle in Luxembourg, this Institute has been established as a *folk high school*, in some ways similar to the *European Folk High School* in Denmark, with which it co-operates.

European Association of Management Training Centres

Established in 1959 with a view to improving management education.

European Baccalaureate (EB) Awarded by schools which have been established in the various states of the European Community and are intended primarily to provide education for employees of community institutions. Usually the students work for this examination in their sixth and seventh year of secondary schooling and in two or three languages. It is regarded as similar to other school-leaving examinations as regards entry to *higher education*.

European Bureau of Adult Education A non-governmental association of national adult education associations of Europe, established in 1953, providing a network for the exchange of information and co-operation within Europe. Its first secretary was *Bob Schouten*. The Bureau publishes a newsletter, is engaged in collaborative projects, organizes an annual conference, and is run by an elected steering committee. Current address: European Bureau of Adult Education, P.O. Box 367, 3800 AJ Amersfoort, The Netherlands.

European Centre for Catholic Adult Education Current address: Nordlaan 96, B–9330 Dendermonde, Belgium.

European Centre for Education (Centro Europeo Dell'Educazione) (CEDE) Established in Italian law in 1974, but not fully staffed until 1982, to collect Italian and foreign educational documentation. It is concerned with *continuing* and *recurrent education*, problems of in-service training, *learning*, and a variety of other aspects. Its Department of *Continuing Education* is concerned with all the work in the education of adults nationally. It has developed comparative work in *adult basic education*, publishes a book series, a quarterly journal, and research reports (in Italian). Current address: Villa Falconieri, 00044 Frascati, Rome, Italy.

European Centre for Leisure and Education Sponsored by *Unesco* with the agreement of the Czechoslovak Academy of Science and established in 1968. This centre is concerned about the development of international adult education and has published a number of monographs on the subject. Address: Jilsá 1, 11000 Prague 1, Czechoslovakia.

European Centre for the Development of Vocational Training (CEDEFOP) Established in 1975 by a decision of the Council of European Communities as an autonomous organization. It works closely with the European Commission, promoting and developing *vocational training* and *continuing education* at the community level. It publishes *Vocational Training Bulletin* and *CEDEFOP News*. Current address: Bundesallee 22, D–1000 Berlin 15, Federal Republic of Germany.

European Community Action Programme A programme dealing with the transition of young people from school education to adult and work life. Has produced a number of publications.

European Development Fund A commission of the European Community's directorate for development, it sponsors projects in *development education*. Current address: 200 rue de la Loi, 1049 Brussels, Belgium.

European Folk High School Established in 1976, it is the first adult education institution which has devoted itself to European issues. It runs two winter courses for students of all nations, a three-month and a six-month course, and a summer school programme. Current address: Europahojskolen, DK–4780 Stege, Mon, Denmark.

European Journal of Engineering Education A quarterly journal which deals with engineering education throughout Europe.

European Materials for the Training of Adult Educators (EURAD) The

Council of Europe established this project in 1980 as a *training/retraining* project for part-time adult educators. The first co-operating countries were the United Kingdom, Austria, and Denmark. The Federal Republic of Germany later joined the scheme. The idea underlying the scheme was that there should be a common core of video cassettes with dubbed national languages and specially written support material for each society. However, there is some indication that countries that produced specific video cassettes tended to use only those that they had produced. This cast some doubts on the value of this form of international co-operation, although a thorough evaluation of this project will help assess these points.

European Society for Engineering Education Publishes its own journal and newsletter. Current address: 51 rue de la Concorde, B–1050 Brussels, Belgium.

evaluation The process of assessing the merit of a lesson, course, or curriculum. There are many approaches depending upon the researcher's purpose. For instance, evaluation might focus upon the aims of the course and whether they have been achieved, or the process of the course (structure and methods) and how it has been received, or the products of the course and the extent to which they are able to perform what is required of them; these are all different approaches to evaluation. Both the criteria of *assessment* and the methods of undertaking the assessment need careful consideration. This is regarded as an essential part of *programming* or *programme planning*.

Evangeleische Arbeitsgeinschaft für Erwachsenenbildung in Europa The Protestant Association for Adult Education in Europe. A European association which seeks to promote *adult religious education* in Europe, to exchange experience and ideas, to promote joint research projects, and to co-operate throughout Europe. Its membership is drawn from throughout Europe. It arranges an annual conference and works with national organizations. Current address: c/o The British Council of Churches, 2 Eaton Gate, London SW1W 9BL, UK.

evangelization Christian churches employ this term to refer to *preaching* to convert people to their way of thinking. It is a form of *instruction* which seeks to achieve a predetermined end-product. See *behavioural objectives*.

evening class A form of *adult education* which is *post-compulsory*. In the United Kingdom it is most frequently organized by the *Local Education Authority, the Workers' Educational Association*, or a *university extra-mural department*, and held in day schools in the evening. The first ones appear to have started in the 1750s in Newcastle. Many of these early classes were in mathematics and the sciences for craftsmen.

evening college Most evening colleges in the United States are institutions attached to universities which offer *part-time adult students* the opportunity to read for degrees. There are a few independent evening colleges, all of which offer degree programmes.

evening grammar school (*Abendsgymnasium*) Established in the Federal Republic of Germany after the First World War, it offers a traditional secondary school-type *curriculum* on a part-time evening basis to people in full-time employment, and has allowed many working-class people to gain access to *higher education*.

evening high school See *Abendsgymnasium*.

evening institute The official term used by the Department of Education and Science for *Local Education Authority adult education* classes in the United Kingdom, even though many of the centres actually called themselves by other terms.

evening school Schools for working people, held in the evening after the end of the working day. 1. The 1814 Education Act in Denmark imposed a responsibility upon the government to arrange evening education (afterskoler) for people who had left school, so that from early in the century most towns and rural districts had evening schools. There were also evening folk high schools in Denmark. It is estimated that about one-fifth of the population of Denmark participates in some form of education, probably the largest proportion of any country's population attending voluntary *adult education*. 2. There were private evening schools as early as 1766 in Philadelphia and 1833 in New York although it was about 1850 before their implementation really seemed to gather momentum. It was not until the end of the century that separate planning, co-ordination, and supervision of these schools occurred in the United States. Often these schools were advertised as *private instruction* and open to anybody willing to pay.

Everyman University The Israeli equivalent to the Open University in the United Kingdom. Established in 1974; admitted its first students in 1976. It provides pre-degree, *undergraduate*, *vocational*, and *adult education* (non-vocational, general interest) programmes. There is a system of *study centres* throughout the country. Current address: Tel-Aviv, Israel.

EWINC See the *Edinburgh Walk-In Numeracy Centre*.

examination A formalized method of *assessment* that occurs at fixed points in some courses. This is practised much less frequently in *liberal adult education* than in *initial education* or *professional education*.

exchange programme An exchange of either students or academic staff in order to work in each other's educational location for the purpose of cultural and professional enrichment.

Exeter Papers Papers of the *First International Conference on Comparative Adult Education* held at the Exeter Inn, Exeter, New Hampshire, USA, in June 1966.

exhibit A collection of items displayed to assist the *learning* process.

exhibitionist A person whose actions are frequently designed in order to display his/her attributes.

existentialism A philosophical theory, first formulated by Kirkegaard, in which being is of fundamental importance. Each person is aware of his/her own self and able to act in the world on the basis of experience and the situation. It is a theory espoused by a number of educational theorists, such as *C. Rogers*, and has consequently been very influential in *adult education* theory.

Expanded Food and Nutrition Education Program An educational programme in the United States in which federal funds are allocated to employ and train people from poor communities. The aim is to enable them to teach their neighbours about food and nutrition.

experience 1. A direct participation in an event. 2. The accumulation of previous experiences. It is this that *Malcolm Knowles* refers to as a rich resource for learning. This is only true if the previous experiences have not inhibited future learning potential.

Experiential Education The quarterly news bulletin published by the *Society for Field Experience Education* in America.

experiential learning Learning in which the learner has a *primary experience* with the reality being studied, or learned about. However, the term is often used to refer to *affective education*.

experiment A research approach in which the researcher sets up the situation and controls the variables so that certain hypotheses may be tested.

Experimental College Established at Wisconsin in 1925 with *Alexander Meiklejohn* as its head. It was a liberal college in which students followed a curriculum in which they related their education to their lives. It closed in 1932 because of lack of funds when people were concerned about its liberal perspectives.

experimental research An approach to research which, through the control of variables, seeks to predict future interrelations between them. This approach tends to be *quantitative* and adopts a *positivist* perspective.

Experimental World Literacy Programme (EWLP) Launched in 1967. As a result of the International Conference on Adult Education in Montreal in 1960 there was, in 1965, a world conference of ministers of education to examine the problems of literacy. It led to an experimental programme funded by *Unesco*, the United Nations Development Programme, and the participating nations aimed at eradicating *illiteracy*. It also measured the impact of *literacy* on social and economic development. The programme consisted of teaching literacy, numeracy, and some vocational skills, which became the basis of *functional literacy*. The programme lasted until 1973 but was not adjudged by all to have been a success.

expert A person whose *knowledge* or *skills* is acknowledged by his/her peers to be outstanding.

expert mission Occasionally, organizations such as *Unesco* will send a group of *experts* in *adult education* to a developing country in order to give assistance and advice in the development of an *adult education* programme.

exposition A systematic, often written, statement about a certain subject.

expository teaching *Teaching* that is orientated to explanation.

expressed need The concept of *need* is common but conceptually contentious in *adult education*. However, some scholars suggest that expressed needs are those which people experience and make known. See also *felt need*.

expressive arts Subjects such as music, art, dance, and drama through which people can express their emotions and/or experience, emotional satisfaction, etc.

expressive leader A leading figure in a group simply because he/she endeavours to ensure that every member of the group is accommodated. One whose purpose is to ensure that the group's dynamics function smoothly. Often second in command. See *task-orientated leader*.

expressive objectives These are process *objectives* rather than product ones, i.e. *behavioural objectives*. They do not, therefore, focus upon the end–product of learning but upon the learning opportunities. Many *adult educators* feel that expressive objectives are much more appropriate for the education of fellow adults.

expressive writing Writing that is creative and expresses the emotions of the writers.

EXTEND A registered charity which endeavours to train people to help the elderly and disabled to retain or recover their physical mobility. Current address: 5 Conway Road, Sheringham, Norfolk, UK.

extended education Education that is *post-compulsory*.

extended education centre A centre for the education of the mentally handicapped who live in the community, usually attached to an *adult education* institution.

extension agent An organizer of *extension education*, especially in relation to work of *agricultural extension* in the American *land grant colleges*. See *agricultural extension agent*.

extension college During the period 1850–80 a number of extension colleges were founded in England as a result of the *extension* work of the Universities of Cambridge and Oxford. These later enrolled full-time students and grew into the civic universities in England and Scotland.

extension education 1. Forms of education that extend beyond the normal boundaries of the educational activity of the organization providing it, e.g. *university extension*. It is a major type of *adult education*. See also *extra-mural department*. 2. Form of education provided by the *extension service*. See also *cooperative extension*.

extension education centre A centre established by an American *land grant college* in which to provide *extension studies* away from the university campus.

Extension Review An American quarterly journal concerned with the *extension service* published by the United States Department of Agriculture. See also *Journal of Extension*.

extension service The organization of *extension education* throughout the United States is often referred to as the extension service.

extension studies Work conducted by a college or university *extra-murally* in *adult education*.

external course A course which is organized *extra-murally*.

external degree The degree of a university, or other degree–awarding body, which is offered to *external students* successfully completing a degree course of that institution. In some cases the *curriculum* is the same for *internal students*, but in others it differs considerably. The external degree of the University of London was one of the only accesses to degree qualification open to adults in the United Kingdom, and elsewhere in the world, for many years.

external examination An examination set by an educational institution for students other than its own. This was one of the early ways in which adults were able to gain degrees through the *London University external examination system*.

external examiner In the United Kingdom system it is normal for colleges and universities to appoint one or more external examiners to a course to ensure that its standard is comparable to that of similar courses elsewhere. It is a part of the system of self-regulation of these colleges and universities.

external student 1. Traditionally a *mature student* who sits an examination, e.g. University of London degree, although the designated course has not been followed within the constituent colleges of the institution. 2. In the *General Certificate of Secondary Education* examination, an external student is one who has followed the syllabus prescribed for external students, which does not meet the national criteria, and who has less that 15 hours of *timetable* study time per week in term time.

external study Study organized by an educational institution for *external students*, often through *distance education* techniques.

extra-curricular activity Activities organized by an educational institution that occur outside the confines of its normal *curriculum*.

extra-mural department (EMD) These have traditionally been university departments of *adult education* which have offered university-type courses to the general public within a specified locality 'beyond the walls of the university'. They were established in England and Wales as a result of the *Final Report of the Adult Education Committee of the Ministry of Reconstruction* about *adult education*. They have often been granted *Responsible Body* status. More generally, an EMD is an educational department offering courses which are outside the educational organization's usual *curriculum* to the general public. See also *Responsible Body*.

Extra-Mural Education Committee In Scotland university extra-mural education is organized by committees which have representatives from the universities, *Local Education Authorities*, and *Workers' Educational Association*. They receive the grant for the administration of extra-mural education from the *Scottish Education Department* and are serviced by the *extra-mural departments* of the Scottish universities of Glasgow, Aberdeen, Dundee, and Edinburgh. The first of these committees was established at Glasgow in 1924.

extraneous variable Extra variables in research which may influence the relationship between the dependent and the independent variable.

extroversion A personality theory in which people direct their attention outwards, away from themselves, and gain satisfaction and pleasure from social interaction and physical fulfilment. See *introversion*.

extroversion–introversion A hypothesized dimension of personality in which there are two poles, *extrovert* and *introvert*, and that all people's personalities may be classified somewhere along that continuum.

extrovert One who has the characteristics of *extroversion*. Perhaps this type of person is advantaged in some forms of *adult education* in which social interactions are emphasized. See *introvert*.

Exxon Educational Foundation American educational foundation. Address: 111 West 49th Street, New York, New York 10020, USA.

eye contact Making contact through viewing, the interlocking of people's gazes. However, staring is regarded as bad manners and the quick glance is good etiquette. Part of the study of human interaction.

Eysenck Personality Inventory An inventory of a self-report nature which tests a number of factors: *extroversion-introversion*, *neuroticism* and *psychoticism*.

face-to-face groups Groups in which there is a direct social relationship.

facilitative teaching An experiential teaching method whereby the teacher provides experiences which result in learning. The teacher is, in this role, a *facilitator* rather than a provider of information and the students learn as a result of either *problem-solving* or *reflecting* upon their *experiences*.

facilitator A teacher who assists in the learning process without being the provider of information or the demonstrator of skills.

facility The equipment that exists within an organization or a location that facilitates *teaching and learning*.

factor A hypothetical construct which is assumed to influence some outcome or phenomenon under investigation.

factor analysis Statistical techniques through which a number of significant *variables* are isolated and correlated with each other.

factory college Established in China, colleges that are established in the premises of large factories and serve a wide geographic region. Students attending these colleges study full-time, relieved of their work responsibilities, but continue to receive their salary.

faculty 1. In universities in the United Kingdom, faculty refers to those groupings of academic departments with similar knowledge bases that form a unit of the university administrative structure,

e.g. the social science faculty. 2. In the United States, faculty refers to members of the academic staff who are employed by the university or other educational institution.

faculty advisor/counsellor Member of *faculty* in a US college or university who is the student counsellor.

faculty exchange programme A programme in which two colleges or universities arrange for an exchange or interchange of academic staff.

faculty load An academic member of staff's *teaching* load, i.e. the number of classes or hours taught per week in an American college or university.

faculty rank The occupational status of a member of *faculty* in an American university or college.

fading Gradual removal of support cues and promptings in order to assist the *learning process*.

Fagbladet Aften og Ungdomsskolen (The Adult and Youth School) Danish magazine concerned with *adult education*, *youth education* and related issues.

failure 1. The inability to complete an assignment, course, or examination to the required standard. The assumption of this term is often that the standard is objective but this does not hold for many types of *assessment*. It is widely agreed that much of the assessment process is subjective, so that the term *failure* needs to be treated with a degree of care within educational circles. 2. Term occasionally used to refer to the fact that a *learner* has not performed at the level anticipated.

failure rate The percentage of students failing an examination or course.

fall semester The *semester* starting in late summer or early autumn in an American college or university; the first semester in the academic year.

family improvement education A form of education practised in Third World countries designed to improve the quality of family life, e.g. *health education*, home care, nutrition, child care.

family life education American form of education designed to enrich family life or to prepare young adults for adult family life. This form of education has a long history in America with organizations such as the *National Congress of Mothers* being formed as early as 1897. In addition, *extension education* has focused upon this area for a great deal of its work.

Family Planning Association In the United Kingdom this association offers advice and assistance to those who require it but also has its own educational programme. The association has branches throughout the country.

farm agent See *extension agent*.

Farm Radio Forum Occurred in Canada in the 1930s when *listening groups* used radio broadcasts for *adult education* exercised in agriculture and policy-making. See *National Farm Radio Forum*.

Farmers' College on Wheels See *Farmer's Cooperative Demonstration*.

Farmers' Cooperative Demonstration An *extension education* enterprise which *Booker T. Washington* started from *Tuskegee Institute*. It consisted of wagons containing demonstration materials for farmers which were taken throughout the southern United States and which educated both black and white farmers

about seed selection and other aspects of farming. After *Washington*'s death farmers donated to the *co-operative extension service* a large agricultural truck to be used for demonstration purposes in his memory.

farmers' institute Started in 1860 in the state of Connecticut, United States. They have served a number of purposes, including education and providing a meeting place for farmers. An early educational venture in agricultural education, which culminated in the *Cooperative Extension Service*.

Farmers' Union 1. Established in the United States in 1902, it offered a broad agricultural educational programme in the south and middle-west of the United States. 2. In the Federal Republic of Germany this union is involved in *further education* in as much as it relates to agricultural work.

Faure, Edgar Chairman of the committee established by the International Commission on the Development of Education of *Unesco* which produced the report *Learning to Be*. He was a former Prime Minister and Minister of Education of France.

Faure Report The International Commission on the Development of Education of *Unesco* appointed a committee under Edgar Faure to examine the place of education in the contemporary world and in the future. This report, *Learning to Be*, was submitted and published in 1972.

feasibility study An initial study in order to examine the practicality of a project.

Federación de Associaciones de Educación de Adultos (FAEA) Established in Spain in December 1984 to co-ordinate the activities of non-governmental *adult education* organizations in that country. Current address: Apartado de Correos 2352, Madrid, Spain.

Federación Española de Universidades Populares The Spanish federation of *popular universities*, founded in 1982 and currently having over 60 members. Current address: Modesto de Lafuente, 63, 2, 28003 Madrid, Spain.

Federación Interamericana de Educación de Adultos (FIDEA) The federation of *adult education* organizations throughout Latin America. Current address: Edificio Capaya Penthoue, Calle Veracruz, Las Mercedes, Caracas 1060, Venezuela.

Federal Academy of Public Administration The central establishment of *continuing education* of the government of the Federal Republic of Germany. Established as a result of decisions taken in 1969. Other federal establishments of *further education* are run by other sectors of the government, including the military (the largest of all), Finance, the Foreign Office, and the railways.

Federal Board of Vocational Education Established in 1917 as a result of the *Smith–Hughes Vocational Education Act* in the United States, its main function is to supervise the federal programme of *vocational education* in high schools and vocational schools.

Federal Broadcasting Act American legislation in 1967 which created the *public television service* which provides *educational television* and other public affairs.

Federal Catholic Workshop for Adult Education The federal body for *adult education* in the Catholic Church in the Federal Republic of Germany. It has both state and federal association membership. It publishes a quarterly journal on *adult education* which deals with the workshop's internal matters and other aspects of *adult education* within the Church.

Federal Communications Act In 1963 legislation was passed in America which allowed for federal funds to be used for the creation of *educational broadcasting* facilities. However, the scheme was co-operative in as much as the states had to match the federal funding.

Federal Emergency Relief Administration (FERA) From 1933, as a relief measure for unemployed teachers in the United States, FERA made federal funds available for projects in *adult education*. Its successor, the *Works Progress Administration*, continued and broadened this from 1935.

Federal Employee Literacy Training Program (FELT) This programme recruits federal employee *volunteers* for work in *literacy* education, as part of the *Adult Literacy Initiative*. Current address: FELT, Adult Literacy Initiative, 400 Maryland Ave SW, Room 4145, Washington DC 20202, USA.

Federal Extension Service See *Cooperative Extension Service*.

Federal Institute for Vocational Education and Training (Bundesinstitut für Berufsbildung) Founded in 1970, this German institute works outside of school education, and deals mostly with in-company *training*. It also conducts research to improve *training* in companies. Established under a 1969 law, it is responsible to the federal government to which it acts as an advisory body. Current addresses: Fehrbelliner Platz 3, 1000 Berlin 31, Federal Republic of Germany, or Friesdorfer Strasse 151–153, 5300 Bonn 2, Federal Republic of Germany.

Federal Interagency Committee on Education (FICE) This committee is mandated to study and make recommendations to the Secretary of Education of the United States to ensure effective co-ordination of federal programmes, policies, and administrative practices affecting education. It co-operates with the *Adult Literacy Initiative* in a variety of ways.

Federal Republic of Germany *Adult education* in West Germany is

125

administered by the federal body and by the states. However, information about adult education in the Federal Republic can be obtained from: The Secretariat of the Standing Conference of the Ministers of Education and Cultural Affairs of the Lander in the FRG, Postfach 20 40, D–5300 Bonn 1, Federal Republic of Germany.

Federatie educatieve omroep See *Federation of Educational Broadcasting* in the Netherlands.

Federatie katholieke plattelandsvrouwen Nederland The *Catholic Countrywomen's Associations in the Netherlands*, of which there are over 600 branches. It conducts *non-formal adult education* in an attempt to make the participants aware of changes in their own life situations and in the wider world. Current address: Postbus 29708, 2502 LS Den Haag, The Netherlands.

Federatie van vormingscentera See *Federation of Residential Adult Education Centres.*

Fédération des Associations et Sociétés Françaises d'Ingénieurs Diplômés Established in 1929, the French association of graduates from schools of engineering. Engineering has always been at the forefront of innovations in *continuing education*. Current address: 19 rue de Blanche, 75009 Paris, France.

Fédération Française des Maisons et de la Culture See *French Federation of Centres of Youth and Culture.*

Fédération Léo Lagrange See *Léo Lagrange Federation.* A leading *public education* movement in France. Current address: 84 rue Saint-Thibault, BP 175, 28106 Dreux Cedex, France.

Federation of Adult Education Associations (FAEA) Spanish federation of associations. A great deal of *adult education* in Spain is organized by regional associations. This federation was founded in 1984. See *Federación de Associaciones de Educación de Adultos.*

Federation of Associations of the Third Age in Catalonia A regional council in Catalonia, Spain established in 1982 concerned with all activities of the elderly, including *adult education.* Contact address: The President, FATEC, Bertran 41, 08023 Barcelona, Spain.

Federation of Dutch People's Universities See *Bond van Nederlandse volksuniversiteiten.*

Federation of Dutch Trades Unions Institute See *Stitchting FNV-scholingsinstitut.*

Federation of Educational Broadcasting A Dutch federation. Current address: Feduco, Postbus 555, 1200 AN Hilversum, The Netherlands.

Federation of 18+ Groups A British federation of the *Eighteen-Plus Groups* that emerged as a result of a report in 1939 on 'Disinherited Youth'.

Federation of Public Programs in the Humanities An American organization concerned with citizenship study and with bringing humanities scholarship within the public policy debate. Current address: 15th South 5th Street, Suite 720, Minneapolis, Minnesota 55402, USA.

Federation of Residential Adult Education Centres (Federatie van vormingscentra) Dutch federation of residential associations. Current address: Postbus 36, 3970 AA Driebergen, The Netherlands.

Federation of Sports' Educational Association The latest Swedish *educational association* to be formed to organize *study circles.* It was recognized by the Swedish government in 1986.

Federation of Yugoslav Adult Educators' Associations This is a federation of state societies. Each state assumes responsibility for the federation in turn. Current address: Andragoski Centar, Vojnoviceva 42/II, 41000 Zagreb, Yugoslavia.

Fédération Suisse pour l'Education des Adults See *Swiss Federation for Adult Education, Shweizerische Verinigung für Erwachsenenbildung.* Current address: Oerlikonerstrasse 38, CH 8057 Zurich, Switzerland.

fee The costs to the student or the student's sponsoring organization of a course of study.

Feed the Minds Campaign A not very successful campaign conducted by the Christian churches in the United Kingdom in the 1960s to assist with *literacy campaigns* in the Third World by providing, through the churches, cheap Christian literature for newly literate people.

feedback The process of giving information about an inquiry, piece of work, or performance. Research shows that this is necessary if effective *learning* is to occur.

fellow Member of a research or teaching staff of a college or university.

fellowship The position held by a *fellow*. Often these are endowed posts but others are funded through grant aid for specific projects and are of limited duration.

felt need A subjective experience of *need*, which may be related to *wants*, but a concept used frequently within *adult education* literature. The distinction between *want* and *need* is blurred and certainly impossible to demarcate empirically.

Fernuniversitat-Gesamthoschule The distance teaching university in the Federal Republic of Germany, established in 1974. It offered its first courses in September 1975. Unlike many *distance teaching universities*, this does not have an *open access* policy to studying: students have to be qualified in the same manner as they would to study at a traditional university if they wish to earn a degree. By contrast, unqualified students can be admitted for the purpose of continuing their studies and they are regarded as *guest students*. Most of this university's educational material is prepared for distance teaching without face-to-face contact although it does operate a system of *study centres*, most of which are still in North Rhine-Westphalia, Current address: Hagen, North Rhine-Westphalia, Federal Republic of Germany.

field 1. Area of study or academic discipline, e.g. 'it's not my field'. 2. Place, physical location, where the actual event(s) takes place, e.g. 'out in the field'.

field agent One who works in the *field*, is associated with the college or university, and is involved in *teaching*, organizing, or researching in the field.

field centre A place where some activity or study occurs, situated away from the main site of the educational establishment.

field course A course of study conducted in the place where the phenomenon under study occurs.

field dependency A *cognitive style* in which the learner is seen as being affected by the whole arena in which the learning occurs rather than just the phenomenon being learned. It is a *global* form of learning. Field dependents are usually people who are gregarious, affectionate, tactful, and considerate. See also *field independency*.

field experience Experience gained by having undertaken a course of study or a period of time of work in the place where the activity actually occurs, as opposed to where it is studied.

field independency A *cognitive style* in which the learner concentrates upon the phenomenon to be learned rather than the whole field; an *analytical* approach to learning. Field independents are socially independent and have a highly developed sense of their own *self-identity*. See also *field dependency*.

field notes Records made during a research *observation* or during a *field trip*.

field of adult education Attempts to draw boundaries around *adult education* have resulted in the occasional use of this term to refer to that which is included within the field.

field of knowledge The *knowledge* about an area of study (see *field of adult education*) which is not the same as an academic discipline. See *field of study*.

field of study A subject for study, research, or teaching which may involve the combination of a number of academic *disciplines*. Rather than regarding *adult education* as an academic *discipline*, scholars tend to see it as a practical area for study, research, and teaching.

field officer A person appointed to work in the field away from the main administrative centre. *REPLAN*, for instance, employs this approach. See also *field agent*.

field research An approach to research which is open-ended and *qualitative*, which does not have a single method of data collection but seeks to incorporate a number as the researcher endeavours to draw close to a natural situation.

field studies 1. Investigations undertaken outside of the classroom or other learning location, usually with reference to the study of the environment. 2. In the United States the term tends to be used to relate to practical experience in the wider sense.

field trip An educational visit to learn about a phenomenon or object away from the educational organization.

field visit See *field trip*.

field worker One who is employed to work in the place in which the activity under study occurs. See also *field agent*.

field work teacher In the United Kingdom this title is used for a practising *health visitor* (an element of public health nursing) who is trained in the art of one-to-one teaching and who is involved in the professional preparation of health visitors by working with them in professional practice. Educational preparation is mandatory in the United Kingdom for health visitors who take students in professional practice. See *teacher practitioner, practical work teacher, clinical nurse teacher*. In addition, it is occasionally employed in the same manner in social work education.

Fiji See *National Association of Adult Educators*.

Film The magazine of the *British Federation of Film Societies*.

film forum The use of a film, followed by discussion groups, in order to create awareness of issues.

film society A local society established both to view films and discuss the film seen. There are many such societies in the United Kingdom. See *British Federation of Film Societies*.

Final Report of the Adult Education Committee of the Ministry of Reconstruction, 1919 Popularly known as the *1919 Report*. This is a classic report with recommendations about the future of *adult education* in Britain after the First World War. Many of its utopian ideals have never been put into practice.

Finnish Folk High School Association Established in 1907, all 89 folk high schools in Finland are members. The association conducts research and disseminates knowledge about the folk high school movement. There is a journal, *The Folk High School Journal* (*Kansanopisto-lehti*) which is published eight times a year. It is a member of the *Nordic Council of Folk High Schools*. Current address: Pohj Rautatiekatu 15B, 00100 Helsinki 10, Finland.

Finnish Library Association Very involved in adult education. It runs its own courses and publishes a journal,

Library Journal (*Kirjasto-lehti*). Current address: Museokatu 18A, 00100 Helsinki 10, Finland.

Finnish Society for Educational Science Finnish professional education association. Current address: Bulevardi 18, 00120 Helsinki, Finland.

Fircroft College Established in 1909, the second residential adult education college in England. It was proposed to commence as a college which recruited mainly rural workers, but this never really occurred. It has a Quaker origin, founded under the influence of *George Cadbury*, and was connected with the *adult school movement*. Its first warden was Tom Bryan. It is now a residential adult college for men and women in Birmingham, United Kingdom which has been supported by the Department of Education and Science. It was closed for five years in the late 1970s following internal disputes and a rent strike but reopened in 1980. Current address: 1018 Bristol Road, Selly Oak, Birmingham B29 6LH, UK.

Firmstart *Training* provided for 16 weeks over a period of a year by *Manpower Services Commission* for people who have successfully started their own business. (Note: the *Manpower Services Commission* changed its name to the *Training Commission* and then to the *Training Agency* in 1988.)

First Act on Further Education The 1975 legislation of the state of North Rhein-Westphalia in the Federal Republic of Germany. This act includes extensive legislation for the provision of *further education*, including *political education*, by the municipal authorities.

first degree A bachelors degree (see *higher degree*). It does not have to be the first in succession, but rather in level.

fishbowl A *teaching and learning* technique in which *group discussion* is employed in two different ways. Initially a small group from the larger class sits in the middle of the class and discusses a specific subject, whilst the remainder of the class sit around the central group and observe and listen to the interaction. Thereafter the whole class discusses what occurred within the smaller group.

Fisher, Dorothy Canfield Associated with the *American Association of Adult Education*, in its early years. Became the author of the first book on *adult education* written for a lay audience in the United States and abroad, entitled *Why Stop Learning?*

Fisher, Welthy (1879–1980) Founder and animator of the Literacy House in Lucknow, India, chairperson of *World Education* in New York, recipient of the first *Nehru Literacy Award* and many other awards for literacy work, Welthy Fisher was an American citizen who settled in India with her husband (a bishop of the Methodist Church in America who worked in India) and who worked unceasingly for *adult literacy* in India where she was known as the 'literacy lady'.

Fisher's Test A statistical test for determining the significance of a correlation coefficient.

Fitzpatrick, Alfred (1862–1935) Born into a Presbyterian family in Pictou County, Nova Scotia, he initially became a Presbyterian missionary in the forest camps in Ontario. After three years he left to experiment with the *Frontier College* idea of having *labourer teachers*. This grew and became established, even though he considered that it should only be a temporary phenomenon until the Canadian government realized its responsibility to those who worked in the railways and forest camps. He started the practice of *labourer teachers* in the camps, using young men and women who would give time to undertake the normal work of the camps and teach as well.

Five Percentage Level of Significance An indicator in social science research, as a statistical measure, that is used to suggest that in the comparison of data that there is only one chance in 20 that the data occurred by chance.

fixation 1. The process whereby an attitude, cognition, etc. becomes rigid and inflexible. 2. In Freudian theory, the process whereby one becomes attached to a stage of development, or to a person or object, so that it inhibits further growth or development.

fixed costs The expenses that have to be met by an educational institution independently of the number of students who enrol or pay *fees*.

fixed interval A schedule of reinforcement.

Flash Formation Continue A magazine published in France by the Université des Sciences Sociales of Grenoble, from *Centre Universitaire d'Information de Recherche et Documentation sur l'Education Permanente* (CUIDEP). Contains information about developments in *continuing education* and about recent publications, legislation about continuing education. Contact address: 2 Place de l'Etoile, 38000 Grenoble, France.

flexibility The ability to adapt pre-arranged and prepared content and method to respond to a potential learning situation and accommodate the unexpected. This is seen to be an essential characteristic of an *adult educator*.

flexible learning A wide range of possibilities offered to students and a degree of student autonomy on choice of what to study, when and how. See *flexi-study*.

flexi-study An approach to teaching and learning using a variety of modes, such as the provision of prepared teaching and learning material with tutorial support. A useful approach for the busy, mature student which has been introduced by a number of different educational institutions, especially in *further education* in the United Kingdom.

Flitner, Wilhelm (b. 1888) German adult educator, influential in the inter-

war period, whose main concern was *popular education* as a means of creating the new state. He founded the German School of People's Research and Adult Education.

Floodlight The Inner London Education Authority in the United Kingdom has for many years published a compendium of all the courses offered in *adult education* in the city, under this title. However, this *Local Education Authority* was disbanded by the Conservative government and a number of smaller authorities created from it.

flowchart Diagram depicting the interrelationships between parts of a more complex whole.

fluency activity In language classes it is quite normal to devote the latter part of a *session* to free speech and discussion to try to help the students employ the grammar, words, and structures that they covered in the session within a more broad context as they also seek to achieve some fluency in the language.

fluid intelligence That form of intelligence which is innate and biologically determined. See also *crystallized intelligence*.

focus of attention The phenomenon to which concentration is directed.

focusing process The process of adjusting topics, goals, etc. in such a manner as to make them more explicit and mutually supporting.

Folk College Association of America Current address: CPO 287, Berea, Kentucky 40404, USA.

folk culture The *culture* of the ordinary people: traditions of art, drama, story, etc. of small regional groups of people within a larger society. This tradition is often neglected by educationalists who present *high culture* or *dominant culture* as the form of culture to be appreciated.

Folk Development Colleges A network of colleges established in

Tanzania in 1975 to support the national *adult literacy* campaign. The network has enabled many people to become literate using mass media and popular culture.

folk education Term used in Scandinavia to refer to *adult education*, although there are linguistic differences that reflect the differing perspectives between Scandinavia and many other countries towards *lifelong education* for all.

folk high schools Adult education institutions which are now spread throughout the world. The following contains information about some of the countries in which they have been established.

1. They started in Denmark in 1844, in Rødding, as a *community education* venture. Folk high schools owe a great deal to the thought of *Bishop N. Grundtvig*. In Denmark there are 166 schools, 28 specializing in home economics and 32 in agriculture, and they are all residential. Danish immigrants to the United States first introduced the idea there in the late nineteenth century. See *Folk High School Association of America*. However, since 1970 there has been a move in Denmark to develop some *technical education* in some of them, but as yet they do not offer credit. More recently they have opened their doors to older, retired people participating in their programmes. Danish folk high schools have to be approved but they are independent, non-profit, self-governing adult education organizations, although some sponsorship occurs among some of them. There have been some *evening schools* which were folk high schools. See also *day folk high school*. An association of such schools exists in Denmark. Current address: Folk High School Information Office, Vartov, Farvergade 27 G DK–1463 Copenhagen K. Denmark. There are also folk high schools in the Faero Islands, Iceland, and Greenland. Current addresses for information: Faroy Fólkaháskulia, 3800 Torshavn, Faero Islands; Knud Rasmussenip Højskoliat, 3920 Qaqortog, Greenland; and

Lýdáskólinn i Skålholyi, 801 Selfoss Island, Iceland.

2. In Holland an *Association for the Establishment of Folk High Schools* was formed in 1931. Now a part of the education of adults in that country, with folk high schools associated with the national body. They are frequently residential and although they do not always aim at certification, nor exclusively at intellectual training, their aim is one of intellectual awakening. Four institutions work in an agrarian context but, significantly, there has been an increase in retired persons attending courses throughout the country. There are also other residential adult education centres in Holland. Current address: Vereniging voor Volkshogeschoolwerk, Postbus 314, 3800 AH Amersfoort, The Netherlands.

3. In Finland there are 89 folk high schools which offer courses for credit and a national *Finnish Folk High School Association*. Current address: Järnägsgatan 15 B 12, SF- Helsinfors 10, Finland.

4. Folk High schools were introduced in Sweden from Denmark in 1868 when three schools were started. They offer courses for credit. There is now a separate organization and special teacher training for teachers in folk high schools. Current address (of the association): Landstingdfögskoleinformation, Box 6606, S-113 84 Stockholm, Sweden.

5. Folk high schools were started in Poland in 1900. By 1914 there were seven but they were all destroyed in the First World War. They were subsequently re-started and some still exist today.

6. There are also approximately 900 folk high schools in the Federal Republic of Germany which belong to a national association, the German Union of Folk High Schools. Many of these were opened in 1947 after the Second World War. They offer *open further education* and are not tied to any particular groups; nor do they espouse particular political positions or causes. It has been suggested that the German folk high schools are more like *people's universities* since they offer courses with their own form of certification. Others see them as more

like *adult education institutes*, since they run mostly *liberal adult education* courses. Certainly, some people do not regard them as folk high schools in the Danish sense of the word. See *People's College*.

7. In Norway there is separate legislation to cover the folk high schools and the schools do not run courses for credit. However, their history here is significant since *Bishop Grundtvig* directly approached the Norwegian people in 1837. However, the first one was not founded until 1864 in Hamar. Current address for information: Nordens Folkiga Akademii, Box 1001 S – 442 25 Kungälv, Norway.

8. In Belgium there are a number of folk high schools, some of which are organized by the *Lodewijk de Raet* Foundation. One, in Kessello near Leuven, is residential.

9. *Highlander* in the United States was originally modelled on the *Danish movement* and would see itself in the folk high school tradition.

10. Folk high schools have recently been introduced into Africa. In 1975, for instance, the government of Tanzania decided to build 85 folk high schools, called *Folk Development Colleges*.

11. Folk high schools were introduced into India in 1948 but only a few have been built.

12. Folk high schools were beginning to emerge in what is now Yugoslavia early in the twentieth century but did not really become established. They are, however, the early precursors of the *people's universities* there.

13. The first folk high school in Latin America was opened in Chile in 1988. See *El Canelo de Nos*.

folk house (Volkshuis) The equivalent to the *university settlements* in Holland, started at the turn of the twentieth century. Their objective was to raise the level of *development*, *culture*, and happiness of the working-class peoples.

Folk House (Bristol UK) Started as a non-residential settlement by the *adult school movement* in 1920 and continues today as an adult education institution. Current address: 40 Park Street, Bristol BS1 5JG, UK.

Folk og Fritid (People and Leisure) Danish journal established in 1966, published four times a year and concerned with *adult education* and other cultural activities.

Folk School Association of America (FSAA) Established in 1977 to provide opportunities for people of similar educational philosophies to communicate, to introduce new people to the folk high school concept, and to develop these ideas in a relevant manner in the United States. The association publishes a quarterly newsletter. Current address: CPO 287, Berea, Kentucky 40404, USA.

folk university These are *adult education* institutions which usually provide adult education on a part-time basis. In some countries they are closely connected to the local *university*, but in others they are more independent.

1. An institution in Denmark formed through the co-operation of the folk universities of the five national universities (Copenhagen, Aarhus, Odense, Aalborg, Roskilde) and managed by a national secretariat. Each local level has its own committee; over 120 exist and each university is semi-autonomous in its functions with its folk university. The first of the local committees was founded as early as the end of the last century when a Folk University Association was formed (1898) between the University of Copenhagen and the labour movement. It has had a troubled history. In 1971 a new national structure was established as a result of the *higher education* legislation of 1970. Now there is a national committee co-ordinating work throughout the country. The courses are non-vocational and not all courses lead to *credit*, although there is a movement towards this. Current address: The National Secretariat of the Folk University, University of Odense, DK–5230 Odense M, Denmark.

2. In Sweden, one of the sponsoring educational associations of *study circles*. It sponsors advanced courses in scientific and technological subjects and has also sought to publish its own materials. It

has a university base and is the only one of the *educational associations* in Sweden located within the university framework. Originally a student movement, it commenced in 1933. Current address: Folkuniversitetet, Styrmansgatan 47, Stockholm 11460, Sweden.

3. In Norway where there is no *university extension* tradition, there is a folk university having branches throughout the country. Current address: Folkeuniversitetet, Sørkedalsvn 10b, 0369 Oslo 3, Norway.

Folkbildningsförbundet The national federation of adult education associations in Sweden. Current address: Industrigatan 4B 1tr, S-11246 Stockholm, Sweden.

Folkehögskolan 1. The journal of the *Swedish Union of Folk High School Teachers* published eight times a year. 2. Norwegian journal established in 1905 and published monthly.

folkeoplysning (general adult education) The Danish word for a difficult concept: it refers to the alternative educational tradition in Denmark and has its roots in the social movements of the country. It might be summarized as enlightenment about the cultural traditions of the people, and as such it receives a great deal of state support.

Fondo de Capacitación Popular A Colombian organization involved in *popular education*. Current address: Inravision, Carrera 14 No 63–09, Bogotá, Colombia.

Fönstret (The Window) A Swedish magazine of *adult education* and other cultural activities, established in 1954 and published 16 times a year.

Food and Agricultural Organization (FAO) A *Unesco* organization orientated to the improvement of farming and the concerns of hunger. It uses many *adult educators* in its work, especially as *agricultural extension agents* working as consultants in Third World

countries. Current address: Via delle Terme di Caracalla, 00100 Rome, Italy.

Food For Thought Begun in 1940, the journal of the *Canadian Association for Adult Education*. In 1976 the association adopted the title *Learning* for its journal. Its predecessor was *Adult Learning*.

Food is Life A *mass campaign* conducted by the *Institute of Adult Education* in Tanzania, aimed at *agricultural development*.

Ford Foundation Established in 1936 as a charitable foundation which has supported education, including *adult education* in America. Current address: 320 East 43rd Street, New York, New York 10017, USA.

Foreign Policy Association Established in the United States in 1918, this association has been concerned to raise citizen awareness by running discussion groups, similar to *study circles* in the United States, concerning foreign policy issues. In 1955 it started the *Great Decisions* programme.

forgetting 1. Loss of ability to recall, recognize, or reproduce what had previously been *learned*. 2. In some forms of psychoanalytic theory, forgetting is regarded as a form of repression.

Forma The journal of the Portuguese adult education association, published in Portuguese three times a year. It commenced in 1982.

formal education The hierarchically structured education system which extends from primary schools to graduate programmes at university. See, by contrast, *non-formal education*.

formal operational thought Related to Piaget's approach to *cognitive development*, specifically to the *adult stage*. Piaget considered that it began about the age of twelve years, although his schema has been questioned by theorists recently.

formal organization This may refer either to a bureaucratic organization or a standardized approach to organizing any phenomenon.

formal training *Training* received within an organization setting.

formalism An approach to the acquisition of knowledge that places emphasis upon the organization, consistency, and development of principles.

formateurs d'adultes The French term for *trainer* of adults.

formateurs jeunes See *youth trainer*.

formative assessment The process of assessing students at the start or in the preliminary stages of a course in order to assess their learning *needs*, through which a teacher can plan, or help plan, a teaching and learning programme. It is unusual for such an *assessment* to be used in a *summative assessment* of the students.

formative evaluation The process of undertaking a preliminary *evaluation* exercise, usually during the process of the course, in order to improve the on-going teaching and learning process.

formative profiling In the *Certificate for Pre-Vocational Education*, all *assessment* is done through *profiling*. This is the initial profile prepared by the students in conjunction with their tutors, to help guide the students through their course, spotlighting both achievements and *needs*. See also *summative profiling*.

forms of knowledge The philosopher Paul Hirst postulated that there are seven forms of knowledge; formal logic and mathematics; physical sciences; human sciences; history; religion, literature and the fine arts; philosophy. These are distinct from *fields of knowledge* and do not constitute disciplines as such. For Hirst, *liberal education* is a broad education that encompasses the seven forms of knowledge.

Forschung der Socialistischen Berufsbildung Publication established in 1967. Published every two months in the German Democratic Republic about *vocational education*.

forum 1. Sometimes called *open forum*, in which participants question and discuss a total *presentation* as a group. 2. A teaching technique in which the whole of a class participates in discussion for a fixed period of time, sometimes in the presence of a specialist.

Forum for Access Studies (FAST) A national body established to promote access to *higher education* for mature students in the United Kingdom. It publishes *Journal of Access Studies*. Current address: South Bank Polytechnic, 58 Clapham Common North Side, London SW4 9RZ, UK.

Forum of African Voluntary Development Organizations (FAVDO) Established in 1987 following a meeting in Dakar in Senegal in which representatives from 23 countries participated. This forum aims at establishing links of communication among agencies, providing support, producing resources, and acting as a lobby for voluntary development organizations. Its general assembly meets every three years and it has an executive committee. Contact address Radi, P.O. Box 12085, Dakar, Senegal.

Forum of African Voluntary Development Organizations Echo The journal of the *Forum of African Voluntary Development Organizations* and is intended to act as a focal point for African voluntary development organizations.

Forum on the Rights of Elderly People to Education (FREE) A forum which has campaigned for the rights of the elderly to education in the United Kingdom. It was established in 1981 and produces its own regular bulletin. Current address: Bernard Sunley House, 60 Pitcairn Road, Mitcham, Surrey, UK.

Forum – Zeitschrift der Volkschochschulen *Adult education* journal published quarterly in the Federal Republic of Germany since 1967.

foundation course 1. In American university study of adult education, the foundations course tends to include the philosophical, sociological, and historical approaches to the study. This differs totally from the United Kingdom, where each of these courses provides a major focus in itself. 2. In the United Kingdom a foundation course is usually the first year of a total course. In the *Open University* it is expected that every student will have completed at least one such course as part of the degree. 3. In the study of art, the foundation course is a course in its own right; thereafter students specialize.

Foundation for Domestic Education in the Rural Areas Established in Holland in 1935 to provide domestic education for groups in the rural population that were most in need.

Foundation for Education with Production A non-governmental organization in Botswana, established in 1982 by Patrick van Rensburg, concerned primarily with developing educational alternatives to challenge forms of education that reproduce the current social structures, including the desire to integrate the educational curriculum with the world of work. Publishes the journal *Education with Production*.

Foundation for Educational Broadcasting and Multi-Media Education A Dutch foundation. See *Stichting Teleac*.

Foundation for Formal and Non-Formal Education and Information A Dutch foundation. See *Stichting IVIO*.

Foundation for Woodbrokers in the Netherlands This is the Quaker foundation which runs *adult residential schools*. See *Stichting ter bevordering van het Woodbrookerswerk in Nederlands*.

Foundation Papers In the short history of the *National Foundation for Adult Education*, these papers were its quarterly publication.

foundation university Term used to describe some universities founded in America from the colonial period until the late nineteenth century.

4-H Clubs Young people's clubs that have formed a backbone of *cooperative extension* work in the United States. The four Hs are: head, heart, hands, and health. The movement's symbol is the four-leaf clover. It provides a major forum for *adult education* in America and also has a training programme to prepare leaders for all its activities.

four-year college American university providing all four years of the bachelor degree programme.

fourth level course In the United Kingdom, the *Open University* has four levels of course for its bachelors degree, with the fourth considered as being the most advanced.

fourth revolution The transformation of post-secondary education by new educational technologies. A term used by the Carnegie Commission on Higher Education in the United States in 1972.

FOVUX Swedish outreach programme in *adult education* in which state funds were allocated to the recruitment of adults in the work place and on housing estates through personal contact. The success rate was high, with as many as 40 per cent of working-class people contacted in the work place and about 25 per cent of those contacted in the home joining an educational programme.

Fowler, James W. Professor of Theology and Human Development at Emory University in Atlanta, Georgia, United States. He pioneered the work on faith development, suggesting that there are six stages in faith development in a manner similar to other aspects of *human development*. See. *L. Kohlberg, J. Piaget*.

135

Fox, Samuel Quaker grocer who was one of the first *adult schools* in Nottingham in 1798. See also *William Singleton*.

fragmentary understanding A partial understanding superficiality of knowledge.

Frandson Award Literature award in the field of continuing professional education administered by the *National University Continuing Education Association* in the United States.

Frandson, Phillip (d. 1981) Internationally acknowledged *adult educator* whose last position was Dean of University Extension at University College of Los Angeles. He was president of the *National University Continuing Education Association* in the United States in 1977–78. See *Phillip Frandson Scholarship Fund*.

Franklin, Benjamin (1706–90) Co-author of the American Declaration of Independence. Perhaps best known in *adult education* because he founded the *junto* in Philadelphia. He was also involved in library provision and in the foundation of the *Philadelphia Society for Promoting Agriculture*, a forerunner of the *Cooperative Extension Service*. He was involved in the provision of the early *subscription library* service and was a scientist of repute.

Franklin Books Program A voluntary American programme to supply books to libraries in the Third World.

Franklin Institute Established in 1824 in Philadelphia for the advancement of science and the education of the public in science and industry. Current address: Benjamin Franklin Parkway, 20th Street Philadelphia, Pennsylvania 19103, USA.

Franks Report A British report into business education, published in 1963, which resulted in the establishment of business schools in Britain.

Frauen Museum See *Women's Museum*.

free association A Freudian technique of association of ideas under the guidance of a trained analyst.

Free Churches' Education Board (Frikyrkliga Studieförtbundet) One of the sponsoring *educational associations* for *study circles* in Sweden. It was established in 1942.

Free Educational Association An educational association in Denmark which provides *general adult education*. It is associated with the liberal political movement.

Free Institution of Education Founded in Spain in 1876 by a group of intellectuals, this organization has played a significant role in the history of education in that country. It tried unsuccessfully to form a free university, promoted the *Pedagogical Museum* and a variety of other educational projects, including the foundation of the *Asociación para la Enseñanza de la Mujer* (Association of Women's Education), *university extension*, and pedagogical missions (travelling teachers organizing cultural activities in rural parts of Spain).

free provider Term used in the Federal Republic of Germany to refer to a *provider* of *open further education* which is in the common interest.

Free School at Tvind The only children's school in the *Tvind* Schools in Denmark, it is both a day and boarding school for children aged between six and fourteen years.

free university Learning networks established throughout different cities in the United States providing adult learning through networking. They are organizations which offer non-traditional, non-credit education to the general public, in which anybody can teach and anybody can learn. They began in the 1960s on college campuses but by the 1970s were established widely throughout America. Some are entrepreneurial concerns whilst others are free and based at *libraries*, etc. It is a concept different from that of the Free University of Berlin, where 'free' refers to a political phenomenon.

Free University Network The national association of *free universities* and learning networks. Current address: 1221 Thurston, Manhattan, Kansas 66502, USA.

freedom 1. Personal liberty. 2. The state of being free. 3. The ability to order one's own actions. 4. The philosophical doctrine of being unrestrained by physical determinants. See *autonomy*.

freelance teacher See *part-time teacher*.

freewheeling See *brainstorming*.

Freire, Paulo Born in 1921 in Brazil, he became leader of the Brazilian adult literacy movement in the 1950s but was also associated with the liberation theology movement. He was imprisoned and exiled after the military coup in Brazil in 1964. Thereafter he worked in Chile, then with the *World Council of Churches*, and subsequently returned to Brazil. One of the original thinkers in adult education, he pioneered important new approaches to literacy and stimulated thought in the philosophy and sociology of adult education. He is the author of numerous books and articles about *adult education* and *literacy*. See *talking books*.

French Education League See *Ligue Française de l'Enseignement et de l'Education Permanente*.

French Federation of Centres of Youth and Culture A provider of *socio-cultural animation for young adults* funded partly by the Ministry for Leisure, Youth and Culture and partly by local municipalities.

frequency The number of occurrences of the same score in a sample or a *population*.

frequency distribution The spread of scores in a sample or *distribution*; often recorded in tabular form.

Fresh Horizons Courses started at the *City Literacy Institute* in the United Kingdom in 1966 to provide mature adults with a new perspective on life. In the first instance these courses attracted mainly women but they were open to both sexes and gradually men started to attend them. Initially they were full-time courses.

Fresh Start The term frequently used for courses especially designed for adults who left school at the minimum school-leaving age with few or no qualifications to help them return to study.

Freud, Sigmund (1856–1939) Neurologist and founder of the schools of psychology and psychotherapy that bear his name. Perhaps insufficient attention has been paid to his work in *learning theory* especially the emphasis that he placed upon the *unconscious*.

Freudenberg, Gideon (1897–1979) Born in Germany but emigrated to Israel in 1935. He was both a farmer and an *adult educator*. Collaborated with *Martin Buber* in establishing *training* for *adult educators* and was the first director of the Training College for Adult Educators. Thereafter he was director of the Martin Buber Centre for Adult Education at the Hebrew University in Jerusalem. He was also active in other aspects of *adult education* in Israel.

Friedrich Ebert Foundation West German political foundation established in 1925 and involved in *adult education*, especially in the fields of political and social self-determination and participation. Also runs *adult education* institutions abroad, in keeping with the international awareness of West German *adult education* generally. Current address: 53 Bonn-Bad Godesberg, Kolnerstrasse 149, Federal Republic of Germany.

Friedrich Naumann Foundation West German political foundation involved in *adult education*, especially in the fields of political and social self-determination and participation. In common with other West German adult education institutions, it has an international interest and runs *adult education* institutions abroad.

Friends First-Day School Association (FFDSA) Many of the early *adult schools* in England were started by the Society of Friends (Quakers). This association became the co-ordinating association for these schools.

Friends of Swedish Primary Schools Corresponds to the *Society for Popular Culture* and also functions in Finland. Runs the Educational Activities Study centre, the Swedish correspondence institute in Finland and financially supports Swedish adult education activities in Finland. It has its own journal, *Swedish Area (Svensk-Bygden)*. Current address: Annankatu 12, 00120 Helsinki 12, Finland.

Friends of the ICAE Although the *International Council for Adult Education (ICAE)* does not have individual membership, it does have a network of 'friends' who are subscribers to and supporters of the association.

Fritid og Samfund Danish journal published since 1977 about leisure-time education.

front-end model of education Term used to convey the idea that education is primarily something that is done for and to children and, by implication, that adult education is not a significant aspect of educational thinking or policy. See also *initial education*.

Frontier College In Canada, these are colleges that are established in the forestry and railway camps to work with labourers and lumberjacks. The Frontier College began in 1899 as the *Reading Camps Association*, by *Alfred Fitzpatrick*, for all the labourers who needed basic education. Frontier colleges existed in every camp and, for a while, among Canadian service men when they served abroad. Employed *labourer-teachers* to reach the people with whom they wished to work and help. They offered *adult basic*

education and *Canadianization* education to the labourers, many of whom were immigrants who often did not speak English. As Canadian frontiers have been pushed back and changed, so the work of the college has changed, so that it is now working at the urban frontiers of society. The college's motto is 'Life without Letters is Dead'. Current address: 31 Jackes Ave, Toronto, Canada.

Fujin Kyoiku Joho Journal of education for women, Published biannually in Japan by the *National Women's Education Centre* since 1979.

Fulbright Act Federal legislation in America in 1946 to promote the exchange of teachers, students, and researchers with specified countries. Some adult educators have received this award.

Fulbright Scholarship An American government award for *graduate study*, *teaching*, or *lecturing* by an American citizen abroad, or for a foreign national to visit the United States. There have been some scholarships granted to *adult educators*. The programme is administered by the US State Department. This programme of exchanges has been established as a result of the *Fulbright Act*.

full-time equivalent A formula for funding employed by many educational institutions in which part-time students have to be adjudged in terms of their equivalency to full-time students. In addition, this formula is used to relate the number of full-time equivalent students to the size of the academic establishment. E.g. for every 15 full-time student there should be one full-time academic staff post.

full-time regular education Assumed to be all compulsory education plus the normal pattern of *higher education*, but excludes what is recognized as *adult education*.

Functional Adult Education National Centre Established in the *Sudan* in 1960. It is a documentation and information centre which collects statistics of *adult education*, undertakes some research, and provides some adult education training. It stresses *adult literacy*. Current address: P.O. Box 71, Shendi, Sudan.

functional literacy Regarded as the level of skills in *literacy, numeracy, oracy*, and *social skills* that enables a person to play an active, independent role in society. *Unesco* has defined this as having acquired the *knowledge* and *skills* in reading and writing which enable a person to engage effectively in all those activities in which *literacy* is normally assumed in his/her culture or group. There was pressure in North America to regard the cut-off point to be a reading ability of less than Grade VIII (about the reading ability regarded as normal for a 14-year-old). See also *semi-literate*.

Fund for Adult Education Established in 1951 in the United States by the *Ford Foundation* as an independent organization to assist all men and women in continuing their education. Until its termination in 1961, many adult education enterprises were assisted by the Fund. The grants had four objectives: to increase *knowledge* and *skill* of those in responsible positions; to recruit and train those who could lead *liberal adult education* programmes; to strengthen university *adult education* programmes; and to assist the use of *liberal adult education* provision in the *training* function.

Fund for Adult Education Fellow One who has received an award from the *Fund for Adult Education*.

Funkkolleg *Courses by radio,* established in the Federal Republic of Germany in 1966. It occurs in different parts of the country where a university, such as the *Deutsche Institut für Fernstudien* of the University of Tübingen, co-operates with the local radio station and with the *folk high schools* to prepare a course lasting some 30 weeks. Material is printed for the students who register for the course and examinations are conducted at its termination. The *folk high schools* arrange *study groups* which are *listening groups* as

well and a certificate is awarded to those who complete the course in a satisfactory manner.

Further and Higher Education Unit 3 The branch of the *Department of Education and Science* of the UK government responsible for *adult education*.

further education 1. In the United Kingdom, this refers to part-time and full-time education at the *post-compulsory* school age, usually regarded as of a lower standard than *higher education (advanced further education)* in the United Kingdom. Traditionally this referred to the 16–19-year-old *young adult* but now it is much broader. *Liberal adult education* is often regarded administratively as a sector of further education and many *colleges of further education* have departments of adult education. Additionally, a great deal of *continuing education* with a *vocational* orientation is undertaken by these colleges. 2. In the Federal Republic of Germany, this term covers *adult education, continuing education*, and *vocational retraining* and is defined as 'all forms of continuation or resumption of studies after completion of the first educational phase of varying duration and as a rule after taking up fulltime employment'. It is for adults of all age groups and educational qualifications, and may be *vocational* or *general*.

further education school (Berufsschule) Established in Germany as a *further education* establishment in which instruction is directly linked to the learning of a trade through a system of apprenticeship.

Further Education Staff College UK college involved in curriculum development, management, organization, and staff development in *further education*. Its students are further education staff. It organizes seminars, courses, and some *distance learning* materials. Current address: Coombe Lodge, Blagdon, Bristol BS18 6RG, UK.

Further Education Unit (FEU) This unit was established in 1977 to develop the efficient provision of *further education*, including *adult education*, in the United Kingdom. Concerned with curriculum, organization, and development, it promotes relevant research and disseminates the findings. It has an advisory Education and Training Committee specifically convened to deal with matters concerning the education of adults. It is also concerned with *PICKUP* in England and Wales. Current address: 2 Orange Street, London WC2H 7WE.

Further Training Establishment of the German Trades Union Federation Concerned with *continuing education* and *re-training*, it assists employees in learning *skills* with which they can be promoted at work. There are many different *training establishments* of this institution throughout the Federal Republic of Germany.

Gabon *Adult education* in this country is co-ordinated through a main organization. Current address: Direction Générale de l'Education Populaire, BP 1560, Libreville, Gabon.

Gagné, R.M. (b. 1916) American theorist of *learning* and performance. Whilst his work is specifically concerned with children, aspects of it, such as his phases of learning, are very relevant to *adult education*.

Galaxy Conference of Adult Education Organizations Conference held in Washington DC in 1969. Twenty adult education organizations in the United States held their annual conference simultaneously with 2,508 people attending. They adopted a joint declaration and planned for the formation of the *Coalition of Adult Education Organizations* which began in 1973.

gaming An educational method in which the students participate in games in order to explore issues of social concern, personal growth, and development. Gaming is one method of motivating reluctant participants in the learning process.

Gandhi, Mahatma K. (1869–1948) Gandhi was intensely interested in education throughout his life; for him it was lifelong and related to the environment. He was concerned to work through groups of people devoted to an ideal, an Ashram, in order to help the masses obtain emancipation and a better standard of living.

Ganga Established in 1969, a Nigerian *adult education* magazine which covers

areas of *adult education* work with Moslem people in the country. Published six times a year.

Gardiner, Robert Born in Ghana he has worked there and in Nigeria in *extra-mural* work, social welfare, and community development. He has held executive positions in the Economic Commission of Africa, leadership positions within the United Nations, and in 1979 was elected president of the *International Council for Adult Education*.

Garnet Foundation Has made many large grants towards *literacy* projects. Current address: Garnet Foundation, Lincoln Tower, Rochester, New York 14604, USA.

Garnett College Named after Thomas Garnett, first professor at the Royal Institution in London. A United Kingdom college specializing in the preparation of teachers for *further education*, it also runs courses for *adult educators*. In 1987 it ceased to be an independent educational institution and was merged with Thames Polytechnic, although it still retains its site and conducts the above courses. Current address: Roehampton Lane, London SW15, UK.

Gasiorowska, Natalia (1881–1964) Polish scholar and *adult educator* who worked as a teacher in a variety of settings including the University for Everyone, the Communist Folk University, the Popular University and the Free Polish University at various times in her life. After the Second World War she was appointed Chancellor of the

Pedagogical College at Lodz and then professor at the University of Warsaw.

gateway club Club for mentally handicapped young people providing leisure, recreation, and *continuing education* for young people with *special needs*.

Gaussian curve Normal curve of distribution.

Gekkan Kominkan (Kominkan Monthly) Japanese monthly journal of the *National Association of Kominkan*.

Gekkan Shakai Kyoiku (Social Education Monthly) Japanese monthly periodical for *social education*.

Gelpi, Ettore (b. 1933) Currently the head of the *Lifelong Learning* unit at *Unesco* and author of a number of books and many papers on *lifelong education*. He is a radical in his perspective, employing a marxian framework of analysis, and has examined such areas as the education of migrant workers. He has an all-embracing concept of education and is concerned that *non-formal* approaches should be used throughout the developed world. He is humanistic and optimistic about the future of education.

gene The carrier of hereditary characteristics from one generation to another, capable of replication.

general ability It was postulated by Spearman that *intelligence* could be divided into a general, or overall, ability and a *special ability*, and that both could be measured.

General Act on Adult Education Legislation passed through Parliament in Holland in 1985, the aims of which are to provide a coherent national and local support system for *adult education* throughout the country. This is to be achieved by introducing local and regional centres, giving provincial authorities the task of co-ordinating *training*, and by having a national agency. Its implementation has been delayed.

General Aptitude Test Battery (GATB) A series of tests used in occupational guidance in America it consists of 12 tests that allow the presentation of results in a profile that can be assessed against the profiles for 22 different occupations.

General Certificate of Education (Advanced or A-Level) Traditionally taken at 18–19 years of age as a school-leaving examination and entry test into *higher education* in England and Wales. See *Scottish Highers*.

General Certificate of Education (Advanced Supplementary or AS-Level) Introduced in 1987 with the first examinations in 1989 to be taken alongside *A-Levels*, but will require only half the study time. They are intended to broaden the sixth form *curriculum* in England and Wales.

General Certificate of Education (Ordinary or O-Level) Traditionally taken at school-leaving age in England, i.e. 16 years, and regarded as a necessary step to entering the final two non-compulsory years at school. Five O-Levels was regarded as a minimum entry for certain jobs and professions. Adults would return to evening classes in order to obtain the requisite number of O-Levels. Phased out in 1987 and replaced by the *General Certificate of Secondary Education*.

General Certificate of Secondary Education (GCSE) A single system of examinations for 16 years-plus introduced in the United Kingdom from 1988. Since the certificate is school-based there are special syllabi for *external* and *mature students*. Five examination groups are involved in setting syllabi and awarding accreditation at this level.

general degree A bachelors degree in which the student has not specialized. May be obtained at either pass or honours standard.

general education The term adopted by the *Advisory Council for Adult and*

Continuing Education to refer to all forms of education that are not specifically vocational. This was an attempt to break away from the *vocational–nonvocational education* distinction in a more meaningful manner. See also *non-vocational education*.

General Education Development (GED) Tests used by adults in the United States as a means of acquiring a pass in the High School Equivalency Examination. These consist of tests in writing skills, social studies, science, reading skills, and mathematics. Each state has its own procedures and policies for their administration.

General Educational Plan Submitted to the federal government and the states of the Federal Republic of Germany in 1973; the first state to agree to its major tenets was North Rhein-Westphalia in 1975. See the *First Act on Further Education*.

general impression method of marking See *impression marking*.

General Medical Council (GMC) The registration body for medical doctors in the United Kingdom. Current address: 44 Hallam Street, London W1N 6AE, UK.

General Nursing Council for England and Wales (GNC) As a result of the Nurse Registration Act of 1919 this Council was established; among its responsibilities was the supervision of the *training* of nurses in different hospitals. This function it fulfilled until it was closed in 1983 as a result of changes in the nursing profession. Its functions were taken over by the *English National Board* and the *United Kingdom Central Council*.

General Secretariat of Adult Education Situated in the Greek Ministry of Culture, it is responsible for providing a framework of all post-school education in that country. See also *Greece*. Current address: Directorate of Adult Education, Ermou Street 15, Athens, Greece.

generalist Person whose interest or occupation involves the spanning of a number of specialities.

generalization The process of drawing general principles from specific instances. It is also regarded by some theorists as a significant factor in learning, since learning begins with specific experiences, some of which may be generalizable.

generation gap The period of time between generations in which cultural changes have occurred, thus making the behaviour and values of different generations diverse and sometimes antagonistic towards each other.

generic social worker A *generalist* in the area of social work.

generic training As more specialities are appearing within the professions, each requiring its own preparation, there is an increasing demand for a *common curriculum* between all the specialities for some professional training.

generic training in social work Courses of preparation for social work which cover the whole field.

genetic fallacy The mistake in arguing that because a phenomenon is the way it is at the present time, it must always have been the same. E.g., because humankind might have descended from the apes it must now retain ape-like characteristics.

genetic principles *Malcolm Knowles* claimed that *adult education* has six genetic principles or features that are peculiar to it and under which conditions it flourishes. These are that: it responds to specific needs; its development is episodic; it survives best when attached to agencies that were established for other purposes; its programmes occupy secondary status within an institution; its stability and permanence relate to an increasing differentiation in its administration, curriculum, finance, and methodology; it emerges and crystallizes without reference to any conception of an institutionalized adult education movement.

genetics The study of heredity and variation in organisms. This has special significance for the understanding of such human attributes as *intelligence*.

genital stage According to *Freud*, a stage in human development when children become interested in sexual organs, i.e. between four and five years of age.

genius Person with exceptional ability.

geography The study of the earth's surface and the relationship between it and population. Two forms of geography have emerged: physical geography, which concentrates upon the earth's surface, and human geography, which is more concerned with the spatial arrangements of its population.

geology The study of the earth's crust, its constitution, and the history of its formation.

geometry A branch of mathematics concerned with aspects of spacial representation, e.g. lines, forms, solids, etc.

geomorphology Morphology is the branch of biology concerned with the form and structure of organisms, geomorphology is the study of these within the earth's crust.

geophysics The branch of *geology* that employs physics to examine the properties of the earth.

George–Barden Act US act of 1946 concerned with *vocational education*, superseded the *George–Dean Act*.

George–Dean Act US legislation of 1936 extending the *Smith–Hughes Vocational Educational Act* of 1917.

Georgi Kirkov Society for Dissemination of Scientific Knowledge The Bulgarian *adult education* body. Current address:

Graf Ignater Str No. 2, Sofia 1000, Bulgaria.

geriatrics Branch of medical science concerned with the diagnosis and treatment of illness in the elderly.

German Adult Education Association (Federal Republic of Germany) The association co-ordinating *adult education* in the eleven Länder of the Federal Republic. This association has supported *adult education* in a number of Third World countries, and has its own department for international co-operation. Publishes the biannual *Adult Education and Development* in German, English, and Spanish. Current address: Rheinallee 1, D–5000 Bonn 2, Federal Republic of Germany.

German Education Council Formed in 1965 as a replacement for the German Committee for Education, it is a body of experts which has close ties with the government of the Federal Republic of Germany. It published a structural plan in 1970 in which *further education* was included. Perhaps the most forceful legislation that has stemmed from this is the *First Act on Further Education*.

German Institute for Distance Studies See *Deutches Institut für Fernstudien*.

German–Maltese Circle This organization offers German language courses for adults in Malta. It issues its own newsletter. Current address: Messina Palace, 141 St Christopher's Street, Valetta P.O. Box 58, Malta.

German Protestant Workshop for Adult Education (Evanelische Arbeitsstelle Fernstudium für Kirchliche Dienste) The federal association concerned with *adult education* in the Evangelical Church in Germany. It is a federation within which a large variety of organizations participate. There are a wide range of activities with which this association is concerned, including family education, discussion groups, study centres, and peace education. It also prepares material for *self-study* and is involved with the Evangelical Academies and in the preparation of its own *adult educators*. It is located in Hanover.

German Trades Union Co-operative Institute for Education Involved in all forms of *adult education*, with special reference to the interests and needs of workers.

German Trades Union Institute for Vocational Training Involved in *vocational education* oriented towards improving the working and living conditions of workers, towards the democratization of society, and helping working people to be aware of the issues of technological society.

German Union of Folk High Schools (Deutsches Volkshochschulverband) Established first in 1927 but re-founded after the Second World War in 1953. The federal body co-ordinating the *folk high schools* in the Federal Republic, with a membership in excess of 900. It has its own *Pedagogical Institute* which issues an information bulletin and is involved in the preparation of *adult educators*. It is active in 37 Third World countries.

gerontogogy The term used in Yugoslavia for *educational gerontology*.

gerontology The scientific study of ageing and of the problems associated with elderly people. See also *educational gerontology*, *geriatrics*.

Gestalt The main idea underlying this term is that of 'unified wholes'. It has become an influential school of thought in learning theory, as the *laws of organization* indicate.

Gestalt laws of organization These laws refer to the manner by which people see 'wholes' rather than parts. There is the law of continuity, whereby people see continuous figures rather than parts; the law of closure, whereby people see a complete figure even if it is not actually complete; the law of proximity, in which people relate separate figures by their distance from each other; and the law of

similarity, whereby people see similar patterns within larger 'wholes'.

Gestalt psychology A school of German psychology which originally sought to challenge the structuralist position. Affected learning theory by arguing that learning is a restructuring of the whole situation which often involves *insight, intuition,* etc. Hardly exists today as a separate school of thought but has influenced *adult education* through *gestalt therapy*.

Gestalt therapy A form of therapy which is usually conducted in *groups* and seeks to broaden people's awareness of themselves by recalling past experiences, emotional states, and bodily sensations. Used in *affective education* within the *humanistic* movement in *adult education*.

gesture All forms of *communication*, verbal and non-verbal.

Ghana National Council for Adult Education Current address: c/o Institute of Adult Education, University of Ghana, P.O. Box 31, Lagos, Ghana. See also the *People's Educational Association*.

ghetto A part of a city or town inhabited almost exclusively by an ethnic minority within the country as a whole. A great deal of *community education* is undertaken in these areas.

Gilchrist Educational Trust Founded in 1841 under the will of Dr J.B. Gilchrist to promote learning throughout the world. Was active in promoting science lectures and *extension work*. Current address: 1 York Street, London W1H 1PZ, UK.

Gilde projects Skills-exchange projects for the elderly in the Netherlands, with the Gilde providing a guide, a newspaper, and advertising in a free weekly newspaper so that older people can advertise their skills or respond to an advertisement. The aim is to get skilled older people to help other older people do jobs and improve their own *skills*. The oldest project was established in

Amsterdam in 1984 but there are now many similar projects throughout the country. Contact address: Gilde Project, NFB Eisenhowerlaan 114, 2517 KM den Haag, The Netherlands.

global learning A technique of *learning* in which the totality of something is studied rather than the parts.

global marking A marking technique in which the assessor seeks to assess a piece of work holisitically rather than *analytically*.

globetrotting-orientation An approach to learning used to describe *learners* who have an individualistic approach to *learning*, who seek to jump to conclusions, or seek generalization without sufficient evidence.

gnosiological cycle This stems from the Greek work 'gnosis' meaning *knowledge*. The cycle is the movement from the act of knowing towards the act of creating new knowledge through learning and experience.

goal-orientated learning An approach to formal learning. E.g., a learner who enrols in an educational course has clear objectives. One of *Houle's* three approaches to learning. See also *activity-orientated learning; learning-orientated learning*.

goal The intended end-product of either a *teaching* and *learning* transaction or a course. Hence, there are *short-term* and *long-term goals*. See also *objective*.

Gold Report Published in the United Kingdom in 1972, it referred to a review of the national patterns and organization of shop stewards' courses in the trade union movement.

Golden Age 4-H Clubs The four-H concept (head, heart, hand, health) has been adapted from its original usage with young people in rural America in *cooperative extension* and is now used in some areas with adults and the elderly. See *4-H Club*.

Goldsmith's College Constituent member college of the University of London since 1988, although it has throughout its history been associated with the University. The college was founded in 1891 by the Goldsmith's Livery Company as a charitable institution providing commercial, craft, and design education for working people. It has always retained its connection with *adult education*, although it is now an institution of *higher education* through its adult centre and its part-time degree work. Current address: Goldsmith's College, New Cross, London SE14 6NW, UK.

Goldsmith's Company This charitable livery company supports education and makes grants towards educational purposes. Current address: Goldsmith's Hall, Foster Lane, Cheapside, London EC2, UK.

grade 1. A position or level on a scale. 2. A mark as a result of an *assessment*. 3. A year-level in a school or college.

graduand One who has been awarded a degree by a college or university.

graduate To pass from a college or university with an award.

graduate assistant A research or teaching assistant. This is a fairly common position in American universities where the assistants are paid a salary in order to undertake this work whilst they are completing their own research degree.

graduate education In the United States this term is used in the same manner as *postgraduate education* in the United Kingdom, that is studies beyond the first degree.

graduate equivalent An award, such as a professional qualification, which is treated as equivalent to a first degree for the purposes of entry to a *higher degree*.

Graduate Record Examination (GRE) Administered by the *Educational Testing*

Service, these advanced tests are designed to provide a common measure of the level of graduates. They are used by graduate schools.

graduate school An educational institution devoted to postgraduate work.

graduate student A student studying for a higher degree in an American university; the equivalent to a postgraduate student in a British university.

graduate study See *graduate education*.

Gramsci, Antonio (1891–1937) Italian Marxist mainly responsible for the widespread use of the concept of *hegemony* in radical analysis of *education* and *adult education*. He was not an educationalist but through his political activities he was responsible for a number of educational enterprises, such as educational classes in factories. He is now known largely because of the publication of his *'Prison Notebooks'*.

Gran Campaña de Alfabetización A massive campaign in *adult literacy* launched by Cuba in 1961 during which approximately one million people were taught to read and write.

Grange Established in 1867 as 'The Order of the Patrons of Husbandry', its aims were to advance education and to elevate the occupation of farmer. It was a secret society and became a national American movement.

Grant Foundation Established in 1936 by William Thomas Grant initially to help children. More recently it has established a commission on *young adults* entitled *Youth and America's Future*.

Grau, Herbert (1916–73) Influential in Austria in founding the *folk high school* in Linz, he was also influential in founding the Federation of Austrian Folk High Schools. He was a member of the *European Bureau of Adult Education*, a member of the Austrian *Unesco* Commission, and a *Unesco* expert on *adult education* working for it in Greece.

Great Books Foundation Established in the University of Chicago in 1947, it published great books in paperback, trained discussion group leaders, organized discussion groups and published training manuals.

Great Books Movement Originated with John Erskine, Professor of English at Columbia University where he ran a programme on the Great Books in 1921. *Mortimer Adler* was a student on this programme who later co-operated with *Robert Hutchins* at the University of Chicago in running a similar course. In 1940 Adler published *'How to Read a Book'* which signalled the start of the programme nationwide. Discussion groups were established and reading programmes undertaken in Great Books Clubs.

Great Decisions Program Launched in 1955 by the *Foreign Policy Association* in the United States, this is a programme to raise citizen awareness about foreign policy through discussion groups. Each year the Association selects a number of issues and the mass media tend to address these subjects, with study groups meeting throughout the country to discuss them. Those who join are invited to feed back their ideas which are then collated and shared with congressional committees, State Department Officials, and others. See the *National Issues Forum*.

Great Tradition A term used by *Harold Wiltshire* to describe what *adult education* offered a nation: a humane curriculum, provision for the reflective citizen, non-vocational learning, and democratic and socratic teaching approaches.

Greece The Greek agency for *adult education* is the Centre for Studies and Self-Education. Current address: 17Ag Filotheis St, 105 56 Athens, Greece. See also *General Secretariat of Adult Education*. In addition, there is a department in the Ministry of Education. Current address: Ministry of National Education and Culture, Directorate of Adult Education, Ermou Street 15, Athens, Greece.

Green, Ernest General Secretary of the *Worker's Educational Association* in the United Kingdom from 1934 until 1950, he was influential at the start of the Second World War in getting *adult education* introduced into the army.

Gresham College Founded in England in 1597 when Sir Thomas Gresham's home was converted into a college on the death of his widow, with funds that he had left. The original college existed until 1768. A new college was built in 1843 and another in 1913. The college was incorporated into City University in London at its inception in 1966.

Grosche, Robert (1888–1967) Early German theorist of *adult education*, especially, as a Catholic, of *adult religious education*. He was also concerned with the churches' involvement in *community education*. Author of a number of books and papers on the subject.

group A number of people who associate for a common purpose.

group counselling Counselling undertaken in a *group* rather than individually.

group development The stages in the life of a *group*. Different scholars recognize different stages in the group's dynamics.

group discussion A frequent *teaching method* in *adult education*. See *discussion*.

group dynamics 1. The way in which a *group* functions and the interactions among its members. 2. The study of the manner in which groups function.

group need The need of a *group*, which might be a *learning need*.

group norm The generally expected pattern of behaviour that evolves when a number of people associate over a period of time for a common purpose.

group pacing The pace of learning set by each *group*, rather than by individuals (see *self-pacing*) or by the *teacher*.

group participant One who takes an active part in the life of the *group*.

group process See *group dynamics*.

group selection technique A method that involves setting for the candidates for a particular post or position an activity to be undertaken as a *group*, so that their willingness and ability to function within a group may be assessed.

group structure As patterns of behaviour emerge in the functioning of a *group*, so different people play special roles, assume specific responsibility, exercise power, etc. The structure lies in the patterns of relationships that occur.

group teaching The practice of subdividing a class by interest or some other criterion and teaching the sub-groups separately.

group therapy The process in which a *group* of people having similar *needs* assist each other through the group processes of interaction and the sharing of common problems, experiences, etc.

group training scheme A scheme in which a number of small employing organizations join together to provide *training* for their employees.

group tutorial The process of several students having a tutorial with the same *tutor* simultaneously.

group work The ability to understand the dynamics of a *group* and consequently to work effectively with one. Group work is usually undertaken with small groups, with an ideal maximum of about 12.

Groupe d'Etudes et de Recherche pour l'Education des Adultes (GEREA – Group for the Study and Research in Adult Education). Formed in 1965, this is an association of voluntary associations concerned with the education of adults in France. It seeks to provide information and other means of liaising with its membership and between its membership and other organizations. Current address: 13 rue la Condamine, 75017 Paris, France.

Groupe de Recherche pour l'Education Permanente (GREP) Founded in 1964 in France in association with the Ministry of Agriculture, with the aim of contributing to the social advancement of farmers in France. Over its years its function has extended to cover *training*, guidance, and technical assistance. Current address: 13–15 rue des Petites Ecuries, 75010 Paris, France.

growth The development of the person.

growth theory The theory which suggests that the aim of teaching is to assist in the growth and development of the *learner*. Consequently the *teaching* and *learning transaction* is regarded as *learner-centred*. This theory is espoused by many *adult educators*.

Grundtvig, Bishop Nikolai Frederik Severin (1783–1872) A poet, priest and theologian, a Norse philologist, philosopher, historian, politician and educationalist whose ideas were significant to the growth of the *folk high school* movement in Denmark. He believed that youth, not childhood, is the best age for education. He also believed that education should be free of punishments, examinations, and all forms of coercion. A biography was published in 1983 by the *Danish Institute* in Copenhagen.

guest lecturer A visiting speaker to the whole or part of a course or for a specific occasion.

guest student In the West German *Fern Universität*, students who are not qualified to register for the whole degree course but who enrol for one part of it are referred to as guest students. See also *associate student*.

guest worker A migrant worker in the Federal Republic of Germany. Many *adult education* programmes have been introduced in West Germany for migrant workers.

guidance The process of providing advice and support to learners, or potential learners, about the suitability of their qualifications, the course that they may wish to study next, and a variety of other matters. Educational guidance has become a very important feature of *adult education* in recent years as the educational system has become very complex. See *educational guidance*.

Guidepost A magazine of the *American Personnel and Guidance Association*.

Guinea Bissau *Adult education* is organized here by the Ministry, as it was when *Paulo Freire* wrote his well-known letters to Guinea Bissau. Current address: Dpt da Educaçion de Adultos, Ministerio de Educaçao Nacional, CP 353, Bissau.

Gulland, Ian Worked in adult education from 1928 to 1970, the last 32 years as head of Adult Studies at *Goldsmith's College*, London.

Gulland Memorial Lectures A series of lectures organized at Goldsmith's College, London, in memory of *Ian Gulland*. They terminated in 1989.

Gurr Committee Committee that examined the practices of *correspondence colleges* in the United Kingdom and recommended the establishment of a *Council for the Accreditation of Correspondence Colleges* in the 1960s.

Guttman Scale A method developed by N. Guttman for the measurement of *attitudes* using attitude statements listed in increasing levels of intensity and specificity.

Guyana Adult Education Association of Guyana. Current address: P.O. Box 10111, Georgetown, Guyana.

gynagogy Some feminists have regarded *andragogy* as a sexist term and have suggested that this term, the art of helping women learn, might add balance to the adult education vocabulary.

Habermas, Jürgen (b. 1929) The leading scholar in *critical theory* in the 1970s and 1980s he has influenced a number of *adult educationalists* especially in his approach to *knowledge* and *interests*.

Hadow, Grace First vice-chairperson of the *Women's Institutes* in the United Kingdom.

Hadow, Sir Henry Chairman of the committee established by the *British Broadcasting Corporation* and the *British Institute of Adult Education* in 1928 to investigate the place of broadcasting in *adult education*. Its report was *New Ventures in Broadcasting*, published in 1928. One of its most significant recommendations was that *wireless discussion groups* should be established.

Hakubutsukan Kenkyu The monthly magazine of the *Japanese Association of Museums*, which has been published since 1928.

Hale Report Report of the committee on university teaching methods in the United Kingdom in 1964.

half-life Technically, the time taken for half the atoms in a radioactive material to decay. Now used to describe the half-life of *knowledge*, which reflects the rapidity with which *knowledge* changes and becomes obsolete in a technological age. This is perhaps more true for professional and technological *knowledge* than for many other forms because of the emphasis placed upon research in these areas. Hence, the growth in *continuing education* can be put into perspective.

Hall, Budd L. Secretary-General of the *International Council for Adult Education*. He succeeded *Roby Kidd* in office.

Hall, Frederick (1878–1938) An advocate of the Co-operative Movement in England and the chief advisor to the first Co-operative Movement college in Holyoake House, Manchester, when it was established in 1915. Throughout the whole of his life he was an advocate for the *Co-operative College*, finally established in 1919 but not housed in its present premises until after the Second World War.

Hallenbeck, Wilbur C. Professor of *adult education* at Columbia University, and a well-known scholar in the field. In 1935 he was the recipient of one of the first Ph.D. degrees to be awarded in *adult education* in America, at Teacher's College, Columbia University.

halo effect The process by which someone is assessed as being more competent than they are as a result of previous good performances. The term originated with *E.L. Thorndike*.

Hampton Clubs Founded in England by *Morse Cartwright* in 1812 and were popular with radicals. They were an early form of *study circle* in England in which radical texts were read and discussed. During this period there were Hampton Clubs in a number of large towns in England. See also the Methodist *class meeting*, for there was close connection between Methodism and radicalism during the nineteenth century.

Handbook of Adult Education in Scotland Annual publication of the

Scottish Institute of Adult and Continuing Education. Formerly called *Yearbook.*

Handbook of Adult Education in the United States First published in 1934 and intermittently thereafter. It now appears about once every ten years. In 1980 eight volumes were published; normally a single volume only is published. Each handbook reviews the state of *adult education* in America at the time of publication.

handicapped person Persons who, for a variety of reasons, physical, mental or social, are unable to participate fully in normal activities and who might therefore have *special needs* in order to learn.

handout An *aid* to teaching and learning in which the learners are given a written or printed supplementary item from which to learn.

Hans Seidel Foundation West German political foundation which is also involved in adult education, especially in the fields of political and social self-determination and participation. In common with other West German adult education institutions, it promotes international awareness and runs adult education institutions abroad.

haptic learner One who learns best through the sense of touch.

hard-of-hearing Descriptive term for people who have a hearing impediment which is severe enough to affect their learning but who can participate in normal educational activities, even though they may require some form of amplification.

hard-to-reach-adult Adult members of the population who are underserved by *adult* and *continuing education* programmes provided by educational agencies. They are the target population of many forms of *outreach education.*

hardware Term used in the computer field to refer to equipment. See also *software.*

Haret, Spiru (1851–1912) Founder of *adult education* in Romania through the organization of a network of *adult education institutions,* He was influential in establishing *study circles* and village libraries. One of the most significant figures in the history of Romanian *adult education.*

Harper, William (1856–1906) Founder of Chicago University in 1892 and its first president. He was closely involved in *adult education* movements, such as *Chautauqua.* When he established the university it had an *extension* division and a publishing house from the outset, together with a department for *correspondence study.*

Hart, Joseph K. (1876–1949) Early American adult education theorist who looked to the community as the basis for education and experience as the foundation of *knowledge.* He, like *Eduard Lindeman,* was influenced by *pragmatism, John Dewey* and the Danish *folk high school movement.* He wrote many books but his work has not received a great deal of attention recently within American *adult education.*

Hartmann, Ludo M. (1865–1924) Founder of Austrian *university extension* at Vienna University in 1895. He started popular evening classes and became a leading figure in the *popular education* movement in German-speaking countries.

Haslegrave Committee Committee established to review technical courses and examinations in the United Kingdom.

Haslegrave Report Published in 1969, the report of the *Haslegrave Committee* led to the establishment of the *Business Education Council,* the *Technical Education Council,* and their Scottish counterparts, in 1973.

Hatch Act American legislation of 1887 which allowed research to be conducted in the *land grant colleges.*

Haycocks Reports The *Advisory Committee on the Supply and Training of Teachers* in the United Kingdom, under the chairmanship of Professor N. Haycocks, published three reports. The first, in 1977, was concerned with the training of full-time *further education* staff and recommended a two–year part-time *Certificate of Education*. The second, in March 1978, was on the training of part-time staff in *further* and *adult education* and recommended a three-stages training (ACSET I, ACSET II, and ACSET III) which followed the pattern set by the *East Midlands* training scheme. The third report, 'Training Teachers for Educational Management in Further and Higher Education', was produced in August 1978. These reports have been particularly influential in the preparation of *part-time adult educators* in the United Kingdom.

head of centre Many *adult education* institutes are situated on more than one site in the United Kingdom, each site being called a centre. The head of centre is the member of staff who has administrative responsibility for the site within the institute – usually a full-time member of the academic staff although there are some part-time members of staff who hold that responsibility.

Health and Safety at Work Act Legislation in the United Kingdom in 1974 which led to many courses of a *vocational and health education* nature being mounted by industry, commerce, and the trades unions. The act specifies adequate standards of health and safety. It applies not only to industry but also to other places of work.

health education With the growing health awareness in the Western world there has grown up a variety of formal and informal agencies offering people advice, guidance, and education about their own physical fitness. Health education may be defined as any series of planned teaching and learning episodes that are aimed at increasing people's awareness of health and well-being.

Health Education Authority Formerly the *Health Education Council*. Current address: 78 New Oxford Street, London W1A 1AH.

Health Education Bureau Established by the Irish government in 1975. Since 1978 it has had a fulltime staff whose task is the promotion of *health education* in the Republic of Ireland. Current address: 34 Upper Mount Street, Dublin 2, Republic of Ireland.

Health Education Council A British government-supported body, having the status of a Special Health Authority, which assists in *curriculum development* in schools and other organizations. It also organizes in-service training and provides lists of resources in *health education*. It became a separate health authority under the Conservative government. See *Health Education Authority*.

Health Education Index The most complete resource reference in *health education*, revised every two years and abstracting from over 500 different sources. Published by B. Edsall and Co. 36b Eccleston Square, London SW1V 1PF.

Health Education News A publication from the *Health Education Council*.

health-related activities The body of subject matter and study of subjects concerned with the promotion of individual health.

health sciences The study of a variety of different disciplines related to people's mental, physical, emotional, and social health. Term more common in America.

health visitor A trained nurse whose role in the community is preventative, rather than specifically orientated to nursing. Health visitors work with all ages, although they tend to specialize in work with mothers and young children. See also *field work teacher*.

hedonism A philosophical theory that pleasure is the sole good.

Hegel, G.W.F. (1770–1831) German idealist philosopher whose theories have influenced many people, including *Karl Marx*. His theory of contradiction, above all else, is cited with reference to Marx, yet his voluminous writings have been less influential upon educational philosophy than perhaps they might be in the future.

hegemony A concept which has a long history within Marxist theory and which has become an established concept within educational thought in recent years, reflecting the views of *Antonio Gramsci*. Its meaning is still not clearly defined although it tends to refer to the exercise of leadership, power, or influence in a non-formalized manner by one group, usually a dominant social class, over another, e.g. the working class. Gramsci claimed that every hegemonic relationship is an educational one.

Heidegger, Martin (1889–1976) Regarded by many, but not by himself, as an *existentialist*. Much *adult education* theory has an existentialist basis and consequently his writings are appropriate to much of that theory.

Hely, Arthur Stanley McNath (1907–67) Director of *Adult Education* at Wellington University, New Zealand. He moved to Australia where he played a similar role at the University of Adelaide. He was also influential in the establishment of the *Australian Association of Adult Education* and some of the early international meetings in this field. He was the author of *New Trends in Adult Education*, published by *Unesco* in 1962. He returned to New Zealand where he became executive officer of the *National Council for Adult Education*.

hemgard Swedish *house of discussion*.

Her Majesty's Inspectorate This British body of officials reports to the Secretary of State for Education on the quality of educational provision in order to improve the quality of that provision. A limited number of inspectors are concerned with adult and continuing education, one aspect of their function is to visit providers of adult education and make reports on their visits. The inspectorate was established in England under the 1833 Factory Act.

heredity The transmission from one generation to another of genetic factors that determine behaviour and physical characteristics. The extent to which it influences intelligence is debatable. See *fluid intelligence*.

hermeneutics Originally the study of the interpretation of biblical texts. Within *existentialism* it has come to relate to the search for the meaning for human existence. In this latter sense it is gaining some currency in *adult education* literature, often as a result of *critical theory*.

Herzberg's Theory Term used in *vocational education* although it is a theory of occupational satisfaction. Herzberg identified motivators/satisfiers which relate to job interest, and hygiene/ dissatisfiers which relate to the environment, as two sets to be considered.

heteronomy The act of depending upon the *authority* of another; the opposite of *autonomous*.

heuristic methods A *teaching technique* in which the work is planned so that the *learner* is enabled to discover the laws or principles underlying it.

hidden curriculum Most educationalists agree that the hidden curriculum consists of the non-academic norms and attitudes that are systematically learned by students within the educational organization, but which are not openly stated within the institution's explicit objectives. Some radical educators go on to suggest that there is a political and ideological element in the hidden curriculum that relates the curriculum process to the power relations of the wider society.

hierarchy of needs Proposed by *A. Maslow*, this hierarchy has five levels:

physiological, safety, love and belongingness, *self-esteem*, and *self-actualization*. The concept is widely cited, but it is not without its critics.

high culture The form of *culture* in which the performing visual and literacy arts that are perceived by an elite to be cultural dominate to the exclusion of *folk culture*.

high school completion Satisfactory completion of four years of high school or its equivalent within the American educational system.

high school diploma The award signifying satisfactory completion of high school in America.

high school equivalency diploma The award signifying satisfactory completion of *high school equivalency examinations* in the United States.

high school equivalency examinations See *General Educational Development* test.

Higher Council for Literacy and Adult Education for Palestinian People A *popular education* association for Palestinians. Current address: Cultural Education Department, Palestine Liberation Organization, Damascus, Syria.

higher education Instruction in *knowledge* and *skills*, the promotion of general powers of the mind, the advancement of learning, and the transmission of a common culture and common standards of citizenship. It fully recognizes the value of research and those areas of learning which have an indirect relationship to the world of work, i.e. the arts, humanities, and social sciences. Commonly regarded as post-advanced level in England, post-highers in Scotland. Higher education is provided in universities, polytechnics, and other designated institutions of learning. All graduates from high school are entitled to enter higher education in the United States and similar students in secondary

high schools in other parts of the world enjoy a similar right. Different countries therefore have different forms of higher education, some are elitist (such as those in the United Kingdom); some are more open to everyone who is qualified to enter and in which a great proportion of young adults enter (rather like the United States); and others have universal higher education where all have the right of *access*.

Higher National Certificate (HNC) A UK award in business studies, science, technology, or agriculture. It was a two-year *higher education* qualification but generally regarded as a sub-degree level. Replaced by the awards of the *Business Education Council* and the *Technical Education Council*.

Higher National Diploma (HND) Qualification similar to the *higher national certificate* but regarded as about *first-degree* level. Replaced by the awards of the *Business Education Council* and the *Technical Education Council*.

higher preparatory examination In Denmark all areas have, by law, to provide *second chance* adult education in single subjects leading to a qualifying examination. This examination is equivalent to the Danish upper secondary school examinations but is designed for adults. It was introduced in 1968.

Highlander Center Founded by *Myles Horton* as Highlander Folk School in 1932 and has had a long and honourable history working with the disadvantaged, the powerless, and the labour unions in Appalachia, Tennessee and elsewhere in the United States. Its work has recently assumed an international dimension. The educational programme is based upon residential education, research, and technical assistance for grassroots leaders. In 1959 the state of Tennessee revoked the Highlander Folk School's charter and confiscated its property. Rather than fight the action the center moved to its present location and reconstituted itself as the Highlander Research and Education Center. In 1982 it was nominated for the

Nobel Peace Prize. The center issues a regular newsletter, *Highlander Reports.* Current address: Route 3, Box 370, New Market, Tennessee 37820, USA.

Highlander Reports The newsletter of the *Highlander Center.*

Highway, The A magazine of the *Workers Educational Association* which was started in October 1908 in the United Kingdom.

Hillcroft College Founded in 1920 in England under the auspices of the *Young Women's Christian Association* and supported by the *Workers' Educational Association,* and located at Beckenham. It moved to its present site in Surbiton in 1926. This is the only residential college for women in the United Kingdom. It was founded to provide women handicapped by lack of opportunity with a chance to study and to develop their skills. Current address: South Bank, Surbiton, Surrey KT6 6DF, UK.

Hill's Cognitive Style Inventory This is an inventory of some 30 style elements, with as many as 100 items, which is used to produce cognitive style maps based upon the respondent's expressed preferences. The length of this test is seen to be one of its greatest problems.

Hinukh Mevugarim Be-Yisrael (Adult Education in Israel) The journal of the *Adult Education Association of Israel,* established in 1972 and published at least twice each year.

Histadrut Na'amnat The Movement for Working Women, a section of the general trade union movement in Israel devoted to providing for every woman in the country an opportunity for *continuing education.* Na'amnat has a scholarship fund for women.

histogram Similar to a graph but in which data are presented in the form of a series of vertical rectangles touching each other. See also *bar chart.*

Historical Foundations of Adult Education: A Bulletin of Research and Information Started in the academic year 1985–86 by the *National College of Education* in the United States, it was envisaged that this would be published three times a year in the fall, spring, and summer. Current address for correspondence: National College of Education, 1000 Executive Parkway, Suite 110, Creve Coeur, Missouri 63141, USA.

History of Adult Education There is a great interest in this aspect of the field of study of adult education, with conferences held fairly frequently and a number of study groups in existence in different countries. There is a study group within *SCUTREA* in the United Kingdom. The first History of Adult Education International Conference was probably held at Oxford in 1986, with a second at Aachen in 1988. There is also a History of Adult Education network sponsored by the *International Council for Adult Education.*

History of the Origin and Progress of Adult Schools An analytical study of the *adult school movement* in England by Thomas Pole until the time of its publication (1816); the earliest known book published on any aspect of *adult education.*

Hofmann, Walter (1897–1952) One of the foremost exponents of the use of the *library* in the education of the people in German-speaking countries, as a result of his work in Leipzig.

Højskolebladet The magazine of the *folk high schools* in Denmark. Published in Danish.

Holbrook, Josiah (1788–1854) Founder of the American *lyceum* movement in nineteenth century *adult education.* Born in Derby, Connecticut, USA. The first lyceum was started at Millburn, Massachusetts in 1826, although Holbrook originally called it a *society for mutual education.*

Holiday Fellowship A UK study holiday organization, in the liberal adult education tradition.

holism A *learning style* in which the *learner* seeks to complete the task and fit the learning in a global context; opposite of the *serialist* style.

holistic education A model of the *teaching* and *learning* programme that focuses upon the whole situation, so that the *needs* of the learner and the teacher are met in a social situation which enables the whole person to be developed.

holistic learning A *cognitive style* in which the learner tackles the whole problem and responds to the whole, rather than learning from and responding to a part of it. This is seen as the opposite approach to *serialist* learning. See also *global learning*.

home demonstration agent An extension agent of the *Cooperative Extension Service* in America whose main responsibility is in organizing extension classes and other activities in such areas as home–making. Agents have themselves usually studied *home economics* and then become *adult educators* in the extension service.

home economics The body of subject matter, and the study of subjects, related to the home and family. Subject commonly studied through the *cooperative extension service* in America, although it is also studied widely in other countries.

home economics school Residential schools in Denmark for young people over 16 years, similar to *continuation schools* but specializing in home economics; there are also some in needlework. Both are of five months duration. An association exists for these schools. Current address: Association of Home Economics and Needlework Schools, Hojtoftevej 20, DK–8240 Risskov, Denmark.

home groups The *adult school movement* introduced the idea of organizing adult schools in the home in 1954, following the ideas of the early church. See also *house group*.

home study education Education designed for students to undertake at home and away from the educational institution. See *distance education*.

Homebound Program Programme launched by the Queensborough Community College in New York City, USA, to enable handicapped people to participate in educational activities through 50 classrooms equipped with teleconferencing facilities. The homebound student is also equipped with the facilities to participate through the system.

homily A form of *instruction*, usually used within the context of the Christian churches when it refers specifically to *preaching*.

Honduras See *Asociación pro Educación de Adultos*.

Hong Kong Association of Continuing Education The professional association for *adult education* in Hong Kong. Current address: P.O. Box 97325, T.S.T. Post Office, Kowloon, Hong Kong.

honorary degree A degree awarded by a college or university to a person of outstanding merit without the necessary completion of an academic course of study.

honours degree A degree taken at a higher level, or a degree obtained with excellence. In some instances the honours degree has a separate curriculum, but in others the level of honours denotes the considered degree of excellence.

horizontal learning Learning from and teaching others in group situations by sharing experiences.

Horton, Myles (b. 1905) Founder of *Highlander* in Tennessee, Horton was influenced by the Christian social gospel and thinkers such as *Dewey* and *Lindeman*. He studied at Union Theological Seminary, went to Denmark where he was influenced by the *folk high school movement*, and eventually returned to Tennessee where he founded *Highlander*. Over the years *Highlander* has been involved in many *community education civil rights*, and *labor education* activities. *Highlander* was closed on one occasion by the Tennessee state authorities but Horton has lived to see the school he founded gain a worldwide reputation, although he himself has published very little.

Hotel and Catering Training Board Responsible for the vocational preparation within this industry in the United Kingdom, it also produces a wide range of educational publications and some open learning materials. Current address: International House, High Street, Ealing, London W5 5DB, UK.

Houle Award The *C.O. Houle* Award for Literature in Adult Education is administered by the *American Association of Adult and Continuing Education*. The award is made annually for a piece of scholarly work in the English language which may be considered as a principal contribution to the whole field of *adult education*. It may be written by one or more authors and must be a printed publication in book form.

Houle, Cyril Orvin (b. 1912) Professor of education at the University of Chicago and thereafter Senior Program Consultant with the *Kellogg Foundation*. He is the author of a number of influential books on *adult education, adult learning*, and *professional education*. Perhaps his most influential book is *The Inquiring Mind* in which he distinguished three types of learning orientation: *activity, goal*, and *learning orientation*. See the *Houle Award*.

hourly rate Many *adult educators* are employed on a part-time basis and are paid at different levels, usually by the hour.

house church See *house group*.

house group The term used by the churches when organizing small church study worship groups in the home. The *adult school movement* in England also adopted the idea and used the term *home group*.

house journal A magazine or journal published for the information of the employees of an organization, department, etc. Also used to publish views of the department or organization to an external readership.

house of discussion The *hemgards* movement (house of discussion) was a traditional method of *adult education* in Sweden employing public places (houses or meeting halls) to encourage cultural and intellectual pursuits. It was a forerunner of the *study circle* and as a movement was overtaken by it.

Hull House An early *university settlement* in America, founded by *Jane Addams* and Ellen Greta Starr in Chicago in 1889.

human biology The branch of biology concerned with the human body.

human capital theory The theory maintaining that investment in human resources to improve the level of *knowledge* and *skill* in a society is the most effective method by which a society can encourage growth and development. See also *screen hypothesis, human resource development*.

Human Employment and Resource Trust (HEART) The Trust Functions as a national training board for non-formal *skills* training in Jamaica, especially with school-leavers. Current address: HEART, 4 Park Pulevard, Kingston 5, Jamaica.

human relations Term used to refer to social relationships. A great deal of *adult education*, especially *continuing professional education*, has been devoted to teaching people to acquire *skills* in this field.

Human Relations The monthly periodical of the *Tavistock Institute of Human Relations*.

human resource cycle A cycle which management might employ in *human resource development*, consisting of recruitment, selection, placement, socialization, evaluation, training and development, promotion and transfer.

human resource developer One involved in *human resource development* programmes, as trainer, teacher, or staff developer.

human resource development (HRD) An American term with similar meanings to the English term *staff development*. This is a central area of concern to many adult educators in the United States but left more to training officers in the United Kingdom. The *American Society for Training and Development* is the professional association to which most HRD personnel belong. HRD is the training, education, and development of employees through job enrichment, job enlargement, and organizational development. It offers the provision of learning and growth experiences within the workplace.

human rights One of the rights specified in the United Nations Declaration of Human Rights is that of education.

human rights education Part of the *non-formal education* programme in Sri Lanka provides opportunity for young people and adults to understand human rights through two approaches: a discussion forum; and adding human rights to the *curriculum* of some of the *vocational education* programmes.

humanagogy Pedagogy and andragogy combined, it represents the differences as well as the similarities that appear to exist in human learning. Humanagogy was proposed as a solution to the andragogy-pedagogy debate in the 1970s–80s in the United States by R. Knudson.

humanism This has two variations. The first is closer to the *humanistic* approach to *adult education* since it emphasizes the potentialities of the human to direct his/her own life in order to achieve a more satisfactory existence, and it applauds human achievements. In this it is perfectly compatible with religous belief. The second is a philosophy that rejects all belief in the divine, claiming that people should be concerned only with human welfare since this life is all that exists.

humanistic An approach to *teaching* and *learning* that emphasizes the dignity and humanity of persons involved in the process. See *humanism*.

humanistic psychology A school of psychology which affirms the human qualities of the person, such as *autonomy*, *freedom*, and *subjective experience*. It has been very influential in *adult education* with such thinkers as *A.H. Maslow*, *Carl Rogers*, and *Malcolm Knowles*.

humanities The study of human culture, especially the classical languages of Greek and Latin.

Hume, David (1711–76) Scottish philosopher concerned about human understanding. He argued that there could be no genuinely scientific experiments in psychology; thus only experience is the basis of knowledge.

Hungary Current address for the national institute in the country is: Népmuvelési Intezet (Institute for Adult Education), Corvin Ter 8, 1251 Budapest, PO Box 33, Hungary. See also *Institute for the Promotion of Scientific Knowledge*.

Hungarian Society for the Dissemination of Knowledge (TIT) The successor of the *Scientific Education Association* which was founded in 1841, it has always been an adult education society and currently has a wide range of activities, from summer courses for overseas students to study Hungarian to lectures for workers about modern technology.

Husen, Torsten (b. 1916) Swedish educationalist, well known for his international perspective on education and for his writings on *lifelong education*.

Husserl, Edmund Gustav Albert (1859–1938) German philosopher; founder of the phenomenological approach to philosophy that is becoming important within some approaches to the study of *adult education*.

Hutchins, Robert M. (b. 1899) A lawyer by training, he became president of the University of Chicago at 30 years of age. There he co-operated with *Mortimer Adler* in running a Great Books seminar. Eventually this resulted in the *Great Books Foundation* and the *Great Books Movement*. Hutchins was also chairman of the editorial board of *Encyclopaedia Britannica*, which is owned by the University of Chicago. He was a *liberal adult educator* and author of a number of books, including '*The Learning Society*' in which his ideals for the future of society are set out.

Hutchinson, Anne Marbury (1591–1643) Born in England and later emigrated to Boston, America where she led religious meetings. This meeting was possibly the first social movement in America and Anne Hutchinson was involved in teaching and group discussion in her home. Later she was excommunicated from the church.

Hutchinson, Edward The only secretary of the *National Foundation For Adult Education* in the United Kingdom between 1946 and 1949 and then secretary of the *National Institute of Adult Education* until his retirement. Holding office in the years of the development of *adult education*, Edward Hutchinson contributed a great deal to its growth and development.

Hvidberg, Flemming Friis (1897–1959) Founder of the *Popular Education Association* in Denmark. He was influenced by *Nikolai Grundtvig's* ideas. He also served as Minister of Education in that country.

hypothesis An untested assertion to be examined during research. See *null hypothesis*. Hypotheses are tested but it should never be the intention of a researcher to prove a hypothesis.

hypothetical–deductive reasoning A reasoning process which starts with a hypothetical position from which results previously obtained could have been deduced.

I

IAEA Newsletter Monthly newsletter published in English by the *Indian Adult Education Association*, started in 1979.

Iberoamerican Distance Education University (UNIED) Current address: Panama City, Republic of Panama.

ICAE News Newsletter of the *International Council for Adult Education*.

ICDE Bulletin Journal of the *International Council for Distance Education*. Published three times per annum in English.

ice-breaker A group technique to enable people to relate to each other in a group, usually used at the start of a course or a session. A variety of different techniques are used, depending upon the purpose of the group.

id One of Freud's three layers of the *self* the other two being the *ego* and the *super-ego*. The *id* is the deepest element; it is self-contained and seeks only to fulfil its own aims. It is the primitive energy of the human being.

idea In Plato's writings this is the intellectual equivalent to the form. Later it became something that was perceived directly in the mind, and more recently it has come to refer to a *hypothesis* or a plan in the mind.

idea inventory The construction of a list of *ideas* as a result of a *brainstorming* session.

ideal 1. An abstract representation of the basic characteristics of a phenomenon,

e.g. *ideal type*. 2. A moral value which is striven after.

ideal self The image, value, or type of person that people think that they could or should be. An element in the *self-concept*.

ideal type A representation of a phenomenon, symbolizing it by its fundamental characteristics only.

idealism A complex concept with a variety of meanings, some of which are relevant to *adult education*. 1. People's ideas are the sole cause of social behaviour. 2. In order for people to alleviate their dissatisfaction all that they have to do is to change their ideas about their *selves* and their behaviour. 3. People are willing to listen to rational thought and act upon it.

idealized self A perfected characterization of the *self*; what the individual would like to become.

Ideas in Action The bimonthly bulletin published by the *Food and Agriculture Organization* about the Freedom from Hunger and Action for Development programmes.

identity A social construction in which a person comes to see how he/she is seen in the social world; also, how each person sees his/herself. Hence there are both social and self-identities. Both concepts are important in understanding how people act and interact in the process of *teaching* and *learning*. See also *self-identity*.

identity crisis An acute sensation of doubt about one's identity. It often calls for people to redefine their identity. Some research in adult education has been undertaken on transition periods in the life cycle.

ideographic A psychological system relating to the concrete or the individual. See *nomothetic approach.*

ideological state apparatus A Marxist concept, formulated by Althusser, to refer to those social institutions, including education, which uphold the dominant *ideology* within society.

ideology Frequently used to illustrate the way in which people conceptualize phenomena, usually of a political or social nature. There are at least three ways in which this term is employed: as rationalizations or justifications of activities of specific groups, e.g. an occupational ideology; as the more political interpretation, e.g. a political statement; and as a worldview or a system of meaning.

Illich, Ivan (b.1926) Born in Austria, he is a priest and was vice-rector of the Catholic University in Puerto Rico. Thereafter he wrote a number of books on deschooling and other subjects, usually presenting a critical perspective. He also co-authored a critical appraisal of *lifelong education.*

illiteracy The inability to read. See *illiterate.* Recognized as a major problem worldwide with many campaigns launched to eradicate it. In some countries *literacy* education is almost synonymous with *adult education.*

illiterate 1. Between 1948 and 1971, it was defined by the Ministry of Education in the United Kingdom as 'a reading ability less than that of the average seven-year-old in 1938'. This is impossible to measure but it does provide guidelines. See also *functional illiteracy* and *semi-literate.* 2. In the *English Language Proficiency Survey* in the United States it was defined as the inability to answer 20

out of 26 questions correctly on the *Measure of English Language Proficiency* test.

illusion False perception of reality. There are many psychological illustrations of illusion but in sociology the concept of false perception is more common. Marx used the term 'false class-consciousness', and Habermas 'false consciousness', to relate to one form of illusion about social reality.

image A picture in the mind, often a construction of reality.

imagery Descriptive language; sometimes regarded as an important element in *teaching* adults.

imagination The process of recombining memories of previous experiences into constellations of new idea or pictures. In addition, it can combine past memories with new thoughts. It is both creative and constructive, although it also has a pathological side.

imitation A form of *learning* through copying another's behaviour, which can be immediate or after a time lapse.

immigrant One who resides in a country other than that of birth. Immigration is one of the major reasons for teaching the host language as a second language, e.g. *English/Danish as a second language.* This is a major form of *adult education* in all host countries of the world. See also *migrant worker.*

immigrant education A major component of the *adult education* programmes of many countries which have been recipients of immigrants. See *Americanization education, Canadianization education.*

immigrant language centre Centres established to provide intensive language tuition to immigrants.

Imogene Okes Award This award is made by the Commission on Research of the *American Association for Adult and Continuing Education* for outstanding research in *adult education*. The award is given in memory of Imogene Okes, whose reports on adult education participation have been widely quoted. The award is for a single piece of work published within five years preceding the award and consists of a wall plaque and a nominal cash grant derived from the Okes Memorial Fund.

impact evaluation The term tends to be used loosely but it is a complex idea about the effect of an educational programme. That effect can be short-term or long-term, direct or indirect, etc. It refers to performance and practice at the end of the educational programme. See also *summative evaluation*.

Imperial Institute Original name for the *Commonwealth Institute*.

Imperial Relations Trust This trust offers a bursary each year to an experienced young (between 28 and 50 years old) adult educator to undertake a study visit to Australasia or Canada for an extended period of four to five months. The bursary was administered by the *National Institute of Adult Continuing Education*. The trust was renamed the *Commonwealth Relations Trust* in 1980.

impression marking A holistic approach to grading, rather than an *analytical approach*.

imprinting A social attachment created between the young and members of the older generation who care for them.

improvident orientation An approach to learning in which the *learner* places emphasis upon fact and detail rather than upon the whole context.

Impuls Swedish magazine which carries information about *study circles*.

impulsive A *learning style* which is considered the opposite of *reflective*. One who responds to a potential learning experience rapidly.

in absentia In his/her absence. E.g., a university award may be made to a candidate *in absentia*.

inaugural lecture a lecture given by a new professor at a university to commemorate the assumption of the chair at that university.

in-basket exercise An exercise given to students undertaking management training to help them consider priorities.

incidental learning The unintended *learning* that occurs through personal interaction and social experience.

inclusive understanding Sometimes used to refer to *deep processing* of information, resulting in *reasoning*, *reflection* and new insights.

in-company training Training conducted by a commercial or business establishment for its employees within the organization.

Independent Broadcasting Authority The commercial television authority in the United Kingdom. It is also committed to an educational content in its programmes, especially Channel 4, through its advisory council on education. Current address: IBA, 70 Brompton Road, London SW3 1EY, UK.

independent learner A *self-help* concept that emerged prior to the emphasis upon *self-directed learning*. The independent learner is one who seeks *knowledge*, *skills*, and self-improvement, in an autonomous manner, often outside the formal educational system.

independent learning Often claimed to have at least four distinguishing characteristics: *self-pacing*, the opportunity to follow alternative routes, individual selection of *learning goals and objectives*, and open *access*. See also *independent learner*, *independent study*.

independent study Programmes of study that have been established by educational institutions for the *independent learner* which lead to the award of an educational certificate. Some scholars, especially in the United States have suggested that the willingness to engage in this is an essential characteristic of an *adult educator* and of the *profession of adult education*.

independent variable A *variable* not dependent upon another variable under investigation. E.g. if the independent variable has a certain value assigned to it, the *dependent variable* will automatically assume a specific value since it is dependent.

India *Adult education* in India is controlled by a directorate of adult education within the Ministry of Education. The directorate also runs an information centre, conducts research and monitors developments, and offers support services for all *adult educators*. Current address: 34 Community Centre, Basant Lok, Vasant Vihar, New Delhi 110 057, India.

Indian Adult Education Association Founded in 1939 as a result of an All-India Adult Education Conference held in India in 1938. Current address: 17–B Indraprastha Estate, New Delhi 110 002, India.

Indian Cultural Education Centers See *North American Indian Cultural Education Centers*.

Indian Institute for Educational and Cultural Co-operation A foundation in India which promotes co-operation and international study. Current address: MW Wadia Trust Buildings, 22d Parsi Bazaar Street, Fort, Bombay, India.

Indian Journal of Adult Education Official journal of the *Indian Adult Education Association*. There is considerable concern for adult education in India. This journal has been published monthly since 1939. Although most of the papers it carries are orientated towards India, many have wider application. Obtainable through the *Indian Adult Education Association*.

Indian National Adult Education Programme Initiated in 1978 to enable the mass of the population to play an active role in social and cultural change.

indicator A phenomenon or variable whose presence and quantitative measurement are crucial for a judgement on the effectiveness of a programme in terms of specified criteria. Originally these tended to be economic in nature but this has subsequently been refined. Now it represents any quantity that can be measured and is regarded as significant to the effectiveness of an educational programme. They are used for evaluation, formation of policy, and the growth of knowledge. Since they tend to be quantitative in nature, it has to be recognized that this approach is suspect for the measurement of quality.

Indira Gandhi National Open University The Open University of India, established by act of Parliament. The stone-laying ceremony was held in November 1985. Current address: K–76 Hauz Khas, New Delhi 110016, India.

indirect methods of teaching See *facilitation*.

individual entitlement A concept proposed by some exponents of *recurrent education* who argue that everybody should have the right to a specific amount of *post-compulsory education* and that they should be able to draw upon it throughout their lifetime. See *drawing rights*.

individualism 1. Personality traits that distinguish people from one another and lead to some people being more prepared to act in an individual manner. 2. A social philosophy which emphasizes the importance of the individual over social action and collectivism.

individualized instruction Approaches to meeting the *needs* of each student during the process of *teaching* and *learning*.

individuation The process whereby a person forms a clearer boundary between *self* and the world during *development*.

indoctrination A process of changing a learner's beliefs, *knowledge, attitudes,* even *skills,* in a predetermined direction. It can occur if the *aims, methods,* or *content* of the *teaching* and *learning* transaction prevent or hinder the learner from considering the propositions in a critically aware manner.

Indonesia The *adult education* association of Indonesia is the Directorate of Community Education. Current address: Jin Kramat Raya 114, Jakarta, Indonesia.

induction 1. A planned programme in which new students are introduced to the learning establishment or the new course. This word is also used for the programme employed to introduce a new teacher into the education establishment. 2. A method of thought in which a general law is inferred from the analysis of specific instances.

inductive reasoning The process of *induction*.

Industrial and Commercial Training: Management of Human Resources A monthly magazine on issues of staff development.

industrial education May be seen as either the provision of education opportunities for workers or the study of education within the industrial sector. See *worker education*.

Industrial Language Training Service Initiated in the United Kingdom in 1974. *Manpower Services Commission* provision, through its *Action for Special Groups*, of language training for members of ethnic minorities. (Note: the *Manpower Services Commission* changed its name to the *Training Commission* and then to the *Training Agency* in 1988.)

Industrial Relations Training Published in 1972 in the United Kingdom, this report by the Commission on Industrial Relations argued that trade unions are responsible

for the *training* of their stewards but suggested that some of this could be carried out in conjunction with employers. It also argued that industrial relations training should be separated from preparation for the role of shop steward.

Industrial Society Provides services to industry on a wide range of areas. The society has an education branch, *Education for Industrial Society*, and publishes its own journal, *Industrial Society*. Current address: 3 Carlton House Terrace, London SW1Y 5DG, UK.

Industrial Society The journal of the *Industrial Society*, published four times a year.

industrial studies The study of the workplace and its problems for workers, the context within which work is conducted and the skills necessary to organize and manage work within the wider society. In short, the study of work in society, especially from a non-management perspective.

Industrial Training Act The first UK government intervention in industrial training of employed persons resulted in this Act of Parliament in 1964, in which the Minister of Labour was empowered to establish *Industrial Training Boards* for any industrial or commercial sector. The objectives of the Act were to overcome a shortfall in the supply of highly skilled labour.

Industrial Training Authority of Cyprus Established by law 21/74 in 1974, it is a semi-government organization, responsible for identifying needs in manpower and developing training systems and policies to implement effective *training*. It is not itself a training authority, it is only the co-ordinator and the organization responsible for the implementation of *training*. It has also implemented a *training the trainers* programme in industry.

Industrial Training Board (ITB) Established as a result of the 1964

Industrial Training Act in the United Kingdom. Twenty-seven ITBs were established, covering some 13 million employees. Each board imposed a levy on employers, some of which went towards the administration of the Board and the remainder was redistributed to employers on the basis of the amount of training that they undertook. This arrangement was changed in 1973 when the *Manpower Services Commission* assumed responsibility for meeting these administrative costs and from thereafter the ITB worked in conjunction with the MSC. In 1981, sixteen of the Boards were abolished and seven retained. (Note that the *Manpower Services Commission* changed its name to the *Training Commission* and then to the *Training Agency* in 1988.)

industrial training organization (ITO) In 1981, with the abolition of some of the ITOs, a considerable number of non-statutory bodies were established to plan industrial training. These are collectively known as industrial training organizations. They receive funding from the *Manpower Services Commission* for adult training. (Note that the *Manpower Services Commission* changed its name to the *Training Commission* and then to the *Training Agency* in 1988.)

Industrial Training Research Unit An independent organization involved in research into selection and training. Runs courses and seminars and publishes results of its research. Current address: Lloyds Bank Chambers, Hobson Street, Cambridge CB1 1NL, UK.

Industrial Tutor, The The title of the journal of the *Society of Industrial Tutors*, published twice a year.

inferiority complex This term originates in the work of *Alfred Adler* and refers to a collection of repressed fears that gave rise to feelings of a more general inferiority. In general speech it tends to be used to refer to any form of inferiority feeling. It could be one reason why some people do not enrol in *adult education* classes voluntarily since their school experiences have given them a general feeling of inferiority in relation to learning and *education*.

informal education Often refers to the form of education that occurs when people learn informally from their environment. However, there has been confusion between the concepts of *education* and *learning*. Hence another definition is where groups of people learn through planned activities in an informal manner, e.g. where there is no overt status role difference between learners, or where the providers of education are voluntary organizations, such as the churches.

informal learning The type of *learning* that occurs when a person acquires *knowledge*, *skill*, or *attitudes* through interaction in an informal situation, even if that situation is a *network* situation. It is often *self-directed learning*, although it can occur reactively as well as proactively on the part of the *learner*.

informal reading inventory (IRI) An informal test used to determine the initial placement of an *adult learner* in reading, used in preference to a formal test. A number of such inventories have been produced in the United States for *adult basic education*; some consist of word lists while others are of short passages.

information 1. Knowledge to be presented to other people. 2. News. 3. Knowledge that is stored but can be accessed. It should be recognized that most information is interpretation of fact even though it might be presented as if it were fact.

information brief A *teaching aid* consisting of a summary of specific information about a given topic. This summary is distributed to participants prior to a session so that they can prepare themselves.

information Bulletin on Adult Education This bulletin, published in English from Hungary, serves as an exchange of professional information about *adult education* in the Balkan and neighbouring countries. It was established with the support of *Unesco*.

Information Center on Instructional Technology American centre for guidance in education technology, with special reference to work with Third World countries. Funded by the United States Agency for International Development. Current address: 1414 22nd Street NW, Washington DC 20037, USA.

Information File Published by the *International Bureau of Education*, these are easy-to-read articles providing information about the state of the art in specific fields of education, such as *adult education*.

information retrieval A branch of computer science concerned with the classification and storage of large quantities of *information*.

Information Service Project for Lifelong Education Started in Japan in 1976, this project seeks to provide a comprehensive information consultation service. It also encourages *lifelong education* through advertising, publishing guidebooks and generally seeking to provide the public with information about education. It is supported by a grant from the Japanese government.

information society Society orientated to the dissemination of *information* through technological means.

information system The methods, materials, media, personnel, and recipients necessary to transfer information within a specified field of activity.

information technology (IT) Computers and other forms of technology that both store and generate information which can be transmitted widely by electronic means. The study of information technology includes the economic, social, political, and moral implications of its use.

information technology centre Established by the *Manpower Services Commission* to provide *training* in new technology, electronics and computing. Mainly for young adults but there have been some courses offered to a broader range of adult students, especially on a fee-earning basis. (Note: the Manpower Services Commission changed its name to the *Training Commission* and then to the *Training Agency* in 1988.)

Informecca The newsletter published by Radio ECCA in Las Palmas in the Canary Islands which includes many articles on *adult education* and *distance education*. Current address: Apartado 994, Las Palmas de Gran Canaria, Spain.

in-group Any group which seeks to distinguish itself from other groups and sees itself as superior to other groups.

in-house training *Continuing education* conducted by employing agencies within the organization itself without recourse to *formal education*. See also *in-company training*.

initial education The first formal education that occurs in the lifetime. It may be completed at the end of compulsory education or it may not be completed until the first break in full-time education thereafter. Differences in definition occur among various scholars. See also *school education* which is similar. However, initial education is a little broader since it may include experiences in further and or higher education.

initiation To introduce someone into a new situation or new knowledge, often through a ritual process. Hence, on occasions *education* is perceived as being a process of initiating the learners into new *knowledge* and *skills*.

ink-blot test A generic term for a number of projective psychological tests using ink-blots.

innate Characteristics that exist or are potentialities at birth as a result of genetic factors. The extent to which characteristics about *learning* ability are innate has not been widely discovered.

Inns of Court These 'colleges' organize examinations for the profession of barrister and organize legal education in the United Kingdom from Gray's Inn, London.

Inquiring Mind, The This book was written by *C.O. Houle* in 1961 and became a seminal work, sparking off a great deal of research into motivation for learning, types of learner etc. In it Houle formulated three types of learning – *activity-*, *goal-*, and *learning-orientated*. This typology has formed the basis of much research since that time.

inquiry-based learning See *discovery learning*.

inquiry methods *Teaching methods* in which the learners are presented with problems and are expected to discover answers for themselves. See *discovery methods*.

in-service education An education programme prepared and offered to employees who are released from their normal employment in order to attend. It is usually vocational in nature. See *in-service training*.

in-service training *Continuing education* given to employees during the course of their working life, which may be *in-house*. It may also take the form of *block release* or even secondment.

Insight The newsletter of the *British Broadcasting Corporation Continuing Education Department* giving information of all future *continuing education* programmes. Current address: Insight Information, BBC, London W1A 1AA, UK.

inspector General term for officers who are appointed to inspect and supervise educators. It has partly been replaced in recent times by the less threatening term of *advisor* in the United Kingdom

educational service, although it is still used within other educational professions.

instinct An unlearned response characteristic of the species as a whole. It may be argued that *learning* is a human substitute for instinct. However, the term is used in everyday speech in a much less precise manner to refer to forms of bodily drives.

Institut Canadien d'Education des Adultes Established in 1952, the French language *adult education* institute in Canada. Most of its membership is in Quebec. Publishes its own bulletin about adult education in French–speaking Canada. Currrent address: 506 est, rue Ste Catherine, Suite 800, Montreal, Canada H2L 1C7.

Institut National d'Education Populaire French national *adult education* association. Current address: Centre d'Etudes de Recherche et de Documentation, 11 rue Willy Blumenthal, 78160 Marly–le–Roi, France.

Institut National de Formation et de Recherche en Education Permanante (INFRED) A French academic institute for both the preparation of adult educators and for research into the education of adults. Publishes its own journal, *Education et Societé*. Current address: 14 rue du Général Humbert, 75014 Paris, France.

Institut National de Recherche Pédagogique. French national research institution into pedagogics. Current address: 29 rue d'Ulm, 75320 Paris, Cedex 05, France.

Institut obscego obrazovanija vzroslych The *Adult Education Research Institute* of the USSR. A large institute undertaking a great deal of research, having over 100 research staff. Current address: Naberegnaja Kutuzowa 8, Leningrad, USSR.

Institut pour le Développement et l'Education des Adultes A Swiss institute concerned with *adult education* and *development*. See also *Centre for the Study of Education in Developing Countries* and the *World Council of Churches*. Current address: Case Postale 2428, 1211 Geneva 2, Switzerland.

institute An educational, research, professional, or pedagogical establishment, or other professional association.

Institute for Culture A great deal of *adult education* work in Hungary emanates from this institute. Information about *adult education* in Hungary can be gained from it. Address: Institute for Culture, Budapest, Corvin tér 8, Hungary – 1251.

Institute for Formal and Non-Formal Education and Information A Dutch institute. See *Stichting IVIO*.

Institute for Responsive Education This institute is concerned with citizen's action and publishes its own quarterly, *Citizen Action in Education*. Current address: 704 Commonwealth Avenue, Boston, Massachusetts 02215, USA.

Institute for Retired Professionals A national network located on specific campuses of education throughout America. The Institute is a peer-taught and professionally-taught *adult education* enterprise in which retired persons can join and explore interests together. Where they are located on a university campus, institute members can also enjoy other benefits from the social and cultural activities of the campus.

Institute for the Development of Educational and Ecological Alternatives (IDEAS) Current address: P.O. Box 7768, ADC-NAIA, 1300 Pasay City, Philippines.

Institute for the Promotion of Scientific Knowledge Hungarian institution. Current address: Bródy Sándor u 16, H 1367 Budapest 7, Hungary.

Institute for Training and Development Professional body for those involved in training. It seeks to lobby on behalf of trainers and training and publishes its own journal, *Training and Development*. This association has recently started a qualifying course in conjunction with the *City and Guilds of London Institute*. Current address: 5 Baring Road, Beaconsfield, Bucks HP9 2NX, UK.

Institute for Workers' Education Established in Holland.

Institute of Administrative Accountants Incorporated in 1916, the first professional body in England to represent internal accounting. It is also the examining body for administrative accountants. Current address: Burford House, 44, London Road, Sevenoaks, Kent TN13 1AS, UK.

Institute of Adult Education Established at Teachers College, Columbia University, USA, in 1941, with a grant from the *Carnegie Corporation*. The first director was *Morse Cartwright*.

Institute of Bankers A chartered institute, established in England in 1879, responsible for the professional preparation of bankers. It runs courses at a variety of levels and successful completion can result in becoming an associate of the Institute of Bankers (AIB). It has its own library and publishes its own journal. Current address: 10 Lombard Street, London EC3V 9AS, UK.

Institute of Bankers in Scotland The Scottish equivalent to the *Institute of Bankers*. Current address: 62 George Street, Edinburgh EH2 2LY, UK.

Institute of Careers Officers Professional institute for those engaged in the careers service in the United Kingdom. Current address: 37a High Street, Stourbridge DY8 1TA, UK.

Institute of Chartered Accountants in England and Wales The professional body for chartered accountants, responsible for accreditation of courses. It is the qualifying association. Current address: Moorgate Place, London EC2, UK.

Institute of Chartered Accountants in Ireland The professional body responsible for the accreditation of courses and the qualifying association for chartered accountants in both Northern and Southern Ireland. Current addresses: 11 Donegal Square South, Belfast BT1 5JE, UK, and 7 Fitzwilliam Place, Dublin 2, Republic of Ireland.

Institute of Chartered Accountants of Scotland The professional and qualifying association for chartered accountants in Scotland. Current address: 27 Queen Street, Edinburgh EH2 1LA, UK.

Institute of Chartered Secretaries and Administrators The professional body in the United Kingdom for chartered secretaries and administrators, responsible for the accreditation of courses of preparation. It is also the qualifying association. Current address: 16 Park Crescent, London W1N 4AH, UK.

Institute of Chiropodists UK professional and qualifying association. Current address: 133 Oxford Street, London W1, UK.

Institute of Commonwealth Studies Current address: 27 Russell Square, London WC1, UK.

Institute of Cost and Management Accountants This professional group was formerly called Cost and Works Accountants but changed its name to reflect more accurately the type of work undertaken by qualified professionals within this occupation. It is both the accrediting and qualifying association. Current address: 63 Portland Place, London W1N 4AB, UK.

Institute of Domestic Heating and Environmental Engineers UK professional and qualifying association.

Institute of Health Education Membership open to professional people involved in medicine, nursing, education, social services, and related fields. The institute is also open to corporate membership. Quarterly journal, regular newsletters and frequent meetings throughout the United Kingdom. Current address: 14 High Elms Road, Hale Barns, Cheshire, UK.

Institute of International Education Affiliated with the University of Stockholm; well known for its studies on comparative education, mostly with *initial education* but it has also been concerned with *lifelong education*. Current address: Institutionen för International pedagogik, University of Stockholm, S–106 91 Stockholm, Sweden.

Institute of Lifelong Learning American society for lifelong education. It is also a *clearinghouse* and related to the *American Association of Retired Persons*. Current address: 1346 Connecticut Avenue NW, Suite 502, Washington DC 20036, USA.

Institute of Municipal Treasurers See *Chartered Institute of Public Finance and Accountancy*.

Institute of Pedagogical Research (Instytut Badan Pedagogicznych) Polish research institution. Current address: Department of Adult Education, ul. Górczewska 8, 01 180 Warsaw, Poland.

Institute of Personnel Management The professional body for those engaged in personnel and training fields in the United Kingdom. Current address: Central House, Upper Woburn Place, London WC1H OHX, UK.

Institute of Quantity Surveyors UK professional and qualifying body. Current address: 98 Gloucester Place, London W1, UK.

Institute of Recorded Sound The British national sound archives. Current address: 29 Exhibition Road, London SW7, UK.

Institute of Road Transport Engineers UK Professional and qualifying association. Current address: 1 Cromwell Place, London SW7, UK.

institution 1. Refers to some form of organization, often a closed one, having a social, economic, educational, cultural, political, or religious purpose.
2. Sociologically reference to the patterned and regulated forms of behaviour that people regard as a norm or commonly accepted value. 3. An organization. 4. Total institution; a closed institution, e.g. prison.

Institution of Chemical Engineers The professional body and qualifying association for chemical engineers in the United Kingdom. Current address: 12 Gayfere St, London SW1, UK.

Institution of Civil Engineers The UK professional body for civil engineering. Current address: Great George Street, London SW1P 3AA, UK.

Institution of Electrical and Electronics Incorporated Engineers UK professional and qualifying association. Current address: 2 Savoy Hill, London WC2, UK.

Institution of Electrical Engineers The professional body and qualifying association for electrical engineers. Current address: Savoy Place, London WC2R OBL, UK.

Institution of Electronic and Radio Engineers UK professional body and qualifying association. Current address: 8–9 Bedford Square, London WC1B 3RG, UK.

Institution of Gas Engineers UK professional body and qualifying association. Current address: 17 Grosvenor Crescent, London SW1X 7ES, UK.

Institution of Highway Engineers UK professional and qualifying body. Current address: 3 Lygon Place, London SW1, UK.

Institution of Industrial Managers Body responsible for *management education* in the United Kingdom and overseas. Current address: Rochester House, 66 Little Ealing Lane, London W5 4XX, UK.

Institution of Mechanical and General Technical Engineers UK qualifying and professional association. Current address: 33 Ovington Square, London SW3, UK.

Institution of Mechanical Engineers UK professional body and qualifying association. Current address: 1 Birdcage Walk, London SW1H 9JJ, UK.

Institution of Mining and Metallurgy UK professional body and qualifying association. Current address: 44 Portland Place, London 4BR, UK.

Institution of Mining Engineers UK professional body and qualifying association. Current address: Hobart House, Grosvenor Place, London SW1X 7AE, UK.

Institution of Municipal Engineers UK professional body and qualifying association. Current address: 25 Eccleston Square, London SW1V 1NX, UK.

Institution of Nuclear Engineers UK professional body and qualifying association. Current address: 1 Penerly Road, London SE6 2LQ, UK.

Institution of Plant Engineers UK professional body and qualifying association. Current address: 138 Buckingham Palace Road, London SW1, UK.

Institution of Production Engineers UK professional body and qualifying association. Current address: Rochester House, Little Ealing Lane, London W5, UK.

Institution of Public Health Engineers UK professional body and qualifying association. Current address: 13 Grosvenor Place, London SW1, UK.

Institution of Structural Engineers
UK professional body and qualifying
association. Current address: 11 Upper
Belgrave Street, London SW1X 8BH,
UK.

**Institution of Technical Engineers in
Mechanical Engineering** UK
professional body and qualifying
association. Current address: 3 Birdcage
Walk, London SW1, UK.

**Institution of Water Engineers and
Scientists** UK professional body and
qualifying association. Current address:
31 High Holborn, London WC1, UK.

**Institution of Works and Highways
Technician Engineers** UK professional
body and qualifying association. Current
address: 125 High Holborn, London
WC1, UK.

Institution of Works Managers UK
professional body and qualifying
association. Current address: 455 Cardiff
Road, Luton, Beds, LU1 1RQ, UK.

institutional care Residential care.
Much *adult education* is conducted with
residents within organizations of this
nature.

institutionalization The process of
habitualization of behavioural patterns
which results in the formation of social
institutions.

Instituto de la Mujer A division of the
Department of Culture in the Spanish
government. Currently concerned with
women's education. Current address:
c/o Almagro 36, Madrid 28010, Spain.

**Instituto Nacional para la Educación
de los Adultos** The national *adult
education* institute of Mexico, established
in 1981. It offers a documentation and
consultation service. Current address:
Alvaro Obregón #273–50, piso, Col
Hipódromo Condesa, 06170 Mexico DF,
Mexico.

**Instituto Português de Ensino a
Distáncia** The Portugese *distance teaching*

institute which later became the
Universidad Abierta.

instruct 1. To direct or order.
2. Teaching method of a *didactic* nature.
3. To authorize. The second of these
three definitions is most frequently
employed within *adult education*,
especially to that part which is often
referred to as *training*. See also *private
instruction*.

instruction The process of *teaching*, but
often used in relation to *training*.

instructional aids See *audio-visual aids*.

instructional design The process of
preparing a course in a specific manner,
utilizing *educational technology* in order to
achieve specific *objectives*.

instructional games See *gaming*.

instructional material Teaching aids.

instructional objectives The teacher's
objectives in a teaching and learning
session, usually non-negotiable and often
behavioural in orientation.

instructional technology See
educational technology The development
and design of *teaching aids*.

instructor One who *instructs; teacher*.
However, the term is often associated
with teaching at a low level, including
helping students to acquire skills.
Occasionally, in the United States it is
used with wider connotations of teaching
to include all that the *teacher* does to help
adults *learn*.

instrument A tool. Often used in the
language of American research to refer to
an accepted and validated *research tool*,
such as a *questionnaire, attitude inventory*,
etc. which is utilized in a new and
different research process.

instrumentalism A system of *pragmatic*
philosophy which holds that ideas are
instruments that should guide actions to
bring about change. Hence, for some

liberal adult educators instrumentalism in education is the very antithesis of the purposes of *liberal education* and even of *education* itself.

integrated course A course in which the theoretical aspects taught in an educational establishment are combined with a practical component experienced in the workplace. See also *sandwich course*.

integrated curriculum A *curriculum* in which all the parts fit into a meaningful whole. There is considerable debate within *adult education* as to whether there is a *curriculum* within it. To some extent this relates to the approach to planning, e.g. whether the course is planned as a whole or whether the educational programme of an institution is offered as separate courses. See also *curriculum*.

integrated education Occurred in America when schools and colleges were no longer segregated by the colour of the learners.

integrated teaching The *teaching* of different subject areas in a thematic manner, so that the different *disciplines* are not emphasized.

intellect The *cognitive* ability of the person is usually the subject of this term, although it originally referred to rational ability.

intellectual 1. A member of a social stratum to which society has ascribed the dominant role of providing it with the solutions to its problems, explications of its dominant *worldview, ideology* etc. 2. One who is employed in an occupation usually considered to be intellectual. 3. One who is learned and has the ability to think critically. This group should be seen as separate from the *knowledge class* since the latter group often seeks and is granted power. Intellectuals generally seek not power but influence.

intellectual development Theories within *initial education* seek to explain how the intellect develops with age (see

Piaget. The term is more frequently used by adults in referring to their past educational or learning experiences. It is similar to the concept of *experience* used by *Malcolm Knowles* in his writing about *andragogy*.

intelligence The ability to respond effectively to experiences within the process of living. However, there are a variety of other definitions which relate to whatever constituent elements the theorists attribute to intelligence, such as abstraction, *learning*, and the ability to respond to new situations. There is no agreed definition. Some debate whether intelligence relates entirely to an innate, biologically–determined ability or whether it relates to the ability to deal with experience, which could be viewed as part of the nature/nurture controversy within the social sciences. It is generally assumed that not all intelligence is fixed at birth but that some of it depends upon experience, especially in early childhood, according to some scholars. In recent years it has been assumed that biologically-based intelligence (i.e. *fluid intelligence*) declines with age, but experiential intelligence (i.e. *crystallized intelligence*) increases for as long as people are still engaged actively in the process of living. Other theorists suggest that there are multiple intelligences (see, for instance, *social intelligence*) whilst other theorists are certainly not convinced by this approach.

intelligence quotient (IQ) A numerical measure of *intelligence*, measured by specific tests. More frequently used in *initial education* than in *education for adults*.

intelligence test A technique devised to assess the level of intelligence that candidates possess, or the stage in mental development that they have reached. There are a variety of established tests. They are frequently used with children and often employed in *selection* processes for courses of study, career and occupational selection.

intelligentsia A term that emerged from nineteenth century Central and Eastern

Europe to refer to radical or revolutionary thinkers. In contemporary society it tends to have the same meaning as *intellectual*.

interaction analysis The study of group processes.

interactionism 1. See *social interactionism* and *symbolic interactionism*. A sociological approach to understanding human behaviour based upon the ideas that the human being is influenced by social pressures that are experienced in social interaction. *G.H. Mead* highlighted the fact that the *self* is itself a product of interaction. 2. The human process of relating with other people, significant in adult education for the use of *group* methods and also for the discussion on *teacher–student* relationships.

interactive learner One who learns most effectively through verbalization and discussion.

interactive technology The type of technological systems being introduced into *distance education* in which the learner is able to interact either with a teacher, through telephone, teleconferencing, etc., or with a variety of prepared educational programmes that have been designed to meet a variety of specific *learning needs*, so that the learners can select relevant educational programmes for their needs, e.g. interactive videos.

Inter-American Federation for Adult Education (FIDEA) A non-governmental, non-profit agency which seeks to promote a democratic and unified educational system throughout the Americas, to promote adult education in the region so that a democratic society may be created. Current address: Apartado de Correos 20016, San Martin, Caracas 1020, Venezuela.

inter-disciplinary A study of a phenomenon that involves the use of two or more *academic disciplines* simultaneously.

interest Often related to *needs* and *wants*. 1. A disposition to engage in certain activities which are appropriate to specific ends. 2. A freely chosen activity. 3. An activity which provides satisfaction and pleasure. Many teachers maintain that creating this is a very important component of *teaching*. 4. Used as 'best interests' to refer to the benefit to be gained from some action. Hence, the *critical theorists* suggest that those people who suffer from false consciousness do not know their best interests; but however they can be taught them.

interest group A group of people who meet to pursue the same or similar activities. Some *non-formal* education programmes provide a teacher free of all charge if such a group can be formed.

interest inventory An attitude test used to assess people's likes and dislikes.

interest test A test used in personnel selection and careers guidance. A number of different tests exist to obtain information on the personal and leisure interests of people or candidates. These are highly developed in the United States, but are also employed in the United Kingdom.

interface A meeting point; some writers refer to the interface between theory and practice.

interference 1. A conflict between *associations* formed between *stimuli* and *responses*. 2. The conflict between *learning* new *information* and the *memory* of previous phenomena or events which inhibits the memorization of that information. 3. The situation in which old information is difficult to recall because of current information. This often occurs with adults in education because much of their educational activity occurs in the midst of other activities. They are forced to try to memorize or recall when they are being presented with new information about other aspects of daily living. Thus it is sometimes claimed that adults cannot memorize as well as younger people.

Intergovernmental Advisory Council on Education (IACE) Established in 1979 to advise the president of the United States on the impact of federal education activities, to assess compliance, and make recommendations on the federal role in education. The president also appoints the membership.

intern An American expression for a new recruit to a profession preparing for a professional position, who spends time performing the professional role as part of that preparation. See also *professional placement, teaching practice*.

internal consistency 1. The logical sequence of an argument. 2. In questionnaire design, it refers to the extent to which all the items measure precisely the same phenomenon.

internal degree A degree of a college or university awarded to successful students who have been registered at that institution. See also *external degree*.

internal examination *Examinations* conducted by the educational institution offering the course of study, rather than by an external examining body. Often these are not the final examinations although on occasions these are the ones which lead to the award or qualification. The extent to which these are acceptable within certain *professional education* courses is debatable. Some professions allow the colleges to conduct the professional examinations internally, whilst others expect to be the examining body.

internal validity See *internal consistency*.

internalization 1. The acceptance or adaptation of beliefs, values, attitudes, or standards as the internalizer's own. It may be regarded as something that happens as a result of *socialization* or because of a deliberate attempt to emulate a group which one has joined. 2. The process of learning is sometimes referred to as the process of internalization, especially if it is the *learning* of a complex procedure or system, etc.

international adult education The study of *adult education* on an international, rather than *comparative*, perspective; seeking to understand the events and trends in more than one country. It also includes the exchange of studies in *adult education* through international gatherings and conferences. See also *comparative adult education*.

International Andragogy Institute A non-profit organization established by the *Inter-American Federation for Adult Education* and the universities of the East and Simon Rodriguez (Venezuela); Federico Villarreal and San Cristobel de Huamanga (Peru); Nacional Autonoma Heredia (Costa Rica); Instuto de Tecnologia (Republic of Dominica); Florida State University (US). Current address: Apartado de Correos 20016, San Martin, Caracas 1020, Venezuela.

International Associates Created in 1975 to further the aims of the *Coalition of Adult Education Associations* in the United States on an international basis. The idea behind this is to establish an international network of adult educators, to facilitate exchange, and stimulate co-operation and research.

International Associates Newsletter The newsletter of the *International Associates*, published quarterly and started in 1982.

International Association for Educational and Vocational Guidance Established as a professional association for practitioners in 1951. Current address: 257 route d'Arlon, Strassen, Luxembourg.

International Association for Integrative Education An international non-profit organization seeking to develop an educational perspective which integrates different dimensions of human life – the physical, psycho-social, aesthetic, intellectual, and spiritual – into an educational programme for adults. See *integrative education*. Current address: C.P. 345, CH-1290 Versoix, Switzerland.

International Association for the Evaluation of Educational Achievement (IEA) Following a conference organized by the *Unesco Institute for Education* in Hamburg in 1958–59, this association was formed in 1961 with organizational membership from a variety of countries and supported by grant aid. It has carried out a considerable body of research but little of it has been directly related to the *education of adults*.

International Association of Universities of the Third Age An association of *Universities of the Third Age*. Current address: Jean Costa Université des Sciences Sociales, Place Anatole-France, 31042 Toulouse Cedex, France.

International Baccalaureate (IB) Awarded by a number of schools and colleges following the successful completion of the years of sixth-form study in a number of world colleges since its inception in 1967. The only college in the United Kingdom offering this course is Atlantic College in South Wales, which is also the oldest college in this system. Current address: International Baccalaureate Office, 1 rue Albert-Gos, CH–1206 Geneva, Switzerland.

International Book Committee Current address: c/o International Reading Association, 701 Dallam Road, Newark, Delaware 19711, USA.

International Broadcasting Trust Involved in supporting educational activities. Current address: 2 Ferdinand Place, London NW1 8EE, UK.

International Bureau of Education Founded in 1925, maintained under the auspices of Unesco since 1969. Publishes many pamphlets and guidelines, including one on *adult education*. It also publishes an *Information File*. The focus of much of its concern is the relationship between education and the world of work. Current address: P.O. Box 199, 1211 Geneva 20, Switzerland.

International Centre for Advanced Technical and Vocational Training Established by the *International Labour Office* in 1965. Current address: 140 Corso Unità d'Italia, 10127 Turin, Italy.

International Centre for Public Enterprises in Developing Countries Established in Yugoslavia in 1974 to promote direct co-operation among developing and non-aligned countries. It now has over 30 member countries. It has a concern for *adult education, human resource development*, and *development education*. Current address: International Centre for Public Enterprises in Developing Countries, Ljubljana, Yugoslavia.

International Charter of Workers' Education Prepared and published by the *International Federation of Workers' Educational Associations*, this charter describes *adult* and *continuing education* as a necessary part of the democratic political process. It calls for further *vocational education* and a widening of *general education*. It also relates its position to that of other world bodies, such as *Unesco*, that seek to provide education for working people.

International Community Education Association A voluntary independent association seeking to draw together people working in the field of *community education*. It holds an international conference every four years and publishes its own newsletter. It has a secretariat in the United Kingdom but may also be contacted at: c/o Briton Road, Coventry CV2 54LF, UK.

International Community Education Association Newsletter The newsletter of the association, published in English.

International Congress of University Adult Education Established in 1960 at Syracuse University after the *Unesco Conference* at Montreal to develop and maintain contact among people involved in university *adult education*. It is involved in seeking to establish *adult education* as an accepted field of university teaching and research. Publishes its own journal, the *International Journal of University Adult Education*, and a newsletter. Contact address: c/o The Department of Extension and Summer Studies, University of New Brunswick, P.O. Box 4400, Fredericton, New Brunswick, Canada E3B 5A3.

International Congress of University Adult Education Newsletter Published in English twice a year.

International Continuation School Started in 1978, a *continuation school* in the *Tvind* schools in Denmark, concerned with educating young people to understand the international problems of the world.

International Co-operative Alliance This organization has a number of divisions concerned with aspects of *adult education* in developing countries, including the *Co-operative Education Materials Advisory Service*. Current address: 15 route des Morillons, Ch–1218 Le Grand-Saconnex, Geneva, Switzerland.

International Co-operative Institute Formed in Saskatchewan, Canada in 1955 in which it was planned to merge all the co-operative educational programmes in Saskatchewan and Manitoba. The first director was Harold Chapman. In 1959 it became the *Western Co-operative College*.

International Correspondence Bureau Established in 1920 by the *adult school movement* as part of its international activities, putting people in touch with others who were interested in *adult education*. In 1956 its activities were transferred to the International Friendship League. However, it was re-started to a limited extent for a brief period in the 1970s.

International Correspondence Schools An organization in Scranton, Pennsylvania, which became the largest organization offering *correspondence tuition* in the United States.

International Council for Adult Education (ICAE) Founded in 1973 by the Canadian adult educator, *J. Roby Kidd*, together with adult educators from other countries. It is a non-governmental international organization with membership from many national *adult education* associations. Individual adult educators are encouraged to become Friends of the Council. The Council organizes international meetings of adult educators every four years, has networks and working groups on a variety of topics of concern to it, and publishes a journal, *Convergence*. The international meetings have been: Dar-es-Salaam, Tanzania in 1976; Helsingfors, Finland in 1979; Marly-le-Roi, France in 1982; and Buenos Aires in 1985. Current address: The J. Roby Kidd Center, 720 Bathurst Street, Suite 500, Toronto, Ontario, Canada M5S 2R4.

International Council for Correspondence Education See *International Council for Distance Education*.

International Council for Distance Education Adopted this name in 1982, prior to this it was called *International Council for Correspondence Education*. An international body concerned to promote *distance education* to conduct research, to provide information, and assist with the preparation of educators involved in this area of education. Many publications, including a *Bulletin* which is published three times a year. Information can be obtained from the 1986 vice president: Dr D. Stewart, Director of Regional Advisory Services, Open University, Walton Hall, Milton Keynes, MK7 6AA; and c/o External Studies, University of New England, Armidale, New South Wales, Australia 2351.

International Council for Educational Development Current address: P.O. Box 217, Essex, Connecticut 06426, USA.

International Council for Museums Established in 1946. Museums have assumed a much more active role in the education of adults in recent years. This council was established to further international co-operation between them. Current address: 1 rue Miollis, 75 Paris 15, France.

International Council of Voluntary Agencies Current address: 13 rue Gautier, 1201 Geneva, Switzerland.

International Culture Workshop Founded in Denmark in 1987 to establish a centre for cultural exchange and development. Its aim is to create new attitudes towards culture based on existing educational programmes: it runs summer workshops, organizes a school of culture and has international workshop groups. In addition, it publishes its own newsletter. Current address: 3, Ved Moellebanken, DK–6720 Fanoe, Denmark.

International Development Association (IDA) Established in 1960 and concerned with education in Third World countries. Current address: 1818 H Street NW, Washington DC 20433, USA.

International Development Research Centre Current address: P.O. Box 8500, Ottawa, Canada K1G 3H9.

international education 1. The term is often used to refer to *comparative education*. 2. The study of international processes, often of a political or policy nature.

International Education Year In December 1968 the United Nations designated 1970 as International Education Year. Education was meant to be understood in the broadest possible terms, which included all aspects of *lifelong education*.

International Educational Reporting Service The purpose of this service, undertaken by the *International Bureau of Education*, is to foster sharing of information and experience among educational decision-makers, practitioners, and researchers interested in new approaches to educational problems.

International Federation of Library Associations Founded in 1927 to promote international co-operation. Current address: The Congress Building, P.O. Box 9128, The Hague, The Netherlands.

International Federation of Settlements and Neighbourhood Associations Current address: Birmingham Settlement, 318 Summer Lane, Birmingham B19 3RL, UK.

International Federation of Training and Development Organisations The international body to which organizations concerned with *human resource development* may affiliate. It organizes international conferences for those involved in this field.

International Federation of Workers' Educational Associations. A federation of *Workers' Educational Associations*, established in 1947 to improve workers' educational opportunities and to exchange information between countries. Organizes conferences, publishes information, and supports existing organizations. Current address: 9 Upper Berkeley Street, London W1H 8BY, UK. Also contact addresses at: Begstraat 37, B 1000 Brussels, Belgium; and c/o International Department of Histadrut, 93, Arlosoroff Street, Tel Aviv, Israel.

International Federation on Aging Current address: International Federation on Aging, 1909 K Street NW, Washington DC 20049, USA.

International Film and Television Council Founded in 1959 to promote international co-operation. Current address: Maison de L'Unesco, 1 rue Miollis, Paris, France.

International Handbook of Adult Education Published in 1929 in conjunction with the first *World Conference on Adult Education*.

International Institute for Adult Literacy Methods Established by *Unesco* in 1968 and supported by the government of Iran. Current address: P.O. Box 13145–654, Tehran, Iran.

International Institute for Educational Planning A *Unesco* institution established in 1963 to become a centre for the study of educational planning. It publishes its own bulletin quarterly. Current address: 7–9 rue Eugene Delacroix, 75016 Paris, France.

International Institute for Educational Studies Established in 1969 to study post-school education. Current address: 74 ru de la Loi, 1040 Brussels, Belgium.

International Institute for the Management of Technology Founded after a recommendation from the *Organization for Economic and Cultural Development* in 1971 by some of the member states to provide courses for senior management. Current address: 59–63 Corso Magenta, 20123 Milan, Italy.

International Institute of Andragogy (INSTIA) Mainly orientated towards Latin America although it has attracted interest in the United States, this institute is committed to the study of *adult education* (which is the way that the term *andragogy* is employed there). Current address: Calle Veracruz, Edificio Capaya, Pent-house No7 Les Mercedes, Caracas, Venuzuela.

International Institute of Communications Current address: c/o Tavistock House South, Tavistock Square, London WC1H 9LF, UK.

International Journal of Educational Development Quarterly journal started in 1983 and published by Pergamon Press, in the United Kingdom.

International Journal of Health Education The journal of the *International Union of Health Education*, published in English, French, and German.

International Journal of Lifelong Education A quarterly, refereed journal established in 1982 to provide a forum for scholars throughout the world to share views about any aspect of *lifelong education*. Published by Taylor and Francis in the United Kingdom. Current address: 4 John Street, London, WC1N 2ET, UK.

International Journal of University Adult Education Founded in 1962, the journal of the *International Congress of University Adult Education*. Published three times a year.

International Labour Office Current address: Route des Morillons 4, CH–1211, Geneva, Switzerland.

International Labour Organization, Convention 140 Promulgated in 1974, this convention called upon all member states to formulate and apply a policy of *paid educational leave*.

International League for Social Commitment in Adult Education (ILSCAE) *Adult educators* throughout the world who share a concern for issues of social justice founded this association in 1984. Concerned with world peace, literacy, the environment. It has an annual meeting in a different country and is organized by an elected committee. The League has a number of local chapters, or groups that meet regularly. It issues a regular newsletter and has initiated correspondence circles.

International Literacy Day Established in 1966, it has been celebrated on 8 September every year since then.

International Literacy Prize Jury *Unesco* administers four literacy awards: the *Iraq Literacy Prize, Nadezhda K. Krupskaya Prize, International Reading Association Literacy Award*, and the *Noma Prize*. One jury decides upon these awards each year.

International Literacy Year In December 1987 the United Nations General Assembly proclaimed 1990 as International Literacy Year.

International Movements Towards Educational Change (IMTEC) Originally established in 1970 as a project of the *Organisation for Economic Co-operation and Development* in 1970. It became independent in 1977 but remains concerned to introduce educational change. The organization has produced a number of studies, one of which is especially concerned with young adults and *learning from experience*.

International Network for Adult Educators Serving the Disabled Person This is an *International Council for Adult Education* network. The network co-ordinator can be contacted at: 5550 Columbia Pike, Apt. 975, Arlington, Virginia 22204–3127, USA.

International Network in Education This centre responds to international enquiries about *adult education* and publishes bibliographies about a variety of educational activities in the United States, including *literacy, non-formal education*, etc. Current address: Michigan State University, College of Education, 237 Erickson Hall, East Lansing, Michigan 48824, USA.

International Newsletter for Independent Study Launched by North East London Polytechnic in 1982 and published three times a year.

International People's College A Danish *folk high school* founded in 1921 by *Peter Manniche* to promote international understanding. It has an international staff and offers two four-month courses each year and some short summer courses. The working language of the college is English. Current address: 1 Montebello Alle, Dk–3000 Helsingor, Denmark.

International Planned Parenthood Federation Involved in education for family planning and family life. Current address: Regent's College, Inner Circle, Regent's Park, London NW1 4NS, UK.

International Reading Association Current address: 800 Barksdale Road, P.O. Box 8139, Newark, Delaware 19714–8139, USA.

International Reading Association Literacy Award Awarded since 1979 and administered by *Unesco*.

International Review of Education A refereed journal published by the *Unesco Institute for Education* in Hamburg. It is addressed to educators all over the world with scholarly studies of educational innovations, research projects, and trends. Current address: The Editor, Unesco Institute for Education, Feldbrunnenstrasse 58, D–2000 Hamburg 13, Federal Republic of Germany.

international standard classification of education (ISCED) An instrument suitable for assembling, compiling, and presenting statistics about *education* nationally and internationally. Designed by *Unesco*, is intended to cover education of all age groups; thus it is useful for *adult education*.

International Union of Health Education Current address: 3 rue Viollier, 1207 Geneva, Switzerland.

International University of the Third Age See *Universidade Internacional para a Terceira Idade*.

International Yearbook of Adult Education Published in German as *Internationales Jahrbuch der Erwachsenenbildung*, although some papers are in English and all begin with an English abstract. Publishers: Bohlau Verlag, Koln, Federal Republic of Germany.

International Youth Centre This centre provides opportunity for young adults to meet, share experiences, and follow a variety of courses in a residential centre with an international perspective. Address: Vestergade 45, P.O. Box 150, DK 5700 Svendborg, Denmark.

internship A professional placement for students which gives them an opportunity to utilize the relevant theory in practice and to observe other professionals in their work situation. An American expression. See *teaching practice, professional placement*.

internship plan The curricular provision of a college or university for the period of *internship*.

Inter-University European Institute on Social Welfare A European institution concentrating upon study and preparation in the fields of social work, community work, and social gerontology. It is situated in Belgium.

Inter-University Labor Education Committee (1951–57) Established in the United States to further the liaison between labour education and the universities. In 1957 it became the *National Institute of Labor Education*.

interview 1. A teaching technique in which an individual or expert is questioned about his/her area of expertise by learners. 2. A method of assessing ability, aptitude, etc. in face-to-face discussion. See *structured interview*. 3. A survey technique in which the researcher questions a number of respondents.

interview schedule The list of questions that are going to be asked during an interview. It is often very carefully prepared so that the same questions will be asked in the same sequence in the course of the research.

introversion A psychological state in which people turn in upon themselves, become pre-occupied with their own thoughts and shrink from social interaction. See *extroversion*.

introvert One who exhibits the characteristics of *introversion*. The introvert is sometimes disadvantaged in some forms of *adult education* that demand *participation*. See *extrovert*.

intuition *Knowledge* or perception which has not been acquired through the processes of reason and intelligence.

intuitionism A philosophical doctrine that certain forms of knowledge are

acquired through *intuition*, as opposed to *empiricism*.

intuitive thought Arriving at conclusions without the normal processes of *reasoning* and *reflecting*.

invigilator The supervisor of a written examination.

Iran The Iranian National Centre for Adult Education and Training, Ministry of Education. Current address: 101/1 Vessal Shirazi Avenue, P.O. Box 14/1602, Tehran, Iran.

Iraq The national *adult education* association is the Supreme Council for Adult Education. Current address: Supreme Council for Adult Education, c/o Ministry of Education, Al Saadoon Street, Baghdad, Iraq.

Iraq Literacy Prize Endowed by the government of Iraq since 1982 and administered by *Unesco*.

Iraq Supreme Council for Adult Education Current address: c/o Ministry of Education, Al Saadoon Street, Baghdad, Iraq.

Ireland, Republic of See *AONTAS*.

Islamic Adult Education Association Founded in 1963, this Indonesian association covers the whole field of *adult education* in Indonesia. It also organizes a documentation centre. Current address: Jalan Cut Muti'ah no. 1, Jakarta, Indonesia.

isolate A peson who does not interrelate well with others. In *sociometric* tests the isolate is one who is chosen by no other person.

Israel The national *adult education* of Israel is the *Adult Education Association of Israel*. Current address: P.O. Box 303, 93 Arlozorov Street, Tel-Aviv, Cod 61002, Israel.

issue The presentation of alternative positions so that the *participants* can decide among them.

Italy There are two Italian associations concerned with adult education:
1. *Associazione Italiana di Educazione degli Adulti (AIDEA)*. Current address: Via Thailandia 12, 00144, Rome, Italy.
2. Movimento do Collaborazione Civica. Current address: Via Angelo Broferrio No 6 (Scala A Int 5), 00195 Rome, Italy.

item analysis Term used in the production of empirical research tools, such as *questionnaires* or *interview schedules* for the examination of specific items within the schedule.

itinerant teacher One who is employed as a teacher but does not remain in the same building to conduct the educational experiences; i.e., a *peripatetic teacher*.

Ivory Coast Current address of the ministry: Ministère de l'Educacion Nationale et de la Recherche Scientifique, BP V 151, Adijan, Ivory Coast.

Ivy League College A small number of elite colleges and universities in America are known by this phrase.

J. Roby Kidd Award An award of $1500 Canadian established in honour of *J. Roby Kidd* made annually to an individual or individuals who, in the opinion of their peers, have made a significant contribution to *adult education*. The award is not made to an association or an organisation and is administered by the *International Council for Adult Education*.

J. Roby Kidd Trust Fund This fund has been established in memory of *J. Roby Kidd* to honour significant new contributions to the field of adult education. The fund is administered by the *International Council for Adult Education* Management Committee and an award is made annually. Applications must be received by the ICAE no later than the specified date each year.

Jago aur Jago Hindi *adult education* monthly published by the *Indian Adult Education Association*. It was established in 1982.

Jamaica Council for Adult Education Current address: c/o 2a Ruthven Road, Kingston, Jamaica.

Jamaica Movement for the Advancement of Literacy (JAMAL) Current address: P.O. Box 60, Kingston 4, Jamaica.

James Report UK educational report published in 1972 on school teacher education, which recommended the introduction of the *Diploma in Higher Education* to the British system.

James, William (1842–1910) Early prominent psychologist whose principal work was on the *self*. He is frequently cited by *humanistic adult educators*.

Japan See the *National Federation for Social Education*.

Japanese Association of Museums Current address: Kasumigaseki 3–3–1, Chiyoda-ku, Tokyo, Japan.

Japanese Society for Studies on Adult Education The Japanese society for the academic study of *adult education*. Address: c/o The Department of Adult Education, University of Tokyo, 7–3–1, Honyo, Bunkyo-ku, Tokyo 113, Japan.

Japanese University of the Air The *Open University* of Japan, established and first broadcast on 1 April 1984. The formal degree courses did not start until 1985 and then served only Tokyo and Yokohama, but with the intention of expanding within a few years. Unlike many of the new approaches to *higher education* this one places a greater emphasis on electronic media. The objectives of the university are: to provide educational opportunity for working people and housewives; to provide an innovative and flexible system of *higher education*; and to co-operate with existing universities. It is an independent four-year institution offering a degree of Bachelor of Liberal Arts. Unlike some *distance teaching universities*, this university has full control of both a television and a radio station. See also the *University of the Air Foundation, National Center for the Development of Broadcast Education*.

Jevons, Frank (1858–1936) Professor of philosophy and well-known writer about religion, he was also committed to *workers' education* in Britain and was a keen supporter of the *Workers' Educational Association*.

job analysis The process of analyzing the elements of a job. It is useful in the world of work and in *vocational guidance*, since it is important in assessing the employment *needs* that an employee might have.

Job Change Programme A *Manpower Services Commission*-funded programme organized by *adult education centres* and run over a period of one day per week for six months, aimed at attracting older people from management and preparing them for a new career. (Note: the *Manpower Services Commission* changed its name to the *Training Commission* and then to the *Training Agency* in 1988.)

job club First established in Canada and introduced into the United Kingdom in 1984 by the *Manpower Services Commission*. The job club is both a formal and an informal opportunity for unemployed people to meet, to learn about each other's experiences, and to receive some educational opportunities relevant to their *needs*. (Note: the *Manpower Services Commission* changed its name to the *Training Commission* and then to the *Training Agency* in 1988.)

job club counsellor A *counsellor* employed in a *job club* to offer support and guidance to the unemployed who come within the ambit of the *job club*. A manual for counsellors was published in Canada which was *behavioural* in its orientation but it does not appear to have been so widely used in British job clubs.

Job Corps Administered in the United States by the Department of Labor. It offers residential education and training programmes to disadvantaged young people, and has over 100 residential establishments nationwide. Current address: US Department of Labor, Employment and Training Administration, 200 Constitution Avenue NW, Suite 4507, Washington DC 20213, USA.

job description A statement of the main characteristics of an occupational post.

job development Identification and creation of employment opportunities within the work environment for persons participating in *staff development* programmes. A term used more frequently in the United States.

job enrichment The process of adding variation to a job to make it more satisfying.

job entry level of employment The occupational level at which a person is equipped to be employed upon entry to the occupation as a result of *training*.

job evaluation The process of deciding the significance of a job within an organizational context.

Job Opportunities for the Business Sector (JOBS) An American plan to finance the training of the long-term unemployed. It was introduced in 1968 by the National Alliance of Businessmen.

job placement An *internship* undertaken simultaneously with professional preparation.

job readiness The possession of the necessary *knowledge, skills,* and *attitudes* to enter employment.

job satisfaction The satisfaction gained from undertaking a certain occupation. There are two types of job satisfaction: that which is intrinsic to the actual work process, and that which is extrinsic to it, such as financial reward or personal status.

Job Tap An assessment programme for those who are going to be involved in the *Job Training Partnership Act* training scheme.

Job Train A publication seeking to offer an in-depth current analysis of employment issues in the United States. It is published by the *Educational Testing Service*. Current address: P.O. Box 243 Hammond, Indiana, 46320, USA.

Job Training Partnership Act Signed into law in the United States on 13 October 1982 to offer job training to unemployed people so that they could enter unsubsidized employment.

Job Training Scheme (JTS) The successor to the *Training Opportunities Programme*, it provides training for unemployed people on a variety of courses lasting an average of 15–19 weeks. The courses are run by *Colleges of Further Education* and *Skillcentres*. The aim of the scheme is to increase the supply of skilled labour power to employers, thus helping them to avoid skill shortages. Training is intended to focus upon higher-level occupations and technical skills and the upgrading of present skills. Eligibility for the scheme is restricted to trainees of at least 19 years of age, who are unemployed or willing to relinquish their employment on commencement of the course. They cannot have undertaken a sponsored training course in the previous three years, and they must be willing to take up employment in the field of training on completion of the course. See *employment training*.

Jodl, Frederick (1849–1914) Philosopher and leader of the *popular education* movement in Austria, where he was especially influential in Vienna.

John Robinson Award Established in 1986 in memory of *John Robinson*. Administered by the *National Institute for Adult Continuing Education* and given to individuals who have made a substantial contribution in the United Kingdom to educational work with adults.

Johnson, Alvin Early twentieth century adult educator. Director of *The New School for Social Research* from 1923, frequent writer in the field, he wrote an early study on *libraries* and *adult education*. He was president of the *American Association of Adult Education* from 1939 to 1940.

Joint Board of Pre-Vocational Education *British Technical Education Council* and *City and Guilds of the London Institute* act together as the Joint Board of Pre-Vocational Education, which controls the *Certificate for Pre-Vocational Education*.

Joint Commission for the Study of Adult Education Formerly the *Joint Committee for the Study of Adult Education Policies, Principles and Practices*. In 1949 the commission recommended that it be enlarged and that the *AAAE* and *NEA* explore the possibility of closer ties. This resulted in the Joint Commission playing a major role as these two organizations rapidly moved towards amalgamation, which occurred at a conference in Columbus, Ohio, in May 1951 when the *Adult Education Association of the United States of America* was founded.

Joint Committee for the Study of Adult Education Policies, Principles and Practices Established in 1946 as a result of a joint conference of the five main *adult education* organizations in America at that time, including the *AAAE*. In 1948 the committee changed its name to the *Joint Commission for the Study of Adult Education*.

Joint Committee on Educational Television (JCET) Established in 1951 and sponsored by the American Council on Education, this committee was influential in getting educational television established in the United States. Later it changed its name to the *Joint Council on Educational Television*.

Joint Council on Educational Television A federation of national television organizations which co-ordinates the field of educational television in the United States. It was formerly called the *Joint Committee on Educational Television*. Current address: 1126 16th Street NW, Washington DC 20036, USA.

joint course provision See *joint provision*.

Joint Examination Board for Adult Education Established in Finland and works within the *Association of Finnish*

Adult Education Organisations arranging examinations for adults on a national scale. In this context, an adult is a person above the age of 16 years. It is anticipated that this system will become the official national examination system, opening an increasing number of educational opportunities to adults, irrespective of their previous education.

joint frequency A statistical measure of the simultaneous occurrence of two or more variables.

joint provision The result of two or more *providers* of *adult education* that combine to provide courses. This occurs in the United Kingdom between the *Workers Educational Association* and *university extension*.

Joint Trade Union Education Committee Proposed in 1961 to be the educational body for the trade union movement, but it was never formed. Instead, the *Trade Union Congress Educational Department* organized a different scheme which resulted in an autonomous education scheme for the movement.

Joint Ventures Center First established in Philadelphia in 1986 as a *Council for Adult and Experiential Learning* joint project supported by a number of charitable trusts. These centres seek to co-operate with employees, labour unions, and employers in providing counselling, returning-to-learning workshops, career planning, training, and re-training programmes.

Jones, Reverend Griffith (1683–1761) Rector of Llanddowrorin in Wales in the early eighteenth century. He was responsible for starting the *Welsh Circulating Schools*.

Jones, Thomas (1870–1955) Very influential in *adult education* in England and Wales during the first half of this century, especially in the *Workers' Educational Association*. He was also a founder of *Coleg Harlech* in 1927.

Jordan The General Union of Voluntary Societies is one of the organizing agencies for *adult education* in the country. Current address: P.O. Box 1635, Amman, Jordan.

Jordanian Higher Committee on Adult Education and Literacy The government committee controlling *adult education* in the country. There is also within the ministry a documentation centre which offers research and training services. Current address: Ministry of Education, Amman, Jordan.

Journal of Access Studies A quarterly journal published by the *Forum for Access Studies*.

Journal of Adult Education 1. First published in September 1926 in the United Kingdom, it soon became *Adult Education* and was the longest-running journal in the adult education movement. 2. The original title of the *American Association of Adult Education*'s journal, established in February 1929, which changed its name to *Adult Education Journal* in January 1942. 3. The journal of the adult education association of Zambia, launched in 1982 and published twice a year by the University of Zambia. 4. Currently the journal of the Mountain Plains Adult Education Association in the United States. The journal was established in 1972 and is published twice each year.

Journal of Adult Education Tanzania Published annually since 1977 in Tanzania.

Journal of Adult Learning The half-yearly journal of the *New Zealand National Council of Adult Education*.

Journal of Adult Theological Education The journal of the *Association of Centres of Adult Theological Education* in the United Kingdom.

Journal of Community Education Published four times a year from the Community Education Development Centre, Coventry, UK. This journal focuses upon issues in action research and community education techniques.

Journal of Continuing Education in Nursing American journal which was started in 1969 and is published six times a year. All papers are restricted to continuing education within nursing.

Journal of Correctional Education Published quarterly by the *Correctional Education Association* in America.

Journal of Distance Education The journal of the *Canadian Association of Distance Education*, also called *Revue de l'ensignement à distance*.

Journal of Education for Women See *Fujin Kyoiku Joho*.

Journal of Educational Gerontology The journal of the *Association of Educational Gerontology* in the United Kingdom. It commenced in 1986 and is currently published twice a year.

Journal of European Industrial Training Established in 1977. Concerned with management and organizational development as well as aspects of *training*. Published eight times a year.

Journal of Extension This journal has been published six times a year since it was established in 1962. It is a journal about the *university extension* service in the United States. See also *Extension Review*.

Journal of Further and Higher Education The journal of the *National Association of Teachers in Further and Higher Education* in the United Kingdom. It is published three times a year.

Journal of Leisure Research A quarterly American journal which occasionally carries articles of interest to *adult educators*.

Journal of the African Association for Literacy and Adult Education Established in 1986 and published by the

African Association for Literacy and Adult Education. Current address: P.O. Box 50768, Nairobi, Kenya.

Journal of Workers' Education One of the publications of the *Workers' Educational Association* in the United Kingdom.

judicial education This form of education covers programmes to meet the needs of all people who are employed within state judicial departments in the United States.

Judicial Education Network An American network of judicial educators which also organizes its own seminars. Contact with the Network may be made through the *National Association of State Judicial Educators*.

Judicial Studies Board This educational board is concerned with the *continuing education* of the judiciary in the United Kingdom. It arranges for judges to be trained in sentencing, summing up at trials and in their initial training after appointment. The Board also organizes refresher seminars, has prepared some *distance learning* material and makes a report every few years about the judiciary.

junior college US college that teaches only the first two years of a four-year college course (the freshman and sophomore years). First established at the University of Chicago. Some are units of a four-year college, others extensions of high schools, and still others are independent.

junior secondary general certificate (MAVO) The certificate awarded at the end of four years study in secondary education in the Netherlands, following primary education in Dutch schools. It is now possible for adults to return to school in the day or evening to gain this qualification; a form of *second chance education*. See also *senior secondary general certificate*.

junior secondary vocational certificate (LBO) Awarded at the same level as the *junior secondary general certificate* in the Netherlands and takes the same amount of time, but contains more technical subjects. It is also available as a form of *second chance education*. See also *senior secondary vocational certificate*.

junior year The third year of a four-year college course.

junto Formerly called the *Leather Apron Club – a Workingmen's Social and Debating Club*. The word means a group of people joined for a common purpose. It was a discussion club, started by *Benjamin Franklin* and 11 friends in Philadelphia in 1727 to explore intellectual problems. It originally met on Friday evenings. However, juntos were not only debating societies; they frequently led to action. From them arose a number of civic enterprises such as the *public library service*, a philosophical society, and a volunteer fire company. This form of association was resurrected in the annual meetings of the *American Association of Adult and Continuing Education*, as in the conference at Philadelphia in 1983.

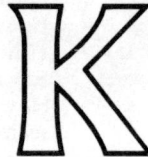

Kageb Erwachsenenbildung
Established in 1962. The quarterly
bulletin of the *Katholische
Arbeitsgemeinschaft für Erwachsenenbildung
der Schweiz und des Fürstentums*.

kandidaati First-degree level in Finland.
See also *candidature, kandidat*.

kandidat First-degree level study for
university education in Denmark. See
candidature, kandidaati.

Kansanopisto/Folkhögskolan The *folk
high school* journal in Finland. It was
established in 1928 and is published eight
times a year.

Kant, Immanuel (1724–1804) German
philosopher. While he did not write a
great deal that relates directly to *adult
education*, some of his discussions on
experience and phenomena that occur in
the mind independently of experience,
and his brief work on education, are
important to the philosophy of the
education of adults.

Kapp, Alexander In 1833 Kapp, a
German teacher, is reputed to have
introduced the word *andragogy* into the
education vocabulary.

**Katholische Arbeitsgemeinschaft für
Erwachsenenbildung der Schweiz
und des Fürstentums** Swiss Catholic
association for the education of adults.
Current address: P.O. Box 2069,
CH–6002 Lucerne, Switzerland.

**Katholische
Bundesarbeitsgemeinschaft für
Erwachsenenbildung** The *Catholic*

Association of Adult Education in West
Germany. Provides a wide range of
courses in *adult education*, with over
100,000 courses a year to over six million
participants. Each area is covered by a
Catholic education organization functioning
like an *adult education institute*. Current
address: Urstadtstrasse 2, 5300 Bonn I,
Federal Republic of Germany.

Kawamoto, Unosuke (1888–1960) A
leading theorist in *social education* in
Japan, concentrating upon the richness of
leisure.

Kekkonen, Helena Finnish *adult educator*
who specialized in *peace education*. Winner
of the Unesco Prize for Peace in 1981.
She has been secretary-general of the
*Finnish Association of Adult Education
Organizations* and the moving force in the
creation of the network of adult
educators working for peace which is
sponsored by the *International Council for
Adult Education*.

Keller Plan A *programmed learning* plan
in which the student studies prepared
material at his/her own pace and then
must complete the end of a unit test
successfully before proceeding to the
next one. See *mastery learning, personalized
system of instruction*.

Kellogg Foundation Philanthropic
organization established by W.K.
Kellogg in 1930 with the intention of
helping people to help themselves. It is
an independent foundation managed by
its own board of trustees. Its
programmes are in health and
educational needs, many in *adult
education*, and grants are restricted to

188

specific geographic locations. Current address: Secretary, W.K. Kellog Foundation, 400 North Avenue, Battle Creek, Michigan 49017, USA.

Kelly's Personal Construct A system constructed by psychologist George Kelly which assumes human behaviour is based upon experimentation rather than reaction, in which individuals construe their world by bipolar opposites, e.g. black and white, good and bad, etc.

Kenny Report A report in Eire published in 1984. See *Commission on Adult Education.*

Kenya Adult Education Association Current address: c/o KNUT Headquarters, P.O. Box 30407, Nairobi, Kenya.

Kenya Journal of Adult Education Established in 1973, the journal of the Board of Adult Education in Kenya.

Keppel, Frederick President of the *Carnegie Corporation* during the period in which it was involved in *adult education* in America. He was responsible for a great deal of the support that *adult education* received from the fund.

Kettering Foundation Established in America in 1927 by Charles E. Kettering, its staff works in partnership with other organizations to establish the links between education, governance and science. Current address: 5335 Far Hills Avenue, Dayton, Ohio 45429, USA.

key participants The use of significant personnel in the *evaluation* of *training.*

keystoning The effect produced when the image projected by an *overhead projector* is not square but wider at the top than at the bottom. This distortion is produced because the angle of projection is not perpendicular to the angle of the screen.

Khaki College A Canadian *adult education* movement during the First World War for the education of men in the armed services. It attracted many enrolments for all types of classes. It was this experience, among others, which influenced *Ned Corbett* to enter *adult education.*

khit-pen 1. Term from Thailand meaning 'to know how to think'; it describes the philosophy of that country's *adult/non-formal education* service. It involves using three types of *knowledge*: of self, of society and environment, and 'book' knowledge. 2. It is also the title of the *non-formal education* journal published by the Ministry of Non-Formal Education in Thailand six times a year. This was established in 1980.

Kidd, J. Roby (1915–82) Born James Robbins Kidd in Saskatchewan, Canada, he was to become one of the leading *adult educators* in the twentieth century. He held many positions of importance, including the first chair of the Adult Education Department at *Ontario Institute for Studies in Education*, chairman of the Unesco International Committee for the Advancement of Adult Education from 1961–67, president of the Second World Conference of Adult Education held in Montreal in 1960, jury member of *Unesco World Literacy Awards Committee*, chairman of the Unesco Evaluation Committee of the Experimental World Literacy Project from 1974–75, and many others. He was the recipient of many awards and author of a number of books, including *'How Adults Learn'*, which became a widely recognized text book. However, he is best known as the founder and first secretary-general of the *International Council for Adult Education*. The first biography of J. Roby Kidd by Nancy J. Cochrane was published by the Centre for Continuing Education, University of British Columbia in 1986. See *J. Roby Kidd Award* and *J. Roby Kidd Trust Fund.*

Kilpatrick, William H. (1871–1965) Professor of Education at Teachers College, Columbia University, New York, who pioneered the *project* method in education.

kinesthetic learner One who learns best whilst moving around.

kinesthetics The study of bodily movement in relation to speech.

kirjeopistot Part-time *adult education* institutions in Finland.

Kjellberg, Knut (1867–1921) A leader of the *popular education* movement in Sweden for many years. He was the first chairman of the Popular Education Association.

Knapp, Seaman A. An *extension agent* who is generally credited with being the first to demonstrate the importance of on-farm demonstration, rather than demonstration in a college, to get farmers to change their practices. See *Cooperative Extension Service*.

Knights of St Crispin The union of shoemakers in Canada in the nineteenth century which, during the 1860s, employed lecturers and readers to expound to the shoemakers whilst they were employed in the monotonous work of making shoes.

knowledge 1. The certainty that phenomena are real and that they possess specific characteristics. 2. The domain of true propositions or statements. 3. Mastery of some principle. A major element in the philosophical debate about knowledge is the extent to which it is objective or subjective. In addition the types of knowledge may be classified according to their condition, e.g. empirical knowledge, pragmatic knowledge, and rational-logical knowledge. The concept of *belief* and its relationship to knowledge has also to be considered. Finally, the *forms of knowledge* constitute another aspect of the discussion about knowledge. See *body of knowledge*.

knowledge class A concept that has become familiar within the social sciences, especially since the emergency of post-industrial society, to refer to four distinct grouping: the scientific, the technological, the administrative, and the cultural sections of modern society. This group should be seen as separate from *intellectuals* or the *intelligentsia*.

knowledge manufacture The processing of information so that it becomes a form of socially produced *knowledge* reflecting certain perspectives, in the media, etc.

Knowledge Network A learning network in Canada.

Knowles, Malcolm S. (b.1913) One of the best known humanistic *adult educators* in the United States. He is a former executive director of the *Association of Adult Education of the United States of America* and professor of adult education at North Carolina State University. He is perhaps best known for his emphasis on *andragogy* and, more recently, on *contract learning*. He also wrote the first major history of adult education in the United States and several other books.

Koch, Hal (1904–63) Church historian and *adult educator* in Denmark. One of the leaders of *adult education* in Denmark during the Second World War when he was chairman of the Danish Youth Association, principal of a *folk high school* and a university professor.

Kohlberg, Lawrence American development psychologist whose work grew out of that of *Jean Piaget*. Kohlberg concentrated initially on conceptual development in children, studying their development in the use of moral concepts.

Kokuritsu Shaken Tsushin (National Training Institute of Social Education Newsletter) A bimonthly Japanese periodical published by the *National Training Institute of Social Education* since November 1971 in Japan.

Kolb's learning cycle D.A. Kolb postulated a cycle of four elements: concrete experience, reflection and observation, conceptualization and generalization, and experimentation.

Kolb's learning style inventory
Consists of nine items with four preferences in each. It purports to indicate four learning styles, but is based upon the validity of his *learning cycle*, and some scholars have suggested that this is too simple.

Kold, Christen (1816–70) An important influence in Danish *adult education*, he was involved in the formation of some of the early *folk high schools*, including the *agriculture schools*. He was trained as a teacher but suffered persecution during part of his life for both his theological and his educational views. He was influenced by *Nikolai Grundtvig*. He was also the first person in Denmark to run courses of education for rural women.

Kom Newsletter of *Komvux* in Sweden.

kominkan An adult learning centre based in a local community in Japan, having some of the characteristics of the community school. The word may be translated as citizens' public hall. There were well over 17,000 of them in Japan, in which *adult education* is based.

Kominkan Geppo Former title of *Gekkan Kominkan*, the journal of the *National Association of Kominkan* in Japan. See *kominkan*.

Komvux Local authority *adult education* in Sweden. It began in 1968, offering higher primary and secondary education to adults. Publishes its own newsletter, *Kom*.

Konrad Adenauer Foundation A political foundation in West Germany involved in *adult education*, especially in the field of political and social self-determination and participation. Also involved in adult education in other countries, in the same way as other West German adult education institutions express an international awareness.

koranic schools Institutes in which Islamic culture is taught.

Korea Air and Correspondence University A *distance teaching* university in Korea. Current address: 169 Dongsung-dong, Chongro-ku, Seoul 110, Republic of Korea.

Korean Association of Adult and Youth Education Current address: c/o Institute of Educational Research, Seoul National University, Seoul 151, Republic of Korea.

Korean Educational Development Institute Current address: Gang Nam Gu Umyeon Dong, San 20–1, Seoul, Republic of Korea.

Korean Women's Development Institute Established in April 1983 as a research centre for women's issues in Korea. It is also involved in training, resource development, dissemination of information, and publishing. Current address: CPO 2267, Seoul, Republic of Korea.

Kosowska, Irena (1879–1945) Polish *adult educator* who worked for the education of rural women.

Kovačić, Alexander (1917–77) Well-known Yugoslav adult educator, involved with the *people's universities*. Editor of the journal *Andragogija* and director of the *Andragogical Centre* in Zagreb.

Krant The Dutch national magazine for those undertaking *adult literacy*.

Kristen Folkehøgskole The Christian *folk high school* magazine which is published in Norway ten times a year.

Krzywicki, Ludwik Oachim Franciszek (1859–1941) Polish social scientist and *adult educator*. He held high office within the university and research fields. He sought to make scientific *knowledge* more widely known, was concerned with *illiteracy* and with people's opportunities for education. He was one of the founders of the University for Everyone in Poland, and was very active and influential in the development of *adult education* in the country.

Kuwait There is no association of *adult education* but there is a Department of Anti–Illiteracy and Adult Education within the Ministry of Education. Current address: Post Box 7, Safat 13001, Kuwait.

Kweneng Rural Development Association Founded in Botswana in 1969 to assist in the process of *development* through the *training* of young people, providing *vocational education*, *adult education*, and *extension education* for the poorer sections of the community. It has a number of different programmes related to the work situation.

kyoiku Japanese *adult education* institutions.

labor college American college for trade unionists.

labor education Workers' education in America.

labor studies The study of labor, its history, problems, and future development in the United States. See *trade union studies, workers' education*.

laboratory Room especially designed and equipped for specialist practical work, e.g. a scientific laboratory or language laboratory.

labour college The first labour college was formed in Oxford in 1909 as a result of disputes at *Ruskin College*. It was more radical than *Ruskin*; some see it as Marxist although other commentators feel that the radicalism was not to be equated with Marxism. With the rise of the trade union movement in England during the inter-war years a great number of labour colleges emerged in different towns, concerned with working-class education and associated with the trade union movement. See *National Council of Labour Colleges*.

Labour Education Established in 1964, the quarterly journal of the *International Labour Office*.

Labour Forum A weekly bulletin established by the *Workers' Educational Association* in Canada in the 1940s.

Labour International The quarterly journal of the *International Labour Office* which is concerned with worker education and was established in 1964.

labourer–teacher The *Frontier College* employed labourer-teachers to reach the labourers in the work camps. They were highly educated middle–class men and women who were prepared to work alongside the labourers in the camps and then offer *basic education* in the camps in the evenings. Often they were undergraduate students; certainly many had received a university education.

laissez–faire *Teaching style* in which the teacher does not seek to impose a specific ethos and discipline in the classroom.

land grant college The land grant colleges were established under the *Morrill Land Grant Act* of 1862 in the United States, when certain colleges were given grants to establish the study of practical subjects, such as agriculture and engineering. Most of them have subsequently expanded their activities and offer a full university curriculum, but they have retained their *extension* activities.

Land Grant College Act The *Morrill Land Grant Act* of 1862 which provided a grant of 30,000 acres of public land to each state for each senator or representative that it had in Congress, to endow a college of agriculture and mechanical arts. However it was not until the *Hatch Act* of 1887 that research was allowed at these colleges.

land grant institution See *land grant college*.

Landelijk beraad van plaatselijk vormingswerk The Dutch national association for local centres of liberal adult education. Current address: Burg. Loeffplein 24, 5211 RZ Den Bosch, The Netherlands.

Landelijke vereniging VJV See *National Association for the Education of Young Adults*. A Dutch association. Current address: Mariahoek la, 3511 LD Utrecht, The Netherlands.

Landsforeningen Aldre Sagan A Danish national association open to all people over 18 years of age but with a predominantly elderly membership. It acts as a pressure group for elderly people. It is divided into regions, with each region organizing local groups that act as political lobbies but also arrange social, guidance, and educational activities. Also known as *Danage*.

language A system of symbols, often verbal (although non-verbal communication might be conceived of as a form of language), which seeks to express ideas, *knowledge*, feeling, sensations, values, etc.

Language Association, German for Immigrant Workers See *Sprachverband Deutsch für auslandische Arbeitnehmer e.V.*

language circle A *study circle* that studies languages.

language codes The forms of speech used by people of different social classes.

language deficit Deficiency in language usage, often caused by cultural deprivation.

language laboratory *Laboratory* especially equipped with teaching machines, audio cassette equipment, etc. so that students can study speech and learn languages.

Last Post The name given to the newspaper produced by the *University of the Third Age* in the United Kingdom; the title was not appreciated and was changed.

late adolescence Stage in development from 16 to 20 years of age.

late adult transition The period between 60 and 65 years of age when the adult moves from a dominant place in social living and begins to get accustomed to being regarded as a member of the older generation.

late adulthood Sixty-five years and older. This is a period about which there has not been a great deal of research but it is one in which the older person seems to move from the centre of the stage of life in Western society.

late bloomer American term for *late developer*.

late developer Term used to describe a person who demonstrates academic, or other, ability after having left school. However, such people may have been *underachievers* at school.

latent function A consequence of the existence of a phenomenon which was neither intended nor initially recognized. However, some latent functions are recognized and used in certain situations. It might be claimed, for instance, that the *hidden curriculum* is about the latent functions of attending an educational institution. See also *manifest function*.

lateral thinking Restructuring the knowledge that a person already has in order to bring about new insights and ideas. See also *vertical thinking*.

Latin American Center for Basic Education (CREFAL) Centre affiliated to the United Nations involved in *adult basic education*. Current address: Pátzcuaro, Michoacán, Mexico.

Latin American Council For Adult Education (Consejo de Educación de Adultos de América Latina). This organization emerged as a result of regional co-operation in *adult education* over a number of years and represents over 60 *non-government organizations* involved in *adult education* in the region. Current address: c/o Castilla 6257, Correo 22, Santiago, Chile.

Latin American Ecumenical Community Education Center (CELADEC) A peasant Christian *community education* group based in Peru.

Laubach, Frank (1884–1970) American founder of the *literacy* movement that bears his name. A former missionary of the Congregational Church. His method is perhaps epitomized by the phrase *each one teach one.*

Laubach Literacy Action (LLA) The domestic arm of *Laubach Literacy International.* It trains and certifies *volunteer* tutors to teach reading and writing, including *English as a second language.* It also provides assistance to its local programme (it operates over 500) and prepares instructional material. Current address: 1320 Jamesville Avenue, Box 131, Syracuse, New York 13210, USA.

Laubach Literacy International A non-profit educational corporation founded in 1955 by *Frank Laubach* to enable illiterate adults and older adults to acquire the listening, speaking, reading, writing, and mathematics skills to solve the problems that they encounter in daily life. Current address: 1320 Jamesville Avenue, Box 130. Syracuse, New York 13210, USA.

Laubach Literacy International News The quarterly newsletter of *Laubach Literacy International.*

laurea Italian first degree.

Law Society Established in England in 1825, the association for those professions associated with the law and responsible for their professional preparation.

laws of learning *Edward Thorndike* postulated a number of laws of learning, concerning effect, exercise and readiness. His work was influential in *adult education* in the inter-war years.

lay leader 1. A *leader* in the Christian churches. 2. Term employed by *Cyril Houle* in his *pyramid of leadership* to refer to the *volunteer* leaders who are *adult educators* by virtue of their work, e.g. youth club leaders.

lay training Term used by the Christian churches to refer to the education and training of lay people so that they can live a more effective Christian life in the society or be a more useful worker within the organization of the church.

Le Conseil Superieur d'Education Populaire The *adult education* association of Belgium. It combines both the French and the Flemish associations. Current address: Galerie Ravenstein, 78–1000 Brussels, Belgium.

leader One who accepts responsibilities to guide, rule, or control a group or organization. There are many types and styles of *leadership.*

leadership 1. The ability of a person to influence the actions, behaviour, beliefs, and feelings of another person or persons and gain their co-operation. 2. The ability to attract followers to the performance of a task.

leadership style The approach to *leadership* adopted by a leader, e.g. *authoritarian, democratic, laissez-faire*, etc. Studies in leadership style have been applied to *teaching style.*

learned goal A goal which is itself acquired through *learning.*

learner One who learns, a student.

learner analysis The identification of an intended audience for a learning activity and of the significant characteristics of those learners.

learner-centred education Education which is determined to a great extent by the *needs* of the student. The *teaching* and *learning* activities involve the active participation of the learner.

learner-controlled instruction (LCI) The process in which the *learner* assumes responsibility for setting the educational *objectives* of a *teaching* and *learning* session, so that the responsibility for *self-development* lies with the learner. Used in certain work situations.

learning 1. Any more or less permanent change in behaviour as a result of *experience*. 2. A relatively permanent change in behaviour which occurs as a result of practice. 3. The process whereby *knowledge* is created through the transformation of *experience*. 4. The processes of transforming *experience* into *knowledge, skills*, and *attitudes*. 5. Memorizing information. There are many other definitions but it will be seen here that (1) and (2) are behaviourist, (3) and (4) are not, and (5) is an imprecise social definition. This is a reflection of the on-going debate about the definition of this process.

Learning Formerly *Continuous Learning*, published by the *Canadian Association for Adult Education*. Published quarterly since 1976.

learning activity centre Part of the *non-formal education* programme in Sri Lanka is to provide learning opportunity for *non-schoolers* living in remote parts of the country. These centres provide alternative education on a voluntary basis.

learning activity package A self-contained set of materials designed to assist the *learner* in mastering some specific area of *knowledge* or *skill*.

learning block Something that prevents a person from *learning*. It may be psychological or situational.

learning community An organized group of people working together to increase their *knowledge, skills*, or *sensitivity*.

learning contract A learning contract may be between a learner and a tutor, or any other person, or even a self-made contract. It is an agreement to learn certain *knowledge, skill, attitude*, or *value*

required by the learner. The agreement is frequently made in writing, but this is not essential to this form of learning. Usually, the contract specifies the objectives, the methods used, the resources, the date by which the contract will be met, and the criteria by which it will be evaluated. Considerable literature exists about the way that contracts operate and the extent to which they are successful – which they generally tend to be with *adult learners*. Known to have been used as early as 1919.

learning curve A graphic representation of the expected or actual rate of acquisition of a *skill* or *knowledge*, depending upon how it is used.

learning cycle A model of *experiential learning* devised and popularized by D.A. Kolb, in which learning is seen as a process of observing and reflecting upon a concrete experience and, having done that, drawing conclusions and generalizations that can be tested in practice. Kolb claims that the learning process can begin anywhere in the cycle, but the model seems more applicable to *learning* from *experience*. *Dewey* made many similar suggestions and Kolb certainly sees his work within this framework. See *Kolb's learning cycle*.

learning difficulty See *learning block*. However, this term is often used in a broader context to refer to any failure to make satisfactory progress through a course of academic study.

learning disability An inability to learn something as a result of sensory handicap or cultural deprivation.

learning environment The total set of conditions that influence learning. This has become a concern for some educators in the professions who are interested in the effectiveness of *internship* or *professional placement* as a learning activity.

learning episode A defined period of time in which *learning* occurs or is planned. The period of time may vary from a moment to a much longer period, although it is unwise to specify time length, except for specific purposes. See *learning project*.

learning exchange An *educational brokering* agency whose task is to match those who wish to teach something with those who wish to learn the same topic. Much of the exchange is conducted by telephone or if there is a centre, then by visits of prospective clients. These are usually private, independent businesses. Many of the early ones were operated from college campuses. They occur more frequently in the United States than elsewhere in the *adult education* world. These organizations make a great deal of use of *volunteers*.

learning exchange network A form of *learning exchange* which has been developed in America to take into account the strengths and weaknesses of the earlier forms of *learning exchange* and also to cater for rural populations. Unlike the earlier approaches, these networks have an implementation plan and are organized by local people.

learning from experience Term sometimes used to refer to that type of *learning* that is facilitated through the provision of primary experiences, followed by reflection. There is also the recognition in this concept that life's experiences are also a basis of much human learning, so that facilitated learning is only employing a natural method of learning. See also *experiential learning*.

Learning from Experience Trust (LET) An educational charity in the United Kingdom which has been established to develop ways in which people can make maximum use of their knowledge and skills. It endeavours to develop methods of identifying and measuring *learning* which has not been formerly examined. It is related to the *Council for Adult and Experiential Learning* in the United States. It publishes its own newsletter, organizes conferences, and

undertakes research and development projects. Current address: Regent's College, Regent's Park, London NW1 4NS, UK.

learning how to learn It has been recognized in recent years that *learning* skills can themselves be learned. *Study skills* courses have therefore become more frequent, in which students are introduced to some of the basic and more sophisticated skills of learning.

learning laboratory Specially equipped room for students with either *programmed* or other *self-instructional* materials for *independent study*.

learning log A record of *learning* undertaken, or a record of *learning needs* discovered as a result of *experience*. This is used in professional preparation, especially during the *practical placement*. See also *diary*.

learning material Term used for the material prepared by *distance learning* institutions for *study packs* and for other study material on *distance education* courses.

learning need Considerable conceptual confusion exists around the concept of *need*, and this term is used quite interchangeably with it. However, it has a more specific connotation when it relates to a deficiency that can be rectified through the acquisition of specific *knowledge, skill* or *attitude*. Some scholars are unhappy with the use of need since there is always the implication of deficiency that ought to be rectified.

learning needs assessment The identification of learner, provider, and community *needs* and the synthesis of these into a specification of the problem.

learning network A matching service of people who wish to *learn* and those who wish to *teach* a subject, skill, or topic in a formal or informal manner. The networks are sometimes established through *educational brokering* agencies, or through some other organization.

Learning Network Established in Australia in the mid–1980s, it negotiates with the media to provide educational broadcasting and, in addition, provides its own curriculum. It is also seeking to negotiate with other educational institutions to provide educational opportunity complementary to the educational broadcasts. Publishes its own magazine.

Learning Opportunities for Adults A report issued by the *Organization for Economic Co-operation and Development* in five volumes betwen 1977 and 1981, covering the following topics: a general report; new structures, programmes, and methods; *non-participation; participation* and widening access for the disadvantaged.

learning–orientated learning One of *Cyril Houle's* three types of learning, reflecting the person who learns for learning's sake. See also *activity-orientated learning, goal-orientated learning.*

learning package A collection of materials prepared by a teacher or educational institution to be used for *self-directed learning.*

learning plateau A period in the process of *learning* in which progress seems slow and the acquisition of new *knowledge* and *skill* seems difficult.

learning process Learning as a process, as distinct from the product of learning, e.g. the learning.

learning project According to *Allen Tough*, a learning project takes a period of at least seven hours of deliberate and sustained effort to acquire new *knowledge* or *skill*, although it does not have to occur during a single period or within any specified period of time. The time-frame seems to be arbitrary to some degree, as he himself is aware. See *learning episode.*

learning resource centre A centre that gathers books and other learning material, usually in a specialist topic, in order to be of service to learners. *Libraries* were an early form of resource centre.

Learning Resources Kit Formerly called *Tie Lines* when it was established in 1966, it has changed its name to Learning Resources Kit. It is published every two months by the *Canadian Association of Adult Education* in English and French.

Learning Resources Network (LERN) Established in 1974, this is a national technical assistance network in non–credit programming. This association publishes ACET, a newsletter on *adult learning.* Current address: 1221 Thurston, Suite 301, Manhattan, Kansas 66502, USA.

learning setting analysis The identification of contextual factors relevant to the design of *learning* activities.

learning society An ideal held by adherents of *lifelong education* in which a society makes ample provision for all its population to learn whatever they wish at any time throughout their lives. Learning, fulfilment, and realizing full human potential for everybody thus becomes a possibility. It might be possible to claim that in those countries where the facilities and support exist for *study circles* that the rudiments of the learning society have been created.

learning style See *cognitive style* The term seems sometimes to refer to the characteristic and preferred approaches to *learning* other than the cognitive, such as strategies adopted to learn more effectively, but it also refers to the individual differences in the way that people think and learn.

learning style inventory Developed by David Kolb from his *learning cycle*, it consists of a nine-item self-description questionnaire which asks respondents to rank sets of four words in order of appropriateness for their own learning. Thereafter, through a system of scoring, the respondents' learning preferences are determined. It is widely used but open to a number of criticisms, including the fact that the cycle may not depict the most accurate research into learning and that it is not always replicable. See *Kolb's learning style inventory*.

learning task analysis An identification of the main *skills, knowledge,* and/or *attitudes* required by a learner and the subdivision of these into their basic components.

learning theory Theories of *learning* often associated with a particular scholar or school of thought.

Learning to Be The title of the *Faure Report* submitted to and published by *Unesco* in 1972.

learning to learn See *learning how to learn*.

Leather Apron Club See *junto*.

leave of absence Period of time during which a person is away, either from work in order to study (see *paid educational leave*) or from attendance at an educational institution.

leaving certificate The certificate granted to successful students on passing examinations at school-leaving age. Often the failure to obtain such a certificate is a hindrance for adults as they seek to progress in their careers. Thus *adult education* institutions often organize courses so that adults can obtain such a certificate or its equivalent later in life.

Lebanon At present there appears to be no organized *adult education* although the American University of Beirut has a *university extension* programme. Current address: Division of Education and Extension Programs, American University of Beirut, Lebanon.

lecture 1. A method of teaching. 2. A discourse on a particular subject given by a person, usually a designated teacher, to an audience whose participation is minimal. 3. To scold or reprimand. See also *public lecture*.

lecture theatre Large, especially equipped room, usually with raked seats so that all *learners* can see the *lecturer*. Not very suitable for many *adult education* activities.

lecturer 1. One who gives a *lecture*. 2. In the United Kingdom, a teacher in an institution of *further* or *higher education*. See *professor* in the United States.

lecturette A short *lecture*, sometimes referred to as a mini-lecture.

legal adult A person who has reached the legally specified age of *adulthood*.

legibility The clarity of written work for reading or deciphering.

Leipziger, Henry M. (1853–1917) British-born American founder of the *New York (City) Free Lecture System*.

leisure 1. Time and opportunity for relaxation. 2. Period away from paid employment. 3. Free time.

leisure centre Specially equipped centre for sports and other leisure time activities in which there is often *instruction*.

leisure class That socio-economic group of people in a society which can afford to live on its wealth rather than its earned income.

leisure counselling Assistance to help people plan their *leisure* time.

leisure education As Western societies have become more leisure-orientated, so there has grown up a concern to help people learn how to use their *leisure* in a beneficial and constructive manner. *Pre-retirement education* might be viewed as a form of leisure education.

Leisure Learning A programme initiated by the Scottish Museums Council to develop *learning* programmes for a wider variety of audiences than *museums* usually attract.

Lengrand, Paul (b. 1910) One of the founders of *Peuple et Culture*, Lengrand taught for a few years in Canada after the Second World War and then returned to Paris. Member of the *Unesco* secretariat from 1948, in 1951 he was appointed head of the Adult Education Division of *Unesco*. He is a most active proponent of the concept of *lifelong education* and his concern is one of the main reasons that *Unesco* adopted the principle. His book on the subject has been translated into 17 languages.

Léo Légrange Federation An organization providing *socio-cultural animation* in France, funded partly by the Ministry for Leisure, Youth and Sport and partly by local municipalities.

Lesotho Association of Non-Formal Education Current address: c/o Institute of Extra-Mural Studies, National University of Lesotho, P.O. Roma, Lesotho.

Lesotho Distance Teaching Centre Founded in 1974, it publishes a biannual report. Current address: P.O. Box 781, Maseru 100, Lesotho.

lesson Fixed period of *teaching* and *learning*.

Lesson Handbook The original title of the annual study notes of the *adult school movement* which started in 1911. The later title *Study Handbook*, was adopted in 1919.

lesson plan The *teacher's* outline of the proposed *lesson*.

Let's Read Established in 1974. Quarterly publication of the *Jamaican Movement for the Advancement of Literacy*.

letters Sometimes used as a synonym for *arts*.

Leverhulme Foundation UK educational foundation which supports and sponsors educational research. Current address: 21–23 New Fetter Lane, London EC4A 1NR, UK.

Lewin, Kurt (1890–1947) American psychologist whose work contributed to the development of *group dynamics* and *activity-based learning*. His work has been very influential in *adult education*.

Lewisham Skills Centre A centre in Lewisham, UK in which young and old together can learn and exchange *skills*. It commenced in September 1984. Current address: c/o Age Concern, 18 Brownhill Road, London SE6 2EJ, UK.

liberal adult education Much *adult education* which is of a non-vocational form is characterized as liberal. However, it is usually regarded as a form of cultural enrichment for adults through a process of *teaching* and *learning*. It is often regarded as the antithesis of *vocational education*. See *Everett Dean Martin* as an early theorist.

liberal arts The study of the fine arts, humanities, and social sciences; a form of *liberal education*.

liberal arts college American college which provides four-year degree courses in *non-vocational education*.

liberal education The form of education that is concerned with the comprehensive development of the mind in the acquisition of knowledge. The theory underlying this is derived from Greek thought and based upon the *ideology* of *liberalism*. In adult education the concept *liberal* is used much more flexibly and at times almost seems equivalent to *non-vocational education*, although a few scholars would dispute this. *Everett Dean Martin* was an early theorist of *liberal adult education*.

liberal progressive A slightly more socialist ideology than pure *liberalism*. *Adult education* is sometime analysed as being liberal progressive rather than merely *liberal*; the reason for this is that the former introduces ideas of equality and redistribution of privilege which the latter does not include.

liberal studies A non-vocational element introduced to *vocational education* courses in order to broaden the *curriculum*.

liberalism An ideology that suggests that individuals are rational, free to pursue their own interests, and independent. The element of rationality has also resulted in liberalism being equated with the development of the rational mind, this was the basis of the Greek ideas of *liberal education*.

liberating education In some ways this is a term similar to *popular education*, especially in its Latin American context. It is associated with the work of *Paulo Freire* and has the following characteristics: it is associated with the people, organized by the people, and critical of the more established forms of education which are provided by the state for purposes other than that of emancipating the people.

Liberia The National Adult Education Association of Liberia is located at: P.O. Box 3931, Monrovia, Liberia.

Libert, Karol (1807–75), Polish thinker, his ideas similar in some ways to *Nikolai Grundtvig's* in believing that education should be given to young adults in a loving manner. He wrote *The Ideas of Educating People* in 1841 in which he maintained that education should develop in people dignity and self-esteem.

liberty The freedom of the will or political freedom. The former is assumed in much *adult education* literature.

library 1. A local or community *learning resource centre* providing information and books for both vocational and leisure learning. In the 1970s, probably following initiatives such as the one taken in Atlanta, Georgia, libraries became much more involved in seeing themselves as learning resource and advisory centres for *independent learners*. 2. May also refer to a collection of books. Many *independent learners* would collect books from which to learn. 3. The first *public library* in the United States was opened in Boston in 1673, although it was not a free public library until 1852. The first free library opened in Peterborough, New Hampshire on 9 April 1833.

Library and Documentation Centre A centre at the *Unesco Institute for Education* in Hamburg which seeks to build a library of books and articles that relate to various aspects of education. See *Lifelong Education Bibliography*.

Library Association The UK association of librarians, it has been concerned with *adult education* in a variety of ways, since it sees the *library* as a tool in adult education. It has a standing subcommittee on *continuing education*. Current address: 7 Ridgmount Street, London WC1E 7AE, UK.

Library of Congress The national library of America. Address: Library of Congress, Washington DC 20540, USA.

Library of Congress classification A classification system for books developed in the *Library of Congress*. See also *Dewey decimal classification system*.

Library of Continuing Education In 1964 Syracuse University received a grant to continue its collection of *adult education* materials which for a while was called by this name. Thereafter it became known as *Syracuse University Resources for Educators of Adults (SUREA)*.

library science The study and skill of collecting, organizing, and utilizing books and other learning materials.

license A legal document authorizing a person or organization to perform specific services.

licentiate in education 1. An academic qualification in education, usually below first-degree level in England but sometimes studied after the completion of the first degree; similar to a *postgraduate certificate*. 2. The qualification awarded by some European universities as the first degree on completion of five years of study. See *licentiture*.

licentiture The last three years of a degree course in some European countries, e.g. Belgium. See also *candidature*.

life change See *life cycle*.

life class Art class using live models.

life crisis It has been argued that major changes in the pattern of a person's life (e.g. a change of job) stimulate other changes, one of which is sometimes a trigger to return to study.

life cycle The series of changes that occur in the life of a person or organism between one stage in its development and the identical stage of the next generation. See *early adulthood, middle adulthood, late adulthood*.

life cycle transition Periods of major change in the course of life, sometimes associated with chronological age but also with changes relating to individual circumstance. See *early adult transition, mid-life transition, late adult transition*.

life history method An approach to the study of learning which became popular in adult education in the late 1970s, based upon *social interactionism*. In this method subjects recount aspects of their life in order that researchers can understand more about the social aspects of learning. Also used in educational gerontology to help the very old come to terms with their life's experiences.

life passages See *career*. Life passages are those patterned pathways through aspects of social living.

life review A normal process in older adulthood of looking back over life, taking stock, and confronting mortality. This type of review has been formalized by some educational gerontologists who run workshops to help people undertake the review in a more systematic manner. There are some similarities to *life history* methods.

life satisfaction A concept found in gerontological literature which refers to a cognitive assessment of one's progress towards desired life goals.

life sciences The biological and related sciences.

life skills Those *skills* necessary to live and interact successfully in the context of social living. Sometimes referred to as *coping skills*.

life style The way of life adopted by an individual, often related to socio-economic position.

life world A sociological/phenomenological concept employed in some theories of learning. It refers to a frame of reference, stock of *knowledge* etc. which provides meaning for an individual's aspirations and actions.

life writing A technique often used in education for the elderly, helping them recall experiences in their past for a variety of reasons, including that of recording for posterity. See *life review*.

lifelong education The proposition that *Education* should be a lifelong process was adopted by *Unesco* although it had been popularized in the early twentieth century by such adult education thinkers as *B. Yeaxlee* and *E. Lindeman*. There appear to be two approaches to lifelong education in contemporary literature: one that stretches *initial education* forward throughout the lifespan using the idea of *continuing education*, and the view of adult educators who seem merely to wish to add the theories of *initial education* to their own. Both approaches have a rather conservative perspective.

Lifelong Education, Assessment and Referral Network (LEARN) A network of the *Council for Adult and Experiential Learning* member institutions involved in developing and disseminating educational services for adults, including enhancing *access*, career guidance, educational planning, and assessment of experiential learning. The initial funding of this network was given from 1982 to 1987, when it was concluded with a number of publications in books, training manuals, and reports.

Lifelong Education Bibliography Published by the *Unesco Intitute for Education* and updated regularly.

lifelong learning The process of *learning* which occurs throughout life. The terms *lifelong education* and lifelong learning are often used interchangeably because there is a tendency to treat *education* and *learning* as synonymous concepts, which is imprecise.

Lifelong Learning A report by the Commission of Adult Education in Eire, published in 1983.

Lifelong Learning Act Title I, Part B of the Amendments to the Higher Education Act (Public Law 94–482) passed by the US Congress in October 1976 and generally known as the Lifelong Learning Act. It was never considered likely that the act would be implemented in the form in which it was passed although it is widely considered that the act made an impact on US legislation about *lifelong education* generally. See the *Mondale Act*.

Lifelong Learning: An Omnibus of Practice and Research Published eight times a year. The practitioners' journal of the *American Association of Adult and Continuing Education*. Discontinued in 1989. See *Lifelong Learning: The Adult Years*.

Lifelong Learning Forum A periodical newsletter issued occasionally by the Department of Adult Education, University of Georgia, USA.

Lifelong Learning Research Conference An annual research conference held at the University of Maryland, USA, each spring. It commenced in 1980. Proceedings published.

Lifelong Learning: The Adult Years Established in 1977, the practitioner journal of the *American Association of Adult and Continuing Education* and published eight times a year. Its name was changed in September 1983 to *Lifelong Learning: An Omnibus of Practice and Research*.

lifespan development The idea that throughout life there is a continual movement from one stage to another. See the work of *Jean Piaget, Lawrence Kohlburg*.

Ligue de l'Enseignement, La (The League for Teaching). Formed in 1866 in France with the aim of providing free education for all outside of the education system. Dissolved during the Second World War but re-established after the war, it was renamed *La Ligue Française de l'Enseignement et de l'Education Permanente* in 1967.

Ligue Française de l'Enseignement et de l'Education Permanente, La The name adopted by *La Ligue de l'Enseignement* in 1967, it has been a major proponent for a system of *popular education* in France. Current address: 3 rue Récamier, 75341 Paris Cedex 07, France.

Likert Scale Scale used in attitude measurement tests. It usually consists of a number of attitude statements with a five-point scale for each. Respondents are asked to indicate which, from 'strongly agree' to 'strongly disagree', approximates most closely their own feelings.

Limat Bedirhre Meserete Timihrt Journal established in 1983 in Ethiopia and published quarterly by the national literacy campaign. The title means 'Development through Post-Literacy'.

limited English-speaking ability Term used in America to refer to those whose proficiency in English is limited.

Lindeman, Eduard (1885–1953) One of the founding fathers of the *adult education* movement in the United States. He was author of the book *'The Meaning of Adult Education'* which is regarded as one of the milestones in the development of *adult education theory*. While he never held an academic position in adult education, he was professor of social work at Columbia University, where he was greatly influenced by the ideas of *John Dewey*. However, he also assumed something of a sociological perspective towards adult education. He was influenced by the Danish *folk high school* movement and was the first American theorist to use the term *andragogy*, in 1927.

Lindeman Center for Community Empowerment Through Education Centre involved in work with the urban poor to make the resources of higher education available to them, by assisting them in solving their own community problems while preserving the initiative of their local groups. Current address: Lindeman Center, Northern Illinois University, 188 W. Randolph, Suite 2817, Chicago, Illinois 60601, USA.

Lindop Report UK report on non-university *higher education* which also concerned itself with *access* courses for adults to this sector of higher education. It recommended multi–outlet *access* courses rather than specific courses in which educational institutions of higher education validate a specific access course and then guarantees admission to its own educational programme to successful students. The report was not totally enthusiastic about such developments in British higher education.

linear relationship In statistics this refers to a specific form of relationship between two variables.

Linga Established in 1976; a publication in the Central African Republic about *adult education.*

linguistic code See *language code.*

linguistic context The speech context within which a word or phrase is used.

linguistic philosophy A school of philosophy which concentrates upon the analysis of language. Not prevalent in the philosophy of adult education.

linguistics The scientific study of language and speech.

lip reading The ability to read and understand what a person is saying

without necessarily being able to hear the words. A skill taught to deaf people.

Listener, The A weekly magazine published since 1929 by the British Broadcasting Corporation which carries articles about serious broadcasts and texts of addresses, etc. It was initially conceived as an educational journal of sound broadcasting to reinforce and support broadcasts and, to a great extent, it still provides this function.

listening group A group of people organized to listen to radio or television programmes and discuss them afterwards. It is a method of mass education whereby the educators organize such groups throughout a country or region prior to the educational broadcasts.

listening skill The ability to listen carefully with insight and understanding. A skill taught to those involved in counselling.

literacy 1. The *Unesco* definition is that a person is *functionally literate* when he/she has acquired the knowledge and skills in reading and writing to enable him/her to engage effectively in all those activities in which literacy is normally assumed in his/her culture or group. 2. Commonly defined as a reading age of 9.5 years. 3. Five years of schooling. Clearly, whatever definition is adopted, it must be regarded as a relative concept.

Literacy – A Newsletter See *Adult Education Information Notes.*

Literacy Advance The quarterly magazine of *Laubach Literacy Action.*

literacy centre Centre which provides *non-school* children with opportunities in *basic education.*

literacy education The teaching of reading, writing, and social skills at a basic level. See *adult basic education.*

literacy test of written English (comp) A British test used in personnel selection and vocational guidance. Part of the National Institute of Industrial Psychology package of tests.

Literacy Volunteers of America
(LVA) Established in 1962, it operates many programmes in *adult literacy* which are supported with *volunteer* tutor training, management assistance, and the development of audio and visual materials. It also organizes national conferences. Current address: Widewaters 1, 5795 Widewaters Parkway, Syracuse, New York 13214, USA.

literary association Historical voluntary association, similar to *mechanics institutes*, although not necessarily as specifically geared to the working people. Offers a formalized education to adults.

literature 1. Written material. 2. The body of writing about a specific topic. See *literature review*.

literature review An overall assessment and analysis of the published research or writing in a specific area of study which is the focus of concern of a researcher or writer.

LITNET A national computer information system developed by the Federal *Adult Literacy Initiative* designed to increase communication among organizations and individuals involved in *adult literacy work*. Provides data and an information bulletin board. Address: The Adult Literacy Initiative, 400 Maryland Ave. SW Room 4145, FOB 6, Washington DC 20202, USA.

Litt.D. Doctor of Letters.

Litt.M. Master of Letters.

Liveright, Albert Alexander (1907–69) Leading American adult educator, director of the *Centre for the Study of Liberal Education for Adults* from 1957 until 1968, when the organization was closed. He then became professor of adult education at Syracuse University.

Livingstone, Sir Richard President of Corpus Christi College, University of Cambridge, and advocate of *residential colleges* for adults in the United Kingdom. He advocated the establishment of *people's high schools* as residential colleges in each *local education authority*, claiming that some subjects, such as *philosophy*, were best studied by adults. He was influenced by the *folk high school* movement in Denmark.

local authority advisor Formerly called a local authority inspector. Most *Local Education Authorities* in the United Kingdom employ a senior person to act as an advisor to practitioners in the field and to its own committees. There are advisors for *adult* and *further education* in most authorities.

Local Collaborative Projects UK *Manpower Services Commission* provision of funding, on a pump-priming basis, towards the establishment or continued development of local partnerships between employers and training providers to analyse employers' training *needs* and to develop the material necessary to respond to them. (Note: the *Manpower Services Commission* changed its name to the *Training Commission* and then to the *Training Agency* in 1988.)

Local Consultancy Grants to Employers (LCG) Companies may receive these grants towards two-thirds of the cost (to a stipulated maximum) of consultancy fees for the analysis of their training needs in respect of the introduction of new technology and improving business methods.

local development councils The *Russell Report* led to a movement to create local development councils for *adult education* in which representatives would be drawn from the major providing bodies, educational institutions, tutors, students, industry, and voluntary associations. Some *Local Education Authorities* started these but many fell into disuse, since the Report's recommendation of a *national development council* was not accepted by government. The *Advisory Council for Adult and Continuing Education* never achieved the status of a development council.

local education agency (LEA) 1. American term used to refer to agencies in specific localities to which educational services may be contracted. 2. In Federal legislation, the local education agency is a legally constituted board of education, or other educational authority.

Local Education Authority (LEA) In the United Kingdom education is controlled by local government, with each local area having its own authority in charge of education. A great deal of *adult education* is also controlled by these authorities.

Local Education Authority Training Grants Scheme (GRIST)/(LEATS) This scheme came into operation in England and Wales in 1987. In it local education authorities have to present their bids to the *Department of Education and Science* for funding for *in-service training* and this is broken down into national priority areas. Approval allows for the year's in-service expenditure to be claimed from the DES, subject to audit and arrears. This scheme was replaced by a similar one with a similar name in 1988 which became known as LEATS. In this latter instance Local Education Authorities receive training grants mainly on a per capita basis, within which national priorities are identified by the Department of Education and Science.

Local Employers Networks Groups of local employers, partially funded by the *Manpower Services Commission* to research their joint *training needs* and identify training programmes with appropriate *providers*. After the initial grant aid they are expected to become self-supporting. (Note: the *Manpower Services Commission* changed its name to the *Training Commission* and then to the *Training Agency* in 1988.)

Local Government Industrial Training Committee (LGITC) Since

the early 1980s most states in Australia have formed these committees, funded by national and local government in association with trade unions and professional bodies. There is also a federal Local Government Industrial Training Committee.

local history The historical study of a specific geographical area; a popular subject in *liberal adult education*.

local learning centre Centres situated in areas where adults go about their daily business, offering opportunities for them to have an initial analysis of their learning needs, advice, and guidance. It is, in essence, an *education shop*. The term was proposed by the *Advisory Council of Adult and Continuing Education* in the United Kingdom.

local school district A *local education agency* in the American system similar in some ways to the *Local Education Authority* in the British system.

Local Training Grants to Employers (LTG) A scheme in the United Kingdom in which employers are paid a grant to train existing employees or new recruits for hard-to-fill vacancies caused by such changes as new technology or the growth of new markets.

locals A term used by students of occupations to refer to those practitioners whose *reference group* tends to be members of the local employing agency. See also *cosmopolitans*.

Locke, John (1632–1704) English empirical philosopher who wrote about *education*. His *'Essay Concerning Human Understanding'*, which emphasizes *experience* in *learning*, is much neglected in *adult education* theory.

Lodewijk de Raet A foundation in Flanders, Belgium, established on 14 October 1952 to provide a wide variety of *adult education* programmes. It runs its own residential *folk high school* near Leuven and other non-residential ones throughout Belgium. Current address:

Stichting-Lodewijk de Raetn
Koördinatie, Liedsstraat 27–29, 1210
Brussels, Belgium.

logic Formal study in philosophy of the
principles of inference and proof. A form
of thought and reasoning based upon
deduction or induction.

logical operations The stage in
conceptual development which *Jean
Piaget* believed was reached in *young
adulthood*.

logical positivism A scientific approach
to the analysis of language to determine
its meaningfulness.

London and East Anglian Group A
group of three examining boards, East
Anglian, London Regional, and
University of London, which have been
grouped together to provide the *General
Certificate of Secondary Education*
examination and which provide *external
and mature* syllabuses. Current address:
The Lindens, Lexden Road, Colchester,
Essex CO3 3RL, UK.

**London Association for Continuing
Education** (LACE) An organization of
adult educators and administrators
concerned with all aspects of adult
education. Publishes its own newsletter.

**London Chamber of Commerce and
Industry** This organization has provided
some examinations in commerce subjects
in *further education* in the United
Kingdom.

London, Jack (d.1988) Well-known
American radical adult educator. He was
professor of adult education at the
University of California and wrote some
of the early studies in the sociology of
adult education.

London Working Men's College
Technically called the *Working Men's
College* but the prefix London is
included here to distinguish it from other
colleges that were started after its
formation. Established in 1854 at 31 Red
Lion Square by *F.D. Maurice* and the

Christian Socialists, this college quickly
gathered a group of the best-known
teachers of adults, including *John Ruskin,
D.G. Rossetti*, and many others. The
college sought to emphasize human
studies and, unlike many of the *mechanics
institutes*, it survived – but not without
many struggles.

long-term goal The predetermined
outcome of a course of study. See *aim*
and *short-term goal*.

long-term memory Once *information*
has been processed in a deep and
understanding manner, it is said to be
stored in the long-term *memory*, as
opposed to the *short-term memory*.

longitudinal study A research
technique that studies one or more
groups or categories over a period of
time. See *cross-sectional study*.

looking-glass self The American
sociologist, C.H. Cooley, first used this
term to refer to the type of *self-concept*
that emerges as a result of seeing oneself
as others do as a result of interaction.

Lorenzetto, Anna (b.1914) Professor of
adult education at the University of Rome
and a recognized expert on *adult literacy*.

low achiever One who underperforms.

low-income level A measure in the
United States below which people are
defined as being of low-income.

lyceum The lyceum movement was
started by *Josiah Holbrook* in
Massachusetts in 1826. They were
associations, normally town-based,
usually for working people, formed for
mutual improvement through the
acquisition of useful knowledge by
lecture, discussion, or any other
appropriate method. They were *self-help*
organizations in which members were
both learners and teachers. The
movement grew to such an extent that
there was a National American Lyceum
and over 3,500 lyceums in different
towns within a decade of the start of the

movement. By 1850 the national movement had disintegrated, although individual lyceums continued to function. The lyceum was originally called the *Society for Mutual Education* and later became known as the *Society for the Improvement of Schools and Diffusion of Useful Knowledge*. The latter name indicates that some of its members assumed a wider concern than adult education.

M.A. Master of Arts degree.

Maatschappil tot nut van't algemeen The Dutch *Society for Public Welfare* founded in 1784. From its earliest days it has been responsible for many initiatives in *non-formal adult education* and *community development*. It has nearly 200 branches through the Netherlands. Current address: Jan Nieuenhuizenplein 9, 1135 WT Edam, The Netherlands.

Macau The *adult education* association of Macau is the Associaçào de Educaçào Permanente de Macau. Current address: Rua Amizade, No. 23, 2F1, G.P.O. Box 3031, Macau.

machine learning The emulation of human knowledge–acquisition processes by digital computer systems. The significance of machines being able to learn from and control their environment has been a significant feature in engineering for many years. These systems have recently begun to appear in *adult education* studies. They are also significant in forms of *education* and *training*.

Mactavish, J.M. The successor to *Albert Mansbridge* as secretary to the *Workers Educational Association*. He had been a shipwright in Portsmouth who gave the celebrated speech on behalf of his class at the Oxford Extension Summer Meeting in 1907. He was involved in leading the WEA in the direction of closer work with the trade unions. He was secretary from 1915 to 1928.

M.Ad.Ed. Master of Adult Education degree awarded by the University of

Zimbabwe, as a result of courses run by the Department of Adult Education in the university. See also *B.Ad.Ed.*

maison de la culture French *community centre* in which a great deal of education for adults is conducted, although the activities of the centre are more broadly social and cultural and do also include children's activities.

major The main subject studied by a student at university in America is called the major subject.

major award A higher-value scholarship

major premise A term employed in logic to refer to the premise containing the major term.

Malaysian Association for Continuing Education Current address: 10000 Jalan Awan Dandan Taman Yarl, Klang Road, Kuala Lumpur, Malaysia.

Malian Association of Adult Information and Training Contact address, c/o CFAR – Union Nationale de Femmes du Mali, P.O. Box 1740, Bamako, Republic of Mali.

Malta, University of This university provides considerable *adult education* in its part-time evening courses, many of which lead to a recognized *diploma* of the university. The university also offers a part-time evening degree course. Current address: Office of the Registrar, University of Malta, Msida, Malta.

Man in Health A *mass campaign* launched by Tanzania's *Institute of Adult*

Education in *health education*, using *listening groups* and local radio.

management committee The group or committee responsible for an educational institution. The constitution of such a group in the United Kingdom consists of local councillors, students, staff, and a number of appointed or co-opted personnel. The functions may be advisory and are often managerial. It is the committee responsible for the efficient running of the organization and to which, in the first instance, the principal or head is accountable.

Management Development The *Manpower Services Commission* developed this scheme to support management education in two types of projects: development projects in which better methods of training and developing management are introduced, and in the introduction of a management development programme. (Note: the *Manpower Services Commission* changed its name to the *Training Commission* and then to the *Training Agency* in 1988).

management education Teaching the principles and practice of management. A wide-ranging and increasingly significant area of *continuing professional education* throughout the world.

managerial economist Term used in Norway to refer to a manager who has successfully completed the *management education* course organized by the *Norsk Korrespondanseskole* School of Management.

managing agent Agent approved by the *Manpower Services Commission* to run *youth training scheme* activities. (Note: the *Manpower Services Commission* changed its name to the *Training Commission* and then to the *Training Agency* in 1988).

Manchester monographs A series of books produced by the Department of Adult and Higher Education, University of Manchester, which have explored some important issues in *adult education*.

mandatory continuing education (MCE) The practice by which members of a profession are compelled to attend *continuing professional education* in order to retain the licence to practise. Usually the profession stipulates the extent of this obligation, e.g. at least one *refresher course* every five years. In America a large number of professions are introducing mandatory continuing education and some states enforce the regulation for those who wish to register to practise in that state.

mandatory grant In the United Kingdom, financial support that is paid to students by the local government as a result of central government regulations. There are few courses for which adults can obtain this, such as full-time undergraduate study and training in the teaching of adults at recognized educational institutions.

mandatory periodic refreshment See *mandatory continuing education*.

manifest function A consequence of the existence of a phenomenon that was intended and is recognized. See *latent function*.

manipulation 1. The management of people for ends other than those of their own choosing. 2. Physical dexterity.

Mannheim, Karl (1893–1947) Hungarian sociologist who settled in Britain. Professor of sociology and the philosophy of education, his main work was in the sociology of *knowledge* – an important area in the study of adult education.

Manniche, Peter (1889–1981) Danish *adult educator*. Founder of the *International People's College* in 1921 and its principal for 33 years.

manpower analysis The analysis of the characteristics of the workforce. Important in *manpower planning* and *needs analysis* in *continuing education* and *staff development*.

Manpower Development and Training Acts A series of federal laws passed in 1962, 1963, and 1965 in the United States that were designed to provide financial aid for *youth education and training*.

manpower planning Analysis of present and future *needs* in the structure of the workforce.

manpower program American term for a programme that combines *counselling, training* and *work experience* designed to place people in occupations.

Manpower Services Commission (MSC) Established under the Employment and Training Act of 1973 to run the public employment and training services. In 1988 it was renamed the *Training Commission* and then to the *Training Agency*. It was accountable to the Secretary of State for Employment in England and also to the Secretaries of State for Scotland and Wales. It was financed by grant from the Department of Employment which was responsible for overseeing its budget. The MSC was located at Moorfoot, Sheffield.

manpower studies The study of the supply and demand of the workforce. See also *manpower planning*.

Manpower Training and Development Act (1962) US federal legislation concerned with the provision of *retaining* for unemployed persons.

Mansbridge, Albert (1876–1952) Founder and first secretary of the *Workers Educational Association*. Born at Gloucester in 1876, the youngest of four sons of a carpenter. Apart from his work with the WEA, he was influential in many areas of adult education, including being involved in the foundation of the *British Institute of Adult Education*, the *World Association for Adult Education*, and others. He was also a member of the Adult Education Committee of the *Ministry of Reconstruction* which produced the famous *1919 Report*.

manual dexterity The ability to control and co-ordinate the physical body in relation to perception.

manual dexterity test An *examination* to investigate the extent of a person's *manual dexterity*.

manual training *Training* in *skills*.

Marcuse, Herbert (1898–1979) American Marxist philosopher and early *critical theorist* whose works have been subject to critical reappraisal recently although his work is significant in the realm of *critical theory*.

marginalization The exclusion of large sectors of the population from central and crucial areas of the economic and power positions of society. The concept can be used to refer to *disadvantaged* groups in organizations and to disadvantaged nations in the world as a whole. See *disadvantaged*.

MARIS (Materials and Resources Information Services) Set up in 1983 to provide a computerized database of *distance learning* materials. It is based at Bank House, 1 St Mary's Street, Ely, Cambs CB7 4ER and in Scotland at Dowanhill, 74 Victoria Crescent Road, Glasgow G12 6JN, UK.

MARISNET A national database within the *Manpower Service Commission*'s *Open Tech Programme* which enables educationalists and employers to call up the entire range of *distance learning* materials on adult vocational education. Access to other databases is open through this network and available by annual subscription. See *MARIS*. (Note: the *Manpower Services Commission* changed its name to the *Training Commission* and then to the *Training Agency* in 1988).

mark The grade given to a piece of work.

market research The process of identifying and assessing likely markets. This is a feature of the life of educational institutions which are expected to offer courses that will attract students. It is sometimes wrongly referred to as a form of *needs analysis*.

marketing The recognition that because a great deal of both *liberal* and *continuing education* is not compulsory the *providers* of education have to promote it among potential students. The underlying idea is that it should achieve a mutually satisfactory exchange of value in the marketplace of *education*. However, there are some advertising devices which should not be used in *continuing education* since they may well compromise the educational value of the courses advertised.

marking The process of assessing students' work. Note that marking may not entail grading, although it usually does. See also *analytical marking* and *global marking*.

marking scheme A set of notes that guides tutors (and students) about specific criteria for marking a piece of written (or other) academic work produced for *assessment*.

Martin, Everett Dean (1880–1941) Influential American liberal adult educator in the first half of the twentieth century. Director of the *People's Institute* in New York City from 1922 to 1934. Author of *'The Meaning of Liberal Adult Education'*, published in 1926 but perhaps not well known today.

Martin, George Currie (d.1938) A leader in the *adult school movement* during the early part of this century, from 1912 to 1930, president in 1932, and one of its foremost historians.

Marwick, William Hutton (d.1982) Scottish *adult educator*. He conducted the first *adult education* class for Edinburgh University in 1931, where he continued to teach until his retirement.

Marx, Karl (1818–83) Founder of modern Communism. Born in Trier in the Prussian Rhineland and educated at the universities of Bonn and Berlin, he

was a prolific scholar and writer. Exiled from Germany, he settled in England where he produced many of his greatest works. He did not write a great deal about the *education of adults*, although it has subsequntly been submitted to a great deal of Marxist analysis by scholars who have been influenced by his system of *radical* thought.

Marxism *Marx*'s thought has assumed a variety of forms, so that Marxism now refers to a variety of radical ideological systems that owe their origins to his work.

Maslow, A.H. (b.1908) Humanistic psychologist whose 'hierarchy of needs' and ideas of *self-actualization* have had considerable influence in the education of adults. His writings are concerned with the whole person, a feature which has attracted those in *adult education* with a humanistic perspective.

mass campaign An educational campaign designed to reach the masses, especially the rural poor, often using local radio and *listening groups*. See *Man in Health* for an example.

mass education The education of all the people in a population, or the education of a large group of people simultaneously.

mass media Media which convey *information* to large numbers of people at the same time. There have been many instances in which both *broadcasting* and *newspapers* have been used in the process of educating adults.

Massnahmen zur beruflichen und sozialen Eingliederung (MBSE) Programme for vocational and social integration for foreigners which is sponsored by the German Federal Institute for Work and local and state governments. It is a one-year *vocational education* programme in which migrants are expected to learn German, become acquainted with such areas of work as vocational preparation, and receive vocational guidance. This programme works in close harmony with *Sprachverband Deutsch für ausländische Arbeitnehmer* and is organized nationally.

masters degree in adult education
1. In the United Kingdom there are two forms of masters degree, both of which are awarded by different universities, and the *Council for National Academic Awards* – a taught masters and a research masters. The first is a higher taught degree while the second is a lower research degree. (In Oxford and Cambridge the masters degree (M.A.) is automatically awarded to those who graduate with good honours on application.) 2. In the United States the masters degree is a taught practitioners' degree.

mastery Demonstrated proficiency of specified *knowledge* or *skills*.

mastery learning A form of learning that entails the successful completion of the learning exercise for one part of the course before progression to the succeeding ones.

mastery test An examination designed to assess the extent to which the requisite *knowledge* or *skill* has been mastered.

matched groups In educational research it is sometimes useful to be able to match groups of people on all variables relevant to the research except the one being investigated.

matched sample Samples selected because they share the same characteristics relevant to the study.

matching funds System of aid in which a donor offers a matching amount of support if the educational institution can raise a related amount.

matching type questions A variant of the *multiple choice question* in which respondents are asked to match a given response, from a number of options, to a set question.

material self Concept introduced by William James which refers to aspects of

the *self-concept* which relate to material objects.

mathetics A term that *J. Roby Kidd* used to mean the study of students' behaviour in the learning process, which he contrasted with *pedagogy*, the study of the teacher's behaviour in teaching.

matna The Israeli centre for culture, youth and sports. These are located in many communities, and are *community centres*.

matriculation Passing to the end of school examinations, which enable the student to progress to university study.

matrix Usually a rectangular display of research results along two axes that facilitates the comparison of two variables.

Matthews, Sir James A *Workers' Education Association* district secretary and an active member of the *National Institute of Adult Continuing Education*. See *Sir James Matthews Memorial Trust*.

maturation The process of physiological and psychological change which occurs with ageing. See also *gerontology, educational gerontology, maturity*.

mature student 1. Any student who recommences education over the age of 21 years (formerly 23 years; in some authorities this later age is still assumed). A number of different categories have been identified: the delayed achiever; those who delayed enrolment until their financial circumstances allowed for it; women returners; those changing careers; those involved in some form of *continuing education*. 2. For adults sitting the *General Certificate of Secondary Education* examination, a mature student is one who is 17 years or older.

Mature Student's Union Established in 1975 to look after the interests of mature students in the United Kingdom.

maturity 1. Within the debate in *adult education*, the concept of *adult* has sometimes been defined in terms of maturity. E.g. a person is an adult when he/she reaches a certain age or is regarded as psychologically or socially mature by his/her fellows. 2. A condition of the highest development in areas of social and psychological relationships.

Maudsley Personality Inventory A psychological test designed to measure introversion–extroversion and the level of neuroticism. It is employed in some *adult education* research.

Maurice, Frederick Denison (1805–72) One of the leading theologians of the *Christian Socialist* movement and author of many books and articles. He held professorships at King's College, University of London, as professor of English literature in 1840 and theology in 1846 (from which he had been dismissed prior to his involvement with the *London Working Men's College*) and later at the University of Cambridge, as professor of moral philosophy. Maurice was the first principal of the *London Working Men's College* and one of its principal architects. His educational views can perhaps be summarized thus: education should liberate, inculcate a sense of divine order, and help create a sense of respect for the person.

M.B.A. Master of Business Administration, an increasingly sought-after degree in management.

McClelland, Donald (b.1917) American psychologist well known for his work on *achievement* and *needs* but less frequently cited than *A.H. Maslow*.

McClusky, Howard Yale (1900–82) First president of the *Adult Education Association of the USA* and a pioneer in American *adult education*. He was at the University of Michigan for 56 years, where he held many offices in the university and in national adult education. Additionally, he was the author of the First National Paper on *Educational Gerontology* for the *White House Conference on Aging* in 1971.

McCune Award The Donald McCune Award for Collaborative Efforts in Adult Education seeks to recognize the individual or group who has implemented a programme or created a product that has promoted collaboration in adult education. The award is sponsored by the *American Association of Adult and Continuing Education* and presented at the *AAACE* annual conference. There is also a state award in California in his memory.

McCune, Donald (d.1986) State director of *adult education* in California, where over the years he made a considerable contribution to the field of adult education, as the *awards* in his memory testify.

M.Ch. Masters degree in surgery. See *Ch.M.*

Mead, George Herbert (1863–1931) American social psychologist and founder of *interactionism*. His work centred around his theory of the mind and the *self*, important ideas in research into adult and children's *learning*.

mean Measure of central tendency. See *arithmetic mean*.

meaning–orientation An approach to *learning* in which the *learner* seeks to comprehend the whole meaning rather than just the facts.

meaning perspective *Jack Mezirow* defined this as the structure of psycho-cultural assumptions within which new experience is assimilated and transformed by one's past experience.

means test Process of assessing whether a student, or the student's family, earns sufficient income to pay the requisite fees for school, college, or university. This is now creeping into *adult education*, especially where there are reduced fees for pensioners or unemployed people.

Measure of English Language Proficiency (MALP) A written test of literacy, consisting of 26 questions which test the individual's ability to identify key words and phrases and match these with one of four fixed-choice alternatives.

mechanical ability The *skills* required to employ and diagnose reasons for malfunctioning of mechanical equipment.

mechanics institutes Organizations that began with the inspiration of *George Birkbeck* at the start of the nineteenth century, probably about 1823, in Glasgow in Scotland. *Birkbeck's* aim was to offer a scientific and mechanical education to working-class people. However, it might be claimed that they actually began in Glasgow in 1799 while he was still teaching in that city. The movement flourished in Britain in the first half of the century, although it is doubtful whether the movement was ever really working-class, since one of the reasons for the growth in some *mutual aid societies* was the failure of the mechanics institutes to cater for working people. They were, however, a worldwide movement, with institutes in Australia, Canada, New Zealand, and the United States. In America, the first were founded in Philadelphia in 1824 and in Boston in 1826. They were democratic institutions, offering lectures and reading facilities to their members. The movement declined in the second half of the nineteenth century.

Mechanics Institution Founded in London in 1817 by *Timothy Claxton* because he was unable to gain admission to a *philosophical society*. It predated the *mechanics institute* in London. Claxton's institution was a weekly discussion group at which members were expected to deliver in rotation a lecture on a subject for discussion. Lectures were to be delivered fortnightly.

mechanistic learning model The behavioural approach to *learning* in which the person is regarded as reactive, mechanistic, and passive, receiving and processing stimuli from without and reflecting it in the learning outcome.

M.Ed. Master of Education degree.

media The means of transmitting *information* to people, often the mass media since the *target audience* is as many people as possible.

media analysis Analysis of the aims, content, and methods of media presentations.

Media and Adult Learning Founded in 1979, this journal is published by Northern Illinois University, Dekalb, Illinois 60115–2866, USA.

media centre An area in an institution in which a full range of materials, equipment, and associated staff is available for those wishing to use either the equipment or the audio/video cassettes which have been collected.

media research As more attention is being paid to *learning* rather than *teaching* in *adult education*, so research into the educational role of the *media* is becoming increasingly prominent. Two areas seem to dominate at present: studies of how the media present *adult education*; and how they present *information* generally.

media university A *distance teaching* university.

median The mid-value in a *frequency distribution* in statistical research.

mediated instruction Teaching conducted through the *media* rather than direct *face-to-face* interaction.

mediated self-learning A form of *self-directed learning* in which guidance is provided as to mastering the information produced, e.g. a reading guide.

Medina, Lorenzo Luzuriaga y (1889–1959) A significant *adult educator* in Spain. He was head of publications in the Pedagogical Museum in Madrid, founder of the *'Revista de Pedagogia'* (Pedagogical Review), and author of one of the most influential books on the history of *adult education* in Spain.

Mediterranean Association of Adult Education Formed at a conference in Zaragoza, Spain in November 1984, this association links national adult education organizations around the Mediterranean.

Meeting in Finland An annual event started in 1970 in which the *Association of Finnish Adult Education Organizations* plans an international gathering of adult educators to discuss important political and educational concerns.

Meeting Special Educational Needs A report which concentrated upon the special *needs* experienced by *handicapped people*, and in which there was considerable reference to the needs of the *young adult*. The commission reported in 1978 and its findings are sometimes called the *Warnock Report*, after Mary Warnock, its chairperson.

Meiklejohn, Alexander (1872–1964) Born in Rochdale, England, his family emigrated to the United States while he was still very young. He became a social philosopher of education, convinced that education had to relate to real life. He was president of Amherst College from 1911 to 1923, but his views found disfavour with the board of trustees. He then became head of the *Experimental College* at Wisconsin and later director of the *San Francisco School of Social Studies*. He collaborated throughout much of his life with *John Walker Powell*.

membership group A group of people with which an individual identifies and by whom he is accepted as a member.

memorizing The process of committing to *memory*. A form of *rote learning*.

memory 1. The mental function of retaining information after having had an *experience*. 2. The storage system itself within the mind or brain. 3. The actual content of what is retained. There has been considerable research on memory and ageing which is significant to *educational gerontology*. See also *short-term, long-term, semantic,* and *episodic memory*.

memory span The number of items immediately reproducible after a presentation. The materials need to be of unrelated sets of symbols; otherwise coding systems will expand the measurement of the span.

mental ability Ability to think, often to think on one's feet.

mental ability test An examination of a person's general ability to adapt to new situations and to learn from experience.

mental coaching A technique employed by *Peuple et Culture* to assist people in developing the art of critical thought. It has three phases: a number of exercises to help participants express themselves; a number of exercises to practice in order to become more aware; and the recreation of the first phase with the implementation of the skills of the second.

mental disorder A form of abnormality or illness.

mentally retarded person People who have been classified as mentally subnormal or those who are significantly below average ability.

mentor One who advises. In adult education this is not normally the official teacher, but one who advises on how *skills* should be performed in the workplace. In the United Kingdom, mentorship has been suggested for the *ACSTT II* training of adult educators as the person who advises on and supervises teaching practice. Often the mentor is assumed to be the advocate as well.

meritocracy Term used to suggest that in any society the most able rise to the top of the social hierarchy.

metaphysics The study of human existence as a whole, as opposed to the natural sciences. Implicit in many theories of the education of adults is a metaphysic, but the *philosophy of adult education* has not yet been sufficiently developed for this subdiscipline of philosophy to hold a significant place in *adult education* theory. However, the religious and theological roots of much adult education in the West is becoming increasingly recognized in recent studies.

Metcalfe Memorial Lectures Frank Metcalfe was a leader of the *adult school movement* who died in 1929 at the age of 38. A memorial fund was established which led to five memorial lectures being delivered between 1930 and 1934.

method An established or systematic order of performing any act or procedure.

Methodist Study Centre The *distance education* centre of the Methodist Church in the United Kingdom. Current address: The Methodist Study Centre, Division of Ministries, 1 Central Buildings, Westminster SW1H 9NH, UK.

methodology 1. The study of methods of research. Often wrongly used to refer to the method of a particular piece of research. 2. Sometimes used to refer to courses in *teaching* methods, but only rarely since this is now often included with *curriculum studies*.

Mexico See *Instituto Nacional para la Educacíon de les Adultos; Unidad Nacional de Educación Basica para Adultos*.

Mexico Declaration Following an international conference sponsored by *Unesco* in Mexico in 1979, a declaration was published about the role of *education in development*.

Mezirow, Jack Professor of adult education at Teachers College, Columbia University, well known for his work on *learning theory*, especially *perspective transformation, reflectivity, emancipatory learning*. He has relied a great deal on the work of *Jürgen Habermas* to work out his ideas.

microbiology Branch of biology involving the study of micro-organisms.

micro-didactical work (mikro-didaktische Tatigkeiten) Term used in the Federal Republic of Germany to describe some of the special features of *adult education*: direct communication in small groups and *discussion* methods.

micro-teaching Literally a scaled-down approach to teaching e.g. teaching a very short lesson to a very small class of two or three, etc. It can last from 2 to 20 minutes but it provides practice in a situation which might not otherwise occur until teaching in a classroom. It provides opportunities to practise new and different skills in a safe environment.

middle adulthood The period in which a person finds him/herself as a member of the dominant generation, a senior member of work and the family. At the same time the early signs of physical decline become apparent. It is a period in which the *adult* has to reflect upon earlier choices.

Midland Examining Group A group of five examining boards (East Midland Regional, Oxford and Cambridge Schools, Southern Universities Joint Board, West Midlands, and University of Cambridge) which offers the *General Certificate of Secondary Education* with the *external and mature* syllabuses for adults. Current address: University of Cambridge Examinations Syndicate, 1 Hills Road, Cambridge, UK.

mid-life crisis The apparent psychological crisis that many people experience in early middle age which can result in depression or change of life style. It has also been associated with career change. This is one of the classical *life cycle transitions* and is a period of reassessment in life.

mid-life transition The period between 40 and 45 years when the *adult* passes from *early adulthood* to *middle adulthood*. It is sometimes called the *mid-life crisis*.

Midwest Research to Practice Conference Started in 1981 at the University of Northern Illinois, this is a regional annual conference of adult educators in the United States.

migrant education The form of education offered to immigrants on their arrival by some societies in order to accustom the immigrants to the culture of the host country. See *adult basic education, English as a second language*.

Mill, J.S. (1806–73) English philosopher who is important to the development of the theory of *adult education* since it was he who first maintained that education was important for *democracy*. He is also one of the major philosophers of *individualism* and *liberty*, concepts employed very frequently in *adult education* literature.

Millar, J.P.M. (b. 1893) General secretary of the *National Council of Labour Colleges* in England from 1923 and for the greater period of its existence. He was concerned that the labour colleges should be the educational division of the growing trade union movement.

Miners' Welfare National Educational Fund A fund which offers financial support in the United Kingdom in the coal industry and their families for educational purposes.

Ministère de la Communauté Française *Belgium* is divided into two cultures, French and Flemish, and this is the ministry responsible for the French peoples. (See *Ministerie van de Vlaams Gemeenschap*). It has a division for leisure and cultural education. Current address: Direction Générale de la Jeunesse et des Loisirs, Service de l'Animation et de la Diffusion Culturelles, Galerie Ravenstein 78, 1000 Brussels, Belgium. See also *Vlaams Centrum voor Volksontwikkeling*.

Ministerie van de Vlaams Gemeenschap The Belgian ministry responsible for the Flemish peoples in Belgium. Within it there is a department responsible for *adult education*. See also *Vlaams Centrum voor Volksontwikkeling*. Current address: Administratie voor

Onderwijs en permanente Vorming, Parociaanssttraat 15–23, 1000 Brussels, Belgium.

Ministry of Church and Education The government ministry in Norway responsible for *adult education*. There is a separate Department of Adult Education which was established in 1966 and which takes advice from the *State Council of Adult Education*. Current address: Kirke og undervisningsdepartementet, Avdeling for voksenopplaering og folkeopplysning, Fredensborgvn 24, Postboks 8119, Dep. 0032, Oslo 1, Norway.

Ministry of Defence School of Electronic Engineering Involved in teaching electrical and electronic engineering. Address: MOD School of Electronic Engineering, Arborfield, Near Reading, Berks, UK.

Ministry of Overseas Development The UK ministry responsible for funding *development* projects, including educational enterprises.

Ministry of Professional Training The ministry which has taken over responsibility for the education of *young adults* in France, having apparently similar functions to the *Manpower Services Commission* in the United Kingdom: education of young adults, training the unemployed, etc. Its work has been decentralized and there are 21 regions throughout France. (Note: the *Manpower Services Commission* changed its name to the *Training Commission* and then to the *Training Agency* in 1988.)

Ministry of Reconstruction Created in the United Kingdom at the end of the First World War to reconstruct the country after the war. It prepared a report on *adult education* which has become known as the *1919 Report*. See *Final Report of the Adult Education Committee of the Ministry of Reconstruction, 1919*.

minor award A lower-value scholarship.

minor subject For a student who is following more than one subject, that which occupies less time and is generally regarded as the second subject is often referred to as the minor subject.

mission A mission statement in the United States is a statement of an organization's purpose or aspirations.

Missouri Valley Adult Education Association Founded in 1938, the first regional adult education association in the United States. It covers the area of North and South Dakota, Nebraska, Kansas, Missouri, Iowa, and Minnesota.

mixed ability group Group of people who are not streamed for their ability. Sometimes there is confusion between ability and achievement within this context.

mixed ability teaching Teaching a group of people of different abilities simultaneously. Again, there is sometimes confusion between ability and achievement within this context.

mode The most common value in a *frequency distribution* in quantitative research.

model A diagrammatic presentation, or some other form of representation, of a *concept* or a *system*. Models are constructed for purposes of understanding or teaching. Every model, being a distillation of reality, is bound to be an oversimplification of it. This approach has been used a great deal in *adult education* literature.

model answer A prepared answer to a set question used as an example. If the question is an *open question* there are a variety of ways of responding to it; thus this approach has limitations as a *marking scheme* but is useful for revision purposes. It is used in some *correspondence courses*.

model learning *Learning* through *observing* and *imitating*.

modelling See *role modelling*.

modem A device that can be fixed to a computer to allow it to receive signals directly through the telephone system. Used increasingly in *distance education* courses using computers as the main means of producing courses and written assignments.

moderator 1. An individual who introduces and guides *discussion* and audience participation during a *panel, colloquy,* or *forum*. 2. A person who acts as advisor to an educational course team. That advisor may represent the body which is validating the course or making the award.

modernization A theory of *development*, largely emerging from Western societies, in which Third World countries are expected to follow the same stages of modernization as has the West. *Adult education* has a role in helping people learn how to introduce these ideas into the country. However, it may be questioned whether this is a development process and whether it is a role *adult education* ought to perform.

modular course A course comprising a selection of *modules* from which the *learner* can select as appropriate to his/her own learning *needs*.

modular instruction A component of a course of instruction, e.g. a *module*, when used in the context of methods of teaching.

module A self-contained unit of teaching and learning that can be used in combination with other units to build a course or courses. An advantage of the modular approach is that the same unit can be used in different courses.

Mondale Act The *Lifelong Learning Act* in America, sponsored by Senator Walter Mondale.

monism A philosophical theory that maintains that there is only one substance, so that the mind-body relationship is not regarded as a *dualism*.

monitor A person who keeps a check on a phenomenon. In the *Open University* in the United Kingdom, staff who are employed to check the teaching or marking of *course tutors'* work are referred to as monitors. They check for the level of *grading* and the amount of teaching that the tutors undertake in the comments that they make on students' scripts.

monotechnic Term used to indicate that a course or programme prepares people for only one occupation.

Monsanto Fund Established to execute the Monsanto Corporation's philanthropy, it contributes to a number of tax–exempt organizations including those in the field of *adult education*.

Montreal Mechanics Institute The first *mechanics institute* in Canada, founded in 1828 as the Montreal Mechanics Institution. The first few years were not very successful and it ceased to function in 1835. It was recommenced under a new name in 1840 and still exists today as the *Atwater Library of Montreal*.

moonlight school *Evening school* for the poor in the United States in the nineteenth century which was only held when the moon was full so that it would throw light on the trails and paths to enable those who came to learn to see their routes home.

moral development A stage theory which claims that people pass through six stages of moral development during their lifetime, with at least some of these being during adulthood. The theory has been developed by *Lawrence Kohlberg*, who extended the original research of *Jean Piaget*. Whether the stages are related to age or *experience* remains as yet an unresearched question.

moral education The consideration of moral ideas and practices. Sometimes this becomes the *teaching* of moral behaviour, which then approaches *indoctrination*.

moral philosophy The study of *ethics*, or moral *value*.

moral relativism The theory that there are no absolute *values* and that all values are relative.

mores The customs and *behaviour patterns* by which people live and to which *conformity* is expected.

Morocco Address of the official government agency on *adult education*: Département de l'Alphabétisation et de l'Education des Adultes, Ministère des Affaires Sociales, Avenue des Heros, Rabat, Morocco.

Morrill Land Grant Acts See *Land Grant Act* of 1862. A second act in 1890 authorized federal support for separate but equal institutions for blacks in American states, thus prohibiting racial integration. See *land grant universities*.

Morris, Henry (1899–1961) As Education Secretary for Cambridgeshire, he proposed in 1924 the creation of *village colleges* in which the college was to become the centre of the cultural life of the village in which child and adult were to be educated together. He was also concerned with their architecture and wrote about their design.

Mortensen, Ernst Gustav (1887–1966) Pioneer of *correspondence education* in Norway and founder of the Norwegian correspondence school.

motivate 1. To impel someone to act. 2. To function as a goal or incentive.

motivation The internal state or the intervening process that drives a person to act in a specific manner. There is a variety of slightly different interpretations, e.g. some postulate general arousal without any specific goals while other theorists claim that motivation is more specific.

motive The reason for acting in a specific manner. It may be conscious or unconscious.

motor skills Physical *skills*.

Mott Foundation (Charles Stewart) Foundation interested in making grants to local projects dealing with *basic skills* for youth. Current address: Charles Stewart Mott Foundation, Mott Foundation Building, Flint, Michigan 48502, USA.

Movimiento Brasileiro de Alfabetización de Adultos (MOBRAL) The Brazilian literacy crusade which started in 1970 and is funded by the state with tax-deductible support for business and industry. Current address: Rua da Alfandega, 214 andar, Rio de Janeiro 20.070/RJ, Brazil.

M.Sc. Master of Science degree.

M.Soc.Sc. Master of Social Science degree.

M.Tech. Master of Technology degree.

multi-cultural Education which considers more than one *culture*. This is very significant in the contemporary world.

multi-cultural education 1. A system of education which considers more than one *culture*. A preparation for the social, political, and economic realities that individuals experience in culturally diverse and complex societies. This is very significant in the contemporary world. 2. A system of education that allows for all ethnic groups within a society to celebrate and learn about their own cultures.

multi-disciplinary The use of more than one academic discipline but without integration of the disciplines (which would make it *inter-disciplinary*).

multi-ethnic The involvement of more than one ethnic group. See *multi-cultural*; however ethnicity and *culture* are not synonymous concepts.

multi-factor tests *Tests* endeavouring to measure a variety of *factors*.

Multi-Faith Resource Unit A resource centre to enable people of different religious and cultural backgrounds to learn about each others' faiths and customs. It concerns *adult religious education* in a *multi-cultural* society. Current address: 1 College Walk, Birmingham B29 6LE, UK.

multiple choice question A form of *examination* question in which the question is asked in the stem and a variety of answers are provided so that candidates can indicate which they consider to be correct. Advantages are in ease of marking but there are difficulties in setting exact questions. They are also open to the criticism that it is possible for candidates to guess at answers. See *objective test*.

multiple regression Statistical technique for analysing the relationship between *variables*.

multivariate analysis Analysis of several *factors* simultaneously. Both *dependent* and *independent variables* can be analysed in this way.

multiversity A concept now beginning to appear in which the differing functions of the university, including *teaching, pure and applied research*, and *service*, are all given emphasis.

Murikka Statement on Adult Education Statement made after a *Meeting in Finland* in 1979 when *adult educators* from 28 countries made a proclamation about the place of *adult education* in the contemporary world in which they saw the role of an adult educator as consciousness raising.

Murphy Report Published in Ireland in 1973, with an interim report in 1970, by the *Committee on Adult Education*. The reports were called *Adult Education in Ireland*.

museum A place in which objects of artistic, historical, archaeological, or scientific interest are exhibited. Frequently a place for *self-help* education but in recent years they have played a much more active role in *formal adult education*.

Museum Training Council An idea proposed in a report, *Museum Professional Training and Career Structure*, published in 1987.

Museums Association UK professional and *qualifying association*. Current address: 87 Charlotte Street, London W1P 2BX, UK.

mutual improvement societies Usually, small groups established on a *self-help* basis for the purpose of *adult education*, with the basic principle of the better educated helping the less well educated. The first mutual improvement societies were established in London towards the end of the seventeenth century and were middle class in origin. But during the period of their greatest popularity, in the nineteenth century, they were mostly working class in membership. They often met in members' homes but also in other premises, while they tended to be independent, there is some evidence of federations of societies. See also the *adult school movement* and the *working men's reading rooms*.

mutable self The *self* which is able to accommodate change and progress and respond to the freedom so engendered.

myth Cultural story conveying *historical* or *metaphysical* propositions. These stories often told the *world view* of a tribe of people. As the conditions of the tribe changed, so some of these stories were adapted to the new situations. Writing prevented this flexibility, but different accounts of the same story revealed how the myths were adapted.

Nabila Brier Award An award made to a woman adult educator in memory of *Nabila Brier*. The first award was made in October 1987.

Nabila Brier Fund Established in memory of *Nabila Brier* to assist in the forging of links between women educators in Arab-speaking countries and the remainder of the world. The fund is administered by the *International Council for Adult Education*.

Nadezhda K. Krupskaya Prize Established by the USSR in 1970 as a literacy prize and administered by *Unesco*.

Narodno Svenčilište A Yugoslav journal of *adult education* which is translated as *People's University*. It commenced in 1954 and was renamed *Obrazovanje odraslih* in 1959.

Narodnoe Obrazovanie A Russian journal founded in 1918 about the *education of adults*. The title means 'people's education'.

narrowcast A form of transmission of *information* to specifically targeted audiences through such media as cable television, etc.

National Academy for Adult Jewish Studies of the United Synagogue of America Current address: 155 Fifth Avenue, New York, NY 13206, USA.

National Academy of Education American association. Current address: 11 Dupont Circle NW, Suite 130, Washington DC 20036, USA.

National Adult Education Association The *adult education* association of Tanzania. Publishes the journal *Studies in Adult Education*. Current address: P.O. Box 7484 Dar es Salaam, Tanzania.

National Adult Education Association of Uganda Founded about 1980, this association seeks to bring together all who are working in the field of *adult education* in *Uganda*. Current address: P.O. Box 8174, Kampala, Uganda.

National Adult Education Centre (Xarunta Waxbarashada Dadka Waaweyn) The national centre for adult education in *Somalia*. Current address: P.O. Box 1032 Mogadishu, Somalia.

National Adult Education Clearinghouse This clearinghouse disseminates information about *professional preparation, curriculum, research*, and commercial and non-commercial materials useful to *adult educators*. Special areas include: *adult basic education, ageing, career education, competency-based education, international education*. Produces its own newsletter. Current address: Montclair State College, Upper Montclair, New Jersey 07043, USA.

National Adult Education Foundation (NAEF) Established by the *American Association for Adult and Continuing Education* in order to provide a funding base to support projects in the field of *continuing education*. Current address: 1112 16th Street NW, Suite 420, Washington DC 20035, USA.

National Adult Literacy Agency The literacy agency for the Republic of Ireland. Originally a subcommittee of *AONTAS*, in 1980 it became an independent body with a grant from the state. It is regarded as a voluntary agency which seeks to promote literacy through Ireland. Current address: 8 Gardiner Place, Dublin 1, Republic of Ireland.

National Adult Literacy Project (NALP) As a result of the *Secretary's Initiative on Adult Literacy* this 14-month project began in late 1983 in the United States to gather, analyse, and disseminate data on model literacy projects, to develop new forms of technical assistance to strengthen existing programmes, to design new ones, and to shape a priority research agenda.

National Adult School Organisation The association of *adult schools* which co-ordinates *self-help* study groups throughout the United Kingdom. See *National Adult School Union*. Current address: Norfolk House, Smallbrook, Queensway, Birmingham, UK.

National Adult School Union The name adopted by the *National Council of Adult School Unions* in 1914 and retained until 1982 when it became the *National Adult School Organisation*. See also *National Council for Adult School Associations*.

National Advisory Board for Local Education Authority Higher Education Established to advise the UK government about non-university *higher education* in England and Wales. Published an influential paper on *continuing education* in July 1984. The organization was disbanded in 1989 as a result of the reorganization of *higher education* in the United Kingdom.

National Advisory Council on Adult Education (NACAE) Established in 1966 as the *National Advisory Council on Adult Basic Education*, it is a presidential advisory council whose members are appointed by the president of the United States. It changed its title to the present one in 1970. The council consists of 15 members, including chair and vice-chair. It operates through committees and advises the Commissioner of Education on general regulations and policy in the *adult education* title in the act, and advises the Office of Education on policies and procedures governing the approval of state plans. The council is also empowered to review the administration and effectiveness of *adult education* programmes and sponsored work under the title of the act, and to report to the president. Current address: Suite 323, Pennsylvania Building, 425 13th Street, Washington DC 20004, USA.

National Advisory Council on Ageing Canadian national advisory council concerned with education about ageing. Current address: Jeanne Mance Building, Ottawa, Canada K1A OK9.

National Advisory Council on Bilingual Education (NACBE) Established in 1974 as an advisory committee to the Secretary of Education of the United States, who also appoints the members.

National Advisory Council on Career Education (NACCE) Official American council, established in 1974, whose members are appointed by the president to advise, prepare annual reports, and lobby on behalf of *career education*. Current address: Regional Office Building No. 3, Room 3100, 7th and D Streets, Washington DC 20202, USA.

National Advisory Council on Continuing Education (NACCE) Established in 1965 as a presidential advisory council whose membership is appointed by the president of the United States, as the *National Advisory Council on Extension and Continuing Education*. It changed its title in 1980 to the present one. It has the mandate to examine all federally funded *continuing education* and training programmes and to make recommendations that will aid the effectiveness of the funding and eliminate duplication. Current address: 200 L Street NW, Suite 560, Washington DC 20036, USA.

National Advisory Council on Ethnic Heritage Studies (NACEHS) Established in 1978 as an advisory committee to the Secretary of Education of the United States who also appoints the membership.

National Advisory Council on Extension and Continuing Education (NACECE) Official council whose members are appointed by the president of the United States to advise, prepare papers, provide an annual report, and lobby on behalf of *extension* and *continuing education*. It changed its title to *National Advisory Council on Continuing Education* as a result of legislation in 1980.

National Advisory Council on Indian Education (NACIE) Established in 1972 as a presidential advisory council whose membership is appointed by the president of the United States.

National Advisory Council on Radio in Education The first council in the United States to examine the place of educational broadcasting, sponsored by the *Carnegie Corporation* through the offices of the *American Association of Adult Education*.

National Advisory Council on Vocational Education (NACVE) Established in 1968 as a presidential advisory council whose membership is appointed by the president of the United States to advise, prepare annual reports, and lobby on behalf of *vocational education*. Current address: 425 13th Street NW, Washington DC 20004, USA.

National Advisory Council on Women's Educational Programs Official American council, established in 1974, whose members are appointed by the president to advise, prepare annual reports, lobby, and prepare policy papers on women's education. Current address: 1832 M Street NW, Suite 821, Washington DC 20036, USA.

National Affiliation for Literacy Advance American association concerned with *adult literacy*. Current address: 1011 Harrison Street, Syracuse, New York 13210, USA.

National Aging Policy Study Center on Education, Leisure and Continuing Opportunities for Older People Established in the United States by the *National Council on Aging,* this centre is a focal point for the study of policy on the elderly. Current address: c/o National Council on Aging, 1828 L Street NW, Washington DC 20036, USA.

National Agricultural Center for Advanced Study Located at the University of Wisconsin, this is a national resource for research and development for the *Cooperative Extension Service*. It is also involved in *professional training* of workers in the field.

National Alliance of Business Independent non-profit, business-orientated organization which seeks to improve educational, training, and job opportunities for the *disadvantaged, disabled*, and displaced. Current address: 1015 15th Street NW, Suite 500, Washington DC 20005, USA.

National Alliance of Voluntary Learning Formed in 1979 by *adult educators* concerned with *continuing professional education* to provide a collective voice for those who want to emphasize the voluntary nature of *continuing professional education*. Current address: Faculty of Adult Education, Northern Illinois University, DeKalb, Illinois 60115, USA.

National Assessment of Educational Progress (NAEP) This US association receives federal support for a variety of work with adults, including studies of *literacy* among *young adults*. Current address: NAEP Educational Testing Service, CN6710, Rosendale Road, Princeton, New Jersey 08541–6710, USA.

National Association and Council of Business Schools Formed in 1912 to promote business schools, it assumed a role of raising standards in private business schools and established the Accrediting Commission for Business Schools.

National Association for Adult Education of China Current address: 37 Da Mu Chang Hu Tong, Beijing, People's Republic of China.

National Association for Human Development An American association for human development. Current address: 1750 Pennsylvania Avenue NW, Washington DC 20006, USA.

National Association for Industry–Education Cooperation American association concerned to foster this co-operation. Current address: 235 Hendriks Boulevard, Buffalo, New York 14226, USA.

National Association for Public Continuing and Adult Education (NAPCAE) One of the organizations which merged with the *Adult Education Association of the United States of America* in 1982 to form the *American Association for Adult and Continuing Education*. Its history is closely related to that of the *National Education Association*.

National Association for the Care and Resettlement of Offenders (NACRO) Established in the United Kingdom in 1966, this is a voluntary agency established to care for those who have left prison. Current address: 125 Kennington Park Road, London SE11 4JJ, UK.

National Association for the Development of Distance Education Swedish association established in Stockholm in 1984 to provide a forum for the exchange of ideas about *distance education*.

National Association for the Education of Young Adults (Landelijke vereniging VJV) The Dutch national association for youth education.

Current address: Mariahoek 1a, 3511 LD Utrecht, The Netherlands.

National Association for the Teaching of English as a Second Language to Adults (NATESLA) Founded in February 1978 in the United Kingdom, this association aims to advance the education of UK residents whose first language is not English by helping organizers and teachers share their experiences and expertise in this area. The association publishes a newsletter and organizes an annual conference. Current address: Fairfield House, 1 Broomfield Road, Sheffield S10 2DN, UK.

National Association for Total Education Sri Lankan association for *lifelong education*, publishes the journal *Adult Education, Development and Peace*. Current address: 176/22 Thimbirigasaya Road, Colombo 5, Sri Lanka.

National Association of Accountants Professional Association. Current address: 919 Third Ave, New York, New York 10022, USA.

National Association of Adult Education See *AONTAS*. Current address: 14 Fitzwilliam Place, Dublin 2, Republic of Ireland.

National Association of Adult Educators The national association in Fiji. Current address: P.O. Box 2448, Suva, Fiji.

National Association of Black Adult Educators American *adult education* association. Current address: 1411 K Street, Room 930, Washington DC 20005, USA.

National Association of Community Action Agencies Current address: 1411 K Street NW, Washington DC 20005, USA.

National Association of County Agricultural Agents National association of *extension agents* working in agricultural extension. Current address:

203 West Nueva, Room 310, San Antonio, Texas 78207, USA.

National Association of County Home Demonstration Agents
National association of all *extension workers* working in the sphere of home and family life.

National Association of Development Education Centres
(NADEC) Established in London in 1979 by the *development education* centres in the United Kingdom to encourage mutual support for those involved in *development education*, to assist and advise existing groups, to provide through a newsletter relevant information, to organize meetings, to lobby politically, and to provide means for members to communicate with each other. Current address: 6 Endsleigh Street, London WC1H 0DX, UK.

National Association of Educational Broadcasters An American specialist professional association established in 1925 which serves as a trade association for its Institutional membership. Current address: 1771 N Street NW, Washington DC, USA.

National Association of Educational Guidance Services for Adults
(NAEGS) Throughout the United Kingdom *guidance* services have been organized. A national association was formed in 1982 with the aims of encouraging the formation of such services and assisting their maintenance and development. It also offers help and advice to *adult educators* who are considering establishing such a service and publishes a directory of *educational guidance* services. Address: c/o ECCTIS Sherwood House, Sherwood Drive, Bletchley, Milton Keynes, MK3 6HW, UK.

National Association of 4-H Club Agents National association for extension agents working in the area of the *4-H Club*

National Association of Kominkan
(Zenkoku Kominkan Rengokai) The

Japanese association which co-ordinates the work of the *kominkan*. Current address: Toranomon 1–17–1, Minatu-ku, Tokyo 105, Japan.

National Association of Local Centres for Liberal Adult Education
(Landelijk beraad van plaatselijk vormingswerk) The Dutch federation for local *liberal adult education*. Current address: Burg. Loeffplein, 24, 5211 RZ Den Bosch, The Netherlands.

National Association of Mental Health UK voluntary association which seeks to improve conditions for the mentally disabled. Current address: 39 Queen Anne Street, London W1M 6HY, UK.

National Association of Public School Adult Educators American professional association.

National Association of State Judicial Educators (NASJE) An American association for judicial education which holds an annual conference, publishes a newsletter (started in 1986), and acts as a clearinghouse for those within each state who are involved in *continuing education* for the judicial profession, i.e. state judicial education officers. This association works closely with the state Justice Institute, which is currently assisting in the funding of its newsletter. Current address: c/o National Center for State Courts, 300 Newport Avenue, Williamsburg, Virginia 23187–8798, USA.

National Association of State Universities and Land Grant Colleges
(NASULGC) Established in 1908, this association is based in Washington and makes direct budget requests on behalf of *cooperative extension* to the Office of Management and Budget. Address: One Dupont Circle, Suite 710, Washington DC 20036, USA.

National Association of Teachers in Further and Higher Education A professional association representing teachers in all non-university *post-compulsory education*. It incorporates the *Association of Adult and Continuing Education*. It also acts as a trade union of these teachers in the United Kingdom. Current address: 27 Britannia Street, London WC1X 9JP, UK.

National Association of Trade and Technical Schools National American association with concerns in *adult education*. Current address: 2021 L Street NW, Washington DC 20036, USA.

National Association of Women's Clubs Co-ordinates women's clubs' activities in the United Kingdom. Current address: 5 Vernon Rise, Kings Cross Road, London WC1X 9EP, UK.

National Association of Youth and Community Education Officers A professional association of youth and community education officers in the United Kingdom. Current address: 19 Thorpe Park Road, Peterborough PE3 6LG, UK.

National Awareness Campaign Launched by the *Manpower Services Commission* in the United Kingdom in November 1984 to make employers more aware of the need for *training* and therefore to invest more finance and time in this aspect of employment. It was not generally considered to be a successful campaign. (Note: the *Manpower Services Commission* changed its name to the *Training Commission* and then to the *Training Agency* in 1988).

National Book League UK body established to promote the use and publication of books. Current address: 7 Albemarle Street, London W1X 4BB, UK.

National Bureau for Handicapped Students Concerned with students with *special learning needs* and involved in educational projects as well as advice-giving. Current address: 336 Brixton Road, London SW9 7AA, UK.

National Business Education Association US association to promote business education. Current address: 1904 Association Drive, Reston Virginia 22091, USA.

National Catholic Adult Education Commission Established in June 1958 by the Roman Catholic Church in the United States.

National Catholic Educational Association Established in 1904 in the United States. Current address: 1077 30th Street NW, Washington DC, USA.

National Center Clearinghouse This centre has three functions: to identify *vocational education* improvement projects, to maintain a data base for *vocational education* curriculum materials; and to record innovations in military education, especially those which might be transferable to wider areas of education. Current address: c/o National Center for Research in Vocational Education, 1960 Kenny Road, Columbus, Ohio 43210, USA.

National Center for Career Life Planning A *clearinghouse* of the *American Management Association*. Current address: American Management Association, 135 West 50th Street, New York, New York 10020, USA.

National Center for Community Education Address: 1017 Avon Street, Flint, Michigan 48503, USA.

National Center for Educational Brokering A *clearinghouse* for those involved in *educational guidance* and *counselling* in the United States. It was established on 1 January 1976 to promote educational brokering through technical assistance, publications, policy studies, and recommendations. It also publishes its own free monthly bulletin. Current address: 1211 Connecticut Avenue NW, Suite 400, Washington DC 20036, USA.

National Center for Educational Statistics American federal body, part of the US Dept of Education, which is involved in the collection of all educational statistics. It undertakes surveys and publishes reports. Current address: US Department of Education, Washington DC, USA.

National Center for Leadership Development in Adult and Continuing Education A centre funded by the *Kellogg Foundation* at the University of Georgia with an aim of developing more effective leadership in the field of *continuing professional education*. Current address: University of Georgia, Athens, Georgia 30602, USA.

National Center for Public Service Internships American *clearinghouse* concerned with *internship* in *professional education*. Current address: 1735 I Street NW, Suite 601, Washington DC 20006, USA.

National Center for Research in Vocational Education Based at Ohio State University, it sees its mission as helping to increase the ability of diverse agencies, institutions, and organizations to solve educational problems relating to individual career planning, preparation, and progression. It generates research, develops educational programmes, evaluates individual needs, provides information services, and conducts leadership programmes. The *ERIC Clearinghouse on Adult, Career and Vocational Education* is part of this organization. Current address: Ohio State University, 1960 Kenny Road, Columbus, Ohio 43210–1090, USA.

National Center for Voluntary Action American *clearinghouse*. Current address: 1785 Massachusetts Avenue, Washington DC 20036, USA.

National Centre for Developments in Nurse Education UK centre established in Sheffield. See *English National Board Learning Resources Unit*.

National Centre for Industrial Language Training Funded by the *Manpower Services Commission* until 1987, it provides English lessons for ethnic minority workers. Current address: Havelock Centre, Havelock Road, Southall, Middlesex UB2 4NZ, UK. (Note: the *Manpower Services Commission* changed its name to the *Training Commission* and then to the *Training Agency* in 1988).

National Centre for Popular and Adult Education (Udviklingscentret for folkeoplysning og voksenundervisning) A *documentation centre* established in Copenhagen by the Danish government in 1985 to monitor and record all *adult* and *popular education* innovations in Denmark. It is to make recommendations to the Danish government about revising the *Danish Voluntary Education Act* of 1968. Current address: Copenhagen, Denmark.

National Centre for Teaching Materials (Landscentralen for undervisningsmidler) A national centre in Denmark which purchases, prepares, and lends teaching materials to teachers. It works in conjunction with county centres (14 of them throughout the country). All teachers may use these facilities, including teachers of adults.

National Centre for the Development of Broadcast Education A Japanese national institution under the jurisdiction of the Ministry of Education and used by all the Japanese universities. It has staff with the expertise to prepare radio and television educational broadcasts and also prepares material for the *Japanese University of the Air*. This centre also has a research function. It is located on the same site as the *Japanese University of the Air*.

National Certificate in Training and Extension (NCTE) The certificate awarded to *adult educators* who have completed their training at one of the four residential adult education training centres in Zimbabwe.

National Childbirth Trust A voluntary educational organization in the United Kingdom offering education in parenthood. Current address: 9

Queensborough Terrace, London W2 3TB, UK.

National Christian Education Council A UK council involved in religious education in the Christian churches. Has an adult unit. Current address: Robert Denholm House, Nutfield, Redhill, Surrey RH1 4HW, UK.

National Clearinghouse for Commuter Programs Current address: 1195 Student Union Building, University of Maryland, College Park, Maryland 20742, USA.

National Clearinghouse on Aging American *clearinghouse*. Current address: Administration on Aging, Department of Health, Education and Welfare, HEW North Building, 330 Independence Avenue SW, Washington DC 20201, USA.

National Coalition for Instructional Telecommunications American coalition of those involved in this form of *educational technology* and *distance education*. Current address: Nova University, 3301 College Avenue, Fort Lauderdale, Florida, USA.

National College of Education Established in 1886. One of the oldest *teacher education* colleges in the United States, this college now offers degrees in *adult education* on a number of campuses throughout America.

National College of Juvenile and Family Law A national college situated in Reno. It provides *judicial education* and has an extensive law library. Current address: Judicial College, University of Nevada-Reno, Reno, Nevada 89507, USA.

National Commission on Accrediting US body concerned with the *accreditation* of colleges and universities. Current address: One Dupont Circle, Washington DC 20036, USA.

National Commission on Cooperative Education *Co-operative*

education has been developed fairly widely in the United States and this national body provides a forum for those engaged in it. Current address: 360 Huntington Avenue, Boston, Massachusetts 02115, USA.

National Commission on Libraries and Information Science American association concerned with *adult education*. Current address: 1717 K Street NW, Suite 601, Washington DC 20037, USA.

National Commission on Vocational Education Established in 1913 to investigate the desirability of federal aid for *vocational education* in the United States. In 1917 it strongly recommended that funds should be granted to establish a nationwide system.

National Committee on Education by Radio A pressure group that existed in the 1930s in America to try to ensure that educational interests were considered within the framework of commercial broadcasting in America. It was not very successful. Perhaps its only success was the establishment of the Federal Radio Education Committee.

National Community Education Association Founded in Michigan in 1966 to advance and support community involvement in public education, it is a non-profit membership association advocating *community education* in the United States. It also advocates that the community's resources should be more equally divided and that there should be democratic participation in the decision-making processes about the use of resources. Publishes a newspaper, *Today* or *Community Education Today*, a journal, *Community Educational Journal*, and a variety of other books. Current address: 119 North Payne Street, Alexandria, Virginia 22314, USA.

National Community Education Day Sponsored by the *National Community Education Association* and other organizations, this was inaugurated in 1982 but was not so designated until

1986. It is one day set aside during American Education Week to recognize and celebrate strong relationships between schools, colleges, and the communities that they serve.

National Computing Centre Threshold Scheme The *Manpower Services Commission* supports training in computer skills for 17–19 year-olds in a scheme operated by the National Computing Centre for training linked to work placement. (Note: the *Manpower Services Commission* changed its name to the *Training Commission* and then to the *Training Agency* in 1988).

National Confederation of Parent–Teacher Associations UK body founded in 1956 linking parent–teacher associations in children's schools. It has also been involved in some educational work with parents.

National Congress of Mothers Established by Phoebe Hirst and Alice Birney in 1897 with a number of aims, one of them being *parent education*. Later this became the *National Congress of Parents and Teachers*.

National Congress of Parents and Teachers See *National Congress of Mothers*. Current address: 700 North Rush Street, Chicago, Illinois 60611, USA.

National Consumer Project A national scheme in the 1970s in the United Kingdom for *consumer education*, utilizing local study groups. It was jointly sponsored by *Workers' Educational Association*, the National Federation of Consumer Groups, and the Education Departments of the *Trades Union Congress* and the *Co-operative Society*.

National Convention for Integrated Lifelong Education Japanese society established to study a wide variety of aspects of Japanese life and education and their interrelatedness.

National Co-operative Education Association The Co-operative

Association is widespread throughout the United Kingdom and has a long history of *adult education* activities, including organizing the *Co-operative College*. Current address: Stanford Hall, Loughborough, LE12 5QR, UK.

National Co-ordinating Body on Adult and Continuing Education The Dutch co-ordinating body. See *Coördinatiegroep projecten volwasseneneduucatie*.

National Council for Adult Education Renamed the *New Zealand Association for Continuing and Community Education* in 1988.

National Council for Educational Awards The national council in the Republic of Ireland that approves and validates educational courses.

National Council for Educational Technology Established in 1967 and later in 1973 to become the *Council for Educational Technology*.

National Council for Technological Awards (NCTA) See *Council for National Academic Awards*.

National Council for Vocational Qualifications Established in October 1986 following a government review of vocational qualifications. The formation of this council was announced in a White Paper, *Working Together*. The aims of the council are to provide a clear framework of vocational qualifications based on standards of *competency* agreed by industry. The council will operate in the whole of the United Kingdom, except Scotland (where separate arrangements exist). The council is initially funded by grant aid but intended to be financially self-supporting by 1990–91. Current address: 222 Euston Road, London NW1 2BZ, UK.

National Council for Voluntary Organizations Many voluntary organizations engage in *adult education* activities, and this is the co-ordinating body in the United Kingdom. It aims to extend the involvement of voluntary organizations in social issues and to act as a *resource centre* for their activities. Current address: 26 Bedford Square, London WC1B 3HU, UK.

National Council of Adult School Associations Started in Leicester in 1899 to advance *adult schools* in Britain and to co-ordinate the work of the local associations. The title was changed in 1907 to *National Council of Adult School Unions*.

National Council of Adult School Unions The association of the *adult school movement* bore this title from 1907 until 1914 when it became the *National Adult School Union*. See also *National Council for Adult School Associations*.

National Council of Aging An American council concerned with professionals and *volunteers* who work with matters affecting older people. Current address: 600 Maryland Avenue SW, West Wing 100, Washington DC 20024, USA.

National Council of Churches in Christ in the USA This council is concerned with *adult education* within the churches. Current address: 475 Riverside Drive, Room 866, New York, New York 10027, USA.

National Council of Educational Opportunity Associations Current address: 1126 16th Street NW, Washington DC, USA.

National Council of Labour Colleges Established in 1921 to co-ordinate the *labour college movement* which grew after the First World War, but which was the result of the break-away from *Ruskin College*. (See the *Central Labour College*.) It sustained the radical labour education movement in the inter-war years but was terminated in 1964 when it merged with the *Workers' Education Trade Union Committee*, with which it had disagreed throughout the inter-war period, to form the *Trades Union Congress Education Service*. One of its great contributions to

adult education was the introduction of correspondence courses in 1923. Perhaps the best-known person within this movement was its general secretary, *J.P.M. Millar*, for nearly the whole period of its existence.

National Council of Negro Women Current address: 1346 Connecticut Avenue NW, Washington DC 20036, USA.

National Council of Senior Citizens Current address: 1511 K Street NW, Washington DC 20005, USA.

National Council of State Directors of Adult Education Current address: 1201 16th Street NW, Suite 429, Washington DC 20036, USA.

National Council of Technical Schools Established to monitor standards in technical schools in America but was incorporated into the Engineering Council for Professional Development.

National Council of Urban Administrators of Adult Education American council. Current address: 1201 16th Street NW, Suite 429, Washington DC 20036, USA.

National Council of Voluntary Literacy Schemes Established in 1977 to co-ordinate the voluntary work undertaken in literacy in the United Kingdom.

National Council on Adult Jewish Education American council concerned with *adult education* among Jews in America. Current address: 114 Fifth Avenue, New York NY 10011, USA.

National Council on Aging Current address: 1828 L Street NW, Washington DC 20036, USA.

National Council on Community Services and Continuing Education Current address: One Dupont Circle NW, Suite 410, Washington DC 20036, USA.

National Council on Community Services for Community and Junior Colleges Current address: One Dupont Circle NW, Suite 410, Washington DC 20036, USA.

National Council on Women and Development Ghana government council involved in women's education. Current address: P.O. Box M.53, Accra, Ghana.

National Department of Education Established in 1867 in the United States, it is now known as the *United States Department of Education*. However, the first known government involvement in *adult education* provision occurred in 1777 when money was spent to provide mathematics teaching to soldiers.

national development council The *Russell Report* proposed that such a council should be established in the United Kingdom for *adult education*, but the UK government established only the *Adult and Continuing Education Advisory Council*. See also *Unit for the Development of Adult Continuing Education*.

National Distance Education University Established in Bangladesh in 1986, this *distance learning university* seeks to provide access to *higher education* for *mature students* who did not enrol in university during their youth. It seeks to use material produced in Bangladesh, but also courses made in other *distance teaching universities*. It takes a maximum of 2,000 students and has two sessions per annum. Current address: Kabil Mansion, Shaheb Bazar, Malopara, G.P.O. Rajshahi, Bangladesh.

National Distance Learning Centre (NDLC) Established by the *Open College* for those who require distance tuition and have not access to an *open access centre*. The centre has been established under a contract with the *Open University*. Current address: Parsifal College, Finchley Road, London NW3 7BG, UK.

National Education Association Established in 1857 as the National

Teachers Association, it merged with other associations in 1870 and adopted its present name. It never assumed a major adult educational role until its involvement in *immigrant education* in 1921. (See *Americanization education*). Its Department of Adult Education in 1924 became involved in the formation of the *American Association of Adult Education*. The department was merged in the *Adult Education Association of the United States of America* in 1951. A Division of Adult Education Service was also established in 1945. Current address: 1201 16th Street NW, Washington DC, USA.

National Education Association Today Special annual journal of the *National Education Association*.

National Education Crisis Committee Established in South Africa in 1986, reconstituted from the Soweto Parents' Crisis Committee, to try to introduce education for blacks through the *night school* movement that would be liberating. See *People's Education for People's Power*.

National Educational Association for the YMCA and YWCA An *educational association* for the organization of *study circles* in Sweden, established in 1929.

National Educational Guidance Initiative This initiative is jointly funded by the *Training Commission* and the *Department of Education and Science* in the United Kingdom to provide information, advisory, and consultancy services to *Local Education Authorities* to help them develop local networks for *educational guidance*. Contact address: c/o UDACE, Christopher House, 94b London Road, Leicester LE2 0QS, UK.

National Educational Television Current address: 10 Columbus Circle, New York, New York 10019, USA.

National Endowment for the Humanities This organization has intervened in a number of ways in American public life. It initiated voluntary state councils for the public to discuss national issues and in 1976 started the *American Issues Forums*.

National Extension Centre for Trades Union Education Opened in October 1984 in London, it has become the centre for much trade union education, although most still occurs in local regions in the United Kingdom.

National Extension College (NEC) Founded in 1963 by Michael Young and Brian Jackson with four aims: to provide a second chance for adults; to use *correspondence tuition* and *educational broadcasting*; to be involved in developmental projects; and to assist with Third World *development*. Initially it had a difficult time establishing itself but with the development of *flexi-study* in which local *colleges of further education* co-operated with the NEC, it has assumed a significant place in the development of the education of adults in England. It has also assumed an international dimension. It sells educational material and liaises with other educational institutions to produce some of its educational programmes. Current address: 18 Brooklands Ave, Cambridge CB2 2HN, UK.

National Extension Homemakers Council Current address: Route One, Box 129, Bunker Hill, Indiana 46914, USA.

National Farm Radio Forum Started in 1939 as one of the methods by which the *Canadian Association of Adult Education* encouraged citizen involvement in Canadian life. See *Farm Radio Forum*.

National Federation of Adult Education Associations In Sweden there are a number of *adult education associations*. See *Folksbildningsförbundet*.

National Federation of Community Organizations This organization seeks to draw together neighbourhood groups in the United Kingdom concerned with the improvement of community life. It provides a support service for local

community groups and publishes its own magazine, *'Community'*. Current address: 8–9 Upper Islington Street, London N1 0PQ, UK.

National Federation of Settlements Established in 1911 to co-ordinate the work of *university settlements* in the USA.

National Federation of Social Education A professional association for *adult education* in Japan. Publishes the monthly magazine, *Shakai Kyoiku*. Current address: c/o The National Education Centre, 3–2–3 Kasumigaseki, Chiyoda–ku, Tokyo 100, Japan.

National Federation of Voluntary Literacy Schemes Association of non-statutory bodies in the United Kingdom involved in *adult basic education*. Current address: 131 Camberwell Road, London SE5 0HF, UK.

National Federation of Women's Institutes A voluntary federation of *Women's Institutes* which is involved in a variety of educational enterprises. It trains many of its own leaders in *adult education*, especially *Stage I*, and has its own college, *Denman College*. Current address: 39 Eccleston Street, London SW1W 9NT, UK.

National Foundation for Adult Education Started in 1946 it changed its name when it merged with the *British Institute for Adult Education* in 1949 to become the *National Institute of Adult Education*. Its first and only secretary was Edward Hutchinson. It published a newsletter, *Foundation Papers*.

National Foundation for Educational Research in England and Wales Non-statutory research body, more concerned with *initial education* than with *adult education* although it has undertaken some research and publishing in this field. Current address: The Mere, Upton Park, Slough, Berks SL1 2DQ, UK.

National Foundation for the Education of Youngsters and Adults (EDUCAR) The Brazilian adult education association. Current address: SCLRN 704/705, Bloco H, Lojas 33/43, 70730 Brasilia, Brazil.

National 4-H Club US Association of *4-H Clubs*. Current address: 7100 Connecticut Avenue, Washington DC 20015, USA.

National Governors' Association Task Force on Adult Literacy The National Governors Association established a task force on *adult literacy* as part of its 'Making America Work' programme. (There were five other task forces on Jobs, Growth and Competitiveness, Welfare Prevention, Teen Pregnancy, School Dropouts, and Alcohol and Drug Abuse.) Its first meeting was held in Kansas City in February 1987. Current address: NGA, 444 N Capitol Street NE, Washington DC 20001, USA.

National Home Study Council Established in the United States in 1926 to raise the standards of private *correspondence colleges*, it created an accrediting commission of *correspondence colleges* in 1956. Current address: 1601 18th Street NW, Washington DC 20009, USA.

National Home Study Council News The newsletter of the *National Home Study Council*, published twice a year. Most of the subjects covered are about *correspondence education*.

National Indian Education Association Founded in 1976, this is the national *adult education* association of North American Indians, established to promote, support, and work towards the improvement of the North American Indians. Educational work with minority groups in the United States is an important although infrequently studied area of *adult education*. Current address: 3036 University Avenue, SE, Minneapolis, Minnesota 55414, USA.

National Information Center on Volunteerism *Adult education* employs a great many volunteers and this centre

acts as a *clearinghouse* on volunteers. Current address: P.O. Box 4179, Boulder, Colorado 80306, USA.

National Institute of Adult Continuing Education (NIACE) The title of the *National Institute of Adult Education* after 1983, thus reflecting the wider role that the institute was to perform in *adult education* in the United Kingdom.

National Institute of Adult Education (NIAE) Established in 1949 as a result of a merger of the *British Institute of Adult Education* and the *National Foundation for Adult Education*. It acts as a centre of information about adult education and a publishing centre for professional literature, including the journal, *Adult Education* and a number of books and other publications. In addition, it has a large data bank about adult education. Membership is primarily associational, but there is a category of individual members. Both types of members are able to attend, or send representatives to attend the annual study conference. It is an independent body supported by a government grant. It changed its name to the *National Institute of Adult Continuing Education* in 1983. Current address: 19b De Montfort Street, Leicester LE1 7GE, UK.

National Institute of Health Administration and Education Indian institution which trains health administrators. Current address: E–16 Greater Kailesh 1, New Delhi 48, India.

National Institute of Labor Education Established in 1957 to expand the scope and volume of labour education and enlarge the co-operation between labour and non-labour organizations in education. Formerly, the *Inter-University Labor Education Committee*. Supported by the *American Federation of Labor/Congress of Industrial Organizations* (AFL/CIO). Current address: c/o Federal City College, 1424 K Street NW, Washington DC 20005, USA.

National Institute of Social Education (Kokuriysu Shakai–Kyoiku Kenshujo) Japanese institute founded in 1965, involved in training of professional *adult educators*, research, and publication. *Social education* is the term used in Japan for certain forms of the *education of adults*. Current address: 12–43 Ueno–Koen, Taito–ku, Tokyo 110, Japan.

National Institute of Work and Learning Current address: 1200 18th Street, Suite 316, Washington DC 20036, USA.

national institutional accrediting association A recognized accrediting agency in the United States, usually voluntary and non-governmental, which administers the procedures for institutional accreditation in a fixed geographical area.

National Issues Forums Started in 1981 and sponsored by the Domestic Policy Association, these are *study circles*, or *town meetings*, that study three national issues selected as a result of polling those organizations which sponsor the forums. The results of the discussions are fed back to policy-makers. There is also a *Washington Week* in which the general findings are discussed with congressional representatives and other relevant personnel. It also organizes a literacy programme. Current address: 100 Commons Road, Dayton, Ohio 45450–2777, USA.

National Library for Psychology and Education Swedish national library offering a full library service to *adult education*. Current address: Frescati Hagväg 10, P.O. Box 50 063, 104 05 Stockholm, Sweden.

National Literacy Day 8 September.

National Manpower Institute US institute which publishes its own free bimonthly bulletin. Current address: 1211 Connecticut Avenue NW, Suite 301, Washington DC 20036, USA.

National Manpower Training Association Current address: 591 Washington Street, Memphis, Tennessee 55414, USA.

National Museum of Ireland Established in Dublin in 1731. Current address: Kildare Street, Dublin, Republic of Ireland.

National Negro Business League Started by *Booker T. Washington* in 1900, who presided over it until his death in 1915. He and other successful black entrepreneurs in the southern states of America encouraged others to embark upon their own business enterprises.

National Negro Health Week Started in America by *Booker T. Washington*, it became a major *health education* exercise throughout the country.

National Network for Curriculum Coordination in Vocational and Technical Education Established in 1972 in the United States in order to reduce duplication in *curriculum* innovation by creating a network of co-ordination centres and state liaison personnel. This involves a linking of potential curriculum resource agencies. They are federally funded through competitive contracts from the *United States Department of Education*.

National Open College Network In the United Kingdom *open college* groups have been established which have a number of foci: education for adults, adult access to educational opportunities, innovation in education, and wider *accreditation* for experience and learning. There is no central organization for this network although most of the local networks are affiliated with it.

National Organization for Women US organization concerned with equal opportunities for women. Current address: 5 S.Wabash, Chicago, Illinois 60603, USA.

National Organization of Library Work (NBLC) The Dutch national association of libraries, which is very committed to *adult education*. It holds *adult literacy* cassettes, co-operates with the *Netherlands Study and Development Centre for Adult Education*, and develops its own bibliography of *adult education* literature. Current address: NBLC, Den Haag, The Netherlands.

National Priority Skills Scheme (NPSS) Grants are made by the *Manpower Services Commission* to *industrial training organizations* which are responsible for their distribution to employers to support the development of pilot training schemes in new disciplines, high-level computer training etc. They are intended to supplement the employers' training efforts. (Note: the *Manpower Services Commission* changed its name to the *Training Commission* and then to the *Training Agency* in 1988).

National Programme for Tele-Education (PRONTEL) Brazilian organization involved in *distance education* through the medium of television.

National Programme on Adult Education The literacy programme of India, designed to reach 40 million people by 1990 and another 60 million by 1995. See also *Rural Functional Literacy Projects*.

National Public Radio Current address: 2025 M Street NW, Washington DC 20036, USA.

National Referral Center The *Library of Congress* supplies data for individual requests. Address: Library of Congress, 10 First Street SW, Washington DC 20540, USA.

National Research Council US body, established in 1916, concerned with research in all areas of knowledge, including the behavioural sciences. Current address: 2101 Constitution Avenue, Washington DC 20418, USA.

National Research Council of Canada A national research agency that sponsors research in all areas of knowledge.

National Retired Teachers Association American association of retired persons. Current address: 1909 K Street NW, Washington DC 20006, USA.

National Rural Career Guidance Network An American *clearinghouse*. Current address: National Center for Research in Vocational Education, Ohio State University, 1960 Kenny Road, Columbus, Ohio 43210, USA.

National School Volunteer Program *Volunteers* have been extensively studied by *adult educators* in the United States. Current address: 300 North Washington Street, Alexandria, Virginia 22314, USA.

National Self-Help Resource Center American *clearinghouse* concerned with *self-help*. Current address: 2000 S Street NW, Washington DC 20009, USA.

National Society for Performance and Instruction An international organization, founded in 1962 and based in Washington, committed to increasing productivity in the workplace through the application of performance and instructional technologies. It was previously called the *National Society for Programmed Instruction*. Current address: 1126 16th Street NW, Suite 214, Washington DC 20036, USA.

National Society for Programmed Instruction See *National Society for Performance and Instruction*.

National Society for the Promotion of Industrial Education Established in 1906 in the United States to act as a pressure group for *vocational education*.

National Society of Quality Circles Formed in the United Kingdom in 1982 by some 20 organizations involved in operating *quality circles* with the aim of encouraging their development in the United Kingdom. The organization was sponsored by the Industrial Participation Association. Current address: 85 Tooley Street, London SE1 2QZ, UK.

National Swedish Federation of Adult Education Associations The federation of the ten educational associations which sponsor *study circles* in Sweden.

National Technological University (NTU) An American consortium of universities and businesses that have combined to provide graduate degree courses in the United States by videotaped and satellite transmission.

National Training Act (1982) A Canadian federal government act which has increased its powers in the provision of *vocational training* by, among other things, enabling it to fund training agencies directly rather than indirectly through provincial governments.

national training awards Launched by *Manpower Services Commission* in April 1987, these awards are made to any organization in United Kingdom able to demonstrate that its training, of whatever sort, has helped it function more smoothly. There are three forms of award: those to employers, to training establishments, and for the innovative use of training methods, Current address: P.O. Box 12, Nottingham NG7 1BR, UK. (Note: the *Manpower Services Commission* changed its name to the *Training Commission* and then to the *Training Agency* in 1988.)

National Training Institute of Social Education Japanese institute concerned with *training* in *social education*. Current address: Ueno-Koen, 12–43, Taito-ku, Tokyo 110, Japan.

National Training Laboratory (NTL) Its first meeting was held at Bethel, Maine in 1947. It later became the headquarters of the *group dynamics* movement.

National Union of Societies for Equal Citizenship Established in 1918 from the *National Union of Women's Suffrage Societies* in 1918 and campaigned for ten years until women gained the same voting rights as men. Thereafter it transformed itself into the *National Union of Townswomen's Guilds* with a greater

educational role for the new women citizens.

National Union of Townswomen's Guilds Townswomen's Guilds offer many educational opportunities for women in England and Wales; this is their national body. This movement emerged from the *National Union of Societies for Equal Citizenship* and assumed its current name in 1933. Current address: 75 Harborne Road, Edgbaston, Birmingham B15 3DA, UK.

National Union of Women's Suffrage Societies A suffragette movement in England which changed its name in 1918 to the *National Union of Societies for Equal Citizenship* when women were granted the vote at the age of 30 years.

National University Continuing Education Association (NUCEA) The national association for adult educators in university continuing education in the United States. Formerly the *National University Extension Association*. The present council is divided into four councils, a number of working committees, and regional divisions. It publishes the journals, *Continuing Higher Education Review* and *Continuum*. Current address: One Dupont Circle, Suite 420, Washington DC 20036, USA.

National University Extension Association (NUEA) Established in 1915 to provide an official and authorized organization through which colleges, universities, and individuals engaged in educational extension work might confer to their mutual advantage and to develop and promote the best ideals and methods of extension education. Twenty-two colleges became founder members of the association, which grew rapidly. It published a monthly magazine, *'NUEA Spectator'* and the proceedings of its conferences. It became the *National University Continuing Education Association*.

National University Teleconference Network (NUTN) Established in 1982, it is an international organization providing a live, interactive, teleconferencing service to universities, colleges, business, industry, and the professions. It provides a means of exchanging information and is also networked with similar organizations. Publishes a newsletter, organizes conferences and seminars. Current address: 332 Student Union, Oklahoma State University, Stillwater, Oklahoma 74078–0653, USA. See *Campus Conference Network*.

National Urban League Current address: 425 13th Street NW, Washington DC 20004, USA.

National Vocational Education Act Passed in the United States in 1963, this act allowed federal monies to be granted to individual states to assist with the development of *vocational education*.

National Vocational Guidance Association Current address: 1607 New Hampshire Avenue NW, Washington DC 20009, USA.

National Women's Education Centre (Kokuritsu Fujin Kyoiku Kaikan) Founded in 1977 by the Japanese Ministry of Education, this is a national centre for the education of women. It publishes its own journal, *Fujin Kyoiku Joho*, and is well known throughout the world, having received visitors from over 100 countries since it was established. Current address: 728 Sugaya, Ranzan-machi, Hikigun, Saitama 355–02, Japan.

native language The first language of a person.

natural philosophy The classical term for physics.

naturalism General philosophical belief that what is studied in the natural world is all that there is, i.e. that there is no supernatural intervention in the world.

naturalistic research An approach to research which endeavours to describe

the natural setting as fully as possible so that a better and fuller understanding of people and their actions can be achieved; a *qualitative* rather than *quantitative* approach.

nautical school An educational institution providing courses in all aspects of sailing.

Necessary Teacher Training College Started in 1972 by the *Tvind Folk High School in Denmark*, this is a novel scheme in teacher training in which teachers are trained in the methods and convictions of the *folk high school*, such as having to travel around the world, find work and save money, get to know about the living conditions of a variety of socio-economic groups of people, teach part-time and study part-time. It reflects the experimentation of the *Tvind School*.

Nedić, Ljubomir One of the first advocates of *university extension* in *Yugoslavia* and the person who delivered the first extension lectures in Belgrade in 1888 on the topic of 'Sleep and Dreaming'.

Nederlands centrum voor volksontwikkeling See *Netherlands Association of Adult Education Organizations*. Current address: Postbus 351, 3800 AJ Amersfoort, The Netherlands.

Nederlandse bond van plattelandsvrouwen A national association of more than 700 branches which aims at promoting women's awareness of their responsibility to participate in society through *non-formal education*. The branches hold lectures and meetings on topics of interest to the groups, which are mainly rural. Current address: Postbus 90652, 2509 LR Den Haag, The Netherlands.

Nederlandse federatie voor bejaardenbeleid (Netherlands Federation for Policy on Ageing). A great amount of education is provided for elderly people in the Netherlands, including attendance at the *folk high* *schools*. Current address: Eiserhowerlaan 114, 2517 KM Den Haag, The Netherlands.

Nederlandse vereniging van huisvrouwen A non-demoninational association with more than 200 branches throughout the Netherlands, it organizes courses and other educational activities. Current address: Jan van Nassaustraat 89, 2596 BR Den Haag, The Netherlands.

need Perceived by many to be the basic rationale for many educational programmes. It is a disputable concept with no agreed definition although scholars offer a variety, including wants, demands, and deficits. Perhaps it is best conceived as a disjuncture between a person's *knowledge, skill,* or *attitude* and that which it is necessary to have in order to perform acceptably within that person's socio–cultural milieu. There are many variations on this concept. See, for instance *learning need, educational need, felt need, expressed need, hierarchy of needs, normative need, comparative need, primary need, secondary need.*

need for affiliation Term used to indicate that people need to associate with others and form relationships with them.

need gratification The satisfaction of *need.*

need to achieve This term was used by *D. McClelland* to reflect the motivation to be successful. It is a similar term in some ways to *Maslow*'s idea of *self-actualization,* although it carried with it a much greater emphasis upon success in the world.

needs analysis This term is used in a manner similar to *needs assessment.* It is about determining exactly what *needs* exist which may be satisfied by an educational programme.

needs assessment The process of identifying discrepancies between the *participants'* current and desired proficiences as perceived either by

themselves or by others. Sometimes called *preparatory evaluation,* needs assessment in *human resource development* is fundamentally about assessing the needs of organization and preparing the employees to meet those needs.

needs meeting A philosophy which emerged early in *adult education* that adult education is a response to situations in which adults find themselves and discover that they require more *knowledge* or additional *skills.* It has led to considerable debate within the field and, on occasions, has been viewed as an excuse for not having any other rationale for the existence of *adult education.* However, there is still considerable reference made to *needs meeting programmes.*

needs meeting programme 1. The theory of *programme* development which suggests that the *curriculum* or *programme* is designed in order to satisfy the *needs* of the intended participants. 2. The theory in *community education* that the *curriculum* of an *adult education* institution is designed to help meet the *needs* of the local *community.* See *program planning.*

negative correlation A statistical term used to describe an inverse relationship between two *variables.*

negative reinforcement Any event or experience which influences people such that they do not wish to repeat it.

negotiated curriculum An approach to teaching in which the teacher plans the *curriculum* in conjunction with the students, taking their *needs* into consideration. It more frequently applies to negotiated content than to negotiated teaching methods, so that it is in actuality a form of negotiated *syllabus,* within specified limits.

negotiated learning A style of *teaching* and *learning* in which the teacher and learners negotiate content or methods of their learning. This style is used frequently in *adult education* but it does depend on the learners being motivated to learn. It becomes more practical with some modern *assessment* techniques such as *profiling*.

Nehru Literacy Award An award made by the *Indian Adult Education Association* for services to adult literacy education.

Neighbourhood Guild The first *university settlement* established in New York in 1886 by Stanton Coit. Now called *University Settlement*.

Neill, A.S. (1884–1973) Progressive school educator in the United Kingdom, many of whose ideas are very relevant to *adult education* theory.

neo-Freudian A term used to describe any modification of orthodox Freudian theory. See *Freud*.

Nepal *Adult education* in Nepal is controlled by the Ministry of Education, which also runs a documentation service and distributes materials to *adult educators*. This was started in 1956. Current address: Adult Education Section, Ministry of Education, Kaiser Mahal Kantipath, Kathmandu, Nepal.

Netherlands Association of Adult Education Organizations (Nederlands Centrum voor Volksontwikkeling) The national association for *adult education* in the Netherlands. Current address: NCVO, Postbus 351, 3800 AJ Amersfoort, The Netherlands.

Netherlands Federation for Policy on Ageing See *Nederlandse federatie voor bejaardenbeleid*.

Netherlands Institute for Adult Education/Friends of Nature (Nivron) A national association with over 100 branches which is concerned with *leisure* activities and camping but which also focuses upon political action, *social education*, and nature conservation. A *voluntary organization* with a *non-formal* educational remit. Current address: Postbus 50561, 1007 DB Amsterdam, The Netherlands.

Netherlands Study and Development Centre for Adult Education See *Stichting SVE*, Current address: Nieuweweg 4, Postbus 351, 3800 AJ Amersfoort, The Netherlands.

network The webs of social relationships which pervade all social activity.

Network of Continuing Medical Education US *network* concerned with the *continuing professional education* of those employed within the medical profession. Current address: 15 Columbus Circle, New York, New York 10017, USA.

Network of Counseling Centers Serving Women Current address: 14 East 60th Street, New York, New York 10022, USA.

Network of Women in Australian Adult and Continuing Education A network that exists to ensure that women's issues are kept to the forefront of *adult education* in Australia. It also seeks to analyse women's issues in *adult education* and to inform practice. It runs *workshops*, publishes a newsletter and can be contacted through the Council of Adult Education. Current address: 256 Flinders Street, Melbourne 3000, Australia.

networking The development and use of contacts, the linking process of individual and collective *skills, information*, and advice.

Networks for Informal Adult Learning UK network. Current address: 8–9 Upper Street, London N1 0PQ, UK.

New Communities Project A Department of Education and Science project co-sponsored by the Department of Adult Education of the University of Southampton, UK. It was an *action research* based on the Leigh Park estate in Hampshire to develop new strategies for increasing *participation* in *adult education* by those groups of people who are not normally *participants*.

241

New Horizons in Adult Education
An electronic refereed journal initiated in 1987 by the Syracuse University Kellogg Project. It uses *AEDNET* and an electronic network using BITNET mainframe communications. It publishes papers about *adult education* and facilitates on-line discussions between participants about the papers. It was conceived and run by the graduate students at Syracuse University.

New Opportunities for Women (NOW) Courses that seek to broaden the scope of opportunity for women, by increasing self-confidence and broadening horizons.

New School of Social Research Established in New York City in 1919 by James Harvey Robinson and colleagues as an opportunity for educated adults to pursue further study. In the first few years there was some dispute among its founders as to precisely what its purpose was. It arrived in 1923 at its present purpose under the directorship of *Alvin Johnson*.

New Start A *return to study* course begun at the Centre for Continuing Education in the University of Auckland, New Zealand. It is also an *access course* to higher education at the university.

New Start Programme for Disabled People A *new start* course in New Zealand for the *disabled* to prepare them for university education.

New Training Initiative A major consultative document published by the *Manpower Services Commission* in 1981. It highlighted the inadequacy of the British system of *training* and set three major objectives: to develop occupational training; to provide more opportunities for young people to continue their education and training full-time until they are 18 years old; and to provide more opportunities for adults. (Note: the *Manpower Services Commission* changed its name to the *Training Commission* and then to the *Training Agency* in 1988).

New Ventures in Broadcasting A report published in 1928 in England as a result of a committee chaired by *Sir Henry Hadow*. It recognized that broadcasting played a significant educational role. One of the results of this report was the establishment of *wireless discussion groups*.

New York (City) Free Lecture System Established in 1890 in New York by *Henry Leipziger*, this movement grew and attracted thousands of people to what was essentially a *people's university*, sponsored by the New York City School Board. The programme was terminated in 1928 through shortage of funding. One reason why its popularity declined was said to be the growth of the cinema.

New York State Study Circle Consortium A programme to introduce the *study circle* concept to the United States. Sponsored by the Rockefeller Brothers Fund, the New York State Department of Adult Learning Services, and the State University of New York at Albany; thereafter other educational institutions joined the consortium. Current address: Room 234M, State Education Building, Albany, New York 12234, USA.

New Zealand Association for Continuing and Community Education Formerly the *National Council for Adult Education*. Current address: 192 Tinakori Road, PO Box 12114, Wellington, New Zealand.

New Zealand Council for Educational Research Current address: P.O. Box 3237, Wellington, New Zealand.

New Zealand Journal of Adult Learning A biannual journal published by the *National Council for Adult Education* from 1983.

Newbattle Abbey Adult College Scotland's only adult *residential college,* offering one- and two-year courses that lead to university entrance. Grant-aided by the Scottish Department of Education; however its funds were withdrawn at the end of 1987 by the Conservative government. There has been a considerable, but not very successful, campaign to save it. Current address: The Secretary, Newbattle Abbey College, Dalkeith, Midlothian, EH22 3LL, UK.

Newland Papers A series of papers published by the Department of Adult Education, University of Hull, to disseminate the research of staff and research students of the Department. Newland is the area of Hull in which the university is located.

newspaper college A system of *distance education*, started in 1978, used in West Germany and prepared by the *Deutsches Institut für Fernstudien* in which some 12 to 15 articles and about one half-page of a tabloid newspaper are published weekly throughout Germany. These form the basis of a course, but there is enrichment material available (a book and study guide) and suggestions for further reading.

Next Step The publication of *Christian Aid* in the United Kingdom.

Nexus A journal for educators and educationalists who are interested in the response of education to unemployment. Published three times a year from the Department of Educational Studies, University of Surrey, Guildford GU2 5XH, UK.

Nicaragua See *Consejo Nacional de Educación Adultos de Nicaragua* and *Asociación de Educadores de Adultos de Nicaragua*.

Nieuwsbrief Published in Flemish in Belgium by *Vlaams Centrum voor Volksontwikkeling*, this is the practitioner's journal. It recounts the activities of *Le Conseil Superieur* and of *Vlaams centrum voor Volksontwikkeling*. It also records other noteworthy events that are occurring in the field in Belgium. It was started in 1985 and is published monthly.

Niger The current address of the national body is: Direction de l'Alphabétisation et de la Formation Permanente, MEN B.P. 525, Niamey, Niger.

Nigerian National Council for Adult Education A voluntary council which, since its inception, has co-ordinated *adult education* throughout Nigeria. It organizes an annual conference and encourages the formation of branch associations in each of Nigeria's states. Current address: c/o Department of Adult Education, University of Ibadan, Ibadan, Nigeria.

night school 1. See *evening school*. 2. In South Africa night schools are the form of education offered to black people. It is not so much an education for the whites, but rather state black educational provision.

Nihon Hakubutsukan Kyokai See the *Japanese Association of Museums*.

1919 Report See *Final Report of the Adult Education Committee of the Ministry of Reconstruction, 1919*.

Nivron See *Netherlands Institute for Adult Education/Friends of Nature*.

Noma Prize A literacy award of $5000 per annum established by Shoichi Noma of Japan in 1980 and administered by *Unesco*.

nominal group technique A variation of *snowballing* in which individuals respond to a question in writing. All the responses can then be read and discussed by the group, with the group leader classifying, ordering, and synthesizing the group's final conclusions.

nomothetic approach Nomothetic refers to the process of proposing or prescribing a law; educational research having this approach assumes laws of human behaviour and seeks to test them.

non-advanced further education This covers basic craft or technician level training and is available to anybody who has left initial schooling in the United Kingdom.

non-award bearing Courses that are organized and run without an award for successful completion. See also *non-credit, non-competence giving*.

non-competence giving A *non-award bearing* educational programme.

non-credit A term which is more commonly used in the United States to refer to an educational activity organized without an award for successful completion. Learning for its own sake, as in some forms of *liberal adult education*. This was first offered by universities in the United States in 1816 when a professor from Rutgers University offered science lectures to the public. See *George Birkbeck, credit*.

non-directive counselling The process of *counselling* in which the counsellor acts as a listener, helping the client decide for him/herself about the decision that should be taken.

non-directive interview An *interview* in which there is a free exchange of views between interviewer and interviewee, rather than one in which the former directs the process.

non-formal education Educational activity which occurs outside of the established formal system and is organized to serve the identifiable *learning needs* of specific groups. The learning context has to be improvised for each of these groups. This is a form of education used a great deal in Third World countries, where it appears synonymous with out-of-school education for children and adults. Some countries have special sections in the Department of Education for non-formal education. In Sri Lanka, for instance, this section publishes its own newsletter, *Sarathi*.

Non-Formal Education Information Center American *clearinghouse* on *non-formal education*. Current address: Institute for International Studies in Education,

513 Erikson Hall, Michigan State University, East Lansing, Michigan 48824, USA.

Non-Formal Education Journal Launched in 1983 by the National Council of Educational Research and Training, New Delhi, India, seeking to cover all aspects of *non-formal education*. Current address: Sri Aurobindo Marg, New Delhi, 110016, India.

Non-Formal Education Periodical Thai journal established in 1980 and published every two months.

non-governmental organization (NGO) An organization that is not a statutory body and not completely financed by the state, which exists to undertake a social or community task. Many *adult education* organizations fall into this category.

non-judgemental An approach which seeks to examine situations without making moral judgements.

non-linear A relationship between two *variables* which is too complex to be depicted by a straight line in a graph.

non-participation Non-enrolment in adult education, called the non-participation issue by the *Organization for Economic Co-operation and Development*.

non-resident One who does not live in the premises provided for the course of study. *Adult students* are often in this category and are often disadvantaged when residence is a requirement for a course of study.

non-respondent An individual who fails to reply to a questionnaire, or complete a test, etc.

non-schooler One who has never attended school; usually from rural areas in Third World countries.

non-structured interview See *unstructured interview*.

non-teaching staff See *support staff.*

non-traditional education An American term which relates to *external degree, credit transfer, experiential learning,* and other aspects of education that were examined by the *Commission on Non-Traditional Study* in the early 1970s. It refers to all forms of flexible and innovative arrangements designed to provide a wide range of *learning opportunities* to adults of all ages.

non-vocational adult education See *non-vocational education.*

non-vocational education All *adult education* which is not specifically orientated to the occupational sector. The *American Association for Adult and Continuing Education* sought to replace the term with *general education* but the suggestion did not get unanimous support from *adult educators.* 'Non-vocational' is often used to refer to non-examination courses mounted by an adult education institution.

Nordborg Conference An international adult education conference organized in 1972 at Nordborg by the Danish Ministry of Education. The conference was significant in that it brought together experts whose main concern was to focus upon comparative methodology in adult education.

Nordic Association of Adult Education The association for *adult education* which seeks to co-ordinate the work of the national adult education institutes in Scandinavia.

Nordic Centre for Research and Training in Adult Education Proposed as early as 1963; it has never been established.

Nordic Council The council of the five Nordic countries, it has conducted some comparative research into *adult education* in those countries.

Nordic Cultural Co-operation Following an agreement signed on 15 March 1971 there has been co-operation among the Nordic countries on all forms of education, including the education of *young adults* and *adult education.* Adult education co-operation began in 1976. Current address: Nordic Council of Ministers, Secretariat for Nordic Cultural Co-operation, Snaregade 10, DK–1205 Copenhagen, Denmark.

Nordic Folk Academy (Nordens folkiga akademi) Established in 1968, this academy arranges courses for leaders and teachers in the *folk high schools.* In addition, it acts as a resource agency for the folk high schools and has conducted research in *adult education* in the Nordic countries. Current address: Box 1001, S–44225 Kungalv, Sweden.

Nordic Folk High School Council The association seeking to co-ordinate the work of the national *folk high school* associations in the Scandinavian countries. Current address: c/o Nordic Folk Academy, Box 1001, S–44225 Kungalv, Sweden.

Nordic Review of Adult Education *Adult education* journal. Formerly the *Norwegian Review of Adult Education,* it has subsequently extended its remit to the whole of Scandinavia.

norm That which is normal, or which occurs most frequently as the socially accepted form of behaviour. It is often the behaviour expected by a group because conformity within a group is often a prerequisite of membership. It is a non-moral term in the social sciences.

norm-referenced testing An approach to *assessment* which seeks to compare one person's performance against the average for the group rather than against specific criteria. See *criterion-referenced testing.*

normative 1. Prescribing to a standard. 2. Behaviour which responds to social pressures in such a manner as to be conformist.

normative need A deficiency which is considered to be a *need* because it falls below a standard or *norm*. This standard is usually subjective and often arbitrary, since it is often almost impossible to determine standards *empirically*.

Norsk Korrespondanseskole The Norwegian correspondence school founded in 1914. Despite the fact that Norway is a small country (population: 4 million) it has about 80,000 to 100,000 enrolments. In 1976, it became a private organization. It runs courses at every level, including university, for both *liberal adult education* and *continuing professional education*. It has its own Business Education school. All courses that it runs have to be approved by the Norwegian Ministry of Education. Current address: Oslo, Norway.

Norsk Pedagogisk Studiesamling The Norwegian education library which provides a full library service in all areas of education. Current address: Bankplassen 3, Oslo 1, Norway.

Norsk Sentrum for Informatikk (Norwegian Centre for Information Science) This centre contains the data bank (FOVU) for a survey on more than 1,000 adult education development projects that have been undertaken in the Nordic countries in recent years. The survey was conducted by a co-ordinating body representing institutions in each country. Current address: Oslo, Norway.

Norsk Voksenpedagogisk Institut The Norwegian Institute of Adult Education. Current address: Lade Allé 60, 7000 Trondheim, Norway.

North American Association of Summer Sessions Current address: Box 1145, Washington University, St Louis, Missouri 63130, USA.

North American Indian Cultural Education Centers Established in Canada to preserve and extend North American Indian culture and language, to continue and encourage research into this cultural heritage, and to produce educational programmes about North American Indian culture.

North East Adult Education Conference An annual conference organized in the northeast of England, it began in 1980. The address of its chairman and secretary are obtainable from the *National Institute of Adult Continuing Education*. Current address: c/o Division of Adult Education, Lincoln Gardens, Scunthorpe, South Humberside DN16 2ED, UK.

North of England Council for Promoting Higher Education for Women Formed in 1867 to co-ordinate groups of women concerned with this ideal. It was these groups who invited *James Stuart* of Cambridge University to give a series of four lectures that are generally regarded as the beginning of *university extension*.

North–South: A Programme for Survival The *Brandt Report*.

Northern College An adult residential college, established in 1978, running a mixture of long-term and short courses, partly as a result of the *Russell Report*. Current address: Wentworth Castle, Stainborough, Barnsley, South Yorkshire S75 3ET, UK.

Northern Examining Association A group of five examining boards (Associated Lancashire, Joint Matriculation, North Regional, North West Regional, Yorkshire and Humberside Regional) which together offer the *General Certificate of Secondary Education* examination, with mature and external syllabuses for adults. Current address: Joint Matriculation Board, Manchester M15 6EU, UK.

North–West International Adult Education Conference A conference organized by adult educators in the northwest of England that, since 1986, has assumed an international flavour. Current address: c/o Oldham Centre for Community Education, Chaucer Street, Oldham OL1 1BA, UK.

Norwegian Adult Education Act Enacted in August 1977 to regulate those elements of *adult education* partly or wholly financed by the government. It recognizes that *adult education* can assist individuals in attaining a richer life style, additional knowledge and skills, and personal and professional development. It is an intention of the act that all people should have equal opportunities of experiencing *adult education*.

Norwegian Association of Adult Education Organizations (Samnamnda for studiearbeid) Founded in 1932 to establish co-operation and co-ordination between member organizations, both nationally and internationally. There are about 40 member organizations, a list of which can be obtained from the association. Current address: Dronningensgt 17, Postboks 560 Sentrum, 0105 Oslo 1, Norway.

Norwegian Association of Correspondence Schools (Norsk brevskolsforbubd) An Act of Parliament in 1948 controls the 30 correspondence schools approved by the Ministry in Norway, giving rise to a *State Council of Correspondence Schools* to assist the *Ministry of Church and Education*. This association coordinates their work. Current address: Postboks 1815, Vika, 0123 Oslo 1, Norway.

Norwegian Association of Employers (Norsk Arbeidsgiverforening) Organizes courses and support training for its various member organizations. It also acts as an advisor to those bodies on educational matters. Current address: Kr. Augustsgt 23, 0164 Oslo 1, Norway.

Norwegian Broadcasting Association (Norsk riksingkasting) The organizer of many *adult education* enterprises, including programmes of *study circle* use. Also concerned with foreign language teaching. Current address: Bjørnstjerne Bjørnsons pl 1, 0340 Oslo 1, Norway.

Norwegian Catholic Association for Study Activities (Katolsk studieråd) The Roman Catholic Church organization which is a member of the *Norwegian Association of Adult Education Organizations*.

Norwegian Christian Study Council (Norsk kristelig studieråd) Member of the *Norwegian Association of Adult Education Organizations*.

Norwegian Directorate for Public and School Libraries (Statens bibliotektilsyn) Governed by an Act of Parliament in 1971, the public libraries are regarded as an instrument for the development of *adult education* in Norway. Current address: Munkedamsvn 62, Postboks 8145, Dep, 0033 Oslo 1, Norway.

Norwegian Federation of Trades Unions (Landsorganisasjonen i Norge) Organizes courses for shop stewards and members, often in association with the Norwegian *Workers' Educational Association*. Current address: Youngsgt 11, 0181 Oslo 1, Norway.

Norwegian Free Churches' Study Council (Frikirkelig studieråd) Free Church *adult education* organization, and a member of the *Norwegian Association of Adult Education Organizations*.

Norwegian Institute of Adult Education (Norsk voksenpedagogisk institut) Established in 1976, funded directly from the *Ministry of Church and Education* to function in research, documentation, and the provision of information about *adult education*. It was the first association in Norway to have a research remit for adult education. Current address: Lade allé 60, N–7000 Trondheim, Norway.

Norwegian National Council for Museums Current address: Grev Wedels pl. 1, 0151 Oslo 1, Norway.

Norwegian Review of Adult Education Formerly, the *adult education* journal of the Norwegian associations. It subsequently extended its concern to cover all the Scandinavian countries. See *Nordic Review of Adult Education*.

Norwegian Societies of Engineers' Continuing Education Centre (NIF og

NITO studieforbund) Throughout the world the engineering occupations have been concerned about *continuing education*. Those in Norway are members of the *Norwegian Association of Adult Education Organizations*.

Norwegian State Institution for Distance Education (Norsk fjernundervisning) Established in 1977 and funded directly from the *Ministry of Church and Education*. It is a *provider* of multi-media materials and an organizer of courses, with the first course established in 1981. It is also responsible for course evaluation.

Not in Labor Force An American category of persons over the age of 16 years but not classified as unemployed; thus all those in full-time education who are over the age of 16 years come into this category.

Note d'Information The French-language adult education journal of the French-speaking association of *adult education* in *Belgium*, published five times a year. It was started in 1982. See also the Flemish language journal, *Vorming Vlaanderen*.

Notizie The newsletter of the *Associazione Italiana di Educazione degli Adulti*.

Nuffield Foundation Foundation which supports educational research in the United Kingdom. Current address: Nuffield Lodge, Regent's Park, London NW1 4RS, UK.

null hypothesis The reverse of the research question in order to avoid bias in the research. E.g. the research question asks if there is a relationship between *a* and *b*; the null hypothesis is that there is no relationship between *a* and *b*.

numeracy Following the concern for *literacy*, a number of schemes to assist adults with basic numeracy were established in the 1970s. The result was an adult numeracy campaign, sponsored by the *Adult Literacy and Basic Skills Unit* in the 1980s. Competence in numeracy became one of the other elements in *adult basic education*.

nurse teacher One who teaches nurses in their *professional preparation* and *continuing education*. The first courses for nurse teachers were begun in 1918 and they were called *sister tutors* for many years. Only after they ceased to be practice-based did this term disappear from usage.

Nyerere, Julius (b.1922) President of *Tanzania* and a powerful advocate for *adult education* throughout the whole of his political career.

Nyström, Anton Kristen (1842–1931) Swedish pioneer of *popular education*. The founder of the first working men's institute in Scandinavia.

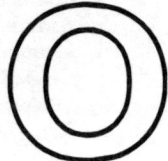

objective 1. The immediate *aim* or *goal* of a lesson or educational course. Used very widely, often synonymously with aim, especially in the United States. However, within *curriculum theory* the concept is refined, so that aim is about the general philosophy whilst objective is more immediate and specific. See *behavioural objectives, expressive objectives*. 2. Descriptive term for *observation, report*, etc. which is undistorted by bias.

objective test *Tests* which may be marked objectively by any marker, such as a *multiple choice* test.

Obrazovanje odraslih A Yugoslav journal which, when translated, means *Adult Education*. It was formerly *Narodno sveučilište* but renamed in 1959 and yet again in 1969 as *Andragogija*.

observation A method of *research* that involves careful viewing of a situation, phenomenon or process. Some forms are more structured than others but in some of the more structured the observer is only looking for specific topics or issues.

observation checklist A prepared list of characteristics that should be viewed during the process of *observation*. See *checklist*.

observation entry A *trainer* interruption in a *group* process in order to focus upon the nature of the group process.

observed score A term sometimes used to refer to the *raw data* in research.

observer 1. One who watches, often someone trained to observe objectively.

2. One who practises the research method of *observation*, and records the process being researched. See also *participant observer*.

obsession Any idea which constantly invades a person's consciousness.

obsolescence The condition arising from use of *knowledge, theories, concepts*, techniques, etc. that are less effective in solving problems than others that are currently available. As the knowledge explosion continues this has become a significant concept in *continuing professional education*.

obstruction method A research technique used in *psychology* in which the subject is obstructed from its goal in order to examine the strength of the *motivation or ability to problem solve*.

Occasional Papers in Continuing Education A series of papers published by the Centre for Continuing Education, University of British Columbia, Vancouver, Canada.

occupation A person's paid employment.

occupational analysis The process of analyzing all the tasks demanded by a specific occupation and specifying them as *competencies* for which *education* and *training* might be given. See *competency-based education*.

occupational education See *vocational education*.

occupational therapy A form of therapy through *learning* and doing.

OECD See *Organization for Economic Co-operation and Development*.

Oeil sur la Formation et son Environment Socio-Economique French journal published every two months since 1983. It is the journal of the *Agence Nationale pour le Développement de l'Education Permanente*.

off-campus programme The programme of courses established by an educational institution away from its own campus, often to accommodate part-time adult students. See also *university extension*.

off-quota Students who are paying a full fee and are in no way subsidized by the government finance to an educational organization are sometimes admitted to that institution and not considered to be part of the allocated number of students to a specific course, i.e. they are off-quota.

off-the-job training Introductory preparation or *continuing education* for employees conducted away from the place of work. See *paid educational leave* as one form of off-the-job training.

Office Français des Techniques Modernes d'Education A French organization involved in the use of *educational technology* in the development of *éducation permanente*. Current address: rue d'Ulm, Paris, France.

Office of Adult Learning Services (OALS) Established by the *College Board* in America to help its members respond to the needs of *adult learners*. It is concerned with the recruitment of adults and assisting adults with college study. It offers advisory services, technical assistance on policy issues, training, publications, and tests. Current address: OALS, The College Board, 988 Seventh Avenue, New York, New York 10106, USA.

Office on Educational Credit A *clearinghouse* about educational *credit* in America. Current address: American Council on Education, One Dupont Circle NW, Washington DC 20036, USA.

Office on Educational Credit and Credentials The office of the *American Council of Education* responsible for evaluating educational programmes. It changed its name in 1987 to the *Center for Adult Learning and Educational Credentials*.

office skills Teaching the practices necessary for the efficient management of a modern office.

older adult One who is 65 years or older, according to the Congress of the United States.

Older People in Folk High Schools in Foreign Countries A project, commenced in 1984, run from a *folk high school* in Denmark. It encourages the old and young to learn about a foreign country and then to travel abroad on educational trips together, with the young unemployed organizing and accompanying the older people. Current address: Brandbjerg Hojskole, Brandbjergvej 12, 7300, Jelling, Denmark.

older worker A working person who is 55 years or older.

olfactory learner One who learns best through the use of the senses of smell and taste.

Olsson, Oscar (1877–1950) Founder of the Swedish *study circle* movement in 1902 at the Lund branch of the International Order of Good Templars. He was a leader in the Swedish temperance movement, and involved in many other activities in Sweden. He wrote material for the *study circles* and believed that books and *libraries* were important in the education of adults. He was also an international figure in other movements.

ombudsman Official who represents the rights of people. In some colleges and universities there is such an official whose job it is to take up the rights of students.

On Adult Training This type of training was enacted as proposition number 92, placed before the Norwegian Parliament in 1964–65, and operative in 1965. It placed *adult education* in Norway on the same basis as other sectors in the education institution and included both *liberal* and *vocational* education with the definition of *adult education* in Norway.

on-course experiential learning *Experiential learning* as part of a taught course.

On-Line The newsletter of the *American Association of Adult and Continuing Education*. This title was adopted in 1983.

on-the-job training A form of *vocational preparation* which occurs in the workplace.

On The Move The title of an early *adult literacy* scheme televised by the British Broadcasting Association for the first time in 1974–75. See also *Your Move*.

One for All The monthly journal of the *adult school movement*, it was originally published by the Midland Association of Adult Schools from 1891.

One Hundred and Fifty Hours (150 hours) The name refers to the amount of time that workers could get in Italy in *paid educational leave*, according to the *Workers' Statute*. However, it has now become the title of the whole programme, rather than just a period of time.

One-Parent Family A family which consists of one parent and children. This family is often *disadvantaged* educationally for both children and the parent.

Ontario Institute for Studies in Education A major educational institution in Canada, which has also contributed a great deal to the theory of *adult education* in that country. It has its own educational publications. Current address: 252 Bloor Street West, Toronto, Ontario, M5S 1V6, Canada.

ontology The philosophical study of existence itself. Some ontological ideas are becoming increasingly important in philosophical approaches to *adult education* and *learning theory*.

Open Access Centre Centres commissioned to support the work of the *Open College*. There were about 100 centres established with the start of the Open College.

open access policy The policy of waiving entry qualifications as a prerequisite of enrolment for a course of study. See *access*.

open admission See *open access policy*.

open book test The type of examination in which the examinees are allowed to refer to books in order to answer the examination questions.

Open College 1. The Open College commenced broadcasting on 21 September 1987 in conjunction with *Channel 4* in the United Kingdom. It is a further-education media institution offering a wide range of courses and learning opportunities, especially in *retraining* and *vocational education*. Current address: Open College, 101 Wigmore Street, London W1, UK. 2. Open College actually had an earlier connotation inasmuch as it was the name given to a network of colleges of further education, usually in a specific geographical area such as South London, linked to one or more institutions of *higher education*. It provided courses for mature unqualified students, leading to *access* either to institutions of higher education or others. Open Colleges should be open to all people of post-school leaving age, whatever their previous qualifications or demonstrated ability; open to enable learners to develop as far as they wish in whatever direction they desire; open to a variety of levels of study inasmuch as courses are offered at these levels; and open to the influence of the learners through a democratic style of management. See *National Open College Network*.

open continuing education Term used in the Federal Republic of Germany to mean the continuation or resumption of organized learning after the completion of any kind of primary or secondary education. This definition is very close to that of *continuing education* in the United Kingdom, although in practice in Germany this term appears to be closer to *liberal adult education*.

open day Scheduled periods during which educational institutions invite visitors often to see the work of students, but increasingly with *adult education* institutions to try to attract future students.

open education Term used in American education in a manner similar to *progressive education*, e.g. open to new ideas and change. In this form of education there is minimal teaching as students pursue their own interests. This is close to what *adult educators* might regard as good practice in the classroom with adult students.

open-ended question The type of question that allows the respondent to develop ideas in answer rather than restrict ideas to a specific area of knowledge. See *open question*.

open enrolment See *open access policy*.

open forum See *forum*.

open further education Term used in the Federal Republic of Germany for those forms of *further education* which are open to all people, as opposed to *closed further education*. In the case of open further education, there are two main sorts of provider – public and private – with the former open to the control of state authorities whilst the latter may be commercial or common-interest providers.

open house See *open day*.

open learning The title given to more flexible methods of study, and teaching in which there is openness in access, content, *delivery systems,* and *assessment*. There are college- or provider-based systems in which learners attend centres; local-based systems with *flexi-study* and support but at which the learning is undertaken in the learners' homes; and *distance learning systems*.

Open Learning Replaced the UK Open University journal, '*Teaching at a Distance*', in 1986. It is a journal published by Longmans in association with the Open University. Current address: Longmans Group Ltd., Fourth Avenue, Harlow, Essex, UK.

Open Learning Federation A network of those involved in *open learning* in the United Kingdom. Current address: c/o Hounslow Open Learning Unit, West London Institute of Education, Borough Road, Isleworth, TW7 5DU, UK.

Open Learning Institute of Hong Kong Scheduled to commence activities in Hong Kong in 1989, this institute is to offer both degree and subdegree programmes.

Open Learning Unit Established within the *Manpower Services Commission* to assume the role of the *Open Tech Programme*. (Note: the *Manpower Services Commission* changed its name to the *Training Commission* and then to the *Training Agency* in 1988.)

open plan Having no, or few, dividing walls between areas. Some schools were planned in this manner in the 1960s and 1970s, but few occurred in *adult education*.

open question The type of examination or essay question that does not restrict the respondent's response too greatly in terms of content. See also *closed question, open-ended question*.

open school A number of open school pilot projects were established in the Netherlands between 1977 and 1980 for *adult basic education*, in which there was an *open* learning approach to education. Since 1980 these schools have continued with government grants for specific projects such as literacy, educational activities for cultural minorities, etc. They also employ radio and television programmes.

Open Tech Directory A comprehensive directory produced by the *Manpower Services Commission* providing information about open learning materials, costs, and support services. (Note: the *Manpower Services Commission* changed its name to the *Training Commission* and then to the *Training Agency* in 1988.)

Open Tech Programme (OTP) The programme, administered by the *Manpower Services Commission*, which started in late 1982 and was financed until 1987. The OTP contracted with single institutions or consortia in education, training, industry, or professional bodies to run projects to produce *open learning* materials and to support services. The MSC grant is regarded as 'pump-priming' inasmuch as after three years the host institution is expected to fund the programme, at least in part. It was subsumed within the *Open Learning Unit* in 1987. (Note: the *Manpower Services Commission* changed its name to the *Training Commission* and then to the *Training Agency* in 1988.)

Open University Established by Royal Charter in 1969 in the United Kingdom to provide university and professional education to those with the keenness and ability to continue their education by study in their own time and in their own homes, particularly those who would not otherwise benefit from university education. It commenced its first *foundation courses* in 1971. It has since become one of the exemplars of university *distance education*. Current address: Walton Hall, Milton Keynes, MK7 6AA, UK. There have been a number of other open universities started since the one in the UK.

Open University of Sri Lanka The recently begun *distance teaching* university of Sri Lanka.

Open University of the Netherlands Opened on 26 September 1984 by Queen Beatrix, it had the aims of providing *second chance education* for adults, an alternative route and cheaper education for adults, and of creating innovations in higher education. See also *Dutch Open University*. Current address: Open Universiteit, Postbus 2960, 6401 DL Heerlen, The Netherlands.

Open University Students Associaton (OUSA) Each *study centre of the Open University* has attached to it a branch of the students' association. The broad aims are to work for the improvement of adult education and for a greater recognition of the role of the mature student within the educational system. Current address: Open University, Walton Hall, Milton Keynes, MK7 6AA, UK.

operant conditioning Associated with the work of *B.F. Skinner*, who claimed that behavioural response can be shaped by the receipt of reward. Skinner's research was initially with rats and pigeons, in the now-famous *Skinner box*.

operant learning An approach to learning in which *learners* are cautious in using evidence but concerned with logical problems and *rationality*. This type of person is not usually good at *problem-solving*.

operational definition A working definition.

operational hypothesis A hypothesis that can be tested.

operationalize To put into practice.

opinionnaire Questionnaire designed to elicit course *participants'* opinions and attitudes about the course. It is an *evaluation* instrument.

Opistolehti-Studieriengen Finnish *adult education* journal published eight times a year.

Opportunities in Retirement An educational *self-help* group which began in 1984 for retired people in the region around Ayr in Scotland. Current address: c/o Room 33, Ayr Academy, Fort Street, Ayr, Scotland.

Opportunities Industrialization Center The first of these centres was started in Philadelphia on 24 January 1964. The movement has spread throughout America and beyond. Many of the centres now receive federal assistance, although *Leon Howard Sullivan*, their founder, insists that they all start without government support. These centres train people and place them in employment.

Opportunities Industrialization Centers National Institute This institute provides technical assistance to the *Opportunities Industrialization Centers*.

option units Some modular courses are constructed of a *core*, which all learners study, and options, from which students make a selection based upon *interest* or occupation.

Options 1. Started in 1986, the journal of the Michigan Association of Adult and Continuing Education. 2. The name given to the *Restart* programme in the United Kingdom in September 1988 when it changed from being a concentrated week-long programme for the unemployed to half-day courses.

oracy *Verbal skills*. Training in verbal communication has become a significant part of the curriculum in some *adult basic education*.

oral examination See *viva voce*. One problem in all oral examinations is the validity of the exercise.

oral history Historical data gathered by word of mouth, a technique frequently used in research with non-literate people. It is also used in literacy crusades.

Order of the Patrons of Husbandry See the *Grange*.

ordinary degree A pass degree, as opposed to an honours degree.

ordinary national certificate One of the qualifications awarded by the *Technical Education Council* in the United Kingdom, it was generally accepted as equivalent to a *General Certificate of Education Advanced Level*. It was a route that some *young adults* took into universities from *colleges of further education*.

ordinary national diploma An award of the *Technical Education Council*, equivalent to two-years of fulltime study, but not usually considered to be of a level different from that of the *ordinary national certificate*.

organic literacy A concept, used by *Freire*, that links words to reality.

Organismic Learning Model A concept of learning that views the person as an active, growing, and developing organism, as opposed to reactive, *mechanistic learning*.

Organization for Co-operation in Overseas Development A voluntary non-profit organization, funded by the Canadian International Development Agency, which sends teachers to Third World countries with specific objectives in basic teacher training, in-service work for school teachers, *continuing education*, and preparation of teacher trainers. Current address: 99 Birchdale Avenue, Winnipeg, Manitoba, Canada, R2H 1S2.

Organization for Economic Co-operation and Development (OECD) This organization was established by a convention signed in Paris on the 14 December 1960 to achieve high economic growth, rising standard of living, expansion of trade, and contribute to the world economy. It has consequently been concerned about issues in adult education and has published the report, *Learning Opportunities for Adults*. See also *Centre for Educational Research and Innovation*. Current address: 2 rue André Pascal, 75775 Paris, Cedex 16, France.

Organizations for Popular Enlightenment Three major organizations, and 17 minor ones, in Denmark which sponsor many of the *study circles* that are organized in that country.

Organization of American States Current address: Department of Educational Affairs, 1889 F Street NW, Washington DC 20006, USA.

organized learning (organisiertes Lernen) A term used in the Federal Republic of Germany to typify *adult education*. It has three main features: a topic, an aim, and a continuing dialogue between teacher and learners.

orientation period Often a one to two week period at the start of a course of study devoted to helping the new students familiarize themselves with the requirements of the course, geography of the institution, and assist those who are returning to *learning* with *study skills*.

orthopedagogy A European term for the study of special education.

Österreichische Volkshochschule The Austrian *People's University*, a quarterly journal published in the German language since 1951.

Osvetoná Práca A Czech journal established in 1961 and published every two weeks in Czech. The title means *Adult Education*.

Oswiata Doroslych Polish monthly magazine on *adult education* published by the Ministry of Education in Warsaw.

Our Right to Learn A campaign which was conducted in Scotland by *adult*

education organizations and individuals demanding positive legislation and *local authority* provision in a variety of aspects of *adult education*. It was launched in October 1981. See also *Save Adult Education Campaign*.

out-centre A subsidiary centre of an *adult education* institution, situated a distance from the main centre.

outcome evaluation See *summative evaluation, impact evaluation*. Outcome evaluation is a term used synonymously with these other two terms in *human resource development*. Compare this with *process evaluation*.

outdoor education The idea underlying outdoor education is that the education should occur where the subject matter exists. Thus it utilizes *visits, field trips, demonstrations*, etc. The emphasis is upon *primary experience* in *learning*.

outline A framework or summary.

outreach education An educational programme located some distance from the premises of the educational institution which is organizing it, aimed at reaching people who do not normally enrol in its programme. A form of *community education*.

outreach teaching *Teaching* conducted off campus.

outreach worker A *community educator*, employed by an *adult education* institution, who seeks to reach people in the *community* who do not normally enrol in the educational programme.

Outward Bound Trust An educational trust that seeks to help *self-development* of *young adults* through participation in adventurous pursuits at sea or in the wilder, more natural regions on land. Current address: Iddesleigh House, Caxton Street, London SW1, UK.

over-educate To provide more *education* than the situation demands. This phenomenon might have been promoted in the West by *professionalization*, in which many more educational qualifications are being demanded by high–status occupations than are necessary for the pursuit of a particular employment. See *over-qualify*.

over-learning An arbitrary concept in which it is claimed that a learner has more than sufficient learning for satisfactory practice.

over-permissive Allowing, even encouraging, a lack of discipline. It might be claimed that some *adult education* practices are over-permissive; however, the response would be that adults should be autonomous and self-directed so that such a claim is necessarily false. This is a part of the debate about the nature of *adulthood* in *adult education*.

over-protective A claim made about some *adult educators* concerning their adult students. See *over-permissive*.

over-qualify In societies in which academic awards and qualifications are highly valued and there is a great deal of unemployment it has become a practice to seek and demand more qualifications than are necessary for the satisfactory completion of *training* or performance of a role. However, the expectation of over-qualification has become a method of selecting applicants for a course or employment.

Overseas Education Fund International Current address: 2101 L Street, Suite 916, Washington DC 20037, USA.

Overstreet, Harry (1875–1970) A social philosopher and for many years professor of philosophy at the College of the City of New York. In his later life he became increasingly interested in *adult education* as a field of both practice and study, writing a number of books on the subject. Included in that number were *'Our Free Minds'* and *'The Mature Mind'*, which were influential, as was the book he wrote with his wife, *'Leaders for Adult Education'* in 1941 and published by the *American Association of Adult Education*. He was influenced by the philosophy of *John Dewey*.

overtime The practice of working extra sessions.

over-training The practice of preparing people to a greater extent than is necessary for the satisfactory performance of a role.

overt response Observable *response* to a *stimulus*.

Owen, Robert (1771–1858) Known as one of the founders of British socialism, Owen sought a better society through education. He provided all forms of education, including *adult education*, when he took over the management of the New Lanark cotton mills as early as 1800. He started *socialist halls of science* which were copied in other places although many of them were soon closed because of financial difficulties. Owen became known throughout the world for his work in all forms of education. He was an early believer in *emancipatory education*.

OXFAM This agency promotes *development education* by providing educational resources, exhibitions, etc. Current address: 274 Banbury Road, Oxford OX2 7DZ, UK.

pacing The speed with which learners progress through educational or learning activities. See *group pacing, self-pacing*.

package A pack of prepared materials for learning a specific topic without requiring the presence of a teacher. There are usually instructions about how best the package may be used.

Pädagogische Arbeitsstelle Deutscher Volkschul-Verband e.V. Started in 1957, this is a documentation centre which is also involved in research, publication, and *training* in *adult education*. Current address: Holshausenstrasse 21, 6000 Frankfurt/Main, Federal Republic of Germany.

paid educational leave (PEL) 1. The opportunity for workers to continue their education during their working life by being released from work with pay in order to continue education. Most paid educational leave is actually *vocational*, although the ideal still remains that people might be released with pay to continue their *general education*. See *recurrent education*. 2. In the United Kingdom the Employment Protection Act of 1975 gave trade union representatives the right to some paid educational leave for relevant *training*. 3. One of the most sophisticated statutory programmes in the Italian *Workers' Statute*, or *One Hundred and Fifty Hour Programme*; another is the law of 16 June 1971 in France which entitles workers to educational leave under certain conditions. Employers having more than ten employees were required to devote 0.8 per cent of their wage bill to continuing training; this was later increased to 1 per cent. 4. In the Federal Republic of Germany every member of the Works Council is entitled by law to three weeks PEL during his/her term of office. 5. In Sweden the Annual Educational Leave Act, which was passed by the Swedish parliament in 1975, gives employees the right to be released from work for *continuing education*. In many instances this takes the form of a *study circle* organized at the place of work. Norway is unlike Sweden in this and PEL is not a right although there have been reports that have suggested that it should be. 6. Much research in a variety of countries shows that PEL is unequally distributed, with the middle and managerial classes getting considerably more than the working classes. See *Convention 140 of the International Labour Organisation*.

Pakistan Association of Adult Education A national *adult education* organization in Pakistan. Current address: 67P–7/2 Margalla Road, Islamabad, Pakistan.

Palestine See *Higher Council for Literacy and Adult Education for Palestinian People*.

Panama The government department responsible for *adult education* is: Departmento Nacional de Alfabetización y Educación de Adultos, Ministerio de Educación, Apartado 2440, Panama.

Pan-American Medical Association Established in 1925. Current address: 745 5th Avenue, New York, New York 10022, USA.

Pan-Cyprian Committee on Adult Education The Cypriot committee of *adult education*, a federation without any executive power for adult education in the island.

panel 1. Two or more speakers who make *presentations* to a class or an audience. 2. Two or more experts who respond to questions from a class or audience.

panel interview An *interview* conducted by more than one interviewer.

Panel of Assessors for District Nurse Training The statutory body responsible for the *education* and *training* of district nurses from 1959 to 1983. Its constitution changed a number of times during this period, as did its responsibilities. The United Kingdom Central Council and the national boards of nursing, midwifery, and health visiting assumed these responsibilities thereafter.

paper 1. A written academic treatise for publication. 2. A research report. 3. A written discussion document.

paper and pen test Any test that requires some form of written response.

paradigm Usually refers to a *model* or example. However, it can also refer to a change in *perspective*, e.g. a paradigm shift.

Paragraphs about Continuing Education A newsletter published by *New Zealand*'s *National Council for Adult Education* since 1974. (The council was renamed the *New Zealand Association for Continuing and Community Education* in 1988.)

Paraguay The Paraguayan association of *adult educators* is the *Asociación de Educadores de Adultos del Paraguay*, Fulgencio Rb Moreno casi Mexico, Asuncion, Paraguay.

parameter The boundaries of a phenomenon.

paraprofessional Used in American education to refer to people employed to assist the professional teacher. Usually paraprofessionals are untrained or perhaps have received a minimum of *training*.

parent association Sometimes called a *parent–teacher association* in which the parents of children in a school form an association in order to assist their children's school. These associations sometimes also run some *parent education* activities.

parent education The process of educating parents to understand the developmental and educational processes through which their children pass. Sometimes called *parenting education*. In the United States this was assisted by many of the educational organizations that began in the nineteenth century such as *Chatauqua* but it was not until 1897 that this movement was co-ordinated in the *National Congress of Mothers*. In the United Kingdom, an example of parent education is the *Open University*'s course on pre-school children.

parent outreach program Organized by American schools to reach parents with *parent education*.

parent–teacher association See *parent association*.

parenthood education Providing the necessary knowledge for and preparing young people generally in the art of parenthood. See *parent education*.

parenting education See *parent education*.

Parker, Cissie (d.1933) An outstanding leader of the *adult school movement* in Britain in the early part of this century. A fund was established by the movement in her memory to provide bursaries to enable men and women to attend the movement's summer schools.

part learning The process of breaking down information to be learned into smaller sections and learning them individually.

part-time adult educator 1. One who teaches, or is otherwise employed in, *adult education* for less than a specified time each week and who is not regarded by the employing authorities as being in full-time employment. In Finland, a distinction is made between the part–time *adult educator* who may teach for the occasional hour each week or who is a voluntary *study circle* leader, and the partially employed adult educator who has other employment which also entails some adult education activity. In some studies, the part–time adult educator has been called the *spare-time* adult educator. 2. In the middle of *Houle's pyramid of leadership* a category exists of those who combine *adult education* with the other duties that they perform.

part-time student An adult who is a registered student, but who has other obligations, such as work or domestic commitments, and so is unable to pursue studies full time.

part-time tutor A teacher who is employed to teach only a specified number of hours each week and has no administrative responsibility in the *adult education* centre unless (s)he has a specific administrative contract, e.g. as part-time head of centre.

participant A course or group member; a member of a *teaching* and *learning* session.

participant observation A research technique in which the researcher plays a role within the phenomenon being researched. An advantage of such an approach is that it allows rich data to be collected within a naturalistic setting; a disadvantage is that if the other *participants* are aware of the research, it may affect their behaviour. However, if group members are unaware of any on-going research on the group, then there are ethical questions that need to be considered by the researcher.

participant observer One who is utilizing the research technique of *participant observation*, that is playing a full role in a social process but also acting in a research capacity at the same time.

participant satisfaction The assessment by *participants* in a course or conference of the extent to which the whole learning experience was of a satisfactory nature. Like all forms of *assessment*, this is a subjective measure but one which *adult educators* have to take seriously since they often operate in a market situation.

participation The attendance at adult education courses. The study of why people enrol has long been a subject of interest to adult educators. See also *non-participation*.

participation research A form of research in which the researcher is a part of the process under investigation.

participation training Helping individuals use the processes and procedures of *group discussion* more effectively.

Participatory Formation A network of the *International Council for Adult Education* which publishes its own newsletter (started 1987). It is available from LEPS Department, Northern Illinois University, De Kalb, Illinois 60115, USA.

participatory research Described in *adult education* as a form of integrated activity that combines social investigation, educational work, and action. A great deal of research in *adult education* has been conducted this way. There is a network through the *International Council for Adult Education* for those interested in this form of research. There are *participatory research networks* organized by the International Council for Adult Education throughout the world.

pass degree A *general degree*, the standard of which is not considered high enough to be awarded an *honours*. Also, a degree with a restricted syllabus in which no honours are awarded.

pass mark The arbitrary *grade* that a course team decides should be considered as having achieved a satisfactory standard.

pass rate The proportion of candidates sitting an examination, or taking a course of study, achieving a *pass mark*.

passive learning The process of receiving information and other stimuli in which the *teacher* directs the process.

pathway A route that a *student* can take through a modular course of study in order to read subjects considered acceptable for specific purposes.

PATHWAYS A programme developed by the *Council for Adult and Experiential Learning* in conjunction with the Communication Workers of America and Mountain Bell to serve employees in seven states of the United States. It has four components: career/education planning; returning to learning workshops; *prior learning assessment*; and organizing courses, certificate and degree programmes. Current address: CAEL, Mountains and Plains Region, 5700 South Quebec Street, Suite 102, Englewood, Colorado 80111, USA.

Pavlov, I.P. (1849–1936) Russian psychologist famous for his experiments with dogs which resulted in his discovering *conditioned reflexes*. These reflexes have contributed a great deal to the *behaviourist* approach to *learning*.

peace corps US programme that *trains* and sends to developing countries *young adults* who volunteer to work on an aid programme. Current address: Professional and Technical Division Office of Public Affairs, Washington DC 20525, USA.

peace education See *peace studies*.

Peace Education Institute A Finnish institute organized by *Helena Kekkonen* and associated with the *International Council for Adult Education*. It organizes

seminars and publishes literature. Current address: Fredrikinkatu 81 B, 001000 Helsinki, Finland.

Peace Education Network A network of adult educators committed to peace education and organized through the *International Council for Adult Education* in association with the *Association of Finnish Adult Education Association Organizations*. It publishes its own newsletter, *Peace Newsletter*.

Peace Newsletter Established in 1981, this is published by the *Association of Finnish Adult Education Organizations* two or three times a year in English and Finnish (Rauhankirje).

peace studies A new study which has emerged in adult education in the 1980s in the United Kingdom although the *International Council for Adult Education* has supported it for a longer period of time. It has been open to considerable attack as being Marxist-inspired. The objectives of peace studies courses encompass the following: understanding the growth and strategy of nuclear planning; assisting peace movements engaging in the public debate; redressing the balance in educational resources made available to knowledge of military studies; and encouraging a greater understanding of the peace movement.

peak experience A term used by *A.H. Maslow* to characterize a profound moment in life; *self-actualization*.

Pearson's product moment correlation coefficient Statistical measure of *correlation* between two *variables*.

peasant schools Commenced in Spain in 1970–71, there are now over 100 such schools. Many have been started by priests as cultural centres and centres for regional *development*. In 1978 they were constituted as *adult schools*.

peasant university A *popular university* which was organized in Zagreb, Yugoslavia between the two World Wars and modelled on the Danish *folk high school* system.

Pedagogical Academy of Cyprus The teacher training institute of Cyprus. It also offers courses in *adult education* to third-year students who wish to work with adults as well as children.

Pedagogical Institute of Cyprus The teacher training institution in Cyprus at which secondary school teachers are trained.

Pedagogical Institute of the German Folk High School Association (Padagogische Arbeitsstelle des Deutschen Volkshochschulverbandes) Established in 1957, it works in close co-operation with the universities to prepare *adult educators* and has produced a *self-study* course to this end.

Pedagogical Musem Founded by the *Free Institution of Education* in Spain in 1884 to update the training of school teachers, provide resources, and support. It is no longer active.

pedagogics The study of *pedagogy*. This is a term employed much more frequently in continental Europe.

pedagogy An activity involving the purposeful creation of learning experiences that will either organize or disorganize the meaning systems or stocks of knowledge of the learners in a variety of ways. Generally assumed to refer to teaching children, although in recent years *adult pedagogy* and *social pedagogy* have also assumed significance in *adult education* in some societies which prefer it to the use of the term *andragogy*. In Sweden, it tends to be used in relation to the *study circles* to mean how adults learn to work in small groups, but this is a relatively rare use of the term.

peer assessment A form of *assessment* in which students or practitioners assess each other's performance, work, etc. without reference to other authorities or experts. It is employed in the education of adults because of the ideology of

egalitarianism and *humanism* that has underlaid a great deal of adult education. It is also one of the criteria that some scholars consider to be an essential ingredient of professional practice, since the professional practitioner should be the expert, with 'outsiders' to the profession less knowledgeable about it.

peer counselling The profession of *counselling* one's peers, usually under expert supervision.

peer culture The subculture that emerges within a group.

peer group Group of individuals who act as a reference group for each member.

peer learning Learning from one's fellows. Often practised in *adult education* when peers teach and learn together without the presence of a *teacher* or an expert, using the experience of all the members of the group.

peer rating The results of one approach to *peer assessment*.

peer review A review by one's peers. Sometimes occurs in some forms of *affective education*.

peer teaching The process of teaching one's peers. If this is a student activity, it is frequently conducted under supervision, e.g. *micro-teaching*. See also *peer learning*.

Peers, Robert (1888–1972) Probably the first professor of *adult education* appointed in any university. He was director of the department at the University of Nottingham from its inception in 1920. There is a Chair of Adult Education named after him at the University of Nottingham. In 1981 the department published a monograph, *'Robert Peers and the Department of Adult Education'*, which summarizes many of his achievements. His best-known work is undoubtedly *'Adult Education: A Comparative Study'*.

pegboard test A test for manual dexterity in which pegs must be placed in holes as rapidly as possible.

Pen and Hoe The journal of the *People's Educational Association of Sierra Leone*, started in 1984 and published in English twice a year.

penal andragogy The term used in Yugoslavia for *prison education*. See also *correctional education*.

pencil and paper test Any form of written test.

Pensioen in Zicht (PIZ) Dutch programme of *pre-retirement education*, translated as *retirement in prospect*. This is an eight–day course for retirees and their spouses which includes an orientation day, a number (3–5) of days in an *adult residential centre* followed by some single days. The programme has not yet become universal in Holland, although it is hoped that all people within two years of their retirement may eventually have the opportunity to participate.

People and Culture See *Peuple et Culture*.

People's College Another name for the *folk high school* in West Germany. These are very common, occurring in most towns. They have three main aims: to provide mental and cultural development opportunities; to give practical help in the process of living; and to prepare people to fulfil their political responsibilities.

People's Education for People's Power A black resistance movement in South Africa. The slogan appeared in 1985 and this organization attempts to create an educational movement through which the participants can gain control of their own lives and lay the foundations for a liberated South Africa. It is sponsored by the *National Education Crisis Committee*.

People's Educational Association An *adult education* association in Ghana.

Current address: PO Box 31, Legon, Ghana.

People's Educational Association in Finland The *study centre* and cultural association of the democratic movement in Finland, established in 1964, with a Marxist ideology. It publishes its own journal, *'KSL Information'* (KSL–tieto), six times a year. Current address: Jarrumiehenkatu 2, 00520 Helsinki 52, Finland.

People's Educational Association in Finland (Swedish) Established in 1964 in Finland to serve Swedish-speaking people, it works as a small but active *study centre* organizing educational activities. Current address: Jarrumiehenkatu 2, 00520 Helsinki 52, Finland.

People's Educational Association of Sierra Leone An *adult education* association in Sierra Leone. Current address: 50 Siaka Stevens Street, P.M.B. 705, Freetown, Sierra Leone.

People's High School 1. See *folk high school*; 'people's' is the earlier translation of the Danish word. 2. The term used by *Sir Richard Livingstone* in his advocacy of *residential colleges* for adults in the United Kingdom. In his writing he abbreviated it to PHS.

People's Institute Established in 1898 in New York City (although earlier ones had been founded in Boston and Chicago) and closed through lack of funds in 1934. It became part of the *Cooper Union*. Its aim was to raise and enrich the culture of working-class and immigrant peoples. *Everett Dean Martin* was its director in its last 12 years, when it concentrated on *adult education*.

People's Library Eleven books published between 1939–40 in the USA for lay people in the broadest sense of the term, in a scheme directed by *Lyman Bryson*.

people's university Established in a number of countries, these are *popular* *universities*. 1. In France they were established in 1898 by middle–class liberals to help meet the educational needs of workers. They did not survive for long as they were criticised as being too much like traditional universities in their approach, especially to methods of teaching, and for being too radical. 2. In Yugoslavia, they emerged during the 1940s and 1950s from the 'sloboda' movement. They are popular cultural institutions in which programmes of both culture and education are conducted. The institutions avoid *vocational education* since that is the preserve of the *workers' universities*. They operate in a manner similar to many other *adult education institutions* with a small full-time staff, usually qualified to degree level in andragogy, which is responsible for the organization. Much of the teaching is conducted by part-time staff. There were people's universities in most towns in the 1960s (over 1,000 were established) when education was free. Now there is a fee charged for each course and there has been a decline in enrolments, with the smaller people's universities being forced to merge with the larger ones. They are therefore perhaps less able to respond to grassroots *needs*. In the Netherlands there is an association of people's universities; see *Bond van Nederlandse volksuniversiteiten*.

per capita allowance Money made available to an educational institution by local or national government, or to a department by a college or university, according to the number of registered students within it.

percentile A one-hundredth point on a *cumulative frequency distribution*.

perception Those processes that give coherence and unity to experience. It includes such factors as *attention*, constancy, *motivation*, organization, and *learning*. It is socially constructed as a result of previous *experiences* but may be expressed individually.

perceptual field The range of *stimuli* of which an individual is aware.

perceptual learning style The preferred means through which people extract *information* from their experiences and are able to commit it and its associated meanings to *memory* and thereafter recall it.

perceptual learning style inventory An instrument designed to test *perceptual learning styles* of respondents.

perceptual skills The ability to process *perception* accurately.

Percival Guildhouse *Adult education* centre founded in Rugby in 1925 and named after Dr Percival, a former headmaster of Rugby School. The term 'guildhouse' reflects the idea that existed in the 1920s in England that *educational settlements* should be regarded as *people's universities* but that since ordinary people would not be happy with the term 'university', the adult settlements would be called 'guildhouses'. A few others were actually called by this name, and none survived.

Performance and Instruction Journal The magazine of the *National Society for Performance and Instruction*, published ten times a year. It includes information on approaches and methodologies about *skills* and effectiveness.

performance appraisal Systematic *assessment* of the way that a worker carries out his/her occupation in order to determine the *training needs*. See *needs assessment*.

performance audit A technique employed in *human resource development* in which organizational behaviour is assessed against the cost to the organization of the activity.

performance-based education The form of education and training which stresses the actual performance as evidence of *learning*. It is *behavioural* in its orientation. See also *competency-based education*.

performance objectives The *objectives* that learners have in relation to those aspects of performance that they wish to change or improve as a result of *learning*. See *behavioural objectives*.

performance-orientated methods Teaching methods that relate learning closely to the practical situation, such as *on-the-job training, learning from experience*, etc.

performance test *Test* which assesses the quality of the performance rather than the knowledge about it.

period A unit of time by which school or college *timetables* are subdivided.

Periodical on Aging Published in English, French, and Spanish by the Aging Unit, Centre for Social Development and Humanitarian Affairs, Vienna International Centre. Current address: P.O. Box 500, A–1400, Vienna, Austria.

peripatetic teacher A teacher who teaches in a number of different educational institutions. Many *part-time adult educators* might be viewed as peripatetic teachers since they are often employed by a number of different educational institutions.

permanent education See *lifelong education*.

person A philosophical concept of the nature of the individual. An important concept for the *philosophy* of the education of adults, in which the nature of *personhood* is discussed. This is an especially important concept for those involved in *humanistic* adult education.

personal chair An academic appointment carrying the title and rank of *professor* in a UK university. These appointments are frequently made to reflect some individual contribution, such as academic scholarship or service to the university. Such appointments are distinct from the professorial appointments which are administrative department heads.

personal development This is the *development* of the individual's own *abilities* and *interests*, often through *liberal adult education*. It can be seen as distinct from *professional development*, although some scholars have argued that the two should be the same.

personal identifier The registration number which the *Open University* in the United Kingdom gives to each student who enrols in its courses.

personal identity 1. A psychological concept about the individual *self*. A person's awareness of his/her continuing self through time. 2. A philosophical problem about the extent to which a *person* retains the same *identity* over time, an important problem within studies of *adult development*.

personal teaching Individual tuition.

personalism A psychological approach that maintains that the individual *person* is the central construct against which all else should be considered. A form of *reductionism*.

personality There is a variety of definitions depending upon the school of thought or research of the writer, so that any definition is bound to fall short. However, it refers to the sum total of aspects that constitute individuality in a broad sense.

personality growth See *adult development*; however personality growth refers to development throughout one's whole lifetime.

personality problem Individual psychological problems, such as negative *self-concept*, etc., as distinct from mental illness.

personality test Scales and tests which seek to measure specific *personality characteristics*, thereby classifying people according to their *personality type*.

personality trait Personality characteristic.

personality type Division of people into categories according to certain *personality traits*.

personalized system of instruction A system of teaching through the use of short *modules* in sequence, with specific *behavioural objectives* which must be met before proceeding to the next module. It is a form of *mastery learning*. See *Keller Plan*.

personhood The concept of person is less used in *adult education* than that of *self*. However, person is body, mind, and self and the development of *person* implies the development of all aspects of the person.

personnel officer A member of staff with responsibility for employees. This sometimes includes *staff development* and *training* although there are often separate officials for these functions.

personnel selection. The process of selection of an individual for employment.

perspective A mental view of, or a cognitive orientation towards, a situation.

perspective transformation 1. A concept popularized by *Jack Mezirow* in a number of seminal articles. Perspective transformation was defined by him as the emancipatory process of becoming critically aware of how and why the structure of psycho–cultural assumptions has come to constrain the way in which people see themselves and their relationships. The reconstitution of this structure to permit a more inclusive and discriminating integration of experience and action as a result of this new understanding is the process of perspective transformation. 2. It will be noted immediately that this definition is only of an emancipatory form of transformation, and that more generally it might be defined as a change in cognitive orientation towards a phenomenon.

Perspectives in Education A quarterly journal which seeks to provide an international forum for discussion on the problems of education, especially in the Third World, from both a theoretical and a research basis, published by the Society of Educational Research and Development in India.

persuasion The process of trying to get people to adopt certain sets of values, attitudes, etc. See *indoctrination*.

Peru The government department responsible for *adult education* in Peru is Dirrección General de Educación de Adultos, Ministerio de Educación, Piso 8, Of 800 – Lima, Peru. There is also an *adult education* journal published in Peru, *Autoeducación – revista de educación popular*.

Peters, Richard S. (b.1919) British philosopher of education whose work has influenced some scholars writing in the philosophy of *adult education*.

Peuple et Culture A French *community education* movement. It was established in Grenoble towards the end of the Second World War in 1944, within the Resistance movement. It moved its headquarters to Paris in 1946. Amongst the main people responsible for its formation were *Paul Lengrand, Joffre Dumazedier,* and Joseph Rovan. Since that time it has acted as a community education service in France, seeking to oppose all forms of inequality. It has a variety of members both individual and affiliated organizations, and is organized through a system of independent districts. It is funded partly by the Ministry for Leisure, Youth and Culture and partly by local municipalities. It represents French *popular education* on a number of international bodies, such as the *European Bureau of Adult Education* and the *International Council for Adult Education*. Current address: 108–110, rue St Maur, 75011 Paris, France.

Pharmaceutical Society of Great Britain The professional association responsible for the *accreditation* and much of the *continuing education* of pharmacists in the United Kingdom. It was founded in 1841. Current address: 1 Lambeth High Street, London SE1 7JN, UK.

Ph.D. Doctor of Philosophy.

phenomenology A philosophical approach to understanding developed by *E. Husserl*, who believed that any analysis of a phenomenon has to begin with a scrupulous introspection of one's own intellectual processes. Thus one's conscious awareness of the phenomenon is what is experienced rather than its objectivity. Central to phenomenology is the idea of one's always being conscious of phenomena.

Phillip Frandson Scholarship Fund. Fund established in *memory* of *Phillip Frandson* to support extension students at UCLA. Administered by the Regents of the University of California. Current address: Dean's Office, UCLA Extension, Los Angeles, California 90024, USA.

Phillipines The government agency controlling *adult education* in this country is the Ministry of Education. Current address: Office of Non-Formal Education, Ministry of Education, Culture and Sports, Palacio del Gobernador, Intramuros, Manila, Philippines. See also *Private Schools National Association in Non-Formal Education*.

philosophers A school of educators and thinkers in ancient Greece, established by Socrates and Plato, which emphasized a transcendental interest in knowledge and which saw the purpose of life to be the improvement of the soul – contemplative rather than participative.

philosophy The study of knowledge, ideas and values, and the logical structure of argument or speech. There are many branches of philosophy, although the philosophy of *adult* and *continuing education* is not well developed.

philosophy of adult education There is little philosophy of *adult education*

although a small number of writers have begun to explore its philosophical analyses.

phoneme The smallest sound unit in speech.

phonetics The study of pronunciation.

physical handicap The inability to function in precisely the same manner as other people because of physical impairment.

Physicians Recognition Award The certification offered to doctors by the *American Medical Association, Council on Medical Education* for successful completion of *continuing professional education* programmes. It requires 150 hours of educational participation and study over three consecutive years.

physics the scientific study of matter and energy.

physiology The scientific study of the functioning of living organisms.

Piaget, Jean (1896–1980) A leading child psychologist who focused his work on *cognitive development*. He has influenced scholars such as *Lawrence Kohlberg* and *James Fowler* who have explored ideas of moral development, and faith development throughout the whole of life.

PICKUP *Acronym for the* Professional, Industrial and Commercial Updating, a national programme started by the *Department of Education and Science* of the United Kingdom in May 1982 to help polytechnics, universities, and colleges meet the updating needs of people at work. It is a vocational, updating, and collaborative exercise between education and industry.

pictogram One or more pictures or symbols used to represent objects or concepts. Often used in displaying basic data in survey reports.

picture storage A technique of *memorizing* whereby facts are related in the mind to a familiar picture or object.

pie chart A method of recording data in which the total *population* is depicted as a circle and the subgroups are recorded as appropriate segments of the circle.

Pilgrim College The *adult education* centre of the University of Nottingham Department of Adult Education, which is located in Boston, Lincolnshire, UK.

Pilkington Report A report in the United Kingdom in 1962 which concerned itself with *educational broadcasting*. It suggested that more channels should be created in television broadcasting so that the education of adults could be extended. It also suggested that local radio should be introduced in the United Kingdom so that people could be made more aware of local events.

pilot course An initial trial course which is usually thoroughly evaluated to ensure that the course responds to the *perceived needs* of the learners.

pilot study An exploratory study.

pilot survey The organization of a small survey prior to the actual research to test the survey instruments and planning.

pilot test The pre-testing of a research *instrument*.

Pitman Examination Institute An institution involved with the examination of secretarial work education in *further education*.

placement Usually refers to professional practical placement, e.g. *teaching practice, internship*.

planned learning experience The provision made for a person to *learn* something relevant to his/her *needs*. Often these are of an occupational nature.

planning In the United States, the term *program planning* refers to the process of preparing the whole of a course, the number of courses, and their implementation. In the United Kingdom, curriculum planning is seen as a similar process. Hence, planning is the process of preparing an educational provision and includes potential clientele, *needs assessment*, context analysis, setting of aims and objectives, planning teaching and learning activities, evaluation, and organizational arrangements. See also *program planning*.

planning checklist A full list of all the aspects that a planner has to consider when preparing an educational *programme*.

Plastics Processing Industry Training Board The body responsible for overseeing the occupational preparation and training within this industry in England and Wales. Current address: Coppice House, Halesfield 7, Telford, Shropshire TF7 4NA, UK.

Plater College A residential college for men and women who are concerned with politics, trade union studies, and social services and who wish to study these topics in the light of Christian principles. The college is primarily Catholic, but does not restrict its entry by religious denomination. No formal entry qualifications are required and the courses lead to diplomas of the University of Oxford. Current address: Plater College, Pullens Lane, Oxford OX3 0DT, UK.

Platform Ouderejaars A *non-formal education* organization for the elderly in the Netherlands with the objective of developing *study circles* throughout the country, supported by the Dutch government. Current address: c/o NCVO, Post Bus 351, 3811 EW Amersfoort, The Netherlands.

Plato (c.428–348 BC) Greek philosopher, many of whose ideas remain relevant to educational philosophy today, especially to the *philosophy of adult education.* See especially *'The Republic'*, in which he discusses *knowledge* and *belief.*

Platonism A philosophy deriving directly from the work of *Plato*. Plato's writing are so complex that they are difficult to summarize as a single philosophy, although central to much of what he wrote is the theory of Forms or Ideas. Another factor that is significant to Plato's thought is *idealism*.

play See *role play*.

pleasure centre Refers to the areas of the brain which when stimulated produce what seems to be pleasure.

Plebs League In 1909 a secession from *Ruskin College* resulted in the formation of the *Labour College*. Its supporters and former students organized and became known as the Plebs League. It published a monthly magazine, *The Plebs*.

Plebs, The The monthly magazine of the *Plebs League*.

Plunkett Foundation A UK foundation devoted to co-operative work, it publishes material on all aspects of co-operation. Current address: 31 St Giles, Oxford OX1 3LF, UK.

pluralism A philosophical theory that reality consists of more than one basic substance or principle. It can refer to the alternative explanations of reality that exist or, in political theory, to the possibility of there being more than one seat of power in society. It is a significant idea for interpreting the place of *adult education* within society.

Pöeggler, Franz Professor and director of the Seminar for General Pedagogics at the University of Aachen in the Federal Republic of Germany. Author of authoritative studies on *adult education* in the Federal Republic.

poets The traditional educators in ancient Greece. They emphasized the importance of community cohesion and health.

Point Four Program Established in 1948 by President Truman to be an agency for technological and educational development in the Third World. It was succeeded in 1961 by the US *Agency for International Development* (USAID).

Poland See *Towarzystwo Wiedzy Powszechnej*, the Polish *adult education* association.

Pole, Thomas (1753–1829) Author of the *History of the Origin and Progress of Adult Schools*, published in 1816. He was born in Philadelphia but came to England as a young man and stayed there. He lived first in London but in 1802 he moved to Bristol. He was a Quaker who performed a ministry, an obstetrician and a writer of 13 books, including the earliest known book on *adult education*.

policy A plan of action adopted by a person or organization. See *social policy*.

political education 1. Considered a priority area in the *Russell Report* as a result of the decline in *civic education*, but not one in which a great deal of time or money was subsequently invested. This education is a form of awareness-raising rather than indoctrination. 2. A very important form of *adult education* in the Federal Republic of Germany, where it is regarded as a form of *citizenship education*.

political science The study of government.

polytechnic In the United Kingdom a polytechnic is an institution of *higher education* which at present does not have the legal right to award its own degrees. The polytechnics were established in the United Kingdom in the 1960s to provide more advanced *technical education*, as opposed to *university* provision.

Polytechnic Association for Continuing Education (PACE) Formed in 1980 out of the conviction that *continuing education* was the mainspring for the development of *polytechnics* and *colleges of further education*. The association runs conferences, seminars, and a newsletter. There is no central office although there is a committee which represents the members and institutions. Details can only be obtained from its officers.

pool of ability A reservoir of *ability*. Usually refers to an untapped source of ability of working–class personnel.

pooling A discontinued method of financing certain advanced courses in the United Kingdom in which each *Local Education Authority* contributed funds to a central pool which then paid the providers of approved courses. This method has been succeeded by the *Local Education Authority Training Grants* scheme.

Popper, Karl (b.1902) Philosopher of natural and social science whose work is well known. Much of what he has written is relevant to *adult education* theory, such as his falsification theory and the nature of *knowledge*.

popular culture The culture of the people.

popular drama The use of drama to portray everyday events, or to depict everyday experiences in a different manner for people to consider. Used in *adult education*, especially in the Third World. It is a technique that liberates the imagination and enables people to conceptualize reality in a different manner. See *popular theatre*.

popular education 1. A term widely used in Latin America, having the following connotations: education is a right of all people, even the masses who were excluded from the school system's benefits; education which is designed for the people by the people; an instrument in the ideological class struggle, radical and often revolutionary; and an education which involves *praxis* inasmuch as the education learned is then put into practice in the class struggle. 2. In Denmark and elsewhere in Europe,

the term is used almost synonymously with *adult education*. However, it may be distinguished under the Leisure Time Act (see *adult education legislation*) *as non-formal education* which a variety of groups can organize. Provided they meet the conditions of the act, they can claim state subsidy for the purpose. Popular education usually takes place in small groups over a short period of time and in a variety of subjects, but does not lead to any form of qualification. 3. In Greece the term is used as in Denmark, and is overseen by a General Secretariat for Popular Education within the Ministry of Education.

Popular Education Association Established in 1947 in Denmark, it is connected with the Conservative Party and provides *general education* for adults.

popular school Established in Spain during the 1970s, they are active in working–class urban areas, staffed mainly by *volunteers*. Since the re-establishment of democracy in Spain some have become more established as *adult schools* under state control.

Popular Schools' Act The 1929 law passed in Yugoslavia establishing a number of *adult schools* in agriculture, home economics, co–operative economics, and *adult literacy*.

popular theatre The use of drama in the *community* to inform and assist people in considering and understanding social, cultural, and political problems. A form of *community education* or *development education*, depending upon its context.

popular university Independent *adult education* institutions in Europe. They have usually been attached to universities and are similar in some ways to *university extension*, although they tend to be a little more autonomous. 1. In Holland popular universities started in the period immediately after the First World War and originated with the *Association for the Encouragement of Popular Scientific Knowledge*. 2. A popular university at the University of Haifa in Israel offers education to the working people. 3. In Spain these have grown in number during the 1970s and there are now over 60 popular universities, which are linked through a central federation, the *Federación Española de Universidades Populares*. 4. In 1907 the first popular university in Yugoslavia opened in Zagreb and was an extension of the University of Zagreb. Many more were formed in the following few years. 5. Université Populaire was also established in France and became a model for the Yugoslav system. See also *people's university, university extension, popular university movement*.

Popular University Movement Began in France after the Dreyfus affair in which there was a drawing together of people from a variety of social strata with the aim of communicating and learning. For a few years it flourished throughout France, but with the re-emergence of social divisons the movement died.

population The total number of people in a society, *community* or *group* to be sampled.

Population Education Clearinghouse Funded by *Unesco*, it supports educational programmes and other activities concerned with the population of Asia and the Pacific region. It keeps large collections of materials and is a resource centre for other organizations. Current address: P.O. Box 1425, Bangkok G.P.O. Bangkok 10501, Thailand.

portfolio A collection of documents, certificates, or publications that verify the professional and academic standing of an individual.

portfolio preparation The preparation of a *portfolio* is a method of demonstrating *prior experiential learning* by means of a folder of evidence which may be presented for *assessment* purposes.

Portugal See *Associação Portuguesa para a Cultura e Educação Permanente*.

positive correlation A statistical measure which indicates that there is an association between two variables.

positive reinforcement Reward for acceptable behaviour in order to reinforce that behaviour. A behaviourist concept. See *negative reinforcement*.

positive transfer The successful transfer of *learning* from one situation or task to another one of a similar nature.

positivism A philosophical approach to *knowledge* which assumes that all knowledge has a scientific basis and that only those questions which are answerable from a scientific method are valid. Hence, much of the *quantitative research* in *adult education* can be seen to be positivistic.

postal enrolment Enrolment of a course conducted through the mail. Many *adult education institutes* advertise their courses and include an enrolment form in the advertisement for students to enrol through the post.

postal questionnaire A *questionnaire* that is sent to respondents to answer; the response is also expected through the same medium.

postal tuition *Correspondence education.*

post-basic education *Education* and *training* after the initial preparation for an occupation. See also *continuing vocational education*.

post-compulsory education Education which occurs after the age of compulsory schooling. It is a term sometimes used to convey all aspects of *lifelong education*.

post-doctoral study A planned study programme that follows the successful completion of a doctorate. This occurs more frequently in the United States than in the United Kingdom.

post-experience vocational education (PEVE) A short course of updating and retraining employees in the United Kingdom, usually organized in an educational institution. This provision is now seen as one of the ways in which education and industry can liaise. It is a form of *continuing education*.

postgraduate education Studies beyond the first degree in *higher education*. See *graduate education* for the American equivalent.

post-hypnotic suggestion Indicates that a person under hypnosis will behave in a specific manner after the hypnosis. It is significant for educators since it shows that not all learning is conscious and that not all of the mind operates at a conscious level.

post-ordination training *Continuing professional education* for clergy.

post-registration education A term used for *continuing professional education* in some professions in which registration signifies completion of initial preparation for practice.

post-secondary education *Education* beyond what is given in *secondary schools*, i.e. after the age that secondary school education finishes.

post-secondary educational institution An educational institution offering education to those who are beyond the legal age of compulsory schooling.

post-test A form of *assessment* that occurs at the end of a *course or module of learning*.

potential The promise of successful performance at a later time.

potted versions Summaries.

poverty A low standard of living; the conditions in which much *radical adult education* has found a great deal of response.

poverty level Demarcates those whose income is below the wage designated by government as constituting a living wage. However, this is an inaccurate means of assessment.

Powell, John Walker (b.1904) Worked with *Alexander Meiklejohn* in both the *Experimental College* and the *San Francisco School of Social Studies*. He became a director of the latter. He was a philosopher of adult education who sought to relate education to social life. Still later he became concerned about the professionalism of *adult education*. He wrote a number of influential books about adult education in the 1950s and 1960s.

power The exercise of control or force, as opposed to *authority*. Teachers frequently exercise this in the process of teaching and the teacher's power has been criticized by *humanistic adult educators* and Marxists.

Power-load-margin model Espoused by *Howard McClusky*, this formula is: Power/Load d Margin, where power is the resources a person can command in coping with the load, load is the demands made on a person by self and society, and margin is the relation between them. It is a model of living in which the extent of the margin becomes important in deciding whether an individual has spare capacity for additional activities, such as adult learning.

power test Any test that measures *ability* by determining the degree of difficulty of material that can be mastered with no time pressures.

practical ability *Skills* as measured by *performance tests*.

practical assessment A form of *examination* in which the practical *competencies* of an occupation can be observed, directed, and assessed. Usually recognized as important within *professional education* and preparation but unless it is undertaken on a *continuous assessment* basis, it may be artificial and place additional strain upon the examinee.

practical work instructor See *practical work teacher* as this is the occupation's title now that more emphasis is placed upon the educational aspects of this job.

practical work teacher A district nurse (similar to a public health nurse) in the United Kingdom, trained in the art of one-to-one teaching, who takes student district nurses with her/him in the professional clinical setting in order to train and prepare them for their clinical role. Preparation for this role is mandatory in district nursing in the United Kingdom. See *field work teacher, teacher practitioner*.

practice 1. The actual performance, as opposed to *theory*. See *practicum, internship*. 2. Repetition of a *skill* until it has been thoroughly learned. 3. The re-ordering of experiences to make them more meaningful. 4. Professional occupation or business, e.g. the legal practice.

practice audit An inspection and analysis of practice before and after a *learning* exercise designed to improve that practice.

practice effect The influence of previous *practice* upon subsequent performance.

practicum Refers to both *professional placement* and on-the-job research experience and is more frequently used in America. It is similar to the English term *professional placement*. See also *teaching practice*.

practitioner One whose work is in the *field of adult education* as a teacher or administrator and organizer, either part-time or full-time.

pragmatics The study of the purposes, effects, and implications of meaningful *language*.

pragmatism A philosophical term relating to the work of C.S. Peirce and *William James* which refers to the theory that ideas become true inasmuch as they assist people in relating them to their wider experience. In a similar manner, one of the conditions of *knowledge* is that the idea, belief or theory is found to be practicable. It was adopted by William James and *John Dewey*, among others.

praxiology In some countries this constitutes a subject in the *adult education curriculum*; it is the study of the practical aspects of the occupation.

praxis A term used in Marxist thought that *Paulo Freire* has adapted to refer to the congruence between individual reflection and the action that results from it.

preach The Christian churches use this term to refer to the process of proclaiming their message, a form of *instruction*. Often used in a derogatory manner to refer to the process of trying to convert students to the teacher's own views.

pre-adult American term for *young adult*.

preceptor A *teacher* or *tutor*. When used in *education*, e.g. the College of Preceptors, it is also a term used in professional practice to refer to a *practitioner* who gives *instruction* to students.

pre-clinical course A theoretical course taken before undertaking a *professional placement*.

pre-coded questionnaire A *questionnaire* which has the answers specified in the form of a code. The respondents answer the questions by indicating which of the prepared alternative answers is/are most applicable.

precognition The hypostatized ability to have *knowledge* about future events.

preconscious A pscyhoanalytical term which refers to *knowledge* or *emotions* which are not within the consciousness but which are easily accessible.

preconscious learning A form of learning in which the learner acquires *knowledge* or *emotions* without consciously learning them but which can at a later date be called into the ambit of the conscious.

predictability The capability of being foretold. In *adult education*, as in the other social sciences, it is usually based upon the *correlations* between variables, or trends that have already occurred, and assumes that events will continue as they have done in the past. Hence, the weakness in all forms of prediction is that it is difficult to take social change into consideration.

predictive validity The extent to which a test has been ascertained to achieve what it claims to test, that is, that those passing a test will meet successfully certain other criteria demands at a later date and that those failing it will fail to meet those criteria demands at a later date.

prejudice A preconceived bias, which may or may not be correct, based upon insufficient consideration of evidence.

Prentice Hall Adult Education Series An early series of booklets on *adult education* published in the 1970s under the editorship of Curtis Ulmer.

Preparation for Retirement A Council of Europe report published in 1977.

preparation period A period of time devoted to preparation.

preparative skills training A basic skills *training* for unemployed people wishing to seek employment in a specific industry.

preparatory evaluation See *needs assessment*.

prerequisite course A course which has to be studied before another can be undertaken within an educational programme or course of studies.

Pre-Retirement Association of Great Britain and Northern Ireland. An association to promote knowledge about education for those who are about to retire and those who have retired. The association provides news and

information about retirement. It publishes a magazine, *Choice*, a newsletter, *Pre-Retirement Association News*, and has a resources unit which is based in the Department of Educational Studies, University of Surrey, Guildford, Surrey GU2 5XH. The current address of the association is: 19 Undine Street, London SW17 8PP, UK.

Pre-Retirement Association of Greater Manchester (PRAGMA) An association actively concerned with the *education* and *training* of both older people and of professionals who work with them. Current address: St Thomas Centre, Ardwick Green North, Manchester M12 6FZ, UK.

Pre-Retirement Association Resources Unit News This is the *Pre-Retirement Association's* national newsletter and is published four times per annum. Current address: c/o Department of Educational Studies, University of Surrey, Guildford, GU2 5XH, UK.

pre-retirement education (PRE) Courses of preparation for retirement, usually organized by educational or employing organizations. See *Pre-Retirement Association*. For Dutch pre-retirement education, see *Pensioen in Zicht*.

Pre-School Playgroups Association (PPA) A voluntary organization making provision for young children in which there is considerable concern for tutor training for its own volunteers, using adult education methods. Also involved in *parent education* in a community setting. Current address: 61–63 Kings Cross Road, London WC1 9LL, UK.

Present Day Papers Published between 1899 and 1903, these papers examined a variety of religious, social, and educational issues. They were edited by Rowntree and Binns, the first historians of the *adult school movement*.

presentation 1. The mode or method by which a teacher introduces students to the *content* to be *learned*. 2. The actual performance of giving a paper.

pre-service training Preparation for an occupation prior to employment within it.

president In America, this term refers to the senior executive of a university or college.

President of the Board of Education In the UK, the former title of the Minister of State for Education.

pressure group A group which seeks to influence power without assuming it. *Adult education* frequently acts as a pressure group or lobby.

pre-test A diagnostic test that is conducted before, or at the start of, a course to assess the *learning needs* of the learner(s). It is an approach to *formative assessment*.

pre-TOPS Preparatory courses arranged to assist potential students of the *Training Opportunities Programme*.

pre-university certificate (NWO) In the Netherlands a certificate is awarded after the completion of six years of *secondary education*. It is now possible for adults to seek this certificate through day school and evening school as a form of *second chance education*. See also *junior general* and *senior general secondary certificates*.

primary education Education for young children, a part of the *initial education* system.

primary need Bodily *need*. See *secondary need*.

prime sponsor An organization which, under the conditions of the Federal Comprehensive Employment and Training Act of 1972 in the United States can contract directly with federal agencies to run manpower training programmes.

primer An introductory textbook.

principal The senior executive officer in a college or institute of *adult education* in the United Kingdom.

principal lecturer An academic post in colleges of *further* and *higher education* in the United Kingdom, perhaps equivalent to a *senior lecturer* in a university. (This equivalency is suggested since in universities, the rank of lecturer is regarded as the career grade, whereas in colleges of further and higher education senior lecturer is regarded as the career grade.)

prior experiential learning *Learning* specifically from informal or uncertified sources such as work, hobbies, or life experiences in general.

prior learning *Learning* that has been acquired, usually outside the formal educational institution, which has not been formerly certified, although *formal education* may sometimes be included.

prior learning assessment (PLA) The *assessment* of *prior learning* is becoming an increasingly important factor in adult admissions and the *Council for Adult and Experiential Learning* has pioneered a great deal of this in the United States. Similar programmes occur in the United Kingdom and in other countries. See *assessment of prior learning* (APL) in the United Kingdom.

Prisnanfe Newsletter The quarterly newsletter of the Philippines *Private Schools National Association in Non-Formal Education*, published in English. This newsletter can be contacted through the University of Baguio, Baguio City, Philippines 0220.

prison education The *adult education* service in H.M. Prisons. See *correctional education*. This service appears to have four main functions: educational, personal growth, amusement, and personal behaviour. There is little evidence to suggest that such programmes actually help people to stay out of prison once they are released. In the United Kingdom all prisons operate a daytime *remedial education* programme; they also organize *vocational education* and an *adult liberal education* programme that can reach postgraduate level. There are *libraries* in each prison and an inter-library loan facility. A deliberate attempt has been made to relate prisons with local *adult education*. In England and Wales there is a separate branch of the prison service related to education. Current address: Chief Education Officer, H.M. Prison Service, Cleland House, Page Street, London SW1P 4LN, UK. See also *penal andragogy*.

private education Education which is financed by sources other than the government.

Private Enterprise Programme A programme of modules relating to business management, operated by the *Manpower Services Commission* for owner-managers. (Note: the *Manpower Services Commission* changed its name to the *Training Commission* and then to the *Training Agency* in 1988.)

private instruction A very early method of *adult education*. Instructors advertised their services as early as 1745 in London, for subjects as diverse as arithmetic and dancing, and in America as early as 1766 for arithmetic and writing. This early private instruction was sometimes on a one-to-one basis but more often it was for *evening schools*.

Private Schools National Association in Non-Formal Education (PRISNANFE) A national association in the Philippines. It publishes a quarterly newsletter in English, *Prisnanfe Newsletter*.

private vocational school A non-public school in the United States which offers *vocational education* to prepare students for an occupation.

proactive Describes an activity in which the actor has assumed the initiative rather than responded to events. See *reactive*.

probability The likelihood of an event occurring. Used in statistics; see *probability theory*.

probability theory The statistical theory of predicting the likelihood of events occurring, given specific conditions.

probation A trial period, often prior to a permanent appointment.

problem An educational problem is a condition or obstacle that *learners* have to surmount during a *learning* exercise.

problem-posing education The antithesis of *Paulo Freire*'s banking *education* concept, it refers to the form of *education* that encourages individual thought and reflection rather than presenting learners with *knowledge* that they must memorize.

problem-solving education A form of education in which a problem is set and the learners are expected to respond to it. Similar to *problem-posing education*.

Problema Na Truda 'Problems of Labour', a journal published monthly in Bulgaria. It was started in 1959 and deals with *training* adults and with the *education of adults* generally.

process Term frequently used by *adult educators* to refer to the teaching and learning procedures within an *educational institution* throughout a course of study, as opposed to the *product*, or the outcome of the course. It relates to such aspects as the teacher–student relationship, the methods employed, etc.

process education A form of preparation in which process *skills* form the basis of the curriculum, e.g. observation, classification, measurement, etc.

process evaluation The *evaluation* of the process of *teaching* and *learning* in either an *educational* or a *training* situation.

process model A *curriculum* model which places emphasis upon the process rather than the *product*. It tends to assume the *humanistic* perspective, and in *adult education* relates to the theories that stem from *John Dewey*, involving the learner in the planning of and dialogic approaches to teaching. See *product model*.

pro–chancellor A senior post in a university in the United Kingdom.

proctor 1. In the United Kingdom, a disciplinary officer of the university. 2. In the United States an officer responsible for supervising examinations.

product Term used by *adult educators* to refer to the outcomes of a course of study rather than the *process* of teaching and learning.

product model A curriculum approach which emphasizes the end-product of the education rather than the *process*. This tends to be *behaviourist* and non-*progressive*. See *process model*.

product moment correlation coefficient See *Pearson's product moment correlation coefficient*.

production school (Produkionsskoler) There are about 60 of these schools in Denmark, similar to *day folk high schools*, in which young adults are taught to make produce that is then marketed. These are mostly non-residential, and some are integrated with the *youth schools*.

profession This concept has defied agreement among scholars of the occupations although there is a general consensus that the word refers to a high-status occupation. Among the characteristics generally agreed for a profession are that it is an occupation founded upon an area of *knowledge* and that it has a service ethic. See *profession of adult education*.

profession of adult education Many of the definitions of *adult educator* include administration as the main area of

expertise rather than teaching and research into the academic area of study of the *education of adults*. Many who teach adults identify themselves as members of their occupation or profession, e.g. as a nurse educator rather than an *adult educator*. Thus at present the *education of adults* needs its own identity before it can begin to claim to be an occupational profession.

professional association An association organized by and on behalf of a high status occupation to control its own affairs, including the *education and training* of recruits and *continuing professional education* of its members. It also acts as a *qualifying association*.

professional code An ethical code of conduct prepared by a professional association.

professional degree A degree which is awarded in a professional subject, as opposed to a discipline of *knowledge*.

professional development 1. *Staff development* resulting in a person's being of greater use to the organization for which he/she works through the acquisition of greater *knowledge, skill*, or different *attitudes*. 2. Building professional competence in a field, such as *adult education*. 3. *Personal development* in which the person gains in *knowledge, skill*, or *attitude* for his/her own benefit.

professional education Term rarely used, but which generally refers to the basic preparation of new recruits to an occupation. See also *continuing professional education, professional development*.

professional institution A professional organization responsible for the *education* and *training* of new recruits, the *continuing education* of practitioners, and the registration of new members. Often referred to as a *qualifying association*.

Professional No-Techniceskoe Obrazovanie The *technical* and *vocational education* journal published monthly in the USSR since 1941.

professional placement Providing students in *adult education* or any other branch of education with the opportunity to observe and learn in the place of work. See *teaching practice, internship, practicum.*

professional training Often used to refer to the initial *preparation* or *education* of recruits into the professions; now used with reference to *continuing professional education*. There is a preference for the term education as it conveys the idea of a higher status, but there has been some movement back to the term *training* as the professions have apparently lost some of their high status in recent years.

professionalization The process of structural change in an occupation as it develops towards its objectives of obtaining public recognition of its status as a *profession*. Most scholars do not agree upon a definition and characteristics of a profession so that this process of change need not be the same for each occupation. However, certain trends have been detected by some scholars.

professor 1. In the United Kingdom, a professor is either head of department in a university or, more recently, in some polytechnics, or a holder of a *personal chair* awarded for services to the discipline or the university. 2. In the United States a professor is a member of the teaching staff in any institution of post-secondary education. There are normally three levels: assistant professor, associate professor, and full professor. In addition, there are a few appointments of higher rank than that of full professor.

professor emeritus An honorary title given to outstanding *professors* on retirement entitling them to take part in the life of the university.

proficiency The capability to perform effectively when the opportunity occurs.

proficiency-based education Emphasizes the achievement of optimal standards of performance through the educational process for the performance of adult roles. See *competency-based education.*

profile A set of measures of different characteristics of a learner that have been standardized to allow comparison.

profile analysis The preparation and analysis of a *profile.*

profiling A general dissatisfaction with the traditional method of examining led to new approaches; profiling was first used in the United Kingdom in the 1970s. It is a 'description' of students' achievements and characteristics on multiple dimensions, e.g. academic or personal characteristics. See *formative profiling, summative profiling.*

PROFITS The Professional Fashion Industries Technology Service, a collection of training videos which can be hired to assist companies with their own in-service training.

Program on Non-Collegiate Sponsored Instruction (PONSI) A programme currently organized by the *Center for Adult Learning and Educational Credentials* which makes credit recommendations on non-collegiate courses. Panels of subject experts are convened to consider specific courses and to make credit recommendations. This is an off-shoot of the military evaluations programme that *ACE* organized.

program planning The study and practice of preparing *adult education*, which starts by assessing *needs*, planning both the process and content of the educational exercise, designing the methods to be employed, implementing the programme, and evaluating the outcomes. Some theorists also argue that since *education* does not occur in a vacuum, it is always necessary to link the process throughout with the organization within which it occurs, e.g. in terms of social effects of the programme. See also the *andragogical cycle.*

programme 1. All the planned *learning* prepared by an educational institution for prospective students; similar to some definitions of *curriculum.* The American study of the practice of *program planning* is very similar to elements of British curriculum studies. 2. An educational meeting or course, based upon the *interests* or *needs* of the expected *participants*. This usage is more common in the United States than in the United Kingdom. 3. A prepared agenda.

programme evaluation An essential part of the *programme planning* exercise in *adult education*, strongly emphasized in American *adult education*. It involves assessing the extent to which the desired *proficiencies* are achieved during the educational process, whether the process itself is considered to be a good educational experience, the extent to which the context within which the programme is organized is conducive to the learning, and the efficiency with which it was undertaken. See *evaluation*.

Programme for Vocational and Social Integration See *Massnahmen zur beruflichen und sozialen Eingliederung*.

programmed instruction The use of especially prepared texts or programmes that guide the learner through a *learning process*. This sometimes occurs in conjunction with *teaching machines*.

programmed learning See *programmed instruction*.

Programmed Learning and Educational Technology A UK academic journal published in London.

programmed text A prepared learning manual, book, or computer programme that represents material in a step-by-step manner for learning.

programming The process of individual and collaborative effort in *adult education* institutions by *adult educators* and adult *students* in *planning*, designing, implementing, *evaluating*, and accounting for *adult educational provision*.

progressive education A form of student-centred education associated especially with the work of *John Dewey*. While the term is used most frequently

with the education of children, there are tremendous similarities between it and the *humanistic andragogical* writings of *Malcolm Knowles*. The connection between the two appears to be *Edward Lindeman* who was both a colleague of Dewey and an early influence on Knowles. It emphasizes creativity, negotiation and individuality.

progressivism An educational philosophy related to the work of *John Dewey*. It was initially child-centred, and orientated towards enabling the child to develop and grow as a result of shared learning activities.

project 1. A learning exercise requiring considerable time and effort, usually *problem solving, research*, or data collection, in which a variety of techniques are employed and in which the outcome is *presented* through one or more media to a tutor or peers. 2. A research undertaking.

Project Literacy USA (PLUS) A multi-media campaign to help combat adult literacy in the United States. It commenced in 1986, combining radio and television broadcasts with community action in which all 525 Public Broadcasting Service (PBS) and American Broadcasting Company (ABC) stations participated.

project method A method of *teaching* and *learning* in which the learner undertakes a task or research exercise usually initiated by the teacher.

Project Share An American *clearinghouse* for improving the management of human resources. It maintains a data base, publishes extracts of papers in journals, and has a newsletter, *Sharing*, which provides a variety of information. Current address: P.O. Box 2309, Rockville, Maryland 20852, USA.

Project 2000 A project set up by the *United Kingdom Central Council for Nursing, Midwifery and Health Visiting* in 1984 to determine the education and training needs of these three professional groups in the light of the projected health care requirements of the 1990s and beyond. The recommendations were finalized in 1987.

projective test A variety of devices used in personality assessment and clinical psychology in which the subject is presented with standardized unstructured stimuli and expected to respond to them in an unrestricted manner.

propaganda Organized dissemination of information, allegations, etc. to assist or decry the cause of a movement or government. The fact that with the growth of the *information society* a great deal of propaganda is issued means that one of the aims of *adult education* should be to produce critically aware individuals.

proposal A term used to refer to something planned, such as a piece of research. Hence a research student prepares a research proposal, a researcher prepares a proposal for the funding agency, a book proposal, etc.

proprietary school An educational institution, approved by the state. In the United States, it is organized to provide education but also to make financial gain for its owners. In the United Kingdom this would be a private school, but in America there are institutions of *higher education* that come into this category.

Prospect Union Educational Exchange The first *educational brokering agency* in America, established in Boston in 1923. It later changed its name to the *Educational Exchange of Greater Boston*.

Prospects The educational journal of *Unesco* published in English, French, Spanish, Arabic, Russian and Chinese. Established in 1970 and published quarterly. Obtainable from Unesco, 7 Place de Fontenoy, 75700 Paris, France.

prospectus The publication of a college or adult education institute containing a list of all the courses that are offered and other relevant information for prospective students.

Protestant Association of Adult Education A West German *provider* with a wide programme. See *Arbeitsstelle der Deutschen Evangelischen*.

Proudh Shiksha The *Adult Education* monthly journal published by the *Indian Adult Education Association* in Hindi. It was started in 1957.

pro-vice chancellor Deputy to the *vice chancellor* in a British university.

provider An organization or individual which organizes and runs educational programmes for adults.

Provision of Adult Education in New South Wales: Roles of the Agencies and Guidelines for Development Official statement on *adult education* in New South Wales, Australia, issued by the Ministry of Education in August 1986, covering all forms of provision in that state. Obtainable from NSW Board of Education, ADC Building, 189 Kent Street, Sydney 2000, Australia.

proxemics Theories of people's use of space as an illustration of the cultural context of behaviour. It is a part of the study of the sensory world of the individual.

psychiatry The study and treatment of mental illness.

psychoanalysis A theory of human behaviour that is associated with the work of *Sigmund Freud*. It is a therapy in which the analyst assists the patient/client in drawing connections and associations between various aspects of behaviour, so that the patient/client begins to understand that behaviour better.

psychodrama A form of group therapy in which patients/clients act out, before an audience, situations from their past lives. See *socio-drama*.

psycholinguistics The psychology of language.

psychology The scientific study of animal and human behaviour and cognition. A great deal of *learning theory* in *adult education* has been psychological in nature since learning is individualistic and psychology concentrates upon individual behaviour.

psychometrics Measurement and testing in *psychology*. It deals with statistical techniques.

psychomotor Associated with physical *skills learning*.

psychomotor domain A *skills* area. There have been proposed lists of educational *objectives* in this domain, but it has not become as well known as the *cognitive domain*.

psychomotor skills Manual dexterity, as opposed to any form of cognitive process. See *cognitive skills*.

psychopath Individual with a personality disorder which causes antisocial behaviour.

psychosexual A term relating to the mental and emotional aspects of sexual behaviour. It is the subject of some *affective education* courses.

psychosis Mental disorder which does not take social reality into consideration.

psychotic One who is in a state of *psychosis*.

Public Broadcasting Service The American association concerned with *public broadcasting*. Current address: 475 L'Enfant Plaza West SW, Washington DC 20024, USA.

Public Broadcasting System Non-commercial broadcasting in the United States, devoted to cultural and education programmes. See also *public television*.

public examination An open *examination*, often administered by an examination body.

public forum The forum was a lecture followed by open discussion on a variety of topics. *John Studebaker*, as US Commissioner of Education, started the public forum series throughout America in the same manner as he had seen in Des Moines. Common in parts of America. See *National Issues Forum, Des Moines Forum*.

public health The health of the community; a subject of much *adult education* in Third World countries and increasingly in the developed world.

public language A term used in linguistic analysis to refer to non-formal language.

public lecture One of the oldest methods of *adult education*. Lectures were advertised, with admission fees, as early as 1584 in London and 1726 in the United States. Subjects such as anatomy and electricity were amongst the early popular ones.

Public Libraries Act Passed in the United Kingdom in 1850, the Act of Parliament which established the *public library service* in Britain.

public library A library that offers a service to local residents free of charge. It is usually funded by local government.

public library service See *library*.

public school In the United States, the public schools, which are not private institutions as they are in the United Kingdom, have been among the major *providers* of *adult education evening classes*. The first evening classes were conducted in public schools in Boston and Louisville in 1834. The participants were mostly working *young adults* although older adults also enrolled. However, the degree of participation of the public schools in *adult education* differs from state to state. See *proprietary school*.

public service Term used in the United States to refer to that aspect of university work in which the university is responsible to the local community, e.g. in *university extension, continuing education,* providing public lectures, and even in the use of university facilities for community activities.

public service employment A US term for a form of employment orientated to the public good, often sponsored by government.

Public Service Satellite Consortium An American grouping concerned with *public service*. Current address: 4040 Sorrento Valley Boulevard, San Diego, California 92121, USA.

public television The term used in the United States for the non-commercial television service devoted to educational and cultural pursuits. See also *Public Broadcasting System*.

Puczynska-Wentlandtowa, Hanna (b. 1906) Polish *adult educator* who has written several books about *adult education* and has specialized in *teaching methods* and *health education*. Held many important positions within the sphere of *adult education* and health education and is the editor of a library of health education books.

Pulse of Public Continuing and Adult Education The newsletter of the *National Association for Public Continuing and Adult Education*. This ceased publication when the association merged with the *Adult Education Association of the United States of America* in 1982.

pupilage The period of *apprenticeship* that a qualified barrister must spend with a senior barrister in the United Kingdom before being allowed to practise.

purpose A declaration of intent for a specific *teaching* and *learning* session. Similar to *objective*.

purposeful behaviourism A theory of learning that suggests that the learner is able to connect means and ends. She/he will, therefore, learn in a purposeful manner by making the necessary connections between the means and ends and act accordingly.

pyramid of leadership *Cyril Houle* suggested that in *adult education* there is a pyramid of leadership consisting of *volunteers* as the base; a tier of those who have a responsibility for *adult education* although they are not primarily *adult educators*; and a tier of those whose primary concern and responsibility is adult education. This pyramid relates in some way to the discussion on the *profession of adult education*.

Quaker Social Responsibility and Education Department The Society of Friends has played a significant and influential part in the history of *adult education* in Britain. It still retains this interest. Current address: Friends House, Euston Road, London NW1 2BJ, UK.

qualification 1. An educational qualification is the formal award that records successful completion and fulfilment of the requirements of a course of study. 2. A recognition of some form of achievement. However, not all qualifications are socially recognized. Hence it is possible to purchase a degree from a pseudo-university which is a qualification but not one that is socially recognized.

qualification inflation The tendency for increasingly higher *qualifications* to be required for entry to the same job.

qualifying association A *professional association* which prepares and tests new recruits to a profession. See *professional institution*.

qualitative research An approach to research in which data are collected in a non-numerical manner, including the researcher's own subjective responses to the research situation. This approach frequently assumes a *phenomenological* perspective.

quality circle See *study circle*. This is a group of people, often between four and twelve, in the work place, who meet together voluntarily to teach and learn from each other about aspects of mutual concern in their work, such as quality.

Popularized in industry by the Japanese. See *National Society of Quality Circles*.

quality control Techniques to ensure that the standards of performance and production are satisfactory. The term used to be employed entirely within the productive industries but in recent years it has been creeping into the educational vocabulary and used in similar ways to *evaluation*.

Quality of Working Life A concept employed by those in *training* and *development*. It may be broadly defined as the process of work organization which enables the participants at all levels to contribute in shaping the organization's environment, methods, and outcomes. This is a broader process than that of merely improving the working conditions and a number of major developments have been made in this field.

quantitative research An approach to research that assumes a positivistic paradigm, in which numerical data are collected and analysed. This approach endeavours to be objective. It is not applicable to many aspects of education of adults.

quarter The division of the academic year into four parts, each called a quarter. Used in American universities, where teaching occurs in three quarters and the fourth quarter is devoted to *summer schools*.

quarter credit hour An American term for the number of hours of class enrolment that a student has throughout a *quarter*.

quartile Every twenty-fifth *percentile*.

question A form of words seeking to elicit a response from another person. In teaching, *questioning* is an important method and there are different ways of classifying them, such as *open-ended* and *closed questions*, information-based, analysis and evaluative, etc.

question bank A bank of examination questions which have been set by examiners but never used on examination papers, stored for future use.

question entry The type of interruption made by a *trainer* when raising a question about the *group* process.

question period A specified period of time after a *lecture* during which an audience can question the speaker.

questioning A *teaching method* in which the teacher poses questions rather than providing answers. See *Socratic teaching*.

questionnaire A *research* technique in which the researcher designs a schedule of questions that is then sent to a sample of respondents. It is a self-administered *quantitative research* approach.

quiet period A period of time devoted to *reflection* to enable a group to discuss a *problem* or issue after a period of individual thought.

Quilon Social Service Society
Charitable foundation established in India in 1960 and concerned with *non-formal education* programmes for adults. Current address: Fatima Road, Quilon – 691013, Kerala, India.

quota sampling A non-random form of sampling in which a specific number or proportion of types are sampled from the *population*.

quota system A selection system more commonly employed in the United States than the United Kingdom in which a specific proportion of those selected for an educational course or job are chosen on the basis of a specific ethnic or racial background.

race A human group having a common genetic inheritance. It is very unlikely that such a phenomenon as a pure race exists today.

racism An ideology which claims that groups of people have different characteristics determined by hereditary factors and which endows some races with superiority over others.

racism awareness training Originated in America, this has subsequently been used in the United Kingdom since the early 1980s. It is an effective form of training people to become aware of any racial attitude that they might have, through self-expression and group interaction. Recently discredited, considered immoral by some, and replaced by *anti-racism training*. The claims against this form of *training* still need to be thoroughly researched.

radical adult education A form of *adult education* based on the premise that education is not neutral; It endeavours to promote *change* and *liberation*. The ideology is usually framed within a critical social science perspective. See *radicalism*.

radicalism An ideology that favours change of a fundamental nature in organisations, institutions, or society at large. Related in education especially to those who embrace *education for liberation* and certain forms of *community education* and *community action*.

radio college A system of *distance education* started in 1969 by the *Deutsches Institut für Fernstudien* in West Germany consisting of a series of about 30 radio broadcasts, with 14 accompanying booklets, *computer marked assignments*, and local study groups.

Radio ECCA (Emisora Cultural de Canarias) The cultural radio station of the Canary Islands, founded in 1963 by Francisco Villen Lucena, a Jesuit, and now run by the Ministry of Education for *adult education*. It provides courses at the level of *literacy* and many more advanced courses. Much of its income derives from student fees for its courses. Current address: Avda. Mesa y López, 38, Apartado 994, Las Palmas de Gran Canaria, Spain.

radio listening group Group established to listen to educational radio broadcasts and to discuss their content. Often, radio stations prepare study *packages* to accompany the programmes. See also *radio study group*. These courses are often part of a formal programme of studies and group members enrol for the course.

Radio Popular University Established in Holland in 1930, the *popular university* of the air.

radio school Radio broadcasts used in parts of the Third World for groups of peasants who, having followed the broadcast, study textbooks produced by the centre with the assistance of a locally trained volunteer. The local structure of the radio school is implemented by the local community and church leadership who organize, control, and encourage participation.

radio study group See *radio listening group*.

Radosavljević, P. R. (1879–1958) The first Yugoslav scholar known to have engaged in the study of *adult learning*. However, he undertook this work whilst a professor of psychology in New York. He discovered not only that adults learn but that their learning is sometimes more effective than that of younger generations – an important finding at the time he was propounding it. He was a contemporary of *Edward Thorndike*.

Raikes, Robert The founder of the first *Sunday school* in England, in the city of Gloucester in 1789, in Sooty Alley among the chimney sweep's children. He publicized his work in the *Gloucester Journal*, of which he was proprieter and editor.

Raising the School-Leaving Age (ROSLA) When the school-leaving age was increased from 15 to 16 years in the 1972–73 academic year in the United Kingdom, the children remaining at school were referred to as 'ROSLA children'. This did not have a great effect on *adult education* although it did place considerable emphasis on the *education of young adults*, since special material was prepared for this group.

Ramsay, Allan Started the first *circulating library* in Edinburgh in 1726.

Rand School of Social Science Opened in New York in 1906 by a trust fund of Mrs Carrie Rand to provide workers with an education and to prepare them for a position with the labour unions, the socialist party, or the co-operative movement. It was owned by the American Socialist Society. However, it ran into financial difficulties and had to be closed. Its address was: 7 East 15th Street, New York, New York, USA.

random learning *Learning* acquired through the process of everyday living; learning from life, but not formalized in any way. It is a type of incidental learning.

random sample A *sample* in which every member of the *population* has an equal chance of being selected every time a selection is made. It is the only pure manner of sampling.

ranking Also known as rank ordering, this entails placing grades or items in order according to certain, usually pre-specified, criteria.

rapid reading Techniques that allow the reader to read at a faster than normal pace.

rate-of-return studies Studies that have examined the incomes of adults in relation to the cost of their education, showing the rate of return on the original educational investment.

rate of return to education A method that seeks to analyse the cost–benefit of education by comparing the earnings of adults with extended education with those whose education has been limited. The findings are then related to the costs of obtaining education. Also known as the *direct-returns-to-education* approach.

rationality The use of reason or logic to think out a problem. The fact that a solution is rational does not mean that it is either correct or the only possible solution to a problem.

Rauhankirje The Finnish title of *Peace Newsletter*. It is published in both English and Finnish.

raw data Unanalysed research information.

raw score Statistical data that have not been analysed by statistical techniques.

re-accreditation The process in which members of a profession have to undergo specified *continuing professional education* and be examined for professional *competence* in order to retain the right to continue to practise.

RE:ACE A newsletter from the Office of Research and Evaluation in Adult and Continuing Education, Northern Illinois University, DeKalb, Illinois 60115, USA.

reactive Responsive. See also *proactive*.

readability 1. The ease of understanding of written materials according to the writing style used. 2. The total of all elements within written material that affect the success that a reader will have in mastering a specific piece of writing. The difficulty of a piece of writing may be used in assisting readers to cope with written material at their own level.

reader 1. A position in a UK university which is usually awarded for high academic achievement. The holder is expected to concentrate on scholarship. 2. A person employed by a publisher to assess the suitability of book manuscripts and proposals for publication. 3. A symposium of articles collected to form the basic reading for a course of study.

Reader, The The newsletter of *Literacy Volunteers of America*, published quarterly since 1972.

Reader's Advisory Service The first specified adult education role within the American library service, started in 1926.

reading ability The *skills* in reading shown by individuals.

Reading Camps Association The forerunner of *Frontier College* which began in the work camps in Canada in 1900. It started as a separate room in the camp devoted to reading and writing. It became a movement with a great deal of support, supplying books and other materials. In 1906 it became a legalized association.

reading circle Used in the Roman Catholic Church in the United States from the 1880s as a means of *adult Christian education*, and to improve the educational opportunities of adults through prescribed courses of prepared reading.

Reading Circle Union Established in 1889 to encourage the development of *reading circles* in the Catholic Church in America.

reading level The level of achievement in reading attained by individuals.

reading list The lists of books recommended for a specific course.

Reading Research and Education Center Established at the University of Illinois, Champaign–Urbana, in 1987 as one of 11 centres to help teachers become more effective instructors of reading in order to help combat *adult illiteracy*.

reading scheme A plan or series of books prepared to assist in *literacy*, each book being a planned development of the preceding one.

reading test Techniques to assess the level of achievement in reading.

Reading With a Purpose Series Published by the American Library Association between 1925 and 1933, this consisted of a series of *reading lists* with introductory essays on 67 subjects.

readings Published collections of articles, symposia, etc.

realism The belief that universals have an actual existence independent of thought.

reason The faculty for *rational* argument, judgement. There are generally considered to be three categories of reason: evidencing (showing why something is true); motivating (providing the reason why somebody did something); and causally necessitating (demonstrating the causes of an event or phenomenon).

recall The process of retrieving information from *memory*.

receiver role A *learner role* in which the learner is the receiver of information.

reciprocal questioning A technique for improving comprehension in which both teacher and students read a passage together. The teacher then invites the students to ask him/her questions and when the students have finished questioning, the teacher does the same to the students. The technique helps comprehension and enables the teacher to evaluate the comprehension level of each of the students.

reciprocity The reciprocal recognition of *qualifications* by professional associations or educational institutions.

recognition The awareness that an event or a phenomenon is one that has been experienced previously.

recollection A memory.

Recommendation on the Development of Adult Education

Sixty-seven recommendations adopted by the General Conference of *Unesco*, held at Nairobi, Kenya in October–November 1976. These recommendations were made to all member states about the way that *adult education* should develop. The Assembly recommended that member states should take the necessary legislative action to put these recommendations into effect.

reconstructionism A Marxist analysis of one of the functions of all forms of education: to reconstruct society according to its present values and form. Hence, some definitions of *education* refer to the transmission of *culture* from one generation to the next.

Record of Achievement It is planned that by 1990, all children leaving school will have a record of achievement which will include curricular and extra-curricular activities, compiled by the school or college in negotiation with the student. This record will be used for job applications and for entrance to *higher education*.

recorder A member of a *group* who has been allocated, or volunteered for, the task of recording the *group dynamic* and/or *discussion*.

recruitment The process of attracting new people or students to an occupation or educational institution.

recurrent education The belief, regarded as a strategy for *lifelong education*, that people have the right to keep returning to education throughout their lives. Exponents of this concept include the *Organization for Economic Co-operation and Development* which issued a number of reports on the topic in the 1970s. There are two broad approaches to this viewpoint: one regards it as a type of *continuing education* while the other, more radical, perspective treats education as a human right. Some exponents have embraced the viewpoint that everybody should be entitled to a specific length of post-school education at some stage in their lifetime. This viewpoint is clearly related to *paid educational leave*. In the United Kingdom, there is an *Association for Recurrent Education*, within which both views are held. In Sweden, the law on *higher education* sets aside a quota of places in higher education for adults over the age of 25 years, so that recurrent education is embodied in law.

Red Latin Americana de Información y Documentación en Educación (REDUC) A bibliographical data bank regarding education formed by 23 organizations in 17 countries in Latin America and the Caribbean. It produces a variety of materials that can be made widely available. It also publishes a comprehensive list of *abstracts* classified by subject and author; the material is published only in Spanish or Portuguese. Current address: c/o CIDE, RUDEC Co-ordinator, Erasmo Escala 1825, Casilla 13608, Santiago 1, Chile. Most of this material is also available in North America and can be read in the library at the Ontario Institute for Studies in Education. Current address: 252 Bloor Street West, Toronto, Ontario, Canada M5S 1V6

Redcliffe–Maude Report (1976) A report on *Support for the Arts in England and Wales* which claimed that 'arts support' and *education* are not separate entities.

reductionism 1. Any doctrine that seeks to explain and reduce a complex proposition to a simpler one. 2. The belief that human behaviour can be reduced to or interpreted by the behaviour of lower animals. Hence, *behaviourism* is a form of reductionism.

redundancy The loss of employment because there is no longer a place for the individual within the employing authority. Sometimes redundant persons are invited to attend *pre-retirement education* by their employers. However, the processes of being forced to leave employment and retirement are different and require different forms of educational programme.

Rees, James Frederick (1883–1967) Professor of history and an early *adult educator*. He conducted the first extra-mural class in Wales, organized by the University College, Bangor, in 1910–11.

refer The process of giving a *student* an opportunity to improve upon a grade or an academic performance in an assignment before the final decision is made.

referee 1. An *assessor* of a paper or book who judges whether it is suitable for publication. See *reader*. 2. One who writes a reference, recommendation, or testimonial on behalf of another person.

reference book A term employed for books such as dictionaries or encyclopedias, which provide general rather than specialist information.

reference group A sociological theory which seeks to explain why people identify with groups (either ones to which they belong or those to which they do not but would wish to belong), and how their reference group shapes their behaviour, values, and attitudes. It is a useful theoretical approach to the study of *participation* in *adult education*.

reference library A collection of books and other primary data which can be used on the premises but not borrowed. This collection may contain *reference books* or it may be a specialist library.

referral 1. Directing a student to improve upon an academic performance prior to the final decision being made. 2. Re-directing an enquiry, request, or a person with a problem to a more suitable person.

reflection The process of thought, usually associated with careful and considered *reasoning*. This has become a much more significant concept in theories of learning in *adult education* than in *initial education* because it has been less influenced by *behaviourism*.

reflective A *learning style* in which the individual thinks carefully upon an experience or information before responding.

reflective learning *Learning* by thoughtful review and analysis of *experience*.

reflective technique Regarded as different kinds of process, of which there are at least six: remembering, repeating, reasoning, reorganizing, relating, and reflecting. See also *reflectivity*.

reflectivity *Jack Mezirow* proposed seven levels of reflectivity: reflectivity (awareness of a specific perception, meaning, sensation): affective reflectivity (awareness of how the individual feels about what is being perceived); discriminant reflectivity (assessment of the efficacy of the perception); judgemental reflectivity (making and becoming aware of the value judgements being made); conceptual reflectivity (assessing the extent to which the concepts employed are adequate); psychic reflectivity (recognition of the habit of making percipient judgements on the basis of limited information); and theoretical reflectivity (awareness of why one set of perspectives is more or less adequate to explain experience). For Mezirow, only the latter three are critical reflectivity. It is these that are most likely to occur in adulthood, although he does not produce a great deal of evidence for this assertion.

reflex Automatic response to a stimulus; a response which is not consciously controlled.

reforming society *Voluntary association* formed in early America with the intention of ensuring that people in the local neighbourhood adhered to the *norms* and *mores* of that community. It is probable that these early voluntary societies were copied from practices in England.

reformism An ideology of change, often found among *adult educators*. Reformist change is gradual, initiated by those in power and certainly not *radical*.

refresher course A course of study designed to assist the learners in relearning or revising *knowledge* and *skills* that they had previously held.

regents The governors of a US university.

Regional Advisory Council (RAC) Responsible for co-ordinating *further* and *technical education* throughout the region. There are ten Regional Advisory Councils throughout the whole of England and Wales, financed by the *Local Education Authorities*. They assist in the planning of further and *higher education* in the area. They are involved in *adult education*, further education, *youth* and *community education*, and adult tutor training. They are also the validating body for *Stage I* and *Stage II* of the *Haycocks Report* recommendations for the training of part-time educators. In addition, there is a *Standing Conference of Regional Advisory Councils*.

Regional Centre for Functional Literacy in Rural Areas for the Arab States (ASFEC) Centre for *adult literacy* which holds seminars and publishes information about adult literacy in Arab countries. Current address:

Sirs-El-Layyan, Menoufia, Arab Republic of Egypt.

regional institutional accrediting association A recognized voluntary agency which administered the procedures of *accreditation* of educational institutions in a region of the United States.

regional management centres Established in the United Kingdom in 1971 to provide excellence in *management education*.

regional office The *Open University* in the United Kingdom is subdivided into 13 regions covering the whole country. The administrative centre of each region is its regional office.

regionally accredited Descriptive term for an educational institution in the United States that has been *accredited* by impartial experts from one of the six regional accreditation associations and found to be of degree standard.

register List of students in a class. See *roll*.

registrar A senior member of the academic staff of a college or university responsible for the academic administration of that institution.

registration fee Fee charged on enrolment for a course of study or in order to become a member of an organization.

regius professor A professional appointment which is in the gift of the Crown in an established university in the United Kingdom.

regression 1. A *psychological* term to indicate a mental state in which the person exhibits behaviours of an earlier age group. 2. A statistical term used to indicate association between one *variable* and other variables in an analysis.

regulations The rules of an institution.

regular education Term used by *Unesco* to refer to the normal and continuous sequence of full-time education from school through to higher education.

rehabilitation The process of restoring an individual who has been physically or mentally disabled, or who has been imprisoned, to readapt to the demands of society.

Rehabilitation Act This federal act of 1973, amended in 1978, mandates that *post-secondary educational institutions* receiving federal financial assistance should provide equal opportunities in terms of access and services to disabled individuals.

reification The process by which an abstract concept is treated as if it had concrete existence.

reinforcement There is a tremendous variation in use of this term in psychology, but for most purposes in *adult education* it may be regarded as *reward* for correct behaviour in *conditioning* theory.

reinforcer The *stimulus* that reinforces acceptable *behaviour*.

relativist 1. One who regards all *knowledge* as relative rather than absolute. 2. A *learning* style in which the *learner* seeks to assess *knowledge* within its context, seeking both meaning and relevance. See *deep processor*.

relaxation techniques Techniques that assist individuals in relaxing their muscles, minds, etc. These may be taught to people in potentially stressful occupations, or to others who face stress, to help release physical or psychological tension. Relaxation classes are run by many institutions of *adult education*.

released time Time which an employee is given to attend educational activities.

relevance Since much *adult educational* activity is planned in response to *needs analysis*, it is important to *evaluate* the activity in terms of its relevance to those needs.

reliability The extent to which something is dependable, that is consistent and stable in seeking to measure a *variable* or other phenomenon under investigation. It is a statistical concept which refers to the level of dependability of a test or instrument of research in the performance of the function for which it was designed.

re-license See *re-accreditation*.

religious education *Education* in the sense of learning about the religions of the world, or about personal religious development. *Adult religious education* is increasing as a relevant area of the education of adults. Often this is regarded as Christian education, but there is no reason why it should be restricted in this manner. See also *lay training*.

Religious Education Association An American association concerned with religious education, including *adult religious education*. Current address: 409 Prospect Street, New Haven, Connecticut 06510, USA.

remedial adult education *Adult education* provided for *low achievers, slow learners* and the mentally handicapped. See also *adult basic education*.

remedial education *Education* offered to those who have not achieved as high a standard in their education as they could have been expected to or would have liked. See *remedial adult education, second chance education*.

remedial loop Term used in *programmed learning* to refer to the additional process which is incorporated into the learning sequence for those learners who have given an incorrect answer to a question at the end of a stage in the programme.

remember To recall, recollect, retrieve, or reproduce *knowledge, skill, attitude*, or other experience.

reminiscence A form of recall of past experiences, often pleasant memories. This is an important element in some forms of *educational gerontology* and in preparing people to face death.

repeated reading A procedure adopted in some forms of *literacy* education which involves the selection of a short piece. The level of difficulty is dependent upon the competence of the learner. The learner reads it to a teacher who times the length of time taken for the reading to be completed and notes the number of errors. The reader is then required to practise the reading and undertake the same process for as many times as is necessary to reach a specified rate of reading speed and then progress to another passage.

repertory grid A technique to measure the relationship of concepts in George *Kelly's personal construct* theory.

REPLAN Commenced in 1984 and planned initially to run until 1987 but subsequently extended to 1989, and funded by the *Department of Education and Science, Welsh Office,* and the *Manpower Services Commission.* See *Adult Unemployed Programme,* which is its formal title. Its objects were to bring about more and better educational opportunities for unemployed people by encouraging and supporting changes in education and training in England and Wales. See also *education support grants,* which were awarded within the project. Address: Room 7/1, Department of Education and Science, Elizabeth House, York Road, London SE1 7PH. (Note: the *Manpower Services Commission* changed its name to the *Training Commission* and then to the *Training Agency* in 1988).

Report of the Special Programme Committee on Education of the Canadian Association of Adult Education (1943) One of the most important reports ever produced by the *CAAE.* It advocated a programme of reconstruction after the Second World War that was more radical than any

previously adopted. It was presented to the Conference in London in 1943 and led to the formation of the *Canadian Citizens' Forum.*

REPORTS Magazine The magazine of *Word Education,* which is published to stimulate thought on emerging issues and to share innovative ideas.

representative sample A sample in which the proportion of each category is the same as the proportion in the total *population.*

repression In Freudian analysis, a process which operates at the unconscious level preventing previously learned *experiences* reaching the conscious level.

reproducing orientation An approach to learning in which the *learner* relates to *syllabus,* and seeks to memorize facts rather than meaning.

reproduction The outcome of *learning* that merely memorizes facts. In social reproduction theory, Marxist and other radical analysts claim that the social processes merely reproduce the same social and power structures. They regard this as the inevitable approach of most forms of *education.*

required course In the United States, this is the compulsory element in an educational programme. See *core curriculum.*

research A systematic investigation into a phenomenon to collect facts, information, or principles about it. There are a variety of types of research, such as *quantitative, qualitative, empirical, naturalistic.*

Research and Practice in Adult Literacy Group (RaPAL) Commenced in 1985 in the United Kingdom, it is a network of practitioners which intends to publish papers about *adult literacy.* Current address: Secretary RaPAL, Department of Educational Research, Lancaster University, Lancaster LA1 4YL, UK.

research assistant A person who is employed to assist a researcher in undertaking a *research project*. Often this person undertakes a *higher degree* during the process and it is one way into a traditional academic career. In these instances it is almost like a form of *apprenticeship*.

research methods A course on techniques in research.

research seminar A *seminar* conducted on a research topic.

research student A student who is undertaking a *higher degree* by research.

research supervisor The member of academic staff of an institution of *higher education* who supervises the research conducted by a *research student*.

Researches in Adult Higher Education Chinese journal, published by the East China Normal University. Current address: 3663 Zhong Shan Road, [N] Shanghai, China.

reserve of ability That adult ability which is lost to a society because of elitist selection mechanisms to *higher education*. These mechanisms initially deny entrance and consequently inhibit unsuccessful adults at that stage from developing their talents later in life.

residential college There are both short-term and long-term residential colleges for adults in the United Kingdom. The long-term colleges are founded on the *folk high school* principle, whereas the short-term colleges tend to run courses lasting a single week or a weekend. Many are privately organized.

residential management centre Private and independent centres offering courses from a few days to three months, catering for management (especially senior management in industry), commerce, etc.

resistance The term used by American *adult educators* to refer to the attitudes of people who appear to *need* education but who show no indication of wanting to enrol in the appropriate classes. Another definition is that of adults who are mature and able to make considered life choices based on value systems, and who are of an age to be socially permitted to act upon these choices, but who overtly or tacitly challenge the traditional educational system.

resource A supply of material, aids, manpower, finance, etc. that can assist in the educative process. Although it is often claimed that resources should not influence the *curriculum* it might be true that these are among the most influential factors in *curriculum development*.

resource allocation The equipment granted to a course or department to cover a specific activity.

Resource and Referral Service This *clearinghouse* seeks to develop and disseminate information about resource organizations, to provide data for clients, and to refer clients to other relevant organizations. It maintains its own data bank. Current address: c/o The National Center for Research in Vocational Education, Ohio State University, 1960 Kenny Road, Columbus, Ohio 43210, USA.

resource-based learning A form of *teaching* and *learning* in which learners are given direct access to *knowledge* that is stored, while *teachers* act as *facilitators*. The growth of this approach to *learning* is related to the growth of *resource centres*.

resource centre A centre in which *resources* for learning – books, journals, articles, pamphlets, records, tapes (both audio and video) – are available for learners to use. Centres usually specialize in one area, such as trades union education. In some instances these centres allow borrowing rights and occasionally they have an information officer who will be able to tell learners where other resources are to be located. Some resource centres publish newsletters to inform interested parties about the resources that are available.

Resource Center for Planned Change American *clearinghouse*. Current address: American Association of State Colleges and Universities, One Dupont Circle NW, Suite 700, Washington DC 20036, USA.

resource cost The cost of resources allocated for a specific activity.

Resource Materials Sharing Program A plan to use resources in a community more efficiently through sharing by the liaison of various agencies. This is expected under legislation in the United States, especially in the Higher Education Act of 1965.

Resource Organizations and Meetings for Educators (ROME) A data base developed by the *National Center for Research in Vocational Education*. It contains descriptions of non-profit professional organizations, research organizations, advocacy groups, and agencies in education.

resource person An expert who is willing to be consulted during a *learning project*. In some styles of *teaching* the teacher night be viewed as a resource person.

Resources in Education Monthly publication containing abstracts of material gathered by the *Educational Resources Information Center (ERIC)* and available in many libraries in the United States and elsewhere in the world.

response The direct effect of a *stimulus* in *behaviourism*.

response rate The proportion of a sample which responds positively to a request to complete a test, *questionnaire*, or other form of enquiry.

Responsible Body Those *extra-mural departments*, the *Workers' Educational Association*, and other bodies which have responsibility for providing *adult education* at university level for the general adult population in the United Kingdom. This designation was first used in 1924 when financial support was given to these organisations designated to undertake this responsibility by the *Adult Education Regulations*.

Restart One-week courses for the long-term unemployed. They were intended originally for those out of work for one year but this was reduced to six months from April 1987. Help is given in job-seeking, training opportunities, personal budgeting, etc. The course is free and benefits are not affected. Renamed in 1988; see *Options*.

restricted code The linguistic code characterized by short sentences, ungrammatical statements, use of pronouns, and concrete expressions, which it has been claimed is used by people from the lower socioeconomic classes. See *extended code*.

résumé Curriculum vitae.

retention The ability to retain and to recall information. See *memory*.

retirement education See *pre-retirement education*.

Retirement in Prospect See *Pensioen in Zicht*.

retraining 1. As the vocational requirements of employees change rapidly, there is an increasing need for *continuing education* which involves more than merely learning new techniques. In West Germany, this is the term used to refer to the process of re-equipping an employee to undertake the work that he/she is already performing. 2. A form of preparation for another occupation as structural change forces employees to change their form of employment.

retrieval The process of recalling information from *memory*.

return to study courses Courses that are organized to assist adults in returning to academic study. They usually consist of *study skills, time management, educational guidance*, and *counselling*.

Reuter, Rudolf (1891–1977) A leading figure in West German *adult education*. He was concerned with the public library system and the training of librarians as well as teaching adult education at the University of Cologne. He was also involved in *adult religious education* and produced a bibliography on adult education in West Germany.

review To look back or re-examine. Formal reviews are conducted in certain forms of *assessment* and *evaluation*.

Review of Environmental Education Published three times a year, the journal of the *Council for Environmental Education*.

review of the literature In research projects, the customary practice of undertaking a review of all published research on, or similar to, the phenomenon under investigation.

Revista de Educación Established in 1928 in Chile, this periodical is published by the Ministry of Education in Spanish ten times a year and is concerned with a variety of educational topics.

Revista Educación de Adultos (Adult Education Review) The quarterly journal, published in Spanish since 1983, of the *Instituto Nacional para la Educación de los Adultos* of Mexico.

Revista Interamericana de Educación de Adultos Established in 1978, this Pan American Review of Adult Education is published by the Education Affairs Department of the Organization of American States. Information may be obtained from: Casilla 16162, Correo 9, Santiago, Chile.

revolutionary organizer A *community animateur* whose main function is to create disenchantment and discontent with the current situation in the community and to produce a more challenging climate than the status quo.

Revue de l'ensignment à distance See *Journal of Distance Education*.

reward 1. Used in the same way as *reinforcement* in *conditioning* theory. 2. Loosely, any prize for correct work.

Rewley House The centre for *extra-mural* studies at *Oxford University*.

Rewley House Papers Academic papers published by *Rewley House* on *adult education* over many years.

Ricerca Educativa (Educational Research) the quarterly journal of the *European Centre for Education*, which is based in Italy. It was begun in 1984 and publishes articles in a variety of European languages.

Richmond, Norman Macdonald (1897–1971) The first full-time director of *adult education* in a New Zealand university, he was appointed to the University of Auckland in 1928.

Right to Learn The declaration of the fourth *Unesco* international conference on *adult education*, held in Paris in 1985. The statement specified that people should have the right: to read and write; to question and analyze; to imagine and create; to read their own world and to write history; to have access to educational resources; to develop individual and collective skills. This is regarded as an indispensable tool for the survival of humanity.

Right to Read The earliest phase in the development of the literacy campaign in the United Kingdom was called the Right to Read. It was sustained mostly by voluntary organizations, such as the *British Association of Settlements*, up until mid-1974. Thereafter, the campaign developed through the involvement of such organizations as the *British Broadcasting Corporation*.

rights Legal entitlement. However, in the United Nations Declaration of Human Rights, the rights to education and work are both included. These are regarded as human rights, that is entitlements as a result of human existence.

rigidity 1. In physiology, a state of muscular tension. 2. In psychology, a personality trait characterized by inflexibility in behaviour or even *perception*.

rite A culturally designated ceremony.

ritual A sequence of patterned behaviours, often socially or culturally designated. Many such rituals exist in the education system.

ritualism To go through the motions of a behaviour pattern without being committed to the end-product.

Road Transport Industry Training Board Responsible for training within this industry in the United Kingdom. It produces its own manuals and other training material, and has its own residential training centres. Current address: Capitol House, Empire Way, Wembley HA9 ONG, UK.

Robbins Principle Derived from the findings of the Robbins Report on *higher education* in the United Kingdom in 1963, which stated that courses of higher education should be available to all who are qualified by ability and attainment to pursue them and who wish so to do. While this referred in part to *young adults*, it also related to *mature students*.

Roberts, Robert Davies (1851–1911) First *university extension* tutor in Wales in 1876. He subsequently held many influential positions in university extension in Cambridge and London, including those of secretary to the Cambridge Board and registrar for the London Board of University Extension. He was a great believer in *liberal adult education* for all people.

Roberts, Thomas Hewitson (1906–79) A leading *adult educator* in Australia, where he was director of adult education at the University of Perth. He had also been a professor of adult education at the University of Iowa in the United States, where he was a founding member of both the *Adult Education Association of the*

United States of America and the *Commission of Professors of Adult Education.*

Robins Report A report on the training and employment of the handicapped in Eire, published in 1975.

Robinson, John (d. 1985) Highly involved with *adult education* and broadcasting. For a while he was Further Education Liaison Officer with the *British Broadcasting Corporation* and later became the link between the BBC and the *Open University*. See *John Robinson Award*.

Robinson, Joyce West Indian *adult educator* who pioneered the development of the Jamaican public library service. She was director of the *Jamaican Movement for the Advancement of Literacy* from 1973 to 1981 and managing director of the *Human Employment and Resource Trust* (HEART Trust) from 1982. She has played a considerable role in the development of *adult education* in her country and was vice president of the *International Council for Adult Education.*

Rogers, Carl (1902–86) American humanistic psychologist, author of numerous books, and a major influence on humanistic *adult education*. He was an authority on *counselling* and *self-development*; many of his educational ideas seem to have emerged directly from his conception of psychotherapy.

role 1. From a functionalist perspective, the rights and duties of a social position. 2. In an interactionist perspective, the manner by which individuals fashion their social behaviour within designated social positions.

role conflict Situation in which an individual is expected to perform two different *roles* simultaneously, either as a result of self-perception or as perceived by different members of the *role set*.

role education Term used especially in trade union education to refer to that form of education which provides a broad background of knowledge relevant to the performance of specific roles.

role modelling *Learning* by observing and imitating the *role* of another person.

role play A participative method of *teaching* and *learning* in which learners play roles in order to experience them affectively as well as cognitively. A useful method in *professional education*, it is similar to, but different from, *simulation*.

role set That group of people in specified social positions with whom a *role* player has to interact in order to perform his/her role. Hence an *adult educator* has a specific role set and there may be similarities in that role set wherever an individual performs a similar role within the same socio-cultural environment.

roll The list of these enrolled for a specific course. See also *register*.

'roll-on/roll-off' curriculum A form of curriculum that allows students to commence a course whenever they wish to and to complete it whenever they desire; it is not controlled by the academic term or year. Courses are usually modular and contain a number of different routes through them so that learners may commence at any time.

Romania The documentation centre in Romania includes *adult education* within the sphere of its work. Current address: Officiul de Informare si Documentare in Stiintele Sociale si Politice, Bd Republici 17, Bucharest 70431, Romania.

Ron South Fund Administered by the *Commonwealth Association for the Education and Training of Adults* to provide opportunities for a lecture or other event to take place within an international conference arranged by the *Commonwealth Association for the Education and Training of Adults*. The Fund is to be given by or associated with a person or persons who have, in the view of the trustees, made an important contribution to the promotion of the practice and theory of the education of adults from an international perspective; to assist individuals working in the international context of the education of adults; and to contribute to the development of adult education from an international perspective.

Rorschach ink-blot test A technique to examine personality traits in which a person responds to a standard series of ink-blots.

rote learning The approach to *learning* that seeks to acquire facts mechanically without necessarily understanding them.

round table An educational technique for creating *discussion groups* in which people from different positions in society sit down together to solve problems and to learn from each other. For instance, it is undertaken in *education for self-management* programmes in *Yugoslavia* where workers, managers, and scholars work together.

Rousseau, Jean Jacques (1712–78) French philosopher whose work has influenced *progressive educational* theory, especially through his book, *Emile*.

Rowntree, Arnold (1872–1951) A member of the famous York family, Liberal MP, and leading figure in *adult education*, especially in the formation of the *Educational Settlements Association* for the first 25 years of its existence.

Royal Aeronautical Society A professional and *qualifying association* for aeronautical engineers in the United Kingdom. Current address: 4 Hamilton Place, London W1, UK.

Royal College of General Practitioners A *professional* and *qualifying association* and educational institution for medical doctors in general practice in the United Kingdom. Current address: 14 Princes Gate, London SW1, UK.

Royal College of Midwives A *professional association* and educational institution for midwifery in the United Kingdom. Current address: 15 Mansfield Street, London W1, UK.

Royal College of Nursing A *professional association* and educational institution for nursing in the United Kingdom. Current address: 20 Cavendish Square, London W1, UK.

Royal College of Obstetricians and Gynaecologists A *professional* and *qualifying association* in the United Kingdom. Current address: 27 Sussex Place, London NW1, UK.

Royal College of Physicians A *professional association* for physicians practising in the United Kingdom. Current address: 11 St Andrews Place, London NW1, UK.

Royal College of Pyschiatrists UK qualifying body and *professional association*. Current address: 17 Belgrave Square, London SW1, UK.

Royal College of Radiologists UK professional qualifying body. Current address: 38 Portland Place, London W1, UK.

Royal College of Surgeons A *professional association* and educational institution for surgeons in the United Kingdom. Current address: 35 Lincoln's Inn Fields, London W2, UK.

Royal College of Veterinary Surgeons Established in 1844, the professional society responsible for the preparation of veterinary surgeons. Current address: 32 Belgrave Square, London SW1, UK.

Royal Cornwall Polytechnic Society Founded in 1833 by Anna Maria Fox and Caroline Fox to foster and encourage the spirit of scientific research among the Cornish mining population. This was closely related to the *self-help* movement in nineteenth-century Cornwall. King William IV was the reigning monarch at the time of its foundation and he agreed to become its patron. It remains under royal patronage.

Royal Endowment for Culture and Education A scholarship fund for Jordanians which also stresses its concern to increase the level of women's participation in Jordanian life. Current address: P.O. Box 927226, Amman, Jordan.

Royal Institute of British Architects Established in 1834, the body responsible for the professional preparation of architects in the United Kingdom. Address: 66 Portland Place, London W1, UK.

Royal Institution of Chartered Surveyors UK *professional* and *qualifying association*. Current address: 12 Great George Street, London SW1, UK.

Royal National Institute for the Blind UK organization concerned with blind people, including their *education* and *training*. Current address: 224 Great Portland Street, London W1N 6AA, UK.

Royal National Institute for the Deaf UK organization concerned with deaf people, including their *education* and *training*. Lip-reading courses, for instance, are run in some *adult education* institutions. Current address: 224 Great Portland Street, London W1N 6AA, UK.

Royal Society of Arts (RSA) Founded in 1754 as the *Society for the Encouragement of Arts, Manufacture and Commerce* under the instigation of William Shipley, it became an examining body in 1856 and is the second oldest examining body in England (see the *College of Preceptors*). It is now, in association with the *Southern Examining Group*, offering *General Certificate of Secondary Education* courses for external and mature students. It is about to form an examination association separate from the Royal Society itself. Current address: John Adam Street, Adelphi London WC2 6EZ, UK.

Royal Society of Health UK *professional* and *qualifying association*. Current address: 90 Buckingham Palace Road, London SW1, UK.

Royal Town Planning Institute The professional institution of town planners in the United Kingdom. It is concerned with both the initial preparation and the *continuing education* of its members. Current address: 26 Portland Place, London W1N 4BE, UK.

rubric A set of instructions. In education, it usually refers to instructions given to a candidate and printed on an examination paper.

rule learning One of the higher order of types of *learning* in *R.M. Gagné's* hierarchy of learning, in which he claims that the ability to respond to a *stimulus* by a series of responses is successful rule learning.

Rural Functional Literacy Projects The predecessor to the *National Programme on Adult Education* in India. It was continued and strengthened with the introduction of a new programme.

rural music schools First formed in 1929 in Hertfordshire, England to promote, organize, and train village orchestras.

Rural Women's Access Grants (RWAG) A programme introduced in Australia to improve the access of women living in rural areas to employment and general services, which includes *adult education* and *training*. Current address: Office of the Status of Women, Department of the Prime Minister and Cabinet, Edmund Barton Building, Barton ACT 2600, Australia.

Rural Women's Union An organization in the Federal Republic of Germany which assumes the following educational roles for rural women: nutrition, health, household maintenance, *general education, family life,* and *leisure.*

Rural Youth Union An organization in the Federal Republic of Germany involved with young people. It assumes a number of educational functions including preparing young people to assume responsibilities within the trade union movement.

Ruskin College 1. Formerly *Ruskin Hall,* founded in 1889. In 1907 it assumed its present name. It is a residential college in the United Kingdom, open to men and women. It is grant-aided by the *Department of Education and Science* and governed by a council which contains representatives from the trade union movement and other bodies. The purpose of its foundation was to equip people for the labour movement. It has two sites, one in Oxford and the other in Ruskin Hall in Headington. While it remains independent of the university, its students have been able to sit the university diploma in economics and political science since 1910. Current address: Walton Street, Oxford OX1 2HE, UK. 2. In Trenton, Missouri, *Avalon College* was opened in 1895, but later renamed Ruskin College in 1900. It was opened as a residential labour college.

Ruskin, John (1818–1900) Associated from the outset with *F.D. Maurice* and the *Working Mens's College,* where he was one of the most popular teachers, seeking always to provide a *liberal adult education.* He was also the first Slade Professor of Fine Art at Oxford University and a very well-known writer.

Ruskin Hall Opened in 1899 for the education of working people, it was concerned with political, social, and economic subjects. It was to become *Ruskin College* in 1907. It was originally located at St Giles Street, Oxford in a room leased from Balliol College, but it always remained independent of the university.

Russell, Bertrand (1872–1970) One of the greatest philosophers of the century, he wrote a great deal about *education,* although very little specifically about *adult education.* Even so, many of his views should be considered more frequently by philosophers of adult education.

Russell Report Formally entitled *Adult Education: A Plan for Development,* published in 1973. The report was made to Margaret Thatcher, as secretary of state for education, in December 1972. The committee had been convened under the chairmanship of *Sir Lionel Russell* in 1969 to assess the need for, and review the provision of, non-vocational adult education in England and Wales, to examine the appropriateness of financial policy in this respect, and to make recommendations. The report produced a list of 118 recommendations which covered the whole range of *non-vocational adult education*.

Russell, Sir Lionel (1904–83) Chief education officer for Birmingham from 1946–68, and chairman of the committee which prepared the report, *Adult Education: A Plan for Development*.

Russia See *Union of Soviet Socialist Republics* and *Znanie*.

RVU Educatieve omroep The Dutch organization of radio and television broadcasting organizations concerned with education. Current address: Postbus 1950, 1200 BZ Hilversum, The Netherlands.

Ryle, Efie Appointed in 1917 by the *adult school movement* to work among women members of the movement. She resigned in 1926 but later rejoined the movement in another capacity.

Ryle, Gilbert (1900–76) Famous UK philosopher whose work is well known in the philosopy of education.

sabbatical The period of time academic staff are released from teaching or administration in order to undertake reading and research. Some academic institutions award it automatically; others expect staff to apply for it. It is a form of *paid educational leave*.

Sacred Songs and Solos The first hymn book used by the *adult school movement* in Britain.

Sadler, Michael Ernest (1861–1943) Influential in *higher education* and *adult education* in Britain. He wrote an influential study of *university extension* and was Master of University College, Oxford University.

Saint Francis Xavier University Located in Nova Scotia, Canada it was from this university that the *Antigonish Movement* was organized.

Saint Kitts Association of Adult Learning Facilitators (SKAALF) A national association inaugurated in March 1986 for the training of *facilitators* in *adult learning*. There are only a few trainers and facilitators on the island. Current address: Adult Education Unit, Department of Education, P.O. Box 333, Cayon Street, Basseterre, St Kitts.

Saint Lucia Association of Continuing Education Current address: c/o The Caribbean Research Centre, P.O. Box 1097, Castries, St Lucia, West Indies. See *SLACE News*.

Saint Mary's Non-Residential Settlement Opened in York in 1909 by the Society of Friends as an attempt to introduce a simpler approach to the *university settlements* than had been established elsewhere.

Sakskarta Sandesh A Hindi *literacy* magazine published in India monthly.

Salaried Employees' Educational Association (Tjänstemännens Bildningsverksamhet) One of the 11 educational organizations sponsoring *study circles* in Sweden, concerned with non-manual workers and civil servants. Established in 1934.

Salzburg Discussions of Leaders in Adult Education Begun in 1956, an annual seminar held in Salzburg each summer.

Sami Educational Association (Samisk Studieforbund) There are about 30,000 Samians, or Lapps, in Norway. This educational association is a member of the *Norwegian Association of Adult Education Organizations* and works with the Samian people to help them retain their culture and language.

sample Proportion of a total *population* selected to be tested. See *representative sample, random sample*. Sampling is used in *quantitative research*.

sampling frame Information on the total *population* from which a *sample* is taken. The construction of an accurate sampling frame is a very significant aspect of research.

San Francisco School of Social Studies Established in 1934 as a private adult education institution with *Alexander*

Meiklejohn as its director. Later, *John Walker Powell* became director until its closure in 1942 through lack of funds. The school had a social concern, seeking to relate education to social life.

Sandler, Richard (1884–1964) Teacher in *folk high schools* in Sweden and later a politician, he was prime minister of Sweden between 1925 and 1926. He was also the founder of the *Workers Educational Association* of Sweden in 1912 and its chairman from 1919 until 1938.

sandwich course A course, often at undergraduate level, for which the learner spends periods of study in an educational institution and periods at the work place. The equivalent in the United States is the *cooperative program*.

Sarah Lawrence College The location of a joint workshop held in 1951 which led to the merger between the *American Association for Adult Education* and the *Department of Adult Education of the National Education Association*. It led to the creation in 1951 of the *Adult Education Association of the United States of America*.

Sãrathi Can be translated as one who shows the path; a pilot or a charioteer. It is the name of the newsletter of the *non-formal education* section of the Ministry of Education, Sri Lanka.

Saudi Arabia The official *adult education* body in this country is the Department of Literacy and Adult Education. Current address: Ministry of Education, Riyadh, Saudi Arabia.

Save Adult Education Campaign A movement started in 1980 in the United Kingdom when it was feared that the then Conservative government would withdraw all financial support for *liberal adult education* within the state sector of education. It gained widespread support but never actually became the sole political lobby for *adult education* in the United Kingdom. It lost its impetus by 1982 and while some hoped to replace it with another organization, *Campaign for*

Adult and Continuing Education, this was never really successful. See also *Start Helping Adults to Real Education*.

Savez Andragoških Društava Jugoslavije The *Union of Yugoslav Adult Educators' Societies*. There are separate societies for each state and region in Yugoslavia; this is the general association that maintains the eight major societies. However, it is administered by each in turn and the address given here is the address of the Serbian society, not the address of the union. Contact address: c/o Andragoško Drutro Srbije, c/o Veće Saveza sindikata Jugoslavije, Trg Marxa i Engelsa 5, 11000 Belgrade, Yugoslavia.

Savićević, Dušan (b. 1926) Yugoslav scholar of *adult education* at the University of Belgrade. Former president of the *International Congress of University Adult Education* and the scholar from whom *Malcolm Knowles* learned the word *andragogy*.

Sawad Magazin A *literacy* monthly magazine published since 1951 in Afghanistan.

Sawston Village College Opened in 1930, this was the first of the *village colleges* proposed by *Henry Morris*. It is in Cambridgeshire in England.

scale Any procedure or device used for the purpose of arranging *data* in a progressive sequence.

scale posts Teaching positions which relate to responsibilities and pay scales in the United Kingdom.

scan To read rapidly for general meaning.

Scan The newspaper of the *Scottish Community Education Council*, published ten times a year.

scapegoating An act of blaming a person or group for another's frustrations, grievances, or mistakes.

scattergram The process of plotting *scores* to see the scatter, or *distribution*, of the *data* in a pictorial manner.

Sc.D. The doctor of science degree is occasionally written in this manner.

scepticism 1. A philosophical attitude that maintains that a sure *knowledge* of how things really are may be sought but not found, so that all statements have to be treated circumspectly. 2. A school of Greek philosophy which maintained that reality was unknowable and should therefore be treated accordingly.

schedule A *timetable*. This noun is used much more frequently in America.

schizophrenia A form of mental illness in which there is a distortion of and withdrawal from reality.

scholarship 1. A high standard of *academic work*. 2. A financial grant or award.

scholasticism An early philosophical form that concentrated upon abstract subject matter, careful logic, authority, and often esoteric debate. For a while it did not enjoy a good reputation, but in recent years some of its work has become more prominent.

Schon, Donald A. Professor of Urban Studies and Education at Massachusetts Institute of Technology. In 1970 Professor Schon delivered the Reith Lecture in the United Kingdom. He is author, and co-author with *Chris Argyris*, of many books on learning, action, and reflection which have been influential in the development of educational theory.

school 1. An institution which provides *education*. It usually refers only to education until about 19 years of age, unless prefixed by 'adult', e.g. *adult school movement*. 2. A group of scholars who adhere to similar approaches to study; similar bodies of knowledge may be referred to as a school of thought.

school education Education that occurs in the early part of life, until no later than about 19 years of age. See *initial education*.

School for Adult Educators Established in 1958 by the *Association of People's and Workers' Universities* in Croatia, *Yugoslavia*, for the preparation of teachers and administrators in *adult education*. This school has contributed to the growth of theory and practice in adult education in Yugoslavia and beyond.

School for Living A radical *adult education* project in Spain in which small groups look for social alternatives to contemporary society. It describes itself as a project of scientific investigation of pedagogic social work in the fields of education and the social sciences. Current address: Escuelas Para la Vida, Apartado de Correos 23075, 28080 Madrid, Spain.

school for self-management The introduction of *self-management* has been a feature of modern life in *Yugoslavia*. Schools are occasionally organized for self-management which are run in conjunction with the *workers'* and *people's universities* in which a full *curriculum* of courses relating to *self-management* are studied.

School of Social Sciences The first institution in Finland to establish a lectureship in *adult education* in 1929; by 1949 it had become a professorship in the University of Tampere. See the *Civic College* and *Tampere University*.

school term A prescribed span of time during which schools are open and students are expected to attend. While this concept refers to school, most other educational institutions employ a similar concept and work to similar time periods, unless they are using a *semester* system.

schooling for social promotion The term used in *Belgium* for adult schooling.

Schouten, George Hendrik Leonardus 'Bob' (1906–81) Dutch adult educator, one of the initiators, and secretary and treasurer, of the *European Bureau of Adult Education*. He was secretary from the founding of the Bureau in 1953 until his death.

Schouten Memorial Fund Established in honour of *Bob Schouten* and administered by the *European Bureau of Adult Education* to acquaint young adult educators with adult education outside of their own country.

Schweizerische Veringung für Erwachsenbildung The Swiss adult education association, it has its own library and consultation service. See *Féderation suisse pour l'education des adultes*. Current address: Oerlikonerstrasse 38, Postfach 8057, Zurich, Switzerland.

science 1. The systematic study of the nature of behaviour of the physical universe, subdivided into a number of *disciplines* and *bodies of knowledge*. 2. Any body of knowledge organized in a systematic manner. Educational knowledge is in some countries referred to as scientific knowledge. 3. A method. See *scientific method*.

Science and Art Department Established in 1853 in England to increase the means of industrial education and extend the influence of science and art on productive industry. It was the first British government department to be established to oversee *technical education*. It organized examination syllabuses in science and arts subjects but was criticized because of the division it created between theory and practice.

Science Museum UK national museum. Current address: Exhibition Road, London SW7, UK.

Scientific Educational Association (Tudományos Ismeretterjesztö Társulat (TIT)) Established in 1841 in Hungary, it is the only national association which deals exclusively with public education in Hungary. It publishes a monthly magazine, *Valóság*, and a weekly one, *Élet és Tudomány*.

Scientific, Literary and Artistic Atteneo of Madrid Founded in 1820, this association has continued under a variety of names to organize courses for adults. It currently does not organize courses but it still runs conferences and is one of the most important libraries in Madrid. Current address: Atteneo de Madrid, Prado 21, Madrid 28014, Spain.

scientific method An investigative method involving several stages: the problem to be investigated is first identified; hypotheses are constructed in relation to the problem based upon existing *knowledge*; and the hypotheses are tested rigorously to examine the extent to which they are correct or incorrect. It is frequently claimed to be the best approach to *research* in *adult education* and other social sciences, although this has been hotly debated by other researchers who claim that the study of people – who are not as predictable as inanimate matter – cannot use this approach.

score *Quantitative data* about some phenomenon, *test*, or *research*.

Scottish Adult Basic Education Unit The Scottish unit which provides support for *adult basic education* schemes in Scotland. It also offers training and helps with programme development. Current address: Atholl House, 2 Canning Street, Edinburgh EH3 8EG, UK.

Scottish Adult Literacy Agency (SCALA) Established to deal with *adult literacy* in Scotland; in March 1979 it was replaced by the *Scottish Adult Literacy Unit*.

Scottish Adult Literacy Unit (SCALU) Established in 1979 from the *Scottish Adult Literacy Agency*, it was incorporated within the *Scottish Institute of Adult Education*.

Scottish Arts Council Current address: 19 Charlotte Square, Edinburgh EH2 4DF, UK.

Scottish Business Education Council (SCOTBEC) Established to devise, prepare, and examine courses of study in *vocational education*. See *Scottish Vocational Education Council*.

Scottish Central Film Library Has a large stock of educational film. Current address: 16–17 Woodside Terrace, Glasgow, UK.

Scottish Centre for the Tuition of the Disabled Established in 1979, this centre has sought to respond to the educational *needs* of *disabled* adults. Current address: Queen Margaret College, Clerwood Terrace, Edinburgh EH12 8TS, UK.

Scottish Certificate of Education Higher Grade Taken at 17 years of age it has some similarities to the *General Certificate of Education* (*Advanced Supplementary Level*) in England and Wales.

Scottish Certificate of Education Ordinary Grade Replaced by the *Standard Grade* during the late 1980s, it was taken at 16 years of age. See *General Certificate of Education (Ordinary Level)*.

Scottish Certificate of Education Standard Grade A measure recently phased into Scottish education, with the first examinations in 1986 for some subjects. Taken at 16 years of age. See *General Certificate of Secondary Education*.

Scottish Community Education Council An *adult* and *community education* organization in Scotland. Current address: Atholl House, 2 Canning Street, Edinburgh EH3 8EG, UK.

Scottish Co-operative Educational Association Current address: 95 Morrison Street, Glasgow G5 8LR, UK.

Scottish Council for Educational Technology Current address: 74 Victoria Crescent Road, Glasgow G12 9JN, UK.

Scottish Council for Research in Education Current address: 15 St John Street, Edinburgh EH8 8JR, UK.

Scottish Education Department The official government department for Scotland. Current address: 43 Jeffrey Street, Edinburgh EH1 1DN, UK.

Scottish Health Education Unit Concerned with *health education* in Scotland. Current address: Woodburn House, Canaan Lane, Edinburgh EH10 4SG, UK.

Scottish Institute of Adult and Continuing Education The Scottish national institute for *adult education* and *continuing education*. It also publishes its own journal, *Scottish Journal of Adult Education*, and organizes conferences. Current address: 30 Rutland Square, Edinburgh EH1 2BW, UK.

Scottish Institute of Adult Education The former name of the Scottish Institute until it became the *Scottish Institute of Adult and Continuing Education*.

Scottish Journal of Adult Education The biannual journal of the *Scottish Institute of Adult and Continuing Education*.

Scottish Journal of Youth and Community Work Replaced by *Community Education* in 1978.

Scottish Pre-School Playgroups Association Current address: 16 Sandyford Place, Glasgow G3 7NB, UK.

Scottish Standing Conference of Voluntary Youth Organisations Current address: Atholl House, 2 Canning Street, Edinburgh EH3 8EG, UK.

Scottish Telephone Referral, Advice and Information Network Started within the ambit of the *Scottish Institute of Adult Education* in the 1970s, but became independent in 1984. It broadcasts support, and deals with enquiries and referral services in *adult education*, especially in *adult basic education*. Current address: Network, 74 Victoria Crescent Road, Glasgow G12 9JQ, UK.

Scottish Tertiary Education Advisory Council Established in 1984 for an initial two years, with a remit to report on a strategy for *higher education* in Scotland. Closed in 1987 by the Secretary of State or Scotland.

Scottish Trades Union Congress Involved with trade union education in Scotland. Current address: 16 Woodlands Terrace, Glasgow G3, UK.

Scottish Vocational Education Council (SCOTVEC) Established on 29 March 1985, by the Secretary of State for Scotland. This is the council responsible for some preparation for *vocational education* for Scotland. It issues a national certificate for students who have followed a modular scheme of study offered in a variety of Scottish schools and colleges, which supplements the *Scottish Certificate of Education* of either *Ordinary* or *Standard Grade*. Current address: Hanover House, 24 Douglas Street, Glasgow G2 7NG, UK. See *SCOTVEC National Certificate*.

Scottish Women's Rural Institutes Current address: 42 Heriot Row, Edinburgh EH3 6EU, UK.

SCOTVEC National Certificate A national certificate, open to anyone in Scotland over the age of 16 years, for both *vocational* and *non-vocational education*. It is a modular course; each module should be completed in about 40 hours. See *Scottish Vocational Education Council*.

screen 1. An instrument used in an audio-visual display upon which an image is projected. 2. In psychological theory, to screen something out is unconsciously to prevent it coming to the conscious mind; or to prevent the meaning of a phenomenon from being recognized or understood.

screening hypothesis As an alternative to the *human capital theory*, this theory maintains that employers treat educational qualifications as indicators of personality traits rather than *cognitive*

ability. Hence as education expands, the educational requirements for entry to an occupation rise.

search committee Committee convened to seek out people for senior appointments in the United Kingdom. In the United States, search committees are convened to fill most academic appointments.

Search for Education, Elevation and Knowledge (SEEK) A remedial education programme organized for *disadvantaged* students at the City University of New York.

Sears–Roebuck Foundation American foundation which provides support for some *lifelong learning* activities.

second chance education A term that has recently been used less frequently to refer to educational opportunities for adults to compensate for lack of success or lack of opportunity during their *initial education*. See also *continuing education, recurrent education*. In the Federal Republic of Germany, this is sometimes referred to as *second route education (2 Bildungsweg)*.

second degree A *higher degree*.

second level course *Open University* undergraduate courses in the United Kingdom are at four levels: *foundation*, second, third, and *fourth levels*. The second level is the only other level generally regarded as ordinary degree level.

second route education See *second chance education, Abendgymnasium*.

Second Thoughts The newsletter of *Basic Choices Inc.*

secondary education A form of *initial education* organized by day schools for children of about 12 years and older, some with a *vocational* strand and others with a more *general education* approach. Often, *second chance* education is directed towards providing opportunities for adults to undertake or repeat this period of their education.

secondary group A social group in which social interaction occurs, but of a less intensive nature than that which occurs within *primary groups*.

secondary memory See *long-term memory*.

secondary need *Learned need* acquired through the processes of living. See *primary need*.

secondary school leaving certificate US certificate awarded after six years of study in *secondary school*.

secondary socialization The processes of *socialization* which occur after primary socialization; among these is adult socialization.

secondment A period of time spent away from work for additional *staff development* or *training*. In recent years there has been a growing interest in seconding teaching personnel to industry and commerce. In this case in the United Kingdom, the company is asked to contribute towards the person's salary as the *Local Education Authority Training Grants Scheme* only contributes a maximum of 70 per cent of the overall cost.

Secondment File Launched in 1987 by the *British Association of Commercial and Industrial Education*, it is a 'market place' for secondments from education to industry and commerce. There is a Secondment File Newsletter.

Secretary's Initiative on Adult Literacy On 7 September 1983, President Reagan and Secretary Bell convened a meeting at the White House to promote *adult literacy* in America. Its two main results have been the *National Adult Literacy Project* and the *College Work-Study Program*. Current address: US Department of Education, 400 Maryland Avenue SW, Room 4145, Washington DC 20202, USA.

selection The process of choosing among candidates for a course or position. It is a process of discrimination in which those who are considered to be the most appropriate are chosen, but the accuracy of selection is frequently doubted.

selector A person whose designated role is to make a choice on behalf of a course, department, or organization.

self A concept frequently used by *humanistic adult educators* to refer to the subject person; often used synonymously with the person. It tends to relate to the conception that the person has of him/herself as a social human being. Sometimes used synonymously with *self-concept*. See *mutable self*.

self-acceptance The acceptance of oneself.

self-actualization Seen as the end product of *adult education* by *humanistic adult educators*. It is the point at which persons have developed themselves so that they are achieving their human potential and fulfilling themselves. In *A.H. Maslow*'s *hierarchy of needs*, it is the highest state.

self-administered questionnaire A *questionnaire* which is completed by the person from whom data are being sought, not by the researcher.

self-advocacy The opportunity for the mentally handicapped to speak out for themselves. Gradually, professional carers are recognizing that those who are so handicapped have something to say and must be listened to.

self-assessment A form of *assessment* in which students or practitioners assess their own *knowledge, skills,* or *attitudes*. This is a form of assessment that is sometimes practised within *higher* and *professional education*, and one that professional practitioners in any discipline might undertake as an element in their own practice.

self-assessment inventory A checklist of characteristics, *skills*, and *knowledge* prepared so that learners and employees might undertake their own *self-assessment*.

self-assessment questions Questions set at the end of a piece of information to be learned to enable the *learner* to test whether the information has been internalized and understood. They are used a great deal in *distance education*.

self-awareness Being conscious of oneself, in a relatively objective manner. See *self-acceptance*.

self-coded questionnaire A *questionnaire* having preset answers which are already coded for computer analysis.

self-concept 1. One's concept of oneself, in as complete and as thorough a description as possible. 2. See *self*. This concept appears to have at least three elements: *self-image, ideal self,* and *self-esteem*.

self-consciousness *Self-awareness*, in a manner which sometimes results in embarrassment in behaviour.

self-control The ability to control oneself.

self-criticism Criticism of oneself by oneself.

self-deception Deceiving oneself about one's own abilities and limitations so that one is no longer able to be objectively *self-aware*.

self-denial Foregoing of pleasure and satisfaction.

self-determination The ability to control one's own behaviour and to act upon one's own beliefs. See *self-directed learning*.

self-development Movement towards maturity.

self-directed learning An approach to *learning*, very common in recent studies in *adult education*, in which the learners assume total responsibility for planning the strategies for learning, motivating themselves to pursue their *objectives* and to complete their plans.

self-directed learning readiness scale A scale devised by Gugliemino to test people's attitudes to *self-directed learning*, it is a 58-item *self-administered questionnaire*. The findings from it suggest that there are eight factors in self-directed learning: openness to learning opportunities; *self-concept* as self-directed learner; initiative and independence; responsibility for one's own learning; a liking of learning for its own sake; creativity; future orientation; ability to utilize study skills; and problem-solving skills. The reliability of the scale has been questioned.

self-disclosure The willingness to reveal aspects of one's own personality, thoughts, etc.

self-discovery See *self-learning*.

self-employment course Part-time training offered by the *Manpower Services Commission* for a period of up to 35 hours, as a start-up business training. After an initial year (1984–85) these courses were subsumed under the new Business Enterprise Programme. (Note: the *Manpower Services Commission* changed its name to the *Training Commission* and then to the *Training Agency* in 1988.)

self-enrichment A form of *non-vocational education* in which the students' motivation is to improve themselves, their knowledge, or understanding.

self-esteem The value that people place upon themselves, frequently relating to the value other people appear to place on them. It is also the desire to see oneself as having certain qualities such as strength, competence, or independence. It is the next to highest level in *Maslow*'s *hierarchy of needs*.

self-evaluation Personality testing in which the subject provides information about him/herself.

self-expression An action which helps to develop one's personality through feeling free to express one's own feelings.

self-financing A policy of ensuring that any course pays for itself through its fee income. This is clearly a policy that favours those who are able to afford the fees; hence it is a policy that has been resisted by some adult educators.

self-fulfilling prophecy A term employed in *education* to refer to those situations in which the cause of an effect may be regarded as the expectation that it would occur. For example, a teacher expects a student to fail an examination, treats the student as a failure, and the student subsequently fails the examination.

self-help A nineteenth-century movement in which people sought to improve themselves intellectually rather than morally, usually through setting their own goals, and pursuing them in their own time at their own expense. The most famous exponent of this is probably Samuel Smiles, author of '*Self Help*', published in 1859, although this movement might reflect the Methodist influence upon Britain. There are similarities between this movement and the present concern in the United States for *self-directed learning*.

self-help groups Groups of *learners* convened without a teacher to assist each other in the *learning process*. Used frequently in *distance education*.

self-idealized The expression of the type of self that a person would like to become. See *ideal self*.

self-identity The characteristics that a person attributes to him/herself.

self-image The impression people have about themselves; largely a reflection of the way that other people view them.

self-instruction See *self-directed learning*, *self-teaching*.

self-instructional device A teaching tool that can be used by a *learner* without the assistance of a *teacher*.

self-learning *Learning* by comparing personal and ideal characteristics as perceived by the *learner* with those characteristics identified by others. This is a process of *self-discovery*.

self-management A term used in *Yugoslavia*, where workers started their own worker management schemes in industry in the 1950s. However, the idea of self-management has grown from management at work to being a responsible citizen willing and able to play a part in personal and collective interests, many of which were once the responsibility of the state. Hence there has emerged an educational programme to help prepare citizens to play their full part in this form of management. See *education for self-management, school for self-management*.

self-managers' clubs Municipal organizations in *Yugoslavia* which provide *education for self-management*.

self-orientation Placing one's own interests first.

self-pacing The opportunity to learn at the pace set by the *learner* rather than by the *teacher*. One of the advantages of *distance education*, it is also found in forms of *competency-based learning*.

self-perception theory A position that suggests that people's *attitudes* and *beliefs* are determined in part by observation of their own *behaviour patterns*.

self-presentation The manner by which one puts oneself forward in order to convey the public image that the actor wishes to present.

self-preservation A term that relates to behaviour patterns that function to ensure the survival of the *self*.

self-realization The achievement of potential.

self-report technique Used in the study of personality to show how descriptions of behaviour relate to one's *self-concept*.

self-starter One who can initiate behaviour without the need for external stimulus. See *self-stimulation*.

self-stimulation The ability to provide one's own stimulus for behaviour.

self-study A course of study organized in the work setting in which members conduct a study of aspects of the work situation, making recommendations to future practice. Requires considerable support from organization management. See *quality circle* for a similar but by no means equivalent programme.

self-study materials Materials designed for *self-directed learning* without the aid of a teacher.

self-teaching The process by which people assume primary responsibility for planning their own learning. This definition tends to confuse learning with teaching, although it is the definition used by *Allen Tough* in his seminal studies on *self-directed learning*.

Selly Oak Colleges The complex of colleges in Selly Oak, Birmingham, which contains a number of *adult education* institutions, such as *Fircroft College*, and *Woodbrooke College*.

semantic memory The general knowledge held by people removed from the social context in which it was learned. See also *memory* and *episodic memory*.

semantics The study of the *meaning* of words.

semester The division of the American academic year into two parts of about 15 weeks. There is a movement in this direction in other parts of the world.

semester credit hour A term used to refer to the number of hours of

instruction per week for a course during one *semester*.

semi-literate Defined by the Ministry of Education in the United Kingdom as 'a reading ability falling above the average seven-year-old but below that of a ten-year-old.' See *functional literacy*.

seminar Discussion focused upon an expert presentation, project report, or paper. Can be teacher-led or student-led. Often very effective with adults without the presence of a *tutor*.

seminar room Rooms which are furnished for *seminar* work.

seminary Theological college.

semiotics The study of signs and symbols, especially *language*. This field has not yet attained prominence in the study of *adult education* to a great extent.

semi-profession An occupation which has lower professional status, often because it demands a shorter period of training for new recruits.

senate The ruling committee or authority of an academic institution; the apex of collegiate government.

Senegal The official *adult education* organization is the Direction de la Formation Permanente. Current address: Ministère de l'Enseignment Supérieur, P.O. Box 11027, CD Annexe, Dakar, Republic of Senegal.

Sengo The title of the *adult education* journal which has occasionally been published in the Congo since 1966.

senior college A four-year college in the United States as opposed to a *junior college*, which is a *two-year college*.

senior lecturer In British universities, the grade above the career grade of lecturer. In polytechnics and *further education* institutions, it is regarded as the career grade since there is a further grade of *principal lecturer*.

309

senior secondary general certificate
(HAVO) A secondary education
certificate awarded after five years' study
in *secondary education* in the Netherlands.
It is now possible to return to school in
the day or evening to gain this award as a
form of *second chance education*. See also
*senior secondary vocational, junior secondary
general* and *pre-university certificates*.

**senior secondary vocational
certificate** (MBO) Certificates awarded
after three years of theory and one year
of *placement* in specific occupational
training, e.g. technical, agricultural,
retail, and health care. This is also
available as a form of *second chance
education* in the Netherlands. See also
*junior secondary vocational, senior secondary
general* certificates.

sensation The apprehension of a
stimulus.

sensationalism In philosophy, the idea
that *sensations* are the real components of
the world and, therefore, the source of
knowledge.

sense data *Data* obtained through the
senses by direct *experience*.

sensory capacity The ability to absorb
experiences received through the senses.

sentence A self-contained, grammatical,
linguistic unit of words relating to each
other in a meaningful manner.

sentence completion A form of testing
in which incomplete sentences are given
to respondents to complete. It is used in
some psychological testing.

sentiment A complex disposition
towards a person or phenomenon.

sentimentality A form of emotionalism
which is usually shallow and to some
extent of suspect validity.

sequencing The ordering of material in
a *lesson* to obtain the most effective
learning.

serial learning *Learning* to make a series
of responses in an exact order; form of
rote learning.

serialist An approach to *learning* in
which the learner learns one aspect at a
time in a linear progression. It is a
cognitive style which is the opposite of
holism.

sermon A period of *instruction* within the
context of a Christian service of worship.

**Service Center for Community
College–Labor Union Cooperation**
American *clearinghouse* based at the
*American Association of Community and
Junior Colleges*. Current address: One
Dupont Circle NW, Suite 410,
Washington DC 20036, USA.

Service–Learning Resource Center An
American *clearinghouse*. Current address:
403 Breckinridge Hall, University of
Kentucky, Lexington, Kentucky 40506,
USA.

**Service Members' Opportunity
Colleges** (SOC) Established in 1972 for
two-year colleges and extended in 1974
to *four-year colleges* under the
sponsorship of the *Carnegie Corporation*
and the Department of Defense, this
scheme enables service personnel to enrol
in courses in colleges within the
network, without having the necessary
entrance qualifications. The colleges are
committed to providing counselling and
flexible arrangements for residence.
There is a small full-time staff to monitor
and organize these arrangements, and a
directory, newsletters, and occasional
papers. The full-time staff also seeks to
resolve any formal complaints about the
system. Current address: SOC Suite 700,
One Dupont Circle, Washington DC
20036, USA.

Servicemen's Readjustment Act
Passed in 1944 in the United States, it is
popularly known as the 'GI Bill of
Rights'. This bill enabled many veterans
to return to school to continue their
education after the war, usually with a
vocational intention. This had an

influence upon education in America because it made educational institutions more flexible in meeting the demands of adult students.

Servicio de Educación Permanente de Adultos A national information and documentation centre in Spain, established in 1977 and offering a service to all in *adult literacy* in the country. Current address: Paseo del Prado 28, 8a Planta, Madrid 4, Spain.

Servicio Nacional de Aprendizaje (SENA) A semi-autonomous organization within the Ministry of Labour in *Colombia* whose function is to develop and implement *training* services for workers in a variety of industries. It organizes training centres throughout the country and runs mobile training units.

Servicio Nacional de Aprendizaje Industrial (SENAI) The Brazilian national industrial training service. It has been involved in a variety of educational innovations, including *distance education*. Current address: Departemento Regional de Sao Paulo, av Nilo Pansanha 5029 Andar, Rio de Janeiro, Brazil.

Sesame The student newspaper of the *Open University* in the United Kingdom.

session 1. A period of teaching. 2. An academic period such as a *term, semester*, or year.

sessional tutor A *tutor* who is employed to teach for a specified period, such as a term. See *part-time tutor*.

set 1. A classification; aggregate of things sharing a common defining property. 2. Any condition or predisposition to respond in a particular manner.

set book A text book for a course which students are expected to study. Educational philosophies vary about the benefit of having a set text for a course.

settlement See *university settlement*.

settlement house A dwelling, general purpose building, or administrative

centre within a *university settlement*, it is a centre for education or recreation within a disadvantaged area.

sex education Education about the impulses and processes of reproduction. This subject frequently includes moral education.

shakai kyoiku Non-formal adult education in Japan.

Shakai Kyoiku Monthly magazine of the *National Federation of Social Education* in Japan.

Shanghai Information Centre for Adult Education One of the central resource centres for *adult education* in China. Current address: Director of Adult Education, No. 2 Institute of Education, 195 Zheng Fa Road, Shanghai, People's Republic of China.

shaping theory A theory of *teaching* in which the *learner* is shaped and moulded into a predetermined pattern. See *behaviourism*.

shared facilities The use of facilities, such as rooms, by two or more organizations, although each facility is owned by only one of the organizations.

shared services An arrangement through which two or more persons or organizations share the services of a providing agency.

Sharing The newsletter of *Project Share*.

short-term goal The predetermined end-product of a *teaching* and *learning* transaction. See also *objective, long-term goal*.

short-term memory The *memory* which results when information that has not been fully processed is stored; the opposite of *long-term memory*.

shut-in personality A person who is extremely withdrawn.

Sierra Leone Adult Education Association Current address: c/o The

Adult Education Unit, Ministry of Education, New England, Freetown, Sierra Leone.

sign An indicator, hint, or clue. More specifically, it is used as a symbol of *communication*.

sign language A form of *communication* using *signs* for deaf people. It is used where lip-reading is not possible.

sign learning A form of learning that relates to understanding the relationship between *signs*.

signal learning Term used by *Gagné* for one of his lowest forms of learning; a form of *conditioning*.

Silliman, Benjamin (1779–1864) Professor at Yale College, he gave a course of public lectures in natural science in 1834, long before the *university extension* movement was established. He continued this course for a number of years.

simulation A teaching method in which a real-life situation is recreated in the *teaching* and *learning* process so that learners can have the opportunity to practise their responses, or their *learning*, prior to performing it in reality. This technique is used in many forms of *affective education* to assist learners in reflecting upon their emotional response to situations.

simulator The person or machine through which real-life conditions are created in *simulation* learning.

Singapore Association of Continuing Education Current address: 13 Dalvey Estate, Singapore 1025.

Singapore Vocational and Industrial Training Board Current address: Vocation Drive, Singapore 0513.

single honours degree A first degree in which one subject is studied to honours level.

single loop learning A concept introduced by *C. Argyris* and *D. Schon* which suggests that people learn to design their actions so that they do not disturb the social context within which they learn; the opposite of *double loop learning*.

Singleton, William One of the two people who opened the first *adult school* in Nottingham in 1798. See also *Samuel Fox*.

Sir James Matthews Memorial Trust Fund established in memory of *James Matthews* to provide financial aid to members of the *Workers' Education Association* to enable them to participate in summer schools and study tours at home and abroad. The fund is currently administered from 37 St James's House, Holyrood, Southampton, Hants, UK.

sister tutor Term used for *nurse teachers* in Britain. It ceased to be used when nurse education became clearly separated from clinical practice.

sitting by Nellie A slang expression used to describe the *apprenticeship* method in which the *learner* watches an expert perform and is expected to learn by *observation* and then by *imitation*.

situated pedagogy A form of teaching that locates the subject in the culture of the learners, so that they can become critically aware of their own reality. It is almost essential to *dialogical education*.

skill 1. The ability to behave or perform correctly and effectively in action-based situations. 2. The ability to perform an applied task.

skill centre 1. The successor to the government *training centre* organized by the *Manpower Services Commission* to provide training in *Training Opportunities Programme* courses. Currently these centres are run by the *Skills Training Agency* and provide training in the crafts and manual skills. (Note: the *Manpower Services Commission* changed its name to the *Training Commission* and then to the

Training Agency in 1988.) 2. established in Holland in 1945 to match supply and demand in the labour market. Dutch skill centres employ self-study and written exercises as well as skills instruction.

skill development leave See *paid educational leave.*

skills analysis The process of breaking down complex *skills* into their component parts so that they may be learned more easily.

Skills Training Agency Organized by the *Manpower Services Commission* to run the *skill centres*. It operates as a commercial concern and is required to break even financially. (Note: the *Manpower Services Commission* changed its name to the *Training Commission* and then to the *Training Agency* in 1988.)

Skinner box An experimental apparatus named after *B.F. Skinner*. It is a small chamber with two components: a device for providing food and an instrument to activate the device. When an animal activates the instrument, it receives food. The psychologist's object is to discover when the animal associates the two.

Skinner, Burrhus Frederick (b. 1904) American psychologist and the foremost exponent of *behaviourism*. His work on *conditioning* and *reinforcement* in learning has been very influential in *adult education* as well as children's learning.

Skinnerian conditioning See *operant conditioning.*

Skinnerism The philosophy of *behaviourism.*

skip programme A *programmed learning* text in which a student making a correct response to a problem omits some of the questions in the sequence.

SLACE News The newsletter of the *St Lucia Association of Continuing Education* which started in 1982.

slide Also called transparency, since it is a positive photograph mounted upon a

transparent surface which can then be used to project the picture onto a screen. A useful *audio-visual aid* frequently used in a variety of educational settings.

Sloane, Hans Collector of artifacts and books, whose collections were opened to the public in the eighteenth century in London and contributed greatly to the British Museum and the British Museum Library.

sloboda This word means 'freedom' in Serbo-Croat and in *Yugoslavia* immediately after the Second World War cultural programmes concerned with culture, music, drama, and speeches arose. These were the forerunners of the *people's universities* that emerged in the late 1940s.

Sloman Report Technically called 'Report of the Inspectors appointed by the Government in March 1987'. Following disputes at *Ruskin College* over a lecturer's freedom to teach his own views, the government appointed a committee to examine the affairs of the college and this was chaired by A. Sloman, who was vice-chancellor of Essex University.

slow learner A term used for someone who, for one reason or another, is unable to learn at the normal rate. See *adult basic education.*

small group teaching A teaching method in which larger classes are divided into smaller groups for purposes of *discussion, role play*, etc.

Smiles, Samuel (1812–1904) Well-known nineteenth-century English author, best known for his book, *'Self Help'* (1859), which reflected the philosophy of the period. It has subsequently been quoted frequently by historians of adult education.

Smith, Adam (1723–90) Scottish political economist and philosopher whose views have influenced theories of liberty and welfare. The central idea is that individuals should be left to promote their own *interest* and welfare free of the state's interference. Hence Smith's ideas are significant in policy analysis and in an analysis of *adult education* in contemporary society.

Smith, Arthur Lionel (1850–1924) Master of Balliol College, Oxford, but best known in *adult education* as the chairman of the *Ministry of Reconstruction* report known as the *1919 Report*. He was a campaigner for *adult education*.

Smith, Henry Percival (1894–1967) Involved with the *Workers' Educational Association* in an administrative capacity after the First World War, he became the tutorial secretary for the Delegacy of Extra-Mural Studies, Oxford University, and also wrote an early history of *adult education*.

Smith–Hughes Vocational Education Act A US congressional act in 1917 which made federal funds available for courses in agriculture, home economics, trades, industries, and commerce, and created the *Federal Board for Vocational Education*.

Smith–Lever Act Passed in 1914, this act established the *Cooperative Extension Service* in America by funding each state annually upon the presentation of a satisfactory state plan. Initially, the concerns were for agricultural education and home economics. The law also required that each *land grant college* should create a separate division of extension. It suggested that the teaching methods should include practical demonstrations and publications. The 1983 amendment to the act included energy and natural resources amongst the educational emphasis of the movement.

Smith, William (d. 1848) A doorkeeper in the Methodist chapel in Bristol, a poor and almost unlettered man, who was the founder of the Bristol *adult school* and the Bristol Institution for Instructing Adult Persons to Read the Holy Scriptures.

Smithsonian Institution A national museum, library, and teaching institution in America, founded in 1846. Address: 1000 Jefferson Drive SW, Washington DC 20560, USA.

snowballing a *teaching* technique in which a question or problem is initially addressed individually and then in pairs. The pairs then group into fours, and so on as the snowball grows. People always remain with their previous partners throughout the process. This is a useful *icebreaking* technique and also a good *problem-solving* teaching method.

social academies Schools for social and cultural work, community work, and *adult education* in Belgium.

social action 1. *Action* designed to influence the *behaviour* of others. 2. Action by groups of people designed to influence policy within a *community*. This is related to *radical adult education*.

social administration The study of organization and *social policy*.

social advancement The term used in France for *continuing vocational education* undertaken by employees in their own leisure time.

social agogy See *social pedagogics*. The term was used by Ten Have in the Netherlands to refer to the process of educating, forming, guiding, or supporting a social event, social behaviour, human relations, or group living.

social anthropology The study of social behaviour, especially *culture* and *beliefs*, in non-industrialized countries.

social audit The study of the impact of the policies of a company or a country.

social behaviour *Behaviour* which is either influenced by or designed to influence the behaviour of other persons.

social change A sociological concept that recognizes that change is endemic and that stasis is a rarity. However, it has a more *radical* connotation inasmuch as it often refers to structural change in society, which may also have revolutionary undertones. It is used in relation to *radical adult education*, in which education is viewed as a process that can produce *change agents*.

social class Also *socio-economic class*. Social class is defined by one's position in relation to the means of production of a country. It is a Marxist concept, whereas *socio-economic class* is more Weberian and the one more likely to be employed in most analyses of *adult education*, except when employed by *radical adult education* theorists.

social climate The atmosphere of a society. The idea of organizational climate has been used in *adult education*, especially within the context of *needs analysis*, and also in setting an ethos conducive for *teaching* adults.

social control Education may be seen as a form of social control when it is used to ensure that learners act in predetermined ways. A criticism often levelled at all forms of education by radical educators is that it is a form of social control rather than a form of *liberation*. See also *reproduction, social reproduction*.

social correspondence education A term used in Japan to refer to *correspondence education* which is recognized by the government and provided by other organizations, such as non-profit bodies.

social disadvantage People who are handicapped either physically or socially, which impedes their educational progress. Much *adult basic education* is undertaken with those who are socially disadvantaged.

social distance The degree of separation between different *social groups*.

social drive Psychological pressures that cause individuals to seek *social interaction*. It has been argued that interaction is important to the formation of the person

and quite central to understanding *learning*.

social education This term is beginning to be used for the more radical perspectives in education which start with the needs and interests of the dominated peoples of the world. In Japan, it seems to be used in a manner similar to *liberal adult education* in the United Kingdom. See also *community education*.

Social Education Law Passed in Japan in 1949, it gives Japanese people the legal right to receive *social education*, which is non-formal education *(shakai kyoiku)*, and makes it mandatory for the government to provide it.

social exchange theory A model of social structure based upon the idea of reciprocal social behaviour.

social intelligence The ability to engage in effective, mutually beneficial problem-solving. This approach to *intelligence* assumes that there are a number of types of intelligence, besides *fluid* and *crystallized intelligence*, and this is certainly not proven. It might be argued that this is one facet of *crystallized intelligence*.

social interaction The process of interdependent behaviour.

social learning *Knowledge, skills* and *attitudes* acquired or needed in the process of social living. See *lifelong learning*.

Social Morality Council This UK organization provides an advisory and development service in the fields of social and personal education. Current address: 23 Kensington Square, London W8, UK.

social movement A common action or trend among groupings of people. A number of classifications exist such as: general (e.g. women's movement); specific (e.g. to make *adult education* a right for everybody within a society); and expressive (e.g. a trend in fashion).

social need Any *need* with a social basis.

social network The web of social relations which provides individuals with security and/or support.

social norm A pattern of behaviour that occurs within a specific community or society. It is a useful concept in discussion of *need* since one way of assessing *needs* is against norms.

social order 1. The totality of institutions which comprise *social structure*. 2. The stability of the social structure.

social pedagogics A term used in Europe for adult teaching skills.

social pedagogy A term used in Europe to cover the areas of *adult education, community education*, and youth work. The term was introduced in 1835 by Diesterweg. There are departments of social pedagogy in a number of continental European universities. See *social agogy*.

social policy In recent years there has been a move to analyse *adult education* in terms of social policy, which is essentially an analysis of the social intentions and effects of government legislation and plans.

social pressure The collective influences of others to induce certain forms of behaviour. It is one of the major means of producing conformity.

social psychology The branch of *psychology* that concentrates upon those aspects of human behaviour that involve interrelationships. It is one of the major disciplines underlying theories of *adult education* and overlaps with *sociology* in the realm of microsociology.

social reality Reality as defined or constructed by a group or society as a whole. It is often wrongly assumed that reality and social reality are synonymous.

social reproduction *Radical adult educators* and sociologists claim that *education*, including *adult education*, reproduces the social structures of a society rather than acts as a *change agent*. The basis of this claim is that a function of education and adult education is merely the transmission of existing, accepted *knowledge* rather than the creation of critical awareness that could liberate the learners and so act as an agent for change.

social role The role performed by an individual within a social context.

Social Science College This Finnish college began to train workers for *popular education* in 1929, with a position established for that purpose. In 1946 the post became a professorship. More recently the college moved to Tampere and became Tampere University, where adult education can be studied at all levels.

social sciences Branches of *knowledge* concerned with human behaviour and human relationships. *Education*, and therefore *adult education*, is a branch of the social sciences.

social self The characteristics of a person's *self*, either seen by others or deliberately displayed by an actor for others to see.

Social Significance of Adult Education A series of 27 short studies commissioned by the *American Association of Adult Education* which were commenced in 1936.

social skills *Skills* necessary to undertake normal living within society. Many courses in *adult education* are designed to improve people's social skills.

social stratification The hierarchical manner in which a society or organization is structured.

social welfare Programmes devised to assist the disadvantaged with society. Recently, *adult education* has been conceptualized within a social welfare framework and this has led to some very interesting analyses of *adult education* from a welfare policy analysis. However, it would be quite wrong to limit *adult education* to a form of social welfare, since not all *adult education* is provided against a *needs* analysis.

social work Activities designed to meet the *needs* of *disadvantaged* people within society. It is both institutionalized and voluntary. It is here, especially with *adult basic education*, that there is an overlap between *adult education* and social work.

socialism Various political philosophies which relate to communal ownership of property and state concern for individuals.

socialist halls of science Established in the 1830s in England by *Robert Owen*, these were organized by the working class for their own education. However, many did not survive for long because they ran into financial difficulties and were opposed by the middle classes.

socialization Generally regarded as a process that happens to children; more recently, however, there has been some emphasis upon adult socialization and a recognition that this is a lifelong process. It is the process of shaping human *knowledge, attitudes,* and behaviour through experience of social situations. It is a *learning process* which is usually regarded as informal in nature.

Society for Academic Gaming and Simulation in Education and Training (SAGSET) A UK society established in 1970 which promotes gaming and simulation exercises in education. A number of publications have stemmed from this society. See *Society for the Advancement of Games and Simulation in Education and Training.*

Society for Arts and Science (Genootschap van Konsten en Wetenschappen) Established in 1784, it was the first large voluntary organization founded in the Netherlands in areas which are now regarded as *adult education* and information.

Society for Common Benefit Established in 1784 as an early voluntary society in Holland committed to disseminating new educational and philanthropic ideas. It started at the beginning of the nineteenth century to reach the working masses.

Society for Education in Film and Television A UK society. Current address: 29 Old Compton Street, London W1V 5PL, UK.

Society for Field Experience Education An American society of those concerned with field work in education. Current address: College of Charleston, Charleston, South Carolina 29401, USA.

Society for Mutual Education The original name that *Josiah Holbrook* gave to the American *lyceum.*

Society for Participatory Research in Asia Participatory research is an important aspect of *adult learning* and *development.* An *International Council for Adult Education* project incorporates research from many Asian countries. It has a variety of publications about its work. Current address: 45 Sainik Farms, Khanpur, New Delhi, India 110062.

Society for Popular Culture Founded in Finland in 1874, the oldest *adult education* organization in Finland. Today it is the largest college for *correspondence tuition* with its own Correspondence Institute. The society publishes the journal, *Adult Education in Finland.* Current address: Museokatu 18 a, 00100 Helsinki, 10 Finland.

Society for Promoting Christian Knowledge (SPCK) Established in 1699 by *Thomas Bray,* this organization is specifically Christian in its orientation. It has had a long involvement with *adult religious education,* circulating pamphlets and creating a lending *library.* It is also now a foremost publisher of religious books. Current address: Holy Trinity Church, Marylebone Road, London NW1 4DU, UK.

Society for Public Welfare A Dutch society. See *Maatschappil tot nut van't algemeen*, founded in 1784.

Society for Research into Higher Education (SRHE) Independent research society which organizes an annual conference and which, in recent years, has been concerned with *continuing education*. Current address: c/o The Department of Educational Studies, University of Surrey, Guildford GU2 5XH, Surrey, UK.

Society for the Advancement of Games and Simulation in Education and Training An academic society concerned with participative methods in teaching. Address: c/o Polytechnic of Wales, Pontypridd CF37 1DL, UK.

Society for the Diffusion of Useful Knowledge Established in England in 1826 by Lord Brougham and disbanded in 1846, this society promoted cheap literature and was aimed at the working classes. However, much of the literature appeared to be far removed from the *interests* and concerns of the target audience. This reflected something of the *self-help* ideals of England during this period.

Society for the Diffusion of Useful Knowledge among the Peasantry and Working Classes Established in Sweden in 1833 to present the people with useful *knowledge* and views on public issues in a moral fashion.

Society for the Encouragement of Arts, Manufacture and Commerce Established in London in 1754 at the instigation of William Shipley, it was to become the *Royal Society of Arts*.

Society for the Improvement of Schools and the Diffusion of Useful Knowledge Another name that was attached to the American *lyceum*.

Society for the Improvement of the Working Class (Maatschappij ter verbetering van den werkende stand) Founded in 1854 by Hartman in Holland,

it was dominated by employers and ran, without great success, an *evening school* for adults.

Society for the Spread of Popular Education Historical organization in Germany which gained much support at the start of the twentieth century.

Society in Scotland for Promoting Christian Knowledge Founded in 1709 on the model of the *Society for Promoting Christian Knowledge*, it contributed a great deal to the growth of *education* in the Scottish Highlands.

Society of Industrial Tutors Founded to provide opportunity for all who teach industrial studies in order to develop common services and to assist in the development of this field of study. The society publishes its own journal, *The Industrial Tutor*, and a newsletter. Current address: c/o 38 Haddo House, Highgate Road, London NW5 1PX, UK.

Society of Public Health Educators American society for those engaged in public health education.

Society of Radiographers The professional organization responsible for the education and training of new entrants into radiography in the United Kingdom.

Society to Encourage Studies at Home Formed in America in 1873 as a very early attempt at *correspondence education*, it sought to form home study groups and provide reading guides. It was not successful and soon ceased to function.

socio–cultural adult education The translation of the term used in Belgium to refer to *liberal adult education*.

socio–cultural animation 1. The term used in parts of continental Europe to refer to the manner in which people can be helped to play their part in society as responsible citizens to help make it a more democratic place. 2. Elsewhere, it seems to carry the connotation of leisure-time *adult education*, mostly the pursuit of hobbies and other practical activities.

socio–drama The simulation of social situations to help people solve problems. Used in *consciousness-raising* and *literacy* crusade activities.

socio–economic class Technical term relating to an analytical system of *social stratification* based upon occupation and the status of the position.

socio–linguistics Study of the *sociology* of language.

sociology A scientific and systematic approach to the study of society and people's behaviour within the social context. Recently, the sociological studies of *adult education* have assumed more significance, although there is a long history of sociological studies of *initial education*.

sociology of knowledge Theory of *knowledge* which relates its creation to the social structures.

sociometry An approach to *social psychology* which uses networks and graphical illustrations to record its results. It is based upon an approach to *social relationships* in which respondents were asked to rank in order of preference people with whom they would like to relate.

Socrates (c. 470–399 BC) Greek philosopher who was born and lived in Athens. He gave his name to the *Socratic teaching* method.

Socratic teaching After the Greek philosopher *Socrates* who was noted for his method of teaching through asking questions. This is a teacher-led teaching method through questioning.

software Computer programmes by which a computer can be used.

Somalia Address of the government agency which directs *adult education*:

Department of Non-Formal Education, Ministry of Education, Mogadishu, Somalia.

somatic learning The learning of a behavioural disposition rooted in the bodily constitution. See *training*.

Somerset, Hugh Dixon Crawford (1895–1968) Leading New Zealand *adult educator* who worked in the *Workers' Educational Association* and Victoria University College in Wellington, where he taught a wide variety of educational subjects. He was a member of the *National Council for Adult Education* and the New Zealand National Commission for *Unesco*.

sophists Group of educators who emerged in ancient Greece around the middle of the fifth century BC. They emphasized human interest and taught the skill of rhetoric.

South East Asian Ministers of Education Organisation Current address: 4th Floor, Darakarn Building, 920 Sukhumwit Road, Bangkok, Thailand.

South East Conference of Adult Educators Regional conference in the United Kingdom providing, on a regular basis, residential periods for study with leading scholars and other *adult education* activities for practitioners. Current address: c/o Dept. of Educational Studies, University of Surrey, Guildford, Surrey GU2 5XH, UK.

South East Regional Forum for Adult and Continuing Education (SERFACE) Established in 1982, it only survived for about three years. Its demise indicates the problems of starting voluntary associations since it had no regular administrative support.

South, Ron (d. 1985) Australian by birth, he was a prominent adult educator in the United Kingdom from the 1960s to the 1980s. He was principal of the City Literary Institute, a major *adult education institute* in London, from 1968 to

1984. He was also chairman of the *Educational Centres Association* and member of many other adult educational organizations. See *Ron South Fund*.

South West Africa People's Organisation (SWAPO) A people's organization heavily involved in *adult literacy* work, as well as political liberation, in South West Africa. It is supported by *Unesco*. Current address: P.O. Box 577, Lusaka, Zambia.

South Yorkshire Association for Continuing Education A regional association for *adult education* in England.

Southern Examining Group A group of five examining boards (Associated, South East, Southern, Oxford Delegacy, and South Western) which works with the *Royal Society of Arts* Examining Board. It offers the *GCSE* examination with *external* and *mature* syllabuses for adults. Current address: Associated Examining Board, Stag Hill House, University of Surrey Campus, Guildford, Surrey GU2 5XH, UK.

Sovetskaja Pedagogika (Soviet Pedagogy) A monthly journal published since 1937 which examines all aspects of *education*, including *adult education*.

spare–time adult educator Term occasionally used for *part–time adult educators*. The term has been employed in an attempt to distinguish part–time adult educators who are occasional teachers from those whose role in *adult education* is much more substantial.

spare–time university Established in China, this type of university serves a part–time student population which has not been relieved of its work responsibilities.

Spearman's rank order coefficient of correlation A statistical technique in which two sets of scores are arranged in rank order and the relationship between the orders is calculated.

special education Educational provision for those having *special needs*.

special needs A term used to refer to the *needs* of the disabled.

Special Temporary Employment Programme (STEP) This project was to take the place of the Job Creation Programme when it was phased out in 1978. Its aim was to provide 25,000 temporary jobs, lasting up to 52 weeks, for young people between the ages of 19 and 24 years who had been unemployed for at least six months. This was a *Manpower Services Commission* initiative. (Note: the *Manpower Services Commission* changed its name to the *Training Commission* and then to the *Training Agency* in 1988.)

specialist Person who is specialized in a specific area of work.

specialist teacher One who is employed to teach a particular topic. Many *adult educators* are specialist teachers.

speech Verbal communication.

speech discrimination test A standardized test to measure the ability to discriminate between speech sounds.

speech therapy Treatment for speech disorder.

spiral curriculum An approach to *curriculum* which entails a broadening and deepening study of the subject matter as the curriculum. It is depicted as a spiral.

split session Many *adult education* institutions function on a three-session day (morning, afternoon, and evening). In a split session a tutor is expected to be in the institution in the morning and evening.

sponsor An organization or person who provides financial and/or other support of learning opportunities.

sponsored experiential learning *Experiential learning* in the form of *work experience* as part of a course. See *on-course experiential learning*.

sponsorship schemes Schemes in which financial support of various types is given to *students* or educational institutions, so that the student can pursue a course of study or an educational institution can pursue a specific course of action. Students are sponsored now to pursue their *higher education*. Educational institutions are increasingly running courses or establishing teaching positions under the sponsorship of a financing agency, usually from institutions outside education, often industrial or financial.

Sports Council Established in the United Kingdom by Royal Charter in 1972 to develop the *knowledge* and the practice of sport. It has a number of regional offices throughout England and Wales and is financed by a government grant. Current address: 16 Upper Woburn Place, London WC1H OQP, UK.

Sprachverband Deutsch für ausländische Arbeitnehmer e.V. Language Association of German for Immigrant Workers. Founded in 1974 in Mainz in the Federal Republic of Germany and funded by the Ministry of Employment, this association has the following functions: to develop *curricula* and educational materials; to produce training programmes for teachers; and to co-ordinate the different institutions which offer programmes for migrants. Current address: Raimundistrasse 2, 6500 Mainz 1, Federal Republic of Germany.

Sri Lanka *Non-formal education* is utilized a great deal in this country and there is a section of the Ministry of Education devoted to it. Address: Non-Formal Education Section, Ministry of Education, Isurupaya, Sri Jayewardenepura Kotte, Battaramulla, Sri Lanka. See also the *National Association for Total Education*.

Stacey, William The first person in the United States to receive a Ph.D. in *adult education*, from Columbia University in 1935. His thesis was entitled, '*The Integration of Adult Education*'.

staff development The provision of *learning resources* or opportunities for staff to attend educational or other institutions in order to learn, so that the staff grow professionally and perhaps advance in their careers. It relates to *personal development* but the two are not synonymous because a person might or might not develop personally as a result of staff development. Debates exist about the extent to which the control of the development process should be the responsibility of the employing agency, and whether the development should be only to the benefit of the company or organization or in the direction that the employee wishes the process to take. Often, the responsibility rests with the training officers or personnel managers, who may or may not see themselves as educators of adults. See also *human resource development*.

staff–student association An association of academic staff and adult students of an *adult education* centre which supports the organization of the centre, suggesting course, assisting with the evaluation of the academic programme, organizing social events, raising money for equipment, etc. Active associations can be a great help to a centre.

staff–student ratio The ratio of the number of academic staff to the number of students in an academic institution.

staff tutor 1. One who is employed by a university but not on an academic scale. Often, extra-mural department staff have been given this status. 2. In the *Open University* in the United Kingdom the staff tutors are the academic staff who are located in the *regional offices* and are responsible in the regions for the academic work of the Open University. They may also have some academic responsibility in course preparation.

Stage I (ACSET I – formerly ACSTT I) The introductory course of preparation for adult educators. It is about 40 hours and often conducted prior to a first teaching appointment, although it was originally envisaged as in-service preparation by the second *Haycocks Report*.

Stage II (ACSET II – formerly ACSTT II) The intermediate preparation for adult educators, seen as equivalent to the *City and Guilds 730* course. It is about 100 hours of *teaching and learning* and approximately 30 hours of supervised teaching.

Stage III (ACSET III – formerly ACSTT III) The final stage of the adult educator training, as envisaged by the second *Haycocks Report*. Together the three stages are regarded as equivalent to a full-time year course and successful completion results in the award of a Certificate of Education (AE).

stage concept Refers to theories of *development* that suggest that people's process of development follows fixed patterns, often associated with biological age.

standard deviation A statistical measure of the extent to which a distribution of scores is located around the *mean*.

standard industrial classification A listing of the main types of industrial activities in which organizations are involved. In the United States there is a manual of such classifications.

standard occupational classification A list of the main types of work performed by people. In the United States there is a classification manual and in the United Kingdom the Registrar General publishes one prior to every census. It is from this survey that the socio-economic class structure of the United Kingdom is constructed.

standard performance A work-study term relating to the output a worker will achieve under normal working conditions.

standardized test A test in which the norms have been established and checked so that there can be a relatively objective measure.

standards The generally accepted levels of performance in academic and other work and behaviour. It is difficult to compare standards across years, despite many claims, since it is hard to achieve a comparable objective measure of any phenomenon.

Standing Committee on Continuing Education Established in 1985 to advise *higher education* in the United Kingdom on continuing education provision in universities, polytechnics, and colleges.

Standing Conference of Ethnic Minority Senior Citizens This body provides training for professionals and others whose work brings them into contact with ethnic minority people. It has a training and resources unit and both develops its own training materials and runs its own training programmes. Current address: 5–5a Westminster Bridge Road, London SE1 7XW, UK.

Standing Conference of Regional Advisory Councils for Further Education The joint forum of the ten *Regional Advisory Councils* in England and Wales. Current address: Tavistock House South, Tavistock Square, London WC1H 9LR, UK.

Standing Conference on University Teaching and Research in the Education of Adults (SCUTREA) This UK conference was founded to provide a forum for universities which had a serious interest in the academic study of the education of adults. Membership is open to university departments which provide regular teaching and research in this field of study and which award academic qualifications for study and research in this area. Membership is also open to individuals. It has always been associated with the *National Institute of Adult Continuing Education* and the *Scottish Institute of Adult and Continuing Education*. It is linked with the journal, *Studies in the Education of Adults*, and organizes an annual conference.

Stanford–Binet Intelligence Scale The first test of intelligence known by this name was prepared at Stanford University in 1916, but it was itself a revision of an earlier scale prepared by Binet in 1911. It has been modified on many occasions and there is now a modification that allows for the measurement of adult intelligence quotient.

Start Helping Adults to Real Education (SHARE) A campaign organized by the National Co-operative Education Association to protest against the financial cuts imposed upon *liberal adult education* by the 1980 Conservative government in the United Kingdom. Its objective was limited to a one-day demonstration against the cuts in November 1980. See *Save Adult Education Campaign*.

state board of regents The management committee of a state university in America.

state centre for political education In the Federal Republic of Germany, some states have their own *adult education* centres in which the main theme is political education. These centres are financed by the state and offer courses in political and topical issues free of charge. Their fundamental intention is to strengthen the ideas of *democracy* in that society.

state college Public college in the United States, similar to a *state university*, offering four-year degree programmes.

State Council of Adult Education (Voksenopplaeringsrådet) First appointed in 1966 as a state body to advise the *Ministry of Church and Education* on *adult education* in Norway. Current address: Skovvn 489, Postboks 8170, Dep 0034 Oslo 1, Norway.

State Council of Correspondence Schools (Brevskolerådet) Assists the *Ministry of Church and Education* in Norway in supervising the approved correspondence schools. Current address: Skovvn, 489 Postboks 8170, Dep 0034 Oslo 1, Norway.

state education agency US term to refer to an organization established in law for the purpose of carrying out some part of the educational responsibilities of the state.

state plan A written description of an American state's plan, submitted to the appropriate authority for the allocation of federal funding.

State Regulations on Adult Basic Education In 1986 the Netherlands government agreed on a set of regulations about *adult basic education* which was to be introduced in 1987. They include the acquisition of language, numeracy, and social skills, advice and guidance into secondary education or other educational activity, and outreach and recruitment in *adult basic education*.

state university Public university in the United States, offering four-year degree programmes.

statistics Branch of mathematics which deals with collecting, classifying, and analysing *data*. Used in *quantitative research* in *adult education*.

status The well-defined prestige ascribed to a person or position within a social grouping.

status deprivation The loss of desired prestige.

status discrepancy The difference between degrees of *status* in different groups. This is a phenomenon of which *adult educators* should be aware since many adults coming into *adult education* fear the loss of status in becoming a student once again. They are often very well aware of the low status that they had when they were children at school.

status group 1. A group of people classified together on the basis of shared patterns of behaviour. 2. A group of people who share a common *status* within society.

status need The psychological *need* to achieve high status.

status symbol Symbols that people display to show that they are members of certain high status groups or occupations.

statutory school-leaving age The legal age in any country before which a child may not leave school. Hence *adult education* may be referred to as *post-compulsory education*.

Steinberger, Josef (1874–1961) Roman Catholic priest and one of the leading Austrian *adult educators*. He was founder of the domestic science schools for rural women, and founder of the Society for the Education of Young Farmers which resulted in his starting *adult residential colleges*. He became a politician after the Second World War and was made responsible for education. Much honoured in his country.

stereotype A set of relatively fixed, often simplistic generalizations about the characteristics of a category of persons.

Stern, Josef Luitpold (1886–1966) Austrian *adult educator*, he was greatly concerned with the *education* of working people.

Stewart, David (1883–1954) A leading Australian *adult educator* and founder and first secretary of the Australian *Workers' Educational Association*.

Stichting FNV-scholingsinstituut The *Federation of Dutch Trades Unions Institute*. Current address: Molenweg 2, 8162 PG Epe, The Netherlands.

Stichting IVIO The Dutch institute of formal and non-formal education and information. Current address: Postbus 37, 8200 AA Lelystad, The Netherlands.

Stichting Lodewijk de Raet A Flemish foundation started by Lodewijk de Raet (1870–1914) which runs *folk high schools* in Belgium. It is also concerned with other aspects of *popular education*. Current address: Liedsstraat 27–29, 1210 Brussels, Belgium.

Stichting SVE The Dutch centre for the study and development of *adult education*. It is involved with study, research, and programme development. It also disseminates the results of its research throughout the country and is regarded as a servicing body for *adult education*. Current address: Postbus 351, 3800 AJ Amersfoort, The Netherlands.

Stichting Teleac The Dutch foundation for educational broadcasting and multi-media education. Current address: Postbus 2414, 3500 GK Utrecht, The Netherlands.

Stichting ter bevordering van het Woodbrookerswerk in Nederland The Quaker foundation which runs *adult residential schools* in the Netherlands using the term *Woodbrookers*. These schools were started in 1908. Current address: Postbus 1148, 3800 BC Amersfoort, The Netherlands.

stigma A mark or blemish which causes some people to be treated as different by others.

stimulation Any event that causes the receptor to become active.

stimulus Any phenomenon or impact that causes an organism to respond.

stimulus–response (S–R) *Behaviourist* approach to *learning* in which the response to the stimulus is regarded as the indicator that learning has occurred. See *Edward Thorndike*.

Stock, Arthur Former director of the *National Institute of Adult Continuing Education* who retired in 1988. He served *adult education* in a number of capacities.

storefront schools These originated in the United States, but now can be found in other countries in which *adult basic education* and other forms of education occur. They are an attempt to take *education* to the people and to remove some of the ethos of the school from the educational process. Also known as shop front schools, or *street academies*.

strategy The art and science of planning. It is often used with reference to *teaching techniques* and *learning styles*.

Strategy Report A report published in November 1980 by the Northern Ireland Council for Continuing Education, entitled *Continuing Education in Northern Ireland: A Strategy for Development*. This report makes recommendations about the future of *adult education* in Northern Ireland.

street academy See *storefront school*.

stress A state of psychological tension which often results in breakdown or *burnout*. A variety of educational *workshops* and *courses* have been devised to help people overcome, or at least cope with, the problems of stress.

Stretched Small Business Course Part-time training, offered by the *Manpower Services Commission* for new businesses expected to create jobs. After an initial trial year (1984–85), these courses were subsumed under the new Business Enterprise Programme. (Note: the *Manpower Services Commission* changed its name to the *Training Commission* and then to the *Training Agency* in 1988.)

structural unemployment A form of unemployment caused by major changes in the social structures of a society, e.g. the decline in primary manufacturing. This occurred in Western societies in the late 1970s and 1980s and has given rise to many *adult education* innovations.

structuralism A method of approach to analysis rather than a distinct philosophy. It starts with the idea that the key to understanding a phenomenon lies in the underlying patterns of relationships of its components. Hence this can be applied to the study of both *language* and the *social system*.

structure An organized pattern of relatively stable components.

structured interview An *interview* in which the questions are carefully planned, often written before the interview. This is a good teaching technique but is also used as a *research method*. Some interviews are partially structured, inasmuch as some main questions are prepared while the follow-up questions depend upon the interviewee's responses. See *unstructured interview*.

Stuart, James (1843–1913) Generally regarded as the first *university extension* lecturer, he delivered a series of four lectures to the *North of England Council for Promoting Higher Education for Women* in 1867. He was a fellow of Trinity College and for a number of years applied himself to extension lectures and to persuading the university to organize an extension programme. In 1875 he organized the first *Adult Education Conference* at Sheffield to examine the university extension movement. He also introduced the three elements that were to become almost standard format for extension teaching: the printed syllabus, written work, and the *discussion* period. Stuart was professor of Mechanism at the university from 1875 to 1889 but he was also interested in politics and was a Liberal Member of Parliament on a number of occasions. Stuart House, the offices of the Board of Extra-Mural Studies at the University of Cambridge, was named in his honour.

Studebaker, John W. Whilst in the US Office of Education he initiated the *public forums* movement for discussing public issues in the United States. It was the prototype of the *Des Moines Forums* and a form of *civic education* similar in some ways to the *study circle* movement in Scandinavia.

student 1. The social role (e.g. undergoing a course of study) and status ascribed to learners who are members of formal educational organizations; students have a higher status than *learners* who function in an informal situation. 2. Sometimes refers to those who are studying or are experts in a discipline, e.g. students of *adult education*.

student association Many *adult education centres* organize an association for their students which supports the centre academically and socially. In some centres it is a *staff–student association* whilst in others the staff are often participants although they are not included in the title. An active association can be a great asset to a centre.

student body The total number of students enrolled in an educational organization.

student–centred learning *Teaching* and *learning* situations which start with the experiences of the student rather than the demands of the discipline. Often claimed to be less rigorous than the more formal approach to teaching but there is no need for this to be true. It is quite central to a great deal of *adult education* and it is here that *progressive education* and *adult education* have similarities, both tracing their intellectual origins back to *John Dewey*.

student loans A system of financially assisting students to study by granting them loans to be repaid after the completion of their studies. In some countries these are made by the educational institution and in others, by financial institutions.

student participation The participation by students in the preparation of educational programmes; a common feature of *adult* and some *professional education*.

Student Potential Program (SPP) A *Council for Adult and Experiential Learning* project in which potential students are assessed by a variety of methods to see whether they should be able to complete a college programme. A *profile* is provided. See also *assessment of prior learning*. This programme was recently tried in the United Kingdom and the UK researchers have been in close contact with the Council for Adult and Experiential Learning in the United States.

student record Information kept on file about a student. In the United Kingdom this file, expecially if it is stored on computer, must be open for the student to see; but this access has not always been granted.

studentship An award to study in some universities, usually at postgraduate level.

Studienytt (Study News) A Norwegian journal published bimonthly since 1952. It contains articles about voluntary education and study.

Studies in Adult Education
1. Established in 1969 in the United Kingdom, this academic journal was intended to be published twice a year but on occasions it only appeared annually. It changed its name and approach in 1984 to become *Studies in the Education of Adults*, thereby widening the field of its academic concern. 2. Established in 1966, this is the quarterly journal, published in English, of the Institute of Adult Education in Dar es Salaam, Tanzania.

Studies in Continuing Education
International journal in *continuing education* published in Sydney, Australia.

Studies in the Education of Adults
See *Studies in Adult Education* its former title before 1984 when it widened its field of academic concern.

Studies in the Social Significance of Adult Education in the United States
A series of 27 books prepared in the 1930s and published by the *American Association for Adult Education* under sponsorship by the *Carnegie Corporation* of New York.

Studieskolen Denmark's largest language school, offering courses in Danish to foreigners at a variety of levels. Current address: 6 Antonigade, DK-1106 Copenhagen K, Denmark.

studio 1. A room in which artists, musicians, or photographers work. 2. A place in which recording occurs.

study centre 1. In the United Kingdom, the term is used to refer to the local centres, often rooms in colleges, which the *Open University* occupies on a part-time basis to run local tutorials, etc. 2. There are 18 study centres for the *Dutch Open University* in which students can obtain advice and counselling, and take their examinations. 3. In Finland, there is a completely different concept of study centre. Nine study centres, maintained by national educational organizations, are responsible for the organizing of *study circles* and other lecture and course activities for adults. They also organize and support lecture activities subsidized by the state. These centres are partially financed by the state.

study circle First established by *Oscar Olsson* in 1902, it is an informal group which meets for the common pursuit of planned studies of a subject or problem which has previously been decided upon or agreed. These are democratic groups with no educational prerequisite for membership, based upon the principle of equality, co-operation, companionship, participation, freedom, and *self-determination*. There is a generally agreed teaching approach in study circles which includes: equality and democracy among participants; an endeavour to help participants feel free to express their own opinions; a freedom for all participants; recognition that all members bring to the circle the wealth of their own experience; a democratic but forward-looking planning process; and a sense of continuity. They were originally founded to provide opportunity for the undereducated and the disenfranchised to have a forum to participate in and discuss public issues. More recently, study circles for the retired have become a feature of a number of European countries. Many different types have evolved, including those with *teachers*, those without teachers, and those which combine their programme with *lectures*. There is also the correspondence circle and those which combine their programme with a media programme. From this it may be seen that some could take the form of a *class*, others as informal social groups, still others as therapeutic groups; all types can fulfil their educational purpose. Study circles occur in a number of societies. In Finland, for instance, a study circle is regarded as a spontaneous group which meets regularly to discuss and exchange opinions in an educational process under a leader, based on flexibility and democratic planning. Membership is open and free, depending upon the country (see below). If the group has over five members of at least 15 years of age and meets at least ten times for a minimum of 20 hours, it can receive financial help from the state which is administered through a *study centre*. The amount of state aid to each circle is determined by the Ministry of Education each year. Such systems also occur in Denmark and Sweden. In Denmark, the cost is usually shared between student fees and contributions from national and local government. In Sweden, grants are not available unless the circle meets for at least 20 sessions, has an approved leader and a study plan, and keeps a register. The movement is sponsored by ten organizations which have formed a consortium, the *National Swedish Federation of Adult Education Associations*. In Denmark, there is less emphasis upon a study plan. This arrangement emerged in the nineteenth century when the study circle was regarded as an instrument of social change. See also *New York State Study Circle Consortium*.

study circle association Also known as *educational association*. This association organizes *study circles* throughout Sweden, is recognized by the government and receives a government grant to undertake this work. There are 11 such associations in the country.

study guide A prepared guide to assist learners in mastering the content of a specified piece of learning. It may consist of guidelines to reading a book or to observing the performance of a procedure, etc. Study guides should contain an explanation of the reasons for learning, the anticipated outcomes, the process and procedure of the learning exercise.

study habits Used in the same way as methods of study.

Study Handbook The title of the annual lesson notes for the *adult school movement*. Formerly the *Lesson Handbook*, when it became the *Study Handbook* it adopted a different title for each year.

study leave A period of release from employment in order to follow a course of study usually, but not always, associated with the employment. See also *paid educational leave*.

study organizations The organizations in Sweden that sponsor *study circles*. They are also called educational organizations. See the *National Swedish Federation of Adult Education Associations*.

study pack A prepared programme of study on a specific topic, often containing booklets, other learning materials such as audio cassettes, video cassettes, questionnaires, and self-assessment exercises. Many *distance learning* institutions prepare and market such packs.

Study Promotion Association (Studiefrämjandet) An educational association which sponsors *study circles* in Sweden and concerns itself with adults who were not successful during their *initial education*. It appeals to *young adults* and leisure organizations. It emphasizes such topics as environmental groups, energy, conservation, etc. It has its roots in the agricultural movement and began in the 1920s.

study skills Those *skills* necessary to be most effective as a student, e.g. the arts of reading and essay writing. With the growth of the education of adults there has been a corresponding development in courses in study skills for *adult returners*.

study week A unit of measurement in academic courses in Finland, equivalent to approximately 40 hours of study time.

styles of learning The preferred manner or techniques of learning. Sometimes refers to the physical location of study or the different cognitive approaches to study. See *cognitive styles, learning styles*.

styles of teaching The different approaches to teaching, such as whether a teacher is authoritarian, etc. See *teaching styles*.

subculture Refers to the *culture* of a group or a category of people. Hence an adult class can develop its own subculture which is in some ways comparable to its ethos, a term used in educational circles.

sub–degree course A course of study which is not considered to be of first-year university level. The traditional distinction between *adult education* classes in the United Kingdom has been that university extra-mural classes should be at university level whilst other classes run by *adult education centres* might but need not be of this academic standard.

subject 1. Recognized topic of a curriculum, it can have either a *problem/ theme* or a *knowledge/skill* base. 2. An individual who is the topic of discourse or investigation.

subject–centred The type of curriculum or teaching session in which the academic discipline is the focus of attention; it stands in contrast to the problem-centred approach of *andragogy*.

subject co–ordinator A senior member of the academic staff of a college or *adult education* institution who has the responsibility of ensuring that a particular subject is well covered in the programme. The job entails hiring part-time staff (in accord with the policy of the Institute and the Authority) and programming their teaching; additionally, it might include *staff development*.

subject matter The *knowledge* content of a course.

subjective 1. Relating to the mind of the thinking person. 2. Perception of *knowledge* or reality from the perspective of the thinking person; the opposite of *objective*.

subjectivism A moral philosophical approach emanating from the person. In its simplest form, all moral values are regarded as a matter of personal preference.

sub-library A *library* situated away from the main building.

sublimation The process by which primitive instincts or drives are redirected into more socially acceptable behaviour.

subliminal learning *Learning* of which one is not conscious. See *preconscious learning, incidental learning.*

subliminal perception The *perception* of a stimulus without one's being consciously aware of the cause of the perception.

subliminal stimulus Any stimulus that occurs below the theshold of consciousness.

submission A proposal for which approval is sought; the process of presenting a course of a validating agency, a proposal to a funding agency, etc.

subnormality A mental handicap.

subprofessional See *paraprofessional.* An American term for an assistant or support person to a professional person, e.g. a teacher aide.

subscription library A voluntary association of individuals contributing towards a fund for the purchase of books which can then be borrowed. The first was organized by *Benjamin Franklin* in Philadelphia in 1731. The first known in Scotland was started in 1741 by the miners of Leadhills in Lanarkshire. In England, the first was started in Liverpool in 1758. See *circulating library, library.*

success case method A method of *evaluation* used in *human resource development* in which those apparently successful products of the process are *interviewed* to assess how they utilized the *teaching* and *learning* process through which they had gone.

success ratio Proportion of students completing a course successfully.

successive approximations A term used by *Skinnerian* psychologists to refer to the shaping of behaviour by rewarding the subject as it approximates the desired behavioural pattern.

Sudan The national *adult education* organization is the Secretariat of the National Council for Literacy and Adult Education. Current address: P.O. Box 2588, Khartoum, Democratic Republic of the Sudan. See *Functional Adult Education National Centre.*

suggestibility The willingness to accept suggestions.

Sukhothai Thammarthirat Open University The *distance teaching university* of *Thailand.*

Sullivan, Leon Howard (b. 1922) Baptist minister in the United States who has been concerned with the fate of black people in America. He was the founder of the *Opportunities Industrialization Centers;* he established the Sullivan Principles for foreign companies investing in South Africa; and he is concerned with unemployment in the United States where he was involved in the Young Americans Job Crusade. He was also a member of the President's Task Force on Private Sector Initiatives. Throughout his ministry he has been an exponent of *self-help.*

summative assessment The *assessment* that usually occurs at the end of a course of study, e.g. end of course *examinations.*

summative evaluation The process of *evaluating* the outcome of a *programme* or *course* to determine its success against its *aims* and *objectives*, and to see the impact that the course has had upon learner performance. See *impact evaluation*.

summative profile In the *Certificate of Pre-Vocational Education*, all *assessment* is performed through *profiling*. This is the final computer statement, moderated by the *Joint Board of Pre-Vocational Education*, which relates to the original *objectives* of the course.

summer sessions Harvard University in America started summer sessions for teachers of marine biology as early as 1869 but the idea of the summer session did not really begin in the United States until after *Chautauqua*. By the early part of the twentieth century the summer school was a feature of many universities. School teachers are the most frequent students. These sessions are generally six weeks in duration.

summer school An educational event held during the summer, usually during the vacation period, and most frequently residential in nature. The *Open University* organizes these each year in conjunction with a number of its courses.

summer university The use of the university campus for the study of academic subjects at university level by a wider general public during the summer period. A method used by *Peuple et Culture* in France.

Summerhill UK experimental school founded and run by *A.S. Neill*, which was a democratic organization in which children were encouraged to exercise full responsibility. The school was run on lines that would perhaps have been approved of by many *adult educators* who favour a *progressive* stance to education.

Sunday school 1. Early *adult education* institutions established to help people read. Its primary focus was the bible but its function later broadened. Founded by *Robert Raikes*, who started the first Sunday school in England in 1780. See also *Welsh circulating schools*. 2. In Belgium, Sunday school was mentioned in the first legislation about education in 1842.

Sunday School Society *Sunday schools* became so popular in England after their foundation that by 1785 it was necessary to have a national association to co-ordinate this work.

sunrise semester Established in 1963, US early morning educational television programme.

superego A Freudian concept; the third element of the *self* which may be equated with the cultural values that a child acquires and which form part of its conscience.

supervision The process of advising and guiding a student in a learning situation. The American term is *advisement*.

supervisor A tutor who is overseeing the professional placement of a student in *professional education* or who is advising the student undertaking research. In the latter instance, the American term might be *advisor*.

supplementary training Additional *training*.

Support for the Arts in England and Wales The *Redcliffe–Maude Report* on the *arts*.

support services Activities which are provided to assist in the functioning of the educational organization, e.g. administrative, technical, etc.

support staff Employees who work in an educational institution but whose role is to service the academic enterprise, e.g. secretarial, administrative, reception, maintenance, 'Non-teaching staff' is the preferred term, as it does not have the lower status implications of the original term.

supportive leadership A form of leadership in which the leader is regarded as a support person for those who are led. It is the type of leadership encouraged by the *human relations* approach to management.

surface processor A *learning style* which refers to the process of acquiring *knowledge* at the surface level, e.g. the acquisition of facts. See *deep processor*.

survey An approach to research by collecting *data* by *questionnaire* or *interview* methods from a number of people. See *sample*.

suspension An interruption or temporary debarment from a course of study or from membership of an organization.

Swarthmore Non-Residential Settlement Opened by the Society of Friends in 1909 in Leeds as an attempt to produce a simpler approach to *university settlements*.

Swaziland Association of Adult Education Current address: c/o DEMS UNISWA P/B Kwuluseni, Swaziland.

Sweden See *Folkbildningsförbundet*.

Swedish Association for Educational Activities Study Centre Maintained by the *Friends of Swedish Primary Schools* in Finland as a *study centre* providing educational and cultural activities. It also trains its own tutors. Current address: Udenmaankatu 17b, 00120 Helsinki 15, Finland.

Swedish Association of Adult Education Associations In Sweden ten *adult education* associations sponsor the *study circle* programme: *Workers Educational Association, Free Churches' Educational Board, Folk University, National Educational Association for the YMCA and YWCA, Citizens' Educational Association, Educational Association of the Temperance Movement, Study Promotion Association, Educational Association of the Swedish Church, Adult Schools Association,* and *Salaried Employees' Educational Association*.

Swedish Broadcasting Company Responsible for Sweden's radio and two television channels, one of which is the *Swedish Educational Broadcasting Company*.

Swedish Educational Broadcasting Company Runs one of the television channels in Sweden and is a part of the *Swedish Broadcasting Company*. This company co-operates closely with the educational associations which sponsor the *study circles* in Sweden. Thus it may be seen that television supplements the programmes of the study circles. See *National Swedish Federation of Adult Education Associations*.

Swedish Federation of Non-Formal Adult Education Associations (Folkbildningsförbundet) *Non-formal adult education* in Sweden includes the *folk high school* movement and the *study circles*. This is the federal body of non-governmental organizations of adult education that receive state financial support. Current address: Industrigaten 4B 1tr, S–11246 Stockholm, Sweden.

Swedish Institute Publishes a fact sheet, *'Adult Education in Sweden'*, which summarizes the provision of *adult education*. Current address: Hamngatan 27, P.O. Box 7434, S–103 91 Stockholm, Sweden.

Swedish Union of Folk High School Teachers and Principals The professional association of academic staff working in *folk high schools* in Sweden. Current address: Box 6087, S–172, 06 Sundbyberg, Sweden.

Swiss Federation for Adult Education (SFAE) The umbrella organization of all private, non-profit organizations of *adult education* in Switzerland. Current address: SFAE, Oerlikonerstrasse 38, 8057 Zürich Postfach, Switzerland.

swot To study.

syllabus An outline of the content, usually for a whole course. Sometimes specified by an examination board, e.g. for professional examinations, but very occasionally used to refer to the content of a lecture or series of lectures.

symbol An object or diagram representing something else. See *sign*.

symbolic learning *Learning* by deriving *meaning* from the translation of *information* from one mode of communication to another.

symposium 1. A meeting to hear and discuss a variety of approaches to a subject or theme. 2. A collection of academic papers on a subject.

synapse The region in the brain in which impulses pass from neuron to neuron.

syndicate *Group work* in which the group is given a task to complete within a specified time and then is expected to report back.

syndicate room Rooms provided and equipped for *syndicate* work.

syndrome Any combination of characteristics which indicates a disorder.

synectics A method of identifying and solving problems that depends upon creative thinking, use of analogy, and discussion.

synergogy A learner–centred teaching method which offers the learner: meaningful direction in the form of *learning* designs and learning instruments; a teamwork situation through the design of learning teams having explicit learning goals; and a sharing of all learning opportunities and outcomes.

syntax Rules of grammar in *language*.

synthesis The drawing together of diverse sources and aspects of knowledge to create a new *knowledge*. A high form of understanding, according to *Bloom's Taxonomy of Educational Objectives*.

Syracuse University Publications in Continuing Education (SUPCE) The largest university-based publications organization in *adult education* in the United States. It also reproduces materials that it has been given by other organizations.

Syracuse University Resources for Educators of Adults (SUREA) Probably the largest collection of adult education material in the world. This collection was started by *Alexander Charters* and developed over many years from 1949. In 1952 a grant was established as a memorial to Paul Hoy Helms of the university and in 1961 it received all the resources of the *Fund for Adult Education* when it was dissolved. Thereafter, other collections were added to it. In 1963–64 another grant enabled the creation of the *Library of Continuing Education*, as it was then known. The collection houses books, a pamphlet file, many periodicals and newsletters, personal papers, photographs, and sound and video recordings. It is now planned to store all this material on video disk and make it accessible throughout the world by computer link-up. This project is funded by the *Kellogg Foundation*.

system A set of variables that are interrelated such that a change in one will have an effect on all the remainder.

systematic reflection Term used to refer to the process of reflecting upon life *experiences* regularly in order to identify what has been learned from them.

systems learning *Learning* by achieving a specific goal through a specific system or plan, either guided by another or by following a plan that the *learner* had formulated.

systems theory A theoretical perspective of the manner by which each part of the *system* is interconnected with every other. It is a theoretical perspective used in organizational analysis and also is quite common in *adult education* studies.

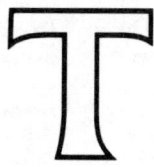

T Group Sometimes used to refer to a therapy group; on other occasions it refers to a training group. In both instances these are small groups of people who come together in open *discussion* in order to learn. They are usually led by a *facilitator*. The *small group* is one of the bases of the *adult education* method.

Taaliem Alkibar (Adult Education) A quarterly journal published in Arabic by the Adult Education and Literacy Department in *Kuwait*.

taboo Any banned or prohibted act or object. The prohibition may stem from religious observances in some countries where taboo means something sacred and set aside for special observance. It is sometimes spelt tabu, reflecting its Polynesian origins.

tabula rasa (Latin, blank tablet) The theory that at birth the mind is completely empty and unencumbered with innate desires, drives, etc. Like a blank cloth, the mind subsequently has imprinted upon it impressions of experience; thus the basis of all *knowledge* is *experience*.

tabulation A means of recording *quantitative data* in table form.

tacit knowledge The type of knowledge that people have who have immersed themselves in a subject so deeply that they appear to understand aspects of it implicitly as well as explicitly. The concept has been expounded most fully in the work of M. Polyani.

Tagore Memorial Award Instituted by the *Indian Adult Education Association* in 1987.

Tagore, Rabindranath (1861–1941) Indian thinker and educator who founded a number of educational institutions in India, all based on the concepts of *non-formal education* and the ideas of *humanistic education*.

talking book 1. A book which has been recorded onto an audio cassette, used with blind people. 2. *Paulo Freire* introduced this term to refer to a book which contains a record of a dialogue.

Tampere University Formerly, the *Civic College* and the *School of Social Sciences*. It was the first school to establish a lectureship in adult education in Finland in 1929. The position later became a professorship in 1949.

Tanzania See *National Adult Education Association* and the *Adult Literacy Centre*. The Ministry of National Education is currently located at P.O. Box 9121, Dar es Salaam, Tanzania.

tape library *Library* with a collection of audio and video cassettes. Many libraries of books now have separate sections for tapes.

target group As *adult education* has been forced to market its courses in a manner similar to companies' advertising their wares, so education has employed the language of advertising. This term refers to that group of people who might respond to a certain course and to whom the advertising should be directed.

target population See *target group*.

task allocation The distribution of jobs by one who has the authority to designate work.

task-based curriculum The *curriculum* of a course in *vocational education* based upon an analysis of the work.

task card Pictures with accompanying directions or assignments.

task-centred group A group which sets out to achieve its aims will utilize principles, acquire the necessary skills, etc. See *process-orientated group*.

task-orientated leader One who seeks always to achieve the specified purpose of the group, irrespective of group dynamics. See *expressive leader*.

'taster' activities A term sometimes employed to refer to adult education centres which provide opportunity for potential students to get to know something about a course of study by offering free introductory sessions.

Tavistock Institute of Human Relations A research and teaching institute concerned with *human relations*. It has influenced *humanistic adult education* and *counselling* in the United Kingdom and further afield. Current address: Tavistock Centre, Belsize Lane, London NW3 5BA, UK.

Tawney, Richard H. (1880–1962) A well-known academic and author of numerous books who, from his earliest adult years, worked in *university settlements* and the *Workers' Educational Association*, of which he later became a leading figure. He conducted the first university *tutorial class* and was recognized as a fine teacher of adults. He was a member of the adult education committee which produced the *1919 Report* and subsequently served on many other official committees. He was passionately concerned about social justice and considered the education of adults to have an important part to play in its promotion. He was undoubtedly one of the most significant people in British *adult education* in the first half of the twentieth century.

taxonomy of educational objectives A list of *objectives*, initially in the cognitive domain and structured hierarchically, proposed by Benjamin Bloom and his associates. Later, taxonomies were prepared in the *affective* and the *psychomotor* domains. These have not become as well known and yet in some ways are just as useful, especially in specialist areas of *adult* and *continuing education*.

teach 1. The presentation of proper bodies of *knowledge, skills, attitudes*, and *values* which can be transmitted to *learners*. 2. The creation of situations in which learners have the opportunity to learn. See *facilitate*. 3. In a *Skinnerian* sense, teaching is about arranging the contingencies of *reinforcement*.

teacher 1. One whose occupation or profession is to teach. 2. Any person who instructs or helps another to learn.

teacher education The professional education of *teachers*.

teacher fellowship A fellowship awarded by a university or college to allow a practising school teacher to spend a *sabbatical* period studying and researching.

teacher mobility The amount of movement between jobs in the teaching profession.

teacher practitioner A professional practitioner who has educational preparation and teaches students in the professional work setting whilst remaining a practitioner. See *field work teacher, practical work teacher*.

teacher preparation See *teacher education*.

teachers' centre An *in-service* centre for school teachers and others in the education institution; it may also have a curriculum development function.

teachers' certificate A professional licence to teach.

teaching 1. An occupation within education. 2. A process by which an individual or individuals provide opportunities through a variety of techniques for others to learn. See *growth, shaping, transfer,* and *travelling theories*. 3. A doctrine.

Teaching Adults A series of pamphlets published by the *National Institute of Adult Continuing Education* to provide help for part-time tutors of adults. It began in the 1960s as a magazine for part-time staff but later became a resource and training package. It was discontinued in 1986, when *Adult Learning Strategies and Approaches* was introduced.

teaching assistant One who is employed to assist a teacher in the classroom. See *paraprofessional*.

teaching hospital A hospital which also has the responsibility for teaching medical students. Thus senior medical staff have not only a medical function but also an educational one. See *teacher practitioner*.

teaching load The workload of a teacher in terms of preparation, teaching, advising and marking time, etc.

teaching machine A device or computer which allows a learner to use a *programmed text* for the purposes of learning without the help or presence of a *teacher*.

teaching methods The variety of different approaches to teaching, e.g. *lecturing, instructing, group discussion,* etc.

teaching observation A period during which trainee teachers observe experienced teachers working in the classroom. This process is beginning to occur in the preparation of *adult educators*

in the United Kingdom, especially during *Stage I* courses.

teaching practice The provision of opportunity for trainee teachers to have some teaching experience, usually under the guidance of a *mentor* or *supervisor*, in the educational institution. See *internship* and *professional placement*.

teaching staff The academic teaching staff of an educational institution.

teaching style Approaches to teaching that are classified by the attitude, expectation, manner, or authority imputed to the teacher during the process of *teaching*.

teaching techniques See *teaching methods*.

team meeting The meeting of a course team, or of those who are to *team teach* a course.

team teaching An approach to teaching in which either (1) more than one teacher teaches the same lesson together, each using his/her own *knowledge* and *skills* to enrich the lesson; or (2) more than one teacher teaches a course, so that one teacher will conduct one session and another will conduct another lesson. Both approaches are used in *adult* and *vocational education*. However, this form of teaching often takes longer to prepare since the co-ordination of the sessions has to be prepared.

Technical and Vocational Education Initiative (TVEI) Started in the United Kingdom in 1983, it is a curriculum project for 14–18-year-olds still in school, and is intended to equip young adults for the world of work. These courses include residential periods and work experience.

technical college 1. See *college of further education* in the United Kingdom. 2. In the United States, the term refers to a community-based institution offering occupational and career-orientated education at *post-secondary* level. See *community college*.

335

technical education Preparation in *vocational education*.

Technical Education Council A UK body established in 1973 and later merged into the *Business and Technical Education Council*.

Technical Instruction Act In 1899 legislation in England enabled local government to spend a penny rate on technical instruction, which altered the role of the *City and Guilds of London Institute*.

Technical Leisure Centre Provides advice, materials, and demonstrations about hobbies which form an important part of the *non-vocational adult education* curriculum of many *adult education* institutes. Current address: 1 Grangeway, Kilburn, London NW6.

technical unit Some societies of the world, like Sri Lanka, attach these units to *formal education* to provide *vocational education* programmes for unemployed young people. It is regarded as a part of the *non-formal education* provision.

Techniques for Teachers of Adults Published in America by the *National Association for Public Continuing and Adult Education* eight times a year until the association merged.

technische Hochschule *Technological university* in Germany or Switzerland.

Technological Horizons in Education Journal Published six times a year by Information Synergy Ltd of Massachusetts in the United States.

technological university A university which specializes in technological subjects. A number were created in the United Kingdom in the post-war period, usually from *colleges of advanced technology*.

technology The application of the practical sciences within industry and commerce.

technology centre A consortium of higher education institutions which provide advice and guidance about research to local industry and commerce on a consultancy basis.

Tehalia (sometimes translated as *tehila*) A Hebrew acronym for a Significant Literacy Programme for the Adult Learner, a programme targeted at mothers. This programme began in 1977 with one study centre and rapidly spread across the whole country; they now number about 80 different study centres. The centres are run on democratic lines so that members are forced to participate in local political activities of the centre as well as literacy activities. Additionally, a variety of social activities are organized to creat dynamic centres.

Tele Université The television university in Quebec, Canada.

teleconferencing A form of *distance education* in which students in different geographical locations can form a simultaneous conference link among themselves or with a tutor, so that a tutorial can be conducted by telephone.

telecourse The use of open-circuit television for educational purposes. It is a modern approach to *distance education*, used exclusively by some institutions and as one element in the provision by others.

telemathic teaching A *teaching* and *learning* programme where interaction between *teacher* and *learner* is conducted through methods other than regular face-to-face contact.

telemathy Learning at a distance.

television university Established in China and similar but not quite the same as the *Open University* in the United Kingdom. In China televised instruction material is used by full-time and part-time students enrolled at the university. In addition, it appears that normal universities, *spare-time universities*, and *factory colleges* all use some of these televised programmes.

temperament A common term for aspects of *personality* that describe how a person usually reacts to situations.

Temperance Movements' Educational and Cultural Association An association which sponsors *adult education* in Norway and is a member of the *Norwegian Association of Adult Education Organizations*.

Temple, William (1881–1944) Leading churchman and Archbishop of Canterbury. Throughout his life he was a great supporter of the *adult education* movement, the first president of the *Workers' Educational Association*, and an active participant in it. He felt that such educational organizations were instruments in the creation of democracy.

tenure The right of permanent employment within an organization.

term 1. A limited period of time during which an educational institution is in session. 2. A word or phrase which describes a phenomenon, situation, etc.

term paper An academic paper that has to be presented by a student at the end of a session and is regarded as part of that session's work.

terminal assessment See *summative assessment*.

tertiary college An institution providing *tertiary education*.

tertiary education Used mainly to refer to education of the post-secondary school student. While it does not refer specifically to *adult education*, adult students are regarded as part of the potential clientele of most tertiary colleges. It includes *higher education* and *further education*.

Tertiary Forum Scottish post-school education launched in 1981 by the college lecturers' associations in Scotland.

tertiary socialization Occasionally used in sociology to refer to a form of *socialization* that occurs during occupational preparation and relates to the *hidden curriculum* of the educational process.

test 1. An *examination*. The term is more likely to be used in reference to a test of a less formal type, seeking to assess students' *knowledge* or *skills*. 2. In the sciences, a procedure to detect the presence or absence of a substance.

test item The individual items in a schedule of questions or attitude statements to be employed in an educational or psychological test.

Test of English as a Foreign Language (TOEFL) Helps institutions determine whether a non-English-speaking applicant has attained sufficient proficiency in English to study in an English-medium instructional environment. Used in the United States.

Test of General Education Development See *General Education Development*.

test of high school equivalency See *General Education Development*.

test of significance A test to examine the level of certainty that a finding is not likely to occur by chance.

Test of Written English A thirty-minute writing test which is part of the *Test of English as a Foreign Language*.

test-study method An approach to *teaching* in which the students are pre-tested to establish the level of knowledge or skill upon which the educator or course has to build. See *needs assessment*.

testimonial A reference or recommendation.

textbook A set book for a specific course of study.

Thailand The administration of non-formal adult education is conducted by the Ministry of Education. From 1978 this department has also run a documentation centre concerned with *adult* and *lifelong education*. Current address: Division of Non-Formal Education Operation, Non-Formal Education Department, Ministry of Education, Bangkok 10300, Thailand.

Thailand Adult/Non-formal Education Association (TANEA) A national *adult education* association in Thailand. Current address: c/o Faculty of Education, Kasetsart University, Bangkok 10903, Thailand.

Thailand's Literacy Campaign The Thai government set a target of reducing Thailand's illiteracy from 14.5 per cent to 10.5 per cent of the population in the Fifth National and Social Economic Development Plan between 1981 and 1986. Research on literacy was carried out by the Department of Non-Formal Education. See *Thailand*.

thanatology The study of death and dying. This is an area of educational concern for professional educators working in the health care professions and for counsellors.

thanatos Freudian concept of the death instinct.

theatre workshops Several theatre companies have established workshops at different times to encourage people studying specific pieces of drama to understand them more fully – a *community education* initiative. See also *community theatre*.

thematic approach An approach to *teaching* and to *curriculum design* that organizes *knowledge* around *themes*. It is sometimes referred to as a *topic approach*.

theme A topic or idea expanded in a discourse, lesson, or series of lessons.

theory 1. A body of generally accepted *knowledge* about some phenomenon or process; this is seen to be distinct from *practice*. Hence there is often a debate about the mutual importance of theory and practice in professional preparation. In a sense both refer to classical

epistemologies: theory focuses on knowledge that comes from theoretical analysis, and practice on knowledge that arises from *empirical experience* through the senses. 2. In philosophy, it refers to a logically deduced construct. 3. An idea or hypothesis.

theory in use *C. Argyris* and *D. Schon* utilize this term to refer to a theory of action which underlies an action, but of which the actor may not be totally aware. The theory in use may not necessarily relate to the *espoused theory*.

theory X D. MacGregor postulated two theories of management style, theory X and *theory Y*, which have been adapted for educational purposes. Theory X suggests that people are basically lazy, dislike work and will avoid it if they can, and that they have so little ambition that they have to be coerced into working. Teachers may adopt a similar approach to learners, thus producing a teacher-centred, *behaviouristic* approach to *teaching*.

theory Y D. MacGregor's second theory is the antithesis of his *theory X*. In it he suggests that people are interested, want to work and satisfy their needs, and are prepared to assume responsibility for their own work. This approach has led to a more student-centred approach to *teaching* and *learning*.

therapy A treatment for disorder or disease, especially of a *psychological* nature. *Humanistic* therapy is a *learning* experience; frequently some of its insights have been incorporated into humanistic *adult education*, raising some conceptual questions about the nature of *education*.

thesis 1. A case or theory maintained in a discussion. 2. A written *dissertation*, or piece of original *research*, usually presented for a higher degree.

think A covert cognitive or mental manipulation of ideas, images, symbols, propositions, memories, concepts, etc; mental activity. There are different types of thinking, which can be described as *cognitive styles*.

think tank a group of people who are called together to solve problems, make policy decisions and projections. These are usually interdisciplinary groups of *experts*.

Thomism A school of philosophy deriving from St Thomas Aquinas.

Thorndike, Edward Lee (1874–1949) Psychologist who taught at Teacher's College, Columbia University, New York. He was responsible for many of the developments in adult psychology, with his work on *'Adult Learning'* (1928) being most significant. He considered that *learning* means connecting. He also concluded that *adults* can learn although their learning ability declines from about the age of 25 years; however he did not think that there was an *intelligence* loss. He was a pioneer in the study of *adult learning* theory.

thought 1. A general term covering the cognitive processes. 2. A specific term that refers to the body of ideas that one thinker has produced.

Thurstone Scale An approach to the measurement of *attitudes*, in which attitude statements are first assessed by experts in the field for reliability and consistency. Occasionally employed in research in *adult education* to test attitudes towards it.

Tie Lines Established in 1966 as a magazine of the *Canadian Association for Adult Education*, it has since changed its name to *Learning Resources Kit*.

time and motion study The study of work which relates job performance to the time taken to perform each task.

time management The ability to plan and control the use of time effectively.

time sampling A process by which a phenomenon is investigated over a period of time. Instead of taking

continuous measurement, investigations are made at periodic intervals.

timed test A *test* that has to be completed within a specified period of time.

timetable The formal arrangement and timing of classes or groups within any institution or organization. *Schedule* is the term often used in America.

Tirelo Setshaba A *community development* project in Botswana for work in the remote areas by young adults who wish to enter *further education*. It is a form of community service that successful young people are expected to give as part of their own education.

To Educate the People Consortium An innovative five-year first-degree programme initiated by Wayne State University, utilizing television, seminars conducted in the workplace, and weekend conferences. The programme is also known as the *Weekend College*.

Today (or *Community Education Today*.) The newspaper of the *National Community Education Association* in the United States.

Tolley Medal for Distinguished Leadership in Adult Education The William Pearson Tolley award is made from Syracuse University, New York, for contributions to adult education leadership. While the award is presented by this one university, worldwide consultations take place before it is made.

Tolman, E.C. (1886–1959) American psychologist, well known for his work on *learning theory*.

Tompkins, Father James Roman Catholic priest and university teacher at *Saint Francis Xavier University* in Nova Scotia from 1902. As an advocate for social justice he was probably the initiator of the *Antigonish Movement*. He was also a cousin of *Moses Coady*, and persuaded Coady to come to Saint Francis Xavier in 1928. Tompkins' radicalism led to his being forced to leave the university in 1922 and to undertake parish work. However, even there he was an inspiration to people and helped his parishioners undertake many projects to improve their *community*.

topic approach See *thematic approach*.

Topshee, Father George (d. 1984) One of the successors to *Moses Coady* and *James Tompkins* at *Antigonish*, Father George Topshee was born in Canada and served the whole of his ministry in the diocese of Antigonish. He became director of the Extension Department at *Saint Francis Xavier University* and director of the *Coady International Institute*. Throughout his life he worked with the poor and underprivileged throughout the world.

top-up Obtaining additional credits or passes in examinations.

total immersion method A method of *teaching* or *learning* a language in which the learner is exposed only to the language and culture being learned for 24 hours a day.

Tough, Allen Studied with *C.O. Houle* in Chicago where he developed an interest in *self-directed learning*. Author of the seminal study, *'The Adult's Learning Projects'*, on self-directed learning. While its methodology has been criticized, the work has been replicated in a number of countries throughout the world.

Towarzystwo Wiedzy Powszechnej The Polish adult education association. Current address: Palac Kultury 1 Nauki XIIP, Warzawa 00–901, Poland.

town hall A method of *training* used by the League of Political Education in the United States in the 1920s to provide citizenship training for adults. See also *town meeting*.

town meeting Community problem-solving, decision-making instruments in a town, initially in New England. The concept has been taken over by the

International League for Social Commitment in Adult Education which has town meetings within its annual gatherings. These are open-discussion, policy-making meetings in which all members are free to participate.

town planning The design of urban areas.

Townswoman Monthly periodical of the *National Union of Townswomen's Guilds*.

Toynbee Hall The first of the university settlements, named after Arnold Toynbee, which were Victorian Christian attempts to serve the poor in London. The founder of the movement, *Canon A.S. Barnett*, placed great emphasis upon *adult education* as an agent for *social change*. He also made use of the newly formed *university extension* classes. The *Workers' Educational Association* emerged from a meeting here in 1903.

track record A record of past performance.

trade test An occupational *test*.

Trade Union Educational Inquiry Committee Established in 1921 as the first major attempt of the trade unions to plan their educational policy and provision.

trade union studies The focus of concern for trade unionists in recent years, it is now advocated as a subject for study in its own right in trade union courses.

Trade Union Studies Journal A journal which focuses upon trade union education.

Trade Union Training Authority (TUTA) Established in Australia as a result of the *Trade Union Training Authority Act*, this is a national body funded by the state to promote, provide and co-ordinate the *training* of trade union members, which is specifically designated as relating to the powers and functions of the trade unions.

Trade Union Training Authority Act
Passed in 1975 in Australia to establish
the *Trade Union Training Authority* and an
Australian trade union training
college.

**Trades Union Congress Education
Department** Established in 1964 with
the termination of both the *National
Council of Labour Colleges* and the
*Worker's Education Trades Union
Committee*. It offers a programme of
courses relevant to trade union officials.
Some courses are national while others
are organized on a more local basis.
There are also some *distance education*
courses. Current address: Congress
House, Great Russell Street, London
WC1B 3LS, UK.

**Trades Union Congress Educational
Trust** This trust offers *awards* for
members who wish to pursue their
education, as supplements to the Local
Education Authority grants where these
are applicable.

**Trades Union Congress National
Education Centre** A *learning resource
centre* for TUC education. Current
address: 77 Crouch End, Hornsey,
London N8 8DG, UK.

Trades Union Congress Open School
Established in the mid-1980s to foster
open learning within the trade union
movement with *study circles* and an
emphasis on educating the membership
of the movement. It has replaced some of
the postal education work that the unions
had formerly undertaken.

traditionalist One whose *attitudes,
behaviour* and *beliefs* reflect past ideas and
practices.

train To *instruct, teach*.

train and visit system (T & V) The
system used widely in *agricultural
extension* over 40 countries. Features of
the system include continuous *training*
and frequent visits by staff, whose sole
responsibility is agricultural extension.
These *village extension workers* receive

strict training and undertake regular
village visitation. In addition to built-in
supervision, there is continuous
promotion of staff, continuous
monitoring of work, and a minimum of
paperwork. See also *cooperative extension*.

trainability The ability to be trained or
prepared for an occupation or profession.

trainee One who is being *trained*.

trainer 1. One who *trains* students or
learners. 2. A sports *coach*. 3. Trainer of
the trainers; one who prepares *adult
educators* 4. In France, one who works in
training in *continuing education*. See *youth
trainer*.

Trainer Support Services (TSS) A
data base hosted by *MARISNET* with
information for *trainers*.

training 1. A planned and systematic
sequence of instruction under
supervision, designed to impart
predetermined *skills, knowledge,
information*, and even *attitudes*. Frequently
contrasted with *education* and used with
reference to *vocational education*. Usually
refers to the shaping of the learner's
habits, *behaviours*, or the acquisition of
skills. It is also frequently related to the
teaching techniques of *demonstration* and
instruction. The definition raises issues of
indoctrination. 2. In the Federal Republic
of Germany, training refers to in-work
continuing education, especially in
medicine. By law, however, work and
training are separate entities. Thus the
right to practice is granted at the end of
undergraduate study and training then
occurs as a part of work.

Training Access Points (TAPS)
Computerized information about
vocational education and training courses,
including date of commencement and
fees, found in Job Centres.

Training Agency When the
Conservative government in the United
Kingdom abolished the *Training
Commission* in 1988 this agency became
its successor, based at the same adress
and having very similar functions.

Training and Development A practical monthly magazine published by the Institute of Training Development.

Training and Development Fund In Norway, an agreement known as the 'Basic Agreement' between employers and the trade unions in the mid-1970s stressed the significance of *lifelong education*. As a result this fund was established for the purpose of enabling both employers and employees to attend *continuing education*. It has resulted in a growth of trade union and industrial *training*, and also an increase in the study of management.

Training and Development Journal The monthly journal of the *American Society for Training and Development*. Current address: ASTD, 1630 Duke Street, Box 1443, Alexandria, Virginia 22313, USA.

training bay An area within an organization set aside for *training*.

training centre Forerunners to the present *skill centres*, at which government training was offered to the unemployed.

training college The term used in the United Kingdom for an educational institution which prepared school teachers. As teaching became professionalized, they became known as *colleges of education*.

Training Commission Formerly, the *Manpower Services Commission*. It assumed its new name and role in 1988. It was subsequently renamed the *Training Agency*. Current address: Moorfoot, Sheffield S1 4PQ, UK.

Training Extension Course (TEC) A US Army *training* technique employing audio-visual, audio, and printed pre-packaged texts. Military personnel can work through their training at their own pace individually. The course is based upon the recognized *learning needs* of the personnel. Each package begins with a *pre-test* and the sessions are *post-tested* by performance-orientated, *criterion-referenced* tests.

Training for Enterprise A scheme organized by the *Manpower Services Commission* to equip people intending to start their own business with the management skills required to launch and maintain a small business successfully. Training is also provided under this scheme for the owners of small companies to increase the efficiency of their organization. (Note: the *Manpower Services Commission* changed its name to the *Training Commission* and then to the *Training Agency* in 1988.)

Training for Jobs A government White Paper of January 1984 which outlined national objectives for the future of industrial training, confirming the *New Training Initiative*.

Training for Skills The follow-up to the *Youth Training Scheme*.

Training for the Future A government publication of 1972 which embraced proposals for the rapid increase of *training* in the United Kingdom. It led to the formation of the *Manpower Services Commission*. (Note: the *Manpower Services Commission* changed its name to the *Training Commission* and then to the *Training Agency* in 1988.)

Training Information Framework (TIF) A scheme in which the *Manpower Services Commission* was to have provided locally based, computerized information about employers, training providers, and types of training facilities available throughout Britain. It was cancelled because of cost considerations in 1985. Subsequently, a computer-assisted, local labour market information system was introduced which was much cheaper and quicker to implement. (Note: the *Manpower Services Commission* changed its name to the *Training Commission* and then to the *Training Agency* in 1988.

Training Institute of the National Employment Service The organization in Belgium that prepares *vocational education* tutors. It also provides additional training for managerial staff.

training needs See *needs*. The term often used by trainers to refer to that *knowledge* or *skill* that workers must acquire to be proficient in their occupational role.

Training of Trainers Committee Established by the *Manpower Services Commission* in 1978 to consider the training needs of those reponsible for training. Two reports were made to the *Manpower Services Commission*, in 1978 and 1980. (Note: the *Manpower Services Commission* changed its name to the *Training Commission* and then to the *Training Agency* in 1988.)

training officer One who is employed to organize the training needed by employees in a company.

Training Officer A specialist journal for *training officers* published monthly. It contains information, book reviews, etc.

Training Opportunities Programme (TOPS) As a result of the Department of Employment review of arrangements for the unemployed, conducted in 1972, this scheme was introduced and became the main adult training scheme until the *Manpower Services Commission* restructured its programme in 1985–86, when the *Job Training Scheme* became the main programme. The aims were to provide training upon request for unemployed adults, subject to the economic need for the skills taught, to enable adults to change occupations quickly, and to promote the concept of retraining. To be eligible for TOPS, adults either had to be unemployed or to relinquish their employment on taking up their place within the scheme; to be at least 19 years of age; to have been away from fulltime education for at least two years; not to have taken another TOPS course in the previous three years; and to have the clear intention of taking up employment in the area of their training on completion of the course. *MSC* paid trainees a small allowance whilst they were in training. TOPS courses were run by *colleges of further education* or at *skill centres* run by the *Manpower Services Commission*. (Note: the *Manpower Services*

Commission changed its name to the *Training Commission* and then to the *Training Agency* in 1988.)

Training Resources Group The group within the *Civil Service College* involved with training the *trainers* in the civil service. It claims to be the largest provider of training in the United Kingdom.

Training Services Agency A UK body responsible to the *Manpower Services Commission*. Current address: 168 Regent Street, London. (Note: the *Manpower Services Commission* changed its name to the *Training Commission* and then to the *Training Agency* in 1988.)

Training Shop Stewards Published in 1968 by the Trades Union Congress, this document is concerned with developing professionalism in the training of shop stewards. It analysed the educational needs of the shop stewards as a result of a survey, and reported upon where the training should occur and what *teaching methods* might be adopted.

Training Standards Advisory Service Seeks to provide objective and independent advice on the quality of foundation and *vocational* training in the *Youth Training Scheme* and the *Job Training Scheme*. It is a *Manpower Services Commission* agency. (Note: the *Manpower Services Commission* changed its name to the *Training Commission* and then to the *Training Agency* in 1988.)

training the trainers The professional preparation of those who will become *trainers, training officers*, or *adult educators*.

transaction The interaction between two people in which there is an exchange process. The *teacher–learner* interaction is likely to be a transaction when it is conducted in a mature manner.

transactional analysis A neo-Freudian theory of personality which suggests that there are three elements to personality and that behaviour is controlled by whichever aspect of personality is in charge at the time that the behaviour occurs. It is practised in a group setting in which the major objective is to have the client achieve an adaptive, mature, and realistic approach to living. Often used in *affective education*.

transactional encounter Underlying transactionalism is the idea that *knowledge* is gained from interactive experiences with the environment.

transactional mode In *adult education* there are, it is claimed, three modes of transaction: individual, group, and community.

transcript The official copy of the course studied and the grades obtained by a student in a college career. This term is much more common in North America and where courses of study are modular in structure. See *profile*.

transduction 1. The process whereby something is transformed. In psychology, sensory processes are transformed into patterns of neural impulses that give rise to sensory *perception*. 2. The process of recoding information from one form to another.

transductive reasoning *Jean Piaget* used this term to describe a form of reasoning which is neither deductive nor inductive, but one in which the thinker moves from one instance or thought to the next.

transfer theory 1. A theory of *teaching* which treats *knowledge* as a commodity to be transferred from *teacher* to *learner*. 2. The term may be more loosely applied to any situation in which the learner's new *knowledge* or *skill* can facilitate the undertaking of subsequent tasks. 3. There are generally thought to be a number of stages in transfer: learning, relating, remembering, and applying to a new situation.

transformative education A concept which refers to the expansion of consciousness and the working towards a meaningfully integrated life. It is a

relatively new concept within the field of *lifelong education* but there are a number of activities within the field of *educational gerontology* which might be conceptualized within this framework.

transformative research Research relating to *transformative education* in which people or communities may gain an expansion of consciousness and more meaningfully integrated lifestyles. A Transformative Research Network was established by the *International Council for Adult Education* during a conference at Leeds University, UK, in 1988.

translation The process of expressing what is expressed in one language into another.

transpersonal psychology A psychological approach to the human being that sees the person within the context of the wider creation; a *humanistic*, perhaps religious, approach to understanding people, not grounded in the more 'scientific' approaches of other schools of psychology.

Travelling Folk High School The oldest of the *Tvind* schools, it commenced in 1970. It is a school in which experience and travel form part of the programme; thus it is a *folk high school* with an ethos different from others in Denmark. There is also a branch called 'On the Road to Victory' in which the participants work in a developing country in Africa on development projects.

travelling theory A theory of *teaching* that regards the subject under review as a terrain to be explored with the *teacher* as the *learner's* guide and support.

Trends in Adult Education An occasional publication of the United States Center for Educational Statistics. Obtainable from: Superintendent of Documents, US Government Printing Office, Washington DC 20402, USA.

Tressell, Robert Originally named Robert Noonan, he later dropped the name 'Noonan'. He was the author of *'The Ragged Trousered Philanthropists'* a book which provides working-class people with a vision of a co-operative commonwealth instead of the evils of unemployment in an Edwardian Britain. The book has been used in *adult education* classes.

trial and error learning A learning process in which the *learner* selects a direction towards a specific objective and modifies the process as she/he moves in that direction, rejecting those elements that are irrelevant to the objective concerned.

triangulation An approach to research in which two or more different methods are employed to study the same phenomenon in order to understand it more fully. It is a useful approach in studying the education of adults.

trimester The division of the academic year into three *terms* of three months each. See also *qiarter*.

Trinidad and Tobago See the *Congress of Adult Education of Trinidad and Tobago*.

TRIST TVEI-related *in-service training* for teachers. See *Technical and Vocational Education Initiative*.

true/false questions A method of testing a group of students by asking questions that require only that they specify that the fact(s) in the *question* are true or false.

trustees The legally appointed governors or managers of an educational institution, fund, or trust.

tuition Teaching.

tuition assistance Educational programmes in which employing organizations pay all or some of the employee's course fees at approved colleges or training agencies. These may be vocationally orientated but they need not necessarily be so, depending upon company policy.

tuition fees Course fees.

tuition reimbursement program A US programme of study in which the employer pays all or part of the fees for the course(s) of study undertaken.

Tuskegee Institute Founded by *Booker T. Washington* in Tuskegee, Alabama in 1881 as a normal school, it soon broadened its base. It acquired funding to become an agricultural college and *George Washington Carver* joined it as director of research. It was here that Washington started many other movements for black people in America.

Tuskegee Negro Conference Founded by *Booker T. Washington* in 1892, this conference continued each year until his death in 1915. It was at these conferences that he tried to teach black people outside the confines of the classroom so that they might raise their living standards.

tutee The student of a specific *tutor*.

tutor 1. A *teacher*; one who instructs. 2. Often, tutoring is a much more personalized teaching function, e.g. one-to-one, or one-to-small-group teaching. 3. In some forms of education the tutor is a personal tutor with some type of pastoral responsibility for the student(s).

tutor-marked assignment The term used, often in *distance education*, when the local *tutor* assesses the students' assignments.

tutor organizer The *adult educator* who has responsibility for planning the provision of the *programme* in an *adult education* institution and who also has a teaching function.

tutorial A discussion between a *tutor* and one or more students, usually with specific reference to academic work.

tutorial class *Albert Mansbridge* recognized that the large numbers of people in individual lectures that were initially provided by the *Workers Educational Association* would not necessarily result in a high standard of *teaching* and *learning*. He launched the tutorial class in 1907 with the intention of providing university standard teaching. Initially, the tutorial class was a two-year commitment (now it is three), and the first tutor was *R.H. Tawney*. The Board of Education gave grant aid to tutorial classes and the first inspection, by His Majesty's Inspectorate, reported in 1910. The first formal regulations for the tutorial class followed this practice in 1913, when it was suggested that the aim should be to reach university honours degree standard. Students were expected to attend two-thirds of the meetings and to complete written work as demanded by the tutor.

tutorial group A group of students which meets regularly with a *tutor*.

tutorial system A method of teaching in which students are allocated to *tutors* for regular teaching and guidance during a course.

tutoring A form of teaching on a one-to-one basis, usually conducted by a tutor or private teacher.

Tutor's Bulletin Begun in 1978, it was intended that this be published twice a year for extra-mural tutors. It was published by the University of Leicester in the United Kingdom.

Tvind An area in West Jutland, Denmark, which has given its name to a series of educational experiments. Schools were built in the Rose Garden in Tvind, and residents have also constructed their own energy power station driven by a large windmill. In these schools the *curriculum* is related very closely to life itself so that the curriculum assumes current significance to all who study there. See *Travelling Folk High School, Tvind Continuation School, Necessary Teacher Training College, Free School at Tvind, International*

Continuation School, Tvind School of Needlework, Arts and Crafts. Visitors are always welcome to Tvind. Current address: Tvind, 6990 Ulfborg, Denmark.

Tvind Continuation School Started in 1974 as a school for the 14–18 year-olds.

Tvind School of Needlework, Arts and Crafts Founded in September 1986, this is a practical school of design, dressmaking, art, decoration, etc. However, it has a more general curriculum as well.

Twenty-one Hour Rule A regulation in the United Kingdom that allows unemployed adults to undertake part-time education whilst still remaining eligible for work and, therefore, for state unemployment benefit.

twilight class *Evening class.* Used with specific reference to those who are regular day students who are expected to attend an evening class.

two cultures Used with reference to the separation between the arts and the sciences.

'two-thirds rule' In studies of speech in the classroom in *initial education*, this 'rule' has been shown to be generally applicable: two-thirds of the time spent in class is speech; two-thirds of the speech is the teacher's; two-thirds of the teacher's speech consists of directing the teaching either through lecturing or asking questions. Research into adult classrooms still needs to test this out.

two-year college American *junior college.*

typescript The typed copy of a document.

typology The study of types or classifications.

UDACE News The newsletter of the *Unit for the Development of Adult Continuing Education* (UDACE).

Udaipur Literacy Declaration Following a major international conference in Udaipur, India in 1982, a declaration was made with a commitment to achieve literacy for all by the year 2000.

Uganda The *adult education* association of this country is the *National Adult Education Association of Uganda*. Current address: P.O. Box 8174, Kampala, Uganda.

ujamaa African socialism. Especially in Tanzania, self-reliance in doing and thinking and also in planning for action. It is perhaps hardly surprising that this term has been associated with Tanzanian *adult education*.

ulpan Residential schools in Israel in which the Hebrew language and culture are taught to immigrants in a *folk high school* spirit for a period of five months. The teaching method is that of *total immersion*.

ulpan Akiva An independent *ulpan* named after Rabbi Akiva, who is reputed not to have learned to read and write until he was 40 years of age. This ulpan is aimed at strengthening an understanding of Jewish culture and at being open to new cultural influences.

ulpanit A non-residential language school in Israel whose courses last for about a year to help immigrants acquire a knowledge of Hebrew.

Ulster People's College Established in 1983 as an *adult education* college in Ulster. Current address: 30 Adelaide Park, Belfast, UK.

unclassified degree A degree at pass level but without honours.

unconditioned response The normal response to a *stimulus*.

unconscious 1. A lack of awareness. 2. Processes in the *mind* that proceed in a manner of which the person is unaware. 3. The primordial repressed desires that *Freud* characterized in his psychology, such as *id*.

unconscious memory The memorization of all events that have been repressed; an important concept for *adult educators* since people come to education with repressed feelings about education in general.

underachiever One who has not attained the level that he/she would be expected to attain in the educational process; one whose performances are far less than would be expected as a result of an *intelligence test*. There are many underachievers who return to *adult education* and who might be classified as a *late developer* if successful at a later time.

underclass The long-term unemployed and unemployable, for whom many educational projects and much *adult basic education* is mounted.

undereducated Those who have not been successful in the school system. However, this term does not imply that the school has failed, since *learning* occurs in the whole of life and school is only one provider of learning. Hence it could be claimed that the social system has failed them.

underemployed Form of employment which demands less than the learning level of the worker.

undergraduate Student in *higher education* reading for a *first degree*.

understanding To *learn, know,* and have the ability to provide explanation about a phenomenon; a form of *deep learning*.

unemployed people's centre These centres have developed in the United Kingdom in recent years, usually run by paid staff and sponsored by the *Manpower Services Commission*, but relying heavily upon *volunteers*. They offer a variety of activities for unemployed people, including *adult education* courses suitable for their clientele. (Note: the *Manpower Services Commission* changed its name to the *Training Commission* and then to the *Training Agency* in 1988.)

unemployed workers' centre A centre established to help the unemployed, often running courses and providing other learning opportunities.

Unemployment Educational Association Established as a semi-autonomous educational organization by the *Workers Educational Association* in Toronto at the time of the 1931 depression.

Unesco (United Nations Educational, Scientific and Cultural Organisation) Founded in 1946. It has maintained a very high profile in both *adult* and *lifelong education,* publishing many documents, reports, arranging major international conferences, and playing a very significant role in the education of adults worldwide. Current address: Adult Education Section, Literacy, Adult Education and Rural Development Division, Unesco, 7 place de Fontenoy, 75700 Paris, France.

Unesco Adult Education Information Notes Published in many different languages and distributed quarterly.

Unesco Conferences of Adult Education There have been four conferences held thus far: at Elsinore, Denmark in 1949; at Montreal, Canada in 1960; at Tokyo, Japan in 1972; at Paris, France in 1985. Each conference issued statements and reports which are available from the Unesco offices, if they are still in print. Current address: Unesco, Division of Primary Education, Literacy and Adult Education and Education in Rural Areas, 7 place de Fontenoy, 75700 Paris, France.

Unesco Institute for Education Institute established in Hamburg in 1951 for the study of education, it is responsible for many research projects in *lifelong education*. It publishes a series of books and monographs, has a *Library and Documentation Centre,* and publishes the *International Review of Education.* Current address: Unesco Institute for Education, Feldbrunnenstrasse 58, 2000 Hamburg, Federal Republic of Germany.

Unesco Institute for Education Newsletter Published occasionally to keep readers up to date with events in the *Unesco Institute for Education.* It carries a list of recent publications.

Unidad Nacional de Educación Basica para Adultos The national union of *adult basic education* centres in Mexico. Current address: SEP, Azafrán 486, 3 Piso, Col Granjas México, México DFC, PO 8400.

Union for Rural Education Established in Finland in 1952 to co-ordinate the work of educational organizations with a rural orientation. It organizes its own *study centre* which in turn is responsible for *study circles,* courses, and lectures. It has eight district centres and 27 member organizations.

Current address: Pursimiehenkatu 15, 00150 Helsinki 15, Finland.

Union of International Engineering Organisations Established in 1951 to promote international congresses and disseminate information. Current address: 62 rue de Courcelles, Paris, 8 France.

Union of Rural Residential School Colleges Educational centres for rural Germany. They work with the *Farmers' Union* although they are independent organizations. They offer both short-term and long-term courses and are in the *folk high school* tradition.

Union of Soviet Socialist Republics (USSR) See *Znanie* and *Institut obscego obrazovanija vzroslych*.

Union of Specialized Agricultural School Graduates A *further education* institution in the Federal Republic of Germany involved with *continuing vocational education*.

Union of Yugoslav Adult Educators' Societies See *Savez Andragoških Društava Jugoslavije*.

unit 1. A module in a *curriculum* 2. A branch or division of a larger organization.

Unit for the Development of Adult Continuing Education (UDACE) This unit was established, following the closure of the *Advisory Council for Adult and Continuing Education*, under the banner of *National Institute of Adult Continuing Education* to undertake a rolling programme of development in designated areas. The establishment of this unit was Department of Education and Science policy and it was funded for three years only. It is significant that it includes the word *development* in its title, as recommended by the *Russell Report*, but not incorporated into the Advisory Council's title.

United Kingdom Central Council for Nursing, Midwifery and Health Visiting (UKCC) Following the Nurses,

Midwives and Health Visitors Act in 1979, this council was established to improve the standards of professional preparation of the various branches of nursing, midwifery, and health visiting.

United Nations Created in 1945 with the principal objectives of achieving peace and security. It seeks to foster international co-operation. Current address for information: UN Plaza, New York, New York 10017, USA.

United Nations Centre for Social Development and Humanitarian Affairs Current address: Vienna International Centre, Box 500, A–1400 Vienna, Austria.

United Nations Decade for Women The decade 1975 to 1985.

United Nations Declaration of Human Rights Accepted by all the member nations, this declaration includes the right to education and work.

United Nations International Research and Training Institute for the Advancement of Women. The objectives of this organization are to stimulate and assist women, through research, training, and the collection and exchange of information, to participate more fully in developmental activities at all levels. Current address: Apartado Postal 21747, Santo Domingo, Dominican Republic.

United Nations University Current address: Toho Seimi Building, 15–1 Shibuya 2 – chome Shibuya-ku, Tokyo 150, Japan.

United States Armed Forces Institute Established in 1942 in Madison, Wisconsin, to provide a variety of services to military and civilian personnel in the armed services. It provides *correspondence* courses, group study guides, residential courses, etc.

United States College Examination Board The board responsible for overseeing the 'credit' system in the nationwide college level examination programme.

United States Department of Education/Office of Vocational Adult Education Administers, co-ordinates, and recommends national policy for improving adult educational programmes. Current address: ROB #3, Room 5028, 7th and D Streets SW, Washington DC 20202, USA.

United States Department of the Army The department responsible for all *adult education* programmes in the US army. Current address: Headquarters US MEPCOM, 2500 Greenway Road, North Chicago, Illinois 60064, USA.

Universidad Alberta The *distance teaching university* of Portugal, which began in 1981 as a result of the *Instituto Português de Ensino a Distáncia*. It is not an *open university* inasmuch as formal entrance qualifications are required.

Universidad Nacional Abierta The Venezuelan *distance teaching university*. It was established in 1977 to offer *higher education* to a wider student body, to assist in the development of the country, and to meet the social demand. The university offers formal degree programmes following an initial year's introductory course. There are regional centres and the university headquarters is in Caracas.

Universidad Nacional de Educación a Distancia The Spanish *distance teaching university*. The initial planning for this began as early as 1968; the university was established in 1970 by an Act of Parliament, and again in 1972. Its first students enrolled on 6 February 1973. The university offers pre-degree courses, degree courses, and *vocational education* programmes. It demands the same entry qualifications as do other universities, but it also offers an admission course for unqualified students. There is also a vocational education programme which uses books, audio cassettes, radio, tutor-marked assignments, and formal examinations. Additionally, it has a

system of *study centres* throughout Spain. The university is situated in Madrid.

Universidade Internacional para a Terceira Idade The *International University of the Third Age*, established in Portugal in 1978. It has a documentation centre. Current address: Rua das Flores 85, lo, 1200 Lisbon, Portugal.

Université du Troisième Age A movement that began in France for education for the elderly, commenced after the French passed a law in 1968 requiring the universities to provide more community education. The first was founded in Toulouse by *Pierre Vellas* in 1973. It is a voluntary movement although it is often closely related to a local university. It quickly spread to other French-speaking countries. Its name was adopted in the United Kingdom where a similar movement began in 1981. There is now an international headquarters of the movement in Belgium. See *University of the Third Age*.

Universities Council for Adult and Continuing Education (UCACE) The title adopted by the *Universities Council for Adult Education* at its 1982 meeting in order to relate to the changing role of university *extra-mural departments*. Membership is open to every university in the United Kingdom and subject to the approval of the council, associate membership is open to any other university.

Universities Council for Adult Education (UCAE) Established in 1947, this council changed its title in 1982 to the *Universities Council for Adult and Continuing Education*. It holds an annual conference and publishes an annual report of the work that universities are undertaking in the field of *adult education*. This body seeks to provide a forum for university *extra-mural departments* and to campaign on their behalf. It was formerly the *Universities Extra-Mural Consultative Committee*.

Universities Extra-Mural Consultative Committee (1926–47) Established in 1926 so that university *extra-mural departments* would have a forum for liaison. It was the forerunner to the *UCAE*.

university extension 1. First suggested by William Sewell at Exeter College, Oxford, in 1850. The first extension lectures were given by *James Stuart* of Cambridge University in 1873 and from England it spread throughout much of the world. Its original intention was to offer university-type education to artisans and others. In common with many such movements, it was the middle classes rather than the working classes which benefited most from the movement.

2. In the United States there were a number of early experiments with university extension, including one at Columbia University in 1889. The first to be formally advocated and funded was a $10,000 grant made in 1891 by the regents of the University of the State of New York to organize university extension in that state. The major advocate of this had been Melvil Dewey, who was at that time the chief librarian of Columbia University.

3. In Canada, the first Department of Extension was established at Queen's University, Kingston, Ontario in 1889, some 12 years after the first classes had started.

4. In Spain, university extension was based on the English model, following an International Pedagogical Congress in Madrid in 1892. Some of these became the *popular university* movement in Spain.

5. In the German Democratic Republic university extension was established in 1946, although it had existed in the united Germany since the mid-nineteenth century. Thus on 23 January 1946, university extension centres were established in East Germany to disseminate general, scientific, and political knowledge amongst adults and young people to enhance the general cultural and educational level of the people. This extension later led to the institution of second chance education for adults, the school-leaving certificate, and other awards.

6. In Yugoslavia, university extension commenced at the University of Belgrade in 1888 when *Ljubomir Nedić* delivered the first series of lectures.

University Extension Outreach The official newsletter of *university extension* in Australia. Published as an insert to the *Adult Education News*.

University for Distance Studies (Fernuniversitat in Hagen) See *Fernuniversitat-Gesamthoschule*.

University of London External Degree System Established as early as 1858, the University of London has been prepared to examine students from anywhere in the world for the award of a degree of the university, although it has not always offered tuition for those examinations. Certain colleges have, however, mounted courses that have prepared people to sit these examinations.

University of Maryland Overseas Program The University of Maryland operates centres throughout the world for US personnel. Current address: University of Maryland, College Park, Maryland 20742, USA.

University of Mid-America Established in 1974 as a non-profit corporation formed by a consortium of mid-western universities interested in teaching adults at a distance using new technologies. Current address: Lincoln, Nebraska, USA.

University of the Air The name by which the *Open University* in the United Kingdom was first popularly known. See the *Japanese University of the Air*.

University of the Air Foundation A public Japanese corporation legally constituted in 1981, it is the founding body of the *Japanese University of the Air*. It is also owner of the broadcast stations used by the university.

University of the Third Age 1. An *adult education* movement in the United Kingdom, which commenced in 1981 in Cambridge, that has adopted the same name as the similar French movement. It functions through local groups which organize *self-help teaching and learning*. Each group is autonomous although they all relate to a national network. Current address: 16 Parkside Gardens, London SW19 5EY. 2. Started in Lodz, Poland in 1979, and rapidly gained a large enough membership to have an Attendants' Council. 3. Established in Australia in 1986 as part of *university extension* there.

University of Wales Extension Board Current address: The Registrar, University Registry, King Edward VII Avenue, Cathays Park, Cardiff CF1 3NS.

university residential adult education Only a few universities in the United Kingdom have residential accommodation, so that this aspect of their extra-mural work is not well developed.

university settlement A feature of *university extension* in nineteenth-century Britain, where men and women from the universities went to live and work among the poor in the large cities in order to help them and educate them. It is an educational and social outreach movement of Christian mission. See *university settlement movement*.

University Settlement Formerly the *Neighbourhood Guild*, the first university settlement established in the United States, in New York in 1886.

university settlement movement Established in 1885 so that the universities could reach and work with people from the working classes, especially in the East End of London. The first settlement was *Toynbee Hall*, but others soon followed. All had an educational element in their work, which varied from one settlement to another. In 1886 a similar movement began in the United States with the founding of the *Neighbourhood Guild* in New York by Stanton Coit.

University Without Walls An *open learning* movement in America which gives academic credit for career and life experiences and organizes *teaching* and *learning* courses.

unlearn The process of having to shed one piece of learning and to acquire a new one in its place.

unlearned Descriptive term for behaviours and acts that occur without having been specifically *learned*.

unstructured interview A planned *interview* technique, as opposed to an informal discussion. The interviewer guides the interview in the planned direction and covers the requisite aspects of investigation. This is a skilled technique; sometimes called non-structured interview. See *structured interview*.

untenured post An academic post for which there is no *tenure*. It is often a temporary position or one filled outside the normal establishment of positions in a department or college.

update To keep abreast with new developments in a field of study or practice.

Update The newsletter of the adult literacy and learning community of the United States. It is published by the *Adult Literacy Initiative* in conjunction with the Office of Vocational and Adult Education. Current address: Update, ALI, Room 4145 FOB 6, 400 Maryland Ave. SW, Washington DC 20202, USA.

upward social mobility Successful individuals tend to rise in the social hierarchy as a result of their success; this may often be expressed in terms of a rise in an individual's *socio-economic class*. However, individual change does not affect social structure; thus *radical adult education* tends to emphasize group loyalty and social structural change rather than individual success and upward social mobility.

Urania 1. A society for the dissemination of scientific knowledge to adults. The first was established in Berlin 1888, although the scientific associations in the mid–nineteenth century may be regarded as predecessors of this movement. The organization is now quite widely spread. It is an early form of *adult education* in Germany and one which is still flourishing in the German Democratic Republic, having been reestablished in 1954. 2. There were also

Urania societies in other parts of Europe, e.g. Vienna and Budapest, which influenced the development of the *popular universities*.

urban education Education provided in inner-city areas.

Urban Theology Unit A UK organization founded to prepare clergy and others who wish to relate their studies to urban theology. The unit runs a study year and a variety of short courses. Current address: Pitsmoor Study House, 210 Abbeyfield Road, Sheffield S4 7AZ, UK.

vacation Holiday.

vacation school See *summer school*.

vade mecum A handbook or other aid carried by a person for immediate usage when needed. Such handbooks are sometimes prepared by educational institutions for professional groups, or in association with them.

validation board A committee which acts on behalf of a statutory body to assess a course submitted by an educational institution.

validation visit A formal visit to an educational institution to assess the extent to which the institution is able to undertake courses that are validated by that statutory body.

validity The extent to which a *test* or *instrument* measures what it is intended to measure.

Valóság (Reality) The monthly magazine of the *Scientific Educational Association* of Hungary.

value The worth of an object or experience. It is often claimed that *education* itself has value. However, it can be argued that nothing has value intrinsically, but that value is placed upon an experience or phenomenon by others. This is a crucial concept since there is great emphasis placed upon *evaluation* in *adult education*.

value judgement A term used in philosophy to imply that an assessment of worth is being made rather than an *objective* judgement.

value learning *Learning* about worth.

value system The interlocking constellation of *beliefs* and *values* that a group, social class, or society normally holds. It forms part of the *culture* of that social grouping.

van Baal, Dr. J. (b. 1909) Former Dutch colonial governor who founded the *Centre for the Study of Education in Developing Societies* in 1963 in the Netherlands. Convinced that *education* is about the transmission of *culture* he considered that recipients should receive education within the context of their own culture, so the Centre has, to some extent, adopted a similar approach to that of *Freire*.

variable 1. A quantity which, throughout an investigation, is assumed to affect the subject under investigation. 2. Subject to change. See *dependent variable, independent variable*.

variance 1. A statistical measure of the extent to which a set of scores are scattered. 2. The square of the standard deviation; alternatively, the standard deviation is the square root of the variance.

Vellas, Pierre French professor who founded the first *University of the Third Age* in Toulouse in 1973.

Venables Committee See *Committee on Continuing Education*.

Venables, Sir Peter (d. 1979) Throughout his life he was concerned with the adult and part-time students. He became vice-chancellor of the University of Aston, from which he retired in 1979. During the period of formation of the *Open University* he was chairman of the planning committee. After retirement he continued to play a large part in the Open University, chairing its *Committee on Continuing Education*. In addition, he was also president of the *National Institute of Adult Education*.

Venezuela See *Federación Interamericana de Educación de Adultos* and *Comité Venezolano de Educación Permanente*. The governmental department responsible for *adult education* is Dirección de Educación de Adultos. Current address: Ministerio de Educación, Esquina de Selas, Edif, Sede Piso 11, Caracas, Venezuela.

verbal behaviour Behaviour involving a spoken response.

verbal intelligence 1. Ability with words. 2. A *test of intelligence* using verbal material.

verbal skills See *oracy*.

verbal test A *test* which involves language.

verbalism Speech which has little substance.

verbatim recall Memory which recalls the exact presentation of the message.

Vereniging van besturen van avondscholen en avondscholengemeenschappen in Nederland (VAN) The *Association of Boards of Evening Schools in the Netherlands*. Current address: Postbus 337, 3440 AH Woerden, The Netherlands. There is also an international secretariat for this organization and VREDA; current address: Noordeinde 1, 2311 CA Leiden, The Netherlands.

Vereniging van instellingen voor schriftelijk onderwijs (VISO) The Dutch *Association of Institutes for Correspondence Education*. The member

institutes have to be accredited by Dutch law. See *Wet Erkenning Schriftelijk Onderwijs*. Current address: VISO, p/a Postbus 9053, 6800 GS Arnhem, The Netherlands.

Vereniging van rectoren/directouren en docenten aan dag/avondscholen (VREDA) The professional association for teachers in both day schools and night schools in the Netherlands. Current address: Damweg 2, 1871 BM Schoorl, The Netherlands. There is also an international secretariat for this organization and VAN; current address: Noordeinde 1, 2311 CA Leiden, The Netherlands.

Vereniging voor volkshogeschoolwerk The association for *folk high school* work in the Netherlands. Current address: Postbus 314, 3800 AH Amersfoort, The Netherlands.

vernacular Common language.

Vernein zur Geschichte der Volkshochschulen Founded in 1987, this is the documentation centre for Austrian adult education. It also has the remit of researching the historical development of *adult education* in Austria. Current address: A–1217 Wien XXI Kürschnergasse 9, Postfach 19, Austria.

Verner, Coolie (1917–79) One of the leading *adult education* theorists of his generation. He was a graduate of Florida State University, professor of adult education at the University of British Columbia, first chairman of the *Commission of Professors of Adult Education*, and an advocate for the development of the *theory* of adult education knowledge. He was a prolific writer, publishing about 275 papers and books about adult education. He was also an authority on Arctic maps and published a book of maps.

vertical thinking Thought processes that are modelled on scientific method, logical deduction, and the addition of more information. See *lateral thinking*.

veterans' education US education of military veterans through federal funding.

videocassette/videotape Educational materials can be prepared and stored on videotapes so that they can be used and re-used at a later time. Videotapes have become a recent and valuable addition to the *audio-video aids* for the teacher of adults. They are also prepared as a part of a *study pack* in *distance education*. They may also be used in the preparation of professionals and in *self-directed* study.

viewbook Books that are stored on a computer disk so that with a search facility, references can be traced. Specific parts of the book relating to the reference can either be transferred to a separate disk for use on a word processor or personal computer, or printed out for the reader.

village college A concept espoused by *Henry Morris* in an early form of *community education* in which the college became the centre of village social life, providing education for children and adults, and also being the location of the library, youth centre, and other local facilities. See also *community school*. The first of these was *Sawston Village College*, opened at Sawston in Cambridgeshire in 1930.

Village Education Resource Centre (VERC) Established in 1977 as a result of the Save the Children Fund (USA) and UNICEF. It is now a national *non-governmental organization* in Bangladesh with the goal of releasing people's energies to that they can participate in the development of their own country through education. The principles of *self-actualization* are taught and the centre is involved in *community development programmes*, training development workers, technology development, *adult literacy*, research, evaluation, and publication of useful information. Current address: VERC, GPO Box 2281, Anandapur, Savar, Dhaka, Bangladesh.

village extension worker In the *train and visit system* in the Third World, *agricultural extension* officers train the village extension workers, who then go into the villages to introduce new ideas to farmers, especially those who are regarded as their 'contact farmers'.

Vincent, John (1832–1920) American Methodist bishop. He was one of the founders of *Chautauqua* in which he retained an interest for the whole of his life. One of the aims of Chautauqua was the improvement of *Sunday school* teaching.

visiting fellow A fixed-term, sometimes honorary appointment in a university or institution of *higher education*.

visiting professor A fixed-term, sometimes honorary professorship within a university or institution of *higher education*.

visiting student A student enrolled in one educational institution but completing part of the course at another educational institution.

VISTA The national ani-poverty agency in the United States. It is heavily involved in literacy work and has endeavoured to create a Literacy Corps, as a result of the Domestic Volunteer Services Act Amendments of 1986, that would train *volunteers* to tutor adult non-readers. Address: 806 Connecticut Avenue NW, Washington DC 20525, USA.

visual ability test A *test* designed to assess an individual's abilities in such areas as visual perception and contrast.

visual aids Models, diagrams, etc. to illustrate the content of teaching. See *audio-visual aid*.

visual handicap Limited vision.

visual learner One who learns best through observation.

visual literacy The ability to recognize and understand at a conscious level the indigenous visual languages used within a particular *culture* and to produce visual messages in those languages.

viva voce An oral examination, common in higher-degree assessment. Since they are person-to-person examinations, they are expensive and time-consuming. Rarely used when there are many candidates.

Viva Voz Portuguese *adult literacy* journal, published in Portuguese monthly since 1980.

Vlaams Centrum voor Volksontwikkeling Flemish centre for adult education, established on 25 October 1984. A non-political association which seeks to be the co-ordinating body for organizations that offer socio-cultural training for adults. The centre is supported by the Ministry of Culture in Belgium. It is involved in research projects and relates to *Le Conseil Superieur* as the respresentative of Flemish-speaking Belgium. It also publishes its own journal, *Vorming Vlaanderen*, and *Nieuwsbrief.* In addition, it has its own library which is open to the public every day. Current address: Visverkopersstraat 13 Bis 2, 1000 Brussels, Belgium.

vocabulary 1. A list of words. 2. The aggregate of words in use, which might also be referred to as an active vocabulary.

vocabulary test Test of a person's store of knowledge about a list of words.

vocation 1. Formerly a calling, e.g. a divine calling. 2. Secularized at present, it tends now to refer to high-status work. 3. The ability to perform a task, as if the ability were a divine gift.

vocational Appertaining to work.

vocational choice Decisions about future work.

vocational education The education and training necessary to prepare a

person for employment or that which is provided during employment to assist the students to undertake their occupational role more effectively. The latter aspect is often called *continuing education, continuing professional education* or *post-basic education.*

vocational education and training (VET) This term is beginning to be used in *competency-based education* literature in order to widen the perspective on occupational preparation.

Vocational Education Committee Established throughout Eire to provide formal *adult education* and *vocational* training. There are adult education subcommittees concerned with non-vocational adult education.

vocational guidance Both *assessment* about ability, personality, etc. in order to 'fit' people for a job, and the guidance offered to people about their occupational prospects.

vocational school A school which is organized for the purpose of training a person for a specific vocation or occupation. In the United States, its functions are defined by the Higher Education Act of 1965.

vocational training Usually refers to the preparation for a low-status occupation; otherwise the name would almost certainly include the word *education* in its title. See *vocational education* and *training.*

Vocational Training Bulletin A publication of the *European Centre for the Development of Vocational Training.*

vocationally qualifying education A nationwide skills *training* programme aimed at unskilled or semi-skilled people, many of them women, who have been unemployed for more than one year to help them update their skills in preparation for work. This programme was started in 1983–84 and its first progress report was published in the spring of 1985.

Voksenuddannelse (Adult Education) Danish journal established in 1978 and published six times a year.

volkshochschule German word for *folk high school*.

Volkshochschule im Westen Founded in 1949 and published bimonthly, this is a German *folk high school* magazine.

Volksopvoeding (Popular Education) An *adult education* journal in the Netherlands established in 1952. It has since ceased publication.

Volkswagen Foundation German foundation established in 1961 to promote educational work and research in the *humanities, science,* and *technology.* Current address: Kastanienallee 35, 3000 Hanover Döhren, Federal Republic of Germany.

Voluntary Adult Education Forum (VAEF) An association of voluntary organizations launched in 1985 in the United Kingdom to give a forum to voluntary organizations which provide *adult education.* It is concerned with the need to develop a partnership within voluntarism, and between it and the state and funding agencies. It also regards itself as a political lobby for its member organizations.

Voluntary Education Act See *Danish Voluntary Education Act.*

Voluntary Service Overseas (VSO) An organization that recruits and sends trained personnel to work with agencies in the Third World, often in an educational capacity. The *volunteers* are usually remunerated on a scale that relates to local rates rather than the UK salary. Current address: 9 Belgrave Square, London SW1X 8PW, UK.

volunteer One who gives a service freely and often without reimbursement.

Many *adult education* and *community education* programmes employ volunteers in a variety of capacities so that the education and training of volunteers has become a significant concern in *adult education.*

Volunteer Centre The UK advisory agency on *volunteer* and *community* involvement. Current address: 29 Lower King's Road, Berkhamstead, Herts HP4 2AB, UK.

Vorming: Tijdschrift voor Volwassencqatie A Dutch journal of *adult education* published ten times a year since 1952.

Vorming Vlaanderen The journal of the *Flemish Centre for Adult Education,* or *Vlaams Centrum voor Volksontwikkeling* (translated as 'Adult Education in Flanders'). It is published six times a year and was started in 1985. See *Note d'Information.*

voucher A document that authorizes the payment of money.

voucher system A financial assistance system in education in which students use *vouchers* to obtain a specified amount of education.

Vrooman, Walter An American, he was one of the founders of *Ruskin College* in the United Kingdom and acted as principal in the early days. Vrooman's wife was one of the other founders, the third being *Charles Beard.*

Vrouw & Wereld (Women and World) The monthly journal of the Catholic Womens Workers' League in Flemish-speaking Belgium.

Vygotsky, L.S. (1896–1934) A Russian psychologist famous for his studies of language.

Wales Committee of the National Institute of Adult Continuing Education Established in 1985 to advise the Welsh Office, Welsh Joint Education Committee, *National Institute of Adult Continuing Education*, and providers of *adult education* in Wales on matters of adult continuing education, including good practice and the quality of provision. Current address: c/o WJEC, 245 Western Avenue, Cardiff CF5 2YX, UK.

Waller, Ross Douglas (b. 1899) Director of Extra-Mural Studies at the University of Manchester before the Second World War, he became an international figure after the war as he sought to assist *adult education* in Italy and Germany. He was instrumental in founding the *residential college* at Holly Royde and was active in many other aspects of the field in the United Kingdom in the 30 years after the war.

wants A term used in *motivation* theory although not so frequently used in *adult education*, in which the term *needs* is used indiscriminately. Wants are closer to *interests* and *demands*.

War on Want This organization promotes *development education* and sponsors projects. Current address: Three Castles House, 1 London Bridge Street, London SE1 9SG, UK.

Warasarn Karnvijai Sonthes The Thai quarterly journal which was started in 1982. It is published by the Ministry and contains information and research reports about *non-formal education*.

warden Often refers to the person who has administrative responsibility for a premises, e.g. the *head of centre* of an *adult education* institute, occasionally the *principal* of a *residential college*, or the head teacher of a *community school*.

Warnock Report See *Meeting Special Education Needs*, published in 1978.

Washington, Booker T. (d. 1915) One of the great *adult educators* in American history. Born a slave, he acquired education and started the *Tuskegee Institute* in Alabama in 1881. It was from this base that he founded the *Tuskegee Negro Conference*, the *National Negro Business League*, the *Farmer's Cooperative Demonstration* and the *National Negro Health Week*. He also recruited *George Washington Carver* to Tuskegee Institute as director of agricultural research. Washington was one of the great workers for the education of the black people of America.

Washington Week See *National Issues Forums*.

Watson, J.B. (1878–1958) American psychologist, professor at Johns Hopkins University and generally regarded as the founder of *behaviourism*.

Wechsler Adult Intelligence Scale (WAIS) An instrument used to test adult intelligence, it consists of 11 subtests grouped in verbal and performance scales, with a built-in age factor. It has been criticized for not providing sufficient testing of adult *learning* ability relative to social effectiveness or problem-solving in areas of life relevant to the *older adult*.

Wechsler, Davis (d. 1986) American psychologist and professor at New York University College of Medicine, responsible for producing the *Wechsler Adult Intelligence Scale*. He also developed a memory scale and a well-known scale of intelligence for children.

Weekend College See *To Educate the People Consortium* at Wayne State University in America.

Welsh circulating schools Founded by *Rev. Griffith Jones*, rector of Llanddowror, as early as 1731–32 for children and adults. The *education* was free, the language of instruction Welsh, and the *curriculum* limited to the barest of essentials – reading and the catechism. The maximum number of schools was in excess of 3,000, but the experiment came to an end before the end of the eighteenth century.

Welsh Education Office The government office through which education is administered in Wales.

Welsh Joint Examination Committee This group offers the *General Certificate of Secondary Education* examination for *external and mature students*. Current address: 245 Western Avenue, Cardiff CF5 2YX, UK.

Wesley, John (1703–91) Founder of the Methodist Church, he put great emphasis upon the teaching of lay people. Hence he started *class meetings*, a *travelling library*, wrote cheap pamphlets, and undertook many forms of *non-formal adult education*. The Methodist Church today still retains his emphasis.

Western Co-operative College Established in Canada in 1959 from the *International Co-operative Institute*, it grew quickly. It is claimed that as it became established it was perhaps unable to serve the ideals of the co-operative movement quite as fully. It was, however, to be the forerunner of the *Co-operative College of Canada* which was formed from it in 1973.

Westminster Adult Leader A quarterly magazine started by the Board of Christian Education of the Presbyterian Church of the United States in 1957.

Westminster Adult Religious Education Centre (WAREC) Established in the United Kingdom in 1977 from the Westminster Catholic Parents Centre, this centre marked the start of the Catholic Church's formal recognition of the place of *adult religious education* within its ministry and mission, where it was part of the Adult Education Committee of the archdiocese. It ceased to exist in its original form in 1984.

Wet Erkenning Schriftelijk Onderwijs The Dutch law governing *correspondence education* which was passed on 1 August 1973. As a result, a correspondence institution can only be accredited if tutors and authors of study materials are properly qualified, the institution keeps courses up to date, the institution takes the previous education of the student into consideration, the institution provides student guidance, and specified information about the institution is both correct and objective. There are about 40 such accredited correspondence institutions in Holland, and there is an *Association of Institutes for Correspondence Education*.

white board The modern equivalent to a *blackboard*. It is a prepared surface, usually affixed to a wall of a classroom, upon which the teacher or students can write using marker pens rather than chalk.

white-collar worker A person employed in a non-manual occupation.

White House Conference on Aging There have been three such conferences thus far: in 1961, 1971, and 1981. They are designed to increase the visibility of older people in the United States and to set policy directions for government and private organisations for the coming decade.

Whitehead, Alfred North (1861–1947) British philosopher who worked for many years in the United States. He started as a mathematician, was a philosopher in the *empiricist* school, and wrote some important books on *knowledge* and *education*. His work is not widely used in *adult education* theory yet.

whole learning A term used occasionally to refer to the technique of teaching from the whole topic to its constituent elements.

whole man A term used to refer to an all-round, broad education. It is also used sometimes by *affective educationists* in contrast to the emphasis placed on cognitive *knowledge* in much education.

Why Stop Learning? Published in 1927, written by *Dorothy Canfield Fisher*, and sponsored by the *Carnegie Corporation* for distribution throughout America and Europe. This was the first book written to try to popularize *adult education*.

Wider Opportunities for Women (WOW) *Manpower Services Commission* provision of *training* courses for women returning to work after a long career break. It is part of the *Action for Special Groups* programme and has been put into operation throughout Britain. (Note: the *Manpower Services Commission* changed its name to the *Training Commission* and then to the *Training Agency* in 1988.)

Wider Opportunities Training Scheme (WOTP) An extension of the *Training Opportunities Programme* work preparation for unemployed adults and for participants in the *community programme*, designed to offer training opportunities for unemployed adults.

Willard, John D. The first professor of *adult education* in the United States, appointed to the post and head of department when Columbia University established its Department of Adult Education in 1930.

Williams, William Emrys (1896–1977) Well-known British *adult educator*, he worked in extra-mural teaching. He was secretary of the *British Institute of Adult Education*, director of the *Army Bureau of Current Affairs* during the Second World War, secretary-general of the *Arts Council of Great Britain*, and very influential in *adult education* generally.

Window, The (Fonstret) The magazine of the *Workers Educational Association* of Sweden.

Winston Churchill Memorial Trust A UK educational trust to encourage understanding among nations in memory of Winston Churchill. It awards the Churchill travelling fellowship annually. Current address: 15 Queen's Gate Terrace, London SW1, UK.

Wireless Discussion Group In 1929, as a result of a committee under the chairmanship of *Sir Henry Hadow* which issued the report *New Ventures in Broadcasting*, the *adult school movement* arranged a number of discussion groups to be established in connection with some of the early broadcasts of the *British Broadcasting Corporation*. This movement lasted until it was abandoned in 1946. One of the weaknesses was the need for a very well-qualified leader to be present at each group.

Wisconsin The University of Wisconsin has been a pioneer in *university extension* work since it began in 1904 to disseminate *knowledge*, undertake research, and provide assistance statewide. It currently provides *cooperative extension*, a phone-in service, and radio and television services.

wisdom 1. The ability to use *knowledge*, *experience*, and *understanding* to act in a wise and common-sense manner. 2. Accumulated knowledge over the years, e.g. the wisdom of the elderly. 3. Wise sayings or teachings. This concept clearly relates to *knowledge* and *belief*.

wisdom of the elders In traditional societies, the seat of *wisdom* was with the elders. While this idea has largely disappeared in a rapidly changing world, it is significant that it has been used as a basis for material in *adult literacy* campaigns in Africa.

Wisher (LaSCAI) Program This programme is based on the US Navy's Language Skills Computer-Assisted Instruction Program (LaSCAI) which was developed for testing the literacy level of navy recruits. It has been selected for use with *volunteers* in *adult literacy* work, and in co-operation with the library service for work with youths and adults whose basic skills are between zero and fifth grade.

Wittgenstein, Ludwig (1889–1951) Leading philosopher whose work centred around language. His work has had some effect upon theorizing within the social sciences although it is not greatly used at present in the philosophy of *adult education*.

WIZQUIZ A computer programme available commercially in America to help teachers develop and improve their testing of students.

Wojciechowski, Kazimierz (b. 1905) Outstanding Polish *adult educator* who was concerned with worker education and popular universities. He was editor of *Oswiata Doroslych* for many years and a leading scholar in the field.

Wolfson Foundation UK educational trust established in 1955 to promote health and education in the Commonwealth. Current address: Universal House, 251 Tottenham Court Road, London W1P 0AE, UK.

Womanschool Opened in 1975 as a college to provide educational opportunities for women in New York.

Women and Development Unit (WAND) Established in the Caribbean in 1978 to act as a *clearinghouse* for the work of women in the region. It publishes its own newsletter, *Women Speak*. Current address: c/o The Extra-Mural Department, University of the West Indies, Pinelands, St Michael, Barbados.

Women Returners Network A network of tutors and organizers involved in returner courses for women. Current address: c/o Luton College of High Education, Park Square, Luton LU1 3JU, UK.

Women Speak The quarterly publication of the *Women and Development Unit*.

Women's Affairs Unit Established by the Government of Botswana to co-ordinate all issues relating to women, it functions within the Ministry of Home Affairs. Current address: The Administrative Officer, Women's Affairs Unit, Private Bag 002, Gaborone, Botswana.

Women's Education des Femmes The quarterly resource publication of the *Canadian Congress for Learning Opportunities for Women*.

Women's Institutes 1. Founded in 1897 in Stoney Creek, Ontario, Canada by Adelaide Hoodless, they increased in number very rapidly in Canada because of the isolation of women in the frontiers. They became one of the largest *adult education* institutions in Canada concerned with legislation, home economics, health, agriculture, and the methods and procedures of the institutes themselves. 2. The first in Britain were started in 1915 by the Agricultural Organisations Society. Each monthly meeting has an educational element and there is often a *community education* aspect involving discussion on local issues. Each local organization is affiliated to the *National Federation of Women's Institutes*.

Women's Museum Established on 7 November 1984, this museum sets out to document the part women have played, and are currently playing, in society. It has an archive, mounts exhibitions, conducts research, and offers programmes for participants. It is supported financially by both local and state governments. Current address: Frauen Museum, Weisbaden, Hessen, Federal Republic of Germany.

Women's Network A Brazilian organization working with women through *non-formal education*, especially in the depressed areas of the world. Current address: C.P. 1803, 01051 São Paulo, Brazil.

Women's Programme of the International Council for Adult Education The *International Council* initiated this programme in 1979 to help mobilize the strengths and experiences of women in a worldwide programme of *adult education* to help advance true participation and equality of women in the world. It is concerned with information sharing, research emphasizing participatory approaches, training, exchanges of people between different regions, and projects.

women's studies The academic study of the place women occupy in society. It concentrates upon women-centred areas of *knowledge*.

Women's Studies International Quarterly International journal of *women's studies*.

women's vocational school Established in several towns in Holland as a result of a programme initiated by the Women's Union of the Federation of Dutch Trades Unions. They offer a variety of programmes, including *information technology* and courses for those starting up in business.

Woodbrooke College Established in 1903 in Bournville, on the same location as *Fircroft College* (which opened later), as a residential *adult education* school.

Woodbrookers Term used in the Netherlands to refer to those residential *adult education schools* patterned on the Quaker schools in Britain, e.g. *Woodbrooke College*, which were started in 1908. See *Stichting ter bevordering van het Woodbrookerswerk in Nederland.*

Woodrow Wilson International Center US educational trust established in 1968 which awards fellowships to educators to pursue their own research projects. Current address: The Smithsonian Institution Building, Washington DC 20560, USA.

word recognition The ability to recognize words and read them aloud.

Work and Life Ten state associations in the Federal Republic of Germany within which the German trade unions co-operate with the *folk high schools*. It has a number of major functions including: working with employees in a political and educational manner, and helping them recognize their place and role in society. It promotes work-based education and is concerned about *paid educational leave*. It considers itself part of the labour movement.

work card A card on which is written a *problem* or a task for a group to undertake in classroom teaching.

Work–Education Exchange The bimonthly newsletter of the *National Manpower Institute* in America.

work experience *Experience* of the work situation, by performing a job as part of a course. This is a form of *experiential learning*. See *internship*.

work sample tests A selection of job analyses, usually carried out on-the-job, which enables a *human resource development* researcher to assess the demands of the job. On occasions these tests are carried out under more controlled conditions.

work study 1. Undertaking a study of a particular occupation. 2. A management technique based upon the theories of Frederick Taylor, who believed that people would do more work if it were scientifically organized. Used to analyse an occupation. See *time and motion study*.

work team meetings A process in which people who work together in a team meet to review their working practices and seek how they may improve them. Subjects may also include interpersonal relations within the group. There are similarities in this method of teaching and learning to *quality circles* and *self-help*.

workbook 1. An exercise or textbook with questions and spaces for answers. 2. A book which provides instructions for work or study to be undertaken, e.g. a type of *study guide*. 3. A book in which work or studies undertaken is recorded, rather like a study diary or a *learning log*.

worker-teacher In Canada's *Frontier College*, a person who is a worker in the daytime and in the evening is the teacher of those with whom he works. See *labourer-teacher*.

Workers' Correspondence University One of the three main *distance teaching* institutions in Yugoslavia, founded shortly after the Second World War. It provides both *secondary* and *higher education*, and has its own publishing house which publishes material other than that prepared for courses. This institution is situated in Ljubljana. See *Birotehnika, Correspondence Education Centre*.

Workers' Education Journal of the *Workers' Educational Association* published twice a year.

Workers' Education Bureau of America (WEB) Established in 1921 to act as a *clearinghouse* of information and guidance, by 1923 the American Federation of Labor had constituted this bureau as the official agency of labour education for its own members. Merged in 1955 with the *Congress of Industrial Organizations'* Department of Education, this organization subsequently became the national educational bureau for worker education in the United States. See *Department of Education of the AFL–CIO*.

Workers' Education News The quarterly publication of the *Workers' Educational Association* in New Zealand.

Workers' Educational Association (WEA) 1. Founded in 1903 by *Albert*

Mansbridge as the *Association to Promote the Higher Education of Working Men*, it assumed its present name in 1905. From the outset it has had three levels: branches, districts, and the national association. Each branch is autonomous, subject to the ideals of the movement, and democratic. The WEA itself is an association of affiliated societies rather than a society of individual members, since Mansbridge believed that individuality is a middle-class phenomenon. The WEA has had a long and honourable history with the *adult education* movement, being responsible for the *tutorial class*, among other achievements. It has always striven to bring university education to working people and remains the largest voluntary adult education association. Its districts hold *Responsible Body* status, receiving government support for their work. The WEA was also established in Australia as early as 1913 and now functions in each state. Current address: 9 Upper Berkeley Street, London W1H 8BY, UK.

2. In Canada, the WEA was formed in Toronto in 1918 and had a particularly close relationship with the University of Toronto, which was its main sponsor in the early years. However, the two did not always agree and the WEA strove for some independence from the Extension Department at the university. It enjoyed considerable success as an organization during the 1930s and 1940s, and spread throughout Canada, inspired to a great extent by the work of *Drummond Wren*.

3. The Workers' Educational Association in Finland was established in 1919 to provide the labour movement with educational services and extensive cultural activities. It has 14 district organizations, 103 local study organizations, and maintains a correspondence institute. It publishes its own journal, *'Time Signal'* (Aikamerkki), eight times a year. Current address: Psassivuorenkatu 5B, 00530 Helsinki 53, Finland.

4. Established in Denmark in 1924, the WEA is the oldest and largest voluntary adult education association in Denmark. It is affiliated to the Social Democratic

Party and to the trade unions. In 1925 *Oluf Bertolt* became its secretary.

5. Founded in Sweden in 1912 by *Richard Sandler*, it was the first *educational association* sponsoring *study circles* in Sweden. This association, because of its links with working people, emphasizes the provision of opportunity for people who had unequal chances earlier in their lives. It publishes its own magazine, *The Window* (Fonstret).

6. In Norway, the WEA is a member of the *Norwegian Association of Adult Education Organizations*.

7. The Austrian association, Arbeiterbildungsverein, was established in 1867 and remains a prominent association for *adult education* in Austria.

8. In Australia, the WEA was founded by Albert Mansbridge in 1913. Current address: WEA House, 72 Bathurst Street, Sydney 2000, Australia.

9. Current address in New Zealand; P.O. Box 6241, Wellington 6000, New Zealand.

Workers' Educational Trade Union Committee (WETUC) Founded in 1919 in England, initially as a partnership between the unions and the *Workers' Educational Association*, it quickly expanded as more unions wished to participate. However, rivalry between it and the *National Council of Labour Colleges* meant that it never enjoyed the total support of the labour movement. It ran a full programme of courses for many years but in 1963 the Trades Union Congress decided that it did not need the two organizations. Consequently, in 1964 both organizations were subsumed under the responsibility of the TUC as a whole, when the *Trades Union Congress Education Department* was formed.

Workers' Statute The Italian law which entitles working people to *paid educational leave*. Initially, it entitled workers to the right to shift work if they were registered for recognized educational courses. In 1973 workers were entitled to the right of day release for 50 hours per annum, provided that they attended 25 hours of study in their own time. This could be deferred for three years, so that workers

could have 150 hours of study. Thus it became known as the *One Hundred and Fifty Hours* programme, although the right was subsequently extended.

workers' theatre The use of drama to educate people about social situations, radical in its political stance. In Toronto, one was established in the early 1930s which became well known in Canada, winning a number of awards for drama. It did not exist for long but by the mid-1930s there were a number of theatre for action groups in Canada.

workers' universities Established in some Eastern bloc countries, especially *Yugoslavia*, with the aim of furthering workers' self-management by providing courses in socio-economic and cultural education. In Yugoslavia, these emerged after the Second World War, and the introduction of worker management in the Yugoslav factory system. They increased in number until the 1960s although there has been some decline since that time. However, as the school *curriculum* has narrowed in Yugoslavia, the worker's universities have gained a new audience in young adults who seek a broader education.

working class Usually refers to those people whose main occupation could be classified as manual labour. Those whose work is non-manual are regarded as middle class.

working hypothesis An unproven hypothesis upon which decisions or policies are made until such time as more evidence emerges to change it.

Working Men's Clubs Established in the middle of the nineteenth century in England by the Reverend Henry Solly with the intention of providing an *adult education* component and of combating the problems of alcohol.

Working Men's College The first of these was founded in Sheffield in 1842 but the more famous one opened in London soon after. See *London Working Men's College*. There were a number of other colleges that adopted this title.

working men's reading room movement An activity of the *self-help* movement which was a feature of nineteenth-century England. Often, but not always, associated with *adult schools*, a number of reading rooms providing newspapers and a small library were established in the nineteenth century. Unlike *mechanics institutes*, these tended to be run by working people for working people, although often supported by the middle classes. They declined in the latter part of the nineteenth century. Those established in Carlisle have been the most thoroughly researched.

Working Together: Education and Training A UK government White Paper issued in July 1986 in which the formation of the *National Council for Vocational Qualifications* was announced.

Workingmen's Institute Established by Johns Hopkins University in 1879 as the first university involvement in working-people's education in America.

workshop In educational terms, a *group* of people engaged in a *project* or other co-operative learning venture.

Workshop of German Educational Centres A co-ordinating body for those educational institutions in the Federal Republic of Germany which have both a political and social purpose, even though they themselves espouse an independent position.

World Alliance of Young Men's Christian Associations Current address: 37 Quai Wilson, 1201 Geneva, Switzerland.

World Association for Adult Education (WAAE) Founded in 1918 by *Albert Mansbridge* in Frederiksberg, Denmark, it was active in promoting conferences of *adult educators* such as the ones held at London in 1922, Cambridge in 1929, and Vienna in 1931.

World Bank The World Bank has supported many development projects which have included an *adult education* component. It has also published a number of books about *adult education* in the context of development. Current address: 1818 H Street NW, Washington DC 20433, USA.

World Campaign for Universal Literacy In 1962 *Unesco* spelt out the cost of a ten-year world campaign for universal literacy.

World Confederation of Organisations of the Teaching Profession (WCOTP) Current address: 5 avenue de Moulin, 1110 Morges, Switzerland.

World Conference on Adult Education The first major world conference on *adult education* was promoted by the *World Association for Adult Education* and held at Cambridge, England in 1929. Nearly 300 members and 33 national delegates attended. A second conference was held at Vienna in 1931.

World Conference on Continuing Education for Engineers and Scientists The first world conference on *continuing education* for engineers and scientists was held in Mexico City in April 1979.

World Council for Curriculum and Instruction Founded in 1970, it holds an international conference every three years; in 1977 it selected the topic of *lifelong education*.

World Council of Churches The World Council has involved itself with *adult education* and *development* for many years. Indeed, *Paulo Freire* was a full-time consultant with the World Council during the 1970s whilst he was in exile from Brazil. It publishes a number of papers and books on the subject and has a separate department devoted to this area of work. Current address: Programme Unit on Education and Development, World Council of Churches, 150 rue de Ferney, P.O. Box 66, 1211 Geneva 20, Switzerland.

World Council of Indigenous Peoples Current address: 555 King Edward Avenue, Ottawa, Ontario, Canada K1N 6N5.

World Development Movement This UK organization promotes *development education* and sponsors campaigns. It is also an educational resource. Current address: 26 Bedford Chambers, Covent Garden, London WC2, UK.

World Education Inc. an American association concerned with a variety of aspects of *community* and *popular education*. Current address: 210 Lincoln Street, Boston, Massachusetts 02111, USA.

World Health An illustrated magazine published ten times a year by the *World Health Organization* for the non-specialist.

World Health Forum: An International Journal of Health Development A quarterly journal published by the *World Health Organization* concerned with issues in health and *health education*.

World Health Organization A specialist agency of the United Nations. *Health education* is one of its major concerns. It publishes a number of journals and newsletters. Current address: Division of Strengthening of Health Services, World Health Organization, CH–1211 Geneva 27, Switzerland.

World Health Organization Chronicle The principal information organ of the *World Health Organization*, published every two months in a number of languages.

World Leisure and Recreation Association This association is concerned with training in leisure studies and education. Current address: 559 King Edward Avenue, Room 108, University of Ottawa Campus, Ottawa, Ontario, Canada K1N 7N6.

World Literacy of Canada A non-profit organization funded by the Canadian government for educational research. Current address: 692 Coxwell Avenue, Toronto, Ontario, Canada M4C 3B6.

World Medical Association Established in 1947 to seek high standards in medical education. Current address: 10 Columbus Circle, New York, New York 10019, USA.

World University Service Established in 1920 for the overall benefit of university education. Current address: 12 rue Calvin, Geneva, Switzerland.

World Young Women's Christian Association Current address: 37 Quai Wilson, 1201 Geneva, Switzerland.

worldview English translation of the German noun 'Weltanschauung'. It means an individual or group system of *knowledge* and beliefs about the world. There are two elements to this: the religious, in its broadest sense, which is about the meaning of the world and life; and the non-religious, which is concerned about ideological issues of daily existence.

Wren, Drummond A Scottish immigrant to Canada who became interested in the *Workers' Educational Association* in the 1920s. He became general secretary in 1927 and when the organization received grant aid for the *Carnegie Corporation* in 1930, he became full-time organizer. He held this post for more than 20 years, building the WEA into a large educational organization. Throughout his career he maintained that the WEA had to be independent in order to be effective but he was often accused of being a communist. He resigned from the movement in the spring of 1951 because of these unproven charges. The WEA in Canada has never been as strong since he left it.

Write First Time Begun in 1975, this is a broadsheet produced by literacy workers, filled almost entirely with the work of *adult literacy* students.

writing school Established in eighteenth-century America to teach writing.

367

X

Xerox International Center for Training and Management Development A large residential centre run by the Xerox company and offering a variety of courses. Much research in the United States shows how seriously *continuing professional education* is taken by industry and commerce. See *corporate classroom*.

year co-ordinator Tutor responsible for the whole year of a course

Yearbook of Adult and Continuing Education 1. An annual publication from the *National Institute of Adult Continuing Education* in the United Kingdom, circulated to all members of the association. It provides useful names and addresses. 2. An annual publication in the United States, which commenced in 1975–76, to provide a wide range of information about events in America in this field.

Yearbook of Adult Education The yearbook of the *National Institute of Adult Education* before it changed its name to the *National Institute of Adult and Continuing Education*. See *Yearbook of Adult and Continuing Education.*

Yearbook of Adult Education in Scotland The yearbook of the *Scottish Institute of Adult Education*. Later this was replaced with a *Handbook of Adult Education in Scotland*.

Yeaxlee, Basil (1883–1967) Awarded a Ph.D. for his study, '*Adult Education and Spiritual Values*', by the University of London in 1922 – one of the very earliest higher degrees in *adult education*. Yeaxlee wrote many books on *adult* and *lifelong education*. His book on lifelong education in 1929 raises many issues which are still significant today. He spent his life in the service of adult education in Britain, having held posts in the *Young Men's Christian Association*. He was also secretary of the *Educational Settlements Association*, secretary of the Central Advisory Council for Adult Education in

the British army during the Second World War, and principal of Westhill Training College. In addition, he was a member of the Ministry of Reconstruction Adult Education Committee which produced the famous *1919 Report*.

young adult Current term for *adolescent*; a person between biological and social maturity. An interesting conceptual question is whether *adult educators* regard young adults as part of their potential clientele, although those involved in initial *vocational education* are constantly involved in their education.

young farmers' club Throughout the United Kingdom there are young farmers' clubs, which function within a national federation, intended to stimulate interest in agriculture and support farming education.

Young Men's Christian Association (YMCA) 1. Founded in 1844 by George Williams in London with an evangelical objective, it did not begin in the United States until 1851. It is also to be found in many countries in the world. Now it is interdenominational and concerned with social issues. Much of its work is undertaken in youth clubs and is of a *non-formal* and *informal educational* type. Many leading *adult educators* have been employed by the YMCA, both in the United Kingdom and the United States. 2. In Scotland, its national offices are in Edinburgh. Current address: 11 Rutland Street, Edinburgh EH1 2AE, Scotland. 3. In the United States, it expanded its work in *adult education* immediately following the Civil War. In 1892 it established its own educational department and educational secretary. 4. In Sweden, together with the *Young Women's Christian Association*, it is an educational association which sponsors *study circles*. It emphasizes family values, music, bible study, social affairs, and international understanding. See *National Educational Association for the YMCA and YWCA, World Alliance of Young Men's Christian Associations*.

Young Men's Christian Association College A professional centre for the study of *informal education*, involved especially in the preparation of youth and community workers. Current address: 642a Forest Road, Walthamstow, London E17 3EF, UK.

Young Women's Christian Association Originally two separate organizations founded by two women simultaneously in 1855, Miss Robarts in the South of England and Lady Kinnaird in London, and united in 1877. The objectives of the organization are similar to those of the *YMCA*. It is especially concerned to provide young adults with the opportunity of self-development. Current address: 52 Cornmarket Street, Oxford OX1 3EJ. 2. In Scotland, its national offices are in Edinburgh. Current address: 7 Randolph Crescent, Edinburgh EH3 7TH, Scotland. See also *World Young Women's Christian Association*.

Your Move The title of a follow-up *adult literacy* programme broadcast by the *British Broadcasting Corporation*. See *On the Move*.

Youth and America's Future A commission established by the *Grant Foundation* in America. There are several research publications and reports on this project. Current address: The William Grant Foundation, Commission on Work, Family and Citizenship, 1001 Connecticut Avenue NW, Suite 301, Washington DC 20036–5541, USA.

youth club Run in many countries in the world for young adults as leisure time activities.

youth culture A *subculture* which revolves around the values and attitudes of young adults. As the period between biological and social maturity has lengthened, this subculture has emerged.

Youth Employment and Demonstration Projects Act (YEDPA) An American programme of the Department of Labor to combat youth unemployment by increasing the opportunities for youth employment and helping to train young adults for occupations.

Youth Opportunities Programme (YOP) Programme devised to provide training and opportunity to acquire *knowledge* and *skills* to unemployed young adults. This is a *Manpower Services Commission* initiative. (Note: the *Manpower Services Commission* changed its name to the *Training Commission* and then to the *Training Agency* in 1988.)

youth schools (Ungdomsskoler) Schools in Denmark for adolescents (14–18 year-olds). They are organized outside of the compulsory school system, subject to the legislation of the *Danish Voluntary Education Act*, and about 60 per cent of Danish young people go in their leisure time for at least one class a week. They are free. It is possible for young people to opt out of the schooling system and attend only youth schools.

youth service There is both local authority and voluntary association provision of educational and leisure opportunities for young adults in the United Kingdom. This dual provision is often referred to as the youth service.

youth trainer In France, those who work with 16–25 year-olds who are unemployed or who have not entered further education are often seen as a separate group of workers. They are referred to as youth *trainers*, or *formateurs jeunes*.

Youth Training Scheme (YTS) A scheme introduced by the *Manpower*

Services Commission to train young people. It was succeeded by the *Training for Skills* scheme. (Note: the *Manpower Services Commission* changed its name to the *Training Commission* and then to the *Training Agency* in 1988.)

youth tutor A teacher concerned with the social development of *young adults*. Such a tutor may be employed within *initial education* or within the *youth service*.

Yugoslavia See *Federation of Yugoslav Adult Educators' Associations*.

Z

Zambia See *Adult Education Association of Zambia*.

Zambia Adult Education Advisory Board Current address: P.O. Box 50093, Ridgeway, Lusaka, Zambia.

Zenkoku Kominkan Rengokai See *National Association of Kominkan*.

Zimbabwe The University of Zimbabwe has a very active Department of Adult Education and awards diplomas, first degrees, and masters degrees in *adult education* by part-time provision and *distance education*. In addition, the department provides research supervision for M.Phil. and D.Phil. degrees. It also awards diplomas in health education and nursing education through the co-operation of its departments of adult education and medicine.

Zimbabwe National Council for Adult and Non-Formal Education Current address: P.O. Box UA 190, Union Avenue, Harare, Zimbabwe.

Znanie The *All-Union Society for the Spread of Scientific Knowledge*. It is a Russian umbrella organization which co-ordinates a great deal of the *adult education* work in the USSR through the provision of lectures, classes, and discussion groups. It also publishes a great deal about adult education in Russia. Current address: Board of Administration, Znanie Projezd Serova 4, Moscow 101 100, USSR.